Lies

Also by Ned Rorem

Lies

A DIARY

1986–1999

Ned Rorem

Introduction by Edmund White

COUNTERPOINT

WASHINGTON, D.C.

The publisher wishes to thank Tom Steele
for his efforts on behalf of this book.

All photographs are courtesy of the author.

Library of Congress Cataloging-in-Publication Data
Rorem, Ned, 1923–
Lies : a diary, 1986–1999 / Ned Rorem ; introduction by Edmund White.
p.   cm.
Includes index
ISBN 1-58243-057-8 (alk. paper)
1. Rorem, Ned, 1923—Diaries.
2. Composers—United States—Diaries. I. Title.
ML410.R693 A3 2000
780'92—dc21
[B]   00-055496

FIRST EDITION

Book design by David Bullen

Printed in the United States of America on acid-free paper that meets the
American National Standards Institute Z39-48 Standard

COUNTERPOINT
P.O. Box 65793
Washington, D.C. 20035-5793

Counterpoint is a member of the Perseus Books Group.

Introduction

by Edmund White

Roland Barthes is right, in his essay on Chateaubriand's Life of Rancé: "Old age is no longer a literary age; the old man is very rarely a novelistic hero; today it is the child who moves us, the adolescent who seduces, who disturbs; there is no longer any image of the old, no longer a philosophy of old age, perhaps because the old man is undesirable."

All the more reason to be grateful to Ned Rorem for this diary, in which, among a thousand other things, he shows us old age, sickness, and death, the three inevitable and edifying truths about life according to the Buddha, and the three great subjects Americans avoid—even consider shameful.

The last third of this diary is the most harrowing, and the most convincing, account of AIDS that I know of. Rorem's lover, the much younger Jim Holmes (JH in the book), becomes ill and dies. As it turns out, there is no better form than the diary for showing the dull, repetitious, demoralizing despair of watching a beloved die from AIDS. The relationship between Rorem and Holmes is marked by sudden gusts of brutality (when Rorem asks coyly which qualities he inherited from which parent, Holmes says the worst from each). At one point Rorem wonders why JH never mentions his love, but toward the end of his life when he does say "I love you," Holmes then immediately wonders out loud what the love of a dying man is worth. Contained in these thoughts and exchanges is at least half the tragedy of AIDS—the inability of men to speak of their affection for one another, and their shame in accepting they're ill and dying.

Around AIDS a whole literature of devotion has grown up, writing marked by noble—noble and *sustained*—sentiments. In these often lachrymose accounts, the dying man achieves wisdom, declares love, suffers courageously, and his help-meet stays cheerful, declares love, and kisses the shrunken, blemished, but still handsome face. This is Tragedy Lite, American-style.

What actually happens is closer to the picture Rorem paints. The dying man withdraws from his lover or lashes out at him (after all, the partner has not received a death sentence), all the while becoming more and more pitifully dependent on him. He contemplates suicide but doesn't act on it. He goes on bizarre, rebellious sprees of self-destruction and defiance (we see Holmes lolling in the tub, the window wide open in freezing weather, smoking cigarettes, listening to Mahler—or Rorem—through headphones). He throws himself into his work when he's well enough—and even when he's suffering; he's racing against the clock. Little things anger him greatly—and he immediately feels bad about his foul temper. The healthy partner, in turn, believes that he is always in the wrong. "I feel impotent, but not useless. If his silences for hours on end, while driving to Hyannis for instance, are sinister, at least he has me to be silent with."

He has me to be silent with—that might well be the title of a book about accompanying someone with AIDS to the grave. The diary is best equipped of all literary forms to show the way the tragic mingles with the quotidian, the way that drama is always partial, botched, and freely adulterated by the ludicrous and the ignoble.

Racine was wrong: tragedy doesn't befall us swiftly, there are no unities of time, place, and situation, our language is never pure, we have no sustained monologues, and we are never permitted a crisis, a revelation or a *dénouement*. Instead, AIDS goes on for a very long time, mixing hope with despair, silence and curse words with elevated diction, and the end is so debilitating, so disintegrating, that there is no wisdom, little tenderness, scarcely any coherence. Whereas Phaedra may be mad, she's not suffering from dementia.

Despite all the horrors of the disease, Rorem does manage to capture the very real heroism Jim Holmes was capable of—his quiet determinism to make ship-shape their house in Nantucket, as if to fulfill a marriage vow "to hold" if no longer "to have" his partner; his professionalism in rehearsing and conducting his church choir up to a month before his death; even his patience in taking care of the dog. Rorem credits himself with no heroism at all, but the reader can only admire his courage in going on with his composing (however fitfully), his voracious reading (even if he complains he "never" reads and watches too much TV)—and the writing of this very book, an undertaking that would have proved daunting to anyone else.

Reading this book plunges one into quick, contrasting reactions: irritation with Rorem's mechanical inversions of normal values and familiar sayings; delight in his unexpected pairing of names (Susan Sontag vs. Harold Brodkey on illness, or Debussy's *La Mer* compared to Ravel's *Daphnis et Chloé*, or the contrast between two German-speaking contemporaries, Kurt Weill and Alban Berg); curiosity about his enthusiasms (I, for one, want to read more by British novelist James Hamilton-Patterson, the one writer he praises the most consistently, and I plan to listen to Messiaen's *Quartet for the End of Time*); impatience with his blind spots and his silliness in defending them ("Emerson dates," he tells us, absurdly, and the Sistine Chapel is less impressive as a whole than in its parts; *To the Lighthouse* is "a humorless bore," the six Bartók string quartets aren't all they're cracked up to be, etc., etc.); and, finally, deep sadness as he traces the decline of his beloved Jim.

What most impresses me is the enormous cultural appetite of these two men, Rorem and Holmes, of a sort the world will not see again, probably, but which was once common enough. Rorem remembers little things his patron and muse, Marie-Laure de Noailles, told him; he refers back to—and constantly quotes—his inspiration, Jean Cocteau. His France of the 1950s is still very much present in his mind, as are his parents ("Mother" and "Father," as he calls them in the High Prissy style). He dismisses *Angels in America*, flying in the face of public opinion; has views about the Heaven's Gate suicide cult; obsesses about his *bête noire*, Elliott Carter, whom he clearly envies; and expresses his abiding hate for the dodecaphonal composers, whom he calls the "serial killers." He continues his life-long comparison of what is German and what is French (telling jokes is French, *explaining* jokes is German, for instance). He reads Updike, Cheever, and Auden, and updates his evaluations of their work. He discusses the great musical per-formers he's known and admired or deplored. He gives us a list of the food (usu-ally quiche) he served on every social occasion. He hands out marks to his compo-sition students.

Into this assemblage of details and *aperçus* creep the first warning signals of JH's illness.

On Friday, 17 February 1995, Rorem writes:

> At noon I returned to find JH in the recovery room, less traumatized than I'd feared, but what he told me was less than Jaffin [Barry Jaffin, JH's doctor] told me a few minutes later in the waiting room. The Crohn's disease is, for the moment, minor, but there's one huge ulcer (and smaller ulcers), which may be a malignant tumor, he won't know until the biopsies are analyzed next Thursday.
>
> "And the blood test?" I asked.
>
> "Positive," said he.
>
> "You mean HIV positive?"
>
> "Yes." He looked at me quizzically and walked off.
>
> Thus began the strange thirty minutes in the near-empty waiting room. One's focus on everything is changed forever. Did JH know? Why him and not me? He's only 55, while I could prepare to die now without too much bile. This sounds unself-ish; in fact, it's pure ego: I want him to take care of me in my old age. What isn't self-ish, since all I care about is his comfort? . . .
>
> On leaving the hospital we walked a few sunshiny blocks down Fifth Avenue. JH has known he's HIV positive for some months, but didn't tell me because I'm "obses-sive."

This passage, unassuming and unannotated as it may be, nevertheless conveys the truth about the *pudeur* that reigns between lovers, the huge realm of the *non-dit* between the positive and the negative (French expressions seem best adapted to this sort of discretion). I can remember the comedy of errors that surrounded the diagnosis and death of a famous philosopher in France. The doctors didn't say the dreaded letters HIV because they felt their celebrated patient must already know the name of his disease. The philosopher never told his lover his diagnosis because, at first, he wasn't sure of it himself, and then, later, because he didn't want to cast the younger man into despair. Only toward the end did it occur to the philosopher that he might have passed the disease on to his lover—a horrible realization, indeed. Here, in the psychological fencing between JH and Rorem, we see a similar series of feints and well-meant concealments.

This diary is Rorem's fourteenth published book, and behind it lie many other efforts at self-preservation. Ned Rorem started off as a gorgeous idiot and has ended up as a somber, suspicious genius. But even as a young man—as his *Paris Diary* (which covers the years 1951–55) reveals—he was already an idiot savant, since he kept such good company, and was as ambitious and inquisitive as he was vain and spoiled. While in his twenties in Paris and at the height of his "beauty" (such a period word requires quotation marks), he was kept by the brilliant hostess Marie-Laure de Noailles, introduced to Picasso, courted by handsome Frenchmen, bedded by sexy Arabs, advised by Virgil Thomson, Francis Poulenc, and Nadia Boulanger, photographed by Carl Van Vechten, Man Ray, and Henri Cartier-Bresson.

He could often be fatuous: "Two years ago I wrote my parents who were worried about how much money to send: 'You have given birth to an exceptional child; you must therefore expect exceptional behavior from him.' I, in turn, was given an exceptional family who have always made every effort to understand and help." He had an eye for the grotesque and blithely tells us that Moroccan cemeteries stink "because Moslems are buried upright, and at night hyenas come to gnaw at their skulls." He mentions that a mouse has just died in his piano, killed "by the hammer strokes." He makes lots of references to his high calling as an artist and accordingly scorns a lady who imagines the beauty of Marrakesh might have inspired him ("If I have written better it's because I've turned my back on the view. It's hard for people to realize that the artist's inspiration is always present and all he needs to express it is concentration; beautiful surroundings are disconcerting").

A Quaker boy from Chicago with indulgent, progressive parents (his father was one of the architects of the Blue Cross insurance company and his mother a dedicated pacifist), Rorem took to the decadent high life of Paris with embarrassing ease: "A cool and languid lobster lunch at Marie-Laure's with Poulenc, who is witty and bright and religious and knows it and you know he knows it and says so and it's a bit spoiled." Gosh . . .

But all teasing aside (Howard Moss did the funniest parody of *The Paris Diary* in *The New Yorker* years ago), one has to be impressed by Rorem's industry between epic drunks as well as by his culture, even by his decision to keep a diary for publication, not exactly an American endeavor. He's a wonderfully companionable writer because we explore the brand-new Old World with him, and for a moment he allows us to see what it would be like to be universally adored: "The writer Miserocchi told me too that when we met at Bestigui's in Venice in '51 he'd left a note at the Danieli saying that since his young friend's suicide I was the only who could give him the *goût de vivre*. I never answered and had forgotten. If we are good to all who love us, what is there left for ourselves? Rome, Rome. Each one says selfishly: 'No one has loved you as I do.' "

If he's silly it's in imitating much older people who were brought up to integrate social charm with erudition, an awareness of rank with an aesthetic acuity. Also, as he has remarked himself, "silliness is germane to the diary-as-genre." Unfortunately, he also learned to imitate his elders' cruelty, as in this unforgivable passage from *The New York Diary*: "I don't like cripples (including especially the blind), or the aged, or children (their self-conscious vanity), or the Chinese, or the irritating and noisy confusion of women's purses, and elbows and voices." (Only Rorem would know how to temper the intolerable with the insufferable.)

His ultimate tribute to the demi-gods of his youth (when he himself was a full-fledged god of beauty) can be found in his 1994 memoir, *Knowing When to Stop*. Now that he is in his seventies he is less concerned by how many hearts he's breaking and more by the fine differences among all those hearts he's collected. Rorem himself might say, "Whereas youth is narcissistic, age is curious." (The epigrammatic style is infectious.) "Youth is personal, whereas age is social. Keats is a young man's poet; Jane Austen is an old man's novelist." By that token, an old man's journal is less *interressé* if the old man himself is interesting and has known enough success to become disillusioned but not bitter. Rorem fits the formula perfectly and brings a generosity (always nuanced, of course) to a re-examination of his past. If in his book from the late 1970s *An Absolute Gift* he gave us a professional musician's assessment of Ravel and Poulenc, in *Knowing When to Stop* he takes the human measure of Marie-Laure de Noailles (whom James Lord has also portrayed in his *Six Exceptional Women*). Such a figure—known only for her taste and her conversation, a faculty and an activity as *insaissisable* as charm—is always particularly difficult to capture in hindsight and through the static rendering of a literary portrait, but Rorem succeeds admirably in catching her on the iridescent wing.

He presents us with a woman fabulously rich, surrounded by Goyas in her *hôtel particulier* on the Place des Etats-Unis, the sumptuous interior decorated by Jean-Michel Franck before the war with white calf leather on the walls. Here she entertained mainly artists, including the painter Balthus and the sculptor Giacometti as well as Man Ray, Leonor Fini, and Dora Maar. Her mother, a descendant of the Marquis de Sade and of Petrarch's Laura, had been one of the two models for Proust's character the Duchesse de Guermantes. Marie-Laure's husband, the Vicomte Charles de Noailles, was largely an absent figure, even though she loved him and even revered him. As Rorem depicts her, she was a strange combination of haughty dignity and a puerile impulse to shock.

When Rorem would one-up her in conversation she would call him by the pet name she'd given him, "Miss Sly" (which she pronounced *Meeze-Lye*). She was a compulsive reader and she alone could compare the use of dialogue in Henry James's *plays*, of all things, and Diderot's novels. She read constantly—as did Rorem, if his diary of the period is to be trusted. Thursday it was Eliot's *The Cocktail Party*, Saturday *The Autobiography of Alice B. Toklas*, Sunday a Sartre play, Tuesday Ronald Firbank and Hawthorne, Wednesday Gogol's "The Nose."

The studious days were followed by bibulous, riotous nights. During one of these sodden dinners, according to Rorem, Marie-Laure said, "Ned is America's gift to France. We all want to bugger Ned. Even Henri." She alludes to the maître d'hôtel, who, pouring more blanc-des-blancs, interpolates without changing expression: "It's an interesting notion, but I'm sure Monsieur Rorem would object. And I'm not made that way."

Rorem's portrait of Virgil Thomson is no less indelible than his picture of Marie-Laure, although a chapter on a composer will necessarily be more technical than one on a woman of the world. When he tells us that Virgil always spoke (even to kids) in "French-style generalities, which are always anathema to literal-minded American children," he's hit the rusty nail on its dull head. When he explains to the reader that teaching composition is as useless as creative-writing courses, he adds, with indisputable authority, "But there is a craft if not an art, the lineaments of which can be imparted, even from one untalented person to another, and that is the craft of orchestration. Instrumentation is physical fact, not theoretical idea. That is what Virgil intended to show me." He presents us with Virgil at work in a clean, pressed pair of Lanvin pajamas, sitting in bed and running the whole New York musical scene over the phone. He gives us a Virgil who is deliciously indiscreet except with regard to his own homosexuality; when Ned brings out his scandalous *New York Diary*, Virgil removes all reference to the confessed pederast in his own forthcoming book. When Virgil's lover the painter Maurice Grosser tells Rorem to help out by setting the table, Virgil announces, "Ned doesn't have to work, Ned's a beauty."

When I met Rorem in the 1970s I had been awed in advance by his legend, that long peacock tail of memories—heavy, encumbering, gorgeous—that accompanies him wherever he goes. Perhaps because he started publishing his memoirs at age forty-three and had by then written so many volumes of them, he held no more secrets for me—or rather, Rorem was for me an open book but a closed life. To commandeer one of W. M. Spackman's titles, he was "A Presence with Secrets." An author one has known only through his writings may seem miraculously approachable, a professional charmer, an idealized version of oneself with his vademecum smile, but the flesh-and-bone man can have a strange accent, be haughtily impatient, tuned to his own past and its denizens like a bird-dog to a pheasant but blind to the present—and to one's own humble, arrogant needs and expectations.

Rorem was not indifferent. He had a harsh way of treating himself and of discounting compliments, but I supposed this was an aging beauty's way of coping with the deceptions of flattery. Or perhaps he was displaying that famous French "realism" I'd heard so much about. But with me he was attentive and observant, which was flattering, and wary, which was even more flattering, especially since I had published only one slim volume at the time and even now would not intimidate a fly. I kept thinking he was like a woman who's just had a face-lift and isn't sure what the effect is and whether those complimenting her are admiring or compassionate.

I suppose what he liked about me was that I was someone younger who still cared about his world—the world of Cocteau, Poulenc, and Virgil Thomson. I recognized the names of the painters who graced his walls (he had a sketch of himself by Cocteau and a painting—was it of boatmen in a clear afternoon light?—by the neo-Romantic Leonid Berman). I was responsive to his idea of conversation—which was serious, cultured, questioning. Any banality I might utter he'd immediately subject to the interferon treatment of his paradoxes, qualifications, second thoughts. Americans (especially Midwesterners like him and me) are routinely more fond of sunny unanimity and easygoing optimism than anything more controversial, but Ned would arch an eyebrow and with an uneasy smile start bombarding any momentary truce with his testing questions. He'd tease and probe, talking with his Donald Duck lisp. He seemed teleprompted by his Parisian ghosts, for surely no American left to his own devices would ever want to break up the first tentative tone of concord (perhaps we treasure peace because so much potential violence is always just under the surface, whereas the French cultivate saucy sallies since under their surface is the all-too-tedious predictability of cultural uniformity).

Once at his apartment I met Janet Flanner and "Darlinghissima" (the pet name of Natalia Murray). They were both old ladies and Ned was very courtly, though still provocative, which I now see he considered to be a social grace. Every soft, furry phrase he uttered had a sting in its tail.

And yet he was a wonderfully gentle, kind man, so different from the moody, childish, Bacchic boor of the early diaries. The source of the difference, I learned, was drink; he'd stopped drinking in the late 1960s and after that his suicidal moroseness, his mood swings, his belligerence, had all vanished. Even to this day if I meet someone who doesn't like Ned Rorem, I say, "You must have known him before 1970." Which is invariably the case.

He represents a vanishing breed, alas. In the States intellectuals are usually dowdy professors on provincial campuses, whereas socialites are power-mad philistines. In France, however, there are still a few of those *salons* where rich and titled people like to mix with artists. Just the other night I was at such a dinner; one of the other guests was an American billionaire stockbroker who, puzzled and offended, asked his bewildered French hostess the next day, "Why did you have all those *artists* to dinner when you could have had a *power* dinner?—there are lots of movers and shakers in Paris at the moment!" Ned is the sort of artist who had his manners and wits shaped in a salon that never witnessed a "power dinner." Now that Paris is no longer in the same league as London, Berlin, and New York, it must be contented with the appreciation of the art of the past. If America is the country of great writers and lousy readers, France today is the land of great readers and bad writers.

In his recent collection of essays and reviews *Other Entertainment*, Rorem has lost none of the confidence that his milieu conferred on him ("Duras is a first-class second-rater," he announces). In discussing Peter Feibleman's *Lilly*, his biography of Lillian Hellman, Rorem writes: "Theirs was unequivocally a mother-son relationship, in which Peter was the mother, Lillian the son." In page after page, Rorem delivers himself of acute, informed judgments; like his beloved Marie-Laure, he is equally at home in the French and the English-language traditions: "Like Cocteau, Auden was an aphorist who monopolized conversation with quips that brooked no argument. Cocteau too, vastly 'official' in his waning years, had been spurned by the very generations whose style he had shaped, and he died, successful and sad, in a mist of self-quotation. When Auden had become a monument he welcomed the interviewers he had shunned for years, but spoke to them solely in epigrammatic non sequiturs." With the same international ease he can tell us that Sarah Orne Jewett did for Maine what Knut Hamsun did for Norway, Louis Hémon for Canada, and Jean Giono for France.

Whenever the subject turns to music, Rorem makes the sort of canny observation only a composer is capable of. He tells us that Libby Holman was the first female pop singer "to exploit the husky purple depths of her vocal register rather than (like Helen Morgan or Ruth Etting) the squeakily poignant top." Or he can toss off a wonderfully illuminating comparison of Billie Holiday and Ella Fitzgerald: "Ella, with her nimbler vocal cords, came through as optimistic even in her plaintive songs; Billie, with her more limited tessitura, came through as plaintive even in her optimistic songs." I wouldn't agree (since Billie always sounds to my ears as though she's suppressing a laugh when she complains) but I admire the kind of observation that Rorem makes and the confidence with which he delivers his opinions.

He returns for a ride on some of his hobbyhorses. He has compared the French to the Germans one time too often (in the present volume he returns to this theme). His dismissiveness of Beethoven is absurd—and when he tells us that Poulenc's song "La Carpe" is worth all of *Fidelio* we can only cringe. He loves to scorn the remarks about music made by most non-musicians (although he should concede that the passionate confusion of a Proust, say, is preferable to the total indifference of most contemporary writers); in this collection he takes a swipe at Kazuo Ishiguro's novel *The Unconsoled*, which is about a concert pianist. And yet how can one resist a reviewer who starts his article with a reminder of Joan Crawford's dialogue in *Humoresque*: "The music I like? Some symphonies, all concertos"? Or who remembers that when someone once complained to Jane Bowles: "The odds are against me: I'm Jewish, homosexual, alcoholic, and a communist," Jane retorted: "I'm Jewish, homosexual, alcoholic, a communist—and *I'm a cripple!* "

Or he recycles once more his notion that if there is a gay sensibility, then some bona fide heterosexuals possess it—James Salter, here as in the past, is the example he invariably gives. (Gay sensibility, perhaps, I can't help but grumble, but no sensitivity to gays. I remember hurling across the room a Salter novel, written in the 1970s, in which one heterosexual man amuses his wife and a straight couple with a mincing, lisping imitation of homosexuals overheard in a bookshop: "Oh, Sartre was right. Genet *is* an absolute *saint*" or something of that sort).

Rorem likes to correct his favorite authors. In a passage of bravura erudition, he tracks down Cocteau's borrowings in his play *Les Monstres Sacrés* and finds the sources of the various characters' dialogue: " 'Happiness is a long patience' comes from Balzac, not Florent; 'All my life I've heard, "Wait 'til you're older, you'll see," and now I'm fifty, I've seen nothing' comes from Satie, not Esther; and 'I don't seek, I find' is Picasso, not Liane." Typically, spanning three cultures and two centuries, Rorem is able to compare *The Sorrows of Young Werther* with *Les Enfants terribles* and *The Catcher in the Rye*.

He tells us in several places that he is "morbidity incarnate" and that he's less in fashion now than previously. I hope my few darts haven't inflamed his morbidity, since he is among the handful of living writers whom I write for and love to read— one of the few, in other words, who count for me. If he is less in fashion (which I'm not at all sure is the case—his concerts and readings are always packed) the decline presages our fall, not his; in any civilized society his views and his art would be essential.

Rorem is a born diarist who feels compelled to comment on—well, not on everything that happens around him, for he is selective, but on the bits of tinsel that catch his eye or rhyme with some earlier preoccupation. We write about those things we know how to render. Isherwood once said that writers are notoriously unobservant, but that when an event enters the range of their talent and interests, their eyes suddenly focus and take a little snapshot. If so, then Rorem's perceptions are hair-triggered; he must use up a lot of film. And he never takes a bad picture.

Lies

1986

Voici que presque rien de ce fil ne me reste.
Sa pelote était lourde et me bondait le coeur.
Et ce coeur si souvent a retourné sa veste
Qu'il croyait ne jamais perdre de sa douleur.
JEAN COCTEAU, Le Chiffre Sept

Never have I been more procastinative, as though work were more a duty than a pleasure. (But work *is* more a duty than a pleasure, to any self-respecting artist out of sophomore class.)

Seeing ourselves as others see us. Jean Stein's misapprehension (or is it my own?). She phoned for the first time in perhaps ten years to ask if I might know some fantastic interior decorator (because of my connections with Marie-Laure in the old Paris days) who could help her with her new pad. Is that where she's always placed me? But that's where I've always placed her—I know nothing of interior decorators.

Trekked north with JH [Jim Holmes] to a vast gymnasium near Columbia University, the only *venue* (as it's said today) sufficient to stage the première of Boulez's *Répons*. Everyone was there, i.e., Elliott Carter, knowing that the writ would be holy. An hour late in starting. All that expensive hype to so little effect, like renting an SST to go fishing in Maine. A few healthy boos would have been in keeping. Not that *Répons* was all that bad. I rather liked it, but for quite different reasons than what Boulez doubtless thinks is in it. It was ornamental, amusing, kind of vulgar, thoroughly non-intellectual, utterly sensual, completely derivative, right in the tradition of French Impressionism and (with those flashing lights and cooing females) the Folies-Bergère. He's not a charlatan, though anything that lavish is suspect, including Wagner.

The other day, when asked by a young Juilliard composer, "What do you think of the so-called New Romanticism in America?" Boulez answered: "You Americans are all so nostalgic." Nostalgic for what? For Mahler, who is the composer most of them are imitating? We never had Mahler in our culture; we're not part of Europe. Boulez's piece meanwhile is vastly nostalgic insofar as it cribs from Debussy, the Stravinsky of *Les Noces*, and Messiaen without the tunes. He takes their filling and ornaments. He takes the gargoyles but not the cathedral.

JH feels that the case of the man killed by 32 hammer blows on the head, defined by the police as self-inflicted, should not be reinvestigated as planned, according to today's *Times*. Suicide knows many forms.

"While the general public may not be expected to respond to new work, other artists should be," claims John Rockwell. "Artists share assumptions about innovative approaches that transcend the boundaries of a given art form."

In retrospect, can't it be seen that even the greatest composers have been as wrong about their peers as critics? It's not for a composer to be right about anything but himself. But it is for a critic to be right. Neither often is.

Is there a young turk or prime mover today, with brains like Boulez yesterday, who singlehandedly will change the face of music? Boulez meanwhile, like Norman Mailer, or like any extremist who as he grows older shifts from left or right toward center, has become fairly benign. Both Mailer and Boulez began as bullies.

Visit at 4 o'clock from Dalton Baldwin (herb tea and an overpriced peach-melba torte from the Éclair). We discuss wet dreams, which the French call *faire une carte de France* and the Italians—less chauvinist—call *carta geografica*. I tell him I've been drawn sensually, if not sexually, to two women in my life, Moira and Leontyne.

Like Moira (at whose house we first met), Rockwell has only one eye—his left is good, her right. They *sit* accordingly. Gunther Schuller also has only one eye. Does blindness affect a composer or deafness a painter?

No one can see his own century. No one, indeed, can see the back of his own head. We can't see ourselves or know what purpose music serves. Music-as-expression-of-the-age is an excuse for horror and formlessness. But every age thinks it's the only and final age, and every age is convulsive, horrid, and formless.

If Dalton is our century's greatest accompanist (but no one can see the back of his own head, etc.), it's because he doesn't underplay, knows the repertory, and lives with Souzay. The least musical instrument is the spoken voice. Question of pitch. Cocktail chatter versus choral intonation, Babylon versus a formal Requiem. But which pitches? Schoenberg choral music is babel.

I don't know about singing. I know about song. ("I don't love music. I *am* music."—Charles Ludlam in *Galas*)

Death of Kate Smith widely covered on page one, and on the TV, which depicts her singing "God Bless America." She does have an accurate and not unpleasant voice, and smooth (smooth like leather rather than like satin). But it's a voice that, with all her facial histrionics and manifest patriotism, is absolutely dead.

Tragedy with a happy ending is true to literature if not especially to life. Forster's *A Room with a View*, for instance, or maybe *Middlemarch* (which isn't a tragedy, though it is a drama of a self-made woman, if I recall). Comedy with a sad ending is true to life but not especially to the stage. Cocteau's *Les Parents terribles* comes to mind.

JH says Dvořák's Fifth is the best symphony Brahms ever wrote.

"It's just me," says Greta Garbo reassuringly to her poodle who is having hysterics at the sound of the key in the latch. Or: Louis the Fourteenth, arriving with his retinue, to his overexcited dog: "It's only me." (Although, of course, he'd have used the royal we—*Ce n'est que nous.*)

The secret of stardom lies in not acting natural—sheer artifice. But artifice comes natural to me.

In eulogizing Roger Sessions for the Academy, Elliott Carter quotes himself from 45 years ago: "Sessions, during his whole life as a composer, has shunned the easy effect and the immediate appeal, has fought to keep music honest, serious, and conscientious to the limit of his power." If immediate appeal is to be shunned, most of Bach and all of Ravel are disqualified. If the easy effect is not honest or serious, all of Tchaikovsky and most of Chopin are disqualified. Implicit in Carter's homage is that Sessions could have used immediate appeal had he chosen. But could he have? *N'est pas joli qui veut.*

Laymen always ask composers: "Why don't you write a good musical and make some money?" What is disquieting is not the assumption that money's the goal, but that a good musical is easy. Inversely, would Carter say that Bernstein sold out by composing all those good musicals when he should have been turning out Sessions-type symphonies?

Elliott and I will never see eye to I. If he feels I misunderstand him, I do.

Do Mongolians have Mongolian idiots?

Speed on. No deeps.

Born of rich but honest parents.

Titles: *Dead and Kicking.*

The Power of Silence. The power, for example, of a lover who doesn't answer letters, a critic who never reviews you, a famous author who adds to his own mystery by ignoring fan mail. The power that Quakers invoke, of course, is the inner silence of a group meeting—he who talks too much seldom says anything. But is this true? Cocteau, Tallulah Bankhead, Anna de Noailles, who never closed their mouths, were worth attending, and a lot of quiet fools are foolish in their quietness.

Nodding Acquaintance. Not just a companion who drowses, but, for example, Andrew Porter, with whom I was on pleasant terms throughout Europe 35 years ago, while today we live a block apart and merely nod when we meet at the A&P. Or Jerry Robbins—we don't even nod. Yet we are the same people. No, we are not.

Just as most people don't realize that Newgate Callender is Harold Schonberg, so they don't know that half my music is for the church.

Troublingly lovely documentary on Billie Holiday. Watching with JH I kept wishing he could share my memories along with my veneration of this creature who, with Jennie Tourel, remains my favorite singer ever. Unlike the current crop of hysterics—Patti LaBelle, Liza Minnelli—forever peddling themselves, Billie just stood there and sang; if, at a climax, she moved a hand or closed her eyes, mountains crumbled. Tracing the years, I seemed to smell her trademark gardenia and taste the very ale of 1939 when I visited Manhattan alone at 15 for the World's Fair, and to watch Billie at Kelly's Stables, the Three Deuces, the Dizzy Club after hours where she sang "Rockin' Chair" (interpolating "she was queer too" between "My dear old aunt Harriet" and "Send me sweet Chariot"). Stingers, and whisky shots, and the fragrance of her thighs as I stooped beneath our table to recover a cigarette butt. Billie's inventive arching and bending of a common tune, her way with a song rather than the song itself, influenced my way of writing songs no less than did Poulenc or Ravel.

The sole jarring note on the PBS film was the advent of one Michele Wallace, self-proclaimed Black feminist, reading a pedantic tract about how Holiday didn't serve the feminist movement. As though the mere fact of Billie bucking the establishment weren't a model for revolutionaries. Ms. Wallace fretted about Billie's texts (but oddly missed the opportunity to point out that Billie's repertory, unlike Bessie Smith's, was almost entirely white). Now, there's scarcely a song in Billie's garland of unrequited love that couldn't be sung by a man to a woman, or to a man, or by a woman to another woman, or to or by just anyone. Love is all the same, like unhappy families, *pace* Tolstoy. Save us from saviors.

The difference between an Art Song and what in America is called a Pop Song is a difference in genre, not in quality. An Art Song is invariable: a Schubert or Debussy song is not rendered in translation, orchestrated, with tempo changed, or key changed, but Pop Song is legitimate with any instruments, for any sex, in any tonality, at any speed.

Discussion with JH about Larry Kert and the closing of his show *Rags*. His singing: the purposefulness, virility, resonance. Yet he's never become a star. Lacks the madness (for beauty limps) that makes his sister, Anita Ellis, unique. Nothing's wrong with him except that nothing's wrong with him. Venus de Milo with her arms restored.

More confusion for the French: He's pretty ugly.

Whenever I complete an essay I reread each sentence asking myself, Is this the shortest route? Writing, like science, is concision, and so too probably is music. (*Le Sacre*, Mahler's Ninth, *Parsifal*, insofar as they are perfect, are also the briefest way of saying what they have to say. Remove one note from a Chopin roulade, and it's no longer Chopin.) So too is everything worth its salt, including eating and sex.

Finished the biography, by Selina Hastings, of Nancy Mitford. During the period when I saw her often, in the early 1950s mainly in Provence but also in Paris, Nancy was at her peak. Although I did read her novels as they appeared—partly because they were amusing, but mainly because she was an acquaintance—I never took her very seriously, nor did I realize that she was famous. Her fame, in fact, like the Sitwells' or the Barrymores', was a collective thing, stemming from the heterogeneity of her sisters. The biography seems dull, limited, and really tells nothing of Nancy's French friends; the person I knew could as well have not existed. But I lost track of her after coming back to America. Through this book I now did learn of her terrible death, a death we all envisage yet pray to avoid, "a rare form of Hodgkin's disease, a malignant enlargement of the lymph glands, in her case rooted . . . in the spine. The pain is known to be one of the two most severe a human can suffer." Poor Nancy. It seems so contrary to all she admired: luxury, culture, nuance, upper-class privilege. She made a profession of super-ficiality, but her death was profound, like Canio screaming through his painted smile.

    Paris as I see it now is decadent, in the true sense of the word. Still the world's most heartbreakingly beautiful city—beneath all is rot. Nothing is happening in the arts (and it's by the arts that any city will eventually be judged): the French spawn theories about art rather than art itself, all is peripheral. This was true right after the war when we went over there, but we didn't realize it yet. Nancy may have.

    She frankly wrote: "I think perhaps I fail to understand the nature of homosex-uality—I am excessively normal myself & have never had the slightest leaning in that direction even as a child." She found "the pansy question" touchy to deal with in her pages, despite Proust, and despite the fact that, like every female in her milieu, most of her male friends were pansies.

Detroit recital in a fortnight with Will Parker. Excerpts from, among other things, *Flight for Heaven*. I never practice my own piano pieces with a personal view-point. These songs, for example, I would perform flaccidly if I didn't imitate Leon

Fleischer's imaginative energy during the many times he accompanied Doda Conrad in 1951. Leon taught me how to play my own music, just as a decade later Richard Cumming (during the song recording for Columbia) showed me how I, as a performer, so often missed the point of my own music. In fact, I had no viewpoint—or, at best, a too modest one. A composer, when he turns player of that which he's composed (this happens rarely in our century), is a separate person.

The vaguest musical designation is *con moto*. The most precise is *presto possibile*.

Local première last evening of String Symphony in Carnegie Hall, preceded by mass dinner at the Fontana di Trevi hosted by Jim Kendrick. (Rudolf Bing, alone at a nearby table, has forgotten his wallet and keeps the management in a dither.) The piece now, under the sculpting baton of Robert Shaw, and after a half-dozen public performances, seems almost too slick for its own good. Nothing's wrong with it—it's donned the chill of perfection—and wrongness of a sort is urgent to all art. (Backstage, Morton Gould: "You're brave, Ned, to write a beautiful piece in this day and age.") Particularly moved by the appearance of Joe Machlis, effusive, despite his phone call at noon saying he wouldn't be coming—quadruple bypasses take their toll.

Unsigned review (presumably by Bernard Holland) in this morning's *Times*. The burden is that my piece "told us nothing new," and is an "attractive work despite— or perhaps because of—its long series of well-worn expressive devices," and "that one comes to admire the String Symphony's very lack of originality." I'm immensely pleased. Originality, the poor man's novelty, has always been the least of my goals, and I imagine that, more and more, my music shall be less and less extraordinary. Still, though Holland probably did not intend his remarks as laudatory, couldn't they have been addressed, just as they stand, to Del Tredici's *Alice* pieces, or indeed to Boulez's *Répons*? (The bulk of the review is on my piece and its familiar tone. Amusing that Holland then proceeds: "The rest of the evening was taken up with more familiar matters . . . ")
    Shouldn't the critic's aim be to seek the individuality, rather than the originality, in a new work? Anyone can be new. Is the newness stamped with personality?

Death of Jean Genet. He was not only the greatest writer of post-war France, he was the most interesting and the most important—attributes that do not always join hands. He aimed high and hit the mark. The aim was interesting in being a broad and raw depiction of same-sex male love. The depiction was important because no one had done it quite that way before. Genet was the Cocteau of the working class. That he should die on the same day as Simone de Beauvoir, who was no less a pioneer for the dignity of females as Genet for the dignity of males, and on the same day as Reagan's bombing of Tripoli portends, at least for the moment, something too bleak to ponder.

Hotel Ponchartrain, Detroit

As always, Will and I alternated in chatting to the hall, he introducing the Debussy groups, I introducing mine. And as always, before *War Scenes*, I explained that although there's no such thing as Political Music—not at least in the sense that music can change rather than merely heighten our feelings about things (music doesn't turn bad people good)—I had nevertheless in 1969 wanted to make a statement about the Vietnam War, as a pacifist and a Quaker. I added that Whitman's prose, although pertaining to the Civil War, could as well pertain to the Trojan War, or to Korea, or to last week's laceration of Tripoli.

After the recital, when the large and mostly middle-aged crowd convened to swallow unalcoholized punch incongruously among the granite lions of Assyria, a mature woman approached to announce that she agreed with all I said, although that if *she* said it she might be thought un-American. "But it's your America too," I said, "and as a taxpayer you have as much right as Jerry Falwell to make the rules." An elderly man interrupted: "Benjamin Britten was a pacifist, just like you, but I have this friend who says that the violence of *Peter Grimes* and *Turn of the Screw* indicates that Britten must have been a real sadist," and he bestowed upon me a look of "Get out of *that* if you can!" At a loss I merely turn my back. Why can I not be patient and helpful like Rosemary or Mother, or like a calm logician answering the wildest questions? It does not require *l'esprit de l'escalier* to grasp that being against violence does not mean that artists must not deal with violence. Britten dealt with matters that concerned him. The elderly man could as easily have construed himself a masochist because he was talking with me.

People (interviewers) act surprised when I profess insecurity. They don't see the perishability of it all. Satisfaction of increasing appreciation is paralleled by vulnerability of simply aging. As he grows more famous (or less famous), a person grows more fragile, until he finally disappears.

A pupil gets most of what he will get during the very first lesson.

Call from manager of Detroit recital. Certain members of "his" audience were "offended" by *War Scenes* and my remarks thereon; they felt I should keep my politics to myself. (Whitman's politics too?)

Jacob Druckman: "We are in transition, and at such a time composers always turn to theater." Now, transition is a historic, not a current, realization; we can only know after the fact where we are (but aren't we always in transition?). Do composers in fact turn to theater during transition? When is transition? The nineteenth century? Chopin, Schumann, Liszt, Schubert, Brahms never wrote, or never successfully, for the stage, but Handel in his "stable" period did in the eighteenth century, and Bach with his masses and passions composed the grandest theater of all time. Meanwhile, if theater in music means opera, then Druckman's series on "The New Romanticism" belies its name. Of course, it's not a stage but an instinct for drama that defines theater in music.

On PBS, *Sunday in the Park with George*, to which I dutifully attend for 150 minutes keeping an open mind, and wanting yet again to get the drift of the composer—why he's viewed with such deference. (*Literary Review* in London: "There are two sorts of American musical now: those by Sondheim, witty, original, usually sad, and the rest.") And yet again I'm miffed. The rhymes are glib and workable, but no cleverer than Cole Porter's, and no "deeper." The music wants profile. The message, about Art and The Artist and Dedication and Sacrifice, is freshman. The sound was awful and so were the performances. I don't mind that the two leads sang badly—stars, after all, don't have to be on pitch, and Miss Peters and Mr. Patinkin, so full of themselves as they gazed into the middle distance through half-closed eyes and deeply concerned with the Importance of it all, did not sabotage the score with their whining. But the chorus wobbled. Everyone was high-class and actorish, like Jean Harlow being a lady.

Phoned Maurice Grosser at Saint Vincent's. Both he and Morris Golde underwent prostate surgery these past weeks, both benign. Morris is home, but Maurice remains in the hospital "with complications." Asked how much of the prostate was removed, Maurice replied, "Enough to make an omelet."
    I dislike soft butter. JH likes it.
    At least twice a day an automobile alarm is set off, to no purpose, throttling the neighborhood for minutes on end, sometimes for hours.

Shuffling through old papers I come across a letter dated July 1951 from the immortal Hélène Jourdan-Morhange. Her words, apropos of the broadcasts in Paris that month of my *Six Irish Poems*, made me smile at the values by which new music was then judged: *J'ai écouté vos beaux poèmes émouvants et sincères. Et je veux vous le dire avant de nous rencontrer. Vous avez évoqué, pour moi, le ferveur de Menotti, et je vous félicite . . .*

Recording of *Sunday in the Park with George*. Revised my opinion. The second of the two acts, which some find a letdown, is singularly touching, personal, and, yes, beautiful. Bernadette Peters's aria about the past is like nothing ever heard before, and haunting with its rising clarinets.

After 83 years Maurice Grosser no longer exists, taken, it will be learned, by AIDS-related problems. So AIDS does not after all discriminate. Virgil dined at Gaby's. On saying goodnight, she asked after Maurice. Virgil explained he'd died in the morning, but had not announced it earlier so as not to spoil the evening.
    What does it profit a cancer cell—or an AIDS virus or any other invader of our system—to gain a human body if, by doing so, it loses its own vitality? A cancer by definition is doomed, since the fact of its being is the cause of death—its own. Doesn't *it*, like everything alive, wish to survive?
    When the virus—the cell—enters the body (but why does it choose to enter a

new body rather than remaining where it was?), how long before it goes to work? Does it look around for a while, as in a hotel room, before using the phone?

Hype, the mask of the ungifted, was never more in evidence than on the PBS portrait of William Burroughs's charmless ego. I watched as much as I could stomach. The weak program was hardly strengthened when slovenly nobodies declared Burroughs "the greatest mind of our time." The Mind read from his bad-boy fiction—a sort of Sci-Fi for queers—in his monotone diction, an unpleasant cross between John Cheever and W. C. Fields. He's the Rube Goldberg of gay porn. Flanked by those other Great Minds, John Giorno and Laurie Anderson, he recounts, not a philosophy of composition but, for the millionth time, how he lived as a junkie in Tangier (regularly mispronounced as Tangiers), and how he accidentally killed his wife with an arrow. Cameos by Brion Gysin and Allen Ginsberg were welcome for their brief flashes of amiability, but when the camera panned back to Burroughs numbness set in anew. Is it his giving drugs a good name that makes young people take him seriously, when they've forgotten Paul Goodman?

Odors of dry sherry, of vetiver, of rye toast, of blond cedar, espresso, citrus, incense, male corduroy: upper-class taste (or smell). Lower-class: odor of ale, of semen, of snake, of salami, locker rooms, lank blue hair, pectorals. No, I've confused the classes.

I can teach anyone to write a perfect song, although the song may lack the blood of life, since only God can give that—the God I don't believe in. Buñuel: "Thank God I'm still an atheist."

Broadcast of Elliott Carter's Fourth Quartet, a hostile, empty, cynical piece, lacking—as the Pornography Commission would say—any redeeming social value. No poetry, no grammar, and, since there's no contrast (all is hyperthyroid), no drama. Yet even Henahan, who clearly doesn't like the work, defers. The Lie surrounding Carter is more contemptible, because more sophisticated, than the Lie surrounding Reagan. Lies of the TV evangelists feed off know-nothings who have nowhere else to turn; the conspiracy of the Carter mafia feeds off intellectuals (including the same intellectuals propelling the conspiracy) who have convinced themselves, in our pale, silly world, that the music's important and profound—importance and profundity being for them the Ultimate Target. But Leighton Kerner and Andrew Porter, more than our Yahoo public, are duped by the Emperor's Old Clothes. As for Elliott himself, why should he not do as he does, take what he can get and play along?

I dream so often of Marie-Laure that she remains a still quick and frequent friend. Thinking back on how I once found her difficult and spoiled, I gasp, for I then was a narcissistic brat. Her patience and generosity, from here, now appear unlimited.

Marie-Laure n'a jamais tutoyé son mari. Et elle ne m'a jamais dit vous, même au début.

Can one truly state that the conspiracy around Elliott Carter is based on a lie? Aren't all lies sooner or later exposed, especially those dealing with art and with the betterment of society?

Well, the plot about women's inherent inferiority prevailed internationally for five thousand years. The greatness of Beethoven is never challenged. We need for women to be inferior, for Beethoven to be great. Human nature is stronger than truth—stronger, that is, than fact. In fact, women are not inferior, and Beethoven is not necessarily great. Nor is Carter necessarily great. The invention of his majesty is as dumb, finally, as the legitimizing of Philip Glass's re-scoring of Czerny exercises.

Wet, windy. Pane fell with a smash from the dining-room window. Replaced soon by super. But all the windows are rotting, and the building itself, though solid, gives off a melancholy dated smell, which I enjoy.

The foregoing 43 entries were compiled for the "musical issue" of Brad Morrow's magazine *Conjunctions*. They were culled from this diary solely for their musical matter. (But since every facet of my life—on stage, at table, in bed—is at least indirectly about my profession, all matters are musical.) Then when I showed the compilation to JH, he found it false and hard. He hopes I won't release it. So I won't.

Meanwhile, in typing the entries, I discarded their dates. Maybe I'll continue without dates, at least for a while. The *Paris Diary* entries listed not only days but hours, until Robert Phelps reshuffled the whole into *his* notion of drama. Those entries, reshuffled, although word-for-word identical to the original manuscript, by definition changed their impact with new replacement. Did they then become Robert's truth, more than mine?

If ever these notes become a book, the book must be called *Lies*. If I have learned one thing in the three-plus decades of publishing diaries, it's that there is no universal accord, nor even a recorded experience that I myself, the day after, can concur with exactly.

I have lost precious friends who say, "I was there too, and Ned's report is skewed, it didn't happen that way at all." Is their truth my truth? Doesn't "truth," as thrown about in law courts, really mean "fact"? Everything is *Rashomon*.

Is my "white lie" to the wife of some friend's infidelity, equal to the Great Lie of Hitler? Who says it's a lie—or great?

Possibly The Diary is a red herring. The author seeks to guide readers away from the essential, which even he ignores.

Can music lie? Certain music can be termed pallid, evasive, even dishonest.

But can it be proved actually to lie?

Honesty? Like happiness, it's a shallow concept. Is any real artist honest? The concept, even though shallow, shifts hourly, and depends on the light. (As for happiness, should that be anyone's goal in this age of mediocrity, cruelty, and war?)

Are the tenets of the Ku Klux Klan a lie? Or those of Christ? Is the moon made of green cheese? Do cows have wings? Are your facts my facts? If a photograph from the west of the Eiffel Tower on Tuesday doesn't jibe with a photograph from the east on Wednesday, which one lies? Are yesterday's falsehoods false when restated tomorrow? We used to burn witches.

Is theater a lie? Are Picasso's goats, Man Ray's portraits lies? Audubon's birds are clearly not birds. Are rouge and wigs and lipstick lies?

Is the angle from which I perceive this vista or that argument now rather than then, a lie? Is art "the lie that speaks the truth," as Cocteau claimed?

Cocteau used to point out that every verse of *Au claire de la lune* was equivocal. You don't have to have a dirty mind, the puns leap out at you.

"'What is truth?' asked jesting Pilate, and would not stay for an answer."

Gosh, I just recalled my essay "Lies: Notes on Craft," published a quarter-century ago in *An Absolute Gift*. Here is the opening page, which states more concisely the points I've just been making:

> My work is my truth. Insofar as that work is also art it is also true for you. That that art may lie makes it no less true. A symbol posing as the real thing betrays itself, yet the betrayal can't disqualify the symbol's status as symbol.
>
> That painting there's not true to life, it's scarcely true to paint. That tune's not natural, not birdsong, not wind's sough, it's false to outdoors. It sounds like nothing else. It lies.
>
> According to who's listening we are all liars. Artist's fables are worth attending. Lies of art ring true.
>
> Am I incapable of truth because I don't know what it is? Whatever truth may be, it's not the opposite of lie. In art it is that which can be cared about, that which we believe.
>
> Those who say, "Look out, he'll quote you in that diary," are the very ones I never notice. The others, they're safe, they can't win, I don't quote, I misquote. Lurking behind the exquisite monster, I'm capable of guidance—that is, of guiding him. The matriarch's mother.
>
> Who most loathe the diary are those depicted within. What they most loathe is not precious archness, not opinions stated as facts nor the urbane reflections posing as pastorale *pensées*, but seeing their life reduced to anecdote, however crass or laudatory. "I was there," they say, "I keep a diary too, I remember what happened, and you're wrong." Of course, there's no such thing as *the* truth, there is only *one's* truth, and even that fluxes with each passing hour. Though I disown nothing, I've come to value discretion, even to claim it among virtues broader than mere truth. Mere truth. Yet in the old days it never occurred to me that friends would feel hurt from my passing verities.

A book's a book, not real life. Yet when offered for real, as a diary, the book must be arranged to seem real. The very arranging teaches an author artifices of life itself, outgrowths which in the telling become more natural than in their larval stage of mere being.

Three years ago on my birthday Lenny Bernstein wrote (in red ink on pale blue paper):

> Very dear Ned:
>   Which shall it be? Or has it already been:
>   1)   Modern? Er . . .
>   And you seek:
>   2)   Eden? Or Mr . . . ?
>   Or are you a Believer:
>   3)   Err? *OM* . . . End . . .
>   Whichever, a very happy birthday, and 60 more.
>   Love Lenny

On 12/1/85, at 1:40 A.M., after having perused my just-published *An American Oratorio*, he wrote (black ink on gray paper):

> "And Ned, a legend urged to flight—" is what you and your new piece are, a piece I have just devouringly read and sung inside, cursing the craven lives [?] of Bernard Holland, applauding all your classy steals (*Peter Grimes, Songfest*), and making, as Ruth Draper says, "one or two *tiny* little suggestions," like rewriting the whole last page (not radically, but so much more beautifully!) and loving every second of it, as I did our dinner-symposium (*very* Plato-ish) on which we touched on 169 subjects each one of which needs and deserves our combined insight which is so powerful because we just frictionate enough in our marginal but real disagreements to inflame each topic so that it acquires urgency, and the warmth of the right-brain informing our hefty intellects (though not always necessarily *lofty* ones), always striking, batting, tickling, trembling for truth that's us. [Illegible: God of sentence] Beginning, I hope, of many more—not only sentences, but hours and notes of days and years. I love you.
>   L
> (To us old lads some thoughts come home
> Who roamed a world young lads no more shall roam.)
>   P.S. I can't shake the illusion that I set *Misgivings*. If not, should have, in *Songfest*. Anyway, it's ours.

(The postscripts refer to my musicalizing of Melville's verse.) Then last year, when my interview with John Simon—apropos of Simon's public remark that "homosexual playwrights should all die of AIDS")—appeared in the *Native*, he wrote:

> Dear good fine smart Ned:
>   I tried to call earlier today, and I leave for Europe tomorrow morning—so this rushed word about your brilliant interview with Simone Simon, in which you and your dog come out total winners. It's fascinating to see what happens when an unRo-

mantic, intellectual, thinker, artist (so rare!) is pitted against a self-styled "severe critic." Bravo.

Love, L 8 May 85

These are samples of Lenny's dozen or so missiles over the years. If not noted here, they'll vanish forever.

JH can't quite buy Lenny. The latter's urban effusions collide with the former's rural reticence. For example, at the "dinner-symposium" referred to, which included the three of us, plus Mendy and Robert Osborne, Jim recalls that Lenny continually attacked me ("Ned, you're so superficial, skipping from topic to topic, without settling on an issue") while lauding his—Jim's—perspicacity ("Jim sticks to the point, and is the most intelligent man in the room."). Lenny does have a penchant for slapping his peers while defending those who, out of taste or lack of notoriety, don't defend themselves.

I don't care much for the Ned portrayed in these pages.

Poulenc never penned an original note: every measure can be traced to Chopin, or Mussorgsky, or Ravel, or Stravinsky, or even Fauré whom he reviled. Yet every measure can be instantly identified as sheer Poulenc, by that mad touch of personal chutzpah that no critic can define.

I am the master in the parlor, the slave in the bedroom. *Le bourreau au salon, la victime au lit.* Which I never write about here. Yet if *The Paris Diary* was a *succès de scandale* thirty years ago, it's pretty tame next to today's ubiquitous gay effusions.

Should this book indeed be called *Lies*? How about *Before I Forget*? Or *Even the Trees* (using Arthur Miller's paragraph as epigraph)?

Do you remember, about twenty minutes into *Psycho*, the cop who questions Janet Leigh through her car window? Do you remember his almost olfactory maleness? the dark goggles which nearly cover his face and which he never removes? how he remains motionless while speaking? and how he eventually drives off after inspecting Leigh's license? Well, I've heard of a certain person who fantasizes about this cop, substituting himself for Janet Leigh, and saying, "I'll give you a blow job you'll never forget." The cop hesitates, then ambles to the other side of the car and gets in. The person instantly gropes him, takes the stiffening dick out of the fly, goes down on it saying, "Don't come too quick," anticipating what Hart Crane named "the warm tonsiling." The person proceeds to moan and gobble the gamy scrotum, while the cop stays silent, and then, after several minutes, comes. End of fantasy.

Now who could that person be! Admitting that it's as improbable today to retrieve that cop as to have an affair with, say, Christopher Marlowe (not for all the tea in China nor all the perfumes of Arabia), is it yet possible to learn who played the role? Is he still alive?

"While you were doing it, did he call you a cocksucker?"

"Yes . . ." Pause. "It was heaven."

"Oh, you know how men are. They're all just great big babies."

Harold Clurman once considered dedicating *The Fervent Years* "To my wife Stella Adler, without whose constant absence this book would never have been written." If our strongest urge is to be with those we love, our second strongest is to get away from those we love. For the artist the second urge is urgent, but he seldom finds legitimate ways to satisfy it.

An artist is never wrong—at least never so long as the essays of his artistry are concerned, if he is a "true" artist and if the particular essay catches fire (for not every essay, even from a genius, bleeds and breathes). By the same token an artist is never right. Right how? Who are we to deem that the added shadow, the substituted semiquaver, the omitted clause on the last page, makes all the difference? Right and wrong are moral concepts, and art aims elsewhere.

Everywhere you hear: Where is our music going? It's a very twentieth-century question, one that would never have been posed by Palestrina or Haydn in days when music served a purpose.

Perhaps music—creative music—is in a quiescent state, our best minds are elsewhere. Maybe classical "serious" music is a thing of the past and all our living composers, you and me included, are barking up a very dead tree. Not that our "best minds" ever cared a hoot about music, or that composers, you and me included, know beans about mathematics. The notion that music is mathematical applies to kindergarten arithmetic; and mathematicians famous for their love of "great music" use that music as relaxation solely.

Ides of March

Visit from Ruth Orkin's daughter, Mary Engel, bringing photographs. At twenty-four she resembles, *en moins fine*, her mother at that age, but with wild dark hair, "highlighted" in bronze, and a determined if innocent notion about her career. (She wants to expand from *Art News*, where she's now in advertising, into editorship elsewhere, including work on Ruth's vast catalogue of photographs. But she knows little about who or what an artist is—even the artists represented in her mag.) We discuss cancer, and Ruth's battle.

The fallacy in the argument in favor of those who have cancer and who, like the valiant Ruth Orkin, can seemingly stay, or even vanquish, the ravages of the disease through the power of positive thinking, is: If they have the power, why did they get cancer in the first place?

Dined at Ellen's with JH, the Gruens, and Darrah Park. On the bus downtown the driver was so hostile to any passenger who presumed to ask him a question

("Where do I get off for West Fourth Street, please?"), that we grew frightened . . . Ellen, as usual, a marvelous meal (roast pork, roast potatoes). John an endless fount of information, gossip, charm . . .

This semester I'm pinch-hitting for David Del Tredici at CCNY. This involves a subway hop to the uptown campus skirting the murderous Morningside Park. The campus itself, the quaint Hamilton House on Convent Avenue, and particularly the music building, look to be appendages of an old monastery. The salary (just one semester, alas!) is thrice that of Curtis, and the students (mainly Asian) are lively and sharp. Yet the hygiene—unlike Curtis, which gleams cleanly—is disquieting. My classroom windows haven't been washed for a year; the wastebasket in which last week I flung some orange peels, still this week contains those peels. As for the men's room, dried semen adorns the seat of an unflushed toilet, while the graffiti are standard if stimulating: "I'd like to suck two cocks at once," "I long for a big dick up my ass," etc. Indeed, the walls are so mono-sexual that it's fun to find in one corner: "It so happens I like grils." But the misspelling has been crossed out by another hand, with "girls" substituted. Beneath this, a third hand plaintively asks: "What's wrong with us grils?"

Nantucket, 2 April
Day after cloudless day of balmy weather for this fugitive week far from urban demands. Sylvia's just left, after 96 hours of relaxed hard work, mostly (I'm embarrassed to say, but not terribly) on setting my affairs in order—a half-dozen commissions, plus contracts for tiny choral pieces, etc. She and JH treat me like a bright nine-year-old. Tantrums of anxiety.

JH's 47th birthday. He's stripping the north bank of its wintry accumulation of dead underbrush, laboring with rake and pitchfork, the eternal cigarette *aux lèvres*, and Sonny roped to the nearby McIntosh apple tree

Reading Barthes again. He always seems nothing more or less than a good-natured and very smart thesis-writer who's thought of a new but ultimately unnecessary slant about an age-old subject. Unnecessary—because there's nothing he says about Proust and Flaubert that Flaubert and Proust haven't already said better.

He hit their Hittite hatter.

My Second Piano Sonata, now 36 years old, is, in hindsight, a solid piece, and certainly, thanks entirely to Julius Katchen, my most popular piece during its heyday in the early 1950s. Today, thanks to publication complications, it is not only forgotten but unavailable, even to me.

For his birthday, I again composed a one-page étude, copied it in colored inks, framed it, and offered it as a gift to be hung on his bedroom wall. I have done this every year since our first, 1967. Has it been nineteen years? If I don't write much about Jim—especially about the nervous breakdown and profound disagreements of yore—that's because I don't want him to read it. But I wouldn't mind his reading that he's "my north, my south, my east and west," and that if it weren't for him I wouldn't be me. Jim is more intelligent than I, and certainly every bit as "musical," even as a composer. (I'd be proud to have signed his *Stabat Mater*.) Our 15½-year age difference accounts, doesn't it?, for his comparative obscurity. He's my dearest friend on earth, and what I feel for him is far deeper than mere love.

One nun to another, while kissing goodbye: "Be good."

Roy Cohn on the Larry King TV show last night put me in mind of that Frenchman who asserts that no one can prove there was a holocaust. Cohn, after buttering up his host by telling King he's one of the few who is fair, exhorts him to name one, just one, innocent person who was ruined by McCarthy. His defense—his *style*—when confronted by the call-in opposition, is to interrupt before the question has been quite posed, roll his eyes impatiently, deny everything (in this case, that he remembered having destroyed the career of the questioner's husband), and to accuse the questioner of stupidity. Cohn, devoid of personality, let alone winsomeness, does have a sort of loathsome force. I don't say this just because I find him wicked. William Buckley is wicked too, yet he's got panache.

JH thinks we've all missed the point of Buckley: that he's a big kidder. Since he's too intelligent to believe his own distortions, his motive for distortion is to keep us jumping, the way a boy torments his kid sister till she bursts into tears of frustration. Buckley's proposition for tattooing homosexuals as potential AIDS carriers has the gay community in a dither. In fact, that community should react as Gore Vidal reacts to Midge Decter: kidding right back. Buckley's having his little joke.

Seeking texts for four works (three choruses—BBC, Franklin & Marshall, a *Te Deum* for Indianapolis—and a voice & orch piece for North Dakota & Bryn Julson). What's left that needs doing? Have I used them all up? Robert Lowell leaves me as cold today as yesterday. There's something wrong about his work that's hard to pinpoint. Not quite a dirtiness, but a willful morbidity, a needless ugliness that's unpoetic (as opposed, for instance, to the *necessary* ugliness of an Alban Berg).

13 April

Awoke from an as-always-light sleep at 4 A.M. to JH's racking cough in the next room. It's a near nightly occurrence (which he never recalls—he sleeps through it), and his morning is often devoted to still more coughing, now less racking than profound, thickly damp, out of control, followed by vomiting *during which* he continues to smoke. (JH consumes nearly three daily packs of unfiltered Pall Malls.) My wakefulness: obsession with how to deal with practical matters (bills, taxes, contracts) after JH has died his hideous death.

The absolute quiet in the eye of the storm. One finds it in certain movies: the silent descent down the stairwell to Hades in *Black Orpheus* (a calm between frantic Sambas); the gentle conversation twixt Hayakawa and Alec Guinness in *The Bridge on the River Kwai* (a calm between frenzied battles). Is this special stillness ever found in music? Yes, maybe in *The Rite of Spring* at the *grande pause* at 71 followed by the Sage's four mysterious measures. Painting can't have it, since it's a sensation of time, of chronology.

Who needs—what is the point of—the Bösendorfer's extension at the bottom of the keyboard? The only time I played one (somewhere with Donald Gramm, maybe in Oklahoma, and *War Scenes*, which opens with the lowest A of a "normal" piano) my left hand continually missed its aim.

Did Marguerite Long play a Bösendorfer? Whatever she played, the playing was wrong—even as Ravel's playing of his own music was wrong—at least to my conditioned ears. A few months older than Ravel, she premièred, under the master's direction, his G-major Concerto as late as 1932, the recording of which was my guide. Not until five years later when I bought the printed score did I realize that, at the soloist's entry on page 4 (*meno vivo*), the last beat of each measure is a triplet, not a grupetto of four 16th notes. Madame Long, true to the Romantic tradition, inevitably let the left hand "announce" the right hand's statement (as, for example, Paderewski does with the "Moonlight" Sonata), thus deforming what appears on the page. Debussy too, according to the old player-piano rolls, misinterpreted his own music. Like Ravel, he composed crisply French phrases which needed no nudging, no interpretation. Both men were twentieth-century composers trapped in the bodies of nineteenth-century interpreters.

Seeking new librettos by rereading (or re-rereading) old plays. *Requiem for a Nun* not only means nothing, is nothing, and has nothing beyond Faulkner's imprint, it's stultifyingly flat. *Tiny Alice*, after the mildly adroit lilt of conversational exchange in the early scenes, has nothing, is nothing, and means nothing beyond the sophomoric discovery that God—that sinister creature—is everywhere and we are all his children getting the short end of the stick. (*Tiny Alice* owes less to Dürrenmatt's *Visit* than to *The Maltese Falcon* with that naughty gang wreaking havoc and skipping town. Alice is Mary Astor, the Cardinal is Greenstreet, etc.)

22 April

Visit from Ben Cheever. Difference in our family backgrounds. He with a drunk and horny parent who preached propriety and was anxious about "effeminacy"; I with sober and orderly parents who were less concerned with appearances than with ideas. It was not so much uncomfortable as merely odd discussing my having slept with Ben's father. But that's why he was here. (JH refused to meet with him, though he'd have had much to add.) Easier to talk with him than with a woman.

On this date in 1938 I lost my "virginity" on a Chicago sofa with Perry O'Neill.

Chicago, 24 April

The so-called Press Lunch this noon at the Arts Club involved me, the orchestra's publicist, and twelve local "entertainment" reviewers of every sex and color, including John Von Rhein and feisty, pontifical, and finally likeable Robert Marsh. I said, "Mrs. Simpson died today," to which the reviewer from *Chicago Magazine* replied, "Dotson Rader claims she was very good at oral sex." Stunned, I could only stammer, "Who isn't?"

28 April

David Del Tredici's huge Alice thing yesterday. Yes, it is about length—if cut, it wouldn't work, in all its tedious splendor. Yet length is its undoing. Nothing much really happens in the piece. The tunes are good, but they don't modulate or (despite DDT's contention) develop.

Nantucket, 5 May

Since the tribute to Eva Gauthier last Friday I've had qualms. My statement, as moderator, was flip, self-serving, anecdotal at Gauthier's expense, and, above all, off the cuff, a talent that isn't mine (accustomed as I am to public speaking). I didn't explain who Eva *was*, or how her individuality and value have only increased with her death. What *was* her value and individuality? It seems silly to have to stress the obvious: that Gauthier knew French literature, knew what words meant, and knew how to construct a song recital. These virtues, taken for granted then, are lost today.

Afterward, with Morris, a minute with Robert and Becki, who gave us gifts of wit and anxiety and Colette's book. Then uptown to Alex Katz's vernissage. Huge portrait of Ada. Ada herself was present. She looks like an Alex Katz.

As in Chicago last week, at the Gauthier thing folks emerged from the woodwork. Little if any feeling about this anymore.

Reagan's utter ignorance of Moslem morality. Assumption that the Libyans, like Reagan himself, are only too anxious to rid themselves of Qaddafi. In my thirty months in Morocco, one thing I learned is that Islam and Christianity are not the same. Reagan on Qaddafi: "The mad dog of the Middle East." But Libya is in North Africa.

The Atlanta Symphony has canceled their Paris performance, including, alas, my String Symphony, not because of bomb scares, but to *deprive* France—a retaliation for France's having withheld permission for our planes to fly over during the Libya raid three weeks ago.

JH says it's time I stopped declaring that opera's future is in film. It's a notion I first posited twenty years ago and have been parroting ever since, while in reality movies and opera have been daily changing all around me. And stop saying I can set anything—even the phone book—to music. *Au point où j'en suis.* I'd give anything for a good phone book.

Frank Rizzo and Morris both phone to say, among other things, that J.J. Mitchell's memorial yesterday was a "success"—that, unlike some memorials, the creature mourned was somehow present. I knew nothing about it. Apparently *Early in the Morning* was sung. It would have been good to attend. But perhaps, like J.J. himself, I *was* there.

Death of Henry McIlhenny, the last of a breed. He was our sole remaining American patron to operate as an individual. And a fabled host. To him I owe my introduction to Ormandy decades ago, which led to so many performances of five different pieces: *Eagles, Design, Sunday Morning*, Third Piano Concerto, *Pilgrims*. Three of these were world premières.

Demoralized by the bad write-ups of the Vln. Concerto in Poughkeepsie. (Miriam Fried.)

The pianist Sahan Arzruni is negotiating with the State Chorus of Armenia for me to compose, *in Armenian!*, a series of unaccompanied songs. To do so, I'll pick from free translations of fourteenth-century verse, then Sahan will transcribe them phonetically as well as read them, slowly, into a tape machine.

Today he brought over a disc of beautiful contemporary Armenian songs he wants me to endorse, which I herewith do:

> A unique contradiction seems imbedded in the typical American music-lover of our century: He likes only what is far in time but close in space. Shunning the music of today, he nonetheless favors old music from his immediate culture. Contemporary American music is as foreign to him as the classics of China, while the classics of Western Europe soothe him more than any nineteenth-century composer from the East.
>
> True, music is not a universal language but an attitude, of one consciousness and of one environment, which does not easily slip past the customs inspector. We are not all the same—it is difference, not increasing similarity, which lends Earth's dwellers their beauty, wisdom, mystery, and, indeed, their identity. But if this identity is never fully grasped by a dweller from another environment, sometimes it can be sensed, appreciated, and even loved, especially if the identity lies in works of art. (Art has little to do with understanding anyway, but with feeling.)
>
> The present disc contradicts the contradiction. This garland of Armenian song—although from far in space and near in time—could satisfy the needs of any fancier of Schubert *Lied*. The arch and ebb of the tunes, although conceived mostly by recent composers, reflect a folkish prosody that borrows, as *Lied* does, from surrounding cultures—Greek, Turkish, Arab, Russian—while retaining its signature as

Armenian. That local signature lies in the ictuses of the native tongue, just as American music—even non-vocal music—can be distinguished from British by dint of mirroring the emphases of its composer's spoken language. My meaning will be clear the moment you hear the virile velvet of Berberian's bass-baritone as it rises and falls (with what passionate intelligence!) to the inspiration of his countrymen, and the caringly expert pianism of Sahan Arzruni as it limns the sad, odd, gay, and above all, flowing melodies to which he was born. I myself was born a Midwestern WASP and weaned on Ives and Griffes. But when I heard these Armenian songs, I felt they too were mine.

Omaha, 21 May

Our house on Wesco Place seen from the air, as we fly away from Nantucket, is not our house but a brownish square in the green, then a smear in a marsh, then a speck, then nothing. But for JH and the animals it remains their abode wherein they may or may not be thinking of me, or gazing toward the sky at the receding dot. Reality, even face to face, is fluid: reference, relationship, proximity.

Here in Nebraska where Leonard plays the Organ Concerto, and where cousin Kathryn is host. Touched by the accent, softer than Arkansans who split vowels into two syllables (Nay-ud for Ned), and by the unashamed friendliness of everyone from the pilot to the chambermaid. I avoid feeling they're hickish . . . Alan B. (whom I met 25 years ago at the Everard Baths), now married with children, phones trying to fix me up with teenagers. No thanks.

Title: "After a Reading of 'After a Reading of Dante' by Liszt," by Ned Rorem.
    What is a "crucible"? a "watershed"?
    More associations: accept, except = potato chips.

Friday the 13th June

Sorting pictures for *The Nantucket Diary*. Have chosen about eighty, including one of Virgil by Tom Victor. Since there is no fiscal allowance for photographs, I must negotiate each clearance. Spoke with Tom Victor, who was not even courteous about saying no. "You'll have to use someone else's picture," said he curtly, and hung up. I too am often asked to lend my talents for this or that, with fluctuating fees, and now have a policy about what to say yes or no to. Surely Tom by now has a policy, if only to say no politely to friends.

JH working on name index for diary. The diary is nothing but names—names of humans. Colette's book of *Flowers & Fruit*. Would that I could concentrate on—commune with—the vegetable kingdom *as a friend*, the way she does.

Paul Goodman once published a small book called *The World I Live in Is Mine*, letters of reaction, cranky or otherwise, to periodicals. (Most of these were not published, or even acknowledged.) I shall do the same. Here now is one to the Sunday Book Section of the *Times*.

"Snob is a purely English term," writes Tom Wolfe in his putdown of Cecil Beaton today, but in fact the original is French (or so the French claim), being the peasant's elision of *c'est noble*—that which is upper-class. (Webster's gives its first—now obsolete—definition as "member of the lower classes, shoemaker.")

"Art and snobbery were inextricable for Cecil Beaton," continues Wolfe. Well yes, and they're inextricable for Wolfe too, as they are—indeed, must be—for every artist who needs to make a living. Haydn was a musician of the court, and Bach's life's blood flowed in pandering, as did Michelangelo's and Picasso's and Henry James's and Proust's. The only difference is that Beaton admits it where Wolfe—with his redneck notion of the Right Stuff and the Painted Word—does not. Wolfe implies, in his antiintellectualism, that snobbism is not "a good thing," at least for him and his kind; yet was he never photographed, in white shantung and jewelled stickpin by America's Beaton, butch Avedon? Like Frederick Brown, who chose to spend years with a subject he manifestly disdained (Jean Cocteau), there is no paragraph of Wolfe's without a sneer, and not a word about Beaton's gifts, his contributions. He's snide about Beaton's anxiety at being called "fairy" and "queer," and giggles about Beaton's youth at Cambridge where "well-born boys jumped into closets during homosexual riots and licked one another's ears." Don't heterosexuals have self-doubts? Don't they, as youngsters, lick one another's ears? Wolfe does compare Beaton to the classical famous—Becky Sharp and Joan of Arc; but why only to women? Why not to Rastignac or Lincoln? Wolfe reacts to homosexuality as to a creature in a zoo—a strict chic creature—and gives Beaton no benefit of the doubt in describing the affair with Garbo (whom Beaton "contrived to meet"—why not just say he met her?) whose reactions Wolfe presumes to know, never suggesting that she too was homosexual. Although Wolfe admits that Beaton's war pictures were "highly praised," he arranges a sentence to imply that Beaton said that "war was not chic," and that once the war was over, Beaton never so much as pointed his camera at the little people . . . again." The same little people immortalized by Proust and Henry James? Wolfe uses French on three occasions (all three phrases, incidentally, using the word *monde*) because for him a French phrase, like a limp wrist, is the height of mockery. In short, Wolfe criticizes a genre for merely existing, rather than for whether the genre is used well or ill. To criticize a genre for itself is of course a specious mode, but ideal for dismissing people more talented than oneself—as Wolfe dismissed the Radical Chic, although Bernstein has demonstrably done more good than Wolfe for "the little people" in his concerts for AIDS relief, for Israel, etc.

Cecil Beaton was a shy, likeable, vaguely silly (to an American) and madly gifted person of a variety that doesn't grow over here. Why are even our own hothouse beauties like Tom Wolfe so leery of . . . and so forth.

Lanford Wilson, pride of our land with his thoughtful scripts and his Pulitzer Prize, states in the current *Village Voice* (June 10): "Dear Editor: What a wonderfully thought-out and well-researched article by Erika Munk. A really good piece of work; and fucking terrifying." How's that for hip writing!

Nantucket, 16 June

Dined last night with Eugenie at 21 Federal, my one annual foray into a public eatery. I hate good food. But I loved the visit afterward to her half-done house in Orange Street, and its Shaker-like spotlessness. Eugenie lent me Auberon Waugh's new (to me) *Literary Review*. Pretty good. Like all such reviews, though, both abroad and at home, it has everything except a classical music column.

Foundering with *Homer*. The decision, after six months of speculating, to set three pages from the *Iliad* for chorus and a few instruments, may end up being too close for comfort to Satie's *Socrate*. Oh well. Just as Literary Reviews have everything except music columns, so devoted Satilophiles know everything about his *oeuvre* except his one great piece. How many could tell the difference . . .

Long talk with Rosemary about whether Mother, at nearly 89, should be taken off Meloril, put onto Lithium, or have shock treatments again. Yet, as JH points out, most people Mother's age are dead.

19 June

"The Supreme Court ruled unanimously today that sexual harassment of an employee by a supervisor violates the Federal law against sex discrimination in the workplace." So reports the *Times*. A good law, so far as it goes, but ill-worded. Sexual harassment is not sexual discrimination, it's sexual harassment, and the law should be against sexual harassment simply. But this law itself is discriminatory. It assumes a male-dominated society, and protects women against that society. Will the law protect a female employee harassed by a female supervisor? or a male employee harassed by a female—or male—supervisor?

sans date

To be continually obsessed with sex, except during the act, when the mind wanders.

If all is vanity, then so is the act of noting that all is vanity.

If, while working at the piano, I hum or sing or squeak as composers do, Sonny, wherever he is, begins to moan.

Since before Shakespeare *tower* and *flower* are noted as one-syllable words rhyming with *hour*. Is *hour* ever made to rhyme with *four*?

> *Olorimes:*
> He's a bad sight reader, but a good sigh treader.
> You need dough — Ewe, knead dough
> for tunes — fortunes
>
> *Toward a palindrome:*
> gnat — tang   speed on — no deeps
> ogre — ergo   stop a slap — pals a pots
> Eton — note   parts — strap

gas — sag
spool — loops
lever — revel
drawer — reward
palindrome — emordnilap
Barab — Barab
Nin — Nin
Dennis — Sin Ned

Gorgeous — gorger

stun — nuts
evil — live
edit — tide
abut — tuba
radar — radar
Evian — naive
Boston — not sob

A torture: His left wrist is fastened to a wall. He is given an ax, the house is set on fire. He can escape only by mutilating himself. (But he will never escape, for the house too is surrounded by fire.)

Nantucket, 24 June

Pandemonium. Before anyone is up Joe B., JH's helper, appears, two weeks late, to paint the eaves which are now overgrown with ivy. Sonny, who hates Joe, yaps uncontrollably while JH has seizures of emphysematic coughing, and forgets to drive me to Dr. Voorhees for my annual checkup. So I take a taxi, and am regaled by the driver, Mrs. Peterson, of her husband's questionable health.

Voorhees finds nothing amiss. The cyst on my inside lower lid, which he injected two years ago, has abated. But after the little list of woes (breast bone, aching thumb, corns, herpes, stinging urine, the incubation period for AIDS virus), I bring up two main concerns: Mother's listlessness and JH's smoking. Well, Mother, who is listless partly because of her daily does of Haldan, is of an age when most people have been dead for ten years. As for JH's smoking, the damage is done (says Voorhees), and to stop would be to call forth ulcers, depression, road accidents, and similar appointments in Samarkand. Does Voorhees, as an objective and presumably heterosexual physician, feel that AIDS may rule what's left of the animal kingdom in another decade or two? Inscrutable as always, he answers that it might not be such a bad idea. I bid him goodbye, saying I thought of him lately while reading Simenon's *L'Ours en peluche* about a highly successful Parisian gynecologist, who arranges nevertheless to commit suicide by shooting the lover of his mistress and then waiting for the cops to come. A doctor, no matter how accomplished, does spend most of his waking hours seeing people at their worst.

After months of wrestling for a proper text (something "uplifting" for the amateur choir of Franklin & Marshall), I've settled on three pages from *The Iliad*—very uplifting, to a pacifist!—and am wrestling now with how to musicalize these pages, in my own translation. Rosemary sent Simone Weil's strong and somber essay, *A Poem of Force*, which compares Homer's subject to the holocaust, and next to her exegesis my tunes seem pallid stuff. I'm proud, nonetheless, of my radically trimmed arrangements, using Samuel Butler's translation mostly.

I also misunderstand the American government, as in the current administration. It's my country too, and I'm embarrassed by what is daily perpetrated. As of yesterday the "sodomy in private" law is firm, and I feel like a Jew in 1944. Not that anyone is committing much sodomy in private these days, what with the horribly constant specter of the plague. More passing friends have been snatched up, Mario Amaya, David Kalstone, Bobby Drivas, all blessed with humor and talent. I, who loathe any change in routine (even to dining an hour late on Tuesdays, here in Nantucket, because of Sonny's weekly training class), dread each new day for its implicit bleakness. The Supreme Court elegantly dismisses as "facetious" the objection that homosexuals deserve a right to privacy. Reagan claims that "too much SALT is bad for you." The noble thinkers of our century, Auden, Proust, Paul Goodman, Henry James, Copland, Simone Weil, will survive long after Meese and Schultz (who ignore even to their names these thinkers) have vanished without a trace. Unless the world's suicide absorbs us all.

Television critics rarely discuss how music is used in the nighttime soaps (the scores for most of them are very "composed," expert, expensive), much less do they examine by comparison. For example, how is the scoring—the orchestration—of *Knots Landing* made to enhance suspense with its movie-type sting chords, as opposed to the more pop frenzy of *Miami Vice*? Yet *Miami Vice*, in a segment once involving a small girl in a large house, enhanced a sustained silence by paradoxically superimposing the sound of what seemed an unaccompanied Russian male chorus in a languid, chromatic, sinuous chant. Was this chant created by *Miami Vice*'s credited musician, Jan Hammer? [Dec. 1990: A week ago, I saw this segment again. Oddly, the male chorus seems to have been rearranged for just orchestra.]

Does Barbara Walters, now that she's God, with her classy clothes and mounded coiffeur, the dropped R's and compassionate gaze, the tone of "I'm every bit as important as these stars," and the illegitimate encroachment on the journalist's code through expressing opinion (as she did, on the exiled Duvaliers in last Sunday's *Times*, rather than simply allowing the Duvaliers to hang themselves on their own rhetoric), does Barbara Walters recall everyone she's ever interviewed? In 1966 I was granted ten minutes on her radio series, apropos of the publication of *Music from Inside Out* (eight lectures on the structure and esthetics of musical composition), and was fitted betwixt—as I recall—a wrestler and a fertilizer salesman. But Barbara was not at a loss, and I liked her a lot.

Does Jacques d'Amboise, now that he too is God, with his ever-so-noble dedication to bringing True Art to the young—does he recall everyone he's been rude to? It would have been in 1956 or '57, the first time Ormandy every played a piece of mine—*Eagles*, or was it *Design*?—in the Philadelphia Academy, and I was elated. Since I was to take my bow from the stage, the manager asked if I'd mind hearing the piece from the wings, offered me a dressing room to wait in, and left. Where-upon d'Amboise stormed in, saying, "Get out of here. This is my room." I was all the more discountenanced in that I was an admirer of the famous dancer.

How many people have I involuntarily offended over the years, by summary dismissal?

Helen Hayes and Fred Astaire, my two unfavorite folks, are co-billed in a tear-jerker.

Janáček and Busoni: two more underrated composers who are overrated. It's hard to get the point of them. But then, I don't get the point of Berlioz either, or of Bruckner.

Respighi was almost as crucial as Ravel, and still (though I seldom hear him—perhaps *because* I seldom hear him) can, like Delius, underline certain experiences of my first fourteen years.

Critics sometimes say, about this or that new work—it should be taken up by all our major orchestras and recorded. It never is. Critics have great power, but they have no power.

If Tom Wolfe had giggled about kikes as he does about fruits, he would . . .

I do feel old. Less old, perhaps, than Father who is not indifferent to the charms of various females at Cadbury, but older than every one on the panel, cited in the current (July 8) *Advocate*, about "Sex in the Age of AIDS." Yet when the younger ones state that "You're less than a whole person if you can survive without sex," while Martin Duberman (who's been without sex for two years) replies, "I have to disagree with the idea that celibacy must always be a form of psychological denial," shouldn't he add that he's many years older than the others, and has had, as the saying goes, his share of kicks?

Bruce Springsteen's painful rasp, hate-filled and talentless, like all the rest (but which Rockwell depicts as the *passion* of youth).

End of the Statue of Liberty celebrations on television. (Had I known that Emma Lazarus's sonnet was so famous, would I have used it to open *An American Oratorio*?) High point: Elizabeth Taylor, breathtaking in white chiffon which the dark breeze twirled about her good legs, as a female ensign escorted her twenty yards across the stage to the podium. Low point: Reagan's cant, and a patriotic duet by Kenny Rogers and Willie Nelson which, had it been submitted to *The Gong Show*, would have been rejected.

The Scarlet Empress (on Frank's VCR), starring John Lodge (Henry Cabot Jr.'s kid brother, who later went into Republican politics), proves again to be odd and arty as hell, but satisfying except for the intrusive score pasted together mainly from Tchaikovsky's Fourth.

Long and likeable letters from Dutilleux and Sauguet, to whom I sent young

Helgeson and Zivian who are spending their summer in France. Nostalgia for Paris, which I shall doubtless never see again.

Struggling—but not savagely, and with little conviction—on *Homer*, treating it strictly as a duty. How, after all, do you put such words to music? In the stark *dépouillé* style of Chávez's *Antigone*? In the witty telegraphic style of Honegger's *Antigone*? If *Pilgrim Strangers* was criticized for lacking the strength of Whit- man's text, isn't that precisely because I avoided mickey-mousing Whitman with groans and screams? How heighten Whitman, or indeed Homer, except by letting the words ride clearly on clear tunes? Those words need not be *interpreted*.

Across from me as I write this, at the long dining room table, sits JH, into his third week of indexing the new book. (What is he incapable of? He's transformed the half-acre surrounding the house into a Maeterlinckian park.) If, says he, there's in fact been less terrorism since the Libyan bombing, it is because terrorists assume they're dealing with rational foes (no pilot will call their bluff, etc.) and therein lies their cunning force. When terrorists deal with the irrational, e.g., Rea- gan, they hush. For the moment.

The diary. Less tough than before. Shallow words in a shallow world.

After a year or so of quiescence, the spastic urethra, which so plagued me from 1980 to 1984, has returned, unannounced, like a terrorist.

Who wrote "Maybe"? Who wrote "I'll Be Seeing You"? Who wrote "As Time Goes By" and "It Never Entered My Mind"?

Nantucket, July

Rosette Lamont's mother, age 88, was murdered in Paris a month ago. Just spoke at length with Rosette, who's beside herself. A drug killing of the elderly, prevalent today in France it seems. Ludmilla, so harmless, intelligent and likeable, was smothered with a blanket. Rosette's reaction today is mindful of the Première Prieure on her deathbed: *"J'ai medité sur la mort chaque heure de ma vie, et cela maintenant ne me sert de rien!"*

Night after night at four A.M., Sam's Siamese yowl peels away my sleep like bark, leaving me flayed and hopelessly awake until dawn.

Nancy Reagan has promised her memoirs, for an "undisclosed sum," to "a major publishing firm." Meanwhile, the White House has again bestowed laurels on var- ious very senior citizens in the arts, including Aaron Copland and Eudora Welty. Copland, unable to grace the official meal in Washington, was represented by Vivian Perlis. Vivian reports that a discussion on writing, between Miss Welty and Mrs. Reagan, was something to hear.

Danny Pinkham has a slick French accent: his American heritage is belied only because the intonation is a little *too* French. Danny also does something I don't do: when speaking a French word within an English phrase ("Poulenc was not basically a *pédéraste*," for example) he utters the word *à la française*, correctly. I'm inclined, when speaking English, to utter the word *à l'anglaise*, for the sake of clarity and flow. Similar, when using an English word while talking French, I'll pronounce it as the French would (birthday becomes *beersday*), although it goes against my nature and I cringe.

Danny's on the island, and so is Virgil, because we're all having songs sung on Tuesday's program. VT very much the old star, and lovable. Picture-taking at Mary Heller's in Sconset.

2 August

Dined with Eugenie, and two of her friends, in her almost-finished house on Orange Street.

Nice anecdote about Peter Benchley and the not-too-bright brother of Mr. Glidden who sometimes sits behind the cash register at the Glidden's Fish Store.

The brother: "Hear you make books."

Peter B. "Well, I write the words. Other people set the type, bind the pages, design the cover."

Glidden's brother (losing interest): "Oh, you have help."

For the catalogue of flawless cameos:

Regina Sarfaty singing Bill Flanagan's "Send Home My Long-Strayed Eyes" in 1959.

Marie Blanche de Polignac singing Monteverdi's *Amor* in 1937.

Flagstad singing Grieg's songs in Paris, 1953.

Tourel . . .

Tiresome hostesses (or, for the sake of feminists, let's say hosts) who are coyly adamant about divulging their recipes for a cheese dip or an orange soufflé. But even allowing the unallowable—that the same ingredients in new hands will taste the same—does a good hostess ever repeat herself? If her dish is so luscious, it becomes famous, therefore never to be repeated.

21 August

Two weeks of sore throat raw and aching, plus a cough and night sweats. Unreassuring is frequent reading of *The Advocate* and the *Native*, which drip with symptoms of AIDS. JH in Kansas for his annual trek. I alone with the cats and with Sonny who, despite my fever and a hurricane, I must take for his 5-times-daily (what's the word? Like thrice for three) promenades. Tomorrow for tea: the ladies from Sconset, plus Eugenie, Martha Lipton, Gerri Feder, and Jean Branch. The Sapphic contingent, also Jewish . . . At least they're not communist.

J'ai vu trois dames de Sconset
Le long les tristes quais
J'ai vu trois dames de Sconset
Voilà un siècle au joli mois de mai

Town ever more crowded, with breeders, by the apparent trillions, and adolescents with transistors on mopeds. Am less annoyed than scared.

The growth which Voorhees removed from my eyelid two years ago is a kind of cyst known as a "chalazion." *On dirait une fleur.* A field of chalazions waving in the breeze.

JH, discombobulated on returning from his annual Midwest visit to his parents: "Either Kansas is real, or New York is real, but they can't both be real."

After more than two weeks he still goes through the tortures of hell with his tobacco withdrawal. When I stopped (the final stopping, that is—I stopped many times) I didn't climb the wall, nor did I grow fat. I had formerly eaten in order to smoke, sweets especially. Cigarettes never tasted good after, say, celery or milk or soda water, but with devil's food cake and coffee. When I stopped smoking, I stopped eating—eating so as to smoke, that is.

Alcoholic. Would I have been alcoholic had I been raised in France? My drinking was conjoined *tellement* to a sense of guilt, a guilt the French do not by definition share, they being raised on red wine from the cradle. (Guilt maybe about wanting to be passive in bed, which, if you're drunk, is acceptable.)

Blue is for boys, pink is for girls. Blue and pink together are lavender.

"Rock me" are the first words Mother remembers me saying. Later she told us the grammatical anecdote about the mother with the demanding child:

"I want to be read to."

"What book do you want to be read out of?" (He tells her, but inadvertently she brings the wrong volume.)

"Why did you bring me that book to be read to out of from for?"

Because we so seldom dine out, JH and I, after a series of shorts and sandals, got all bathed and shaved and be-suited with new shirts—but no neckware—to join Mimsi Harbach and her other guest, Jean MacAusland (widow of *Gourmet* magazine), at the Yacht Club, where we'd never been. No sooner were we seated than the waitress told us that ties were *de rigueur* for men, and that the management would provide some. I gazed at the surrounding tables of mainly septuagenarian clients whose sensibilities were presumably outraged at our unclad necks, told the poor waitress that we were not about to sport someone else's greasy ties, that we were "makers of manners," that at sixty-two I had certainly learned to dress, that her silly law was already out-of-date a generation ago, that it never applied to women, and this was one hell of a sordid welcome. Meanwhile Jean went to the desk, and actually purchased (for who knows what extraordinary sum) a pair of dotted *noeuds papillon* which we docilely donned. I did apologize to Mimsi, who had planned a special evening, for I'm not given to public scenes. But after all that, the cuisine, which should have been splendid, was mediocre, leaving a sour aftertaste.

Glimpsed a hummingbird this afternoon, the second one in twelve years here, whirring amidst the overabundance of blood-red impatiens in our six white window boxes. During a split second it shot up twenty yards to the telephone wires, tremored a moment, then vanished.

Most of the season's reading has been blurb books, bound proofs (those wobbly unmanageable galleys now, thank God, are a thing of the past) of other people's soon-to-be-published masterpieces whose editors are now soliciting free publicity: Purdy's novel, Coleman Dowell's stories, Meryle Secrest's portrait of Dalí, Stambolian's collection of Gay Fiction, and other bonbons that go unacknowledged. But, other than *Barchester Towers*, most of my chosen *livres de chevet* here have been non-fiction (mainly periodicals three hours a day) except for Alison Lurie's *Foreign Affairs*, presented as a house gift by David Sachs.

Frances Fergusen's mammoth pair of essays on *la chose* (as Gide named it) must be considered a breakthrough for *The New Yorker*, which has been squeamish hitherto. She does for gays what Nero did for Christians: casts them as the scapegoat for the spread of evil. That *New Yorker* readers should now for the first time be exposed to homosexuality via Fergusen's ugly misrepresentation (she implies that gays brought AIDS onto themselves) seems nonetheless not accidental, given the right-wing turn taken by the magazine since the sale last year, viz. Renata Adler's garbled account of CBS vs. Westmoreland.

Five weeks since Jim gave up smoking. Result—a depression has set in which he likens to the one eight years ago which he hoped would never return. Man, because unlike animals he attaches a meaning to life, looms like some horrid mutant. In fact (Jim feels) man is alone among the beasts to see life as the senseless mediocrity it is. His sentiment is gloomy and infectious. I try to pretend that life "gels," and that I get joy from "simple pleasures," but really I continue *faute de mieux*. Played my new motets for JH who found nothing better to say than that they're "difficult." With each new day I wonder how I'll get through it—how *he* will. He, meanwhile, retires to his basement hideaway and watches TV wrestling matches, or plays the PacMan game in the VCR.

It is important not to succumb too early, for we'll all die anyway. Animals have infinite faith in us. The clematis seethes with fragrance on the side deck as I perform my morning calisthenics. JH has gone back to New York at dawn this morning on the ferry with Sonny in a rented car (the truck broke down). Tomorrow I too leave, for a week to get the classes started at Curtis. Then back here for three weeks. Summer is over, yet scarcely begun. Last night JH came back to life as we played a new recording of his beloved Messiaen (an English organist, Jennifer Dunn, rather butch and rife with conviction, in the *Méditations sur le Mystère de la Sainte Trinité*).

Joe LeSueur's sordid story of the wake of JJ's death. Like the wake of Poulenc's death. Everything went wrong.

Arthur Danto, who writes so expertly, so readably, on art in *The Nation*, is the only critic of painting that I read. But when he calls Franz Kline a great man, what am I to think of him? (More on Kline, whose back window faced mine when I lived at 213 West 13th in the late '50s.) Franz Kline and all the others: mudpies. Miss Nevelson: mudpies.

Entrenched again in Simenon. *Le Train* is worthy of Dostoevsky, Graham Greene.

Write sometime on Jacques Février. On Mompou in Barcelona in May 1952.
    Write on how, but for some fortuity, a song might not exist. It was Paul Moor, in Munich in 1954, who loaned me Hillyer's poem "Early in the Morning," and suggested it would make an apt setting. It's become my hit tune. (And from where did I filch that tune?)

The anxiety with every rental of Mrs. Quigley's house on Wesco Place, which, since her death, has become . . .
    Spongy gums, ache, bleed, need tending.
    Charm and class are not the same thing. Sandra, for instance, has the one but not the other, while Jessica has the other but not the one. Martita has both, Helena has neither.

New York, 14 September
Back in the city, the first things noticed are the certifiable crazies on every corner, and the non-WASP emphasis of Columbus Avenue. Nantucket seems safe, antiseptic, remote. Central Park rife with beauty and idiocy, women overreacting to "their men," the Daniloff affair an expensive waste of time, bombings in Paris. And on the radio *The Wanderer Fantasy,* the one piece which, when I hear it coming, makes me run the other way. Schubert's touted humility is unapparent in this boisterous fustian whose coda insults, etc. . . . On the television George C. Scott's *Patton*, an oaf we now compare to Olivier, who's something of an oaf himself perhaps. If Scott's the best we have, we don't need any worst. Tomorrow, Curtis. And the new students.

Under the desk I found a scrap of paper, dropped no doubt from these diary notes many years ago: "At the *Éclair*—in this very store—had tea, the child's father, breaks the heart in passing—never saw him again."

Another sound-alike: The fugitive five-note motif at measure 64 in the last movement of Mahler's Ninth, and "Why Can't You Behave?"

Long day. Down to Philadelphia for second session with new Curtis students, all eager, serious, conservative, prolific. Discussion of song-writing. Assign three poems for them to set (Whitman, Gertrude Stein, Hopkins), with a taboo against using twice any phrase used only once by the poet. For a composer to repeat words in a sung version of a sonnet is to repeat the punch line of a joke.

At 4:30 promptly Rosemary and Per pick me up at Locust Street and we drive to Cadbury to dine with parents. A table in the little library, that lies midway between Mother's "wing" and Father's, has been set up for us, and Father's friend Mrs. Peacock (a youngster of eighty-four) has contributed a huge white & pink cake with a thick 7-minute frosting of the sort I used to burn my hands making in our Chicago kitchen half a century ago. Mother, looking alert with a well-done "flapper" haircut, asks, "Are you Ned?" Father, over-agitated because of his continually sore foot, and because he wants things to go smoothly, both does and doesn't want Mother and Mrs. Peacock to cross paths. Various black female interns bring us trays, and businesslike nurses are up and down the halls, more or less ignoring the sometimes gentle, sometimes violent, keening of nonagenarians— "Let me out of here, I want to go home." Yet Cadbury no longer depresses me. Mother's wing is, yes, institutional and weird, but also epic in span and even affable—hardly a snake pit. Father's wing is oaken, Swiss, lofty, like the Magic Mountain.

Father no longer quotes "Ol' Man River"—"I'm tired of living and scared of dying"—but does announce that Yarnell finally succumbed after a six-month bout with what sounds like a pneumocystis pneumonia, or another AIDS-related affliction. I had a notion Yarnell was gay when we first met four years ago. Who was Yarnell? He was the nice-looking social worker, age 31, who officially greeted and advised the new renters of Cadbury. "We of the administration," I distinctly recall him saying, as he showed me around the nine-acre property, "are chosen partly because of our experience, but also because we are young—which reassures the residents."

Per and Rosemary drove me back from New Jersey to 30th Street Station, whence I caught the 8:26 back to Manhattan where I write this.

Eight-hour marathon, called *American in Paris*, yesterday at Merkin Hall to honor Virgil's pending ninetieth birthday. Will & I performed *Banalités* (which I've been playing beautifully since before Will was in diapers, but which he said I "rushed"), two songs of mine (including "Early in the Morning," appropriately, which Crutchfield calls my "best" song, but which, of course, isn't), and two by Virgil (including "The Little Black Boy," in his best hand-crossing antimacassar style, on Blake's vaguely racist verses, during which a Negro in the front row arose and walked out). Brought Shirley back later for herbal tea, and we talked glumly of AIDS and the hopeless bombings in Paris. Gray clouds all over the sky like Valhalla's filthy laundry. Spoke this morning with Virgil, agog with the (deserved) attention he's getting from all over. Says that many of our old friends (Roger Baker, Theodate) are now in A.A., which he refers to as the Prayer Meeting.

Nantucket, 25 September
After a long week in New York, mainly to get class started in Philly, am back for a short month in Nantucket, mainly to orchestrate *Homer*, and to write the Baudelaire choruses (in the English of Richard Howard) and a piano piece for the Kapell competition.

Sarraute portrait to *Yale Review*.

In the intervening week autumn has fallen grandly upon the island. Nature is fading, although roses are making a highly perfumed last ditch stand of perfect pink on JH's patio trellis. Our little apple tree, planted three years ago and which bore fruit copiously last October, is barren this fall. Everywhere pruning goes on with large signs announcing: MEN IN TREES.

Nantucket, 27 September
Phoned Phyllis late in the evening (her voice sounded thick but she swore I hadn't awakened her) to show interest in Gene's memorial, which took place this afternoon in Boston. How commendably like Phyllis to have programmed only twentieth-century music: Shostakovich's Eighth Quartet, and "the pizzicato movement" from Bartók's Fourth. I told her I'd get out my copy of the latter as soon as we hung up, and think of Gene. And so I did, concentrating on the Fourth but perusing them all (as I do every few years), especially the First—which I'd known so well when rooming at the Gabis' in 1943 during the chamber-music orgies in the living room—and the Fifth, which George Perle first showed me, circa 1945, suggesting that those twenty-two crucially irrelevant measures, *con indifferenza*, from the last movement reminded him of a lost child (Wozzeck's son?) or a demented organ grinder.

What models, those six quartets! After them, all others seem superfluous. (Carter revived the genre, and Diamond and Milhaud.) Yet, although whenever I hear it I am filled with admiration, Bartók's music as a whole is a music I never think about when it's not around. It's impeccable, it's theatrical, it's even great. It dazzles, thrills, horrifies, sometimes irritates, but also moves me. But I'm not *touched* by it, as by, for instance, the outset of the quartet by Ravel—Ravel, supposed to be icy, formal, above all that. The notion that French music is objective, nose-thumbing, brittle, anti-romantic, is a notion I've never grasped. French music makes me cry.

Russell Oberlin phoned, returning a call from JH who was anxious to find a counter-tenor for the Purcell *Te Deum* in November. Russell hadn't called back sooner because he'd been in Akron where his old mother had died. He seems undone. I empathize. In three weeks I'll be 63. Three weeks later Father will be

92, and three weeks after *that* Mother turns 89. We're getting on. Yet it's inconceivable that they'll ever die—that I'll become an orphan with no one to turn to.

My herpes—my *harpies*—have sprung out again, five days ago (shortly after the quarrel with JH), this time with an angry maroon imprint the size of a fifty-cent piece on the left buttock. If it runs its usual course, the tiny pustules will explode tomorrow, smear and seep, dry up, and vanish gradually during the next ten days. Meanwhile, JH has taken up smoking again ("Oh, just lightly") after six weeks' abstinence. His mood is better, alas.

Reagan's assertion, on the simultaneous release today of Sakharov and Daniloff, that "this is not a swap," calls to mind Magritte's painting of a pipe called *"This Is Not a Pipe."* Magritte is more forthright than Reagan since *"This Is Not a Pipe"* *isn't* a pipe, it's a picture of a pipe.

Meanwhile, Dalí's famous *trompe l'oeil, Mae West Apartment*, reproduced in the current *Smithsonian* (apropos of Meryle Secrest's upcoming biography) doesn't quite work, because Mae West's mouth—portrayed as a sumptuous double sofa—is closed. Have you ever seen Mae West with her mouth closed? The person here looks like Miss Piggy.

Here is my answer to Meryle Secrest's letters about Dalí two years ago:

Dear Meryle Secrest—

Yes, since I lived in her house for five years, I did know Marie-Laure de Noailles (note correct spelling) well, and also husband, Charles, Vicomte de Noailles. They sponsored, as you know, the early Dalí movies. As for the two-dimensional works by Dalí which I gazed upon daily, I recall specifically the early portrait of Marie-Laure (circa 1922), an absolutely exquisite oil, no larger than 15 x 15. In this, Marie-Laure's right cheek is a large pink rose; she always felt that Dalí had foreseen the auto accident in which years later she smashed her cheek. This portrait is honest, unaffected, free of self-promotion or willfulness. M-L also had a much larger, very "surrealistic" oil of a "meditator" with a frightening face emerging from behind a sheet hanging on a line in a desert. I recall no other Dalís except a series of lovely pencil studies of a nurse, seen from behind, sitting on a beach. Where are these pictures now? The Noailles family is dead or mad or dispersed, and those that survive are not especially interested in art.

At best you might try to see Marie-Laure's one surviving daughter, who has reverted to her maiden name of Natalie de Noailles, and whose address is simply Hôtel de Pompadour, Fontainebleau. But she is apparently not too well, or rather vague.

James Lord, an American novelist and biographer of Giacometti, is a canny and intelligent resident of Paris, and would know as much as anyone about these matters. (Perhaps you know him already?) He's on rue des Beaux-Arts at, I *think*, number 5. I'm in Nantucket until September 15 when I return to New York where my address books are. . . . He'll be useful. And though I'm not sure he's sympathetic to Dalí, he'd know some who are. But, as you well know, nearly everyone is dead.

My own relation to Dalí is restricted to two meetings, the first at Bestigui's ball in

Venice, 1951, when I was drunk and brash and blind, the second at a lunch chez Marie-Laure (later same year), described in one of my books. Rereading this now, I see that my feelings were colored by extra-painterly feelings (not insincere) rather than by Dalí's quality as an artist. Still, I'm hardly the first to point out that he sold his soul to the devil. . . . I knew Gala rather better, but still only slightly. She'd been married to Éluard, who was a friend, and I found her warm and vaguely licentious.

I do hope you will investigate Breton's policy on homosexuality, and how that may have affected not only Dalí, but Crevel, Lorca, and other "borderline" cases.

I've written at this length because I already know your work and like it, and feel that (except for your penchant toward Nin) we have similar tastes and values. Perhaps we can meet one day.

Most cordially,
Ned Rorem

10 October
Bought a supply of high-priced pink soap and of sachet potpourri made, they say, from local herbs and heather, so that the house will smell pleasant when JH's parents visit later this month.

New York, 12 October
The decay in Iceland is inexcusable but predictable. Reagan, like a petulant schoolboy, threw up the whole venture because Gorbachev wouldn't accept the Star Wars misadventure. Yet Star Wars is what any right-thinking American disapproves of. There is no physical deterrent to nuclear war: records are made to be beaten.

To impose a life-support system in a brain-damaged Mongoloid or in a senile cancer patient, rather than let nature take its course, is to go against the way of God. The God I don't believe in.

13 October
JH's parents. I remember Virgil's mother (who would be 121 years old—she was born two years before Satie), very rural, in New York in 1944 and meeting Maurice Grosser for the first time—Maurice, whom I, age 20, already knew. It's a bit like Daron, who's known me now from since he was 18, six years ago, but JH's parents meeting me for the first time.

16 October
Night after night of insomnia. Finally dropped off at six this morning, only to be awakened at seven by deafening rivets across the street which have gone on like a dentist's drill without anesthetic all day long. Showered at noon (in preparation for a photographer who was due at two), then lay down for a nap. Phone rang. Hélène Rémy. Before she spoke I knew that Guy Ferrand was dead. He died last Saturday, quietly, but not in pain, while lying down during a diabetic seizure. (This was

Hélène's report, in faulty English.) Two weeks ago I tried unsuccessfully to reach Guy in Paris. Then I wrote him.

More and more my Moroccan past is literally entombed. Clear cool weather.

To prepare for a speech at Curtis in a few months about *The Rake's Progress*, bought the record of Stravinsky conducting the opera made in 1964. Program notes off-putting. The whole-page quotes from the diaries of both I.S. and of Vera, in perfect if high-flown English (presumably by Craft), are so defensive, arch, snippy, ex cathedra, un-funny, and mean-minded, that one wonders how they could have seemed cogent two decades ago. Like Tennessee Williams, those compassionate depths in which we once drowned, today simply embarrass me. Esp. that anti-gay speech in *Small Craft Warnings*.

Finally listened to Simon Rattle's recording of *War Requiem*. Disappointing. Sopranos in the full chorus are beefed up by the boys' chorus (at least in the *Recordare*), lending an unneeded needle of mean purity to the women's voices. Boy's voices, solo or ensemble, are, with the guitar, the musical sound I most abhor. Sodestrom, so wonderful elsewhere, here with her blandness can't hold a candle to Vishnevskaya's apposite stridency in the *Lacrimosa*. And Britten as always errs when he repeats shreds of verse which Wilfred Owen felt no need to repeat. The repetitions, as always, have no urgent musical explanation. Yet as a whole the piece transcends etc. etc.

18 October

Call from Oliver Daniel. We reminisce about Nell Tangeman. Oliver claims Nell's death was due not to liquor and pills, as I believed when it transpired in Washington 21 years ago, but to a beating by a person or persons unknown. Like Bill Flanagan, she rotted for days before police invaded the apartment. Nell: one of the unique mezzos of America, now forgotten and unrecorded except for her sole published disc, Leibowitz's version of *Gurrelieder*.

21 October

The new four-volume American Grove has arrived, a river of information, and what hours of fun I've had swimming in it, seeking first (like probably everyone is seeking) the sprinkled references to myself. If there's an overemphasis on pop music (Sinatra having a photo and Diamond not), with yet glaring omissions therein (entries for Madonna and Loretta Lynn, but nothing on the more crucial and tragic Libby Holman or Helen Morgan), one can't censure by adding that all these pop numbers will be forgotten in thirty years, since most of the classical numbers will be forgotten too. Commendable is the emphasis on composers above performers (though nothing for pathfinder Janet Fairbank, and little on Nell Tangeman). I'm content with my entry by JH, and with the extended list of works.

No one can "see hisself as ithers see" him, or know the effect of his walking into a room, or even *what he just is*. A Grove's entry is no more representative of any individual than Karl Haas's daily lessons in Germanic sensibility are representative of great music.

Startling how familiar are the nightly perusals of *The Rake's Progress*. I've not thought of it in fifteen years. But during the week of its première in Venice, September 1951, I must have studied it thoroughly. Members of the cast return like old friends in the Piazza San Marco (Tourel, Tangeman, Cuenod), and the hills of Hyères echo Auric's *déchiffrage* of the score which I brought back to Marie-Laure. If I still feel now what I felt then about the libretto—that it's too arch, like Kallman himself, and at the same time too obsequious—I like the music more. Pastiche though the opening unarguably is, every one of its two dozen set numbers is a winner. Cornucopia of tune, and *long* tune, unlike all the motivic Stravinsky before and aft. True, the prosody's foreign, and the edition by Boosey & Hawkes is unforgivably faulty in syllabic division. But the melody's contagious.

The three questions . . . like those in *Turandot*.

23 October

Sixty-third birthday. Visit in early afternoon from Tomas Tichauer. Late afternoon to the movies with JH. Blier's outrageously original but unsatisfactory *Tenue de soirée* with the forever beguiling Depardieu. Unsatisfactory, because the unpredictable ending to the unpredictable film is not *the inevitable* unpredictability. It's a heterosexual's solution (and a French heterosexual at that) to a story that, in fact, has no problem, and so needs no solution: the treatment of gay sex as a given in a wild society.

Quiet evening with JH, who gave me a silver bathrobe and a little mocha cake. Sonny and the cats, TV in the early night, with, during 90 minutes of channel-flipping, four more statements of homosexuality: Gay Cable Network's earnest but mediocre reporting on "the scene" by nelly reporters who roll their eyes; Gena Rowlands portraying a lesbian mother on the witness stand, monosyllabically answering loaded questions of a sneering prosecutor; fag-bashing, on a police soap called *Night Heat*, pictures the whining fags as no more prepossessing than the bashers; and an interview on California's LaRouche initiative advocating a multi-billion-dollar AIDS testing campaign. Our ever-more-aware society that winces less than it did thirty years ago at calling a spade a spade, is scarcely, for that, more tolerant of spades. Queen of spades.

Miriam Gideon, seventeen years older than I to the hour, gave us her music at Merkin Hall. The new little Piano Sonata, pleasantly played by Sahan Arzruni, was a novel delight. But the aesthetic of her vocal music so goes against my own (gratuitous repetition of words and verses, undifferentiated tone from song to song, gimmicky switching from language to language within one song, and the offensive new translation of Saint Paul's letter to the Corinthians, wherein "charity" smarmily is mistranslated as "love"), so put me off that I couldn't hear the music. Andrew Porter, whom I pretended not to see, finally came and sat with me for a few minutes. We spoke about our respective barbers.

27 October

Nonplussed, to put it mildly, by a call from Maggie Mills. Glenway Wescott's had a stroke. A memorial at the Academy & Institute is already being planned, perhaps for next month, and do I know a good singer who, for a not too discouragingly high fee, might sing one or two of Glenway's favorites? Meanwhile, the patient lies paralyzed but nonetheless communicative in New Jersey, and may bury us all.

Apropos fees, when I announce to JH that the Chicago Symphony is feeling me out for their hundredth anniversary in 1990–91 and might pay up to forty thousand for a thirty-minute piece, he says he's just read that Perlman's fee for one concert is forty thousand.

Their hundredth anniversary? Like yesterday I recall the season of their fiftieth in 1940 when we heard Milhaud conduct his First Symphony and play his Piano Concerto. And Chávez's Concerto for Four Horns, and Stravinsky's Symphony in C, and . . .

Andrew Porter's predictable dithyrambs around the *Malcolm X* opera and Berio's new works at the Philharmonic (predictable, because anything Henahan derides will be defended by A.P.) ring false if only because he has recourse to that all-purpose adjective "brilliant." Anything is brilliant. The word's without meaning, except to describe a diamond—which, except for David, hardly needs description.

Tea party here Saturday, so that David Diamond and I, who had both missed her 80th-birthday concert last month, could hear Louise Talma's tapes. Also present: Shirley, Will Parker, Russell Oberlin, Leonard Raver, George Cree, and Pia Gilbert. Played my String Symphony, and two cassettes of Louise's. Then we all sat around the table to ingest my *gâteau au Grand Marnier* heaped with raspberries in a mound of crème Chantilly, three other kinds of cake, blue grapes and white pears, wine and espresso and fruit juice. Very pleasant. Louise, contrary to all other composers, asks that her tapes be played at half the volume I played mine at.

Halloween

No taxis. In the early morning, JH put me on the crowded Columbus Avenue bus where with my luggage I sat scrunched twixt a young woman and an old man. Standing before us was a male creature around forty, earrings, a subtle white wig beneath a black pirate's cap, mascara highlighting a crazed stare, Dracula fangs so understated that I didn't at first see them as fake, and a huge protuberance—a pickle? a ballet slipper?—jutted from his dirty leotard into our faces. Thence to Port Authority and another bus to Newark Airport through the Jersey wasteland. During these rides with my stinging urethra, I felt near death. (What's the use, et cetera.) Will Parker showed up in the nick of time and we boarded Continental flight #145 for Texas.

Singers aren't readers. Noted a few hours later, feeling better after a skyborne snack, as Will snoozes on my left and I, to write this, set aside Simenon's *Le Petit Saint*. Like Donald Gramm, Will is of a deep musical culture, dealing continually and fiercely with a special literature—Heine, Verlaine, Buchner, Apollinaire, Paul Goodman, Wilfred Owen, Whitman, Ashbery—but I've never caught either of them with a book in their lap or heard them utter an opinion about writings other than those they intone in the line of duty. Exceptional in themselves, they are typical of a breed. Singers have no need to be readers. (I myself never read poems for pleasure—only with an eye toward song-making.)

Houston, Marriott Hotel.
Dined chez Tobias Picker with his friend, Aryeh Stollman, a swarthy neurologist from Mount Sinai, Cynthia MacDonald, another woman, Richard Howard, and David Alexander. Six Jews and me.

Tobias says the latest rumor is that Helen Carter writes the music, Elliott writes the letters.

Dorothy Rosenberger flattered that in my "busy, famous life" I should remember her. But why would I not? Would busy fame oblige my 18 months in Buffalo to merge into monochrome blob? Why live, if only to forget?

Philip Johnson, Trasco Tower, & Fountain. Tobias's huge symphony, a white elephant—both bland and heavy, overorchestrated, tragic. The sadness I felt with his boyfriend. Tobias's "AIDS Symphony."

Ransom Wilson's nostalgic (but anemic) program of old friends. Bowles, Barber, Copland.

Carlyle Floyd, looking quite piqued.

Houston Airport, 2 November
Rain. As a switch, a late Beethoven quartet is piped through the mikes as we board Continental flight 144 for Newark, but this music is as irksome as the usual rock fare. Who wants *any* music—even mine, even yours—at such trying moments?

When I first arrived at Curtis, 1943, imbued with Debussy and Stravinsky, I learned that the great music was Beethoven's last quartets. I listened and waited. I'm still waiting.

Will Parker tells me that Bill Dansby, who sang so admirably as alternate lead in the 1979 revival of *Miss Julie*, has died of AIDS.

3 November
Back from Houston depleted. Rushed nevertheless to Tully Hall box office, since Mary Heller had begged me to come to the Sunday-afternoon concert and said she'd leave a ticket. No ticket. Returned home, collapsed, wrote letters, napped, dined on leftovers JH had left in the fridge. He meanwhile, en route to Nantucket

with Frank & Sonny, had promised to call, as usual, before boarding the 9:30 ferry at Hyannis. He didn't. Worry. Stared at television until midnight when I knew the ferry was to arrive, and when (if he were still alive) he'd phone.

At midnight, yes, JH phoned, so I retired relieved. This morning, several calls to several answering services. Depression, assuaged a bit by work: Richard Howard's translations of three Baudelaire poems to be made into choruses for the BBC.

The one weekly TV program I try not to miss is *Apostrophes*, intellectual and well-choreographed. It is also French to the core. For example, tonight: each of the five guests managed to substantiate some thesis by quoting Racine (a playwright unknown in America). Meanwhile, the hyperthyroid theme music is Rachmaninoff's First Piano Concerto. The French literati know all about their culture and only their culture; but, like the American literati, know nothing of music.

I loathe boy sopranos, individually and collectively. The sound, so adored by Britten, to me is mean, snotty, imperious, grating. *Amahl* disgusts, as does *El Retablo*. Child molestation, so in the news these days (a craze, like hula hoops) is far from my mind. Yet as I think back, my sexuality—and that of everyone I know—was keen by age fourteen. I *arranged* to be molested.

Does my paranoia provoke the damaging *amertume*? and does that *amertume* in turn fire my forever stinging urethra?

Here's a letter which JH forbade me to send to Will Parker:

Dear Will:

Excuse the absence from your Schubert runthrough tonight. I'm overwhelmed with deadlines and dare not spare the time.

That said, let me add that I was not thrilled by the show in Houston. Two blackouts during *War Scenes* were enough to subvert the seamless tension needed to project the drama. A composer is always dependent on his interpreter—who can make or break a piece. In this case, as composer acting in tandem with singer, I'm as dependent on you as you are on me. And you let me down. In the note slipped under my door, you blithely wrote, "I'm terribly sorry my concentration lapsed *twice!*" I don't wonder! I'd let it pass if the occasion were unique, and if I didn't feel there were contributing circumstances.

Already on the plane Friday you said you were weary from Thursday's opera appearance followed by a late party, and that you also had bronchitis (which was nevertheless under control, thanks to some wonder doctor). I thus felt uneasy—even vaguely insulted—when, as you tossed down an array of antibiotics, you announced plans to attend some Halloween celebrations that evening. Alcohol on top of penicillin, not to mention late hours, hardly seemed indicated when you had a performance next afternoon. Indeed, next afternoon you were the worse for wear; my music, and by extension my reputation (and, of course, yours), suffered accordingly.

Your life is your life, and I would not presume to tell you how to lead it except insofar as it intersects with *my* life. . . . Of all the singers I've ever worked with, you are the most casual. When Donald Gramm and I traveled together, I hardly saw him except to rehearse. He holed up, rested, gave no interviews, went to no parties—not even after our recitals. If he was sometimes not up to snuff, at least that couldn't be blamed on a regimen like yours, which would daunt a singer half your age.

In the more than two dozen concerts we've shared over the past decade, virtually all have come about through my recommendation. The recommendation continued to be inspired by my convictions about your rare musicality, your passionately beautiful sound (on good days), and your unquestioning commitment to the music of your time. Is it unfair to expect that you owe me the best of yourself? Yet I always ask myself, before we walk on stage, What will go wrong this time?

Whether your memory-slips and vocal problems (the rasping, unfocused, "dropped-out" middle notes and the strident top) also account for the various engagements which you sometimes lament have slipped through your fingers, it's not for me to say. Nor will I dare to contradict your countless fans who tell you you're sounding better than ever. But I, for one, feel used. Although I believe in the notion of you, I can't really rely on the fact of you. It's excruciating for me to have to write this, but it's been on my mind for some time, and finally had to come to the surface.

Your friend

4 Nov.

Coming out of the bank on 57th I dropped in to Rizzoli's where the piped-in browsing music became more important than, say, Zeffirelli's autobiography or Jackie Collins's novel, which were on display. It was an old disk of Piaf, remindful again of how no one today holds a candle to her. I'd forgotten the excessiveness of her rolled "r"—on the tongue *à l'Italienne*—and of her low notes, like Billie Holiday's, *à la baritone*. Without budging, she moved mountains. If she lacks the purity, the iced aloofness of, say, Judy Collins, Judy has none of Piaf's vulnerability. Liza Minnelli poses as vulnerable, yet one feels she could defend herself very well, thank you, with all that belting. Great singers don't belt, don't sell themselves. Piaf, from song to song, is always the person who *caused* the song—the protagonist—never Piaf. Back home, got out her records, spent an hour in the past, one thing leading to another—to Léo Preger's affecting *Etude* which so swayed my nights at the Reine Blanche, and Sauget's *Les Amoureux sont seuls au monde*.

JH says I should stop swiping towels from hotels, not because it's necessarily a tacky habit, or because I might risk the electric chair, but because in all likelihood the chambermaid is held accountable.

Stalin: One death is a tragedy. A thousand is a statistic.

4 Nov.

Smells evoke the past more than do sights and sounds.

Documentary on toucans, mysteriously filmed by a pair of cameras simultaneously inside and outside the nest in the hollow of a tree. Three eggs hatch at two-day intervals, and the chicks remain conditioned by the hiatuses. When the first one is ready to fly he rips open the small feeding hole, while the second tries to patch the hole with droppings, and the third has hysterics from the excess of light. Forty-eight hours later the second is in the position of the now-flown first, while the third tries to patch up the hole.

Visit from Neil Baldwin to borrow my Man Ray portraits for his biography. JH on phone from Nantucket makes me swear not to lend any originals—the archives are already depleted, in a mess, and I no longer have anything like a complete collection of my own published music or records, let alone photographs. I comply. Baldwin promises to return the picture by special messenger. The copies I do have of Man's portraits were made by him, and in my madness (not knowing in 1953 that age both mellows and yellows), I stuck them in a scrapbook. They're smeared with glue.

Dined on three fried eggs, dropped—one, two, three—into the sizzling butter. Like the toucans they reached maturity at separate moments, but because they were melded into each other, like Siamese triplets, I brought them forth with a spatula at the same moment.

Met Russell O. at the Y for "Musical Elements" program of five new works, of which Robert Beaser's *Songs from the Occasions* seemed the most promising, partly because it resembled my music. It was the only vocal piece, and very damaged. Why must a young American choose six poems by Montale? (If *we* don't use our own literature, who will?) Of these, why does he set the middle four in Italian, and the outer ones in English? Why does he repeat words that the poet, surely no less sensitive to echoic intensity than the composer, found no need to repeat? (When the poet *does*, in one instance, repeat a word—*ritornerà ritornerà*—that fact is lost on us, since the musician repeats the word, and in English, *five* times.) Why must the music italicize, instead of letting phrases already heightened by the mere fact of his notes, speak for themselves? Mickey-mousing—i.e., literal imitation, or the onomatopoeia of notes—is embarrassing or comic. For instance, at the close of the first song, when Sperry, full of Deep Meaning, *speaks* "And hell is certain," we smile and lower our eyes. Yes, Beaser's music in itself reminds me of mine, but more primitive: It's energetic, bluesy, roughish Respighi, but uses texts with a lack of slickness and no authority. This reaction's colored somewhat by the fact that before Beaser's piece was played, Russell told me of two friends of his, brothers, each with AIDS, who committed suicide, leaving their parents childless.

5 November

To the Academy in the rain with Ellen Adler. During the meeting I sit between Paul Cadmus, still sexy at eighty-two with his frost-colored leonine mane, and a dozing Arthur Schlesinger in a red bow tie with small white dots, which I coveted. Cadmus as always asks me to nominate Mompou, now ninety-three—but I already have—while Schlesinger, like most literary types, admits unashamedly to knowing little about music, but likes Verdi.

Pleased but disconcerted, during the peaceful cocktail interlude, when Ligeti, who, despite an affably grinning visage, appears hoary and wizened, tells me that as a student in Budapest he had studied my piano music. Then I tell him how much I admire Rostropovich's recording of his Cello Concerto, realizing even as I speak that I mean Lutowslawski (or is it Penderecki?), while Ligeti's features grow quizzical, though the grin grows broader since he, with his faulty English, imagines I'm announcing a new recording. (Later, checking in Grove's, I learn that Ligeti's just my age, and that he does, yes, have a Cello Concerto.)

At the dinner, which consists of a red and repellent venison which I decline (". . . the indigestible portions/Which the leopards reject"—it is Wednesday!) followed by a satisfying Paris-Brest, I find myself between Vincent Persichetti and Allen Ginsberg. Noisy. I manage to catch about five of every six of Vincent's words, so that his language has the same askew connotation that mine must have had for Ligeti. Vincent, his Mephistophelian eyebrows skimming the rim of his fourth beaker of yellow wine, seems anxious to impress on me that his compositional standards are noble. "I never write on commission," he states, "do you?", but admits innocence on the subject of AIDS. I advise him to buy, tonight, a copy of the *Native*, for the disease is gobbling us all up, and if he and Dorothea and their pet raccoon, Raquel, aren't wise to the facts, how much less so is middle America? He pretended to hide his shock when I don't agree that sex and love are always and inevitably intertwined. At seventy-two Vincent seems as naïve about homosexuality as—though more benignly—our Supreme Court. Meanwhile, Allen table hops, to my disdain and envy, and without raising his voice allows bits of himself to rub off, individually, on each of the hundred guests. To Persichetti, for example, Ginsberg whispers (with the incongruity of that famous photo of Edith Sitwell and Marilyn Monroe), "And what do *you* think of Robert Wilson?" I tell Allen how I disapproved of the Burroughs movie. He replies, forever cool, by snapping my image with his ubiquitous little Kodak, and doesn't turn a hair.

Also at our table, Peter Matthiesen, suffering a lawsuit of forty-odd million dollars by the FBI for his writings, chez Viking, about the South Dakota Indians. Like AIDS, this dilemma is merely grazed, and I feel guilty not to have pursued it.

Limousine in the rain with Ellen, Joan Peyser, Charles Wuorinen, Chaim Gross, Louise Talma.

Often I repeat that we have no Sacred Monsters anymore, that our era is not geared toward Masterpieces (a 19th-century concept), that since the death of Picasso, Great Men have vanished, and that there never *was* a Great Man in America, except maybe Martha Graham. (Copland and Auden weren't superstars in the massive pop sense.) But now even Martha can't *tenir le coup*. She dates badly, like most everything. Billie Holiday dates well. Is Britten, *en fin de compte* (*pace* parts of *War Requiem* and all of *Peter Grimes*), as great as we remembered, or simply a peppery cut above his blandly mortal countrymen? Stravinsky almost never disappoints. They are few.

7 November

Paul Goodman came back in a dream. Tears at a bar, haystacks in the sky (perhaps my tooth, all drilled to powder at Swee's yesterday), a dark house at night with groups of people.

Long visit last night from young Ron Caltabiano, who gave off a dizzying sexual smell.

Curtis students here all afternoon. Apples and hot croissants.

12 November

Lunch here with three young (how very young!) performers who drove up from Philadelphia to confer about my *Water Music*, which they'll perform at Curtis on the 25th. The violinist, Charles Wetherbee (*un beau laid*), turns out to have been a student, in Buffalo, of Thomas Halpin, who was the soloist, at age 16, in *Water Music*'s première twenty years ago. *Plus ça change . . .*

Pretty girl on 68th Street chewing bubble gum like a hemorrhoid twixt her lips.

Four Saints in an East Side school, one of the dozens of deserved homages for Virgil's ninetieth birthday. Mediocre voices, but a pleasant production. Nothing can subdue this oddly good-natured opera. Two hours of strong tunes, all tonic-dominant but never dull, no heights really, but touches of depth, as in the "dead, led, wed, said" duet in Act III. JH feels that Gertrude Stein's text (ingeniously split up into a libretto by Maurice Grosser) is, as he calls it, pre-Sartrian—existential. Questions are continually being asked—"How many saints are there in it?" "How many saints can remember a house which was built before they can remember?" "If ten thousand Chinamen could be killed by pressing a button, would it be done? (Saint Teresa: not interested)" "How many acts are there in it?"—questions like those posed by barkers at the country fair (if you can guess the fat man's weight—or how many nails are in this barrel—you'll win a prize) or by children as they discover, day by day, universal puzzles. But the answers really don't make any difference.

Lenny B. in the row in front of ours, talks loudly to us and his date (a pretty female violist) throughout the show. At intermission we discuss smoking—how LB and JH, both on the brink of emphysema, persist with unrepentant relish. We agree to break pizza together afterward, but Lenny is so leisurely about giving his all (autographs, advice, moist kisses to strangers) that JH and I sneak off. Tomorrow is an early day, and I have dental surgery.

13 November

Called Lenny to explain (through a mouthful of Novocain) about our disappearance last night. He was impeccable, declaring in turn that he couldn't resist . . . such warm words about JH ("He's the most beautiful thing in the world, tell him to smoke more") and Daron . . .

JH upset, having overheard a brat in his church refer to him as "that old homosex-ual." "Homosexual" seems more wounding, more sordid than the usual "faggot." "Old," for me, strikes the more hopeless note.

Sauguet's reaction, decades ago, to the German putdown of the French as *vipères lubriques: "Lubriques, oui, mais pourquoi vipères?"*

On the apparent premise that a column is not complete without a plug—no mat-ter how farfetched—for some fellow Britisher and for Carter, Andrew Porter is now a self-parody. In his current survey of Rimsky-Korsakov we read: ". . . his music's response to nature is as quick and fresh as Schubert's, Delius's, Elliott Carter's."

Ballet goers are more of a family than any other audience because they can return, again and again, to the same menu, and because there can be as many as four intermissions per program, as opposed to but one, or none, at concerts.

I'm physically attracted to everybody here except one person?
    Who?
    Myself.

13 November

To Michael Schnayerson, of *Vanity Fair*, re. "AIDS in the Arts":

> Although we now know, more or less, what causes it, AIDS nevertheless remains the most mysterious catastrophe since the Black Death of the 12th century. Cer-tainly nothing positive can be said about it, nor, for the moment, does the fact of it seem to bring out the best in the general international population, starting with the Pope who uses sexuality, as the Ku Klux Klan uses racism, to cultivate hate, igno-rance, and panic among his billions.
>
> As for the particular subject of AIDS in the Arts, nothing positive can be said there either. The greatest works of art do not proselytize, they reflect, and the reflec-tion comes well after the fact. The two or three plays I've seen on the subject are stronger as propaganda than as art; but insofar as they are persuasive at all, they can't compare in intensity and pathos to the weekly medical reports and lists of statistics in the *New York Native*.
>
> In my specialized field there have been noble fundraising demonstrations among performing artists, notably the one at Madison Square Garden led by Leonard Bern-stein, and another last summer at East Hampton organized by Robert Jacobson and Matthew Epstein. But these consisted of opera stars voicing the tried and true, and had nothing to do, artistically, with living statements. Living statements, so far as cre-ative music is concerned, don't seem to exist. How could they? Nothing can be said through music that cannot be said more strongly, more hopelessly, by the mere spec-tacle of one's acquaintances daily being kidnapped. Certainly the horrors of our present world will one day be reflected in our creative arts; such expression may

already inhabit the muse of our composers even as the virus itself may inhabit all our bodies. But the muse is as yet invisible. To speak of AIDS in the Arts is to speak only of what the performing arts can do to raise money, not what the creative arts can do to raise consciousness. The fine arts themselves are having a hard enough time just staying alive, in a government that is as soporific about art as about AIDS.

Even as our young composers will have to make their own new rules about the dissemination of their music in a society that doesn't care, so young people from all walks of life will have to adopt their sexuality to conditions set forth by the pestilence. In the art of literature, in subject matter if not necessarily in quality, there's been a shift. Look at the collection of stories in New American Library's *Men on Men*. The writers, whatever their eventual worth, have expanded the dimensions of all literature. By being beleaguered they emit the courage, ghastliness, and wit that stems from camaraderie, like Boccaccio's pilgrims, telling stories to keep the mind off the bubonic plague.

17 November

Father's 92nd birthday.

The AIDS Show, a California troupe more lively when ad-libbing during intermission than in the fairly sentimental skits. Yet the actors are touching: they speak from the horse's mouth and it makes a difference. (Jules Feiffer's eight cartoons in the *Voice* on the other hand, usually so pointed, this week fall short of their mark: A 10-year-old straight male enviously evokes the promiscuity of his ancestors and bemoans being trapped in a relationship with one girl: "AIDS has murdered my youth." The conceit misses irony because heterosexuals have not yet come to this, and homosexuals have already gone beyond.) One could wish sometimes that *The AIDS Show*, like about a third of the *Native*, were a bit less giddy, less willfully outrageous. Gays in their leisure, when not dealing capably with Major Issues, appear to be, all of them, endlessly silly.

18 Nov.

Lunch at ASCAP with forty other members, plus guest-of-honor (because of his support of the fight against the blanket licensing bill), Senator Edward Kennedy. Introduction by the experienced Morton Gould in a clear voice enunciating sympathetic bromides, answered by the comfortable unison low-keyed laughter always heard at official gatherings, followed by a five-minute statement from Kennedy. Kennedy's oral projection is so ringingly stentorian, like Boris Christoff at his peak, that one forgives the horse's ass accent peppered with dropped R's and interpolated uhs.

Afterward, walked with John Corigliano through the gray cold down Broadway to 57th, where we entered a branch of Manufacturer's Trust. A decade ago, when his father, concertmaster of the Philharmonic, died, John sold the Stradivarius and placed the other family violin, constructed in the early nineteenth century by one Jean-Baptiste Vuillaume, into a vault of this bank. John hadn't been there since, and, fearing the fiddle might have decayed in the strongbox, invited me to check it out with him. ("Not even a whole violin, just a piece of one," I quote ruefully from *The Little Foxes*.) In fact, when we adjourned to an inspection cubicle, and John drew forth the instrument from the frayed silk wrapping, it shone in all its deep red glory and cried out to be played.

Thence alone to Boosey & Hawkes, to deliver the manuscript, completed last night, of the three unaccompanied settings of Baudelaire for the BBC Chorus. (Corigliano tells me, somewhat annoyingly, that he too has used "Invitation to the Voyage"—in Wilbur's translation—for a choral setting.) Jim Kendrick joins us in Sylvia's office. Small talk. I mention to Kendrick that Sylvia's coming to Nantucket for a few days to celebrate the New Year. "Do you want to join us?" I throw out, half meaning it. To my surprise, he says yes, adding that he'd like to bring a friend.

Walked back through Central Park, stopping at Gristede's for a head of iceberg lettuce. Weary. Instead of attending the reading at A Different Light, JH and I dine on leftovers and play our two thousandth game of backgammon. Correct the parts of *Homer*, read more of *Le Petit Saint*, and look at Joan Rivers, whose guest is Martin Sheen. Sheen is the first participant on a late talk-show ever to say something worth heeding. The audience laughs edgily, certain he's kidding when he advocates Civil Disobedience (a phrase new to them), but he remains firm, unsmiling, patient, removed from his own navel, and shows us clips from current films about what we can do to avoid nuclear war—maybe.

Maureen Stapleton on the same talk show. Speaks exclusively about how she takes trains instead of planes because she's afraid of planes. Doesn't she get bored during those cross-country treks? No, she drinks in the club car and picks up strangers to play poker. Ten million people attend this blather.

For 18 years, I've lived across the street from Stapleton and can, should I choose, watch her comings and goings. This eminent actress has worked close to the eminent minds of our time.

All this for a handful of dust, wailed Antigone, and millenniums later was echoed by Waugh. All this for a handful of (happy) dust, theme of *Porgy and Bess*, or theme-song for *Midnight Express*.

At midnight a movie in the kitchen. Winter's here.

Fair. Another word to confuse the French. Its meanings are generically unrelated. Pretty; blond; a circus; just.

John Corigliano says his opera's now scheduled for the Met's 1990–91 season. How long has it been brewing? A decade? What once seemed a jackpot has turned unreliable. In a better world, wouldn't John in these intervening seasons have composed two or three operas, had them produced, learned from their failure, gone on to others? Instead, he treads water, and the dead years pass.

Reagan news conference on TV, a pathetic performance defending arms sale to Persia. Fumbles for words, as Father does. Yet Father says later, "I don't feel sorry for him, but for us." And Father Lawrence Jenco, the hostage freed in exchange for the arms, says, "Trading of arms symbolizes violence. To prevent that I'd have preferred to stay in my cell"—a response showing a third, and to my thinking, a correct viewpoint.

Successful, plotless story about the Hopeless Disease by Susan Sontag in *The New Yorker*. Skillful, mannered, depressing. Images of patients in a ward, bristling with tubes, watching television. Susan's avoidance of the word AIDS (which activists will call a cop-out) is actually a question of taste, and echoes the avoidance of mentioning her own cancer in her long essay, *Illness as Metaphor*, ten years ago.

Dined Thursday at Sahan Arzruni's. Janet and Martin Bookspan, Constantine Cassolas, and three others I didn't know. Armenian cuisine, of which the best part was spinach-and-feta fritters, and the worst was figs in cream imbued with rum. Talk of song and singing mostly—the sad state thereof. No doubt I've been invited because of my endorsement of Sahan's recordings.

Friday, late-afternoon visit with JH to the Phelpses, fresh back from two months at Royaumont. Robert, frail and shaky, but with a healthy face. Becki, stalwart, protective, with always her great posture. Many new and fine paintings from her. Always a strange pleasure (because it brings back, possibly, Hyde Park Bohemia) to be in their raftered pad. Later, dined two blocks away with Maggy and Joe Rosner at their new apartment in an old building, 13th Street. (Good pork roast, baked yams, homemade applesauce, and an acidic Key lime pie from Jon Vie.) Joe, anecdotal and very *bonne mine* for 72. Maggy, a touch arthritic, witty but self-conscious. Above them lives a recluse who paces the rugless parquet with a sound of crackling eggshells.

Today, Sunday, at JH's church, Purcell's *Te Deum*, a tightly made piece with good tunes, fairly well sung (better sung certainly than *Four Saints*, but that says little), and snappily conducted. Several friends there. As I note this JH is driving, worn out, to Nantucket. At five, alone to the Frick for Kurt Ollmann's recital. Perusal of the galleries beforehand meant little: the fact of the pictures seemed somehow less pertinent than the memory of them. Identical to the memory, but not so real. Ollmann is bemusing: good German, good French, good program, good English, the voice satisfying if never gorgeous, and good taste. He has almost everything, but I shan't be quick to scorn Will for Kurt.

Spot on *60 Minutes* with the un-winsome Marvin Hamlisch (refers to himself as "the kid") apropos his new show, *Smile*. Cast, producer, composer, and director have worked valiantly against the odds and are praying for a successful Broadway opening tomorrow. I pray for its failure. Snippets of song divulged on the television seem no more than vamping à la *Chorus Line* interjected with Kern's "I Won't Dance." ("The thing I can't bear to think about . . . is someone dying with the TV on." —from Sontag's story.)

JH phoned at midnight from a Hyannis motel. Ferry broken. He'll proceed to Nantucket tomorrow morning. Imagine his fatigue, the anticlimax.

Jack Larson came to lunch on short notice. (Leftovers of salad, and canned minestrone.) Here for some of VT's ninetieth festivities. Californian and sexy as ever, but older, looks oddly like Jerry Falwell. Told of Gore Vidal's last visit to the crucially ailing Christopher Isherwood. When Christopher nods off, Gore laments to Don Bachardy that the best part of the world is fading, there's no justice, life is evil, we get what we deserve, and the earth's going to be taken over by grasshoppers. Christopher opens his eyes and says, "What's wrong with the grasshoppers?"

Letter from a Dr. C. A. Tripp, whose *The Homosexual Matrix* was apparently newsworthy a dozen years ago. Wants my opinion about who "is" and who "isn't" within the various musical categories. He asked for a sentence, I sent four pages, not having the time to be more brief. Based observations partly on what I told Kinsey in November of 1948 juxtaposed on those same versions now.

When JH isn't sleeping, as usual, in the room next door, somehow the burglar alarms in the street don't explode at four A.M. Instead, at four A.M., Sam, who's now alone in the room with Princess, emits a *meow!* piercing my dreams like a corkscrew and leaving me pointlessly adrift until around seven.

The high point in our European summer of 1936 was seeing *Show Boat* six times in Oslo. The recent TV replay brought back each frame like yesterday. Helen Morgan is as moving as before, Paul Robeson's mere presence is overwhelming (not least in "Ol' Man River," one of the great songs ever, in shape, scope, inspiration, and also in Hammerstein's lyrics), while Irene Dunne remains silly throughout.

  Just looked in my diary of fifty years ago—the close of an entry dated Friday 8/6/36 Grand Hotel, Oslo, Norge: "I like this city more than any other we've been in so far, in Europe. It's terribly nice. Tonight the whole family went to *Show Boat*. Pa and Ma thought it was swell. I sure love Helen Morgan. I'm going to write her a fan letter."

Jack's AIDS theory. The virus came from Cuba with the inmates of lunatic asylums and other unfortunates "freed" by Castro. These in turn had been infected by Cuban military stationed in Haiti and in Central Africa. The dates jibe, says Jack.

Deliver = reviled

Weak piece on Genet by Edmund White in *The Advocate*. Undigested rehash of Sartre for Yankee hicks. At the outset Genet is called "the author of a handful of the most sumptuously stylish novels of this century." Sumptuously stylish? "He seldom bathed or changed clothes but he was an exquisite literary dandy . . ." Literary dandy? "He could speak confidently about Boulez's music." Boulez's music? Well, confidently, perhaps, like White on Genet. The latter is a great author, but we need a Paul Goodman to tell us why—if we need telling.

Barclay Hotel, Philadelphia, 24 November
Two-hour delay at Penn Station. Switched to Metroliner, but still arrived late for classes at Curtis. Dined here with Rosemary. Orchestra concert of student works, plus David Loeb's oboe *Cantata* and my *Water Music*. Rosemary's reaction: dazzled by the youthful virtuosity (indeed, the teenagers play as well now, technically, as they'll ever play—from here on it's all downhill), but not especially moved. Last time she was moved by an event on a stage was the Lunts in *The Visit*—their interplay. I tell her, well, even that would doubtless fall flat if she could see it again tonight, knowing what she knows. We sit in the hotel room 525 and talk about Mother & Father. R. feels mortality ever more heavily, longs to be "surprised by joy" (in the words of C. S. Lewis, whom she's reading with joy). I tell her it'll come with death—that the quadrillionth of a millisecond between the gunshot and the expiration, there looms an eternity in which we float over a field of yellow roses.
    Title: *Person to Person*.

Nantucket, Thanksgiving
Elsewhere apparently there were vast snarl-ups at depots, but I arrived here yesterday (from Philly via Boston and Hyannis) in the holiday madness only two hours behind schedule. Hemorrhoids. Today, mild and clear, back yard flooded. We plant jonquils around the little apple tree. Dine on chicken, Stove Top dressing, onion and lettuce salad, and strawberry meringues. Sonny as usual gets sirloin.
    Answer letters. Between two works—*entre chien et loup*. If I should die tonight, at least I'll have completed and sent off the BBC choruses.

28 Nov.
Listened again to Schwantner's *Magabunda*, four settings of some lousy Spanish poetry full of Meaning, beautifully sung by Lucy Shelton. Identical flaws as in the Beaser a few weeks ago. (Ah, Crumb, what hast thou wrought!) The nicest movement, because it has a clear tune, is the third, *Black Anemones*, which combines Ravel's *Nahandôve* with Barber's *Despite & Still* glued with a Mahlerish orchestra playing Bergian fifths. Although sympathetic to the musical language, I'm virulent about Schwantner's word-settings (as opposed to, say, Boulez's word-settings, which are so esthetically far from my own as to have their own kosher esthetic).

Other non-vocal pieces by this youngish composer I've liked for their color, but his Martin Luther King thing a couple years ago was pale rot—an impossibility. (Why white men can't set black words. Etc.)

Telecast of Gian Carlo Menotti's *Goya*. A fortnight ago reviews of the Washington première were so vile I sent him a condolence plus a copy of a ten-year-old letter (never mailed but printed nevertheless in *An Absolute Gift*, which he doubtless never read) to Donal Henahan, who had publicly chastised the composer without granting him any benefit of doubt. Menotti was the third "grown-up" composer— after Leo Sowerby and Paul Bowles—I ever knew. I was nineteen, at Curtis, where he taught a class in Dramatic Forms. Wainwright Churchill and I were assigned to compose brief theatrical sketches. We had to get special dispensation from Scalero, who disapproved of creative composition, as opposed to counterpoint and more counterpoint, but Menotti persuasively arranged that, as he has persuasively arranged many another deal in the ensuing years. I wrote a 12-minute dialogue between the Sphinx and the Chimera, as quoted in a scene of Huysmans's *Against the Grain*, wherein a female ventriloquist evokes Flaubert's original scene in *The Temptation of Saint Anthony*. I accompanied fellow students Ellen Faull and Kenneth Remo in this little "opera" (my Opus minus one), which, to this day, is the only piece of mine that Gian Carlo, on the rare moments that we meet, ever mentions having heard.

I've always made a point of hearing everything, almost, he's done. However history may ultimately cast him as a composer, it is not opinion but fact that Menotti single-handedly revitalized the concept of living opera for Americans. *The Medium* and *The Consul* still pack a wallop, as do *The Glass Menagerie* and *Streetcar*, even if, as with Tennessee Williams, Menotti's ensuing operas have grown increasingly embarrassing. Without him in the forties no one else would have taken the plunge.

So, if I feel more charitable than Henahan toward Menotti, *Goya* still strikes me as worse than Henahan indicated in his recent review, if only because the review, in its glee at disqualifying Menotti the composer, neglected to treat Menotti the librettist. The libretto is a *Reader's Digest* simplification of what it means to be an artist in general, and an undignified burlesque of what it means to be Goya in particular. We learn more of the painter during a preliminary two-minute filmed stroll through the National Gallery than during two hours of overwrought histrionics. *Bland* histrionics. The music, as usual, owes all to Puccini (this time it's Turandot's 3-note motive for the Three Questions). The audience was fun to watch. (Importunity knocks.) But the stage show was as dull as the dated *Mogambo* last night on the VCR (the title is never explained, nor are the continually discourteous interchanges between the stars), or the pretentious *Winter Kills* the night before.

As *The Nation* said of Roy Cohn during his last months: Ordinarily we won't hit a man when he's down, but in this case we'll make an exception.

Reading Sartre's *The Freud Scenario*, having hoped there might be an opera in there. Now *Goya* is again a reminder of how librettos just can't be cut from the lives of artists (what can we say of them that Goya and Freud can't say better?). Sartre's screenplay, meanwhile, seems not that much above Menotti, or *Mogambo*, or *Magabunda*, or all the other information that rushes helter-skelter into the half-alerted brain.

Ticks, like bedbugs, can survive twenty years without blood, but a tick on a daily diet of blood lives only two or three years.

As in New York, mice are coming into the house here. Last night we set a trap in the broom closet. Yes, I was aware of a vague scuffling at around 4 A.M. This morning, sure enough, the trap had sprung, and the result was horrible. Blood, intestines, a bad smell, semi-decapitation, the poor creature had wrenched himself out of shape. The pair of city mice last week seemed to have been killed outright, without contortions. JH insists we must set traps yet again.

His smoking—I'll never get used to it. He's a mite sadistic withal: I must live with it, but mustn't complain. He says eyether and I say eether. He favors overheated rooms, soft butter, salt; I favor cool rooms, hard butter, sugar. I have no one else in the world.

2 December

He feels that I can't divorce my mind from my body—that *he*, when he has an ill, merely says, "The old sonofabitch is acting up again," blaming it on age. Well, perhaps he doesn't complain. But he does make his ills known: the continual coughing as he smokes in bed, the sinus seizures, the overweightness. Meanwhile, I visited Voorhees yesterday. Says my body will mend itself. Five hours later, while walking Sonny in the freezing darkness, flashes like neon splinters on outer periphery of right eye. Also spots before the eye, like swerving amoebas. Continued all night, again this morning. Sonny has fleas, which we cannot dispel with collars or baths or unguents many.

Write of Mrs. Peacock at Cadbury. Her poems to, and new lease on life at eighty-three because of, Father.

Jim Bridges's *Mike's Murder* on VCR. Steadily interesting and low-key sordidness about cocaine and dumb love. Debra Winger, whom I've previously disliked, is understated and appealing, plain looking, *une belle laide*, a type nonexistent forty years ago.

The exposure of the Iranian arms-sale comedy unfolds as engrossingly as a detective story—or, indeed, as Watergate twelve years ago. Reagan's probably telling the truth when he pleads ignorance. He was told; he just didn't hear.

Back from Nantucket by plane yesterday (JH and Sonny by truck today, a twelve-hour trek) to shop for tonight's guests—the first little party we've given since spring. Frankie & Bill Schuman, and Eugene Istomin. Meal, not good but quite expensive, included doughy filets from Nevada market, carrots in honey, arugula salad, and a terrific devil's food cake with fresh raspberries and clotted cream.

Always miffed by how one corner of the music world ignores another. Eugene shocked that Bill and I should talk about performers as trained seals; Eugene's usual society, performers take the driver's seat. . . . Nice talk about baseball, Greek to me, but I'm not proud of that. (Paul Goodman once compared the game to Ravel's *Sonatine*. And in grammar school I was a pretty good outfielder; although alone in that field, when no ball sped our way, Bruce and I spoke of Marlene Dietrich.) Brief discussion of our prostates. Eugene, who had earlier mixed some potent martinis, then killed a bottle of Bordeaux with the meal, played some of Robert Schumann's F-sharp minor *Sonata*, and *Hommage à Rameau*, his too-long fingernails clicking. For twenty years now, when he goes to the piano to show us something, Eugene, perhaps hiding behind the excuse of cocktails, gives a purposefully unlush display, light years removed from the buttery tone of his youth, eschewing the pedal, speaking out loud, and making harsh sounds, as though to give in to the sensual demands of even Rachmaninoff would seem somehow . . . effeminate. Why? Then he turns around and plays a heartrending Chopin nocturne.

13 December

Everyone gets it wrong. On Gay Cable Network Brandon Judell, with his unsmiling know-it-all pose, tells us that now that Cary Grant is dead the truth about Grant's gay past will out, and shows us stills of Randolph Scott, whom he repeatedly calls Zachary Scott. My two pair of new glasses, after a week's delay, are meant to be ready yesterday; lenses were placed in the wrong frames, and the whole had to be redone. The new bomber, promoted by Reagan (the Judell of the White House), turns out to be a trillion-dollar Edsel. It's a wonder that the little planes shuttling us back & forth to Nantucket (at a higher fare than a trip to Jamaica) don't crash oftener: One trip in four there's a crisis amounting to more than a minor delay. The cover, glossy and lush, for *The Nantucket Diary* arrived from North Point this morning. The designer clearly hasn't read the book; the picture chosen of me resembles a fatuous partygoer, which, whatever else I may be—I am not. No one consulted me.

Gave up on Lore Segal's too-arch novel. Reread Paul Goodman's *Five Years*, which remains what it was twenty years go—an articulately poetic auto-elegy for and by America's best mind, still unappreciated. Oddly dated too, with the anti-feminist stance, the Oedipal view of homosexuality, words like "hep." How would Paul fit in today? What would be his reaction—or Bill Flanagan's, or Marie-Laure's—to this aging mire?

The new critic on the *Voice*, one Kyle Gann, seems like a dud judging from his first two write-ups. A review of Glass is based on flimsy givens, comparing him to Stravinsky, misrepresenting the forties by quoting Morton Feldman, elevating Glass who "never fails to ask difficult questions" (like Schubert's questions?), using gobbledygook jargon like "objectivist mindset," and praising the "raising of arbitrariness to an art form." "We misunderstood from the beginning," says Gann of Glass's "thinking," and goes on to admire the use of "enharmonic intervals (say, a diminished third [*sic*]) to imply an unstated pitch."

This week Gann's flimsy given is that "regional artists" are still, as always, given short shrift by New Yorkers, who make the national rules. This will come as news to Crumb, Paulus, Argento, Schwanter, Harbison, Wernick, Adams, and the multitude of out-of-towners who are stating the premises, especially as regards opera, that New Yorkers seek impotently to follow, and to the array of worthy young New Yorkers who can't get to first base. To set John Becker against his colleagues— Ives, Riegger, Cowell, and Ruggles—because he was "regional" and they New Yorkers is meaningless. They were just as "unsuccessful" as he, nor were they Manhattanites. Gann adds: "One reason why Becker has never taken his rightful place among the precursors of the avant-garde was the Depression, which diverted funds away from experimental work in favor of the populist conservatism led by Copland—a regressive movement from whose influence American music still hasn't fully recovered." Regression is not inherently bad (viz a cancer) anymore than progress is inherently good (viz a cancer); anyway, Copland was every bit as "experimental" as the others, although it is precisely his "conservative" leanings that today are out of fashion. If we've not "fully recovered" from a movement, it's from the infiltration in the fifties of *Bouleziana*—*that's* what took America out of American music. The serial killers.

Visit from Tracey Sterne, still doggedly devoted to Paul Jacobs's ghost. I agree to write liner notes to Paul's rendition, with Gilbert Kalish, of *"En blanc et noir,"* although it's not my favorite Debussy piece, for I too am doggedly devoted to Paul's ghost. What Paul so admired in this piece is exactly what puts me off: a sense of patriotism and defiance in the face of certain death. The performance is perfervid and imprecise, the music self-imitative and propagandistic.

Tracey believes we bring cancer on ourselves through latent bitterness and resentment. Maybe. JH would agree. But I don't have cancer (not yet), yet I'm bitter. What's the cause of the return, since last summer in full force, of my "condition"—the seven-year-old urethral stinging, and twenty-two doctors? No one suggests it might be congestion (congestion of what?) or muscle spasm. The pain is continual.

Wrote a letter, then another, to Jack Shoemaker about the jacket photo for *The Nantucket Diary*. A book *is* its cover. That my prose should be judged by this smug and empty photo, not of my choosing! At least let me choose my own smugness.

Debussy looks like Mandy Patinkin.

14 December

Sunday. JH at church. First cold weather. Brief stroll in the bright park with Sonny. Growls at other males, wags friskily at females, leads me a merry chase, boopsies (as we call it) after a little dance of semicircular essays, ignoring the chill. A dog that spends his beginnings among humans tries to act—thinks of himself as—human. After four months he succumbs to innate caninity and becomes a dog. (But Wallace never thought of himself as a cat.)

The Central Park rats in broad daylight are ubiquitous as squirrels. Some sit on their haunches and beg.

Local première Wednesday of *The End of Summer*, which the Verdehr Trio first played last March in Bombay. Thea Musgrave and Peter Mark (who recall Sylvia and Léonid, or Dominique and Éluard, in that she's the husband, he the wife) sit with us in the Tully box, and, after our pieces, Thea and I bow self-consciously to the scant audience. We join the Verdehr entourage at O'Neal's for club sandwiches and a steaming apple tart, inappropriately topped with Reddi-Whip. All five of the new pieces (the others were by William O. Smith, Ida Gotovsky, Peter Dickinson) quote literally from the past. Thea's *Pierrot* is a charmer, purposefully virtuosic, and visual in the sense that each instrument represents a character: clarinet Columbine, violin Pierrot, piano Harlequin. JH dislikes my piece, feels it's self-indulgent (I use old tricks) and mad (fragments that don't fit together). He later asks Chuck if Sam Barber ever wrote music that he, Chuck, disapproved of. "No."

Father at 92, disconcerted because a certain Mrs. Bevins, 82, claims to be in love with him, and Mrs. Peacock, also 82, who heads the choir in which they both are participants, seems hurt. I do and don't approve. Father does lead them on. Mother unaware. Then again, maybe not. Father says she sometimes asks the name of D— E—, her one infidelity, circa 1932.

Call from Rosemary this morning. Dick Jacob died last night. A relief. His ironic melted look. More later.

Thumbing the Bible this morning, in search of dramatic, conversational texts (I found none) for my students to musicalize as I once musicalized Flaubert for Menotti. I bow again to the majesty of the King James translation. The French simply don't have an equivalent to the Old Testament. "Behold now Behemoth" becomes "*Voici l'hippopotame.*"

Elliott Carter's new quartet, unrelentingly chaotic, leaves nothing to listen for. When all is chaos, nothing is chaos.

But doesn't it reflect our woeful times?

All music reflects its times, and all times are woeful.

It will be interesting to read what Andrew Porter makes of it. Andrew, *knowing in advance* that a new Carter is great, is able to pinpoint the greatness—how Carter sets this word, inflects that phrase, contrasts these notes. The setting, the inflecting, the contrasts are commendable by definition; we have only to inspect them to see God in Man.

Phone Maggy to tell her about Dick Jacob. We reminisce about our first meeting, in 1938, when Dick appeared at the door with Don Dalton, both unknown to us, and invaded the apartment on Dorchester. Don died in his early twenties, decapitated by an airplane propeller, our first war casualty. Dick and Maggy's history was collegiate, centering on Chicago University theatrics. I think back on Dick and Don with equal affection, though 43 years divides their deaths. Maggy and I talk of this, and then we talk of other things. Other things. These phone calls, which lead to "other things," occur more and more.

18 December

At midnight JH called me to the kitchen. Another mouse was trapped, but only by its hand (its tiny child's hand) reaching toward the bait from under the icebox. We released it with ambivalent reaction as it scampered off. Should we catch mice henceforth in a benign cage, and release them in Central Park? Or just live with them? Even rats and roaches somehow have rights.

At 9 A.M., during calisthenics, tuned in radio a split second after Ravel's Trio had commenced, and realized within another split second that things were askew. Forty-five years ago, when I first heard this most wrenching of the composer's works in a listening room at Lyon & Healey's (who was playing? I remember only the deep aqua cover encasing the three old 78 rpms) it was instantly clear that the sole mode for such sensuous crystal—indeed, for all French music—was straightforwardness: just play the notes, please; their "meaning" is in their distribution on the page. Here now, this morning, the mysterious piece was being *interpreted* to within an inch of its life, much too slow, *très senti*. An obstinant masochism made me stick it out. 'Twas the Beaux Arts Trio.

There's no one right way to play any piece; there are as many right ways as there are gifted players. But there *are* wrong ways.

Opening of the refurbished Carnegie Hall on the evening news. Betty Allen refers to "The Star-Strangled Banner."

19 December

Through sleet yesterday to tea chez Ferro-Grumley, gave them a gold box of Perugino chocolates that Mrs. Roush had given me. Taxi with Walter Clemons, who's doing a biography of Gore Vidal. Though Gore may ultimately be seen as the most expert of the triumvirate, with Capote and Williams, he has less anecdotal paraphernalia than they. Except for his upper-crust lineage (the only dull thing about him, but which he pushes), what's there to say?

Students all this afternoon.

JH, as always during this season, extremely pushed, nervous with church work, aching. Asked him if he believed in God, surprised that in nineteen years I'd never posed the question. Answer: For those connected with the church, except the clergy, there's no question, yes or no, of belief. One believes in the encouragement of belief.

Heifitz on radio, Walton's Fiddle Concerto. Reminiscent of Nat King Cole's "Nature Boy."

Half-finished with *Te Deum* for Indianapolis. Yes, I do write to the nature of commissioners, not only making a piece harder or easier according, but layering the very *quality*. Which doesn't mean the quality is higher here than there, simply more viable. *Gebrauchsmusik*. I don't believe in God, yet half my music's for the Church. I don't conceive the same harmonies for a *Te Deum* as for a symphony. Then again, yes, I do.

20 December

In a letter from Nora Jacob, whom I've never met: "I also wanted to tell you what a blessing your sister, Rosemary, has been. Even in his final days, Dad was comfortable around her and drew pleasure from her steady and affectionate concern. She has been a great comfort to both Dad and Mom."

The insertion of "you know" into any spoken phrase, no matter how inappropriate, has during the past generation become a mannerism of every class. Over the past 12 hours, in diverse interviews—with sculptor Nakian, actress Jane Fonda, violinist Miriam Fried—the locution was interpolated as many as *three times per sentence*, even though the "you" could not possibly "know." Paul Goodman, though deploring the habit, had it. The function of the locution, I suppose, is to give the speaker time to think. Yet many a speaker has spoken lucidly off the cuff without resorting to . . .

Dined chez Ronit and Jerry Lowenthal, cozy, with Lucy Mann and her spouse, Robert—he of the constant grin. I vowed beforehand that I would not (nor did I) speak of Elliott Carter. The one previous time I'd talked with Bobby Mann (at Ruth Laredo's a dozen years ago), it was with awe at how his group's recording of Elliott's Third String Quartet deviated not a hair from the printed score. Today my awe at such precision has disintegrated into "All that for a handful of dust"—hardly the thing to say here now. Instead we speak of Dr. Wilhelm Reich, under whose tutelage he pursued a way of life in the late 1940s. JH finds them uncouth.

Christmas Eve, as always, at Saint Matthew's and Saint Timothy's. JH led his choir in the première of the first of my new *Seven Motets for the Church Year*.

Visit to Cadbury. Mother's wing, a prison de luxe, tolerable now, each patient familiar: she who moans ceaselessly "I want to go home," she motionless in her wheelchair except for the trembling purple tongue forever protruding from the very root, and she of the Saint Vitus Dance. Mother, amidst this, benign. Father, thanks to female friends, is leading a life.

23 Dec.

Death of Maurice Grosser, of AIDS, at 83. The ugly riddle of death now. Long talk with Virgil.

Gay Men's Chorus in the new Carnegie Hall.

Death of Celius Dougherty. Crutchfield calls for a statement. Next day, Brandon Judell phones: "Was Dougherty gay?"

The Howard Beach "lynching" with its "victims" refusing to testify, may do for blacks what AIDS has done for gays.

Every year or so, I propose a suicide pact to JH.

1987

Nantucket, 3 January

Stratas's new recording of Weill songs. Worries the tunes to death with expressivity. Why can't these people just sing?

Odd—then again, not odd—that Henry James, America's premier author, certainly a master storyteller, has served our composers so little: one or two operas, and no ballets at all.

Tone poems: "The Great Good Place," "The Beast in the Jungle," "The Bench of Desolation."

Title: *The Seasons*

Barbra Streisand "special." Many mistakes. Plays with her hair too much, distracting us from the song. Reptilian fingernails. Gives no credit to any songwriter, lest, it would seem, her charisma be deflected. (Juliette Gréco, with respect and glamour, used to announce both lyricist and composer before every number.) Lets tension flag by introducing an uninteresting male crooner for a duet or two. Pleads for a better planet that belongs, after all, to "black & white, old & young, male & female, rich & poor" (but not gay & straight). And a cringe-making "America the Beautiful," which she invites her star-studded audience to sing along with.

Still, who's better? When she wraps that tongue around a single tone ("*Vénus toute entière à sa proie attachée*"), warming it from an icicle to a tear, like Anita Ellis before her, it's not a trick but a means to an end, an intelligent end, and moving. I doubt that she, either, could do Weill, but then she doesn't try.

11 January

Virgil phoned to Nantucket last week. There's to be a memorial for Maurice Grosser on February 8, and could I perform his portrait of Maurice, plus four of his songs (three Blakes, plus "Pigeons on the Grass") with "one of those baritones" of mine? Will Parker turned out not to be free. Called Alan Titus. His wife, Janet, said he's in Chicago, and gave me the number there. Before I could call him—though I didn't plan to—he called me, and agreed to do the job for my sake. (He doesn't know Virgil.) Victorious, I phoned Virgil. "Oh no, we don't want Alan Titus," said he. "He's much too famous. Besides, he turned down a role in *Lord Byron*." Exasperated, I told Virgil to find his own damn baritone, called Alan back, embarrassedly explained that Virgil thought he was too big a star for so small an occasion, and besides VT wanted a black singer. Alan took it in his stride. "I'll sing for Virgil's memorial," he said.

Daron shows me a new piece. Although no longer my student, our roles are still defined enough (and I admire his work enough) for me to feel free, even in front of others, to criticize. In 1951, when observing how the *grand monde* functions in Paris, I was not unimpressed when, during an intermission, Jacques Fath came up to Marie-Laure, yanked up her bodice with his right hand while with his left he thrust her ample breast down into her *corsage*. "*Tu es trop décolletée*," he said coolly, and she thanked him.

Re JH: I'm a nag. He's a scold. But he's seldom a nag, and I'm never a scold.

Although I admire much of his music for its terse humor and pathos, Francis Thorne's Fifth Symphony trudges on without a smile and with too much unintegrated percussion—drums used strictly as decoration, like exclamation marks!, or like perfume on a corpse. And it's too long.

Virgil claims Bach never wrote a piece that lasted more than ten minutes (including the great organ fugues) and that twenty minutes is as long as any musical event needs to endure, at least when used as background, as for weddings or funerals. Defensible, if you assume that the *Matthew Passion*, or *Le Sacre*, or *Don Giovanni*, or Verdi's *Requiem*, is made up of sections, each under ten minutes. Sex averages out to twenty-minute bouts. If Mahler's long movements fail, they fail insofar as they exceed the limit. Although, as with Del Tredici or Glass, length is the very point of them.

Bill Bolcom's Violin Concerto, meanwhile (on last Sunday's Jan. 11 ACO concert), seems a Jewish Ives. Upon the Yankee morass of Ives's canvas a clean hymn tune is limned. On the Yankee morass of Bolcolm's canvas are limned augmented seconds and little glisses. Harmless, like the *Chairman Dances* goody of John Adams. But harmless isn't enough for all the fuss. What are they doing that their teacher Milhaud didn't do more "harmfully" 65 years ago?

13 January

Call from Bill Schuman, on behalf of the MacDowell Colony. Leonard Bernstein is to receive the Colony's prestigious Medal of Honor next summer. Will I present the medal, and give a 15-minute speech? Feeling like Groucho Marx ("I wouldn't want to join a club that would have me"—and if I'm the best they can get, then Lenny can't be that important), I nonetheless agree, feeling honored in my turn.

To New Haven in a blizzard with Jaime Laredo, who plays my concerto there.

To the eye doctor: "floaters" & flashes.

Villains often have charm, but it would be hard to include Marcos.

Was it as far back as 1959 that Bill Inge and I discussed turning *Picnic* into an opera? What remains clear is Bill saying: "Just remember Hal—he's the one with the cock." It seemed less strange then than today to delineate among his male characters—all of them heterosexual—according to those "with a cock." Inge was a homosexual misfit, more because he was physically plain than because he was shy. Though he was ten years older than I, I still feel sociologically nearer to him than to today's "liberated" gays, for whom turnabout is fair play, all roles reversible. But would a woman, then or now, distinguish between men as those with or without cocks? So-called gay life in the 1940s was far more open, casual, uncomplicated, than today. But then, I was in a not exactly standard milieu: Paul Goodman, Roditi. And musicians wrestled everywhere.

18 Jan.

Visit to Robert Jacobson in TriBeCa, with Joanna Simon, she of the silver lipstick. AIDS, a sorrily inappropriate acronym, too late to change. The AIDS "look" comes early in the game: the drawn, haunted stare of a concentration camp inmate.

Colette's *Enfant*: Struwelpeter contrite.

Russell Baker's compendium of Light Verse. All of it rhymes. How can it not? Is there an example of humorous poetry unrhymed and unrhythmed? Surprised at how many of the poets I've set to music over the years (unaware that they were "Light Verse"): Stevenson, Dickinson, Burns, Roethke, Frost, Cummings, Eliot, Auden, Blake, Yeats, Butler, Hardy, Byron, Coleridge, Peele, Shakespeare, Graves, Donne, Herrick, Aiken, Carroll, Browning, Pound, Emerson, Landor, Crane, Shelley, Twain, and Kenneth Koch.

I don't stand on my head anymore. Ophthalmological discouragement: it may aggravate the retina.

Profound embarrassment (guilt) at the profound enjoyment of sugar, Ravel, and of being "bottom man" could once have accounted for alcoholism.

31 January

Visit from youngish Richard Danielpour, whose choruses attracted me several years ago at a student concert at Juilliard. He represents his generation in being eclectic utterly, and solidly heterosexual, although the musicians that influence him, with the exception of Stravinsky—*et encore!*—are mostly not: Britten, Bernstein, Diamond, Copland.

Every year or so some perverse sense of duty obliges me to plod through the score & disk of Bruckner's Eighth. And from year to year, although I have a strong memory, I never recall a note.

No one old thinks old—or even thinks of himself as old. You don't recognize me because I'm disguised as an old man.

Reading Philip Roth's new novel. He, yes, is a born author and writes like an angel (especially like angels who write), but it seems more of same, and he's now too old for such gamy talk. (Sexist talk as well, being about how women deal with his organ, not he with theirs, and there's little straight screwing, much less a concern for the state of the world.)

Jane Freilicher, amused, once explained why Elaine Lorillard didn't buy a picture. "I love your paintings," Elaine said to Jane, "but I'm just not into green." I love Roth's writing, but I'm just not that involved with Jews.

5 Feb.

Reread all of Bill Flanagan's letters, with their hot generosity and their ever-growing paranoia, their wild wit. He comes more alive than anyone, and how I miss him, more even than Guy Ferrand. So many letters! Followed by mine to him. All this, before we thought of posterity. (It'll soon be twenty years.) There's enough vitality there to consider publishing them, but could anyone care?

Roth's final paragraph is too close for coincidence to the final paragraph of *Notre Dame des fleurs*, wherein Genet writes from prison: "I once saw a guy who had an erection while writing his girlfriend place his heavy cock on the paper and trace its contours. I would like those contours to portray Mignon." Roth writes (from his prison): "It's fitting to conclude with my erection . . . reminding you of what you said when you first had occasion to hold it . . . 'it just seems a rather rapid transition.' . . . I'd like those words to stand as the coda . . . "

"Child molestation": What would the French think, when even the slightest pressure of a parent's hand on a child's scalp or a priest's embrace of the dutiful choirboy, make crowds cry Wolf? Are children so weak, really, and grownups so strong? When do we grow up? Is sex so harmful? Can't a twenty-one-year-old male "defend" himself against his old professor? And what difference does it make? Who seduces whom? By the time I was twelve I knew my powers, and used them. Am I mentally the worse for wear than your average fag-basher?

Rehearsing VT's songs, for Maurice Grosser's memorial tomorrow, with a 24-year-old ebony baritone who was "anxious to work with the great Ned Rorem" (Virgil's sardonic slogan). The ebony baritone is clearly miffed by the elderly spectacle I represent. Certainly I speak no longer of my body as an erotic object, but rather as an ailing object.

Touch of the flu again, and continually have to "go": diarrhea. (Go dye a rhea!) Nonetheless, drove with JH to Queensboro College where The After Dinner Opera presented *War Scenes* (not badly intoned) as the second on a bill of three tiny operas. Returning via East 36th I said, "Oh, there's the Morgan Library," which JH heard as "the morgue and library."

Two hours as formal guest of twenty-five undergraduate composers at Columbia (23 males, 2 females), and another hour as informal guest for wine & cheese with the same group, minus twenty but adding Jack Beeson, chainsmoking and trim in tight fawn corduroy. They didn't talk much, it was mainly my monologue, which began: No one knows who he is, it's a matter of opinion, a viewpoint that changes every second and is never right on target. Still, we can know *what* we are—it's a matter of fact. I'd describe myself by five nouns: Composer, alcoholic, homosexual, atheist, pacifist. But the sole adjective that comes to mind is: shy. Yes, shy, although I discovered early that shyness doesn't get you far, that anyone with brains is shy, not wishing to rush in with fools. And I discovered, in my shyness, that I was no less smart than most of these witty extrovert loudmouths voicing notions here & there. Et cetera.

Later, when I tell this to JH (who's often embarrassed, probably justifiably, by my "public" stance), he feels that the homosexual label is gratuitous, showoffy, while my saying I'm shy is like a prisoner insisting he's innocent.

At least I no longer talk of my beauty. Coming unexpectedly upon the image in a store window I wonder who that old thing is.

Received today from Virgil a pencil portrait of him by Maurice, drawn a few weeks before Maurice died.

Una Giornata particolare on television, strong as it was ten years ago. The rhythm, the décor, and the acting—by Mastroianni and Loren, underplayed and never off-key—are seamless and sad, hopeless, scary. The "music," or rather, the *fond sonore*, is like that in *Orfeu Negro,* which used the faraway but ceaseless sound of sambas in manic celebration of Mardi Gras. Here it's the faraway but ceaseless sound of radio reports on Hitler's 1938 visit to Rome. I was upset by the expertise. (Leonard Maltin's useful guide, *TV Movies,* states "Fine performances bolster this pleasant but trifling film.")

Dick Cavett's first guests on his PBS series ten years ago were this pair of actors. Dick asked Mastroianni, "How did you learn to portray a homosexual so convincingly?" Mastroianni, who in fact merely played a subdued unshaven version of his own manly self, could have said, "I modeled myself on you, Dick," but instead replied, "Some of my best friends . . . "

The Bishop of the diocese composed of Brooklyn and Queens has banned the use of Catholic facilities by groups that either engage in homosexual practices or condone them. Bishop Mugavero asked his priests "to withdraw any support" to organizations such as Dignity. Homosexuals will nevertheless "still be welcome at regular services open to all Catholics and could continue to receive treatment at Catholic hospitals."

"Youth is joy . . . it is the passion for the useless," wrote Giono. Well, maybe. But if age has any redeeming quality at all, at least in my case, it's to get rid of the *anguish* of youth, the competitive "iffiness" of Love, the loneliness in skirting the supposed joy of others. Which is surely one reason I drank: to face these dangers without which one merely played at living (if, as Sporting Life said, you call that living). Meanwhile, the fact of JH is as solid a joy as I have known, nor have I ever had a passion for the useless—unless all art, to quote Wilde, is useless.

John Cage once said he couldn't abide the Dominant Seventh, and the saxophone.

Sunday 22 Feb.

Afternoon at American Composers' Orchestra with Morris. The four pieces, conducted with cogent vitality by John Nelson, were worth it: Loeffler, William Kraft's Timpani Concerto (just long enough), Hugo Weisgall's early *A Garden Eastward* (opulently blooming and good diction), and Christopher Rouse's more than rousing *Gorgon* (twenty minutes of shrieking four-four). Intermission with Hugo, and with Frankie Schuman, to whom I chat about eye doctor. Because my flashes and amoeba-like visions recurred, Friday I saw Dr. Weisberg, who set me at ease. Frankie, meanwhile, has had a detached retina, and says it's no joke. (Am no longer at ease.) "It was as though my vitreous had fallen into a criss-crossed wood through which I couldn't see," said Frankie.

JH and Sonny have driven to Hyannis to spend the night before ferrying to Nantucket tomorrow at dawn.

Boiler's broken down again, the whole building's without heat and a snowstorm's announced. Sweet potatoes for supper. Lonely, cold.

TV announces David Susskind's death. Then, more flamboyantly, the death of Andy Warhol. (Liza Minnelli: "Future history will prove that there've been two great artists in our century, Picasso and Warhol.") *Malgré tout*, a wistful feeling for Andy.

Midnight. Robert Phelps just phoned to say that Glenway Wescott died an hour ago. Christ!

Began *La Cousine Bette*.

23 Feb.

Apartment freezing. Electric heater. JH phoned, stranded in Hyannis motel, ferry postponed till tomorrow because of gales.

Reread some of the big file of letters from Glenway, but stopped after these sentences:

"I never wish that I were religious, do you? But I sometimes wish that I could write something religious, so that I might constitute a sort of funeral for me in due course." (Oct. 17, 1963) "My left eye has gone on the blink; a little wreath of tiny shadows, and occasionally little sparkles . . . " (Nov. 16, 1963) Too close for comfort.

Call from Maggie Mills, then from Monroe Wheeler. Will I arrange some music for Glenway's memorial at the Academy on March 11? Trying lucklessly to contact singers. But there aren't any anymore.

Later. Debra Vanderlinde has agreed to sing Bach. But who will speak? asks Monroe, addled, 88 and grief-stricken. My life seems taken up with memorials. Grosser two weeks ago. Tonight, Janet Flanner, who would have been ideal to speak for Glenway, who would have worked fine for Flanner.

The heat's back on.

In literature, to make a point through repetition is to weaken the point, as when an aphorist restates his aphorism, lest you missed it—like the car owner who finds his vehicle blocked by a double-parker, and frustratedly honks and honks, leaving the whole neighborhood mad. In music, paradoxically, repetition is crucial. Where would the first movement of Beethoven's Fifth be without it, or any Bach fugue? A double paradox is musical impressionism, which forgoes repetition—with the still *more* paradoxical exception of Debussy, most of whose piano *Etudes*—his works most touted as asymmetrical breakthroughs—rely doggedly on literal repetition. Composers of *la ligne courte* (Debussy, Beethoven) need it to survive. Composers of *la grande ligne* (Puccini, Ravel) will state their long melody but once.

Father used to explain his silence at my reiteratively shouted questions from one end to the other of our apartment on Dorchester Avenue. "Either I don't hear you, or I don't choose to answer."

Some pieces don't need to be heard—at least not by me. Bach's *Inventions*. Debussy's Mallarmé songs. My imagination fills in where even the greatest performance fails. I can't bear another's personality superimposed upon such perfection—not even the composer's.

Alice Toklas, when her great collection was removed against her will by the Stein estate and placed in a bank vault, said: "My old eyes are bad anyway. I see the pictures more clearly in memory than if they were still here on the walls."

26 Feb.

Thursday early evening. Dined last night *en ville* with Earl Wild, who says Jack Roman has AIDS. Letter this morning from Ron Knapp, who writes: "Alas, I am in quite poor health (ARC) and surgery forthcoming. Not a pretty picture, but let us hope Medical Science can help us all in the near future!"

Spent afternoon examining Peter Maxwell Davies's *The Number 11 Bus*. It is something. One of its singularities, at least to American ears, is the constant violence of the instrumental canvas supporting the constant suavity of the British elocution—even at its most cockney—with those flipped R's and long vowels. (Precisely in this suavity is where the King's Singers vaguely betrayed my *Pilgrim Strangers*. It's a cheap shot to say this: I composed the work, after all, for them; yet I long to hear a rougher Yankee bunch intone it.)

Lay down at five to relieve my body, maybe to drift off, when the phone rang and the voice of a woman, after introducing herself, said that Robert Haddad died in a fire in his apartment yesterday. Robert's friend, Larry, who escaped, is alone now after thirty years and without his cats or his papers (his life's work), and without a place to live.

Procrastinating. Interest no sooner rises than it falls in the piece of Schuyler poems. The piano, tuned a month ago by an *accordeur* found through the ads in the *Native*, is already hopelessly off-pitch. JH, to whom I give this news by phone to Nantucket, says the piano up there is hopeless too.

Harcourt Brace has accepted the new book of essays. Seeking a title—a mere three words that seem always harder to find than the three hundred thousand within the book. I *would* like to use a pair of epigraphs:

> *Without music life would be a mistake.*
> FRIEDRICH NIETZSCHE

> *Music is a mistake.*
> QUENTIN CRISP

Just spoke with Joe. Peter Hujar has AIDS.

27 Feb.

Infringement upon the hours. Endless stream of letters of recommendation, letters to the editor (solicited), and of course, letters of condolence, blurbs for books, homages to the dead, citations, unsolicited manuscripts by young composers asking for approval. Rehearsing for Maurice Grosser's memorial recently, for Glenway's next month, composing and delivering the éloge to Flanner on Monday, now a squib about young Beaser for the Institute, another for Bill Coble, another for Chuck Turner, "to whom it may concern," and then tomorrow . . .

Turned down *New York* magazine's invitation to make a statement about the city. An undergraduate-type assignment. *Vanity Fair*, on five occasions (re. Paris, Bernstein, AIDS, Claus von Bulow, R. Tobin), has not used unpaid-for material they requested and which I provided.

All this requires entire days for which, by definition, I'm not given a nickel. And for Will Parker, letter to Boston. One of America's great recitalists, who has *not one* recital booked for next season.

Jasper Johns receives for one early painting at auction three million six hundred thousand dollars. A composer of equal age and reputation might receive fifty thousand for a large orchestral work or opera. Is the composer 72 times less good, or at least less valuable? Ours is an age of investment. A commissioned piece of music can't be hung on the wall to glorify its owner.

Letter from Jean Marais acknowledging the two Cocteau articles, which, nevertheless, because they're in English, he can't make head or tail of. *"Je suis un pauvre demeuré,"* he writes, the Tower of Babel twixt old acquaintances. How much more pernicious, then, the lack of correspondence between, say, Oliver North and Khomeini.

1 March

In an *NYT* puff piece for Pollini, Keith Botsford today declares, as though it were undisputed fact, that Debussy's late piano works "are precursors of atonality and amazing for the times in which they were written." If ever music were tonal to the fingertips it was Debussy; and atonality was firmly entrenched—and itself "amazing"—fifteen years before Debussy's late works of 1916. Why must the Botsfords of our world feel it necessary to claim Debussy for their own, as though to bless him with the possibilities of atonality were to rescue him from a banal fate? (It's unrecorded what Debussy & Schoenberg thought of each other, if they even knew or cared.)

Philadelphia, 3–4 March

At Graffman's $11,000 apartment on Walnut Street (on Fifth Avenue it would be thrice that price) with the lofty bay windows in every room and glamorous views in all directions. One of Naomi's subtly weird meals. As power behind the throne, she calls herself the Imelda Marcos of Curtis, and pours tea on Wednesdays. Does she crook her little finger the way Mrs. Bok used to? "Yes. And I make them crook theirs." Intense lemon-flavored coffee that kept me wakeful all night at the Barclay. Naomi's paintings of huge yellow taxis, original and real. Gary's talk of the Galápagos, where they recently spent a fortnight. View of hideous nearby skyscraper, failed and empty, shaped like an accordion. God's accordion.

Master class of singers in my songs. Four of the dozen quite good, all of them (touching in their long skirts and double-breasted suits) expert, and performing by heart. (Pianists, except for one, so-so. Have they no pride?)

Peasanty lunch chez Rosemary, with Rachel, and Rachel's Brian, age one month. R. says Mother seems increasingly vague. Can't connect a carrot on a plate with a carrot on a fork. Like *The Incredible Shrinking Man*, her frame of reference grows ever more distant from ours.

I'm tired of learning anymore.
    And so I teach.

Boulez declares: "Any composer of our time who has not felt the necessity of the serial method is worthless." Omit the word "not," and I agree.

8 March

Sunday. In his Gershwin article today Rockwell speaks of "the iron hand of modernism" that came to America in the '40s. "Composers who felt instinctively hostile to that movement (men like Virgil Thomson and Ned Rorem) could cling to the French neo-Classical tradition . . . "

He called me a man!

Less offended than touched by a call from the Fund for Human Dignity. Could I suggest someone—perhaps myself—to provide music for their annual dinner, play the piano, say, during cocktails, before the main post-prandial rock group starts playing? I explained that the kind of musicians I know wouldn't play the kind of music they want, so ask Marvin Hamlisch.

Cheese, coffee, cake here cozily this afternoon for Joe Machlis and the Hellers, Chuck Turner, and Joan Peyser.

Un beau laid.
    He's pretty ugly.

Monday, March 16

A cold, caught perhaps from JH, who's been sneezing virulently for days, yet who arose at dawn yesterday (always on Sunday) for his church services and rehearsals, then drove Sonny—and with a fever—to Hyannis, thence to Nantucket by ferry. Yet the apartment remains full of him, and of the infectious beauty of Messiaen's *Joie et clarté des corps glorieux*, which he's been practicing. He phoned at midnight to assure safe arrival. I spoke of being imbued with Joe Orton, whose works—diary, plays, an early novel, and Lahr's biography—I'm reading in preparation for a review in *The Advocate*. I told JH I hoped he wouldn't kill me one day. This put him in a bad mood. Understandably. Tactless of me. He called back a few moments later to tell me to try to learn to be calm, that a calm approach can cure many an ill, or at least arthritis. That I'm overly agitated about who to choose from the bad crop of Curtis applicants. (Two of my composers are dropping out in June: Eric Zivian, after three years, and Kurt Rohde, after just one. Which leaves two openings.) Simply choose the two least bad, and start with scratch. One can tell as much, maybe more, from their written application as from the scores submitted, despite the dumb non-questions printed in the form (*What is your ultimate goal in studying music?*), which can only inspire smarmy non-replies. The least promising pupil is often the best, in that, like the tortoise, he perseveres.

We have no Family Doctor in Manhattan. JH much against. Feels it encourages my hypochondria.

Fiercely sunny day, of the kind that presages spring, which for many brings elation, but that also accentuates the aging process. Ghastly scent of springtime.

Evening. Around 7:30, dining alone at the red table (a big baked yam, applesauce, salad) and reading Orton's diary (engrossing: a redskin reflection of my own paleface), I suddenly began to vomit. The nausea arrived so quickly that I scarcely got to the bathroom. Heaved up some lettuce, which may have been rotten. The nausea vanished just as quickly, but my arms still ache as with arthritis. Returned to the red table for a chocolate sundae, cookies, and coffee. I simply never vomit.

Saturday 21 March

If, within the same minute, the water main bursts in kitchen unstoppably inundating apartment, your upper molar begins to ache piercingly, your lover dies in the bathroom, what's your first action? To see janitor? Call dentist? 911? Meanwhile, your dog, who cannot be left alone, howls to go out. It's 4 A.M.

I'm never, as the saying goes, blocked; my head's always full of organized notions merely awaiting notation. Yet I can't work, and those organized notions loom ever more menacingly. Continual phone clanging. People wanting things. I long for naps only. Perhaps the flu, now in its eighth day, has something to do with it. But JH's flu is worse than mine, and he copes. Dried out.

22 March

Immersed not unpleasurably for a week in the complete works of Joe Orton for *The Advocate*, which has asked for a review of his diary. How appealing that diary is with its smart virility, and how remote from my own with its effete exegeses. "My writing is a deliberate satire on bad theater," Orton says. And his sexy presence still throbs from beyond the grave, it having been a deliberate satire on the Good Life. I wish I could, but won't, mention how resemblant his rapport with Kenneth Halliwell—who murdered him—was to Bill Flanagan's with Edward A., which was simultaneously playing itself out across the ocean. Orton's work: black comedy; his life, white tragedy, etc. A queer Ionesco. His unsentimental promiscuity in a pre-AIDS society makes us gasp, though was I any more chaste? treating people like things? The insouciant iconoclasm, etc. Beckett as camp. (Unless Beckett too is camp of the most rarefied vintage.)

The early novel is supposed to be funny, about unfairness pushed to the point of silliness, but I cringe. The Beatles in Wonderland, or Grendel. Is his title, *Funeral Games*, borrowed from Genet's *Pompes funèbres*? A true *petit maître*, the best thing before Charles Ludlam, whom I've seen only once (in *Galas*, three or four years ago), but who upset me more than any tragedienne since Mary Wigman in 1932.

25 March

Crash course in Smoke-enders for JH last night. Three hours at a clinic for a cynical $350 (about which the staff was evasive), with injections, tranquilizers, moralizing. Now, a day later, JH feels more urge than ever for a cig. We both hack away with our unstoppable flu.

27 March

Three days ago Rosemary called to say that Father had had "a mild stroke." Had been moved from his residence into the medical section of Cadbury. Trouble breathing. X-rays don't indicate pneumonia. Last night she said he's now in the hospital. Perhaps pneumonia. JH spent hours going over papers. (He's got power of attorney in case Father . . .)

Spring weather. Feeling dumb, empty, still coughing. At 3 A.M. heard JH go into kitchen where he had peanut butter, then came into my room, crawled into bed, put an arm around me. After a while, he said, "What did they call Queen Anne's Lace before Queen Anne?" Today he's smoking again. Tonight, a little dinner party (salmon) for Bobby King and other organist friends.

"Personally, I like words to sound wrong."—Wallace Stevens

Stravinsky's Piano Concerto, third movement, is an assemblage of college football songs.

Sheaf of reviews for Jaime's playing of my Fiddle Concerto in Scotland, "wise and compassionate," a far cry from England's contempt for my music—what little they know of it.

Michael Feingold's write-up in *VV* of *Past Tense* is generally laudatory, except: "Ned Rorem's flossy and misguided introduction (the American edition's only real mistake) unwisely tries to link Cocteau's work to the great French tradition of diary-keeping, arrogantly throwing in excerpts from [his] own diary as an uncalled-for *bonne bouche*." Feingold then proceeds to base his whole essay on a confirmation of my introduction, while willfully missing the point of the introduction. (And why is it arrogant to "throw in" excerpts from my own diary? It's simply a device, like any other, for providing explicative symmetry. As a diarist, *d'ailleurs*, I am certainly better known than Cocteau in America, which is one reason Harcourt Brace invited me to preface the book in the first place.) It's Feingold's privilege to be repelled by my "flossy" tone; but it's unprofessional for him to translate that tone as "misguided" when in fact he is saying the same thing I am saying in different words. No less often than I, he throws out French terms to italicize his English affirmations (but what does *bonne bouche* mean?). His closing line—*Jean, étonnez-nous encore*—should, of course, read: *étonne-nous encore*. (Diaghilev's command is too renowned for a switched conjugation.) Should Feingold protest that he didn't know the poet, hence could not *tutoyer* him—well, maybe *he* didn't, but some of *nous* did, and Feingold's feeling is just not French. Nor is it "French" for me to have to explain that one can *tutoyer* the past, myths, anyone we poetically adore, or, indeed, anything within the rules we ourselves fabricate, even though *we* are not French.

28 March

Sheaf of Church Musicians to dine last night (salmon, parsnips, and praline ice). They all profess to use regularly "Sing My Soul." My hit tune. Choirmasters in the sticks, who have no notion of "what" I otherwise am, often thank me for this unaccompanied 32-measure trifle, which has sold 15,000 copies a year for over a generation. But it's my accident—like Borowski's *Adoration* or Barber's *Adagio*. Written, along with two other anthems, during an August morning in Hyères, using texts from a random hymnal found at Marie-Laure's, I sent it off to Carlton Sprague Smith, who gave me a hundred dollars but never "did" anything with it.

Cadbury by truck with JH & Sonny. Saw mother before she saw us, dozing in her wheelchair in the center of the vast dining room, and around the walls other wheelchairs with moaning women. We called out, and her face lit up when she saw us. She is sorry Father doesn't feel well. The thousands of hours she spends alone, without reading! Is she sad? She no longer complains. Kept staring after us as we left, down the long hall. To Father, a mile and a half away in JFK hospital, room 302, shared with a prostrate Mr. Davis whose visiting wife lacks forearms and has a badly charred face. A smarmy priest sits with them. Father confused, hooked up to hanging cords and bottles, a tray on his lap containing an unimaginable and uneaten lunch (fried chicken, mashed potatoes, a big hunk of thickly frosted devil's food cake, some of which has left a moustache). Introduces me to nurse as John Marshall, head of the family. The customs, the habits, of our family have all dissipated. The older a parent becomes, the less—paradoxically—we assume his death. JH feels that father will not recover. Later I profess depression, which JH says is selfish. "Why don't you worry about what you can do for your parents, rather than lament what they've done to you by being sick?"

Sunday 29 March

Call from Audrey Topping. Long talk about God, whom she believes in: just spent some weeks with Shirley MacLaine in Colorado. I feel above it, but try—not too hard—to disguise it. She puts Top on the line. Discussion of a decent obit in the *Times*. Spent sterile day phoning Father's various living colleagues.

JH discouraged because Tower Records contains nothing, *nothing*, in their bins. Only moneymaking CDs are displayed. A losing battle for us all.

Ran into Elizabeth Hardwick on the sidewalk as I was about to enter the splendiferous new Food Emporium on Broadway and 69th. Embarrassed at her seeing me there. "Isn't it a scream," she says. "Well, I like the clean aisles," I say. "But it's overpriced," she goes on, "and I want to stay faithful to the Koreans on the corner." We talk about the weather, which is fine.

As a guest of honor at the Library tomorrow, I'm meant to wear a black tie. (Eugenie looks forward to dressing up.) JH has insisted that I simply buy a new tuxedo, the velvet *complet* in which I've been performing for the past fifteen years being now—at least the pants—too tight. But Father's state, plus the flu, plus indifference, have postponed . . . etc. I'm depending on the maroon cummerbund to disguise not only my pot but also the safety pins at the waist, and the zipper that won't close.

Should composers own tuxes? Yes, even though it's only once a year. But have I truly gained such weight since last I recitalized with Will Parker?

More "buzz-words" I can do without:

Postmodern	*as verbs*:
heartland	to diss
gridlock	to downsize
bottom line	to party
supply side	to bankroll
private sector	to offload
venue	to galvanize
sound bite	
grunge	
infrastructure	
cutting-edge	
grass-roots	
pundit	
workplace	
baby boomer	
couch potato	
perks	
user-friendly	
reader-friendly	
anti-hero	

30 March

Afternoon visit from a Ms. Leslie Holmes, from Boston, for a radio interview on Writing Songs. After half an hour, it turned out that her tape recorder wasn't functioning, so we began again. In two out of three of such interviews-in-the-home the tape recorder doesn't function, and the interviewer invariably says, This is the first time it's ever happened. ("Why is that needle not moving?" Ms. Holmes had exclaimed. Reminded of the 19th-century Swahili grammar which JH was studying a decade ago, in which one found the useful phrase, "Why is that man not buried?")

Evening with Eugenie, cool and lovely in Fortuny garb. Three grotesqueries in an otherwise affable, even glamorous soirée at the Library of Performing Arts where I was one of nineteen "Lions" at a splendidly decorated—all in pink—fundraising dinner. Fame and money seethed. Mr. Vartan Gregorian, beguiling and energetic teddy bear, flattered us all, not only Getty and Horowitz and Isaac Stern (who played, rather hardly, one of the more pedestrian Beethoven sonatas, the first one in D). Ceremonies, appetizing and purposeful. Mostly. But they culminated in an irrelevant and self-serving turn by Cy Coleman during which, because no end seemed in sight, Eugenie and I left. So doing, my velvet pants ripped and (I realized this on reaching home) a sky blue shard of my formal shirt emerged from my fly. On the rainy street the car ordered by Eugenie failed to appear, so in our drenched finery we searched for a cab in which Eugenie delivered me home, my cough worsened. Headache.

Academy Awards. Weary of Wm. Hurt. He's intelligent, capable, but not v. interesting.

31 March

Heavy rain. Calls to the hospital are unavailing. Father delirious most of the time.

Call from a Steven Rosenthal in Buffalo. Wants to commission a concerto for four saxophones & orch.

My favorite American song composers? Oley Speaks and Ethelbert Nevin, for "Sylvia" and "The Land of the Sky Blue Water."

Just wrote a Song Without Words, and now will copy it with India ink and orange crayon as customary gift for JH, whose forty-eighth birthday's tomorrow. Beyond this, I've been unfertile for half a year. Occupied presumably on the Voice & Orch. Suite, to Jimmy Schuyler's poems, I average five minutes a day, no more, on it. As the deadline draws near, things will . . .

David Plante's portrait of Sonia Orwell is more than merely skilled, it's "stippled in silver fire" (as Lionel Abel depicted the fingers of Rimbaud's lice pickers), and does what a memoir should—revives her image like a moving snapshot. *My* Sonia dates from a generation earlier. Was it at the Flore or the Deux Magots that we first met in 1950 through Barbara Howes and Bill Smith? It was before she became "difficult"—or, at least, cranky—and she effused the same blonde vivacity as Valerie Bettis, but more cultured. Sonia was vital, and Plante makes me miss her, but although we were solid acquaintances for ten years, we ended on a sour note in 1961 and never saw each other again.

April 2

Each day commences not with elation but with dread. I feel like crying all the time.

Call from S., whose malaise, like mine, malingers. Long chat, from bed to pained bed. She's filled with apprehension about Joan Peyser's forthcoming biog. of LB. "I wish I'd never given her those letters. She's so exploitive." But what biography, from Plutarch through Boswell to Leon Edel, is not exploitive? And if suddenly Joan's book were withdrawn, wouldn't Lenny be the first to mourn?

Even the writing of a song is exploitive. The poem already exists, in all its pristine perfection. Who are we to seek to improve upon it, to change it, to use it for our inspirational purposes, and finally cull more glory than the poet?

Sunday. Twenty-four hours in Philly for concert of works by the comp students. Proud of Erick Zivian (now, after three years, all of eighteen)'s Wind Quintet, and of Kam Morrill (who dyed his ponytail copper for the occasion)'s Suite for Two Cellos and a set of songs on Yeats poems for tenor and three instruments. Invited Ruth Jacob and Rosemary to dine at the Barclay. With tip, $125, which I charged to the Curtis Institute. Was that wrong? Sick all yesterday with reeking dysentery, returned to New York aching in the rain.

JH to Nantucket with Sonny today. Daylight Saving's begun.

Hugues Cuenod for tea at four. He'll be 85 next month, and just debuted at the Met. *Quelle gloire.* Can I whine about my health when he sits there for nearly three hours (having come from lunch with one, off to dine with another) indefatigably? Hugues' hands, arms, head, torso are always in economical motion, gangling theatrically, projecting. As a pure singer he's as savvy as they come, probably because, never really having had a voice, he still has a voice, and uses it intellectually, not sensuously. We talk of old friends, mostly dead, Nell Tangeman, and *The Rake's Progress* in 1951 in Venice where he called me The Rimbaud of Music (I being drunk at the Caffè della Fenice). He's never heard of Phyllis Bryn-Julson, nevertheless. Before he left he asked if I could play Poulenc's "C"—he has some new words for it. I accompanied him through a parody which began, *"Je suis entré dans un W.C., c'est là que tout a commencé,"* and grew predictably more lewd, while playing suggestively, as Aragon does, with the sound of the sibilant "c" (sucer, etc.). I said, *"Francis l'aurait adoré,"* but was in fact vaguely embarrassed.

JH phoned to say that, as usual, he's stranded in Hyannis. Perhaps the ferry will leave before midnight.

David Plante quotes Jean Rhys: "I'm nothing but a pen . . . Oh, to be able to write like that [the Bible]! But . . . it's not up to you. You're picked up like a pen, and when you're used up you're thrown away, ruthlessly, and someone else is picked up . . ."

Plante succeeds in his depictions of three Difficult Women because, like all true writers, he has device as well as skill (perhaps they're the same). His skill is to echo absolutely *their* voice through *his* voice. His device is to portray them solely, without the distraction of other names—especially of other famous names. We know that Rhys, Germaine Greer, and Sonia see dozens of people a week. These people are suggested, but not named. It is as though the heroines appeared in a group photo in which all the others have been blacked out. Yet those others continue to affect—like a halo—Plante's stars, even though stars may have been only on the outer edge of the picture.

Cuenod says Doda Conrad no longer speaks to him (join the club), and confides that during their half-century acquaintance he never really cared for Doda, whom he refers to in Italian as a *grande pavóne*. It's always a relief to discover that one is not alone *en boîte*. Like Philip Ramey, who swells up some imagined slight until it eats him alive, Doda has judged his friends and found most of them wanting. It takes one to know one, I do it too. But surely I don't let their bad points outweigh their good.

Are there still active W.C.s, functioning as meeting grounds, or even as seats of action? Well, the men's room of Philadelphia's 30th Street Station the other morning, when I stopped in as I often do to rinse my hands of printer's ink from the *New York Times*, featured four male backs side by side in a row of thirty urinals. Despite an occasional backward glance, they were unfazed in their obvious play. In this same area at least two cinematic bloody murders (Travolta's *Blow Out* and Harrison Ford's *Witness*) set the plot in motion.

The teenaged male performers on the Curtis stage Friday all sported neat-fitting tuxedos.

Cuenod, who still patronizes, though not often, the baths of Bern and Geneva, says, "At my age [he's the age of Alice Tully, with whom he's staying here] I needn't worry about AIDS, since normally I'd be dead anyway." As he leaves he says, "Well, we'll meet next in another world," then quickly *il se reprend*, remembering we'd already made a date for next spring when he's to sing in *Turandot* again at the Met.

6 April

Rain. Acid rain. Not so bad as upstate where that bridge near Amsterdam collapsed in a trice hurling four cars to hell. Who of us was not in those cars literally? Literally our land wastes away.

Five hours yesterday at the Academy where Hortense acquits herself with tact and expedience in her first public show as president—a step up from Galbraith's pontifical wit. Sit with Paul Cadmus, who looks a decade younger than his 82 years, despite a recent prostate siege, and Allen Ginsberg, now a photographer, who presents me with a bizarre portrait of myself taken in converse with Vincent Persichetti in these same lofty halls last November. (Vincent did not then know what he now knows: that he has lung cancer.) Allen and I discuss Paul Bowles, who seems to need money in Tangier, he too in failing health. We bring this up to Maggie Mills, who immediately declares that the Academy can provide $3500 from their fund for such "cases." At the dinner, sit between Nora Beeson and Bill Gaddis, the former warm and wifely without, she says, being acquisitive, the latter drunk in a blue cloud of anxious smoke with appealing heterosexual eyes. S. there too, as always stylishly but quietly groomed with her pretty legs and silver laugh. After coffee we are treated to a superfluous reading by Bella Akhmadulina, preceded by a grotesque poem uttered by its maker, Harrison Salisbury. He cites the Great of the past (Pushkin et al.), of the present (Yevtushenko et al.) and adds, "I do not know the poets of the future, but they will be dead in hotel rooms with bullets in their skulls," or words to that effect. Akhmadulina, slight, good looking, and theatrical in the genre of Suzy Delair, declaimed in Russian for forty minutes despite a racking cough. The histrionic tradition is not mine.

Rode home with Vincent Persichetti (bald from cobalt treatments, but spirited), Elizabeth Hardwick, and John Cage. John and I talk of Satie. No two Americans are more closely bound than us to *Socrate*, about the manner of performance of which we disagree totally.

Home late. Long phone talk with JH in Nantucket. Then S. called around midnight (her birthday, and I'd bought some gardenia soap so that she'd think of me when naked, but wasn't able to slip it to her at the Academy). She leaves for Bermuda today, but wanted me to know that Lenny is unhappy about Peyser's book, which he's not read but has heard about from Mendy, who hasn't read it either. I'm apparently quoted as having "gone to bed" with LB when we first met in 1943. Well, I've not read the book either, nor has S., who nonetheless distrusts utterly Joan Peyser. Didn't have the nerve to say that Joan interviewed me last month for the *Times* and that I liked the interview.

This morning spoke with Roditi. Paul Bowles doesn't need money, at least not for the moment, for health reasons. I'm keeping out of it.

Recurrence of flashes on periphery of vision.

S. for forty-four years has had a way, surely involuntary, of belittling aspects of my behavior—of making me feel guilty about whatever doesn't coincide with her morality. Her morality, in part, is one of extreme privacy (though she's had her flings like the rest of us) and of putting art before life. Every five or ten years she lashes out at my little ways, while I've never once torn open for her edification the proprietary *lubies* and smug egotism that drives me, and many another, up the wall. She wouldn't understand. (After a point we must accept our friends' "faults"— those faults are *us*—and hush up or run off.) Nor have I ever divulged, "for her own good," certain incidents which today would simply and uselessly hurt her. People don't change.

But I roundly resent her maternal shielding the world-famous Lenny, and Lenny's own whimpering at my evildoing. Lenny too had his flings, and I was one of them. Had I been a girl would anyone think twice? Lenny and I were 24 and 19 when we met, and we did what young people do. There's an unintended homophobia in S's hopeless attempt to pull a screen around this madly public figure, a homophobia all the more uncharitable in that today, of all days, the dignifying of gays is crucial for us all, including her, and she knows why.

13 April

Wet weather again. A mosquito all night.

JH, rehearsing with his chorus Messiaen's *Sacrum Convivium* for next Sunday's service, says: "Think of a reformed whore. She basks in the light of the cross, but retains her old bangles." Then he requests that they whine on certain phrases. The singers were not amused.

Stravinsky called Messiaen's music a crucifix of sugar. I do love sugar.

Weekend with Sylvia in Lancaster for *Homer* première, maximally rehearsed and replete with good will. Yet I was taken aback, not hearing it through their ears. The chorus of fifty was composed of amateurs, the three soloists were mediocre, and the eight instrumentalists were toneless. Their perspective was pride in their progress throughout the semester, mine was from the opposite vantage—this lacks all professional veneer. If I had not misjudged my technique (the 30-minute piece could sound marvelous with other forces), I *had* misjudged my ability to write for the inexperienced. It's hard to be easy.

Lead article in the *Times* by Paul Goldberger on The Risks of Razzle-Dazzle, and based on a false premise. "The rise in visual literacy," he contends, "has been accompanied by an almost desperate desire to be stimulated." He means visual illiteracy. For when he says that in the 1950s "people were not particularly attuned to the way things looked," he forgets the feats of Noguchi, Ter Arutunian, Philip Johnson, et alia. Far be it from me to defend Zeffirelli, but if ever a Puccini score asked for blowing up, it's *Turandot* (as opposed to *Bohème*), and Goldberger goofs when he says the spectacular sets are "grand beyond all connection to Puccini's delicate music." Oh well, the Arts & Leisure needs to fill space.

9 April

Here is the program note for *Three Poems of Baudelaire*, composed for the BBC Chorus, which Boosey & Hawkes telexed to London:

Is it brash for an American to set Baudelaire to music—and in English, at that? Well, it makes more sense than setting him in French, in view of Debussy and Duparc. We are what we speak. Despite my long years abroad, I've always felt that if I and my composing brethren in America do not create a song literature in our native tongue, no European will do it for us.

Yet nostalgia forever lurks at the door. Thus, when in 1982 my friend Richard Howard won the American Book Award for his translation of the complete text of *Flowers of Evil*, I sensed that a legitimate compromise was also at the door. Just as Howard, in his choice of words and word order, bathed this quintessentially Parisian verse in a New Yorkish perfume (a Londoner's or Dubliner's translation would by definition swerve in other directions), so now could I, while retaining my national integrity, render homage to Baudelaire through his very poetry.

My three unaccompanied settings are easy but hard. That is, knowing they would be created by the world's greatest chorus, I cast the vocal lines in my habitually "accessible" style, while feeling free to curve these lines higher and with more rhythmic nuance than if written for *n'importe qui*. "Invitation to the Voyage," surely Baudelaire's most familiar poem, is marked "meltingly slow." "The Cat," in three brief divisions, moves from brisk triplets to a meditative chorale, then back to the triplets. "Satan's Litanies," using a sort of question-and-answer device, pits the greater chorus, singing generally in unison and always free and warm and involved, against three solosits who remain rigid, cool, remote. At the end, the two forces join in a loud prayer.

More sound-alikes: Micaela's air, *"Je dis que rien ne m'épouvante,"* and the second theme of Chopin's B-flat minor "Scherzo." Turandot's "Three Questions" and *Vanessa's* "Quintet." Ellis Island. Ella's Island.

Rosemary's international offspring: Christopher has had two Jewish spouses, Paul's wife's Chinese, and Charity has two daughters by a quite black man. . . . JH, as always at this time of year, beside himself with my taxes, Father's taxes, his own taxes, and the daily pre-Easter services. Sunday we drive to Nantucket for five days . . . Sonny, more than ever, has taken to biting people.

People say: When you run out of all those commissions you're working on, you'll be able to compose what you want. Assumption: What's paid for can't be quite honest. But composing is how I make a living. Isn't it better to arrange to be commissioned to write "what you want" than not to be commissioned to write it?

Morning with a new doctor named Melester. Reassured. Afternoon at Alice Tully Hall posing in front of the organ for an Irish photographer.

18 April

For 37 years, ever since enjoying it with Henri Hell in a little cinema near the Luxembourg, I've wished to see *La Ronde* again, with its all-star cast and infectious waltz by Oscar Straus. Last night the wish was granted by Channel Thirteen. The lovable cynicism now seems coy, the philosophy cheap, the actors self-conscious.

The Rake's Progress, heard now after an equally long *recul du temps*, dates much better, though the libretto by Auden—who is no less deft than Max Ophuls—and Chester Kallman, now seems merely hard and campy. But Stravinsky's garnishment of that libretto is more "inspired" than I'd recalled. Cornucopia of tune! Model of orchestration, using so little, yet in such a novel way! Authority! Chances taken that always succeed!

Most reassessments show that what we once adored has turned dusty, without taste, like a dear old movie re-seen on TV. Far rarer is when the past is *better* than you recall. *The Rake* is as heartening today as the visit recently from Cuenod, the original Auctioneer.

Boning up for a lecture on I.S. a week from tomorrow. Meanwhile tomorrow, Easter, we leave by truck from this isle to that.

Someone will say, "We really have a great deal in common," at precisely the moment I've decided we have nothing in common.

Irony. In the next decade AIDS will devour a huge mass of humanity, with nature thus solving the dilemma of overpopulation. In America AIDS's initial victim was the gay male, whose rising visibility in the previous decade was a sign, some claimed, of nature solving the dilemma of overpopulation.

Conspicuous consumption. With a decline in musical excellence at the Met comes the rise of expensive decoration, like an old courtesan seducing through her magnificent couch rather than her magnificent body. (Can one get it up for a couch? Yes, some.) Henahan locates the decline as beginning two decades ago with the Met's move to Lincoln Center "when décor specialists such as Cecil Beaton were invited into the picture." But Beaton designed *Vanessa* at the old Met ten years earlier.

May Day

Visit yesterday from one Robert Giard, a fulltime photographer of gay men and lesbians. What the hell.

At six, reception at library for Adrienne Rich, who, except for our one song in *Women's Voices*, I don't know well enough to see again in this mob of fearsome sapphists; after ninety seconds I wonder what I'm doing here, and abscond with my lame soul, which should never leave home alone.

Brief meal and backgammon with JH, then a party at Pia Gilbert's for Gary Samuel. John Cage, ever pleasant, is there, and again we discuss Satie together, this time in French for the benefit of another guest who doesn't know English. John's French is rocky in both sound and sense, belying the untruism that all musicians have an ear for tongues.

Noisy filming of a TV commercial until dawn on 70th Street with violent lights, throbbing trucks, megaphones, and "extras." The company had a city permit which costs nothing, while we, the taxpayers, were required to get our cars off the streets or have them towed away at our own expense. At 4 A.M., JH called the cops, no soap; this morning he called a Deputy Mayor, who sharply stated, "The streets belong to us, not you." The whole mess begins again this evening. "It's only two nights out of your life," says the Deputy Mayor.

Dizzy with sleeplessness, at 10 A.M. I open the door to yet another photographer, Arnold Newman, who had called me last week to ask if he could do my portrait while being interviewed for *American Photographer*. Sleepily I pose, almost in pain, for three hours while Newman cracks jokes for his entourage.

Rosemary flew last night to Hong Kong with Paul & Jackie, who hope to adopt a baby there.

Skimming bound galleys of *The Nantucket Diary* I note my strong impression of Carter's 1976 Concerto for Three Orchestras wherein, with a few orchestral crunches, he "eradicates the infinitely expressive solo strings." Isn't that precisely what I myself did, twenty-four months earlier at the end of *Assembly and Fall*, when my muscular solos were smashed into whimpering—and finally silence—by a series of hideous dry fortissimo tuttis?

Back from a wet five days in Nantucket (by truck both ways with JH & Sonny), where I worked mostly on *A Few Days*, and from 36 hours in Philadelphia, where I did the Stravinsky lecture plus a little speech about seeing the première in Venice of *The Rake's Progress*, which Curtis is offering twice next week.

Unlike the opera itself, which today, at least for me, takes on an impeccable glow it lacked 36 years ago, Robert Craft's notes for the recording are smug, dated, and, as usual, smell specious. For example, the irrelevant pages quoted from Vera Stravinsky's diary ring false; one assumes that Craft himself had more than a hand in them, as in the phrase: ". . . the list of old friends who have come to 'assist' at the performance (that odd French expression which seems to suggest an intention to help move the pianos or fill in on fifth bassoon) is too copious to be continued." "Assist" is not an odd expression for one who has learned English through French, as is the case with Vera. Indeed, to "attend" (a performance) sounds odder to French-trained ears, for whom "attendre" means "to wait." And does Vera keep her diary in English?

The forever unsettled question of updating, as with Corsaro's *Carmen* or Chéreau's *Ring*: Should we properly do Shakespeare's *Tony & Cleo* in Elizabethan dress, as was done at the Globe, or in Egyptian dress, or in modern dress, or in modern Egyptian dress "re-thought" as Elizabethan, or maybe in Russian dress as the latest in cogent timeliness (since Slavic women today seduce gullible American militaries to find out secrets)?

Like *The Rake*, which has mellowed, how would Jenö Zádor's delicious "Hungarian Caprice" strike these ears today?

Peyser's *Bernstein*. Would she'd said more rather than less. If, for example, she must depict my "sleeping with" LB in 1943, why not embellish the dimension by adding that LB conducted the world première of my *Third Symphony* just a few blocks away, sixteen years later? In fact, Peyser doesn't even mention that I'm a musician.

Poll of various musical personalities (but not me) in the *Times* about who's underrated and who's overrated. Naturally Vivaldi is deemed overrated in the light of Bach. Since everyone *knows* he's overrated, I'd have said he's the most underrated of overrated composers.

Death of animals versus vegetables. Our death is singular and utter; plants renew themselves each spring (*Si le grain ne meurt*, etc.). Is a tree its own child? Idle— since eventually it too vanishes.
    There's just too much water. There's water to burn.

2 May
To Cadbury, where JH discusses taxes for two hours with Father while I go to the "other side" to see Mother. At each visit, roughly every six weeks, Mother seems to have grown more remote, retaining her lonely, large, sad, intelligent eyes. She repeatedly asks when we're going to have lunch, although we've just had it. Then, while I'm in the midst of a sentence, she turns in her wheelchair and heads toward the drinking fountain. Or tries to—her coordination is vague.
    Suicide in Houston of Howard Barnestone. Why should this faze me—who had a mere bagatelle with him so long ago?

I do love women, and even love to touch them (as much as I love to touch anyone— we're not of a tactile environment). I'm just not excited by them. Yet three I've fantasized about. Moira. Leontyne. Mrs. Aquino. Have they something in common? Each is excessively what she is, with a heart-shaped mouth.

JH making tapes of his various church concerts to send his mother. He feels his choir sounds not good, that most choirs sound not good, and reiterates that only with a large group can you get a truly soft sound. Sure, a solo fiddle can hold its own against a hundred fiddles: a hundred fiddles are never a hundred times louder than a solo at the same dynamic, since there's no such animal as "a same dynamic," or even a true unison, except by computer. But a hundred fiddles can play *softly* more convincingly than three: by the nature of things they're more in tune.

3 *May*

To the Y with Pia for Barbara Kolb's new piece (effective, i.e., filled with effects which happily work), after which, as we walk toward Central Park along 86th we are solicited by a bum, whom we ignore. Pia says that last week while strolling with John Cage he was approached by three bums in one block. To the first two he gave a quarter each. When the third asked for money, John said, "I was just about to ask you the same thing."

Four o'clock *goûter* at Alice Tully's. We were to have attended the local première tonight of my Organ Concerto, but the concert was cancelled (Little Orchestra Society, no ticket sales).

Have I ever been here by daylight? The view from her 27th floor remains heart-stopping—Central Park being the eighth wonder of the world. The apartment itself, though less grandiose, is as luxuriant as Marie-Laure's *hôtel* with every last *bibelot* a work of art, and the works of art being Corot and Magritte. Alice claims to be crippled from arthritis, but appears hale with her lipstick and pearls, and I always enjoy embracing her solidly. The pair of adorable female Maltese—Sophie, the smaller, with blue bows, and Tati with her pink bows—join us on the sofa for the smoke-tasting tea and Pepperidge Farm cookies served prettily by two elderly women in white.

I had forgotten that Alice subscribed to a group called Unity—not a church, not Unitarians—which keeps her going. She also believes in reincarnation and has several well-told anecdotes to confirm her credo. In moments of great melancholy (as when her longtime lover, heldentenor Edward Gaeffe, died), a consoling and logical voice speaks aloud to her, and that voice is her own from millennia ago. I listen with interest as she explains that she concurs with one of the Unity founders whose theory it is that if six million Jews perished in the Holocaust, that's their recompense for having precipitated the Spanish Inquisition. When I say that the theory is outlandish as well as disproportionate, and that it sounds like a rationalization (the way English colonials used to tell their children that the poor were poor because God was "testing" them), as well as a wee bit anti-Semitic, Alice replies, "Not at all. After all, you and I may have once been Jews, or may yet come back as Jews in an afterlife."

Am reminded of George Cree's anecdote. When Alice returned from Calcutta, he asked her if the poverty didn't bother her. "Poverty?" said Alice, slack-jawed, deep-voiced, and self-contained. "I didn't see any poverty."

Like most gentile middle-class urban males born in 1923, I was circumcised at the age of three days.

Dialogues des Carmélites in English on the tube. During the final "Salve Regina" tears stream down my face, as much for the memories of the Paris première exactly thirty years ago (at the party afterward chez Dugardin, rue de l'Université, I saw Cocteau for the last time), as for the vital performance tonight. But Jessye Norman is quite a presence.

Vernal heat. Rosemary's 65th birthday. Phasing out of the city (we'll truck to the littler island on the 17th for the summer) through final checkups. Monday, a new retinal specialist named Freilich, in whose anteroom I waited for two hours along with various well-off likeable yentas and scared middle-aged gents (including me)—who should lumber in but Diana Trilling, grand and blind, she too there for the first time, a reassuring friend. Flashes and floaters in both eyes apparently don't indicate a detached retina . . . Wednesday, Miss Tully *chez elle.* See above . . . Yesterday, Swee, whose X-rays can't explain aching molars, upper left, but who says my gums "remain shocking"—as though 'twere my fault. Then visit from Sahan Arzruni inviting me to compose, in haste, a few short unaccompanied love songs, *in Armenian*, for the American tour next September of the Armenian State Chorus. Quite a bit of money ($7,500) for what will be a mere seven pages of music. Sylvia thinks I should . . . Tea at Daron's, who plays his expert new Trio.

Today, final *séance* of the scholastic season with the Curtis flock, here in New York. Erick Zivian graduates tomorrow, after three years with me. Despite his pronounced and quite facile gifts, and his sizeable catalogue from the two first years (I did make of him a composer, though he might not put it that way), he gets a mere P, for passing, as does the new one, Kurt Rohde, since neither did much work this year. Ironically, Kam Morrill, originally the least promising, has shown the most promise with his lyrical impulses and instrumental combinations as odd as his gaunt features and peroxided ponytail.

Small dinner party at Virgil's, prepared from scratch by the host and by Paul Sanfaçon, Gerald Busby, and Sam Byers (he of the applesauce-colored hair and matching glasses), with me and Pia as uptown outsiders. Mushroom soup, chicken roasted on a bed of kosher salt, potatoes mashed with garlic, crushed cucumber and tomato salad, and strawberry shortcake like your Aunt Mabel used to make.

Virgil, overweight but nevertheless recovered from diverse ills, is clad in beige & chocolate. He both listens and "pronounces" with the agility of forty years ago, and there's a feeling of deferential and almost too-thick good will as we mutely evaluate these dear moments. But the moments *are* dear. Yes, he pronounces, but not always infallibly. He's amassing a book of letters, uncensored, from the Yale files, and writing a new book based on lectures about what he used to call "the song dodge" (the métier of those who can do nothing else, a term now inapplicable), now called "how to write songs." He emphasizes the need for knowledge about *word groups*: it's not just words we set to music, but sensicle combined with cellules of same: "When I consider" "how my light" "is spent." Can't any fool see that? While the young folk wash dishes gaily laughing, Pia and I request decaffeinated coffee, but there is none. "It's like asking for whisky without alcohol," protests Virgil, a quip that makes sense only if it's assumed you drink for the effect rather than for the taste. Yet the mushroom soup was delectable, and everyone knows that mushrooms contain no particle of nourishment. Indeed, when I once pointed this out, Virgil replied, "Well, neither does a cock."

V.T. thinks it's time for a book to be written about me.

Male homosexuality is chastised, yes, while female homosexuality is ignored by those who make rules. But not because, like Queen Victoria, we won't admit the existence of lesbianism. It's because those who make rules are straight males, uninterested in the image of two men fucking. They *are* interested in the image of two females fucking, since they can, in fact, identify with one of these females. What we enjoy we approve of. (Except in America, where what we enjoy must necessarily be wrong.)

And myself? I'm vaguely repelled—uninterested in the image of any two persons fucking, although I find women as beautiful as men.

Richard Howard's translation is seamless, mostly. To find an occasional run in his hose is thus the more jarring. As when he Englishes *dîner en ville* as "dinner in town" or "dining in town." *Dîner en ville* means "dining out," inevitably at someone else's home—it's a High Society term. "Dinner in town" would be the translation of *"dîner au restaurant."*

14 May

Call from John Myers detailing his most recent chemotherapy. His hair doesn't fall because "the bladder is an exterior organ" (he claims). A tube is inserted, sans anesthetic, into the penis as far as the kidney, and the treatment consists of provoking a rumpus in the bladder, causing clots, which wash out during the ensuing days. John screamed no less than the baby that was being treated simultaneously in the same room. The baby's anxiety soothed John's, "but only just a little bit." Then, he adds, "O, the democracy of pain!"—a phrase he's surely used in conversations of a similar nature this morning. I empathize.

Six hours cleaning house. Layers of soot on every possible surface—the soap, the toilet tissues, between every last row of books. But the glistening new windows seem pristine and tranquil after yesterday's tornado, with a zest of pungent aftersmell, like Dorian Gray's attic after Alan Campbell, with his chemicals, caused a murdered corpse to disappear.

Finished piano-vocal score of *A Few Days* and delivered it to B. & H., going on foot through Central Park, on this most perfect of days, passing the azure azaleas of the admirable Tavern on the Green, remodeled by Warner LeRoy, who caused me much professional anguish three decades ago at the old York Theater.

Thumbing through the folders marked "F" of the obituary drawer in the white filing cabinet, searching for memorabilia of Marya Freund, my hand fell upon the mass of letters from Henri Fourtine. The preoccupation we (we, the young) once had for games, for suffering, for gobbling up time with sex and more sex and recriminations and insoluble jealousy! Could we live it all again? No, because youth is defined by its ignorance of itself: Once we realize we're young, we're no longer young. To squander is a prerogative of the young.

On certain days I think so intensely of Henri that he seems to live again, the rooms fill with the fact of his voice, his odor, his clothes, his crotch, his coffee, like the rooms at 75 Rue de Vaugirard in 1952. But what Henri was—or at least what we were together—now exists only in my memory, and that too must decay.

JH questions the final value of Gertrude Stein, contending that her best works were probably by others. Was the *Autobiography of Alice B. Toklas* in fact by A.B.T., as Maurice Grosser claimed, the voice being so much Alice's? What of Maurice's own workable version of *Four Saints* drawn from Gertrude's unworkable version? Or "When this you see remember me"—doesn't that remind you of Nahum Tate's *Dido & Aeneas*, or maybe of a priest's incantation at Communion? Others penned her prose as others penned Stravinsky's.

Of course, it's incorrect to compare Stravinsky's ghost writers to Stein's, since Stravinsky was not primarily an author. As incorrect as Zeffirelli's public complaint about those criticizing his production of *Turandot*. Verdi, says he, "was so crushed by the critical reception of *Aida* that he wrote nothing for the next seventeen years." Yes, well, but what did the producer of *Aida* do during those seventeen years?

Insomnia is a nightmare.

My domineering passivity. I command you to rape me.

Nantucket, 18 May
Arrived for the summer last night by truck and ferry. The unprecedentedly heavy snows of February have battered the plants and bent the trees, some irremediably. Eight or ten 100-pound branches sadly surround the cluster of elms, and the row of pines perpendicular with JH's basement room are twisted epileptically. Nature in a month may re-shape them happily.

24 May
The deaths for which we are "prepared" often catch us up short. We have waited so long in the desperate shade that the shade itself comes to seem permanent. AIDS with its ironic highs and lows gives the illusion that where there's life there's hope. Then suddenly the hope is gone. On this note I just completed an obituary for Robert Jacobson, who, more than a friend, was, as *Opera News*'s editor, the source of my every word on music during the past decade.

Finished *Bouvard et Pécuchet* (does one "finish" an unfinished book?) with mixed reaction. Flaubert out-Flauberts himself with accurate realistic research. It's an inventory novel. Yes, there is a unique mood, especially in the long, odd, vaguely homophobic first chapter, and the feat (far superior to *Les deux greffiers* from which it stems, as virtuosically as Gide's *Sequestrée de Poithiers* stems from a mere *fait divers*) is impeccable—not a word out of place—especially in depiction of the boredom of farm life in winter. But what does it add up to? What—as the French say—does it rhyme with?

Nantucket, 25 May

For the first time we've planted petunias, blackish purple with a glaucous sheen, like scores of finch-sized peacocks. Fragrance inebriating. Jonquils the size of tubas.

In seven days here I've begun and completed four unaccompanied SATB Armenian Love Songs, *in Armenian*, based on Sahan's phonetics, and using the sixteenth-century verse of one Nahabed Kouchag.

Sleeping *par à-coups* in the too-cool nights.

Documentary on Horowitz, *l'idiot savant du clavier*, whose Mozart (the C-major Sonata I used to play with Belle Tannenbaum) I would have found vulgar forty years ago, but now find aptly rhapsodic, novel, Landowska-like.

29 May

Showed *A Few Days* finally to JH. How did he like the music? "Expert," he said, merely. And the words? A pause. Then: "Stifled. They're stifled, as though Schuyler were exerting himself to appear prosaic so as not to show his real insanity, as opposed to Ashbery who, being basically sane, lets his poems take off in madness."

Showed him also the Armenian choruses. He feels there should be a fifth one, not only to round out the set, but also because their première (a Soviet Choir two nights in a row next October in Avery Fisher Hall) is so auspicious.

Summer weather after weeks of cold. The first peonies, so deeply blood-hued as to be nearly blue, are already fully blossomed and shedding. JH has shorn the lawn so that it looks chic as a golf course, yet he's sorely against *Architectural Digest*'s doing an article here next month. It's my utter greed for publicity, says he; our house just isn't what they're about. JH perhaps takes it too seriously. Publicity, *Architectural Digest*, etc.—it's all just a game. It amuses me to play it.

His coughing at 3 A.M. was so paroxysmal that I went to his room to perhaps give him a back rub. Only to find he was coughing *in his sleep*, as well as grinding his teeth and raving, with Sonny cowering under the bed.

Re. The "game" of publicity: various Chicagoans have sent me Von Rhein's article of a couple of Sundays ago, in the *Tribune*, about "who will last." It's flattering to be pictured, with Boulez and Bernstein, as three of the "fourteen master composers who will score a place in history." (The others are Schuman, Shapey, Feldman, Nancarrow, Lutoslawski, Penderecki, Ligeti, Henze, Messiaen, Birtwistle, and Taverner.)

Dined with Eugenie and Christopher Idone at 21 Federal. When I came home, JH showed me a documentary he'd taped on polar bears. The cubs, with their snowy fur and inexperienced coal-black eyes, resemble Sonny. Sonny & JH drive tomorrow to New York.

Received yesterday a copy of *The Advocate* in which my essay, badly edited, on Orton has finally appeared. In the final paragraph I state that, since Orton, there is simply no theater, at least not that I believe in, with the exception of Charles Ludlam. Today, page one of the *Times*: Ludlam is dead of AIDS.

Call from Father. Says he read Mother a poem today, Leigh Hunt's *Abul ben Adam*, and while doing so, he began to cry. Mother didn't react. I asked him to read it to me over the phone. He did, and began to cry.

Sunday 31 May

Third day of heat wave, the whole town looks wilted. Not just tulips and people, but the very bricks melt dispiritedly. In what shape will JH—who arose yesterday at dawn after a wakeful night (who can sleep in a furnace?) to catch the ferry, and who arises this morning in New York at dawn to lead church services, then heads back to Hyannis with Sonny in the non-air-conditioned Mazda—in what shape will he arrive on the midnight ferry?

Forty years—*forty years!*—this summer I wrote "Mourning Scene" at Tanglewood. Four or five of my very best songs were already three years old.

Thirty-two years ago in Hyères I composed a fair amount of music to my own libretto based on RLS's *The Suicide Club*. The impetus was a house gift from Felix Labisse to Marie-Laure, *Le Livre du suicide*, copiously illustrated, about the more ornate manners people use to kill themselves. Often it's in their national form of capital punishment. A butcher from Vanves, for example, a family man with six children, in 1928 did this: attached a scythe blade to the bottom of an armoire, hoisted this "machine" onto a table, and then, after donning an ash-blonde wig and a confirmation dress, lay down beneath the table and decapitated himself.

Cannot abide Maurice Chevalier.

Composed yesterday a fifth "Love Song" to append to the other four in the Armenian Suite. Sahan Arzruni told me by phone that the Soviet choir that will première these on tour (plus two performances in Avery Fisher next October) plans to use the "fact" of me, an American etc., as publicity. Well, my suite needed a bit more weight, although all a pastiche of modal native tunes. Like Poulenc, I write my own folk songs.

Architectural Digest will not come.

Whatever else may be said about it, Joan Peyser's book has the power to turn old friends against each other. Chuck T., killing the messenger rather than the message-writer, has sent me one of his letters of such meanness that who would dream we'd been pals for forty years? "You and David Diamond were wrong to tell her about Lenny's private sex life, and she was wrong to print it," he writes. "I find it grossly selfish and narcissistic of you not to give any thought to the feelings of others. You are the only person I know who wants to advertise every sexual adventure you have in print for money and notoriety, and I condemn this strongly. Chuck T."

Forgetting that he can't know what I did or didn't tell Joan, that he can't know how she edited it, and that Lenny's sex life is not only quite public but an urgent and scarcely shameful part of his being, Chuck's tone is so unforgiving and Godlike that he will surely want no further recommendations, handouts, or hospitality from me. Most surprising is his American layman's notion of why authors write books: for money! Could I subsist for one year on what I've made from my entire published literary catalogue? If money were what I'm after I'd change my tune.

Chuck's letter (one of many that he writes often, to me and to others, slapping us down without appeal) makes me sadder for him than for me.

The constant reminder that AIDS's chief "risk groups" are gay males and drug users implies no crossing of categories. Has no gay male caught AIDS from a needle? What about a drug user who caught his or her AIDS not from a needle but from sex?

If peonies are in full season, like infected cabbages in all their sanguinary splendor, or like pink swans and Renoir bellies, asparagus is in season too. JH, who relishes asparagus as I relish fudge, steams sheafs each evening—sea green, tender, succulent, and expensive. And ticks are in season, conspicuous on Sonny's milky coat as the beauty spots affected by Dolores Del Rio in her role as Madame Dubarry. Nectarines, too, are in season, but hard as rocks, unless you buy the "tree-ripened" ones at 60 cents apiece.

It's the best season, nevertheless, when JH and I are here alone, before the onset of summer guests, transistors, impositions. Heat gives way to cold again. The impatiens have died.

Do you remember that melancholy field, those dozen satisfyingly unkempt acres across from The Grange (a recreation center where Sonny took—not successfully—his "obedience lessons") and bounded by New Lane and Upper Main? Well, that field's torn up, and soon will contain twenty condominiums. In only two years Nantucket has spawned whole townships where a grandiose no-man's-land once flourished.

Publication of *The Nantucket Diary* is eight months overdue. North Point has postponed it consistently since the delivery nearly two years ago. "It's a big book," they say. "Everything must be perfect." Yet JH has saved them thousands with his expert index. It's now scheduled for September, long after the chief purchasers, Nantucketers, will have left the island.

Publication does not legitimate dumbness. Once an author sees his silly remarks in print they don't suddenly look sensible, though his profound remarks can look senseless. Like hallucinogenic drugs, which cause everyone except artists to think they're artists, but which show artists only wherein they've cut corners.

Discussion with JH this morning, while coffee brewed, about why Andrew Porter's current appraisal of Boulez seemed so lackluster. For Andrew, if Boulez does it, it's the right thing to do (just as Andrew never doubts that, say, a song by Carter merits a column of exegesis). "It," in this case, is Boulez's practice over the years of presenting the same work in different versions, as though a work were forever in the making, acquiring new meaning not only in time but—because the composer continues to tamper—in space, in shape. Perhaps. But Valéry's notorious *dire*, "A work of art is never finished, it is only abandoned," is a damaging slogan. What does it say? Are Mozart's symphonies, Bach's fugues, Michelangelo's ceilings, Tolstoy's novels, abandoned, unfinished? Art is art precisely because it *is* finished, honed into the one form that only it can bear, unrepeatable and forever. The question of works-in-progress being nevertheless offered to the public at odd times is a legitimate question, but Andrew doesn't examine the question.

From behind the hedge comes a sound similar, but not identical, to a fairly unhappy but prosperous child stroking the white gravel with a bunch of last year's wisteria.

Because one of the two new Curtis students wants to begin the fall semester by modeling a quartet on Bartók's Sixth, I've been restudying that piece. The more I hear it the less I hear in it. For all its perfection and glamour, it remains arid and charmless, a robot version of the other five quartets. Rather than being a forerunner, like so many of Bartók's other works, it palely echoes those he foreran (Stravinsky of *Histoire*, Grofé, Strauss, Saint-Saëns, Ravel).

9 June

My bed hugs a slanting corner on the second floor. Two feet off, outdoors beneath the eaves, red sparrows nest. For thirteen Junes I awaken each morning to the chirp of birdlings being fed. (This intimate—this *private*—family is as unaware of me as are people fucking behind a partition in a public sauna, or, indeed, as strangers in the next apartment one yard away.)

Then I arise with an ever more racking sacroiliac hinting at a lopsided day. Touch of herpes again. And they're growing more pronounced—those fireflies on the periphery of both eyes' vision whenever light is dim, as, for example, during a late-evening stroll. I'd say I were getting old, if it weren't that "symptoms" have been asymptomatic my whole life.

Talk of AIDS everywhere, much more than even a month ago.

Nearly one-third done with *A Few Days'* orchestration.

10 June

Bedtime reading still *La Cousine Bette,* one chapter a night, which, since I'm on chapter 43, leaves 91 nights to go. It's all about money, like *Pride & Prejudice,* or like Virgil's autobiography, which is actually an economic history of American music since 1910. But Balzac knew a thing or two about evil-for-it's-own-sweet-sake as well. The characters of *Bette* and of *Madame Marneffe* derive from the *manigances* of Laclos a generation earlier, as—a generation later—Wilde's theme for *Dorian* derives from Balzac's own *Peau de Chagrin.*

I'm not yet the Older Generation so long as my parents survive. But this diary, the earlier volumes, like books by everyone I know, has dealt with pre-AIDS concerns that must seem ambiguous as pre-nuclear military concerns to the young of today. REPENT, FOR THE END OF THE WORLD IS AT HAND. I don't know about repentance, but *for the first time ever* the end of the world is not a religious metaphor. Young people for the remainder of this century at least, will not be able to enjoy love and sex with the rapture that we, even at our most oppressed, did. The tonality of Love Poetry will shift, and even of pornography. Music? Is it demonstrable that music (sheer music, not texts by Cyndi Lauper) can be AIDS-aware?

The first nectarines have arrived at the A & P, the first rosebuds have appeared on the back trellis, and our six snowball bushes are heavy with blooms. Ticks rage.

11 June

PBS Special on Beethoven last night, hosted by Peter Ustinov reciting a bathetic text by one Israela Margalit who also played the piano, curving her digits neatly, the way we're taught to do. Nothing in the text suggested that Beethoven was other than the greatest genius who (in Mae West's words) ever walked the street: thus, a viewer learned little. Ms. Margalit offered a lesser series of variations on an Italian theme, her eyes convulsed by the profundity of it all—the profundity of that Alberti bass and the predictable tune. I waited for "it" to happen. Even in the Philadelphia days of 1943, when Shirley and Eugene were indoctrinating me to the glories of Ludwig, I would listen over and over and over to the late quartets (and diligently learned every one of the thirty-two sonatas), while I kept waiting for "it" to happen. I'm still waiting.

How he hammers at primary triads, peeved at being glued to those root positions, as Mozart, flowing through a rapid series of modulations, unravels, with what ease! the thorniest of knots. JH calls Beethoven the Philip Glass of his era.

Living composers are again becoming linked to living choreographers. Torke, Perle, Glass. The publicity's healthy, but there's a confusion. Neither Glass nor Perle nor Torke have actually composed for dance.

Since *Appalachian Spring* in 1944, how many ballets, good or bad, can you name wherein the music was written specifically for the dance?

"Can't you just leave him alone? Hasn't he suffered enough?"

"Of course he hasn't suffered enough. The whole point of suffering is that there's no apparent end."

A day in June is not so rare when the month is June.

The Thin Man on VCR, astonishingly my first viewing ever. Had it gone a mite farther, it could strike us now as Buñuelesque, especially the party and the final dinner scene. As it stands it's dumb. Myrna's at ease. Her "secret" for that all-knowing look is to turn her eyes to the left while not moving the head, or conversely, to turn the head but not the eyes.

Mood swing: term loved by analysands. For weeks I feel what's called, I guess, happy—unconcerned with matters beyond walking with Sonny or sun on the sidewalk. Then come the hours, especially in the morning, when nothing—neither sunlight nor pet Bichon—seems untinted with horror. This morning contained those hours. And when JH left for New York I felt forlorn, like Sonny when he raises head, opens eyes, and flattens ears, as we prepare to leave him alone, even for a few minutes. Of course, if I were *really* depressed—as Mother has been, or JH—would I bother to write of it here? Orchestrating. Rain.

I'd so looked forward, as always, to JH's call to announce safe arrival, but when he phoned at nine we quarreled. The scolding's daily, incessant, unkind, and based on impatience at my "getting everything wrong." Tonight it was exasperation at what he'd assumed was my mismanagement with North Point about the postal express system. For the first time ever, I nearly hung up on him. When he called back some hours later I was still seething (straw that broke the camel's back, etc.), and we were both unhappy. To each other we are all that matters, and I don't doubt for a second his affection. But even the longest-term set-up is fragile, needs daily cajoling, and must never be taken for granted.

Model new symphonic piece—the piece for Martin Segal's festival next summer—on *Mario and the Magician*.

Sunday 14 June

The point is that it has no point, like those non-developmental open-ended vocal marathons that children adore. ("Nineteenth verse, / same as the first, / the fly sat on the wall"). It couldn't pertain to a Bach-Balanchine ballet, or to a diary, but it could pertain to a Jackson Pollock. Yes, you can psychoanalyze a Pollock, but that's . . . well, cheating, or at least old-fashioned, like analyzing nursery rhymes.

Four weeks today since we arrived, and, except for Cousin Myrtle, not one visitor in the house. Nor, except for a few hot afternoons, have I worn shorts.

Johnny Carson is never less effective than when trying to upstage a guest that happens to be non-human, a cheetah, for example, which yawningly ignores its host's witty remarks. "I wouldn't trust that cat around the block." Animalist?

Around 1939 Rosemary and an acquaintance, Mimi Swedberg (not to be confused with RR's best friend, Miriam Cary), double dated—double *blind* dated—with two boys furnished by Mimi's brother. How pretty the girls looked, like blonde posies, Rose in her cream taffeta formal bought for the junior prom, and Mimi in electric-blue organdy. Next day Rosemary got a phone call from a male voice: "Do you want to get fucked?" Instead of hanging up, she replied typically, "Aren't there more important things to think about in this world?"

The daisies on our north bank began to come out last Wednesday. First, just five or six. By yesterday, perhaps a couple dozen. Now this afternoon, with the sun, there are easily a thousand brass coins glittering in the wind. They'll be healthy for a month, then a new crop comes up and stays till September.

Erotic (very) dream of Lincoln Kirstein.
   Thirty summers ago with Pierre Quézel, we took our tour of western Italy. Was it fifty autumns ago that Maggy Magerstadt entered U-High (or Jew-High, as rival schools named it)? In succeeding seasons, for the record, the Chicago queer bars we frequented (when we could pass for eighteen) were The Club Gay, whose proprietress, Babe, later became pianist at The Ranch on Oak Street; Waldman's, on Michigan Avenue, where Ella Fitzgerald's "Cootchie Coo" set the tone; Gana Walska's, at Polk & Damen—a no-man's-land—where once at noon, between sessions of a final exam in June, we had a beer or two; and Simon's on Rush Street. I entered Northwestern in September of 1940, age sixteen.

Another person in the house is another person in the house, and when they leave the house is (sometimes pleasurably) emptier, but they don't know it. We each inhabit our envelope, not imagining the house as not containing us. Seeing is not believing, nor is believing seeing.
   There are those who speak of having returned from the dead. But if they must return to tell us about it, what's the purpose of death? The illusion of miracle is the base of Belief; all religion is modeled on a need for the reality of unreality. But it's just that—a need, an illusion. When Father hallucinated so hotly in the hospital

last winter, *he was visited by mother as a young girl*. A few days later, he recalled the visitation as more real than real, yet admitted, with the effort of logic, that it was hallucinated. For Father is not religious.

Carol Zaleski, author of *Otherworld Journeys*, claims that "being born is like dying from a previous existence—for the child and the mother too." Well, any rite of passage contains a touch of death, but isn't that strictly metaphoric, as with a girl's menstruation, or a boy's change of voice, or anyone's first broken heart? We believe what we're ready to believe, whether it's "there" or not, from Luther's ink stain to UFOs to Jim Bakker's blather, or to the branch falling in an empty wood and making or not making a noise.

I've just re-reread *Mario and the Magician*. Every sentence is exquisitely contrived metaphor for fascism, but the monstrous magician's tricks are real. His self-presentation as a pretty girl to the hypnotized Mario is the presentation of an illusion, true, but Mario's bullets are real.

The pack of preemptive young people who've just taken over the Quigley house across the lane, with their thunderous hi-fi and compulsory shrieking—they can't know that heretofore the neighborhood had been a residential workplace and that house a tomb. They stare at us in disbelief as we complain.

Sum all this up, please, as Madame Lidoine says to the Première Prioress.

19 June

"Do you hear that bird?" asked JH, who had climbed two flights from his basement lair in the dead of night, although he must arise again at 5 A.M. to catch the ferry. "What bird?" I wonder. He opened my window. Sure enough, after a minute, a dull, stifled warble sounded in the dark. "It's either another baby fallen from the nest," said JH, "or the mother of the dead ones." And he returned to bed downstairs, aching from lack of sleep.

Yesterday afternoon Princess went on a rampage: here and there on the scorched lawn in back we found the mutilated cadavers of three half-grown yellow sparrows. Last summer she was pretty good; now again she's red in tooth and claw, and happy with herself, purring. Later in the day Robert Convery and friend, Andrew, came to dine, bringing a homemade pear strudel.

Decaffeinated tea, plus the threat of neighbors' hi-fi, induced insomnia. Intermittent awakenings, always with the bird's lament, commingling with Sam's endless plaint that drives us mad. At dawn I hear JH vomiting downstairs. Often he thus begins a day.

Now he's en route. It's eleven. The day will be passed alone.

20 June

Starting each day with Haydn, as during the previous fortnight I drenched myself in Bartók. The Bernstein versions of the six "Paris Symphonies" combine austerity with élan, loveliness with snap (with Scotch snap?), and extreme slowness with extreme fastness—they come alive. Still, I find them hard to hear, to concentrate on. So steeped are we in such classics on the radio that they've become wallpaper. Except for the "Minuets," which, like Bartók's "Marches," actively get on my nerves. The nasty regularity of the beat, like rock, is a Chinese water torture.

H. C. Robbins's notes for the Haydn, meanwhile, emanate his enthusiasm but are hardly chiseled prose. The word "brilliant," for example, which should never be used at all since it means nothing, is used four times in two columns. The word "use" is used twice in adjoining sentences (no, it's not for balance or echo, it's an oversight).

Elliott Carter's notes for his own pieces are always original, alluring, necessary. Witness the strange appositeness of his "diagram" for the First Quartet, based on Cocteau's falling tower in *Sang d'un poète*, or his thread of a seagull-trumpet for the Symphony for Three Orchestras. But the music itself? I like everything about it, except it.

The Nantucket Diary, a year behind schedule, is now due for publication in mid-September, at nearly 700 pages (including JH's labyrinthine index) and thirty dollars. How many reviews will mention that much of the first third is drawn from the diary sections of the various essay books? None, I'll wager. People seldom recognize, in a new context, what they reread.

Another sound-alike: Measure 64 of final movement of Mahler's Ninth, and "Why Can't You Behave?"

The last four notes of Milhaud's *Création du monde* and the first four of Gershwin's "I've Got a Crush on You."

21 June

Father's Day, start of summer. Toward midnight, waiting for JH, who arrives on the twelve o'clock ferry. Deep fog. Have I ever missed him so much (though it's been just two days)? The room's filled with roses, white enamel teapots jammed with blood-red, bordeaux, and coral-colored roses, like candy, like Fantin-Latour confection, and wondrous to know they're *our* roses, from our trellis, from our patio.

Inanity on TV. Cyndi Lauper, depressing. Millions upon millions delirious for her art, consisting of pre-Copernican tantrums, like a demented rag doll with no gifts. Though perhaps it's less depressing than the camera on a neighboring channel which draws back to depict an amphitheater engorged with empty faces ecstatic in their sin at the admonitions of Jimmy Swaggart.

23 June

Finished orchestration this morning of *A Few Days* (which title JH thinks should be changed to the less bland *The Schuyler Songs*), 141 pages in just three weeks.

Call from Rosette. Says that, contrary to the slogan, *le temps ne change rien*, she, at 63, is as upset by her mother's murder last year as though it were yesterday.

Call from *Architectural Digest*. A month ago they asked about doing a feature on the house here in Nantucket. JH felt adamantly NO—it's an invasion of privacy, and anyway they just want rich people's houses. I agreed, nevertheless, if I could write the text. Then I changed my mind. Still, rather than have a "test" photographer come and take trial pix, I mailed them snapshots. Understandably, they'll think . . .

26 June

Insomnia. Bright wakefulness 3 to 5 hours per night. Neighbors at 2 A.M. Sam whining and fussing. Worried about both my eyes, lightning flashes in darkness, detached vitreous.

Sunday 28 June

A 34-year-old man in Florida is sentenced to life for having seduced a 14-year-old boy. Boy's mother: "He got what he deserved." (Meaning the boy?) In ten years, when the boy's 24, will he gaze back at the incident as so terrible? In twenty years will he visit the man in prison, perhaps take him books? In thirty years will he still think of it, or, like an adopted child, will the occurrence have become not even an exquisite scab or gold medal? Meanwhile the man rots in a cell.

At fourteen it was I who seduced the 34-year-olds. Or tried to.

While the scrumptious bulky cabbage roses wane on the trellis, the first tiger lilies ebb overnight, hundreds, clashing with the daisies on the bank. The bismuth-pink roses on the back fence hint at their outburst for tomorrow or the day after. Yet no sign of the long-promised thunderstorms, and lawns all over town are scorched. "The veins within our hands betrayed our fear. / What we had hoped for had not come to pass."

Rosette dined with us here last night. Salmon, asparagus, broad and pretty open tart made up of six fruits, including ruddy gooseberries, on a golden custard. Talk of her mother (the pointless anxiety's worse now than a year ago), and of France in our respective heydays.

Not working. Discouraged. Haven't penned even the brief hommage to Bernstein.

Recurrence, on his palms and soles, of JH's "secondary" syphilis indications after seven years. (He first had it ten years ago.) We're both dulled with gloom. Tomorrow, if possible, he'll see Dr. Voorhees. Today, clarity, indolence at Nobadir beach. Reading Mary McCarthy's *How I Grew* . . . "A Clear Day and No Memories." If only.

JH, petting Sonny—whom he loves above all—with his pocked hands: "Strange how animals don't contract our diseases."

29 June

Voorhees says it's ringworm.

1 July

Death of Mompou at 94. Remembering with pride our afternoon together in Barcelona in May of 1952, and treasuring the little song cycle, in Catalan dialect, he inscribed to me. Paul Cadmus for five years has urged me to keep renominating Mompou as foreign honorary member of the Academy-Institute. Now it's too late. But we do have his music forever.

Reagan meanwhile has nominated for the Supreme Court a lawyer named Bork, who, for sheer right-wingery, out-Rehnquists Rehnquist. I never write of politics in this notebook. Why?—when I feel so strongly about the hopeless farce of our current situation (the "Iran-gate" investigation, the PTL scandal, etc.) Probably because, as Virgil says, *les faits divers* are always with us but change every day, while art remains, or at least is supposed to.

None of us understands, really, how others interpret this or that. But to "get it wrong" in the right way is art.

Mary McCarthy's book: brittle, icy, but, to me, absorbing, in its obsession with the books that formed her, and its utter obliviousness to music, an obliviousness which tokens intellectuals in America.

Mother loved to walk. It was her favorite, almost her sole, form of locomotion, and she moved with vigor, keeping always ahead of us on the sidewalk. As late as 1960, when she & Father lived in Pittsburgh, the *Post Gazette* did an article on "local walkers," with a photograph of "Mrs. C. Rufus Rorem, who does three miles a day," striding down the street. Today she keeps to a wheelchair, though there is nothing apparently wrong with her legs. She's obsessed with *not* walking. When I push her down the halls of Cadbury and we pass an unused wheelchair, she'll mutter, "Help me into that wheelchair."

During the decade before moving to Cadbury (already five years ago), Mother had the habit of—if she needed to—peeing on the sidewalk. She simply stopped at the curb and, lifting her skirt without squatting, let go. My youngest nephew, Per, assumed that this was the way of all elderly women.

3 July

The Quigley house on Wesco Place is, this summer, occupied by eight 20-year-old females, from colleges in Virginia and North Carolina, who are contrite when I complain, nicely, about the throbbing rock issuing through their open door after midnight. Mary McCarthy's groups of adolescent girls, though hardly musical, were required four years of Latin before being eligible for Eastern seats of learning, and they talked about culture as well as about boys. These females have a regular procession of boys dropping by, but who knows about their culture? Don't young people anymore ever, ever, ever play Mozart or Ravel? (I used to turn on *Daphnis* full blast fifty years ago because it "fit" the countryside.) One rarely overhears even opera, let alone Carter, through other people's windows. Who indeed buys the records of "our greatest living composer," or, for that matter, who buys mine, let alone listens to them? Well, I've paid cash for Elliott's disks, even for

Philip Glass's. But then, I'm not a Music Fancier—I do it to keep up. And not often.

5 July

Annual perusal (quite thorough) of Bruckner's Eighth. From one year to the next I can never recall a note, and I have a good memory; the Symphony always comes to me as something new, if not exactly fresh, and somehow worthless. Not worthless mudpies, like, say, Louise Nevelson (although it's not proper to compare artists of different centuries), but worthless still. There's no music there. As with Berlioz, or G.B.S., I don't get the point.

In the mid-Fifties I asked in these pages, "What ever became of Nellie Lutcher?" Now, thirty years later, the answer is: She's singing at Michael's Pub.

A diary is the response to an impulse—as opposed to an instinct—for self-preservation.

22 July

Spider bites that don't abate for days.

Father, when I ask about Mother, says she frequently expresses interest in old friends. Like who? Well, like Miss Ring and Davis Edwards. So she's still obsessed with that. (Have I written of it here?—their respective infidelities?)

Song and Dance, my compulsory piece for the Kapell Competition, was played by 24 pianists in one day, down in Baltimore.

A summerish touring group, three singers and a pianist who call themselves A Night at the Opera, passed through here at the Actors Theater at the Gordon Folger Hotel. Included were my *Three Incantations from a Marionette Tale* and *The Fox and the Grapes*. Not embarrassing. Also one of Schoenberg's *Cabaret Songs*, sung, as Marni Nixon does, by a soprano *en travesti*, in this case with a handlebar moustache and a silly T-shirt. Heaven forbid that these songs, which are all on poems from "a man's point of view," be sung straight. But why not? Marlene Dietrich, without apology, recorded, "I've Grown Accustomed to Her Face," without changing "her" to "his," with delicious effect, but Tony Bennett inappropriately sings "The Man I Love" as "The Girl I Love," a far dumber betrayal. Music is higher than sex. Let Bennett use the true words, and the chips fall where they may.

Still no rain.

JH working on choral transcriptions of Poulenc.

Andrew Porter's weekly columns should be named, "On Elliott Carter and Other Matters." It's no longer curious, it's embarrassing, to see Andrew weave Elliott's name, no matter how inappropriately, into any discussion at hand.

3 August

For Stambolian's *Advocate* interview:

Let me state right off that, as its author, I find it paradoxical, even superfluous, to talk about The Nantucket Diary. A diary by nature is an open-ended arrangement: The writer can't explicate the structure as novelists do, or defend research as biographers—even memoirists—do. Theoretically a diary is written for just oneself, to unload daily obsessions, burdens, joys. In fact, of course, a published diary is presented as literature, and if its author is alive he must defend it as such. Still, it always seems weird to give public readings from my diary. Why should I now be grandly showing my navel, for pay, to an audience when precisely what was put on the page was propelled by fear or shyness or, at any rate, a sense of privacy?

Stambolian asks if my diary isn't actually a meditation on mortality:

It hadn't struck me that the diary was necessarily a meditation on mortality, and I'm bemused that it strikes you that way. For I'm a happier person—certainly a stabler one—today at 63 than thirty years ago. Yet I do ponder death, and even the tempting logic of suicide, every single day. It's hardly original to claim that death is scary and disgusting. An artist's work is *not* himself, it's his work. We know really nothing of Chopin or Sophocles or Augustine—of their blood and breath and horniness—through their nocturnes and tragedies and treatises. The notion that I cannot bequeath my ever- throbbing body is untenable. Does this sound ungrateful, or even unimaginative, since my music and books will remain, at least for a time, in libraries? But where are the snows of yesteryear, the slaves of Egypt, or the orchids and tigers and thrushes and, yes, the roaches of millenniums ago? All gone, and what difference does it make? There is no God, no afterlife, of that I am sure. Yet at the same time, although I also know the future will never produce a less stupid world, I do retain—I *think* I do—a sense of the present, of each perfumed second, which can somehow be stretched into its own millennium, and a sense of wanting to be useful now, right now.

You can dip your foot into the same stream an infinite number of times, if you accept the Big Bang theory. Everything comes from nothing. A popsicle of tears.

"What is an artist? An artist is a tortured being who, when he opens his mouth to scream, only beautiful sounds emerge." (Or something like that.) –Kierkegaard. Check with opening of *Either/Or*.
Do I believe this at all? It was John Cage who first exposed us to this gorgeous phrase. In 1945? Cage the Romantic?

6 September

Finished and mailed the review of Marguerite Duras's *L'Amante anglaise* to the *Washington Post*. Notions not absorbed into review:
Like Gide, she pushes *le crime gratuit*, while implying there's no such thing— that we are all murderers by nature. Like Gide's victim in *La Sequestrée de*

Poithièrs, who repeats forever the undecipherable "*Mon bon grand fond malampia*," Duras invents a word for her Hindu beggar woman: Battambang.

Could she have concocted *L'Amante anglaise* quite that way had not Pinget concocted *L'Inquisitoire* a decade earlier?

Le Square: Brief Encounter sterilized. Or, a platonic *Brief Encounter*.

Anonymous letters. Could Cocteau have concocted *La Machine à écrire* had not the film *Le Corbeau* been concocted a decade earlier?

Her works are games, puzzles. Duras is the nom de plume—or, as the French (in this case aptly) say, nom de guerre—of Donnadieu. God given. Is *The War* her best book?

Duras is the other side of Françoise Sagan's coin. She's heads to Sagan's tails. Sagan has more heart, but not fair to play them against each other. (Janet Flanner in December 1965 writes, re. the elections: "Françoise Sagan, who chose de Gaulle, and Marguerite Duras, who chose Mitterrand, had a long tape-recorded argument, which was published in the weekly *Match*—rather good political talk, too.")

Simenon: the thinking man's Piaf. Or rather, Simenon: the non-intellectual's Proust.

Just as Simenon, France's greatest living writer, is much of the time the thinking man's Piaf (viz. *Le Petit saint*, his Portrait of the Artist from *enfant* to *vieillard*) in that his scene is set in working-class districts with low bourgeois actors who suffer and kill and sometimes love and die with all the ardor, but without the leisure for self-indulgence, of the upper class, so in reverse Duras is, much of the time . . . (What is she?)

Three errors of grammar in as many paragraphs appear in Virgil's essays on Brahms, on tempo, on MacDowell. (See Sam Morgenstern's *Composers on Music*.)

What have I taken from Sam Barber, whose music I don't often think about? The vocalise line in *The Silver Swan* owes itself to the wondrous complaint in *Anthony O'Daly*.

10 September

The MacDowell Colony flew me to Peterborough Saturday so I could honor Lenny Bernstein with a speech on Sunday, medal day, at 11 A.M. Bill Schuman was there already, overly friendly, as were all the inmates and personnel of the ranch. By 10:55 there was an overflow crowd, but still no Lenny, who was due on a plane from Tanglewood. Schuman, official and edgily pleasant as we waited, did not tell me what I learned later: that Lenny had been ambivalent (because of the Peyser ruckus?) about my giving the speech in the first place. When he finally arrived in a blaze of picture-taking, he was extravagant to all, but merely civil to me. Schuman was no help when, in his prologue, he warned the audience that although Ned was a brilliant musician and a convincing prosifier, he was not shy of bringing sex into the fray. I felt vaguely offended, having worked very very hard on the lecture, which was in no way lubricious.

But I spoke well, standing, with the honoree seated at my right. Then, during the next twenty minutes, an almost audible warmth issued from Lenny. When I finished he was in tears. He took a full sixty seconds before his acknowledgment, then talked for maybe ten minutes, professing how moved he was by Bill's comradely words about me, and by my "beautifully formed oration" on him, adding it was the first time he'd heard such "penetrating eloquence from one composer about another."

At the open-air lunch we sat together with my two guests, Sharon and Jaime Laredo, and he was all kisses. Margaret Carson immediately xeroxed the speech for the upcoming LB catalogue. By evening, back in Nantucket, a call from Harry Kraut, plus others, with congratulations etc., all effusing. In other words, good news travels fast, the dogs had been called off, and Lenny's entourage could be nice to Ned again.

The little essay is honest, original, skillfully worded, affectionate, and wise. How could all *les petits amis* reconcile that with Ned's mean-minded slander?

12 Sept.

Bill Flanagan was my best friend among composers. From our first encounter in the autumn of 1946 until his death twenty-two years later, Bill and I had an intense (though always platonic) relationship, mostly happy though often rivalrous. Bill envied my slicker musical know-how and the footing I already had in the professional world. I envied his Jesuit education (my own non-musical training had been catch-as-catch-can) as well as an intellect that was quicker than mine. Decent looking if not handsome, he was vain of his person, and certainly his blue, blue eyes, as violent as they were kind, remain unforgettable, offset as they often were by his pale lavender T-shirts and tinted blond crew cut. Once he joined the American Composers Alliance in 1959 and became an "official" published composer, Bill lopped three years off his age, as Tennessee Williams had done, on the grounds that those years had vanished into the bottle, as well as into the thin air of vain aspiration. Actually he was two months older than I. When I returned for good from France in 1957, we grew closer. Between 1959 and 1961, acting on the premise that the simple Art Song might still prove vital in a period (this is apparent in retrospect) of highest instrumental complexity, we launched a successful series in Carnegie Recital Hall called "Music for the Voice by Americans." The common current practice of composers presenting themselves as stars was then unprecedented. We had guest stars, too, notably Copland and Thomson, accompanying their own songs, and our vocalists included Patricia Neway, David Lloyd, Phyllis Curtin, Regina Sarfaty, Reri Grist, Veronica Tyler, all in full bloom, and representative of a now-vanished breed—the recital singer. If we were partners in art as well as in crime, criticizing each other by day, cruising Eighth Street bars together by night, there were no emotional entanglements. Bill lived much of his adult life with Edward Albee, whose phenomenal success as a playwright became an obsession with him. When Edward rose, Bill, on a seesaw, sank. This is clear as I reread his old letters. The early years of our correspondence were in the formal, arch, rather pristine tone of eighteenth-century pornography. This tone shifted, on Bill's side, to one that combined envy with self-laceration. Although Albee was . . .

27 September

Rosette's interview with me in local paper. Walk on the town beach in late afternoon with JH and Sonny. We find Rosette there reading. Says daily ocean baths are the one thing that saves her from the ongoing depression *"au sujet de maman."* To JH the reason is clear: Mother Sea is, even more than the sun, the exquisitely indifferent medication we can all return to and be embraced by.

What do you think of Kyle Gann? I ask JH. Oh, I never read him because I see what he's up to—championing third-rate composers in the name of the academic avant-garde. Who cares.

Dream. (A libretto.) Mardi Gras madness, with a black couple in silver masks and a white couple in ebony masks. During the melée the black man kisses the white woman. They're all liberal. But they are overseen (by a KKK member?). Result: black man lynched. White woman shot by black woman. Black woman kills self. White man left alone for aria at end.

29 September

Composers compose. If that's the case, I'm no longer a composer. Why let my self say yes to so much periphery? Because . . . Weeks have been spent licking and stamping, brochures for the new book which none acknowledge.

I fantasize about taking an ad, or sending an open letter to periodicals: "I do not wish my music to be reviewed. I am not interested in, nor have I ever learned from, the opinions of paid critics. I compose for two reasons: 1) to earn a living; 2) to please performer and hearer. The music does not ask to be graded, nor does it pose as art (there's no longer any such thing) but as a function. Whether it succeeds at what it attempts is not for a critic—but only for me (and whoever commissions it)—to know.

Mary Gordon, regarding the loss of the Latin mass, and the hip up-to-dateness which quickly dates: "Better to get stuck in the thirteenth century than in 1965; better to get stuck in '*Pange Lingua*' than 'Blowin' in the Wind.' "

A. N. Wilson in *The Healing Art* (p. 51): "I hate jokes in sermons . . . There are quite enough things in church to make you laugh without prompting from the pulpit."

In Carson McCullers's bio, pictures of McCullers's père, looking so much like Tom that the years disappeared back to 1952 at the Chelsea when we lay in each other's arms.

Fantasy of showing Bach the music of our time. Fantasy of explaining the vacuum cleaner to Nero.

Truman Capote (Sept. 1949) telling us about Denim Fouts: How if Fouts—who had "slept with" the Aga Kahn and many another crowned head—had succumbed to the implorations of Hitler, perhaps World War II would have been averted.

No matter how it comes, it won't be as you expect.
Tuez moi. Tu es moi.
Drowning the fish, for overdoing.

"His" is an inclusive possessive pronoun, and less grammatically clumsy than the recent deferential-to-feminism formula—everyone and his or her brother. The his-or-her formula, what's more, is prejudicial: it excludes hermaphrodites.

Just as during my first weeks in Paris in 1949 I thought that the Black Market was a gloomy arena you could take a taxi to, so ten years later I thought that to be a member of Alcoholics Anonymous meant signing a card and paying dues.

There is no one truth, and even facts alter each second according to a viewer. The current *Interview* (Nov. 87), next to a huge photo by Man Ray of Marie-Laure, quotes one Philip Core in a book called *The Original Eye* (1984): ". . . friends who enjoyed such sumptuous up-to-dateness were varied but artistic: Cocteau, first of all . . . Jean Marais . . . Breton . . . Aragon . . . the Broglies, Greffulhes . . . Cecil Beaton; and the star-crossed young American composer Ned Rorem, with whom Marie-Laure had another peculiar, unhappy relationship. Such people spread a gospel of style to the four corners of Paris, if not the world . . . "

George Garratt used to say that the word "boy"—the very word—smelled good. In *The Tall Men* it's to a sex-starved rancher who tells her he likes her perfume that Jane Russell exclaims, "That's not perfume, that's girl."

JH upset by mention of him in reviews of my book. Because I don't tell the whole story (re. Stella Adler for instance). Is there possibly, ever, a whole story?

JH's title, *Perfect Pitch*, is perfect for the new collection of 62 essays that Harcourt Brace is to bring out in May. Now Marie Arana has learned that Slonimski's autobiography, due out in March, has the same title. JH has already come up with a new name, *Music Matters*. He meanwhile has spent 95 hours copy-editing the copy-editing, a thankless chore that's left him dizzy. He entered my room around midnight and said, " 'Eureka!' shouted Arnold Schoenberg, 'I've found the cure for the common chord.' "

Terribly disappointed by the brief, bland review of *The Nantucket Diary* in today's *Times* by some woman nobody seems to know. I'd thought that by now the book would be the talk of the town, prominently displayed in every store. Instead, except for good notices by Alan Rich and Michael Dirda in *Newsweek* and the *Washington Post Book World*, it's sunk without a trace. It's my best and longest work of prose, higher class and better penned, certainly, than Capote's unhappy collection, *Answered Prayers*, so widely advertised, or . . . But will it have made a dent on either the literary or musical worlds? I won't take the blame—although it's probably true that "they" find my tone less curious, less in need of airing, than of yore.

Sunday 8 November

JH has left, as so often, by truck with Sonny for the Hyannis ferry (nine hours door to door from here to West Chester Street), and as always I miss him terribly. I allow myself to think that his agitating presence keeps me from work, but a whole day in the empty apartment has produced not much beyond shuffling papers. His tirelessness. Now, having proofread the new book, he's taken on all the responsibility for Father's papers.

Yves Salgues on *Apostrophes*. Fourteen years since I've seen Yves, and he's unrecognizable as he plugs his new book, about heroin addiction, for Bernard Pivot. Something dishonest about his mien and declarations (all heterosexual, like Kubly's a generation ago) decreases any nostalgia I might have felt. Françoise Sagan, sharing the program with Yves and three others, looks and sounds witchy.

(An hour later.) And yet, rummaging through his letters from 1950, and those from 24 years later evoking that summer, I'm shattered. The never-to-be-retrieved past wherein Yves was disintoxicated from heroin as I from alcohol, our handsome youth with weeks to waste, and the violent work. His seven rhymed stanzas called "1950 *pour* Ned Rorem," sent to me in 1973, are very very good, and belong in my treasure chest.

The early published diaries are undated or misdated. The first Cocteau visit, for example, was Oct. 10, 1950, but, thanks to Robert Phelps, who reshuffled entries and years, it would seem to have been in 1951.

12 November

My article "Cocteau in America," written as preface to Arthur Peters's beautiful coffee-table picture book, *Cocteau and His World*, has been amended slightly for the English edition. The title has been changed to *Cocteau Viewed from Abroad*, and, to references to the mixed bag of American artists who doff their hat to the poet (Edith Wharton, Louise Bogan, Pauline Kael, et al.) have been added names of Britishers. To my sentence, "So, Jean Cocteau is not a fact of cultural life in America any more than, say, John Cheever is in England" has been added, unsymmetrically, "or A. N. Wilson in France."

But who is A. N. Wilson? By coincidence Maggy sent me two months ago some paperbacks of his and I've just finished, with pleasure, *The Healing Art*. It's light reading of the highest order, plotted to within an inch of its life (like Iris Murdoch), with "ordinary" people suddenly being lesbians, or quite literally going up in flames. A. N. Wilson's a natural—a born—writer whose sense of dialogue is so easy that one is jarred by what he *can't* do, e.g., emulate American speech. An American reader, no matter how dull, sees his countrymen's speech, in these pages, as filtered through an Englishman's ear; what is normal to us is eccentric to him, but he's not noting this as eccentric, merely as colloquial. Also he has one newly arrived American say "in hospital," and another "producing a cheque book" to write a check in pounds. Nothing is riskier than to presume to denote, in fiction (as opposed to a diary where anything goes), a foreigner on the foreigner's terms, rather than as foreign *tout simple*.

Andrew Porter chides me for chiding Charlotte Brontë for not knowing that robins migrate, when in fact European robins do not migrate.

Queens will say, "He's divine—too bad he's straight," implying that if he were gay he'd go for them. In reality, someone divine and straight might be more likely to put out (for pay, perhaps, or for compassion) than someone divine and gay. Again: Would a straight man find it easier to screw a cute boy than an ugly crone? Depends. If you're not attracted to sex *as* a sex, do you make distinctions between individual examples of that sex?

Mick Jagger last night, in a documentary on the Sixties, being interviewed by Londonian higher-ups after his arrest for drugs. What a beautiful face, what a sensible quietude in his replies. And what a difference—in a flash—in my viewpoint toward him. How nice to know that I can still change viewpoint.

1 December
While re-rereading Mann's *Tobias Mindernickle*, I answer the phone to Tobias Schneebaum's ring about a new doctor. Then Tobias Picker calls.

In the current (Nov. 23) *New Yorker* shines Harold Brodkey's long tour-de-force called "Family," as rednecky a palliative for heterosexual breeding and standard values as any Pat Buchanan might proffer. Plus the calculated smarm of the final phrase, "I feel so permeated by the world and by relationships in the world . . . I

. . . have tried to describe . . . by marriage and example that I don't quite know what to do except to think, My God, how bitterly and deeply I want the world to go on." The world, of course, cannot "go on" through the work of painters and musicians and thinkers, much less through the cavortings of homosexuals whose ways Harold knows well, but which he never falls back upon, which could explain the forever unrelentingly leaden tone of his prose.

Similar *malhonnêteté* glimmered through each utterance of Yves Salgues last fortnight on that *Apostrophes* program as he opined that during a heroin disintox-ication—not to mention intoxication—sex is out of the question. *"Les femmes ne m'interressaient plus."* No doubt because women simply never interested him. Who'd have thought I'd wave a flag for gay lib; but this hypocritical pandering to the norm, even in the highest of intellectual circles (i.e., the circles of Woody Allen, who, in his latest, *Hannah and Her Sisters,* manages his share of fag-belit-tling) fills me with despair, because, My God, I want the world to go on—but a better world.

3 December

Reading my umpteenth Simenon, this one called merely *Maigret* and dealing with a straightforward case that the inspector comes back from retirement to inspect— although the book seems to have been written in 1934 (it's impossible to tell from the Fayard edition), twenty years before the heyday of the Maigret series. With what terse cruel genius Simenon depicts what it would never have occurred to us to depict, yet which seems so inevitable *après coup.* In a mere dozen pages of huge print we watch Maigret, motionless, as he sits for twelve hours in the Tabac Fontaine watching in turn the various habitués and passers-by, overhearing the criminal persiflage during a game of belote, and the light ebbs and alters in this louche locale, as noon succeeds to three, then to six and nine and midnight, the crowds thin out, then thicken, and though nothing happens we can't stop reading.

What do you think of Steve Reich? Well, there's nothing to think.

Long puff piece in the current *VV* on Reich. The apocalyptic breakthrough when the composer decides to amplify his ostinati with a modulation here & there, and with shades of actual development. So I reread (remembering like yes-terday every line, after 29 years, as uttered by Hortense Aldan when it was co-billed with *Suddenly Last Summer) Something Unspoken.* Cornelia, on the phone, asks Esmerelda about the Confederate Daughters luncheon which she decided not to attend. ". . . and afterwards I suppose there was lemon sherbet with lady-fingers? What, lime sherbet? And *no* lady-fingers? *What a departure!* What a *shocking* apostasy."

Am finishing what for the moment is called *Chamber Music for Five Instruments* (has Chamber Music ever before been used as a specific, rather than a generic, title?) by writing the first movement last. It should sound like a rat in an ashcan, commencing with spasmodic little flurries, starts and stops, then gusting into a raucous mazurka. Is this serious? What's serious? Is Reich, or Poulenc, or Mozart, or Carter? Well, it's not solemn. Don't tell anyone, but the effect I'm after is how I recall—after one hearing two years ago—Boulez's *Répons*.

Hard to shake the post-Californian cold. Two weeks of total insomnia, throbbing temples, and one stuffed nostril which from time to time, like a slowly rolling hippopotamus, destuffs itself by gushing its content into the other nostril.

Heterosexuals, even at this late date, are as foreign to me as, say, Estonians or stupid people (not to mention stupid Estonian heterosexuals). Do they, for instance, like peanut butter?

Describe the Edwin Denby myth. The abjectly misdirected sanctification by such as Ron Padgett (see *OINK!*). Describe the Chelsea Hotel in 1944.

Gianni Schicchi: The anxiety and tears of Rosemary re. Father's descent. The will. Money. Mrs. Peacock & Mother. JH.

I gave you the best years of my life.
    Yes, and it's I who made them the best years.

JH, explaining that epileptics have long been known for their icy humor, declares as we hike to the bank in this tingling weather, "It's cold as a twitch's wit."

Should I be annoyed or flattered that Fizdale & Gold allow me to be listed (in Grove's, among other places) as one of the three or four composers they've commissioned and performed, when they've never performed or commissioned anything of mine, including the *Four Dialogues*, which were nevertheless written for them?

Fantastic review of *Winter Pages* by McLelland in Washington.

For two months—more than two months—the intercom non-functions in whole building while a TV system is being non-installed. Meanwhile, in the easily accessible lobby, murder, rape, and incest are rampant.

JH attending, with his Power of Attorney, to Father's affairs. *The Consul*. Kafka. Papers, papers, papers. And the buck forever passed.

December

Notes for End of Year
    Hemmoroids. (After all these years of suffering, I still can't spell it.) A call to Kiehl's on Third Avenue, the first and best herb store in Manhattan, reveals they no longer carry extract of Indian chestnut (the natural *extrait de marrons d'Inde*

which any French pharmacy stocks for varicose veins, and which works within hours) because "we're trying to phase ourselves out of that, and strictly into pharmaceuticals." Similarly, an attempt to buy manuscript paper at Patelson's, the first and best music shop in Manhattan, reveals they no longer carry 14- or 16-staff, or indeed any such stock, and don't know when they'll get more in.

Discussion about "children" at Sono Osato's. The young, 18 to 28, offspring of educated, subtle, engaged musical intellectuals, care solely for hair style, "peer group" approval, and shun ballet and mathematics. Who'll run the store when they come of age? E. M. Forster, "The Machine Stops."

Bernheimer's interview—snappy and fair—quotes JH's entry in Grove's, "all of [Rorem's] music may be characterized as lean and firmly elegant," explaining that JH is my closest friend, then using the phrase over and over to illustrate aspects of my social manner. He can't know that it was I who interpolated that phrase into JH's entry.

My sole claim to fame: second cousin Elaine Rorem is married to Jack Lalanne, and second cousin Audrey Ronning is married to Seymour Topping.

Being moved when the Three Wise Men, JH's black protégés on Christmas Eve, wove their way through the pews unto the crèche carrying high the precious trophies from our household, including the golden Tiffany bowl given to Mother & Father on their fiftieth anniversary.

Young people again. To A.A. with Judy. I can't stomach the self-congratulatory smarm and Jesus chat. Drugs vs. Alcohol. Alcoholism is a disease, but is a drug addiction? Yes, yes, claim the alcoholics. But isn't there a difference in kind? Anyone can be made into an addict, even against their will, by injection, but no one can be made into an alcoholic who isn't innately alcoholic. Drugs are habit-forming. Liquor is not. *N'est pas alcoolique qui veut.* Mother used to have her one beer a day, year in year out, but if she missed a day, no big deal.

New on the AIDS list: Sefronus Mundy, Paul Sanfacon, Robert Joffrey, Aladar Marberger. And of course Maurice Grosser (whom Melester said was the oldest victim he knew).

Nantucket, 30 December
Because the phrase "Do I dare to eat a peach" was a clue last night on *Jeopardy!*, this morning for old time's sake I reread "Prufrock" and found it incomprehensible. Well, I've spent my life with poetry, and of course I never understand it and usually think it silly ("I, too, dislike it . . . "), but I never used to question it.

> *In the room the women come and go*
> *Talking of Michelangelo.*

In what room? What women? Do they talk while in motion, and solely of Michelangelo? Is their talk of Michelangelo evoked with contempt or with sympathy?—is he high culture or snobbery merely? Are "the women" like Sondheim's Ladies Who Lunch, who enjoy Mahler? Are they wrong—or superficial—to enjoy Mahler? What should they be doing instead?

And, in search of choral texts, I'm rereading Revelations in the little Bible Rosemary gave me forty Christmases ago. Then it meant everything to me. Today, like "Prufrock," I just can't grasp it. The titillating King James translation remains Greek to me. I can no longer think in metaphor.

Bitterly, dangerously cold. Listened to Milhaud's Trombone Concerto.

Visit in late afternoon from Eugenie with Scott and Evan, during which Paul phoned to say that Rosemary had an emergency operation for her gall bladder.

Watched *Amadeus*—or part of it—for the first time. What an embarrassment. Interpreted by flat Yankee accents, the *donnée* is to flatter the layman's notion of art. Is it beneath contempt? Not at all, says JH, it's quite worthy of contempt.

So I reread *Equus*, which Peter Shaffer filched from *The Paris Diary*, and sigh . . .

When fantasizing on intercourse with the long dead, it is of course Bach with whom I talk about musical trends, Henry James with whom I discuss gay rights and AIDS, and Cleopatra to whom I explain how to light the stove.

1988

Nantucket, 1 January

A new year, and those dearest are more or less quick: Rosemary in the hospital, Father and Mother in *their* hospital, and JH still coughing his lungs out each morning. Massive blizzard and exceptional cold have abated and the island is mute.

Reading Ackroyd's life of T. S. Eliot. Working on orchestration of *A Quaker Reader*, and, knowing Gerard Schwarz will conduct it next summer, am using small forces. JH feels I'm making it too plain, but it is Quaker, after all. Seeking texts for the choral giants, one to be called *The Society of Friends*. No distractions for the moment. "My time is all broken in little pieces," wrote Eliot's grandpa, a Unitarian preacher, and that's how it is for us all in the city. One thing leads to another, and the biography of TSE leads to Edel's of Henry James (I'd wanted to see if there were references to TSE, who could just possibly have met him—he didn't), learning that HJ did know "the Stephen things," meaning Virginia Woolf and her sister, very well. Hated music. Loved Rupert Brooke.

Phoned various people to invite them to dine next Wednesday, including Eugenie, Denny Koch, Marguerita Sutro, and Patti Claflin, whose son (Ned), age 6 (?), answered, saying Happy New Year, and to whose Mother I said, "To think I knew him before he was dead."

Title for essay on death: "The Distinguished Thing."

If Casals's claim were valid—that every day he finds something new in a Bach suite—then Bach's whole oeuvre could consist of but a single work.

A Quaker Reader is an orchestration of eight of the eleven pieces from my solo organ suite of the same title, composed in 1975. The music of each version is identical—the actual notes and their spacing remain unchanged. But the effect is doubtless radically different. By its nature the organ is gorgeous and grand, even in simple phrases. This second version is comparatively Spartan, using an instrumentation no broader than Haydn's, and eschewing the entire percussion family, including timpani. Also, large areas conceived as virtuosic turns for keyboard present no problems when played by orchestra. The difference, then, between the two suites lies in the psychology of the performer. Let me stress, though, that the plainness of the new version stems less from a need to emulate the plainness of a Quaker meeting than from the practical knowledge that it would be premièred by a group of modest size. Under other circumstances I might have been tempted to color my palette with drums and gongs and harps and bells. Sonority depends on circumstance.

Sunday morning, 3 January

The stillness, the utter stillness, while walking with Sonny into town for the *Times*. Only the far caw of the occasional crow around Old North tower (why there?)—otherwise you could hear a pin drop through the ether. No one in sight—so when Sonny "boopsies" on the slope of Center Street I pretend not to notice, and walk on without cleaning up. I'll do this in the city too (do you?), but am not proud of it.

Toward the Coffin House, a truck with a sticker stating "Shit Happens," and beyond, on Broad Street, a tin sign admonishing "Don't Even THINK of Parking Here." If the sticker were even mildly funny for the moment during which the buyer ponders its purchase, does it remain funny month after month? The philosophy's tiresome, the sight offensive. Offensive too is the tin sign because, I suppose, it's *personal* in scolding us (in our exhausted presumption) for thinking. Silence is broken as we arrive at the Hub.

A half-hour with tapes of Leslie Bassett. The three pieces seem directionless. I keep waiting for It to happen—It being generally a point of theatricality, but in this case a moment of reflection amidst the fustian. Festooned with bombastic percussion, it's all decoration (as distinct from decorative), loud *remplissage* with no melodic distinction amongst those augmented triad chords. Had I liked it when, months ago, Bassett asked me for a recommendation? Did I write the recommendation?

Pondering in a dream Mark Bucci's perfect song, "The World Ended Last Night," of thirty years ago. And dreaming too of that Polish boy met at Jacques Catelain's (Marie-Laure saw often the Catelains then—was it Avenue Henri Martin?) thirty-six years ago, the Polish boy who kissed me.

New York, 8 January

Bette Davis, otherwise quick and witty with Johnny Carson, claims that her recent honor at the Kennedy Center made her "proud to be an American." Why an

American?—why not proud to be an actress? It's not as though China and Russia and France and Norway and Uruguay were loath to bestow praise on *their* performing artists. Then this morning I received—from someone, met a few weeks ago in Los Angeles, who knew I was searching for texts about peace—an odd and awful harangue, by Sarah Bernhardt, called *Du Théâtre au champ d'honneur*. The dumb gist is about a wounded French soldier, a *porte drapeau*, who while dying recites the vicious anti-German *Prière pour nos Ennemis*. "*Seigneur, ne leur pardonnez pas, ils savant ce qu'ils font*"—sanctimoniously reversing Christ's admonition on the cross. Ah, the dumbness of actors without a script. Oh, the sadism of one-dimensional sadism, Debussy's *Noël* included.

Pleasant tea with Arthur Peters, who proudly brings a cassette of a radio interview on *Jean Cocteau and His World*. The interview—rather stuffy—opens and closes with minute-long themes from *Eleven Studies for Eleven Players*, with nary a word that I am the composer, much less that I wrote the preface for the book.

Cocktail chez Claire Brook to toast Tobias Schneebaum's *Where the Spirits Dwell*. Welcome sight of Elliott Stein after how many years! Same brash teenager as in Paris 1949.

The Schneebaum book is bemusing. The subject is so unusual—"An Odyssey in the Jungle of New Guinea," where Tobias lived and loved, and came to grips with his homosexuality—but its treatment so bland. Too much on the author (and Brooklyn), too little on *them*, and not much felicity amongst the verbs and nouns. But I'll persevere.

25 January

Reaction to *The Phantom of the Opera*, for Bernard Holland of the *N.Y.T.*:

> I recall enjoying *Jesus Christ Superstar*, although it was a showbiz pastiche of everything from Palestrina to Penderecki. What it lacked in originality it made up for in the infectious chutzpah of youth laid forth with skilled clarity. The tunes were corny, yes, but corn in itself is not unhealthy.
>
> Well, seventeen years have passed, the chutzpah's soured into commerce, the corn into smarm. In *The Phantom of the Opera* the charming vulgarity of *Superstar* has become merely vulgarity.
>
> The hype surrounding *The Phantom* centers almost exclusively on its unprecedented financial success; nobody mentions the poverty of its score. Despite Andrew Lloyd Webber's vast fortune, I can't think of one serious composer who would change places with him.

Poulenc's music—some of it—is *about* vulgarity, but is itself never vulgar. On the contrary, even such earthy cycles as the *Chansons gaillardes* and the *Chansons Villageoises* are refined to a tee.

Bernstein's music is almost always vulgar (i.e. heart on sleeve), though seldom cheap.

1 February

Amusing, *The Nation's* snappy drama reviewer, Thomas Disch, taking the *Voice's* equally snappy reviewer, Michael Feingold, to task for assuring us that Richard Foreman's "wonderful works remain as elusive as ever . . . and the most dignified thing a critic can do is indicate . . . the general preoccupations and imagery . . . and then bow out gracefully." "Such critical loophole-making," says Disch, "amounts to a Nixonian ploy for establishing plausible deniability." Wasn't it precisely Feingold who, a few weeks ago, found *Nixon in China* an indefensible whitewashing of a villain? Indeed, he was the only critic to object—as I do, sound unheard—to the morality of Adams's opera. I defend Feingold utterly, despite his occasional slurs at my very identity, and should I ever meet him, would be ever so cordial. There's no connection, really, betwixt social and professional intercourse, as Europeans suavely realize and Americans don't.

19 Feb.

For well over a generation, ever since the raising of Leonard Bernstein's *Candide* and *West Side Story* (later, certain works of Sondheim and Kander) to a level of "high art," the question has been asked: "What's the difference between an opera and a musical?" The question, plaintively American, implies that we're secure in knowing our so-called musicals are better than Europe's, but are they on a par with opera? That magic word: Opera.

Although she didn't know it in 1921, Edith Sitwell, with her intensely rhymed nonsense called *Façade* designed to be uttered aloud with a synchronized score, paved the way for today's rap singing, a mode akin to melodrama (free speech with musical accompaniment) but more precise and invariable, like talked song or rhythmicized talk. The mode has been adapted by Stephen Sondheim in the best moment of his new operetta, *Into the Woods*, when the evil Witch, with a tongue like a breakdancer's torso, scats through a series of recipes casting a spell on both fellow players and the public. Unlike Sitwell, who had William Walton to immortalize her verses, lyricist Sondheim has only composer Sondheim to work with.

> *Alice, rather malade, looking pallid,*
> *without malice sang a ballad eating salad*
> *from a chalice at the palace*
> *on a Monday afternoon,*
>
> *while Curly, rather burly, looking surly,*
> *in a surrey, fair and furry,*
> *ate his curry in a hurry*
> *with an alabaster spoon.*

Valentine's Day

Stuck out the whole of *Don Giovanni* on TV Friday, with the stupendously apt Samuel Ramey, and the crisply unhumorous Karajan. Next day dragged out the

Kierkegaard essay—the one on musical erotics we so devoured in 1945, basking in Søren's basking in Mozart. How like old-hat Freud, a century before the fact, it now reads. One good quip: Eros was not himself in love.

Five hours of pupils yesterday, plus Daron with the copied parts of *Bright Music*.

Spoke with Lenny. It's definite: he'll conduct the Violin Concerto with Gidon Kremer and the NY Phil next November, and record it then with Deutsche Grammophon.

Becki Phelps on the phone says they received record of *Letters from Paris*, and when they put it on, it was "like peeling open a large navel orange."

JH, as always in the pre-Easter lenten weeks, works twelve hours a day (currently on an expedient 4-part adaptation of Pergolesi's vital and tragic 2-part *Stabat Mater*), and scolds me a lot.

I do not care for Marlon Brando, Paul Newman, William Hurt. They embarrass me with their greatness, their conceited introspection. Dull, dull. (Hurt's leaden oh-so-honest turn as the drag queen in *Spider Woman*.) Bored too by not only the mystique but by the fact of Chaplin and the Marx Brothers. They're good, but not *that* good, and scarcely bear re-seeing.

March

Ways of the tongue:

Untranslatable French word game that consists of using one formula phrase ("I was in such-&-such city and saw such-&-such happening") based punningly on the sound-alike replay of another formula phrase ("Hail Mary, full of grace"). For example, *"J'ai été à Grasse et j'ai trouvé une Marie pleine,"* which presupposes familiarity with *"Je vous salue Marie, pleine de grâce."* Untranslatable partly because English is not rich in "olorimes," and partly because we aren't Catholics.

Magic movie moments: When the miniature human, inches high, slithers glistening to the rug through the tinsel of a Christmas tree, to proceed with his unseen nefarious scheme in Tod Browning's *Devil Doll*.

For meaning in prose, punctuation is all:

John had had had Frank had had had had had had had been right. (That is: On the exam for the conjugation of the verb "to have," John had had "had," Frank had had "had had." "Had had" had been right.)

For meaning in music, rhythm is all:

when "punctuated," becomes Tchaikovsky:

to which Lenny rhythmically appends the words: "Everyone out of the closet."

March

Some things last forever. Nothing lasts forever.

Returning to New York after years in Europe, how reassuring to find that same stony-faced cashier at Loew's Sheridan. Now Loew's Sheridan is Saint Vincent's garden.

Ida Mae Balaban's father invited our whole freshman class to a preview of *Hurricane* at his Randolph Street movie palace. That palace today?

The universe, it seems, tends toward right-handedness. Observe all mammals, who tend to lead with their dexter paw. Is it anti-nature for certain written languages, like Japanese or Hebrew, to proceed from down to up and from right to left, instead of as God intended?

If all printed music is engraved in the "western" style, how are the verses of Hebrew or Japanese vocal music notated beneath the left-to-right-flowing notes?

With age I increasingly forgo percussion in scoring. Any orchestration book will tell you that the battery is effective in inverse proportion to how often it's used. But, except in rare cases (Varèse, for example, where percussion is integral and not ornamental), any piece that uses drums and gongs and mallets would be just as effective and much less trite without the drums and gongs and mallets. They generally act as maquillage, doubling what's there: mascara and earrings on a healthy skull, with a slash of crimson lipstick like a timpani stroke.

The artist answers questions that have not yet been asked.

11 March

The fourteen-year-old, accused of bludgeoning a classmate to death, has been tried as an adult (he's now fifteen), found guilty, and sentenced to life. Would he be considered an adult if a 21-year-old male were "found guilty" of making a pass at him?

Daily I consider penning an essay comparing Arthur Gold, George Perle, David Diamond, Sheila Silver, and maybe Mary Peacock, if only because their last names together resemble a pirate's trove. That leaves for another day a comparison of Fux, Schütz, and Suk.

Against censorship, I'm for self-imposed fetters. There is no free art; form's stationary. Schoenberg put his new wine in old bottles, while Gershwin revamped the pop song from within the venerable cage of thirty-two bars.

14 March

The first sentence of Robert Craft's review of various books on Balanchine (*NYRB* 31 March) is specious—"No other European émigré artist of the 1930s had as great an effect on American culture and bequeathed as rich a legacy to it as George Balanchine"—since it posits opinion as fact. The third sentence (the second explains that other arts flourished)—"But in this country, classical ballet, that international transplant, indigenous nowhere, was not for certainty considered an art at all, much less a respectable one"—is specious and for the same reason. In Chicago, classical ballet was considered a respectable (whatever that signifies) art by all of us who, year after year, impatiently awaited the three-week Christmas stint at the Auditorium of De Basil's cornucopia of high art in the shape of Lichine and Debussy, Riabouschinska and Rimsky-Korsakoff, Tchelitchew and Hindemith, Massine and Shostakovich, Baronova and Falla, Picasso, Danilova and Offenbach, each close enough still to Diaghilev to breathe *his* respectability across our lake. The fourth sentence—"At the time of his death fifty years later, the émigré with, more truly than the author of the phrase, nothing to declare except his genius, had won recognition for ballet as a great art . . . "—is specious for the same reason: many hold Wilde higher than Balanchine, nor was it Balanchine who, alone, "won recognition for ballet."

Something about the dicta of Craft (a bit like the lyrics of Sondheim) always smells bad, in his icy ex cathedra invulnerable sniping at disbelievers.

The very few times he's mentioned me in print have been with a sneer; yet twice Craft's publishers have asked me for—and I've provided—blurbs. Can he have it both ways?

17 March

Dreamed that in dreams white means black—snow means pitch, for example. The dream turned to nightmare with the sight of a mulatto at dominoes.

St. Patrick's Day, with a smear of green gold on Central Park West where Sonny obliviously scatters his waste and—all sixteen pounds of him—pulls me along like a racehorse.

Rereading the all-purpose Whitman diary in search of texts for the new oratorios. You'd think that with such *telling*—such *italicizing*—texts the world would have *learned* by now. But Reagan, as though to soften the blow of the indictments of Oliver North (sobbing like Swaggart all over the TV) et alia, is shipping four battalions of American troops to Honduras to "protect" that country from Nicaragua. "*Il est près de minuit,*" sang the Prince Golaud, under other circumstances. "*Ne jouez pas ainsi dans l'obscurité. Vous êtes des enfants.*"

. . . Quels enfants! . . . Quels enfants!" Big butch *enfants* at such dreary but dangerous games.

The most repellent smell I've ever enjoyed—other than the smell of just anything before vomiting—was 39 years ago in the *quartier des tanneurs* of Fez, where a half-acre of freshly (and not so freshly) flayed pelts steamed in the winter sun. One of the pleasantest smells spills forth any time you pass The Sensuous Bean, installed six months ago down at our corner: a mélange of a dozen coffees plus chocolate, clove, cinnamon, and apple-flavored tea.

20 March

Sunday. Sleet, then cold sun. Last night, during one hour on the television screen: Two British soldiers are dragged from a car during an "incursion" into an Irish Republican Army funeral, beaten by what looks like a crow-bar and a sickle, then shot dead. A young Arab, arms fettered, is beaten by Israeli soldiers with a brick. Iran and Iraq bombings with, in foreground, "innocent" children and women— and equally innocent military teenagers in panic. American soldiers parachute into Honduras; then close-ups of them mounting special helicopters (which resemble blimp-sized mollusks), their faces as expressionless as those of the Hondurans or of the Nicaraguans. Three simultaneous detective shows (*Spenser for Hire, Hunter,* and a warlike soap opera in Japanese) all boasting handsome faces contorted with hate and revenge, and with bodies of mammals tossed about by bullets and pitchforks with the casualness of a Monopoly game. Morton Downey Jr. on his own show, outshouting his guest with contempt and loathing. From this I turn to the Good Gray Poet, seeking yet again texts for an oratorio. Page after spectacular page of prose reiterates, in the central part of *Specimen Days*, the senseless unquestioning slaughter of adolescents by adolescents. Have I the right to set to music, as in *Pilgrim Strangers* four years ago, such words as these, describing the Rebels indiscriminately stabbing their prisoners, and who, a few minutes later, are murdered by the Secesh cavalry:

". . . seventeen corpses strewed the hollow square. I was curious to know whether some of our Union soldiers, some one or two at least of the youngsters, did not abstain from shooting on the helpless men. Not one. There was no exultation. Very little said, almost nothing, yet every man there contributed his shot"? Because writing music is a game—something to do while passing the years before death. But Whitman's words, and his war too, are games, macho games, like the Trojan War or the one in Vietnam, or Morton Downey Jr.'s games, which add up to nil.

Yet, in the streets nearby where I daily shop and walk with JH and Sonny, between 69th and 72nd, Broadway and Central Park, suns rise and set, daffodils start their giggly apparition, nothing dramatic occurs. People may be dying behind those curtains, but more likely just gazing at their hate-filled screens.

23 March

Saint Matthew Passion last night with Bobby King and JH at Saint Thomas's where, despite hemorrhoids, I sat unbored nearly four hours. Gerre Hancock's version was all-male, in German, with a sensational Evangelist (Jeffrey Thomas), suavely hooting boys together and alone, a smattering of strings, Oboi di Caccia sounding like husky saxes in the "Golgotha" number (69), and a full house. How small they make me feel, these 78 songs with nary a dud amongst them, and their inevitable, cruel interaction, building, building, into such resigned sweet power—and yet how big, too, with such a model to swipe from. The craggy choral bass lines plunging to E's below the staff, and for the tenors, those matter-of-fact A's above the staff. The chromaticism. The Stravinsky in the scoring of the #40 recitative (used too in Ellen's "Embroidery" air from *Peter Grimes*), the Tchaikovsky, the Mozart, the Bel Canto, the Blues. I recall hearing the *Passion*, live, only twice before: first attending with Morris Golde on Sunday afternoon April 9, 1944, as directed by Bruno Walter in Carnegie Hall (I know this from the yellowing program tucked into my old score); then in Munich, February or March of 1954, Peter Pears as the Evangelist. Yet every inspired note's as familiar as one's pocket, so insistently has it become sewn into the public semi-consciousness.

The vastness—though short on humor—of Walt Whitman.

26 March

Some professionals look terrific in pictures or on a stage, but shed charisma in spite of themselves when seen up close. Christa Ludwig and Ellen Zwilich, for example. Others look dynamic and sexy in the parlor but lack glamour when they climb on stage. Ruth Ford and Andrew Gordon, for example.

27 March

Music cannot make a good person out of a bad person (or vice versa) half so effectively as a mere rabble-rousing speech, for art is not moralistic, much less is it propaganda. Insofar as art succeeds as propaganda, as when a military march inspires soldiers in battle, it fails as art. (As a pacifist, however, if I were able to write a march that would inspire soldiers *away* from battle, I'd do so in a trice, art be damned.)

Now we have come into an unprecedented age: the age of nuclear fission and of AIDS. More than ever, no man is an island. If a composer cannot know the effect his music ultimately will have on others, he can know the effect he hopes it will have. Whatever the circumstances of an individual piece, that piece by definition comes from the whole creator. I don't know if my musical language has changed since the advent of AIDS, but I do know that everything I compose now issues from a concern for AIDS, because I am part of my world. If the music of all composers, in intent if not in effect, helps that world even peripherally, we shall not have lived in vain.

28 March

Checkup at Dr. Melester's. The hemorrhoid, shrunk now, doesn't explain the massive ache. The ache stems from internal herpes—a splattering of small lesions, of which some, externally, are sharply painful, as they've been off & on for thirty-five years. Spooky-sounding, but, although AIDS can bring on sieges of herpes, herpes does not bring about AIDS. Stroll through the old Village haunts, and a very pleasant visit to Robert & Becki Phelps (he'd wanted to borrow my copy of Parker Tyler's *Divine Comedy of Pavel Tchelitchew* for his editing of Glenway Wescott's diary). Their third-floor windows wide open to the perfect spring light. Oh, for a fraction of Becki's energy! R. presents me with a piece of typewriting on a sheet the size of a calling card: *"L'important n'est pas de guérir, mais de bien vivre avec ses maux"* (L'abbé Galiani), no less apt for me than for him with his Parkinson's. He's just learned that his doctor will not proceed with the treatment that R. was so counting on.

I'd thought of inserting here the program notes for the two new big pieces, the quintet *Bright Music* and *The Schuyler Songs* for Phyllis Bryn-Julson and the Fargo Symphony. Such notes are the bridge between my prose and my music, the two unrelated halves of my melancholy life. But I can't find copies (the scores are with Boosey & Hawkes), and anyway . . .

Tuesday 12 April

Mother died at the dinner table at Cadbury, 5:25 P.M. Sunday. A Dr. Dougherty phoning at 6:20 with the impossible news, said Gladys Rorem had "expired." I had just put two yams in the oven. At 5:25 I had been working on *A Farm Picture* for the Whitman piece. Tears, shaking, soft warm weather.

Coincidence of Rosemary in New York. Spent night. We all—with Paul & JH and Cory, later Charity—convened at Cadbury. Lunch. The seven of us then to funeral home in Merchantville. Browns. Discussion of costs and cremation details. Visit then to Mother, the strangest hour of my life. The so-familiar face ("arranged" by the *croquemort*), the dear pathetic body, marbleized and still, still and icy, the body from which my sinful hulk had emerged 64 years ago. A house no longer inhabited. Mother was there (with Father & me and Rosemary) but not there. She had vanished from the universe. I cried. Charity cried. Father cried, and said she'd had "a rough few years." Another beautiful spring day. Thanks God for Mrs. Peacock. Father speaks hesitantly, and loses track quickly. But he won't collapse, at least not because of Mother. Suddenly at 64 I'm another person.

Returned exhausted with Paul and JH to New York.

Mother declined because she had the answer to stopping wars (don't wage them), and nobody listened. Robert Miller, her baby brother, interred at Belleau Wood in 1918.

All through this, JH's rich and furious laryngitis, his voluptuous continual hacking as he chain smokes those unfiltered Pall Malls. Solidarity of RR. She's my closest relation, since we're of identical flesh & blood. The crucial cliché is cliché precisely because it's so true & needed. What an important day. And for elegant Charity too.

Musicians' Accord concert. My *Ariel*. Elliott Carter's fallacious program note, re. meaning of *esprit*. The Carter's so polite, but unthinkably, amusingly rude to D. Collup & JH. Elliott's harmless piece. *Esprit* simply doesn't mean breathing. Etc.

At Quaker Meeting, Philadelphia, April 16
In my whole long life not an hour has gone by when I haven't thought of Mother, no matter where in the world I was. For the past week I've thought of her even more, of course, mostly with sadness, but sometimes with joy, and even silliness. It's strange how one can know another person so long, yet suddenly discover that some essential knowledge is missing. For instance, I'm not certain whether Mother believed in God. I do know she believed in poetry, and maybe that's the same thing . . . Let me read a brief passage, which refers to Belief in general, and to Mother in particular.
   This from William Penn:

> He that lives to live ever, never fears dying . . . For tho' Death be a Dark Passage, it leads to Immortality, and that's recompense enough for suffering it.
> And yet Faith Lights us, even through the grave, being Evidence of Things not seen.

19 April
Messiaen's *Des Canyons aux étoiles*, gaudy and long, with Loriod's transcendental piano playing. Florence Gould Hall.
   JH: Well, it's still the same old thing . . . thank God!
   Me: Isn't he a bit senile?
   JH: He was senile at nineteen. That accounts for those unembarrassed program notes, and endless but necessary repetitions.

Interviewers from the sticks usually turn out to be not only the local music critic but also the local sports critic. Typical question: "How do you feel about writing a piece for this particular group, rather than composing something as the spirit moves you?" But the question's no different from "Why are you eating that cabbage when you could be eating brussels sprouts?" or "Why are you sleeping with X and Y when you could be sleeping with A and B?" Commissions go to people whose music is already known, and inevitably specify, in a very general way, something that the composer is known to be good at.

I get the P.E.N. newsletter and the ASCAP newsletter and various other literary and musical newsletters. How mutually exclusive are music and literature in America!

Eyes the deep hazel hue of Scotch whisky.

Radisson Hotel, Fargo,
Sunday morning, 24 April

In the dream we were listening to the première of William Schuman's new symphony. The climax was scored (a theatrical stroke of genius) for a young couple who jumped from a scaffold onto a springboard 500 feet below, then bounced in unison over to the log cabin where we were attending.

This after *The Schuyler Songs* première, which I should report on eventually.

Phyllis Bryn-Julson was superb, as always, but the audience wrecked the flow by clapping (lamely) after each movement.

26 April

Slight stiffening between me & JH re. his re-harmonization of "Come Pure Hearts" for the May 11th concert. I feel he's trivialized an already over-accessible tune. He feels my harmonization is too remote for church hearers. But who hears what? What does he hear?

To be in the subway for the tenth time this week or in a taxi whirling you through Central Park on the gentle first day of spring; to be sitting with your father who is lonely and sad or at a party laughing with someone you've just met but aren't listening to; to be loitering in the pastry shop or chatting with your life's mate; and suddenly to feel a shiver down your spine, for you realize yet again that you're absolutely alone in the world.

18 May

To the Academy in the driving rain with Marie Arana-Ward. Reynolds Price says that James Dickey once said, "I'm not homosexual, but if I were it would be Reynolds Price and Ned Rorem I'd be most interested in."

21 May

Dined à quatre with the Perles. George's attractive *Sinfonietta*. His anecdote about Virgil in the hospital a few months ago. On coming out of the ether VT asked the doctor, "Am I going to live?" "Yes," said the doctor. "Well, if I'm going to live, I'll need my glasses."

I always heard "The Londonderry Air" as "The London Derrière."

No critic ever mentions Paul Goodman's crucial influence on Frank O'Hara's "I do this I do that" poems. Indeed, no critic of poetry ever mentions Paul Goodman.

Nantucket, 1 June

Finished *Hemlock and After* by Angus Wilson, whom I've not read for a generation. During that generation the genre—what might be termed the Campus

Novel, inherited from Gide and Huxley—has been used so effulgently by successors, mainly female (Mary McCarthy, Alison Lurie, even Patricia Highsmith), that the source now seems a bit stale. Angus's prose, unlike the crystalline prose of, say, A.N. Wilson, seems clogged and over-emphatic. For example, in a single half-page paragraph on page 148, to impose a sense of sourness at a public academic midsummer "do," he uses not one but thirty-one nouns or adjectives, some of them twice ("evil," "cruelty"), to evoke the mood. This is a sophomore ploy. And his relationships are icy, even vague. Despite careful descriptions, and a *dramatis personae* of the 25 principles listed at the start, I retain little of the characters. On the other hand, toward the end, at the opening of Book III, there is good writing, accurate, surging, sad, and specific. But by then it's too late. Englishisms, especially in dialogue, ring like a foreign tongue to American ears (eyes), as they do in A. N. Wilson's conversation, even when he's writing *in American*. And the title? Never explained. Is Angus's hero Socrates?

Some of the singers one sees nightly on the video stations are pretty cute. That's just the trouble. They're selling themselves, not a transferable music. Where is the music here so championed by Sandow and Rockwell? Not certainly in a composer. Springsteen (pretty cute) pains me physically with his "Born in the U.S.A." rasped from a strep throat. Even when composed music's involved, a Natalie Cole appears (as she did last week on Irving Berlin's 100th anniversary program), to sing "Suppertime"—Ethel Waters's old "social-conscious" ballad of injustice and sorrow—dressed in a satin mini-skirt, and making the syllables into "expressive" vowels, not sensical.

Terse but thorough, Robert Craft's write-up of Virgil's letters, in the current *New York Review*, is readable and mostly fair. As usual he makes a gratuitous crack about VT "perhaps [dancing] at the Mardi Gras Bal des Tapettes," whatever he thinks he means by that. As usual he snipes at Cocteau. And to end, he asks, "Who can match Thomson when he's writing really swell[?]" and quotes the composer: "I did not notice the misprint 'Angus Dei.' Theologically the cow might as well have been adopted by the Deity as the lamb. Both are peaceful beasts." JH reacts: That shows how much Virgil and Craft know about theology. Throughout the Bible the lamb is shown as a creature nurtured, individually and in the flock, by a shepherd. It is also a dainty sacrificial creature—"Worthy is the lamb"—which the clumsy cow is not.

Hemlock and After—was it daring for its time? Well, not the subject, nor even the treatment of the subject. All the queers (as Wilson calls them) giggle, except Bernard, and he more or less commits suicide.

Virgil, needless to say, includes no letters to me in the book, although some are surely more interesting than . . . etc. I'm represented solely in a footnote as someone (along with Dalí and Buñuel!) whom Marie-Laure "helped support."

Cold and rain, nourishing the window boxes of impatiens, lemon- and coral-colored, and the sensationally bloody peonies. Princess still up to her old tricks, scratching to be let in through the kitchen door so as to go to the basement and thence outside again where she scratches to be let through the kitchen door. Sam, now eighteen, with his never-ending rusty screech and hangdog stance, but otherwise hale. Neither cat has for ten years been allowed upstairs privileges (although Wallace was), reserved only for Sonny, who nevertheless acquires more ticks and fleas than they.

La veille, quand la vieille vétilleuse, lavée de lavande, tournait la vieille vielle dans la vallée.

7 June

Plagued by ticks, Sonny rolls in the tall grass and acquires more ticks. He could be trained to avoid rolling in tall grass, but not to grasp cause & effect: no rolling, no ticks. Likewise we humans are conditioned by slogan-babble to avoid (or at least to know the value of avoidance of) cholesterol or vodka or nicotine, not to mention the avoidance through trial & error (animals know this too) of ingesting perfume or poinsettia leaves. But how many times a minute do we commit errors of cause & effect that hurl us to our death? Not Star Wars, but rather ignorance of universal theorems. Is knowledge itself our downfall—although animals die too, without knowing they're going to?

If I didn't know—hadn't learned—that "qu" in English is sometimes preceded by a "c," I could sit for a month with a dictionary and still misspell the eleventh word in the above paragraph. Similarly, I could sit for a month with a Zulu and, despite gestures, not get to first base unless cued for 5 minutes in a grammatical jumping-off place. This morning in Larousse I sought the phrase *par mégarde*, which I've known how to use, but not how to translate, for thirty-five years. For thirty-five years I've suffered from *herpes simplex*, which, eight years ago, spread from anus to urethra. If I didn't *think* about it, would I have it? Is it *bad* to have it? Is it bad to die—to *know* about dying? What's bad? Indeed, is it *good* to compose music?

Why don't you look where you're going?

For the same reason I don't go where I'm looking.

"The more the universe seems comprehensible, the more it also seems pointless." –Steven Weinberg, 1977. "Why does the universe go to all the bother of existing?" –Stephen Hawking, 1988.

Gervase's clarinet, cool as an iris.

Dullness of the expensive campaigns. Should intelligent prospectors be spending so many months touring the land and slamming each other, rather than staying home and working? Bush isn't a man, he's a Republican. Dukakis seems to be a first-striker.

8 June

The New Yorker refers bluntly to Elliott Abrams's "lies to Congress" (p. 30, June 6, 1988). Is Elliott Abrams a liar, or someone who (like all of us) sometimes lies? What's a lie—the other side of Truth or the other side of Fact? Is Reagan a liar when he says *n'importe quoi* which even a fool knows cannot be corroborated? Is Daron a liar in saying he has four oranges when he clearly has five (or three)? Daron says what he thinks you want to hear. ("Daron, do you agree that the doctor in *Nightwood* is a reflection of Hába's quarter-tone music filtered through the esthetic of George Sand's novels on love?" "Yes, Ned, I've always felt that.") To call a lie a distortion of some larger Truth is to dignify the word. Yet the greatest fiction—the greatest art—is truth that's more than Truth, or rather, Truth defined. A person can be a liar today, to save his skin, but not tomorrow. But once a prevaricator, always a prevaricator. Fact and fancy are one coin, lies and truth another. But a fact can be truth too, and truth can be fancy.

14 June

New Hampshire's slogan: "Live Free or Die." Free of what? cholesterol? bigotry? a nagging spouse? Freedom is what you call it, and all formulas (even recipes) are shaky, since their sense depends on who's running the show. And why "die" rather than correcting the issue? Last week in Boston the press announced that I've been commissioned by WCRB to write "a symphony with chorus and the theme of peace and the human condition." Now what specifically (I asked my commissioners) is the human condition, other than everything human?

The banality of death.
The ubiquity " "   .

21 June 88

Dear Mr. Gottlieb:

All my life I've been reading *The New Yorker*, with an admiring enjoyment of its unique integrity. Suddenly the tone has changed: there is a pandering yuppie tackiness in both the advertising and the essential content.

As a musician, I am of course especially dismayed by the new preemptive "Popular Music" column. True, *The New Yorker* has always had an intermittent Jazz column, but that column was supplementary—not used in place of the regular music column. Indeed, *The New Yorker* was unique among American journals of every stripe in not having a pop column; reporting on pop music is so rife that it has preempted reporting on the increasing fragile domain of concert music in every magazine except *The New Yorker*.

The pretentious pseudo-meaningful gobbledygook of the new pop column can be found in dozens of other magazines. Do you truly feel that your readers ache for it? Do you really need the money?

Nothing is inviolable. But insofar as *The New Yorker*, which was once the source of many a spinoff, is now itself a spinoff, it is no longer *The New Yorker*.

Sadly yours,

21 June
Another sound-alike: Puccini's string quartet, *Crisantemi*, and "Moscow Nights."

Everything eventually ceases or changes (friends go to surgery and are repaired of their horrors; tortured loves become bagatelles of yore, the old—and AIDS-stricken young—die; music gets composed, performed, forgotten) except my "condition." It's been eight years.

Toward an essay on *Music Now*:

Dialects have always, like spores floating in air, throbbed in the worlds of art awaiting a cross-pollination that will render them into languages. Otherwise put: new wrinkles (once known as innovation) have always been the work of lesser artists taken up uncredited by the Great and made their own. At the moment the situation seems reversed: the innovators—the lesser artists—are already world-famous, while those incorporating their ideas into something more solid are, for the moment, obscure. Not that Philip Glass and Steve Reich are especially original; it's merely that their language was a relief to what had preceded it. But without them the young straightforward composers would be different. Torke in dance, Adams in opera, Beaser in song and chamber music, Conte in choral (especially sacred) music. These categories are undergoing revival.

1 July
Tried to watch some of the much-touted (especially by Rosemary who loves collective living) Bill Moyers's conversation with mythologist Joseph Campbell. But it turned out to be statements of the obvious—what a college education used to try to demonstrate: that all religions stem from the same impulses and no one of them is *the* religion. After Mohamet, Jesus, and Buddha are summarily disposed of, we get long cuts from *Star Wars*; indeed, we stopped the TV when the program (filmed chez George Lucas) seemed to be becoming a commercial for that film. For Campbell, the hero is a warrior (but what about Christ, and Buddha, if not Mohamet, who preached peace?); we, of the twentieth century, knowing our earth too well, now explore outer space (but what about Valhalla, Olympus, Jules Verne, or our own dear unexplored oceans and jungles and the psyche of leopards and ants?). The smug vulgarity—and I use the noun in its true sense of *earthy*—pandering to the uninformed, made us turn off the TV, as we turned it off on Moyers's previous series on Creativity, another shudder-making vulgar concept.

Finished 3 *Chambres à Manhattan* (my thirtieth? fortieth? Simenon), a 2-character romance combining Proust at his most jealous, Piaf at her most mawkish, and the author himself at his most sordid. Now reading his massive memoir, wildly *bon vivant*, with none of the hard-boiled gloom of each and every one of his novels.

The Old Maid in the VCR. Like all old movies seen "when," I recall it indelibly but with a double dimension, experiencing it still with an adolescent ken, but finding it dated, far-fetched, one-dimensional, even ungrammatical. (Miss Davis declares to Miss Hopkins, about their disgusting double-duty daughter: "She's been living with you and I for eighteen years.")

Cold soaking weather continues, as do the Midwest droughts.

Finished first third of the huge Chicago oratorio. Needs a title. *Now, Voyager's* ideal, but . . .

. . . like coming in the door, arms filled with groceries, your gleeful dog leaping, you have to pee, the phone rings.

I myself destroyed certain of Bill Flanagan's snappiest letters—those in the style of a pornographic Moll Flanders. And destroyed Joe Adamiak's voice on a love-tape he sent to Utah in 1965. Destroyed in the name of discretion, how times change.

Simenon's lack of discretion in the memoir, compared to my own sexual decorum in the diaries, is notable. But because he is heterosexual his extravagant promiscuity and tribal life depicted in gluttonous detail is laughed off, while my unashamed homosexuality (though never described—no one knows what I liked to "do") is deemed, or was deemed, if not disgusting at least infantile . . . Ought I to describe tastes and fantasies? The time is passed. Yet those fantasies and tastes are a crucial part of me.

Does art stem from its maker's experiences? Probably, although too much experience leaves little time for art. Many an author has been sedentary, creating not from fact but from imagination: Baudelaire's India, Kafka's Amerika, Emily Dickinson's travels into love. Again, with music, who can say that *any* experience is cogent? Terms like sad or happy or lascivious music? The terms are stationary so far as pictures and poems are concerned, but with music they shift with the century. (C-major was lewd in Sparta, minor was merry in the Renaissance.) But admitting there is sad music, does that sadness stem from the composer's feeling while in the act, or from what he's learned years ago about the feeling? It's hard, after all, to write about tears in the eyes with tears in the eyes—the salt water smears the ink. Nor can the pitch of tragedy be maintained for long in a sane human. Now an artist more than anyone is the definition of sanity, at least during the time he's *in the act* of being an artist—which, for a true artist, is all the time.

July 1

JH has clipped back the indoor hanging ivy, in what he calls the Gertrude Stein cut, to make it sprout more evenly.

Hordes of glittering screechy sea gulls, each with its own character, descend from nowhere whenever we fling leftovers into the backyard.

What are the dreams of a man with a stroke? Does Father, who always took lots of naps, awake from them now into a nightmare—or into *another* nightmare?

To Pocomo Beach on this perfect afternoon with JH's protégés Oscar and Augustina, both 18. I'm deeply uninterested in them both, and, though they're here to work, they behave like rude guests.

Daily action all over the house. The kids—JH's Dominican entourage—are lazy, quarrelsome, handsome, constantly running the dryer. Sonny, barking at any slight deviation from routine, and who must constantly be considered if anyone leaves him alone for even five minutes. JH really runs the house, and excellently, though the atmosphere churns. I desperately need a studio: here, I'm obliged to compose with listeners (who, of course, don't listen) forever at hand.

8 July

Sheer stillness after two weeks of motion. Not quite nine in the evening, the sky stays streaked with pale green, though days grow perceptibly shorter. Thirty-five summers ago in Hyères we'd be sitting on the still bright veranda with little canary-colored cups of strong coffee as mosquitoes began assembling. Tonight I've dined alone on leftovers. Yesterday a crew of five from Toronto television, with their cute Canadian accents, arrived at 10 A.M. by ferry and filmed me all day (in the garden, on the streets, in the whaling museum, at Straight Wharf), apropos of a documentary called *Whales in Art*, which will use my String Symphony plus interviews and music of others—Cage, Takemitsu, Xenakis, and various poets and savants), then boarded the late ferry back to Hyannis. JH, deciding, with some justice, that I'm "a lousy host insofar as niceties are concerned," prepared, despite myriad chores of his own, a lunch of prosciutto & melon, chicken in apricot sauce, a miraculous ratatouille, herb bread, ice tea, while I made a huge mixed garlic salad, and a strawberry & nectarine sauce for the vanilla Häagen-Dazs, which we served with espresso. Now JH has driven back to New York, as usual for the weekend, with the two lively but sullen Dominican brats, the piano tuner's come & gone ($75 for a good job on the old Henry Miller grand), so I've had the leftovers on the front porch while continuing with the Simenon memoir. Then, alone, watched *Jeopardy!* as I do ritually with JH after supper throughout summer (never in winter) while playing backgammon.

Judy Clurman phones to say that, yes, Caroline Stoessinger plans a celebratory concert of my music, including Judy conducting NY première of *Homer*, on October 16 (which conflicts exactly with première of *Hail & Farewell*—but things get ironed out). The hitch is that, at my now-forgotten suggestion, Stoessinger wants to economize by making it an AIDS benefit, which is a sort of blackmail for the dozens of choristers, instrumentalists, and Boosey & Hawkes, to donate their services. I'm of two minds. Usually impresarios decide to give a benefit, then look around for musicians. Here, Caroline decides to give a Rorem recital, then looks for a benefit. Is AIDS, this year, how you rake in funds?

Serebrier phones to say he's doing *Frolic* (two giddy minutes) on my birthday with the American Symphony in Carnegie at 3 P.M., the very hour that Curtis in Philadelphia has scheduled a long-planned two-hour all-Rorem chamber concert—couldn't Curtis switch it to the evening? Jesus!

Since seeing Voorhees when suicidal about my "condition" two weeks ago I feel better. Voorhees says it's tension. But every body on earth makes its separate rules, which is why doctors are no more canny than in Hippocrates' day. I worry about JH, overweight, overeating, fairly sedentary, and smoking even when he takes a shower, coughing, and with recurrent dysentery. Yet his graying 49-year-old head, like that on a Roman coin, is handsome as ever with nary a sign of a sagging neck.

Donald Windham calls. I'd invited him to do just this in the condolence letter a week ago. Details of Sandy's demise. In 43 years of cohabitative life they almost never missed a meal together. Sandy, age 66, with a belly like JH's, overblown, died in a matter of minutes, painless apparently, in front of several guests.

The luxury of being alone in the house, being able to work without being overheard, yet not working, waxing the embarrassingly dusty piano, and typing these words to keep busy. It's ten. At midnight, or shortly thereafter, JH will phone to say he's arrived. Unless there's an accident. Now I'll read till the phone rings.

Except for what I've noted here nothing remains of today. The entry could have been shorter or longer. Yet whatever anxiously dreary information it contains will be recalled by me only through the written words. Experience vanishes without a trace.

9 July

Simenon, who averaged five novels a year, claims he no longer recalls them once they're off the griddle. I can recall the very smell and time of day of the composition of certain of my earliest songs, or of nearly everything composed in Morocco; partly that's because I simply noted this data at the end of the piece. But yesterday when Judy Clurman was discussing my *Votive Mass of the Holy Spirit*, I couldn't— still can't—remember a note of this good-sized piece. Simenon forgets plot, probably, but recalls surrounding circumstances. Does music have plot? Certainly. I can usually retain sonic plot, but not tune.

Call from Sedgwick Clark, for whose *Keynote* column, called "Artist's Life," I last week penned a thousand words. His sole editorial suggestions are the substitution of parentheses for dashes here & there, and twice the substitution of *that* for *which*. I've published close to two million words over the years, but have never learned when to use *which* and *that*—and never listen when grammarians explain.

12 July

Suicide on Saturday of Tony Holland because of AIDS. The sadness. Death yesterday of Robert Ferro from AIDS-related pneumonia. On May 11, Robert came to JH's service and looked sturdy, serious, and sexy, as he did a month earlier when Michael Grumley died.

JH says more people die of lung cancer than of AIDS, but their obituaries are less prevalent. Conclusion: It's not that AIDS is more publicized and more . . .

well, odd, than lung cancer (lung cancer's a "normal" choice for JH, who still maintains his three packs a day), but that homosexual males have, in fact, contributed more to our culture than average obit readers may have suspected.

Two-thirds finished with the piano-vocal sketches of the Whitman oratorio.

The WASP backyard swarms with Caribbean bodies. Of the four eighteen-year-olds—two from Dominican Republic, two from Puerto Rico (though all raised in Manhattan)—none has expressed any interest in the fact of Nantucket, much less explored the byways on their bikes. No questions have been posed; rather, in spare moments on a bright day, they retire to their basement quarters (I call it the slave ship) to watch Kiddy Cartoons on the VCR.

Puerto Ricans have sweeter, less conniving, natures than Dominicans. Yes, I have biases, though no prejudices, except against male homosexuals with their thin mean lips, their above-it-all quickness, their defiance that's nasty rather than compassionate. Does the breed (it's my own breed) exist anymore among the newer more open generation?

Nagging arthritis, hips and left crotch mainly. Aspirin helps some.

19 July

I had thought the cherry would dominate. But in a compost mixed for lunch, of green grapes, plums, bing cherries, and raspberries, it was the raspberry—my fragile, unassuming beloved raspberry—which quite neutralized the other perfumes. This information on a steaming day seems somehow more urgent than the opening in Atlanta of the Democratic Convention.

Ruth Ford has been here since Sunday. She looks well, in face and posture, and speaks in the bigger-than-life mode of actors. Has it been really 43 years since her brother and I concocted puppet shows for John Myers? I still have the record.

Father still gets invitations to accept medals or offer advice here & there. No question. He cannot locomote, his speech is incomprehensible, and he cries too much. Rosemary says, Let him simply be a legend from now on.

Re. his crying: JH says he's always been shocked at how we four Rorems are obsessed with ourselves. Such introspection was unseemly in his Kansas childhood.

23 July

The "greenhouse effect" hot spell has given way to torrents. Everything's soggy. Magazine covers curl. The transparent paper on which I incise music won't "take" the lead. Copying the texts of Whitman beneath the notes, according to correct syllabic division, makes me realize exasperatedly yet again how often the poet used dashes for parentheses (generally erroneously, even as he used commas, at least by twentieth-century rules), and how impossible it is to know how to notate the dash as distinct from the divisional hyphen.

Mopeds everywhere. (It's the past tense for mope. She moped on the moped.)

Reading without much excitement *Fifth Business* by Robertson Davies. I note it merely to note it, having noted from the index of *The Nantucket Diary* I seldom mention books read. (For instance, in 1979 I had an orgy, pleasurable, of V. S. Naipaul. Four or five of his books. Never mentioned.) Is it fair to say that, like his native Canada, Robertson's prose is sprawling and bland?

With Ruth, the two kids (and last week *four* kids), Sonny, the two cats, plus the cat belonging to Susan (the woman from across the street) *en pension*, there's been a house full of creatures for some time, all at JH's instigation without consulting me beforehand. (Well, he likes a position of authority, a position that I don't covet.) Now, alone, I don't really work better, but waste time with a less guilty conscience.

Just as young people must make their own rules about AIDS, and about how to make it as composers in a world that doesn't care (sex and culture being on quite different wave lengths than when I was a . . .), so the greenhouse effect deranges the very air we inhale.

27 July

Populism wins out, not only in TV but also in the realm of Serious Art. Of course I'm envious and could use the money, but when a certain Ran Blake is granted the half-million-dollar MacArthur award for his featureless improvisations, and who states his willingness to "pass on his genius" to students while lamenting that the award came too late for, say, Billie Holiday (isn't the award just for "creators"?; would Billie have been Billie if such an award could make her a Good Girl?; what about Bessie Smith or Rimbaud?; where do you begin or end?); or when a certain Jenny Holzer's picture looms large on the front page of today's *Times* as the Artist to Represent U.S. at the 1990 Venice Biennale, and who "argues that art in an accessible language, presented electronically and blended into a public environment, can be as profound as traditional painting or sculpture," I feel what's the use. They invent the rules according to non-standards which fit, after the fact, their pap, and money giants fall for it.

—I hate watermelon, and I hate anyone who likes it.

—Morning dew, mourning due.

—Title: *Asking for Trouble*

—Do the mealy peaches and watery tomatoes that look lovely but taste like nothing contain the same nutrition as tomatoes and peaches that don't look like much but taste like something?

—The most excruciating sound imaginable, other than the throb of nearby rock over which one has no control, is Sam's pained mewing Siamese screech, at any time of day or night, consisting of eleven 3-second ejections like a faucet of static or a nail on slate.

3 August

Andrew Holleran may be persuasive as muckraker and nostalgia-peddler, but he can be sloppy and misrepresentative when it comes to high art. Consider this

gambit from the current *Christopher Street*: "American homosexuals have a curious relationship with England: we treasure its movies (*My Beautiful Laundrette,
Maurice, Brideshead Revisited*), its plays (*The Importance of Being Earnest,
Entertaining Mr. Sloane, Breaking the Code*), its writers (Waugh, Forster, Acker-
ley, Orton, Wilde, Auden, Isherwood, Firbank), its music (Frankie Goes to Hollywood, Bronski Beat, the Communards) . . . but England doesn't lure Americans
the way Paris, or Berlin, or Amsterdam does."

I'm not too put off by two grammatical eccentricities in a single phrase: "we"
for "they" as a pronoun for "American homosexuals"; "it" for "she" to identify England. I'm not too put off by the several categories where one would do (at least
four of the writers—Waugh, Orton, Wilde, and Forster—are subsumed in the
earlier slots). Nor am I too put off by the implicit *donnée* that the artists listed are
gay, although Waugh's sexuality comes as news. However, Holleran should speak
for himself without ghettoizing his readers. I am an "American homosexual," but I
do not "have a curious relationship with England," nor do I restrict my admiration
of that island's culture merely to gay products.

I am certainly no less informed than Holleran about musical matters, and cringe
for him when he equates some of the greatest literary figures of recent times with
fly-by-night rock groups, like equating Stravinsky with a comic strip. Is Auden's
equivalent really Frankie Goes to Hollywood, and not, say, his contemporary Benjamin Britten? Is Oscar Wilde of the same esthetic as the Communards, rather
than, say, Delius or Bax? If Holleran feels compelled to balance his literary array
with hip young gay "classical" composers, why not name Robin Holloway, Peter
Maxwell Davies, or Richard Rodney Bennett? But he has doubtless never heard
of them any more than I've heard of the pop groups he mentions.

Charity forces me to allow that there may not be a difference in quality
between a pop group and a concert composer, but there is a discrepancy in genre,
and Holleran errs in balancing pop groups with serious writers.

These words are less an aspersion on Holleran in particular than a frustrated
lament on current general ignorance which, internationally and amongst otherwise sophisticated intellectuals, acknowledges all the arts except contemporary
classical music. Yet in America and England today there is a multitude of thoughtful and talented composers active in providing a culture that represents their
countries with every bit of the panache of passing rock musicians.

The V Sound. And the vulva's square curve. (And the rocket's red glare.)

To those screaming kids whom I asked to turn down their transistors on the beautiful and savage beach: Yes, I do know what it's like to be young, but you don't
know what it's like to be old. Even if I were stupider than you, my frame of reference is, by definition, longer.

Bright Music première in Bridgehampton. JH came too, and the quintet performed with glowing care: Marya Martin, Ani and Ida Kavafian, Fred Sherry, and André-Michel Schub.

Pix of me in *The Nantucket Journal* = small mean eyes, tight egocentric lips.

Spoke with the redoubtable Mr. Gillett at Cadbury re. Father's lost teeth. Mrs. Peacock's music program has done as much as anything for the morale of Cadbury, yet Gillett treats her like an upstart.

How often I've compared Virgil and Aaron to Avignon and Rome. Couldn't they as aptly be compared to Garbo and Dietrich? All four are still quick, and Virgil at least is still kicking.

13 August
They say: leave an ape alone with a typewriter long enough and he'll write *War and Peace*. (They do not say in what language, or whether the ape will first write *Mildred Pierce*, or indeed whether he might not write his very own disconcerting treatise.) More likely, if you leave even a zillion apes alone for a zillion years, and assuming they don't destroy their typewriters in the first hour, not one will come up with so much as T-H-E. Or they might write the Bible, but backward and without prepositions.

This endless heat leads to thoughts of our globe in the first hour, or in the next zillion years. Nuclear fission. AIDS, the "greenhouse effect," all unheard-of a half-century ago, render our seared ghost as bereft as the apes. We're all we've got. No amount of groping the universe and elsewhere (". . . and elsewhere": term in the ironclad contract for filmed rights of *The Little Foxes*) for *"mon frère, mon semblable"* will avail us. Earth will float dumb forever with no thing aware of it. "Dumb," "forever," are already futile terms. We can no more retrieve ourselves in the future than in the past.

If the past continually re-exists, how about the simultaneous moments of, say, Cleopatra one minute before the asp, and one minute after? Or one minute before her birth, and one minute after?)

I used to chide Francine for listening to Mozart quartets through headphones while jogging, as though jogging were a mere chore without a Nowness to be savored or worked at, and as though Mozart could be absorbed with half an ear. But I listen to *Erwartung* while doing the dishes. Why? It' s a chore—anything to avoid just pure attendance. And Virgil used to say that his best reviews were penned about pieces he heard during his notorious public dozing.

20 August
In the current (September 5) issue of *The New Republic* Richard Taruskin, while taking to task a book about Music in Fascist Italy (he claims that under Mussolini

music didn't thrive, or at least no first-rate composers were working although Il Duce encouraged musical work, while in Germany despite Hitler good work was being done, and even Stravinsky was sympathetic to both Italy and Germany and was anti-Semitic, etc.), nevertheless declares that fascism "was intimately bound up with some of the most significant tendencies in 20th century art. First among them was neo-classicism." He quotes T. E. Hulme: "If you asked a man of a certain set whether he preferred the classics to the romantics, you could deduce from that what his politics were." (By "that" I suppose Hulme means the man's answer.) "It was romanticism that made the revolution; they [who] hate the revolution hate romanticism." Taruskin concludes that artists "of a certain set" in all media, in the aftermath of the Great War turned to classicism, and cites Stravinsky's "prickly piano pieces," played in Venice in 1926, which Prokofiev compared to the music of "a pock-marked Bach."

Taruskin takes Hulme at face value, although Hulme would have been writing about poets. The "certain set" is never defined. Romanticism is never defined. And the implication that fascists were anti-romantic unsupported and shaky. But doesn't revolution mean recurrence—something that comes back? Wasn't Wagner, the anti-Semite, romantic par excellence? And didn't Nazis "of a certain set" play "romantic" music (Wagner, Beethoven) to drown out the shrieks of their victims?

24 August

"I've had a revelation," said JH to Rosette in the lobby of Old North Church after Ruth Laredo's recital. The recital's second half—the first half was Chopin mazurkas, Beethoven *Appassionata*, Rachmaninoff trifles—was Ruth's signature: Rorem's *Song & Dance*, Ravel's *Valses Nobles* and *La Valse* played as a continuing whole, and (as sole *bis*) Debussy's "Girl with the Linen Hair" (as Virgil calls it). "I've had a revelation. The reason Debussy's greater than Ravel is that he cares more. Debussy's little 'Prélude' contains more conviction than all the tastefully cold banality of Ravel's bluster." Well, JH goes on the assumption that of course Debussy's greater than Ravel, and everybody knows it—he's just explaining why. Surely *Daphnis* and *L'Enfant* are heartbreaking despite their "objectivity," although not heartbreaking as Debussy is. The mistake is to compare the two musicians, like saying a mango is greater than a papaya. Yes, Debussy probably does wear his heart on his sleeve more than does Ravel, but if he too is an iceberg compared to Rachmaninoff, he's an iceberg that brings forth hot tears which for me Rachmaninoff doesn't. Yet comparisons are not only fragrant, they are perhaps the most cogent means for (among other things) situating a genre.

What a piece of fustian is the *Appassionata*. The triadic material throughout is uninspired, and the slow movement one of Beethoven's least beautiful.

(What kind of oven does a beeth go into?)

Yet there *is* a shred of wit in Robertson Davies's novel. This, on page 242: "A dear old friend of mine once told me he wanted a God who would teach him to grow old. I expect he found what he wanted. You must do the same or be wretched. Whom the gods hate they keep forever young." And this, a bit lower: "I have never thought that traits that are strong in childhood disappear: they may go underground or they may be transmuted into something else, but they do not vanish; very often they make a vigorous appearance after the meridian of life has been passed. It is this, and not senility, that is the real second childhood . . . "

But artists, insofar as they remain artists, retain their *first* childhood unto death.

John Simon, re: Randall Jarrell: "He passes the supreme test of critics: he sees the good in what he dislikes and the faults in what he reveres."

28 Aug.

Last night reread *Letters to a Young Poet* for the first time in 45 years. I never quite bought it in 1943 while a student at Curtis, and I still don't buy it. Humorless biblical clichés about dedication and sacrifice. But Rilke was not that much older (only 27) than the Young Poet when he penned these truths, and still no doubt felt there were formulas for a good life.

1 September

Finally finished and sent to Washington the review of Feibleman's memoir of Lillian Hellman. What a chore. With a diary there's no obligation to concision (though brevity is next to cleanliness), but essays *must* be the length they must be. Mine was too long ("didn't have the time to be more brief," etc., except that I did); lacks the pro's eye for knowing what not to include. Well, JH says, "it will do," but as with the Myrna Loy review—the only one I never completed—it's hard to write aptly about the work of someone one has known.

For a biographer likewise. To know or not to know, that's the question. Of course, the point of Feibleman's book is that he did know Hellman—his document is reminiscence in the guise of vindication: there's really not much information, just reconfirmation of the quotidian irk. But would, say, Steegmuller's *Cocteau* have been stronger, weaker, otherwise different, had he not met his subject for that one fugitive minute? And what does "know" mean? Hasn't it less to do with longevity than with intensity?

Scotch ballads are supposed to be as pentatonic as Chinese ballads. But in the wee hours I awoke to realize that you can play the American ballad "My Blue Heaven" all on the black keys.

And yet—Rilke. Rereading the *Duino Elegies* and, of course, they are something. Had forgotten how, despite years of discouraging other Americans from setting Rilke, especially in German, when we have such a rich trove here to mine (if we don't create our own song literature nobody will do it for us), I myself used his words in *The Poets' Requiem*. Surely Paul Goodman's was the most original, forceful, and worthy mind of our mid-century. Doesn't his translation surpass in clarity and nuance that of Spender or of David Young? Here's Young:

> With its whole gaze
>   a creature
>   looks out at the open.
> But our eyes
>   are as though turned in
>   and they seem to set traps
> all around it
>   as if to prevent
>   its going free.

The original:

> Mit allen Augen sieht die Kreatur
> das Offene. Nur unsre Augen sind
> wie umgekehrt und ganz um sie gestellt
> als Fallen, rings um ihren freien Ausgang.

Here's Spender:

> With all its eyes the creature-world beholds
> the open. But our eyes, as though reversed,
> encircle it on every side, like traps
> set round its unobstructed path to freedom.

And Paul Goodman:

> All eyes the Creature sees the Open.
> Free of death, the free animal
> has always its decline behind it
> and God in front,
> and as it goes it goes into
> Eternity, as brooks run on.

I lived with those verses in Rome's via Massina during the winter of 1954–55; a longer span from then till now than from the Eighth Elegy's composition (1922) till then. How stultifying even wise laymen can be when explicating a poem. Dr. Eberhardt Kretchmar allows himself to elaborate on Rilke's precision, and misses the point through sheer anthropomorphism: "If . . . we look any animal in the eyes . . . we shall see that their look, their outlook, simply does not meet our eyes and our look, and that even the 'true dog-eyes' keep only just on the surface of this animal's real . . . being, and that every animal's look, even when it is looking at us, looks out beyond us . . . [the sentence lasts much longer]." In fact, Kretchmar is referring to how people, bored to distraction, regard one another, while precious Sonny gives up his whole being into his single-minded clear-focused beseeching.

Scriabin's ten *Piano Sonatas* were not yet complete when Rilke's ten *Elegies* were just begun.

Proust's madeleine, spoons, and the clanking on the pavement. Rilke's raging winds and seas on the battlements below the Triestino castle of Duino. Breakthroughs. The open . . .

The boredom of great works. With difficulty I now reread Rilke (or Valéry or Mallarmé or . . .) when with ease I read them then.

Rilke and animals. But Paul G. wrote: "I cannot live among the birds and bees as though they were like us / if I do not associate with man, with whom shall I associate?"

Paul Goodman and Virginia Fleming, when I took him to see her, circa 1955–56, about her commissioning us jointly to write a *scena* for her. Beforehand I explained how rich and stupid she was. "Nobody's that stupid," the ever-wise Paul had said. After we left Miss Fleming, he said, "I was wrong."

Title: *Getting Through the Day*
    Sequel: *Getting Through the Night*

Thursday 8 September
For days the air's been blue as Greek spring water. Impossible to recall the unbreathable August, or to decide that summer will be already over on Saturday when we catch the dawn ferry, with Sonny and the two boys, and proceed, in a rented car, to Manhattan. The island is still. Fifty thousand tourists vanished. Just the plink and sough of crickets and mourning doves, plus Sonny's scratching for fleas worse than ever. Fall cleaning. JH paints the parlor for the first time in fourteen years. In depths of storage closet the *Boston Post* of July 12, 1927 (I was 3½), as yellow in content as in appearance. Monday, classes start at Curtis (one new student, a young Romanian pianist recommended by Lenny B.), after which with Rosemary we'll drive to Cadbury where I'll see Father for the first time in four months. Be prepared, says R., he's all skin and bones . . . At loose ends. Disoccupied, as the French say. *Le temps pèse aux gens désoeuvrés.* Walking from room to room twiddling my thumbs while everyone else does "useful work," painting, etc., so that I can inhabit a still pleasanter abode (to twiddle thumbs). Yes, I've finished the piano-vocal scoring of *Goodbye My Fancy*, probably my longest single work— about 55 minutes—except for *Miss Julie*. If I died tomorrow, Daron could possibly orchestrate it from my notes. Fifty years ago Mrs. Lee (our art teacher at U-High, and *married*—exceptional for then), in her sweet inability to deal with adolescence, declared, "Well, if anyone finds this class boring they can leave." Everyone left—except Bruce and Maggy and me. But the rest of the day we were *désoeuvrés*. This fall a dozen first-rate concerts in New York will honor me. But that's work done—have I a right to dessert unless I eat the spinach? (Recollections of embarrassment in front of grammar-school pals when Father would do his imitation of a Norwegian farmer in heavy iambs, weak-to-strong + high-to-low, "I *tank* I *go* to *town* now.") Between works—like *entre chien et loup*, or the dark and the

daylight, or *le marteau et l'enclume*, or the devil and the deep. The eleven move-ments of my *Scenes from Childhood* were originally titled after eleven gay bars from the late 1930s and early 1940s: in Chicago Waldman's on Michigan Avenue, Simon's on Rush Street, the Club Gay on Polk & Damen; in New York—the Main Street, the Old Colony, Julius's, etc. Fink, I retained only Mary's and the San Remo. Do you remember? Autobiography: use Markevich's device as opener: events occurring in 1923, name of those born on October 23 (Liszt, Bernhardt, et al.).

20 Sept.

Father died last evening at ten minutes before nine.

Emergency call from Rosemary to Curtis. I quit classes. Six hours at Cadbury, the windless perfect late afternoon with RR in the garden, acorns or something falling on our heads. A stroll to the E-wing where Mother lived and died, familiar faces of certain of the crazies. RR said: "Last week he said, 'I thought I was dead.'" 7 weeks shy of his 94th birthday. His recent medal, only last Thursday. Mrs. Pea-cock's fruit juice, etc. Her pastel gowns & rosewater. Mother died 5 months ago. Their sex life even recently. His pathetic little emaciated body now, like a concen-tration camp victim. The gasping, the unseeing eyes. The breathing, quieter & quieter. The nurse, friendly & efficient. The dark falling outside. Rachel & Mike & Sara & Mary bring lasagna. They leave, Mary stays, also Charity. My mind wan-ders. I read (*The New Republic*). Time passes. What if we threw him on a flaming pyre? Would he awaken? Father's eyes roll up into his head, just the whites show. Breathing quieter. Slower. No odor. But I still didn't realize what RR realized—that *it was happening*. Thank God I stayed. Then we realize there were just twenty more breaths in his body, then 19, then 12. The twitching of the mouth (like Wallace's rictus) twice at the end, a minute apart. Was he dead already?

RR: I think that's it.

RR (to Father): Well, you finally made it. (She's been with him five hours a day for months. The discomfort.)

Tears all around.

Charity: Let's pray.

Mary. Reading from Corinthians. Let's get Mrs. Peacock.

25 Sept.

Obit in the *Times*. Condolences from all over the country. A shocked and respect-ful world. Handwritten and unwavering letter from Virgil Thomson. Another from David Diamond.

8 October

Zinman pinch-hit for Schwarz at the eleventh hour. When I visited him at the hotel yesterday he knew the score better than I. Does the orchestral version of *A Quaker Reader* come off? Like the other pieces on the concert tonight—

Appalachian Spring, Trouble in Tahiti, each by a gay composer, though surely it wasn't planned—this wasn't meant for concert orchestra. Bernstein's and Copland's are theater works about WASP marriages, and mine in a way is too.

Tomorrow JH goes to Nantucket, and I'll hear *QR* again, this time with its Onlie Begetter, Leonard Raver . . . Is the piece a dud? No. Does something happen? No.

Did Howard Swanson in 1978 die of AIDS? Our mutual dentist, Dr. Swee, says there was no explaining his blood count all askew. JH feels that AIDS has been around for seventy years, or maybe seventy thousand.

Where is my song on the Joyce poem (the only one I ever wrote) for Nancy Reid in 1946 or '47, with an accompaniment swiped from *Persephone*? It's in none of the boxes or files.

18 October

Played *The Santa Fe Songs* at the Y, with me at piano and Jaime Laredo, Sharon, and baritone Ben Holt. Jaime's violin tone resembles his voice, smoothly nasal, like Tourel's vocal timbre. Is this to some extent true of all instrumentalists? Holt is not Will Parker but he's conscientious. Anyway, the first performer of a work, even if mediocre, is always the one by whom succeeding performers are judged . . . While playing (excellently) at the Y with these confrères, my thought is: Who am I that this crowded hall should hush for so long at these sounds?

During this performance, on the other side of town, the world première of my *Fanfare and Flourish* (organ and four brass) took place in Alice Tully Hall. A curtain-raiser for the Chamber Music Society.

For the record, surrounding my birthday will be 33 major performances of my music in the vicinity. Try to remember to list them as they come up.

23 October

Sixty-fifth birthday.

Fifteen years ago, for my fiftieth, Lou Harrison sent me four 4-line "Sapphic stanzas" ending:

> *As only a few years older, & not more*
> *wise at all, still joyous & still most lusty,*
> *we send together from our later Eden*
> *to you in your city of towers & thunder*
> *much much joy —.*

(The "we," of course, includes Bill Colvig.)

Nov. 5

Correcting proofs of a musical score. It's not the forgotten accidental or mis-aligned counterpoint that make for the occasional wrong note, but the overlooked metronome mark which makes *every* note sound wrong. In the "Bal Musette" movement from *Picnic on the Marne*, I, like so many composers, allowed the indication of a quarter, rather than a dotted half, to equal 60. The resulting performance is three times too slow. Like a hidden virus that destroys the whole organism.

6 Nov.

There is no such thing as advice—*workable* advice—between generations, there is only example. Advice is useless unless the person advised sees a reason for it, in which case the advice is superfluous, because advice is simply logic (the best way to avoid wars is not to fight them; if you're going to live in France, learn French). Example, on the other hand, is unspoken inspiration. When we respond to a work of art, we are responding to what we did not know we knew. If we can't respond, no amount of instruction—of "advice"—will help us. Even the children of many a true artist are oftimes rebellious toward their parent's example. I could hope that the next generation, and the next, would profit by the errors and glories of the past, but I see no support for such hope.

Interpretation of music, including my own music, interests me hardly at all once I've heard the piece rehearsed, performed, and often. Yet interpretation (which performers must live with all their lives) can make or break music, including my own.

NYC, 18 November

Twice in a row the *Times* daily crossword features my name: yesterday the four-letter clue for 44-across was "Beatty and Rorem"; today the five-letter clue for 34-across is "Pulitzer music prize winner: 1976."

There is no such thing, says Gore Vidal, as homosexuality, there are only homosexual acts, and he's sort of right. Yet, although the last eighteen of the twenty-one years I've cohabited with JH have been non-sexual, hasn't the union (the understanding, the empathy, the style) been homosexual? I could never have lived with a female as I have with JH, yet I adore females. Is our union, then . . . well, homo-*philic*? But the love a woman feels for a man, and vice versa, is also homophilic. (Old joke: "What's the definition of a fairy?" "One who likes his vice versa.")

In autobiography: details on Kinsey in 1948.

The young today don't know about malted milk.

Our dietary cravings are unsynchronized. JH likes starch, red pork, peanut butter, potato chips. I like salads, baked potatoes, all desserts.

The young don't know me, nor I them, nor do we care. I've had almost enough, but don't want to die.

Ellen Adler's story about Kolodin, who had a crush on her, and who occasionally took her to the opera: When she told him that Marlon Brando had phoned from Tahiti inviting her for an immediate visit, and that she had accepted, Kolodin said, "But you had a date with me next Tuesday!"

JH called me to the piano to display his arrangement. Rightful contempt of the translation beneath the original Czech words in the Dvořák songs he plans to use for the service next Sunday—the willy-nilly superimposition of King James (meaningless on the continent) at the expense of the vocal line. JH, with his own new free churchy translations, keeps Dvořák's note values quite intact.

29 Nov.

Jim Kendrick is to be thanked for putting the bug in Lenny's ear about conducting the NY Philharmonic première of the Violin Concerto. It would also be Lenny's return as guest conductor. Since Gidon Kremer was to be soloist, he learned the piece and played it in lesser venues here & there beforehand. JH and I attended his Avery Fisher recital three weeks ago. His diffident intellectual smallish tone was disconcerting. His female "assisting artist" in Berio's *Sequenza* seemed solider in heft and presence than Kremer. They also played Prokofiev (which Mother used to pronounce *Pro*-ko-fife)'s slick and delicious Sonata for Two Solo Fiddles. During *Sequenza*—an empty demonstration of sound effects—JH whispered, "Last summer Kremer called her up and said, in Russian, 'I've got some good news for you, and some bad news. The good news is that you're going to play on my New York recital. The bad news is that we're going to play the Berio.'" Kremer was cool when we introduced ourselves in the Green Room.

I did go over the score chez moi with Gidon; then he went off to Europe, returning one hour before the final rehearsal. Meanwhile, meetings with Lenny. He changed order of movements. I changed them back. Insufficient rehearsals, without the soloist, a demoralized orchestra. Lenny at midnight called to ask for Jaime Laredo's tape. Next morning he confessed that Laredo should have been the soloist, that Gidon was absolutely wrong, he's Brahmsian, I'm Ravelian. I told this to Gidon, who was miffed. Première Thursday riddled with errors. Lenny had decided to repeat the end of the fourth movement after the closing fifth movement so as to have "a rousing finale." Sounded like the concession that it was, and the orch. played it twice too slow. Other faulty entrances. On second night, taking my bow, I nearsightedly fell on my face against a horrified second-violinist. Last performance L. forgot his baton and conducted without it, also dispensing, thank God, with the tacked-on ending. Such is the saga of the mysterious perfection of mores behind the scenes.

Backstage some dull fan asked, out of left field, "What's the difference between rhythm and meter?" Long pause . . . Meter is rhythm contained. I seldom notate in eccentric signatures anymore, but try to *contain* 5/8 rhythms within a steady 4/4 meter. It's easier to read.

Finished setting of Paul Monette's *Love Alone*, for men's chorus and piano four-hands.

Visit from Herb Gold, very centered on homosexuality for one admitted all straight. Asked if he'd ever "done it" with a man, he says no. Asked if he were forced by the Gestapo to choose between an 80-year-old harpy and a handsome lad, what . . . But of course, it depends on the acts required.

My sex life has always been experimental with its vast promiscuity. My musical life conservative.

Susan Sontag's reasonable, thorough, and scary essay on AIDS in the current *NY Review*.

Rearrangements must be made by the young. Big publishers, big recording companies, big orchestras are taboo today to them, yet there are more good young composers than ever, so God must want them. (Lenny says, "He wants cock-roaches too.") As with AIDS, they must make their own new rules. Sexually I'm a virgin in the present age, having been monogamist (i.e., faithful to my own body) for about 18 years, before AIDS was a given.

From Thos. Mann's diaries in 1938, when he lived in Beverly Hills: ". . . took a rather long walk along the glistening blue-and-white ocean at ebb tide. Many con-doms on the beach. I didn't see them, but Mrs. Huxley pointed them out to Katia." Today, a half-century later, this entry would be penned in approbation.

30 November

Sunday prime time. Sickened by a bloody auto chase, I flip the dial to the bland murders of Angela Lansbury, who, says Jack Larson, stands to earn tens of millions in residuals. Thence to a made-for-TV Kenny Rogers opus showing two men spread-eagled in the sun where they will perish of thirst by dusk unless, as is sug-gested, they're scalped beforehand. So I switch to a Chuck Norris replay wherein, for only fifteen seconds, the following is depicted: a brave American military has been strung up by the feet, by "Orientals" in a jungle, his head covered by a gunny sack containing a voracious rat. Sometime later, dead, he is cut down, the sack removed, and we see his face eaten away by the rat, also dead, and stuck like a fly in crimson amber to the coagulated gore. The image, so biased and uninstructive, hovers.

Now the phone rings at 9 P.M. and a female voice asks for me. "The League/ISCM is raising funds for their 75th anniversary" (or something) "and we know you'd be interested in contributing." I tell her she's come to just the right person to expose an exhausted plot, explaining that a) composers should not be asked to support each other financially, and b) what's the League/ISCM ever done for me?

Podhoretz, as quoted in the current *Native*, explains that AIDS is due to men act-ing like women with other men. I hadn't realized that heterosexual women were so given to buggery, or that Norman himself, by his own implication, likes to blow Midge Decter.

Nantucket, 10 December

Death of Henri Peyre. The *Times* quotes him: "When we teach, we teach what we are, not really what we know and not always what we think."

Tackling Gore Vidal's new essays, *At Home*. Inferior to his previous collections, arch, mean, stale. Even when he writes of an excursion into Mongolia we learn little, since he's above it all. Too much repetition, lest we forget they're his coined contribution to our language, of terms like Lit Crit and Bookchat, and too much reference to his noble lineage, despite coy disclaimers: "I shall never write a formal memoir (I have never been my own subject, a sign of truly sickening narcissism)." With all his sarcasm of others' mistakes, his grammar errs here & there; and when he claims that Tennessee Williams—a claim he makes elsewhere about Whitman—"loved to sprinkle foreign phrases throughout his work, and they were *always* wrong," we lift an eyebrow, since Gore himself often writes *cri de coeur* (not the correct *cri du coeur*), and garnishes a page in *Judgment of Paris* with a dutiful but superfluous exercise in French. The piece on Paul Bowles is extremely weak, since he—Gore—is musically uninformed. He suggests that only an Anthony Burgess "knows enough to do [Bowles] justice . . . [being] the first critic able to deal both with his music and his writing." He adds that PB is known to composers as a writer, to writers as a composer. That certainly doesn't obtain today—since no one remembers him as a composer, certainly not young composers who don't know his prose either, and writers—including GV—don't know his music, and never did. John Simon's new essay collection, *The Sheep from the Goats*, is a wiser and kinder volume.

Sometimes, though, the aloofness pays off, and certainly I agree politically with all GV professes. (In *Dress Gray*, his otherwise expert TV adaptation, GV seems to end up allowing that a military school is, *in itself*, not a bad idea.) As when, instead of venting righteous indignation about, say, the Podhoretzes, he simply pretends not to take them seriously—"that wonderful, wacky couple."

The Atlanta Symphony's recording of my orchestral work prompts this from Kyle Gann in *Fanfare*: "Rorem's career has been one of continual decline . . . devoid of soul or backbone." And this from Terry Teachout in *High Fidelity*: "Rorem has emerged at the age of 65 as quite possibly the best composer we have."

Like dentists or waiters, critics aren't real people, they're critics; unlike waiters or dentists, they're likely to move in circles that include real people (i.e., you and me). Conversation with them is as wary and mannered as with another species.

To love. To be able to hurt someone. The urge that E. M. Forster avowed in his dotage. And which guided me through many an erotic foray. To be able to hurt: to prove to oneself that one counts.

An aard-vark's fart.

For the partita
take a seat a-
way from Martita.

18 December

Expensive documentary on Elliott Carter on Channel 13 (Chanel No. Thirteen), which, if nothing else, gets an "A" for arrogance. Most every utterance by Elliott— who looked marvelous, fresh and pink—was specious or superfluous. The canard that Creative Artists, like the one about not repeating themselves, was mouthed by Elliott as though it were new—as though, indeed, newness were in itself a virtue, and as though even the grandest C.A.'s had more than five or six ideas in their whole lives. All of Carter's "inspirational" talk dealt with image, never with craft; he could have been an impressionist so much did he harp on Man and Nature and his need to reflect the time he dwells within. But if he believes his music depicts peoples' interrelationships, or lack thereof, this is belied by the background of wheat fields and rivers rippling in the wind. If, in fact, his music does depict human relationships, the fact of having instruments simultaneously not merely disagree, but not even attend one another, doesn't solve *the problem through music* of depicting such relationships. Meanwhile, as soundtrack substance, the producers erred in featuring Shostakovich's actual movie music, since it fared so much better than E.C.'s. The latter's *Holiday Overture* is hollow fustian coming after *Billy the Kid*. And the remarks about Elliott's influence by jazz ring hollow too. Did he really, like Bernstein and Copland, haunt the 52nd Street bars in the thirties? The shot of Art Tatum at the keys is sensational as he out-Horow-itzes Horowitz. But this shot, shading into a shot of Charles Rosen's hands on the keys playing the Carter Sonata, belies the jazz influence. Rosen is too smart to make remarks like, "Not until the twentieth century did composers invent their own rules." Every composer, good or bad, who ever lived, has made his own rules. The film is self-serving PR.

Emperor's old clothes. "I wrote for an audience—no one listened." Does EC not write for an audience now?

We heard his three-minute "Fanfare." I longed to like it. But after the intriguing first second (fluttering winds), it quickly gets overwrought and heads nowhere. Could last an hour, or less, or more. It has no length.

From Cocteau's *Le Livre blanc*:

> The homosexual recognizes the homosexual as infallibly as the Jew recognizes the Jew. He detects him behind whatever the mask, and I guarantee my ability to detect him between the lines of the most innocent books . . .
> . . . A faultless body, rigged with muscles like a schooner is with ropes and whose

limbs seemed to radiate out like the rays of a star from a nuclear fleece whence would rear the one thing in a man that is incapable of lying and which is absent in women who are constructed for feigning.

Uncredited translation, not bad here, ghastly elsewhere. But the master sounds uncharacteristically antifeminist; and the male organ *is* capapble of lying, as the morning "piss-hardon" unrelated to sex, or the inability to erect with someone who is very attractive.

Early I perceived the unsexy handsome queers, their eyes focused inward, not out. (Their eyes looking in, not out.) Thin mean lips. The narcissism, which is a lack of eroticism.

Reading at Tom Wolfe's bulky novel. Not since our high-school literary magazine, *The Blue Mirror*, have I seen so many dots and dashes and stuffing.

WORDS & MUSIC. All painting is representational, even the most abstract. And all music is abstract, even the most concrete (like the Strauss and Debussy tone poems). Yet all music, even non-vocal "abstract" purely instrumental utterances, is based on the language spoken by the composer. Thus, is all music, like all painting, fairly representational?

NR by Inge Morath, behind the house in Nantucket, 1978
(Photo: Inge Morath © Magnum Photos)

Alexie Haieff, Gore Vidal, and NR in 1982 *(© Camilla McGrath)*

With Judy Collins, Nantucket, August 10, 1998

NR with Jaime Laredo and Murray Sidlin after performance of NR's *Violin Concerto,* January 20, 1987 *(© David Ottenstein)*

With Gloria Vanderbilt 1992 (© *Jack Mitchell*)

Leonard Bernstein, NR, Mary Carswell, and William Schuman at the MacDowell Colony, where NR gave the gold medal to LB, summer of 1987 (© *Nancy Crampton*)

Leonard Slatkin with NR, after the premiere of *Goodbye My Fancy* with the Chicago Symphony, November 8, 1990

NR in New York, 1992
(*© Nancy Lee Katz*)

Alice Tully and Ned Rorem, 1988 (Miss Tully commissioned the organ suite *A Quaker Reader* twelve years earlier) *(© Peter Schaaf)*

Ricky Ian Gordon and NR, April, 1995

Robin Holloway, NR, Claire Bloom, Lee Hoiby, and pianist Brian Zeger after world premieres of three works for spoken voice and piano, in 1995 at the 92nd Street YMCA (© *Nancy Crampton*)

NR, 1996 *(© Arnold Newman/Liaison Agency)*

Gary Graffman after NR's commencement address at the Curtis Institute, May 8, 1999
(© Don Tracy)

With Daron Hagen, 1992
(© *Star Black*)

NR in doorway, 1992
(© *Nancy Lee Katz*)

Erick Sessler, NR,
David Diamond
in 1993

Gary Graffman,
Emanuel Ax,
Andre Previn, NR,
1992, backstage at
Carnegie Hall for
New York première
of NR's Left-Hand
Concerto
(*© Steve J. Sherman*)

The music panel at the American Academy of Arts &Letters, January 14, 1998.
(Top Row) Olly Wilson, Robert Ward, Ezra Laderman, Mario Davidovsky,
(Bottom Row) Steve Reich, NR, George Perle (© *Benjamin Dimmitt*)

NR with the Emerson Quartet—Lawrence Dutton, David Finckel, Philip Setzer, Eugene Drucker,—after première of NR's *Fourth Quartet,* October 8, 1995

NR seated, with Andrew Wentzel, Gran Wilson, Cynthia Hayman, Hugh Wolff (conductor), and Katherine Ciesinski, after the world première of *Swords and Plowshares* with the Boston Symphony, November 15, 1992

(Top Row) Richard Lippold, Jack Beeson, NR, (Middle Row) Will Barnet, Cynthia Ozick, John Updike, John Guare, (Bottom Row) Hugo Weisgall, Elizabeth Hardwick, Ada Louise Huxtable. The Centennial Committee of the American Academy of Arts & Letters, 1994 *(Portrait by Timothy Greenfield-Sanders)*

Susan Graham and NR, 1999

Jim Holmes, 1981

NR with Paul Bowles in 1995, Rob Schwarz in background *(© Phillip Ramey)*

NR with Virgil Thomson
in Nantucket 1986
(© Mary Heller)

With Jim Holmes, December 15, 1997 (© John Jonas Gruen)

James Holmes, 59, Composer, Choir Director and Organist

By ANTHONY TOMMASINI

James Holmes, an organist and choir director long associated with the Episcopal Church of St. Matthew and St. Timothy on West 84th Street in Manhattan, and a sometime composer of considerable skill, died on Thursday at his home in Manhattan. He was 59.

The cause was cancer, which he had had for several years, said his longtime companion, the composer Ned Rorem.

Mr. Holmes was born on April 2, 1939, in Pittsburg, Kan., and brought up in a musical environment. As a boy he studied violin and piano and later continued his studies at the University of North Carolina at Chapel Hill.

In 1967 he moved to New York City. Late that year he met Mr. Rorem and the next year they moved to the Upper West Side of Manhattan. Inevitably, he lived in the shadow of his older (by 16 years) and celebrated partner. But he won admiration in his own right for his professional services and achievements.

His first major post as an organist and choir director was at the Chapel (now Church) of the Intercession in Washington Heights. There, in 1972, he presented a well-received series of organ recitals, each devoted to a modern composer, including Messiaen, Poulenc, Satie and Virgil Thomson.

In 1973 he became the organist and choir director at the Church of St. Matthew and St. Timothy, where

James Holmes

until his illness intervened he never missed a Sunday or feast day service. It was his custom to feature a 20th-century work in his musical selections. His own "Stabat Mater," an unaccompanied choral work of austere beauty, is published by Boosey & Hawkes. In September the church unveiled a plaque honoring him with "thanksgiving for 25 years of devoted service."

In addition to Mr. Rorem, he is survived by his mother, Lora Eastwood Holmes of Corvallis, Ore., two brothers and two sisters.

Jim Holmes obituary, January 9, 1999

Alone in Nantucket *(© Mary Heller)*

1989

1 January

Madness prevails in the New Year. Qaddafi, Shamir, Arafat, Reagan's playing footsies again with Libya plus semi-pardoning Oliver North, and terrorism in Scotland. Holy Moses! JH says the only sane man left is Gorbachev. Who'd have thought that even two years ago?

Doda Conrad's 1950 code-phrase for homosexual: Egyptian royalty.
   As I yank a coat from the hanger, other hangers clatter to the floor.
   No sooner is milk poured onto the cornflakes than the phone rings.

Padding's everywhere. Would Lear's five *Nevers* have been five, rather than perhaps a sufficient three, had not the pentameter imposed that number? Still, the *excess* of "too many" *Nevers* makes Shakespeare Shakespeare, whereas

> *The grave's a fine and quiet place,*
> *But none, I think, do there embrace.*

being merely Marvell, is thick with verbiage. "Fine" and "I think" seem superfluous, inserted to flesh out the requisite eight syllables. (Graves are not "fine"; and "I think" is implicit.) Why not simply:

> *The grave's a quiet place,*
> *But none do there embrace.*

Similarly, in Kander & Ebb's "Life is a cabaret, old chum, / Come to the cabaret," "old chum" was surely tacked on after the fact, for rhythm, not meaning. Both "Tea for Two" and the big choral turn in Britten's *Peter Grimes* ("Old Joe has gone fishing / and You Know has gone fishing") were built on dummy lyrics improvised by an impatient composer until the real thing came along, which never came along.

Incidentally, might Marvell's invitation for us to sport "like amorous birds of prey" steam from Racine's "*Vénus à sa proie toute entière attachée*"?

Alexandrines versus iambic pentameter. In English we speak in fives. Are 5/4 meters in music easier therefore for our ears to grasp, than for French ears?

4 January

For *Seven Days*, what are my hopes for the Met in the coming year?

> Although I contribute one major article yearly to *Opera News*, the Metropolitan's literary organ, I seldom go to the Met itself. Less because of the low vocal standards and high prices than because of the repertory. The Metropolitan Opera is to living music as the Metropolitan Art Museum is to living painting: From the standpoint of a contemporary artist nothing occurs there. The roster and fare of many an outlying company are more vital. As for hopes in the coming season, I have none. The programs have been solidly planned for the next five years.

Unrelated people with the same name, often, for whatever reason, look alike. Gianni Bates and Alan Bates. The Mendelssohn quartet's violinist Nicholas Mann and the Curtis violinist Nicholas Kitchen. Others too.

A lisp. His tongue's a living cedilla. Sibilant. Opposite of me—I can't say an *s*.

Solzhenitsyn: show-biz martyr.

How many folks, especially when I'm wearing steel-rimmed glasses, say I look like George Bush!

Though we've played four thousand games of backgammon as a post-prandial *digestif* over the years, there's always a whiff of suspense. Last night all my men— my "stones"—but two were home, while JH had two men out and the others scattered pell-mell. I asked, gloating, "Could you possibly win with this setup?" He won.

Chance and skill are evenly divided.

Susan Sontag to Nadine Gordimer on a long TV dialogue: "It's well-known that we writers, more than any other artists, must work in solitude, and we hate it. Painters have apprentices to mix their colors, but we writers, more than any other artists" (she repeats), "live mostly in solitude." (No word about composers.) Well, how many painters do *you* know with apprentices mixing their colors?

Julia Child, while demonstrating an Escoffier menu, once announced: "It's an elaborate preparation, I know, with those potato peels all over the floor, but in Escoffier's day, there were all sorts of little boys in the kitchen to clean up as you went along."

All sorts of little boys.

Flipping channels, I pause to glimpse Keith Jarrett fingering what sounds like a simple improvisation on "Over the Rainbow." Such anguish for such modest results, like Portnoy's *père* finally emitting an agate-sized turd. *The New Yorker* 45 years ago carried a cartoon of an amphitheater where ten thousand spectators soberly beheld a distant figure shouting into a mike: "Hold tight, hold tight, hold tight, hold tight, foo-der-ee-yack-a-sacky, want some sea food, Mama . . . "

10 January

January *Friends Journal*, sent by Rosemary, contains joint obit of Mother & Father, brief but thorough and caring. The bulk of the issue, *comme si par hasard*, is devoted to "Essential Lessons of Same-Gender Marriage." Is there another protestant faith that would come so clean? Yet it's precisely the faith as distinct from the philosophy in Quakerism that makes me quake. Of the witnesses, both the pros and cons speak for God in declaring homosexuality a sin or merely a way of life. Since I don't believe in God, I'm put off by each stance. If I'm a "good" Quaker on my terms, and am proud to be one in the world's eyes, the God part still annoys as it does with Alcoholics Anonymous. (It annoyed Mother too—she disliked God—but at least she never talked of the Virgin Mary).

It's the Quakers'—unlike the Catholics'—concern for temporal chaos, their downplaying of Goodness and the Afterlife, their pacifism, that appealed to our family. But I don't seek the religion's sanction of my private manners any more than I shun its disapproval.

21 January

To the Met to see—I mean hear—Jessye Norman in *Erwartung* and *Bluebeard* in a shoddy pretentious production. The Schoenberg décor seemed to be an "expressionist" Viennese drawing room complete with Steinway grand and red maple boughs thrusting in through the casements. JH whispered, "To paraphrase Chekhov, don't bring a piano onstage unless you play it. And is it a forest or a parlor? Either depict a real forest that we understand as her mad mind, or a real parlor wherein she imagines the forest which the *music* depicts."

Do we need a beautiful instrument for *Erwartung*? How did she memorize all those notes? Then we realize that, really, any notes will do. In *Bluebeard* she plays a pushy yenta to Samuel Ramey's passive monarch, as opposed to a creature of feminine wiles wheedling a desperate but powerful sage. But the voice! A sensation—Ramey's too—and Bartók's orchestration (lustrously enlivened by Levine) a model to envy. Blegen's husband's the concertmaster. He told me this morning that the orchestra's still "swimming" in the Schoenberg (last night was the second of a half-dozen performances), and that Levine had installed many a fermata for Ms. Norman. This—on top of the 228 tempo changes in the piece's 425 measures.

Nantucket 23 January

Arrived by rented car and ferry last midnight.

The "condition," a dot of fire in the anus. Anus, a penny or a wild strawberry. Hate anuses—other people's.

Susan Sontag's *AIDS and Its Metaphors* is receiving respectful dismissals. "By comparison with earlier diseases," ends Paul Robinson's *Times* review, "the metaphors associated with AIDS have tended to be both tame and apposite. The disease itself, and not the way we talk about it, is the true source of its horror." How natural it might still seem to agree with the fundamentalists and their Punishment theory, had not Crazy Jane affirmed to the Bishop of a pre-AIDS congregation what we've all been thinking for ten thousand years—that "Love has pitched his mansion in the place of excrement."

Concocting a pallid and derivative (of Poulenc) *scena* for contralto and keyboard from *Anna La Bonne* for the Cocteau centenary by using material from my backgrounds for *The Lady of the Camellias* a generation ago. A generation before *that*, in the winter of 1943, during one of my drunken treks to New York from Philadelphia, Paul Bowles in the Chelsea Hotel at four A.M. played me a recording of Marianne Oswald reciting *Anna la Bonne*.

JH's article on my sacred choral music is expert and thorough, although he calls me (echoing Vaughan Williams's remark about his father) "a cheerful agnostic"— doubtless to placate readers of *The American Organist*—when actually I'm a cranky atheist.

"Born to Dance" again on TV 53 years after the fact. Weird Buddy Ebsen, a rag doll, could be a Twyla Tharper.

In musical composition one cannot lie without eventually being found out. That sentence is meaningless metaphor.

The Music Lesson

I long to travel
When I hear Ravel,
Though I'm less fussy
About Debussy.
I start hoppin'
When I hear Chopin,
And literally snatch
At the strains of Bach.

> *I want to joust*
> *After reading Proust.*
> *And smile with pride*
> *While reading Gide.*
> *Buxtehude:*
> *Mere tutti frutti.*

Nantucket 23 January

Last week, dismay throughout the land about Sex in Schools—pre-adolescents, some of them retarded, who diddle each other. This week, linking throughout the land of Bundy's interest in pornography to his serial murders. Is sex truly so shocking that the shocked forget how they once played doctor? Is it so damaging to a retarded child that in his loneliness he seeks some fun? If there's cause & effect between pornography and murder (as distinct from TV violence and murder), then 99 percent of adult males would be murderers. If murderers enjoy pornography (but what of those who don't?), do most of them also enjoy chocolate milk shakes and boxing matches and sunshine? Am I naïve in answering these questions?

Do I know a bond from a stock? What happens if I'm left alone to deal with that?

The horror of buying clothes, of being pawed by charmless strangers. After procrastinating for a year I'll enter the store, buy anything expensive, then leave in three minutes.

Struggling with my first Paz: *Convergences*. (Those one-word multisyllabic solemn titles, like Martha Graham's 1930s ballets!) I'd expected an intelligence of fancy, blooming and spreading like a good plot. It's mostly intelligent pederasty à la Chomsky-Lévi-Strauss, scratching around word origin and bromides about poetry. "I too dislike it." Having because of my songs dealt with poetry every day of my life, I've never (except for the songs) needed it. Do I need music? I can't afford to answer.

Paz talks of the beauties and perils of translation. Being itself a translation, the talk falls flat. Goytisolo too I find stultifying.

The only poem I ever set to music according to the poet's reading of it was Parker Tyler's "Dawn Angel" in 1945. Parker read it to me with all those swishily effective swoops, and each swoop was entered into the vocal line.

In Memoir: Chapter on Sex, beginning:

I'm looking at a page in the family album, circa 1932, of that . . . No outsider knows the unthinkably time-consuming rigors of cruising. See *The Grand Piano*. "Looking for love where it can't be found"—as title of song. And Goodman's "Waiting for love where it will not come."

It's the waking, not the sleep, that for me is a dive into the mysterious pool. Each morning I ask . . .

Sandy McClatchy writes that "Translating the poem [is] / Helping it out of its disguise of words" . . .

JH says he's always taken the story of Lot's wife with a grain of salt.

7 February

Death of Barbara Tuchman. I never cared for her researched prose, her humorlessness, her vague homophobia, or her herself. But her mother, Alma Morgenthau, was good to me in the autumn of 1952.

America's foremost diarist? Well, if I *am* the only one regularly publishing a diary—every volume of which remains in print—I am never mentioned in essays on diaries (any more than I am automatically included in programs of American song, as I was twenty years ago), and sales of my books are negligible. More wounding is the new *Antæus*, a 450-page assemblage of forty contemporary diarists writing in English, with nothing of mine. Rather than admit to an oversight, Halpern explains that he wanted only previously unpublished portions of diaries (have I none?), and that he had nevertheless invited me to contribute. His lie is like Broido's a few years back when he explained why I was not included in an ad for Presser's favorite composers: He didn't want to offend Boosey & Hawkes! Then why not give to Boosey & Hawkes my few marvelous works that he, Broido, publishes, rather than being a dog in the manger?

The real world knows just what it knows. A composer at a performance of his own music hears only what goes wrong, not what goes right. The small but curious public that cares about (this or that aspect of) me is unaware of the weekly rejections, cancellations, ignorances.

When Gail Godwin writes, "Art, fiction, if it is to be public, must tap the universal. A diary by its very nature is the unfolding of the private, personal story . . ." Her statement is too filled with open assumptions to be valid.

When I asked them to sign their book last night at the Gotham, neither Kenward nor Joe had a utensil. Title: *Poet without a Pen. Painter sans Brush.*

Leafing through *Antæus* is a disappointment. Or should I say a comfort? None of the diaries packs much clout. Mailer's at first glance seems the most interesting when he announces, "Perhaps the writer is less sensitive than his audience," concurring with my oft-voiced "An artist is like everyone—but no one is like him. Like everyone else, only more so." But then one realizes that Mailer's using "sensitive" in two ways, while ostensibly in just one way. A writer is of course *more* sensitive than his audience or he wouldn't be able to hit the nail on the head by writing what the audience—in its sensitivity—*identifies* with. But the writer is *less* sensitive than his reader to the shock value of this or that. "The reason 'insensitive' people react negatively to sex or shocking matters in books," says Mailer, "is it is actually more real to them. They are more sensitive to it." But isn't the reason rather that the author, having *written* of the shocking matters, is simply more inured by the time the reader gets to them? All considered, an intelligent writer is no more and no less sensitive than his reader; he is merely more capable of articulating what the reader did not know he knew.

In the movie *Love Story* years ago, there was a continual unstated conflict in the corny and untrue truism, "Love means never having to say you're sorry." To be sorry can mean to be apologetic, but it also means (in Ray Milland's inference at the end) to be sympathetic with.

Auric's description of Jules Dassin's "musicality" involved an *absence* of music. For the famous safe-cracking scene in *Rififi*, Auric composed his most insinuating score. Dassin: "Let me project the film for you twice, first with the music, second without, and if you feel music adds to the tension, we'll keep it." The music went.

New York 4 February

Long talk with Rosemary. As usual the question of what to do with Mother's & Father's ashes. Their grandparents were crucial to the growing up of RR's kids; they in turn are less keen on my placing the ashes in the Nantucket plot than in having some communal ceremony in Maine or Philadelphia. RR meanwhile feels that since Mother left no will, and never really had a say in major decisions (despite Father's seeming magnanimity, he ran the show), she nevertheless did write down, on two occasions, crosswise over the names in her address book, that she wanted cremation and to be flung to the Hudson River. Well, Jesus, I concur. Rosemary feels we all should convene in New York, go down to Battery Park, maybe board the ferry, and sing "The Lordly Hudson" while performing the act. As to how simple, not to say legal, the act might be (the ashes, which in fact are laced with heavyish bone fragments, might blow back into our fresh faces) is anyone's guess. Anyway, now that Mother & Father are both gone, I feel less strongly about their remains—or my own—than I felt a year ago.

In the time it took to inscribe the notes—about forty minutes—I composed fourteen themes for McNeil Robinson to improvise upon next week at the Stations of the Cross in Saint Paul's Cathedral, while Michael Barone declaims Claudel. Claudel's texts, while heavy, are more inspired and less pompous than the dull dull dull Claudel I once . . .

In most dance reviews one searches in vain for any mention of music used for new ballets, much less for a discussion of *how* the music is used.

Kyle Gann of the *Village Voice* has dismissed my entire musical output as worthless.

Michael Feingold of the *Village Voice* has dismissed my entire literary output as worthless.

14 February (for Symphony Space)

With Donald Collup for an anti-Trump Valentine's program:

> *Spoken:* When asked to join the party, we were given two words of advice: Sing about love, and keep it short. Since most poetry and all music is about either love, death, or the weather, the love part was easy—although *optimistic* love poems are harder to find than sad ones.
>
> These songs date from the 1950s, when romance was a viable theme for me. "Root Cellar" is about the love plants feel for the earth. "Snake" is about the love a poet feels for a serpent's liberty. "Early in the Morning" is about having been young, in Paris, and in love. "To You" is about love for a passing stranger. "An Adam Early in the Morning" is about love for pure nudity. "O You" is about the tingle we feel when our lover comes in the room. And "To a Common Prostitute" is about the love for what Whitman would call the common man.
>
> Sung as a group without pause, the songs last ten minutes.

15 February

Youth, by definition selfish, is at the same time unaware of itself, insouciant, even ignorant. Dumb beauty. "Being young," in the sense of being innocent. Yet the recall of having been young is forever vital, perhaps even accurate.

How well I remember using my youth as manipulation, the calculated pretense—wide-eyed and seductive—of naïveté. Cruelty of kids. Certain tribes, pondering on how most painfully to deal with the captured enemy, throw them to the children, who, with no conscience, burn them up slowly.

How many billion breaths have those children between today and their death—profligate breaths? Whereas with Father last September, we gradually, then suddenly, *knew* he had only so many respirations left in his body . . . twenty, then nineteen, then twelve, then three . . . and then he stopped. But looked the same, after a (when he was already "gone," the nurse later confirmed) nervous twitch of the lips.

Perlman, who gets for one hour in concert what a composer gets to write a symphony, played badly last night at the Valentine affair against Trump. But even had he played well the dreary self-important Kreutzer, could I have discerned his greatness? I simply don't know why one great violinist is better than another great violinist. I can't tell the difference.

Seeing a casual neighbor approaching down the block but too distant to greet, then the vague dread of the forced salute (we don't really know each other that well)—"Hello," "Nice day." This can happen thrice in one day with the same neighbor.

JH who mumbles—always has—mumbles also while emptying the clattering ice cube trays into their container. I don't even pretend to hear.

We are Jack Sprat and Wife. He likes starch, I sugar. I love walking, he loathes walking (he'll unpark the car and try to park it a block closer to the house, to avoid walking that block). He dwells in a closed-windowed overheated room, I in an unheated room.

21 Feb.

Once a pervert, never a pervert. Phrase from a dream, meaning, I suppose, that you can't make jam from a fruit who's not interested.

Another dream: A chapel, pews, many people, very clean, JH's church, but also Paris today where I know no one but must at my ripe age try to get to know people, as in school. On either side above the aisles, guillotines, beneath which, face up and close to the blade, clean young girls who, when their heads are sliced off, fall into bathtubs of clean water. Cleanliness is the keynote.

In the current P.E.N. Newsletter, conversations on Henry James between Hardwick, Gass, and Sontag. Surprisingly (because I don't incline toward his fiction), Gass seems the most heedable. The question of whether HJ is translated is broached, and no one seems quite to know. Susan says that only in the past 15 years has he come to be read in Europe. Yet in June of 1956 *L'Âge difficile* (which Marie-Laure said should have been *L'Âge ingrat*) came out in Michael Sager's translation. Also *La Bête dans la jungle*. M-L had read every word of him by 1952. And now I learn that Marguerite Yourcenar translated *What Maisie Knew* (*Ce que Maisie Savait*) in 1938.

Proust was hardly the first to stress that our yesterdays, once lived, vanish forever—that the past exists only inside the head (even a holocaust?), and that attempts to retrieve it are *current* impulses, which distort, of necessity, since we know more now than we knew then. So the past is by definition embellished—just as we can't hear Haydn as he heard himself, because Billie Holiday, whom he never knew, blocks the way. But last night I saw *Waterloo Bridge* for the first time in nearly fifty years and recalled every frame, each strain of music, even the sense of silliness I'd sensed at sixteen, as though they'd just occurred.

A conservative isn't necessarily a conservative. I am against "progressive" music (admittedly out of self-protection and vested interest—I'm not sure I permit *you* to be against it), aspects of the Working Class *comme c'est*, aspects of abortion. I'm not sexually attracted to certain breeds (can I help it?), and I'm an aristocrat. But I'm also a gay atheistic pacifist. Catholics, Jews, even heterosexuals are "the other" to me, although the French aren't quite.

5 March

Never ever, certainly never in our century, has a non-political figure attracted such political attention as Salman Rushdie. The worldwide call for his lynching suggests that the world suspects art contains a power to persuade.

But art contains only a power to reaffirm: It doesn't change us. Especially in Rushdie's unique case when his accusers, like his sympathizers, have not read his book. Khomeini's call for death is slightly more horrific than the Vatican's call for marital fidelity. And torture rife in Iraq. "Will we ever have a better world?" I ask JH. "No," he says. These periods come in waves (like contrapuntal vs. harmonic periods in music), and the Great Enlightenments of Athens and Voltaire are divided by millenniums of Dark Ages.

Of course, who can know his own history as it is transpiring? Like that ever-dumb statement (uttered even by smart ones like, say, Charles Rosen): We are currently in a state of transition.

Maybe the perfect world would be bland beyond belief.

As Sartre once said about Paris Polytechniciens, *"Ils savent tout, mais ils ne savent que ça"* ("They know it all, but that's all they know") quoted by Edward W. Said in *The Nation* (April 10, 1989).

Ils savent tout, sauf tout.

Cocteau, on Mauriac's death: *Il aurait tout eu, sauf tout.* He had it all, except it.

12 March 1989 for *Bright Music*, spoken before the Tully Hall première:

A composer usually takes one of three stances when talking about his own music: 1) The sentimental or esthetic stance, when he tells you about inspiration, emotional convictions, even sunsets. 2) The gossipy or historic stance, when he gives you practical cues—for whom did he write the piece, and when? Was he in love or otherwise ailing during the feat, and if so, did this affect the content? (People always want to know how such happy music can be penned by one so sad.) And 3) the shop-talk stance, when the composer tells you how the piece was put together.

I revile the first method as irrelevant, and favor the second method as being the most useful in the long run. But it's the third stance I'll adopt today, since we're lucky to have the performers before us. It was for their singular and combined gifts that *Bright Music* was composed during the second half of 1987. As to technical devices, not to mention "meanings," that went into the compositions, only God and I knew about them at the time, and today only God knows.

This morning, examining the score as an outsider might, I was struck by how the composer—who, insofar as he is known at all, is known for his vocal music which is spacious and non-repetitive—by how the composer here has constructed not from themes but from motives, from fragments. For example, the first movement, which is a rondo, is built from a ritornello of but four adjacent notes. Et cetera.

The secret, the *history*, of how a work comes to be is unfathomable, except by outside authorities who invariably give intelligent and irrelevant replies. That history is like the placenta, which has both shielded and coaxed the development of the work; but once the work is delivered, the afterbirth is devoured and forgotten by the no-longer-pregnant parent.

As a skilled prosifier lets fall a rare verb that fans out and changes the meaning of a paragraph the way a drop of iodine alters the color and content of a glass of water, so I seek a needed note that etc. . . . My music may be sometimes trite but never vulgar, although I do aim for vulgarity and avoid triteness.

I am the playwright and you, fiddlers, are the actors—the talking dogs. But talk can never be music. Examples: Part-writing with simultaneous voices at different pitches and speeds, versus the chaos of a cocktail party.

12 March

Sunday morning. Phone calls. Bobby Lewis is 80 and never felt better. Robert Phelps, with his Parkinson's woes, now learns he has cancer of the colon. He's 65. Barry Brook, 71, has cancer of the colon. Third and last performance of *Bright Music* this afternoon. Tomorrow they record at the Academy. Ends and middles and beginnings all at once.

Dick Cavett as guest on the newish Sajak program looked anachronistic. To remind tonight's viewers of his talk-show-host heyday, he projected on the studio screen a replay of the scrumptious exchange, eighteen years ago, between Janet Flanner, Gore Vidal, and Norman Mailer. That was when Janet, bored by the bickering of the others, had interjected that she was fed up with their bad manners. Her studio audience went wild with joy. Tonight's studio audience greeted the replay with a polite but glazed stare: What does Bad Manners mean now when TV discussions are based on the premise of making a point solely by outshouting your opponent?

14 March

Visit from Bill Weaver. I'm struck by how he has no recollection of Kay Starr's "Comes Along a Love," which he played for me in Rome in 1954 and which I've been singing to myself daily ever since, but recalls only the other side of the record, which featured "Wheel of Fortune." Similarly, I'm struck by how Shirley had no recollection specifically of Monteverdi's "Amor," which she played for me in Philadelphia in 1943 and which changed my life, but recalls many of the other madrigals in the classic Boulanger recording.

JH, back from a recital by a choir member featuring Dowland and Campion, notes that these two composers bear the same affinity to each other as do Debussy and Ravel (although they're almost the same age, while the Frenchmen are thirteen years apart). One, who is all froth and charm and formality, speaks the identical language as the other, who is all depth and wistfulness and freedom. Therefore the composers should not be alternated—as the choir member did—but separated into groups.

30 March

Rosemary comes to New York this afternoon with the ashes (not ashes, really—more like chunks of teeth and mineral and sharp largish metal in gray dust) of Mother and Father stored in two boxes of five pounds each. We mix them in a wide urn of biodegradable pottery which R herself had fired in the kilns of Pendle Hill. We conjoin our parents (holding a bit aside which I put in two small spice jars) and tie them up in an old towel. And our cousin Sara Watts. Cold, windy, rain. The illegal bleak cliffs of Jersey, the Palisades parallel with the Cloisters. No one in sight for miles of melancholy icy space, at water's edge we fling forth the remains using as little shovels the sides of the now-broken urn. To *The Lordly Hudson*. We weep, and can scarcely read the 23rd Psalm, asked for by Mary, or her own little statement, typewritten and sent from California:

> Your granddaughter Mary offers prayers to God that your journey may be peaceful and full of joy and that she may meet up with you again in some form, at sometime, somewhere in the universe.

Rosemary too had written a "dear folks" letter, chatty, wistful.

We walk a mile upstream, and are approached by a pair of Canadian geese, later by a pair of mallards, for whom we have no crumbs. It was all soon over. These distinguished long-lived citizens disappeared forever in the choppy waves, and no one knew about it but us.

April Fool's Day

She floundered, then foundered. That is, she flailed, then failed. But what's the difference between careen and career? Aren't the verbs interchangeable here: "The car careened down the road, then careered into the ditch"?

I urinate about thirteen times a day—once or twice at night. Always a dribble, after a preliminary wait of from 40 to 60 seconds. Slight sting lingers. Voorhees says absolutely no surgery—that his reason for being on earth is to keep me from seeing doctors.

There are no composers in America between the ages of 35 and 50. Or almost none. Why? Because that age bracket was weaned in an "inspirational" anti-fine-arts milieu.

Louise Nevelson? Mudpies. Poets of Saint Mark's in the Bowery? Mudpies. The Kitchen composers? Mudpies. Mostly everything is mudpies: uncrafted, deeply felt, shapeless, self-directed graceless mudpies. The Bush administration? Mudpies.

2 April

Fifty years ago this morning JH was born.

For Cocteau speech: I may not know *who* he is (I don't know who anyone is, including myself), but I can offer one version of *what* he is. I do know what I am: a dessert-loving gloomy gay francophilic composer.

9 April 1989

Letters Department, *New York Times*
229 West 43 Street, NYC 10036

By confusing disturbance of the peace with freedom of speech, and by blurring the line between art and politics, Peter Yarrow makes merely self-serving what might be a solid argument about the case of Wade vs. Rock Against Racism (editorial, April 8). The city, seeking to regulate the volume at outdoor concerts, proposes to supply a sound person of its own, unaware that—according to Yarrow—"performers can no more accept the assignment of a 'one night' mix person than Picasso could have accepted a mandated prescription for his choice of colors."

The question is not one of artistic integrity but of noise pollution. One can look away from a Picasso painting, but one cannot *listen away* from a rock concert where one is captive by dint of living near Central Park. When Yarrow claims that "had someone told the big bands of the 1940s to play more softly, the people dancing would have rightfully complained—they needed that honking energy to ease the pain of the sad war years," he forgets that those bands never played on public property within earshots of fifty thousand unwilling residents, including musicians like myself whose privacy was invaded and whose working hours were curtailed.

"Rock and roll needs its sound energy to convey its truth," he goes on, "to roar out its message whether we agree with it or not." Never mind that the "message" enters my window as deafening babel, stressing its point not by "democratic dialogue" (as Yarrow would have it) but by shouting me down. With a flick of the dial I can silence the bullying of a Morton Downey or a TV evangelist whose self-promotion is as righteous as Yarrow's, but against a live rock concert I have no recourse.

When he asks that the Supreme Court "address the critical issue of the role of music in politics" and suggests that the louder the music the more its "truth" will prevail, Yarrow ignores that art, as Auden wrote, never changes anything (the more an artwork succeeds as politics, the more it fails as art), and that raising the decibel level amounts not to friendly persuasion but to coercion through force.

Monday, 24 April

Alone in the city. JH back in Nantucket after 20-hour weekend here.

Child molestation, or discussion thereof, is the current rage. Definitions of, and notions about, it are as conveniently flimsy as witch-hunting, as voguish as cholesterol. *I* was never "molested" as a child nor do I know anyone who was (and I know a few people), though when I was a child I molested some adults. I do not believe in child molestation. I realize that the statement makes me suspect were I to lay a chaste hand on the shoulder of some burly twenty-year-old capable of felling me with one blow, thank you.

Molesting *by* children has been in the news this past week. A gang of thirty adolescents went on a rampage in Central Park, one block away—went "wilding," they call it—and, among other things, gratuitously raped and disfigured a female jogger. How do we convert to a finer life these molesting children? JH attempts it, but in vain.

Tea party yesterday, with a pretty good raspberry cream cake.

But Irene Worth was made uncomfortable by John Simon, or so I sensed. When she rose to leave, I took her aside for a half-hour *tête-à-tête*. She stands up for what she believes etc. Finds Albee self-defeatingly lofty.

For two months, a spastic neck. Feels like strep throat, but is merely a new nervous tic, of constantly wrenching my esophagus muscles, pointless as the *crimes gratuits* of the Central Park youngsters.

The surfeit of Beethoven and Mozart on the "better" stations is as irritating as the unvaried din of rock music.

30 April

Supreme Court brouhaha on abortion.

If life legally begins at conception, can we claim our unborn child as a dependent on the IRS forms? If an embryo is a valued life, why are there no funerals when a woman miscarries?

Write a thesis on *Pale Fire*—a fearsome, learned, post-Reichian explication of Nabokov's text, and of his text within a text—and then set it to music.

4 May

Rostropovich "creates" my *Fantasies & Polka* in Evian. The piece is lush and vulgar (I try, but am never really vulgar, nor am I lush) and should be played: *Dirty but Clean.*

13 May

Alone for a day on the rainy isle I spend a few hours with some of the dozens of tapes, from colleagues or students or strangers, that have accumulated. John Adams's *Wound Dresser* moves me—all the more surprising in that I'd viewed it with a jaundiced eye, like Robin Morgan's famous berating of my Sylvia Plath settings nineteen years ago: "Leave Plath to us. Stick to your male poets." Adams has set the prose of Whitman from the same "Specimen Days" context I've so often

drawn from (for *War Scenes, Pilgrim Strangers, Goodbye My Fancy*). I feel proprietary, even jealous, stupidly offended that anyone, not less a heterosexual, should touch that Great Gray Poet who has nonetheless been used by musicians internationally more than any other bard. Poetry belongs to no one, not even the poet, once it's penned, and Whitman is so temptingly settable precisely because he still springs from the page into our arms. The reference to "sweet death" never made sense until last September when Father died before our eyes. Adams's strange but common, subdued, controlled sounds brought that scene back, and I cried.

Less successful, more overwrought, is Jay Riese's setting of Whitman (incongruously for a female voice—the poet is *not* all-embracing, and his mention of women always seems patronizing), though professional. I covet Adams's understatement: twenty minutes of slow speech, which I must emulate when it comes to what must be mostly the monologue in Sandy McClatchy's potential libretto.

Rereading Denton Welch's *Maiden Voyage*, which Morris Golde, forty-five years ago, used to read aloud as I copied Virgil's music at the Mexican table on the fourth floor of 123 West 11th and we swilled from quart jugs of Schaefer's beer. It's a diary of undeveloped observations that need no further discussion, of details, of "fine writing" à la Elizabeth Hardwick but less self-conscious, of keen and original images with nary a word out of place, and it all adds up.

Do the Dutch make movies?

Nantucket, Sunday 14 May

I've never been interested in talking dogs per se. It's not the fact of their speech but what they say that gets my attention. JH comes back exhausted from 36 hours in New York (he did my unison Votive Mass at Church this morning). After supper (canned minestrone, garlic & tomato salad, orange Jell-o, espresso decaf), we gaze at a segment of *60 Minutes* featuring three examples of idiot savant. The first of these retarded adults carves foot-long horses out of wood, realistic and skillful if ordinary, impersonal—gift shoppe stuff. Asked if he's ever seen such horses, he claims it's all from his imagination. The second idiot can quickly tell you on what day of the week any date in history fell. Once you get a system, is this useless gift so remarkable, especially when you've nothing else to do all day? The third, not only retarded but blind, is a pianist. He just began playing one night, on that untuned upright of his foster parents, rendering Tchaikovsky's First Concerto. Whatever does it come from? marvels the interviewer. "It's because I'm a musician," explains the savant. To "test" this talent, the interviewer plays for him—and for us—the opening of Debussy's *Soirée dans Grenade*, which the savant immediately replays on his upright. The replay, which satisfies the interviewer and, presumably, ten million viewers, is in fact a coarse echo, an iterated C# ostinato with some Cui-type D-naturals and augmented seconds. The wonder is not that the

savant could imitate Debussy even this well, but that Debussy himself once honed from a trite tango, with the merest of "displacements," a nuanced and tasteful masterpiece. This boy simply plays by ear, no better and no worse than the urchins at JH's church. The 60 Minutes program goes on to inform us of the high fees these idiot savants now claim for their gifts. Savants, perhaps. Idiots, hardly.

19 May, Nantucket

Forty years ago today, I set sail alone for France.

After seeing the documentary of Agnes de Mille last night one can think less of her. She's charming, smart, articulate, a bit schoolmarmish (like Virgil), and surely her own best publicist since (except for Martha Graham, whom she quotes continually, and Alfred Frankenstein, who apparently once named her "The Mark Twain of Dance") she and she alone tells us why this or that ballet of hers is a masterpiece, a breakthrough, a joy. Which is o.k., except the ballets speak louder than her words, and they don't add up. As for her solution for the climax of the Lizzie Borden dance called *Fall River Legend*, she hangs Lizzie, because "that's what she deserved," whereas in reality Lizzie was acquitted of the murder of her parents, and lived thirty-five more years, a wealthy recluse abhorred by the neighbors. Since deMille's moralistic fiction is less intriguing than the truth that she wasn't up to dealing with, shouldn't she have chosen a simpler subject?

Probably one reason, beyond the privacy needed for an unbroken chain of thought, that I have no close or even regular friends on the island, is that none of my acquaintances, with the exception of Rosette, has an interest in music, or any real sense of me as a composer (as distinct from a diarist). Does the privacy needed for an unbroken chain of thought guarantee quality?

I wasn't quite sixteen when Freud died.

Red-gold hair the color of a Bible's edge.

24 May

As early as 1945 through the auspices of the *Tribune*, Virgil was able to fly to France for a brief visit. He returned home with—I clearly recall—two nuggets of information. 1) Paris's current rage, a church organist named Olivier Messiaen, "opens up the heavens and brings down the house." 2) The French have a new way of fixing chicken: Don't do anything to it, just bake it till it's done.

These quips come to mind while hearing tapes of David Horne, my new student from Scotland. His concerto playing (Rachmaninoff's *Paganini*, Beethoven's First) is accurate, glittering, self-assured, utterly controlled. Like most of the teenagers at Curtis he technically plays rings around Horowitz. (But of course, instrumental performance, like sexual drive—as Kinsey stressed two generations ago—is pitched highest, at least in the human male, during adolescence; from then on it's all downhill.) Just play the notes please, just sing the words clearly, and *we*, the listeners, will interpret. Similarly, in his own flashy string quartet (which,

for an eighteen-year-old's effort, has a blazing sense of motion, of push, of how to make a piece go), he uses every device except straightforward bowing: *col legno, slap-pizz, non vibrato, ponticello,* harmonics, *glissando,* high melody on the violin G-string, et cetera. (Susan Sontag wrote that *Flaming Creatures* portrays every imaginable sexual expression, with the notable exception of straight screwing.) Let him learn Bach without pedal, let him compose without color. As with the unspiced chicken, one can later add salt or sauce or saffron, which taste good without being nourishing.

25 May

By rights I'd be in Athens today. Why did I & Ellen and also Lukas & Cornelia, Shirley & George, and the Kircheners all renege?

High-jacking. Jet lag. Laundry and bathroom. Nor do I feel a need any longer for foreign exploration. Yet Greece and Austria are the sole countries I've never visited that I want to visit. No longer Japan.

Phyllis Curtin, alone of us all, went.

I know it's impossible to play. What I want is the effect of your trying to play it. Re. "Yellows" in *Day Music.*

11 June

Hours, months, go by when I say "this afternoon" I'll catch up on the diary, but I don't. I *do* make notes, so that the on-the-spot impulse won't be lost later when I collate them, though of course that impulse gets lost. For example, the drama in Peking: The unique assembly of students in Tienanmen Square peacefully petitioning for democracy (*The Nation* reports that CNN television didn't film the pro-Soviet banners); the touching intercourse between the students and the recalcitrant soldiers; the unprecedented vastness of a land in the *act* of change, as we observe this on our screens. Then the sudden reversal, the military tanks flattening the hundred tents of sleeping students. Dan Rather: "There are those who would die for freedom, and those who would kill to prevent it." (Could he have stated with equal justice, "Those who would die for totalitarianism, and those who would kill to prevent it?")

Then Khomeini expires. All is flux. JH spends a fortune at the vet to verify Princess's leukemia—what the doctor calls Animal AIDS—although there's nothing to be done about it. Now she seems livelier. The sty in my eye that I planned to discuss has vanished. The hermit's life here shifts, Eugenie did come to dine, during which the wooden salad spoon fell on the floor and I didn't clean it off. (There was nothing to clean off since the floor is clean, but Eugenie demurely declined more salad.)

Thinking continually on JH's death: Will tobacco or an auto crash kill him before I die? It's Sunday night, I'm 65 and sad, but less sad maybe than at 35. Over-

whelmed with commissions through 1993, and with self-doubt. Is that mass of music since the *Sappho Madrigals* in 1946 . . . is it worth it? Well, it's all I can do. In the past five weeks on the island I've completed the Organbooks—sixteen pieces (four or five originally written as gifts for JH over the years) that JH has coherently titled and split into three suites, one for Spelman, two for Eileen Hunt. Now I read poems and prose with the sole purpose of finding a proper text—a theatrical narrative text—for the tenor-plus-trio piece. But I have trouble with poetry. The older I get the less I comprehend the pose behind which most poets hide. Eliot's out. William Carlos Williams (who's just too . . . hmmm, well, too heterosexual for me) is out, because he's never, never moving. Maybe Auden's in. Or maybe Thoreau, or *Oedipus at Colonus*. Meanwhile JH is due back on the ferry that arrives at 10:30. It grows dark. Sonny searches already for him in basement corners. He left Friday by plane with Oscar, who, at nineteen, has no ideas, no awareness of who's President, of what's happening in the world—in China, for instance. Like all Puerto Ricans, says JH, since he has no past he has no future.

Ideas. This journal has none anymore. Like Thoreau, like the young Denton Welch, I'd like to notate only terse observations, and to hell with philosophy. Philosophy is for collegians. (*Walden*: "Could a greater miracle take place than for us to look through each other's eyes for an instant? We should live in all ages of the world in an hour . . . ")

The nectarines are good, while the peaches are mealy and flavorless. Do flavorless peaches contain the same vitamin quota as flavorsome ones? It's June and we take Sonny to Nobadeer Beach, but no one is there despite the sand the same sunset-omelet color as Tom's belly. JH seems both absent and edgy, with a major discombobulating dispute each day: His church makes decisions without consulting him; the airlines are grossly run; the Finast stamps produce with tomorrow's date. Mostly he's right, but overly critical, certainly with me, if not with the three animals. He's too heavy, his upper right incisor has been gone for six weeks, he smokes. But perhaps if all were well, he'd die. The garden looks beautiful because of him, and his Sunday work is more responsible and organized than mine. Democracy is but a word, and means to the Chinese and Nicaraguans something different from what it means to Barbara Bush. Imagine an Italian as democratic! Are Norwegians?

After three months, no alleviation of the nervous muscle spasm in the throat. Wrench, semi-willfully all day long, into a blue strep tangle, contorted and strained.

Thinking of the early 1950s. Those I taunted for the sheer reason that I could: Jean Grémillon, Shura Cherkassy. (Write these up before it's too late.) JH has devoted his life to me. I've devoted mine to him, too.

12 June

The season of ticks and bloody peonies is abating; now is the season of ashen hydrangeas and fleas.

Listening to music. Like Fauré, Vaughan Williams's catalogue is all slow. But if Fauré wrote fast music which was really slow music played fast, Vaughan Williams

didn't even pretend to write fast music (i.e., metronomically fast). As for the *Oxford Elegy*, I have a constitutional allergy to the accompanied spoken voice—to melodrama. Pomposity. If the sung voice is the most musical of instruments, the spoken voice is the least.

The endless updated "relevant" versions of *The Ring*. Directors taint everything—in their anxiety to make the operas comprehensible to "people of today," and to draw attention to themselves—except the music. Why not change the music too (as someone once did with the *Well-Tempered Clavier* accompanied by drums)? Because, well, yes, why not? But then, why not just compose a new opera?

Resentment at hearing John Adams's *The Wound Dresser*, because, in its use of Whitman's prose, it seems a spin-off of my *War Scenes* and *Pilgrim Strangers*. Plus how can a heterosexual use such words? Then, on rehearing, and rehearing again, I'm moved—and not least because Adams *is* heterosexual. (I *think* he is.)

15 June

Received tape of Rostropovich conducting première of my *Fantasy & Polka* last month in Evian. Not my finest moment: If unalerted I wouldn't recognized the *Fantasy* as mine, so much as a cast-off of Shostakovich, while the *Polka* is cheap Sousa. Not Rostropovich's finest moment, either. This Russian, whose commissions in the sixties did more to augment international cello repertory than any American in history, conducts my piece hickishly, with neither elasticity nor vigor. Am I to blame and taking it out on him? I've never met the man.

Re-rereading for the umpteenth time *Oedipus at Colonus* I find the Dial Press edition of 1947 teeming with marginal notes made around 1951 when I was considering a series of scenes for Cuenod. Those scenes are exactly what I'd have chosen now for Aler, except I've changed my mind and will use Auden. Still, I go on to reread *Antigone*, in the good Fitzgerald/Fitts translation, and it too seethes with flytracks, including in Ode II:

> . . . *but now a passionate word*
> *And a handful of dust have closed up all its beauty.*

Obviously Evelyn Waugh could not have been concerned with this *Antigone* in 1934. (Going now to the shelf to check that date, I see that Waugh's epigraph is plucked from *The Waste Land*—"I will show you fear in a handful of dust"—itself dating from 1922. Ives could well have known Emerson's *Sphinx*:

> *"Thou are the unanswered question;*
> *Couldst see with proper eye,*
> *Always it asketh, asketh;*
> *And each answer is a lie . . . "*

But he never admitted it.

New York, 18 June

Visit to Virgil. Took him two rare Simenon books and a bar of cucumber soap. "Cucumber soap," said he. "Just imagine, someone recently gave me some tangerine soap, which I never use." (Since it was I who gave him the tangerine soap, I felt ruffled.) From there to see Robert Phelps.

Few days later: Called VT about the death of Sauguet. "Well," said Virgil calmly, "Our friends are leaving us." And how did he like the Simenon books? "Oh, was it you who gave me them? We were wondering. Haven't looked at them yet."

New York, 20 June

To Greenwich House last night for rehearsal of *Love Alone* and of the five Whitman songs I'm supposed to accompany with the Gay Men's Chorus. At the first sound I was miffed. Was this what I'd been writing for? I'm used to more professional mixtures. There's a bigger difference between singers than between instrumentalists (sight unseen you always knew Callas from Tebaldi, Gramm from Milne, and, of course, Callas from Milne; while even Glenn Gould couldn't always tell his own recordings from another pianist's), and thus between choruses than between orchestras. And it's not just in pronunciation (non-vocal instruments do not pronounce, though they do announce), it's in timbre, balance, brains.

JH is filching 50-pound cubes of gray granite left downstairs by Con Ed, for the Nantucket garden.

JH in Kansas for 6 nights.

Paul Monette, whom I had never met before reaching across the intervening seats in Row L to shake his hand after the première of *Love Alone*, I liked on the spot. Not staying for the rest of the concert, I invited him, his friend Steve, Larry Mass, and Morris Golde back to 70th Street for vanilla-&-raspberry ice cream, which they refused in favor of vodka. Paul and Steve had arrived at Tully Hall straight from the airport and were exhausted. (Both harbor the AIDS virus.) They asked whether I still kept a diary. Well, I do note daily doings in shorthand in an agenda which at the end of each month I collate, divide into entries, and postdate. For instance—I told him—I might make a memo to describe an impression of him; but the description, being kept on ice, would lack the heat of on-the-spot reporting (I'm typing this four days later) because of what may occur in the interim.

   (Recount the Gay Men's Chorus. My lousy piano playing, especially of "Full of Life Now," all three evenings. Jean Leuvrais and his report of Paris: reactionary, anti-gay, moribund, as it was indeed in '84. And last night Ellen, RR, SXG, and Arnold Weinstein. Today Arnold comes over to interview me about Larry Rivers. Recall Jay Harrison's review of Larry's set and costumes for *Oedipus Rex*: "Still waters may run deep, but lazy Rivers don't.")

Rosemary asks this morning (she spent the night), almost shyly, if my conversation with Arnold and Ellen was similar to conversations I had in the old days with Marie-Laure—whom she calls Maria Laurie. What she meant was, I guess, are we always so gossipy, so skimming-the-surface, so evasive of heavier subjects, like the horrors of China, Persia, flag-burning, and discussions of, say, Samuel Lipman's anti-pornography stance apropos of the cancellation of Mapplethorpe's exhibit. I suppose that artists together don't talk much about art (except from the perspective of finance and fame), leaving that to sophomores seeking Meaning. Our meaning, if we have any, is in our work.

My work, enough now for three years, piles up while I look at TV and do crosswords. But while correcting the just-finished-by-Daron parts for *Goodbye My Fancy*, a labor that will involve another two weeks of around four hours a day, I say to myself—I should really be composing.

Jean Leuvrais (in America for the first time, and whom I took to the Gay Men's Chorus), who loves Brahms but hates Chopin, says of the latter: *"Tant de notes pour dire si peu."* Very pretty—but it obtains more properly to Liszt.

Ciel, mon mari! = Sky, my husband.

To Jean Leuvrais: How do you find Americans physically these days—we, who were the belles of the ball in Paris forty years ago? *"Il n'en reste rien."* Yes, and months go by that I do not see (even among the golden youth of Nantucket) a living soul I'd like to sleep with. At the Gay Men's Chorus, not one of the 150 choristers, or during the three evenings, of four thousand attendants, was handsome, much less sexy or tempting. Why? Is it AIDS that has removed the narcissism, the flirtatiousness, the self-confidence that attends carnal emanation? Or are we just getting older? There are many beautiful women, but it's unarguable that beautiful men, at least in America, are no longer abroad.

Was it Democracy that lured the students in Tienanmen Square, or Capitalism?

What did Paul Monette's friend Steve, 28 and AIDS haggard, *lui aussi*—what did he think of my setting the poem about Monette's lover dying of AIDS? What, in fact, is the *etiquette* of such a situation?

Not having seen Francine in ten years, I ask JH if he thinks she's dropped me. "No, you merely used each other up: Some friendships are meant to last only a certain time."

In the current fuss, right and left, about flag-burning, no one points out that the act is not one of desecration against the country but against the country's sometimes misplaced patriotism. Now Bush actually proposes to amend the Constitution. Supposing his bill passes. When you burn a flag—but with only 49 stars, or with eight red stripes and seven white, or you don't burn it but rip it, or douse it in acid—are you convicted? Bush takes the symbol for the real thing; what's desecration for one is consecration for another. Should the crucifix dipped in urine be banned? Then ban the Ku Klux Klan's flaming crosses. What is meaning, and where do we start?

5 July

Toward a program note for *The Shield of Achilles*:

Composers compose. If they had trouble in kicking off their musical ideas, or even in finding ideas to kick off, they would not be composers. "Trouble," at least in the case of song composers, lies in finding apt non-musical ideas to develop. The months spent in searching for a theatrical text, via Homer and Sophocles' *Colonus*, etc., to use for a tenor to find a through-moving narrative.

J. D. McClatchy, John Ashbery, Mark Strand, Paul Monette, all rejected. Finally only Auden spoke to my condition. Even then, the choice of *which* Auden required days of rereading.

The poems are each from "middle Auden." Why choose them? His objectivity which nevertheless surges. His verses' odd mixtures of force and hopelessness, of cynicism and vulnerability, of hot sadness and cold joy. The smallness of life is nonetheless sanctified, made bigger: There's something to sing about.

A cool, even nippy, 4th of July.

JH's tooth—or lack of it—after five full days, still requires sixteen Advils a day. Gloom. Good meals. Frank.

At sixty-five I still walk daily across the room—on my hands.

Because Denton Welch's material is so introspective, vaguely sensual, non-malignant, we are shocked at his recounting of a stroll in the Chinese countryside where he stumbles across a rotting human head. Then we think, well, human heads are as odd as China itself in 1933. What about a head in the paths of Nantucket? I guess Emlyn Williams anticipated this in *Night Must Fall*.

JH irked by anthropomorphic pronouncements of veterinarian "experts"—that our cats think of us as their mothers, or that our dogs think of themselves as part of the human family. Animals are animals. Sonny, as we watch a thousand visitors descend from the ferry, reacts solely to the one dog amongst them. Yes, he wags his tail (or growls) at certain humans, but does he think of himself as human any more than the children who find him so cute think of themselves as dogs?

Why does he, where there's a dead toad or dried worm fading into the road, day after day, always choose that very spot to roll in? To absorb their shades? Or give them strength in purgatory?

Does Sonny have an Adam's apple?

One morning out of three I simply say, "Another day"—how to get through it? Other days I take the cue from JH, who copes, perseveres, in a manner one could not have foreseen ten years ago during his collapse.

Moral from Woods Hole: Never overestimate your audience.

Shakespeare's signal errors: Music—a succession of sweet sounds.
Music soothes the savage breast.
A rose by any other name.

No twentieth-century composer is more theatrical than when he's writing for the theater. A true theater composer wouldn't wait till 70 to pen his first opera.

10 July

JH has set off an insect bomb in his basement room. All three animals seethe with fleas; within hours after their delousing baths, their itching begins anew. Sonny's the only one visibly affected—the cats don't scratch.

Three of the eight movements in the Auden piece are done, all within the past week. (Of course, the hardest work came before the actual composition began—in deciding on Auden in the first place, then concocting an "inevitable" sequence for the unrelated poems.) Whether the cycle will be "as good as" the Wallace Stevens *Last Poems* eighteen years ago, who knows? But Auden means more to me than Stevens.

No social life on the island. Brief chats in the street with various denizens, that's all, or brief visits from New York acquaintances. The few people who came to dine last summer (the Conroys, Mimsi Harbach) never returned the invitation. I work, read, do crosswords, watch TV soaps, write letters, and work some more. David Del Tredici, invited a month ago to spend a few days here starting yesterday, has neither written nor phoned to announce his plans.

New housing laws passed by the State Supreme Court of New York allows legal possession of a rent-controlled apartment by one member of a gay couple if the other member dies, provided they've lived together for a decade. Good news for JH, if I go first. (We've been *en ménage* for 22 years.)

Is it bigoted to declare that a certain kind of homosexual male repels me? Not the madly effeminate nor the comically macho, but the tight-lipped, smart, bossy, humorless, teacherly brand—"One of those mean ones," as Ben Weber used to say. These can be found too among fringe heterosexuals like married parsons and congressmen and even William Buckley. Meanwhile, many butch bigots excite me.

And certain straight movie actors of highest credentials seem neither winsome nor erotic: Donald Sutherland, Jeremy Irons, Michael Caine.

Asked to name a prevailing mood I'd say sadness. Not just the sadness of our erring world, but of each morning, as I stroll with Sonny in the clean air on Sunset Hill, wondering what difference it makes. Afternoons are better. Nights I arise once or twice, sometimes thrice, or not at all, to urinate, slowly, in the silence.

Brigitta Lieberson, acknowledging my brief condolence note: ". . . but then I think of others—younger—suffering—alone. At least Jon was with us—at home— and died in such a beautiful way that death became friendly .. . . " ("Show me your face, why the eyes are kind!" wrote Charlotte Mew.) Her words are comforting. For Father, who dreaded death, death came gently last September, finally, after no illness.
    But with AIDS?

Brouhaha continues about the flag, the Constitution, and Mapplethorpe's photographs. Well, maybe art *can* evoke what is hidden and unexpressible within some of us. But I still claim it cannot *change* us. Sermons and politics change us. Art merely confirms.

Stella Adler featured on PBS. Better than Clurman's gobbledygook special last Monday. I know Stella strictly socially, when she commands attention by speaking so softly that the whole room must be hushed, so it was amusing to watch her hollering at the class. Mostly commonsense clichés ("You must listen with your blood"; "Plays aren't made of words, but of the imagination underlying those words") that don't scrutinize too well, and mean different things to different people. Her ego imposes upon every demonstration as the cowed ungifted students do their best. But with all her talk of technique—no demonstration (illustration) of it. I was appalled at her approval of the confrontation scene, between child and parent, from *All My Sons*. Acting is not yelling; nor do gentile sons physically touch, much less throttle, their fathers, especially over moral issues (as distinct, perhaps, from self-defense). Yet the more undifferentiatedly these actors screamed, the more Stella applauded. Interesting to see how strongly the same scene might play if understated.
    Stella may be right—that American actors don't move outside themselves, that they are tied up—but could have added that they are therefore the best interpreters of American plays. For the plays of Miller and Williams don't insist on Yiddish histrionics. (I couldn't stop thinking of Ellen through it all, Ellen, a real person, growing up with this glittering monster.)
    Stella must be near ninety now. So is Julien Green, who, according to Jean Leuvrais, is piquant and puritan as ever on French television. (Describe first meeting with Green, in 1951, and the ensuing meeting, that afternoon, chez Julius Katchen, with Leuvrais. Crème de menthe. Leuvrais, who a few years later, played in *L'Ombre*.)

Mel Gibson has taken up broad farce. Since he earns millions a minute, it would be difficult to tell him he's miscast. Do I miscast him by typecasting him? He's versatile, intelligent, and a true actor. But he's too handsome for farce, tries too hard: a Romantic proving he's not a Romantic. Sexy males can do farce (Chevy Chase) but not handsome males, unless, like Olivier, they make themselves up to be strange-looking. Beautiful women (Lombard, Harlow) can. Or could.

Death of Olivier. (Noted a few hours after above entry. The television is full of his wild features.) With what awe I saw him on stage as Romeo, with Vivien Leigh, in Chicago's unaccoustical Ambassador Theater in 1940; *Titus Andronicus* in Paris in the fifties. And forever in the movies where I loved him except for that awful mannerism of rolling his eyes up into his head.

Reading galleys of Harold Norse's silly memoir called *Bastard Angel*, but could as well be called *Little Me* with all its boasting of famous people he's refused to put out for. If years ago I blurbed Salter's first novel with "Can be read with the heart, the head, and with one hand," this book can be read with one hand on the TV remote control.

16 July

"What was he like?" asks Laurence Olivier of Jean Simmons toward the end of *Spartacus*, which I watched last night for the fourth time. "He was a simple man," she answers, speaking of the complex Thracian who managed against all odds of language, logic, and strategy, to mobilize 90,000 fellow slaves and to hold off the Roman armies. "Simple" here is used, I suppose, as distinct from "fancy," rather than from "intellectual" (the *plain man* would have been a model for Dalton Trumbo, who wrote the script), the way "truth" is often meant as "fact" as distinct from an irrefutable philosophy. But probably, in the largest sense, great men *are* simple insofar as their accomplishments are unique. Stravinsky's complicated *Rite of Spring* is finally simple, since the alteration of but one note would diminish it.

Alex North's score is addictive. Ten years ago I filched a minute from it for "Remembering Tommy." Today I'm ready to do the same.

JH, with whom I spoke last night (he's in New York as usual for the weekend), is very, very upset—"feeling friendless," as he puts it—by my taking over the Grove's entry. But since the entry (on my operas) involved only 200 words, and was two months overdue, I completed it myself and sent it to Sadie with a note that JH found cold. Was I wrong? Now I too feel awful.

Sent a postcard last week to Bernard Holland apropos his charming article about music in the open air. Now today, in a mere aside during his review of Glass's *Usher* opera, he writes: "Debussy knew how to deflect emotions from the normal straightforward opera channels. We hear this in *Pelléas*—as the conversational tone of its protagonists rides insouciantly atop the huge waves of menace and mystery generated by the orchestra." I could never have phrased it so succinctly.

Is incest between brother and sister more taboo than between parent and child, siblings being genetically identical, while parent and child are only 50% of the same makeup? Is sex with oneself by definition homosexual?

17 July

Brochure for Pepsico Summerfare is proudly decorated with utterances by Peter Sellars, all specious:

> The only things we know about this world . . . are events within our own lifetime. I have to take these operas and treat them through characters I know . . . say yes, there are people who live this way.

By definition, then, his "events" are not my events, so how can I identify? But perhaps I have more imagination than he.

> Opera . . . has always been about real life . . . Mozart wrote about terribly precise questions and events he witnessed in his life . . . that same sense of witness must be present today.

If there's one thing opera is *not* about, it's "real life." Even if it were, it would be, like all art, a condensation of real life. In any case, if the libretto is not relevant to our time, then neither is the music, so why does Sellars bother?

> If somebody is so offended at what I have done with the piece, that at least means they have to think about what they think the piece is . . . Then I've already done my job.

So he's got you, coming or going. The assumption that I've never thought about what I think about the piece is, at the very least, unmannerly. Nor has offensiveness ever been a springboard toward *appronfondissement*. Sellars' defensiveness is his rationale for his narcissism—for drawing attention to himself and away from the Mozart he feels needs his transliteration. And if Mozart does need transliteration, why does Sellars sing him still in Italian?

Impossible and unfair crossword puzzle again today, with clues like: Latvian slang for drayhorse.

18 July

Rigorously against rules, it was nevertheless leaked to me months ago by nominator Sandy McClatchy, and by Lenny B., Bill Schuman, and Eugene Istomin, each of whom wrote a recommendation—that I was up for a MacArthur. The *Times* this morning announces John Harbison, and a 66-year-old jazz musician named George Russell of Boston, as recipients. I don't begrudge them a cent. But would I be less disappointed had I not known? JH says I'm "too established." Hmmmm.

Anyway, we won't make the major improvements on the house, plus other reassuring expenditures we'd semi-consciously planned.

Received three glowing copies of Arlys McDonald's finally finished 284-page *Ned Rorem: A Bio-Bibliography* from Greenwood Press. What a flattering massive chore of research! Have I really set to music 122 different authors? Of these I've used most frequently Paul Goodman with 20 separate works, Whitman with 13 poems, Roethke with 11, the Old Testament with 14 (as distinct from the New with 3). But these statistics don't account for, say, James Schuyler, whose one listing is actually a 25-minute voice & orchestral cycle of eight poems, or Kenneth Koch, whose two big settings come to an hour's worth of music, or Frank O'Hara, whose two settings amount to a half-hour.

The discography lists fifty different records (most now unavailable), and the bibliography lists 784 items, with quotes—some ecstatic, some dismissive—from reviewers as far afield as Herbert Gold and Paul Henry Lang. Peter Davis says in 1967 that *Sun* is a blinding jewel—"beautiful, fascinating, and totally heartless" (do jewels have hearts?), while in 1971 he allows that *Letters from Paris* is "certainly one of Mr. Rorem's most lovable efforts." And so forth.

Yet the whole seethes with errors of fact (of course, Truth as a concept is irrelevant to such a venture), like listing someone named Joyce Castle rather than, correctly, Sherry Zanoth as soloist in *Sun* with Howard Hanson, under "selected performances"; or misleading shifts of emphasis, like no review for a major work, and a large review for a small work; or misdatings and misspellings. How much vaguer is an actual biography, with or without its subject's permission. Biography is mainly about the biographer.

> *Dost thou know who made thee? . . .*
> *Gave thee such a tender voice . . .*
> *Little lamb, I'll tell thee . . .*
> *He is meek and he is mild . . .*

Do lambs have tender voices, rather than grating bleats? Is Christ meek and mild, rather than strong and purposeful? A lamb *is* cuddly and guileless, but imagine his vast cruel teeth from a flea's eye-view. Sharks shock us as they rend their fellows. Are the spider's fangs, in slow-motion close-ups, more dreadful than the 12-eyed fly it stings, the fly that stung our innocent baby? And Burns's darling louse? The roach we seek to step upon knows the surest route to safety, but meanwhile goes berserk, his wee heart thundering in self-preservation. That innocent baby? At seven, he's quick to torture his parents' captives. Perspective's all.

Allegro. Andante. Con affetuoso. These terms just won't apply. If I indicate simply *Insincere* for the musical mood of "Lay your sleeping head, my love, / Human on my faithless arm . . ." will that be useful?

Is it racist to be attracted to just one type, Semites, for instance?

I refuse the universe.

26 July

Are the best of times always the worst of times? Is there always some mortal who finds total fascism the height of joy, another who in Eden sees naught but suffering? Is politics like music, which, from generation to generation, never actually improves (art hasn't "improved" for a thousand years) but merely shifts stress from harmony to counterpoint to harmony to counterpoint—the harmonic periods being simpler? Is art under a censorious regime necessarily poorer than under a relaxed regime when "fuck you" and "down with Christ" and "burn the flag" can be shouted impuniously from the housetops?

Our liberal society changes wildly from week to week; I feel ashamed in the eyes of, for example, any Frenchman, to be dwelling in the same land as a yahoo like Jesse Helms, who decides what's good or bad in art by showing it to his wife. (Though wasn't it Madame de Gaulle who persuaded her spouse to rid Paris of its *pissotières*?) Once I wrote that the function of art is to satisfy that indefinable area within us that can't be satisfied by the senses, or at least by the grosser senses: taste, touch, smell. Today I'd say art's function is just to help us limp through life.

So many people (even Richard Goldstein) these days enunciate the predicament more succinctly than I, and, as in the case of Arthur Schlesinger in the *Times* last Sunday, more patiently. He is "surprised" by the revival of blasphemy in our secular age. He confesses "to a certain amusement [at hearing] the Judeo-Christian tradition praised as the source of our concern for human rights [when] in fact the great religious ages were notable for their indifference to human rights in the contemporary sense." He quotes Swift: "We have just enough religion to make us hate, but not enough to make us love." But the dissenters wail about "the taxpayers' dollars" that support Mapplethorpe, with never a peep about their dollars for war, or about the violence at any flip of the dial.

Golf = Flog Desserts = Stressed

A female collie—one only—has so permeated West Chester Street with her heat that Sonny, for three days, has been out of control at the window.

Harmony is French, counterpoint is German.

Metaphor is French, simile is German.

We dine at the Rosettes. I sit next to a 19th-century beauty who promises more than she gives. "Why," she wonders—while admitting she mustn't say such things in thoughtful society—"are Blacks not on the same scholastic level as Whites?" Well . . . but they *are*, although they've never been given a chance. "But they *have* been given a chance." Since I'm not black, how should I take this, I who, despite liberal training, thought the same thing for years, and am not stupid? In a fan letter to Alison Lurie I once wrote that *Foreign Affairs* was tainted only by a faint tint of homophobia. She replied coolly that she was *not* homophobic, but didn't ask me to specify. Larry Mass, in his interview about opera with me, which I've just reread with alarm, suggests that I'm anti-Semitic because I feel Anne Frank's diary was ghost-written by her father. Since he's Jewish and I'm not, then he's right. I must ask, If women have proved themselves after five thousand years, why not blacks?

We rent videos. I could never have gazed upon *The Thin Blue Line*, because of its insistent pain, had not its protagonist, in reality, been released last week from his Texan prison. But I wanted to hear Philip Glass's score. Glass has found his niche. The Rashomonian repetitions in the script would have been boring were it not for Glass's boring music, music which *because* of its monotony ties up, locates, and heightens an otherwise banal scene. His name today, Philip Glass, seems designed for dropping, like John Cage's or Susan Sontag's yesterday. It's neat, compact, glimmering, memorable, and his music could not have been penned by someone called, perhaps, Elmer Stuckenschmitt. Are we our names? All's in a name. A fuck by any other name would feel less good.

Planet of the Apes, which neither of us had seen, is unwatchable with Heston's tomcat smirk robbed from Gable, and the sophomoric script. The only compelling image is the final one of the Statue of Liberty, when he realizes that after three thousand years he's back on Earth, the very Earth he'd presumably quit because "brothers kill each other." On realizing the planet had been demolished way back when, is he thoughtful? Silent? No, he is not. He has a tantrum. "They *did* it, the bastards," screams he, hitting the beach with his fists.

Yes, I too sneer at television, but watch it probably two hours a day. How many half-hours have dwindled away? But how many half-hours mount high in reading.

28 July
Twenty-four hours at Martha's Vineyard. The Perles. Off to San Francisco for two years. Rae Gabis, age 94. But I knew her *mother*. And Virgil's mother, in 1944. And Grandfather Rorem was born in 1857, five years before Debussy. Shirley's swordfish. We listen to Wuorinen's Piano Concerto, over-long and non-reflective, aggressive, even mean. But it's something. After the clattering first movement JH says, "It's music that says: 'No one's going to call me a fairy.'"

George composes according to a computerized printout. I ask if he dreams, as I sometimes do, of music as vines.

S.'s somewhat right-wing stance vis-à-vis Judge Bork and Oliver North's acquittal.

While waiting for the ferry back to Nantucket we pause in the absolutely still Disneyesque Baptist park of Oak Bluffs with gingerbread houses like candy bananas and pink Turkish delights.

Beauteous blond youth of Nantucket, on their features no stamp of experience, no ability to comprehend. But is there anything to comprehend? Living with *The Shield of Achilles* one "could not hope for help and no help came."

2 August

Rare spat with JH last night. He feels he does all the work around here—mows lawn, lays bricks, bathes pets, drives, shops, does laundry, irons, cooks—and he's somewhat right. While I loll about with my music or mess up crosswords. When I do lend a hand, he contends it's all wrong. (This kind of nervousness is at its most cynical when guests loom. Jim Kendrick and Jane Burwell arrive this afternoon.) Then I went to bed and dreamed I observed—and took notes about—two murders near Times Square. The police were seeking me as a witness. Or did I myself commit the crimes, one by gun, the other by strangulation? The conflict was compounded by F-major imposing itself upon E-major, uninvited, over and over, like a cheese slicer.

7 August

Unbreathable weather. On a day like today twenty years ago the city morgue phoned to announce Bill Flanagan's death. And it will soon be twenty years since Marie-Laure disappeared. How often I think of them both! Have I ever had closer friends? Meanwhile crucial lovers vanish—Henri Fourtine, Guy Ferrand, Joe Adamiak—and, of course, Mother and Father. Now Robert Phelps is gone. What I owe him is incalculable. Or, rather, wondrously calculable.

10 August

Parents' 69th anniversary.

Two and a half days in Woods Hole for something called "Shaping the Future: An Arts & Sciences Symposium," with John Hollander and four others.

My "presentation," following that of the likeable Nobel laureate Baruch Blumberg, was able to feed off his. Prefacing his speech on the etiological role of the hepatitis B virus in the prevention of primary hepatocellular carcinoma, he doffed a token hat toward the arts by declaring that, in science, one thing always leads to another, and cited Pasiphaë's union with the white bull, which produced the Minotaur, which incited Theseus to the maze, etc. Naturally, I said that in art the goal is an end in itself, the Minotaur, like all crossbreeds, is a mule and cannot reproduce, and thus, as in Gide's version, is a harmless work of art munching gardenias at the end of the tunnel. (In Paul Goodman's version, there is no minotaur at all—except in the maze of the heart.)

Played parts of *Sunday Morning*.

One of the scientists repeatedly referred to Darwin's *Origin of the Species*, and his wife asked me if there was a Mrs. Rorem. I patiently answered, "No, I'm homosexual."

When my 19th-century beauty last week turned to me—"I know one's not sup-posed to say this in some circles, but I believe Blacks *are* inferior. Why do they con-sistently get low grades?"—this was in response to my stated disappointment in the Chinese and the Jews, whom I'd always felt to be superior but who now, in Peking and in Israel, were settling problems with the sword like everyone else. When I report this to Mimsi & JH, they say that, yes, on New York subways black mothers don't talk to their children. Even in the deep south, where white trash spends the evening reminiscing, what have the blacks to chat about except horror?

Suddenly I realize where Paul Bowles's Mahlerian "dying fall" stems from: That drooping minor-third used in "The Lamp Is Low" section of Ravel's "Pavane" was acquired by P.B. for his air, *Te de llevar*, from "The Wind Remains"—an air that's haunted me for forty-six years. And the professor who falls from comparatively high in *A Distant Episode* echoes the professor in *The Blue Angel*.

23 August

Tomorrow from Boston on the boat come emissaries Leslie Holmes and George Brown of WCRB as they came two years ago and gave me a hefty downpayment on an oratorio I've not yet written one note of. Now they want their pound of flesh, and I've no ideas. JH will make them a ratatouille from thirty unflawed tomatoes in the garden, and a pecan pie. Meanwhile he is able to concentrate for hours at a time on the outdoor brickwork. I get up (from desk or piano) every fifteen minutes, and putter. For Boston, all I know is what I *don't* want to compose: Not another solemn, meaningful, gorgeous, deeply moving cantata. Humor is more complex than tragedy. Is there no way to write something witty, that's at once high litera-ture and worth singing about? (Weill and Brecht.)

Within hours after shelling the house with insecticide bombs, and bathing Sonny in sprays and infectious lathers, he is again covered with as many as two hundred fleas.

For me, hemorrhoids again, and diuretic pressures night and day. The ailments rise and wane, like Piranesi doors opening and closing in remote corners of the lower abdomen.

Finished, in seven weeks, *The Auden Poems* and sent it off to B&H. With three organ suites, that makes about 70 minutes of music completed this summer. Yet I feel I don't work enough. Just turned down a young pianist, Neil Rutman, who wants a concerto, and the Franciscan (all female) string quartet, because I must write, in the next three years: 1) Brass Quartet; 2) Trio for the Beaux Arts; 3) Eng-lish Horn Concerto for the NY Philharmonic; 4) Left Hand Concerto for Gary G.; 5) The vast Oratorio for Boston; and 6) The Whitman opera with Sandy for the NY City Opera.

If God had to rest on the seventh day, can he have been all-powerful? Perhaps he's resting when you pray to him.

Thirty years ago I began my first teaching stint as a full professor at Buffalo University.

6 September

A note on Simenon for the *Boston Globe*: Considering he was the most widely published writer who ever lived—at least the most widely published great writer—it's disconcerting how unknown Simenon was. Beyond the famous but formulaic Maigret series, he wrote dozens of what once were termed "psychological novels." As Balzac and Proust described the ills of the entire Western world by refracting those ills almost solely through the upper classes, so Simenon, like Genet, reflected the world as seen through the eyes of criminals or the very poor. There was nothing he did not know, and nothing he could not describe. His knowledge embraced every branch of human learning, and his description came through the use of the specific, as distinct from the general, adjective. In a single sentence he could depict et cetera.

His prolificity was dumbfounding. Josephine Baker among his ten thousand women. With Gide, Cocteau, and Sartre, he is among the four greatest French writers of our century. No one living in France today to hold a candle to him. I've often asked, in the past year, is he still alive? People don't know. No Nobel Prize.

"I consider myself an impressionist, because I work by touches. I believe a ray of sun on a nose is as important as a deep thought."

Roger Norrington's authenticity (ancient instruments and tempos—but what do we know of what the music *meant* to Bach's listeners?) *versus* Peter Sellars's updating of Mozart—of all but the music. Two publics, with their devotion to the music of the past, yet facing opposite directions.

29 September

A word before catching the noon ferry to New York. For JH, every morning of the year begins with a coughing spree so wrenching that he actually vomits. During this process an already-lit cigarette waits on the edge of the sink (JH seldom uses ash trays); after the process he inhales voraciously, and begins another day of chain-smoking. The cough, he contends, is due solely to nerves—his "tension cough" as he considers coming pressures—and maybe he's right.

I'm working on three pieces at once: the brass quintet called *Picasso*; the Boston cantata called *Swords and Plowshares*; the Beaux Arts Trio called nothing for the moment. Also practicing daily on Mahler songs (and Ravel, early Debussy, and my own) in preparation for a first rehearsal with Arleen Auger, end of October.

Ankey Larrabee, circa 1948, said she and John Cage made love to the steady beat of a metronome. But the slug loosened, slipping from 63 to 76 to finally 200 beats per minute.

Death of Virgil. Suddenly I wish I'd kept notes on our dutiful visits over the past
year; he had grown so benign, almost affectionate. He had concerns, but not anxieties. V.T. wasn't morbid, which accounts maybe for his longevity. (Though
Mother was morbid & she lived long.) He wasn't warm but he was dear. Paradox
of love: coveting vs. sharing.

1 October

> They say
> You have no lips for a fool such as I
> They say
> You just believe in a hello and goodbye
> And they say that the one I admire
> Isn't even remotely concerned
> And that I'll go on playing with fire
> Until I have learned
> My heart has been burned . . .

So flows the 1930s ballad in its non-developing masochistic route. Oughtn't the
"fool such as I" grow vengeful? Oughtn't he/she kidnap the "you," imprison him in
the *basement*, though which he escapes through a *casement*, but "though you
depart," you're ever in the "dungeon of my heart."
   This greeted me toward 4 A.M. during the insomnia accompanying my continuing low-grade headache.

2 October
Jesse Helms announces that art that is prurient isn't art. (Webster's: *prurient*, adj.
Having or arousing lascivious thoughts or desires.) In other words, sex is bad—at
least a sexual notion incited by art is bad.
   Cocteau, in *Démarche d'un Poète*, claims that the greatest art triumphs over
our intelligence when sexuality speaks, and if "this moral erection does not occur,
the pleasure a work of art affords is of a merely Platonic or intellectual order and
without the slightest elective value." Okay, so far as it goes; even a crucifixion or
battle scene, depicted by a great artist, can probably incite a moral erection. But
do women identify with moral erections?

Peter Shaffer's *Equus* (have I noted this elsewhere?) could have been inspired by
the early pages of my *Paris Diary*—the scene about a child destroying a horse with
sharpened prongs. In his preface Shaffer admits to having forgot where he first
read of this "crime." The *Paris Diary* was published in England just when he
would have been writing the play.

Nobody sings my songs anymore. A generation ago nearly every vocal program
listed in the Sunday *Times* included in its American group at least one Rorem song,
sometimes a whole group or cycle. Season after season now passes with nary a

mention. Barber is still sung, but among living composers it's mainly Argento and Bolcom today. Like Yeats's romancer, I "loved long and long / And grew to be out of fashion / Like an old song." I note this wistfully, without bitterness. Times change.

16 October

People speak of World War Two as "a necessary evil." Webster defines evil as "morally reprehensible," but surely it also means the "absolute bad," as opposed to the absolute good toward which man aspires. Can evil ever be necessary? Pacifists say war is never necessary—there's always an alternative. But if war *is* necessary, then it should not be termed evil unless one agrees that the Allies were as ungood as the Axis. Are there, then, layers of evil?

Essay on Debussy's form. So much expository statement comes in pairs. Use *Mandoline* (every pair of measures, plus the whole piece being divided in two identical parts) as an early example, a piano *Etude* as a late example, and nine out of ten pieces in between. He was not formally inventive, or even ambiguous.

Practicing on seven beautiful but sweaty Mahler songs in preparation for rehearsal with Auger next week. Despite their beauty, I take little pleasure in them, unless I find some French kinship. Chopin, perhaps, occasionally? Certainly the saddish aimless modality of Chopin's A-minor mazurka is refracted six decades later in Mahler's *Erinnerung*, measures 19–21.

18 October

As we were watching, after supper last night, *Destry Rides Again* (a simpleminded version of *High Noon*: When the chips are down fight fire with fire, not with reason; and Dietrich tries too hard in her dumb role), the earthquake hit San Francisco, just three weeks after Hurricane Hugo hit Charleston. Implacable meanness of nature. Irradicable image of happy (or unhappy) families in cars suddenly flattened like bloody pancakes. On November 1st, I fly to West Coast for a week. Or do I?

29 October

Prostate ache, in anticipation of California later this week. Sixth suave day of Indian Summer.

Lunch here (two kinds of quiche and a pear tart) with Arleen Auger and her business manager, Celia Novo, then a long first rehearsal during which I play the Mahler songs better than she sings the American songs. She's not a child. But her voice is silvery, clean, elegant, and sweet as an icy stream in summer. I feel as she gives her all, that perhaps she is squandering those perfect lilts on a mere rehearsal. On the other hand, as red brews in a green tomato and will emerge no matter what, or as semen is in a male body and will always spout at necessary dreamy intervals, so a soprano, who admittedly has only so many high Cs in her, between now and her downfall, *must* emit those high Cs even if wasted on the desert air.

A fundamentalist, regarding Michelangelo, as quoted in *The Advocate*: "The Sistine Chapel ceiling is a disgrace, and the painter is burning in hell because of it."

Words are symbols for what isn't there at the moment. Painting depicts three dimensions in two dimensions. But if music is symbolic or representational, I don't know of what, and I've been dealing with it for six decades.

Do the Jews count the number of gays who come to their parties, as JH and I sometimes count Jews? (Jean Stein's uncle, rue Bassono, 1953, with his quota on homosexuals.)

I don't know any lesbians. None.

Finished writing a substantial and heartfelt reminiscence of Robert Phelps for next Sunday's memorial, which alas I can't attend.

13 November

I've always hated the phrase "The Six Million," it being preemptive, elitist, discriminatory of ten million others who vanished in vain. Gay Cable Network broadcast a dinner by (I guess) a gay & lesbian group. Eli Wiesel, and none too soon, speaking as honored guest, begins: "True, the Bible has never been very tolerant of you . . . " (*You*, he says, distancing himself.) If he means well—and he does—it's hardly a tactful way to start, especially since he has only a few more lines to his speech. Worse, he neglects to add—*everyone* neglects to add—that the Old Testament was written for Jews only. The Leviticus dicta couldn't care less about African goyim or Norwegian Quakers. Even Cardinal O'Connor cannot legitimately call on the Bible to back his anti-gay cause.

Also on the program, Dinkins, committing himself. Although I've hitherto mistrusted his icy political eyes, now because of this stance I'd vote for him, if I voted.

The Ascension last night with JH to hear the first of three Duruflé homages. Performances of grand clarity (by organists McNeil Robinson and John Walker, and by Dennis Keene's big choir with Maureen Forrester, age 59 and hardly the worse for wear) but the music doesn't merit the attention. (Well, maybe once.) It's at all times gorgeous, but over-solemn and soundtracky. Like Les Six, without the camp or control, or like Messiaen without the outrageous harmonic sedition. The *Requiem* is slow from start to finish, using Gregorian chant exclusively for its tunes. Well, with Gregorian chant you can't lose. But neither can you win. The melody is inherently appealing, but impersonal by definition. Duruflé is Gregorian chant in thirds. He is to Poulenc as Cilea is to Puccini: The same thing but less good.

Madame Duruflé at party later was the very definition of Gallic charm.

Another tongue-twister for Francophones: "Sit tight, thick shirts."

If Steve Reich is "Fred Waring without the tunes," serial music is "just a lot of notes."

Vivian Perlis's second "autobiography" of Copland is as lively and real as the first: her circumspection and his tone of voice leap from every page. Yet (except for a tactful hint in my own interview) Aaron might as well be a eunuch, for all we learn of his personal temperament, or a lucid professor, for all we're told of his advancing senility.

"Nature, the gentlest mother . . ." begins his first song on Dickinson's words. If ever Mother were harsh, or rather, indifferent, it's Nature. Regard the earthquake, AIDS, and thirst in the desert.

With the German wall coming down, and Russia's reversals, America, with her caution and self-censorship, is being left behind. We've become *the* conservative land today. Frohnmayer, as new head of the National Endowment of the Arts, is more than disappointing. Artists, meanwhile, instead of pitifully decrying the NEA at every turn, ought simply to ignore it. The pathetically small amounts of money granted by government to art in this country do not merit the publicity. The taxpayers' dollars? Rather, the taxpayers' tenth of a cent.

JH says, as to abortion, that if government has the right to deny abortion, it also has the right to impose abortion under circumstances it might deem appropriate, i.e., unmarried mothers.

Beethoven's "Spring" Sonata on WNYC this morning. I never fail to be surprised at how unsurprised I am at how little surprise figures in even Beethoven's most proven chestnuts (those endless root position tonics & dominants). Just as I'm always surprised at my own lack of surprise in America's Puritanism.

Because I admired the original energy of his *Hundred Years of Solitude* long ago, I tried to cut García Márquez's *Love in the Time of Cholera*. But with the very opening paragraph, the translation is so littered with ambiguous modifiers and antecedents ("He told him he had only six hours to live . . . ") that I gave up in confusion after page 14. *Dommage*.

I hate the sound of ice cubes in a glass, and of the over-loud laughter of women. I love the taste of iron bars in a jungle gym, with the faint rustle of sweat from glowing fellow children. I hate the taste of Brussels sprouts and oysters. I love the sight of any cloisters. I love the sound of any classical sequence. I hate the sight of decapitated heads in bathrooms. I hate the smell of babies. I love the touch of grape juice, and the smell of wet leaves and pencil shavings. If I hate the touch of wet hands, I do love the aroma of grown-ups.

Pink waits in the green peach as the next earthquake lurks under Haight Street, or as ill health stalks the back of the brain. Never completely out of consciousness, the earth could open at our feet in forty years, or before we reach the next corner.

26 November

Describe Virgil's vast memorial yesterday at Saint-John-the-too-too-Divine as Latouche used to call it. JH's Satie on the organ, plus his playing of Thomson interludes, holding together the whole service. Phyllis Curtin stayed with us for 36 hours. Exhaustion. JH slept on kitchen floor with the three animals, his early schedule, self-pressure, and the terrible abscess beneath his left incisor.

An hour or two with Phyllis going through songs, Mahler and early Debussy and Poulenc. Her continual anxiety and apologies for her frayed voice. The songs she chose of VT's are about the only right thing for her to come out of retirement for. We sang through songs, and at Vilmorin's, *Mais comme j'étais loin de lui / Et que sa voix ne portait plus / Il est mort seul dans le bois*, I felt tears rise. She sounded, not too long ago, so beautiful, *et ainsi vont toutes choses* .. . .

Describe the *Temps retrouvé* tone at the Century Club, with Minna Lederman, Theodate Johnson, Vittorio Rieti, Elliott Carter, and all of our little declarations. (Try to recall all this later.)

JH feels that in fifty years there'll be nothing left of Virgil.

Sick with worry about JH, his morning vomiting, the cough, the abscess. It's Sunday, we're in New York, his dentist's in Nantucket. Called emergency dentist. Will see about an extraction tomorrow at one. Fever. Then he goes to Kansas. Then Nantucket. Always the church. Never stopping. In twenty years he's never missed a Sunday. And his over-eating, and of junk food.

His tapes of, nevertheless, good performances this morn at church of Handel and Palestrina. *L'esprit du choeur* is thrilling. He is loved.

Doriot Dwyer played beautifully—a solo line is all that can carry in the cathedral, with its nine-second reverberation, the length of an earthquake. Says she's often played *Book of Hours*, but was unaware of *Romeo & Juliet*. When I got out the score to send to her, I realized that—not having looked at it for ten years or so—I scarcely recalled it. If you'd asked me yesterday, How does it begin, how does it end?, I could not have answered.

At the Coliseum Bookstore, thumbing Quentin Crisp's new book, I find my name several times therein. I want to buy it, but don't want to be seen buying it (what might people think!), so I buy a second book (Herbert Leibowitz's *Fabricating Lives*) to soften the blow, thereby spending 45 dollars instead of 24. How's that for adjustment?

I don't commit suicide partly because of the inconvenience it would cause. Death as inconvenience.

Crisp: "In tones drenched with pity, people say of someone, 'He died alone.' I have never understood this point of view. Who wants to have to die, and to be polite at the same time?"

Nantucket, 20 November

In the rented car that brought us here yesterday the radio played a Vivaldi Psalm for alto, in several movements, called *Nisi Dominus*. But one of the movements isn't Vivaldi's, it's by Villa-Lobos. Sly fox: his famous fifth *Bachianas brasileiras* isn't filched from Bach at all, but note for note from Vivaldi. Yes of course it's his too, like Borges's *Don Quixote*.

Lou Harrison, when he lived in that walk-up on Bleecker, was the first to play me Bidú Sayão's record of the Villa-Lobos. Who wrote the text of the central section? Over and over, until it cracked, we played the final measures of that section, to pin down the harmony.

He ate eight. Wait, weight.

30 Nov.

Tried to buy the *Nisi Dominus* at Patelson's today. No luck. Forty years ago, many a store in Greenville or Omaha had all oddities in stock. You just walked in off the street and purchased the orchestra score of this or that Messiaen. Today, nothing anywhere. Not even a store.

Diversions for Brass Quintet
2 Trumpets in C, Horn in F, Trombone, Tuba

At first my plan, like Mussorgsky's, was to compose a series of pictures, with titles drawn specifically from Picasso. But that device soon seemed both overwhelming and parasitical. Music cannot be proven to mean anything beyond itself; if the arts could convincingly represent each other, we'd only need one art. So I assembled my series of "abstract" pieces into a theatrically feasible order, and gave them non-programmatic titles. Two of them, *Pastorale Quartet* and *Chorale*, were originally conceived for an Armenian chorus. As for *Bach's Tomb* (originally called merely *Largo*), not until it was finished and copied did I realize the theme was taken from the composer's name.

The current *TLS* (Dec. 1–7) carries a long and mostly credible review, by one Jeremy Sams, of *Satie: Seen through His Letters*. Credibility crumbles toward the end when Sams states: "If one listens to, say, *Mercure* or *Socrate* (although it is hard to imagine anyone doing so for pleasure) it is possible to hear the Satie of the future hidden behind a Glass or in a Cage." I, for one, have found more pleasure in *Socrate* than in any other work of this century. *Socrate* is all about words and tune, with those being set in relief and given a frequent wrench by a poignant harmony or a switch of rhythm. There is no humor, much less camp, in the piece, but a great deal of awe and of . . . well, Socratic beauty. That Sams should hear the simplicity of the three movements as inert like Glass or silly like Cage makes me wonder yet again: Who hears what and when? Are there no absolutes?

22 December

Perused once, but carefully, John Ash's poem "In a Rainy Country" (in the current *New Yorker*), and understood it all. Perused it a second time and understood nothing.

Call from Sylvia to say the Guarneri wants a quartet from me. (Also a Pro Musica group in Ohio: short orchestral piece.) I can't not do it. After two quartets, in 1947 and 1950, it's time for a first real one.

It occurs to me that my oeuvre alternates chronologically between the light and the heavy. (Light & heavy for me, that is.) The recent three *Organbooks* are light by being collections of brief bits. Next, *The Auden Poems*, is heavy, i.e., "serious," in its text. The just-finished *Diversions* for Brass Quintet are desserts. The upcoming trio will be an entrée. The quartet will be heavy too—although perhaps light might be a change. God has had enough of deep quartets, or of English-horn concertos with string accompaniments.

Are my light pieces better than the heavy? What's better?

"I don't believe you really have those dreams, you make them up," Henri Fourtine used to say.

Then who makes up the dreams I do have?

Christmas Eve (Sunday)

"Brilliant," to describe literary style and content (like "delicious" to describe food), is too overused for meaning. Yet the *Times Sunday Book* reviewers know no other adjective. One Robert Ward, identified as a "television writer," today employs the word six times in his one-page write-up of H. L. Mencken's Diary. The write-up is also otherwise inept, fallacious, literal-minded, and dull.

In Rome, early 1954, when Elliott Carter's First String Quartet was played, I'd never heard anything like it before, and told him it sounded like the end of the world. To this day is incised on my brain the device, in the Adagio, of two impassive muted violins juxtaposed with the savage viola and cello—a device devised by Ives in *The Unanswered Question* (disparate simultaneity), and, before that, in *Nuages*, where Debussy's Cor Anglais rends the cloudily indifferent strings. Of course, in the quartet from *Rigoletto* too—or in any vocal ensemble singing in what Virgil calls "differentiated counterpoint"—each voice voices its own thoughts, as opposed to the undifferentiated counterpoint of, say, a fugue.

Listening again now to Elliott's quartet, in anticipation of writing another of my own maybe next year for the Guarneri, I'm again struck with fear and displeasure. It's not a nothing piece, but . . .

EC's need to be "important," to make important statements. I've never felt the need. Enjoyment (on some level) is more important than importance.

26 December

Words on the death of Samuel Beckett, for the *Boston Globe*:

He was a master in the lineage of the 19th-century Greats, and his subject matter, like Dostoevsky's or Kierkegaard's, was despair. But unlike them, his identifying property was economy—leanness to the vanishing point. He made of human loneliness a subject of high camp, yet despite his virtuosity he created no enjoyable characters or any real catharsis.

His ultimate value will lie not so much in his own works, which aren't especially likeable, but in his influence. Without him there would be no Pinter or Albee, no Ionesco or Orton.

His work lent itself well to music: the minimalism with words, sentences, paragraphs, allowed for refurbishing by composers. Many of his plays have been made into operas with more or less success.

When I first saw it in 1953 in Paris, *Waiting for Godot* seemed arty and dated. Ten years later, when I listened to it not for content but for sonority, the echoes and rises and falls of language seemed pure music, and I revised my opinion.

I never met him. But he seems to have been a decent and humorous type. Madeleine Renaud, the actress, told me that when she toured in his monologue, *Happy Days*, Beckett would phone or telegraph her several times a week, wherever she was in the world.

He was one of those rare ones, along with Joseph Conrad, Vladimir Nabokov, and Isak Dinesen, who wrote exclusively in a language not their own. Beckett, an Irishman, gave to French a tonality absolutely new. When this tonality was translated back into English, English ironically took on a clipped Gallic resonance of brevity and wit, a resonance that is "the Beckett sound," and by extension, the sound of all theater in our mid-century.

Nantucket, 27 December

Noriega on Christmas Eve gave himself up to the Vatican Embassy in Panama City, clever guy, outwitting the Bush pursuers, which shouldn't be hard. (You don't announce you're going to kidnap someone, then arrive three days later and expect him to be waiting.) Meanwhile Nicolae Ceausescu and evil wife have been executed in Romania. So Eastern Europe is now almost entirely rid of tyrannical rule. *And in so short a time.* Meanwhile, the *Times* and other easy-going mouthpieces object to the crass tactics of ACT-Up, saying the Gays and Abortion Rights Activists have "set back their cause" by demonstrating during Cardinal O'Connor's high mass. That's what blacks were told a generation ago: Be patient, don't set back your cause by acting up. If Communist Europe can do it (though revolutions are never achieved on empty stomachs—what happened in Romania?) so can we. By acting up. The older I get (admittedly thanks to JH's prodding), the more radical I grow.

Usually, just as one begins to resemble the opposite sex as one ages (hormonal redistribution, or something), so does one verge toward the political center, away from left or right. The reverse seems to obtain chez moi.

Tested yesterday for new reading glasses. $205. Rather steep. JH pays fifteen dollars off the rack for his . . . Prostate acting up.

Steegmuller writes in *TLS* (Nov. 24–30), regarding Proust's *Correspondence:*

> The final letter in the volume, apparently written the last night of the year, is to Cocteau, consoling him on the reported disappearance of Garros [the pilot], 'If, as it would grieve me to learn, Garros is dead, my consolation is to think that you will have the comfort, you who loved him, of having made him live forever, in a sky from which nothing ever falls, and where the names of human beings live on like those of the stars.'

Title: *The Sky from Which Nothing Falls.*

1990

The two questions composers most often hear are:

1) When do you compose? In the morning? On weekends?

Answer: We are never not composing: in the dentist's chair, on the subway, even standing here now. Composers compose, that's their business; the actual notation is merely the final step, the tip of the iceberg.

2) How do you hear all those notes in your head?

Answer: If composition were taught in grade school, the way poetry and painting are (or used to be), the question would be moot. Any child can daub, or rhyme cat with rat. If he could learn the rudiments of musical script (which, yes, is the least realistic art), the process would seem less mysterious.

Afternoon visit from Eugenie with Christopher Idone. (At 4:30 it is still dusky enough to turn on the Christmas bulbs around the front arbor, but noticeably lighter than a week ago.) Discussion of the word "literally" used metaphorically, as in "I was literally dead," or "her voice literally shatters glass." I mention that Julius Katchen once claimed that he "literally had an orgasm while playing the Andante of Brahms's *F-minor Sonata* on a public stage." In my memoir of Julius (reprinted in *Setting the Tone*) I amended this to "he felt that he was fertilizing the universe." Now in *The New Yorker* [Jan. 8, p. 95], a reviewer, Edmund Morris, writes:

So freely did this vast harmony of foreign notes mix with his own that [Liszt] must have felt at times that he was "fertilizing the universe"—to borrow a phrase from the late Julius Katchen.

The phrase is not Katchen's (he had a high IQ but no knack for word play) but, of course, Mr. Morris can't know this.

Undersung prose writers: Denton Welch. Coleman Dowell.

3 January

We're sure we see evil in the faces of the evil. Yet Klaus Barbie resembles my dear grandfather who was a congregational minister and loathed violence, while Marie Ceausescu looks like Madame Curie (to name but two who are everywhere reviewed these days). If you can't judge a book by its cover, you can judge a cover by the book. It's rare that a stupid-looking man turns out to be intelligent, yet often an interesting-looking man turns out to be dull. Intellectually dull. With women it's harder to judge, at least from before the Enlightenment. Marilyn Monroe, dumb blonde, longed to be taken seriously, and killed herself. Ona Munson played Belle Watling in *GWTW*, married Leonid Berman, and killed herself. The stupid-looking can be canny: viz., Sylvester Stallone. Slobs can be neat thinkers, viz., Auden. None of this pertains to sexual appeal. And so on . . . Thoughts from this morning's walk with Sonny as he sniffs dog shit on the first warmish day in weeks.

We hate to lose consciousness in our dreams. (Recurring notion during long patch of wakefulness last night.) I haven't had a good night's sleep in thirty years.

5 Jan.

In car en route for NY: JH describes as "collegiate" the U.S. Army's playing loud rock outside the Vatican Embassy to drive Noriega mad. "They could as easily, and to the same effect, have played Elliott Carter's Double Concerto."

Sex has all the senses except sound. Sex has no sound, at least for me.

There's no "right" way to interpret a piece—there are as many right ways as there are true performers; even the composer's way is not definitive—it too can alter with the years. (This is especially so with singers, since there's obviously a bigger difference between a male and a female singing the same chanson than between female and male pianists with the same mazurka.)

Now I've changed my mind. There may be many right ways to conduct a Mahler symphony, but there is only one way to conduct *La Mer*. There may be many true ways to play a Chopin *Ballade*, but only one way to play *Reflets dans l'eau*.

Can the vase be nicer than the flowers?

Howard Moss spoke of visiting Lamb House, Henry James's home in Sussex, now a museum. From the bedroom dresser Howard picked up the master's hand-mirror, and for a long, long time gazed into it. No answer was forthcoming.
  Memoir title: *The Lamb House Mirror*.

18–19 Jan.
Judging at the Academy. Jacob Druckman asks for five minutes of our precious time (not at lunch, but during the judging) to "tell a story." We expected something. It turned out to be a mere scatalogical play on words (about how Lukas, on Dick Cavett's show, inadvertently referred to rock music as defecating), and we all roared.

27 January
Is what we produce already in our genes? Is every splayed sentence, or gush of notes, or ooze of oil *there* from the start—including the revisions we would have made a year later, or ten years later, or the notion that we don't believe in revisions? Is the fact that we died before making the revisions also in our genes?

Listened anew to *The Desert Music*. I'd forgotten—among its other attributes (so few)—how nicely vulgar Steve Reich's music is. Philip Glass is pristine by virtue of using mainly triads. But Reich, with his female chorus cooing, evokes the 13th-chord harmonies of 1940s dance bands filtered through Debussy's *Sirènes*.

Not everyone is bisexual at birth. *I* wasn't.

Homosexuality and alcohol. Alcoholism in itself is bad (although to be a permanently recovered alcoholic is illuminating and multidimensional) while homosexuality in itself is neither good nor bad (same as heterosexuality). Causes, or reasons, for alcoholism and homosexuality have never been agreed upon, even by people like me who've pondered the questions forever. But I do know the relation between the two, at least in my case: how alcoholism results from homosexuality. (Shyness, the guilty longing for passivity, etc. Not true, though, of other very aggressive gay drunks.)

Homer. The terms of the contract from Pennsylvania's Franklin & Marshall College, which commissioned this work, were that it be "uplifting" (to celebrate the 200th anniversary of the school's founding), preferably on an American text, performable by students with optional solos and a very small instrumental group, and fifteen minutes long.
  Celebratory texts that are also good literature don't grow on trees. After a year of false starts with apparently logical choices—Benjamin Franklin, William Penn, Herman Melville, even the Preamble and the Amendments to the Constitution—

I concluded that "uplifting" is in the ear of the beholder. When finally I opted for *The Iliad* my worries were over, and the music flowed forth in six weeks. If the piece is twice longer than bargained for, and if the text is not American, Homer nevertheless seems apt because for three millenniums he has formed the core of Western culture.

The words for the outer movements are from the opening page and the closing page of the epic, and for the central movement from Book Three. The translation draws from various 19th-century prose versions, mainly Samuel Butler's. The composition was realized in Nantucket between June 9 and July 27, 1986, and the instrumental score (devised to have a "primitive" ring without resorting to drums) was finished a month or so later.

January

Connie Chung, sophisticated and responsible newscaster, is guest on a pop talk show. Because she's just like the rest of us, she allows herself to conjecture whether Tom Selleck, whose shoe size is 11½, is "big all over." JH seeks to fault this crassness, but says, "She'll only claim to be getting back at men who always joke about women." (That is, she has every right to be low-class.) Her actual error lies, in fact, in betraying her "class." We don't want her to be like the rest of us. Joan Rivers could get away with the quip, but it's unlikely that, say, Dan Rather would, on a talk show, conjecture about Dolly Parton's boobs.

Finished program note for Eileen Hunt on the *Three Organbooks*. Didn't say that some of the sixteen vignettes are truly not hers but gifts to JH. He's worth all my music to me, and I'd never compose another note if that would save his life.

JH, who's been listening to Mahler with increasing testiness, says it all sounds like Ice Capade music.

Bought Andy Warhol's *Diaries* at Penn Station, surprised to find myself therein:

> (1984) . . . I was reading the Ned Rorem diaries while I was up there. From the Sixties to '71. He missed the whole scene that *we* were part of, though—he was back in the elegant Forties and Fifties still. He puts me down a couple of times I guess. . . . Ned Rorem met Anaïs Nin just so he could be in her diary and she could be in his. And I want to do that, too—I want to find somebody who does a diary now so we can be in each other's. . . .
>
> Oh and in Ned Rorem's diary he talks about some girl named Jean Stein being so terribly in love with him. Something like that. I'd like to mail her that page anonymously, let her see how it feels to be put down in print. I think I will.

Well, having made it into Andy's book, it's downhill all the way. Actually, the very little I knew of him I liked, as when he with such gentle skill filmed me and Kenward Elmslie walking up and down stairs at Kenward's in, I guess, 1963.

Sunday 18 Feb.

Having seen Marcel Schneider, like a long-lost sister, on French TV's *Apostrophes*, and heard him talk of Gide's early *Les Nourritures terrestres*, it occurred to me that I'd never read that book. Have I a copy? Yes, with yellowing pages, all of them uncut. So I spent a quarter-hour slitting the paper. Inexplicably, on page 294, the phrases which Paul Goodman translated for *The Poets' Requiem*, have been underlined with a ruler (" . . . *le lièvre ou le cerf poursuivi . . . trouve joie dans sa course et ses bonds et ses feints . . . mais je la crois, dans son ensemble, . . . le bonheur d'être, dans toute la nature jusqu'à l'homme, l'emporte de beaucoup sur la peine. . . .*"). And on 192, the famous opening spoken lines from Stravinsky's *Perséphone* are versified, but with no mention of their being used in the cantata:

> *La brise vagabonde*
> *A caressé les fleurs.*
> *Je t'écoute de tout mon coeur,*
> *Chant du premier matin du monde.*

Of course, these two extracts are from the *Nouvelle nourritures*, which date from the mid-Thirties. But how did an uncut book become . . . ?

28 Feb.

With JH to Arleen Auger's recital. She sounds beautiful, if careful, with a selection that lacks energy, or at least histrionics. A Schoenberg group from 1899 predates certain Strauss songs also included. But Arleen sang them with a touch—inappropriate—of *sprechstimme* and darkness, thinking doubtless that Schoenberg is Schoenberg after all, and that's what you do. But she knows now what Schoenberg didn't know in 1899—that he would be "wildly modern"—and such knowledge is superficial.

A waste, somehow, for an American singer to offer an entire concert in German. Would a German singer ever, *ever*, give an entire concert in English?

3 March

Titles, like the trends of harmony versus counterpoint, float by and return with the generations. Fifty years ago Modern Dance works had solemn one-word Greekish names like *Monody* or *Epiphilathium* or *Anxiety* or *The Masses*. Musical pieces were just called *Sonata* or *Suite*. Then thirty years ago musical pieces were called *Monody* etc., while Modern Dance works were called *Circe* or *Every Soul's a Circus*.

Anyway, I need a title for the new trio, other than Trio, because I've written several trios (the one with flute, cello & piano is plainly called Trio) and that's confusing. Even Beethoven and Schubert had subtitles: "Archduke," "The Trout" (or is that a quartet?).

JH suggests *The Unquestioned Answer*. Pretty good, especially for me. When Lenny B. adapts Ives's wonderful title, *The Unanswered Question*, for his book of lectures, he (Lenny) uses it in a vast Romantic extra-musical sense of "What does it all mean—what is the secret of the universe?" For me, music asks no questions, it provides an answer. Questions are philosophical, and art is not philosophy; art is an end in itself, an *answer*. However, everyone thinks the title a touch cute, even fascist.

In recent pages here had I discussed finding the phrase "The Unanswered Question" somewhere? in Wordsworth? or Wilde? The Sphinx? (It's in Emerson.)

Mother. Her racial tolerance. Her pacifism. But her intolerance of foreign languages, and of Puerto Ricans. "They sound like little birds, and look like them too."

God and I have an understanding. He doesn't believe in me, and I don't believe in him.

4 March

"Although I hold to the opinion that music is the most noise conveying the least information, I could be said to have experienced a musical weekend," writes Quentin Crisp in the current *New York Native*. "In a convoy of editors, I went to tea with Mr. Rorem to deliver him copies of Mr. Steele's opera magazine, which has Mr. Rorem's picture on the cover. I first met him when he gave a talk in a room behind the church on Second Avenue, which we have now renamed the Church of St. Ned. He is the kindest of hosts, but I was frightened by his attitude toward the world in general. When he said of somebody that he despised him, I was so shocked that I could not refrain from pointing out that we are free to dislike other people, but that, if we despise them, it raises the question, 'Who are we?', or, worse, 'Who the hell are we?' To this he replied, 'I'm better than they are. That's who the hell I am.'"

I'm not so much insulted as squashed by Quentin's glib definition, which in a phrase disqualifies my life's work. But should he not distinguish between "dislike" and "despise"? Each of us knows ourself to be better than others *in certain ways*. All men may be created equal, so far as worth and desire are concerned; yet surely Quentin knows he's superior to, say, Cassius Clay as an aphorist (if not as a poet), just as I know myself to be superior to, say, Jesse Helms as a composer (if not as a manipulating logician). JH feels I'm overreacting to what was, after all, tea-party outrageousness.

JH meanwhile has reread (as much as he could take) of the Stravinsky/Craft conversation books. Meretricious. The sarcasm of, for instance, "The Cure for V.D." (what's wrong with Vernon Duke's "April in Paris," that the song should be so sniffed at?) stems transparently from Craft's once-tenuous and now-vanished situation as Stravinsky's mouthpiece.

3 April

Lively meeting and deadly meal at the Academy where Hugo Weisgall, on his first full day as president, acquitted himself with brevity and patience. Rode home in a stretch limo with the Beesons, Ralph Ellison, and John Updike, who's at the May-flower. Updike and I, the last to be dropped, had ten minutes of conversation to invent. When he said that, yes, he had indeed written a libretto (with Gunther Schuller) but that music was a mystery to him ("Can you really hear all those notes in your head?"), I, with uncalled-for huffiness, replied that *littérateurs*, even high-order ones like himself, are never embarrassed about making such remarks, but can you picture a composer admitting "Novels are a mystery to me." I added that I'd once mentioned his limitations in a book (see *Nantucket Diary*, p. 500). Was he annoyed? He said that sometimes unknown composers mail him taped settings of his verse. Does it sound odd to him? "Yes, like taffy, stretching phrases out of shape."

How "real" people hear music is as wondrous to me as, to them, how composers hear. Like taffy—that's terrific. And comprehensible. Elliott Stein once said that music on the page—whether right-side-up or upside-down—looked like Klee. Since he couldn't hear those visible notes, he was free to *see* them. Like a foreign language: once we learn and understand it, we can no longer hear it.

I asked Updike why he didn't write a homosexual story for a change.

5 April

Having attended both David Del Tredici's *Steps* (world première by Philhar-monic) and David Diamond's 1965 *Fifth Symphony* (the Juilliard Orchestra) this past fortnight, I'd say that Diamond's music is dramatic but not theatrical while DDT's is theatrical but not dramatic. DD's seethes with portentous content skill-fully worked through but without color for color's sake, while DDT's is shy of con-tent but gaudy to a fault.

Drama without theater. Theater without drama. Britten, at his best, has both.

8 April

What does one conclude about the much noted comparison between Europe's emerging democracies and America's increasing fundamentalist repressiveness? It's been so few months since the Berlin Wall was sundered, yet already furtive right-wingery replaces dogmatic left-wingery, while in Cincinnati the exhausted and unimportant Mapplethorpe issue still rages. Even today's *NY Times* declares on page one: "The seven photographs at issue include images of homosexual acts; two are of children with their genitals exposed." Only that scarcely visible semi-colon spares the children from being implicated in the homosexual acts! If the "acts" were heterosexual would they offend? If the pictures were paintings and not photographs would they offend? If the children's exposed genitals were on Renaissance cupids would they offend? And isn't the phrase "with their genitals exposed" suggestive of "exposing their genitals"—as in exhibitionism? And so what?

JH feels that Europe's new democracy is really a mild fascism replacing communism, that is, the people's self-censoring conservatism, as distinct from censorship from without—from the government. We in the USA put pressure on our self-censorship from the eternal urge for order, for being told what to do, for avoiding the poetic threat of overflowing our borders. Liberalism, to the right, means chaos.

Most wistful of all, at least for me, is Václav Havel's wondrous key position today, like Paderewski's or Claudel's of yore. Yet, left to his own devices during a recent visit to Washington, he dons blue jeans and heads for a disco because he "loves rock." What difference can that make? say my colleagues, since after all he is instigating policies of High Art in Prague. But High Art is not "democratic," and, at least as represented in music, bores Havel no less than it bores Bush. (As an aristocrat, or at least a non-populist, I seem to fit into no viable category either here or there.) And Havel's plays? Have they a voice of their own? No one disputes their nobility of purpose, but are they more than lukewarm Kafka?

How can one judge Mapplethorpe by a single picture? Any Mapplethorpe photo is by itself less charged with sense or implication than in context with its neighbors. The innocent, non-erotic, decorative patterns of his nudes and fornications are echoed in lewd inhuman lilies. Plants here are surely more suggestive than human flesh.

I don't mean anything I say. Including that sentence.

24 April

TEACHING

In general, teaching's a healthy infection. It leads a horse to water and makes him drink. But with musical composition teaching comes only after the fact. A student must produce his work before the teacher can comment. Now, to produce a work is cause for panic in one who is not a composer. Ask a piano virtuoso to write a simple piece, and he flees.

The teacher doesn't necessarily "know" more than his student. He simply hears with a different ear (as do the student's comrades, or, indeed, the student himself when appraising his teacher's music). David Horne, age 19, knows more than I about, say, the notation of string harmonics, and dares to say that all musicians "should" know about the notation of harmonics (although string players themselves are often in the dark). What David will not yet grasp, and won't for another forty years, is that after a point a composer gets rid of excess baggage. I'm no longer interested in notation of string harmonics since I am not interested in harmonics *tout court*—my music doesn't, and never will, require them. Similarly, I'm less interested in reading masterpieces today, than reading . . . et cetera. *J'ai lu tous les livres.* In a half-hour I could master harmonics notation, but David will need more years before he dispenses with this. Learning is not the accumulation of knowledge, but the application of knowledge. (Larry Rivers: "I get a new idea every three or four years.")

Listened with JH and Donald Collup to Argento's *The Water Bird Talk*, an hour-long solo turn by Collup himself. Argento's language by its nature demands tune-fulness, for he is harmonically sparse and tonal (if instrumentally rich). But do I remember a thing about his music from year to year? He is afraid to take a chance, a chance with a tune perhaps for fear the tune will prove tacky. David Horne takes nothing but chances. His work is all bravura and daring. He won't take the chance that not taking a chance is already a chance: i.e., write something spare. No sooner do I tell him this than he draws from his pouch a handful of Blake settings. They are perfect: pure, sweet, and true.

I never had a Special Teacher—a guiding master—except in the dead. Debussy and Ravel were more crucial to my education than Sowerby or Nolte or Scalero or Wagenaar, or even, later, Thomson and Copland and Honegger.

26 April

Plays, the stage, legitimate theater. Magic words when we were young. Mother and Father took us to the best. Why now do I see a play only once every four years, and that only through coercion? Because I can't believe it and probably never did, and because even the greatest actors seem like silly children.

The hiatuses between my playgoing are long enough for whole new trends to becloud the mystique. Tonight at the jam-packed claustrophobic Helen Hayes Theater I would have fled during the entr'acte, had I not enthusiastically accepted Craig Lucas's offer to supply a ticket to his *Prelude to a Kiss*. So geared was the lowbrow mob to a laugh-track, and so slick was the direction toward this mob, that the already unfunny lines were stretched like slow motion. Nothing elliptical, nothing unspoken. Everything spelled out. Spelled out slowly. Lusterless actors in a coy plot drawn from *Our Town* via *Peter Pan*. (Anything you wish for, even your old life relived, or a new life from scratch, can be had if you wish hard enough.) Uncalled-for-vulgarity solely for cheap laughs. (Example: the uptight bourgeois New Jersey mother, during the wedding scene, admonishes the guests posing for her camera to say, not "cheese," but "bullshit," and they all say "bullshit.") Well, I guess theater needs to pander, for without the simple audience there is no theater. How would Duse seem today? Were there redeeming features? But last night I simply couldn't believe it—and was relieved when Craig said that because there was a backstage fire, he couldn't join me for ice cream after all.

Yet it's had unanimous rave reviews.

I penned the above as a fan of Craig Lucas, whose earlier play *Reckless* (which

I've read but not seen—seeing is disbelieving) seemed original, painful, theatrical. It could make a good opera, with a slow fadeout at the end, while they're still talking.

Alexander Nevsky on TV last night. Like most remembered masterpieces, it does-n't hold up. The theirs-is-not-to-reason-why patriotism, the smug justification of sadism that dissolves from the rendering of a German foe into the smile of right-thinking peasants, the black-and-white politics, the overlong battle scenes, all this can't be made easier to digest for all the artiness of the photography. The photog-raphy, and indeed the recording of Prokofiev's pretty good score, seems oddly raw for 1938. Hard to realize that *Nevsky* postdates *It Happened One Night* by five years.

S&M. Sadistic slaves. Masochistic master.

I've asked myself why it is that Frank O'Hara inspires so much more of a legend than other such recently dead poets as Paul Goodman or Theodore Roethke or Randall Jarrell—poets who are certainly as "good" as Frank (if these things can be measured) and perhaps even technically better, if technique means honing mate-rial to a minimum so that it will have maximum impact. Certainly one of these poets, Paul Goodman, influenced Frank overwhelmingly, and Goodman (and, for all I know, Roethke and Jarrell as well) still has his coterie of widows. But these widows don't "do" as much as Frank's, and are themselves less *influenced*.

There are two answers, one nice, the other less nice. The less nice answer is that Frank's poetic tone is deceptively easy and thus dangerously imitable. His diary format—the "I do this, I do that" verses—is something anyone can pick up without half trying. Frank has more no-talent mimics than anyone except Allen Ginsberg.

The nice reason has to do with Frank's generosity, a warmth that extends from beyond the grave, not only to those who knew him, but to those who did not—who, indeed, were not even born when he was felled by that fatal dune taxi.

He was the least selfish of artists. Most artists are out for themselves, like every-one else. They're interested in other people's art only as that applies to them-selves. Frank O'Hara was interested in other people's art for its own sake. He could spend hours, months, helping other poets, even bad poets. Or writing blurbs for painters, unsigned blurbs that did nothing for his own posterity. Thus his poetry was generous too—not because it was about other people. He's written lots of lazy junk, but at their best those split-second on-the-spot odes are good precisely by virtue of being split-second on-the-spot, and they melt your heart. The most suc-cessful example is, of course, "The Day Lady Died," uncopyable but oft copied. The Masturbation School of Poetry declares: "Anything is valid because it happens to us and we are poets." But what makes a poet a poet? It's the one undefine-able profession. Frank's poems had at their best the blood of life, while *their* pens are dipped in embalming fluid, yet the subject matter is identical.

A NOTE ON MY ORGAN MUSIC

In the United States the organ is an acquired taste, not only for musical laymen but for most professional musicians. Laymen connect the sound with churchgo-ing, an extra-musical occurrence irrelevant to the concert hall. Professionals (except, of course, for organists themselves) can find the sound over-rich, blurred, remote from the incisive linear flow they were taught to parse in counterpoint class.

Do I fall into both categories? Although raised in a musical milieu, my ken did not include organ literature. Yet over the past fifteen years I've composed four good-sized works for solo organ (mostly from James Holmes's urging), and before that, any number of choral pieces with organ accompaniment. Which comes to about four hours of music for the instrument, more than any other American has produced except for those out-of-the-mainstream specialists of so-called Sacred Music.

How has this come about? Mainly through an intellectual, rather than an emo-tional, impulse. True, as a student in 1946 I experimented briefly with a four-minute Fantasy and Toccata, sent it unsolicited to the Boston virtuoso, E. Power Biggs, and never thought of it again. (Forty years later Eileen Hunt exhumed the manuscript from among Biggs's trove and programmed it with some success.) And in 1950 I concocted and published a brief Pastorale. But these were minor forays. When Jim Holmes, a choir director by trade, suggested in 1974 that I could do worse than contribute something meaty to the organ repertory (after all, he explained, organists, more than any other breed of instrumentalist, are prone to feature new music), I jumped at the challenge. A *Quaker Reader* resulted, and proved to work in public. This led to a commission from the American Guild of Organists, and four years later I composed another suite, *Views from the Oldest House*, inspired by scenes of Nantucket. Five years after that, the orchestra of Portland, Maine, asked for an organ concerto.

Another hiatus. Then, just this past year I finished three Organbooks. The first was commissioned by Leslie Spelman; the second and third by Eileen Hunt, specifically to be premièred on the 150-year-old Goodrich instrument of Nan-tucket's Unitarian Church, the only organ by that maker still existing on its original site. Together the Organbooks contain sixteen pieces, and their object, I suppose, is simplicity. The previous works have all been complex and hard; it seemed time to write something more technically plain. These pieces are nonetheless gradu-ated from very easy to quite thorny. Played consecutively they form a sort of Pil-grim's Progress of forty-odd minutes. But the three books can be dipped into as well, like jewel boxes, offering what's useful for this or that occasion.

Though I flatter myself that I compose with an experienced flair for the organ,

I still hear it as an amateur. The timbre of all organ music, including my own, remains mysterious to me: I never know quite what to listen for. This ambiguity is at once irksome and thrilling, and will keep me forever intrigued.

Nantucket, 16 May

Yesterday, the Ides of May, annual planting of begonias and impatiens, hued like stained glass. Today the window boxes seem already more radiant. How easily I recall, from fifty years ago, Miss Campbell (she's still quick at 95)'s class in Roman literature, and these lines from Lucretius:

> *Observe this dew-drenched rose of Tyrian grain.*
> *A rose it is today, but yesterday*
> *It was the earth, the sunshine, and the rain.*

Reading autobiographies. The margins of Russell Baker's are strewn with blue-pencillings. Likewise Arthur Miller's, which has a marvelous ending. Coyotes watch his house from afar at night: "I am a mystery to them until they tire of it and move on, but the truth, the first truth, probably, is that we are all connected, watching one another. Even the trees."

"Even the Trees," what a great title! I wrote Arthur about it. In his answer he said, "You mention that I am an activist who thinks good plays can change people while you feel that art can only make people more of what they already are. I am sorry to have to agree with you, but I can't help trying somehow to act as though I don't . . . "

My book, after the terrific social consciousness of Miller's, or the moving arguments in Paula Fox's fiction, or maybe Tom Wolfe's sprawling arrogant new novel, will surely be smeared for its oblivion to the world. What world?

JH, on learning of Sade's notorious death while fucking a goose with its neck in a drawer, says: "I suspect fowl play."

25 May

Phone interview with a journalist in Colorado. Two inadvertent gaffes from him. "Are you," he asked, "yet seventy?" A minute later: "Here in Boulder next week we're having a festival of American song, and I think one of yours is to be sung." Two decades ago such a festival would revolve around me; now years go by without one song—never mind a cycle—being heard in New York. I say this wistfully, not bitterly. Things change, and yes, I'll be seventy in 3½ years. One is replaced.

A sunset on my songs.

Apostrophes last Sunday featured journalists, including a cartoonist named (I think) Cabot, and a collection of his called *Les Cabot Defendu*, caricatures that never made it to the paper, because of his editors' sense of taste or libel. No, he has never regretted anything he's printed: front-page news is so much more vicious than his poor cartoons, etc. He's a young-looking fifty-five with a Cheshire grin and a giggle, not butch. He recounts this anecdote: *"Après la guerre j'ai cité Peyrefitte qui disait, 'Je n'ai pas été collabo. Je n'ai jamais couché avec un allemand.' "* The all-male enclave chuckles from out their comfortable heterosexuality, as my rusty ears miss the point—why would "I never slept with a German" sound gay, since the noun in English comprises both sexes? But of course in French it means German *man*. Yet the joke's not a mockery of Peyrefitte (the French all know he's gay) so much as a mockery of all homosexuality, which in Paris is still good for a laugh.

For the 50th anniversary of U-High's graduating class in Chicago:

On that June morning in 1940 we emerged from the Chapel as graduates—that is, as grown-ups. But judging now from snapshots my parents took, we looked awfully innocent, dolled up in maroon & white, dutifully clutching our diplomas, grinning, shuffling. During the ensuing 200 seasons some of us have covered the globe, speaking different tongues, writing symphonies, having love affairs. Others have stayed in Illinois, gotten rich, gotten divorced, or just gotten along. Still others have died—from the wars, from natural causes, or from their own hand. And the years fly by like a snowstorm. Yet don't we just become more of what we always were? Don't you feel a seamless continuity?

Off the top of my head, what I recall today about my time in the Lab School is a non-scholastic sequence of flashbacks: How Edith Harris dotted her "i's" with circles. How her sister wore high heels. How pretty Dorothy Goes published a story in *The Midway* about raiding the icebox, and how handsome Charles Kahn forever excelled at track. How Monsieur Bovée pointed out our mistakes with his forefinger and its terrible wart, and how Miss Lemon sported a natty suit of gray & pink linen. How Betty Gray sprinkled a perfume called Danger on her handkerchief while Dr. Frank took a bite from a snow apple to show us the fruit's ultrawhite flesh as we watched hungrily. How Miss Shepherd required us to parse a dry phrase on a golden afternoon when through the open window came a scent of lilac in Scammons Garden and a tinkling from the season's first Good Humor cart. How intense, and how sad, remain the smells of pencil shavings in math class, of okra soup in the lunchroom, of sweat in the lockers. How bright the sun shone on the day Billy Stickney died.

I covet these extracurricular minutiae more tenaciously than the educational program we were offered at our parents' expense, for the simple reason that, for an adolescent, the senses seem more urgent than sense. Yet I remember (sometimes more clearly than the day it was imparted) the classroom data too, even to what I did not know I knew. If Madame Green accorded me the very lowest grade in her sophomore course, what I nonetheless gleaned came in handy when, in 1949, I sailed for France and Morocco to begin a decade wherein each aspect of my verbal life would be conducted in the French language.

Except for Maggy Magerstadt, whom I see regularly, and Bruce Phemister and Perry O'Neil, whom I see occasionally, I've lost touch with the class of '40. But sometimes in strange cities I run across their children. Recently in San Francisco the manager of the Symphony, Kay Akos, announced: "You used to know my mother, Marian Weinberg." With an embarrassed thrill I recalled a hideous tango performed for some school show by Maggy and me, accompanied by Marian's skilled and witty pianism.

The reality of the past may change imperceptibly with each receding day, yet nothing's tougher than our concept of that past. For without memory, the present and the future could not exist.

At *Moses und Aron*, the young couple in front of us was rapt. "Hicks from Jersey," muttered Morris. When the curtain came down the audience rose up, including the couple in front of us, applauding wildly—everyone but Morris and me (we find standing ovations hickish).

"Would you mind sitting down," said Morris to the couple. "We can't see the stage."

Abashed, they complied. Minutes later, when the clapping subsided, they turned to say: "You are the rudest man we've ever seen."

To which Morris, unfazed, replied: "Yeah, well. You're probably from New Jersey."

19 July

Sondheim sent a tape of *Assassins*. It makes an iffy first impression. JH likens Sondheim to Paul Bowles. Neither gives an inch toward allowing affection into their work. An aloof meanness is ever there, not as a device but as an end in itself. Never let it be said (they seem to infer) that they are *susceptible*.

Well, JH's right, and he hates it. I like it. It's a pose (is it a pose?—yes, it's a pose—everything's a pose) that nevertheless asks to be admired or they wouldn't strike the pose in the first place. So yes, they *are* susceptible, they want appreciation.

Harold Arlen, though he probably never knew it, employed the same rhythm in "The Man That Got Away" as did Satie in the last movement of *Socrate*: in 4/4: and/one, two, three rest and/ one, two three, rest and/

She is a hasn't been.

Pardon = hard on.

Nantucket, Labor Day

JH can't bring himself to have Princess killed by lethal injection rather than take her back to the confines of the city apartment where she'll spend another winter peeing everywhere but in her box. I'm no less touched by JH's anguish at Princess's suffering, or worse, at the prospect of Sonny's eventual death and what it will do to JH, than by the untold suffering that Saddam Hussein (or for that matter President Bush) is prepared, as I write this, to cast over the globe. Am I a compassionate being? Not especially.

What *is* compassion? and how? and for how long?

14 October

Responding to a request about "The New Tonality," I submitted this reaction to the *Contemporary Music Review*, which they didn't print because I refused to sign an unthinkable copyright agreement.

I'm not very taken with the subject of tonality, my own or anyone else's. I've always assumed that the whole of music—indeed the whole of the universe—is tonal, and that assertions to the contrary "protesteth too much." All music, including Boulez and Babbitt, is tonal to my ear, and I'm convinced (but can't prove it) that everyone, including Babbitt and Boulez, hears music tonally. Should a score appear wildly complicated, I listen simply by imposing a subliminal pedal-point beneath the wildness, and the complicated filigree then falls into place. By tonal I mean, of course, derived from the overtone series—a cosmological given. To deny the inescapability of this series' power is merely to admit the power through denial.

As to the term "the new tonality," I confess in good faith that I don't know about it. Is it a current trend? It feels suspiciously like a reversion, and quite un-new. I am old enough to retrace the trends of my own generation, and to realize that they recapitulate ontologically the trends of music's history for the past 1500 years. The history is not one of progress (art doesn't progress, at least not in the sense of improving), but of continual back-&-forth: the Eternal Return. We evolve perpetually from harmonic periods into contrapuntal periods, into harmonic, into contrapuntal, into harmonic, forever. A contrapuntal period is always complex, and is always superseded by the antidote of a harmonic period like the one we're currently enjoying. I would suppose this was common knowledge, and that "the new tonality" is but another incarnation.

Listened to *Assembly and Fall*, the 25-minute unrevised version, for the first time in a decade. What an overreaching, pretentious mess. It's my most diffuse, willfully ugly piece, aimless and exasperating. But the last five minutes are masterful, frightening and original in their evocation of hopeless eradication.

A 20-year-old says that in London "they're talking about the New Complexity." After a shock of disbelief, my reaction is ho-hum. The wheel turns forward, then backward, and I'm too old for the redundant trip. Similarly, when the Persian Gulf "crisis" began last August, I felt—leave me out of the same age-old macho mistakes. The earth won't learn until Homo sapiens evolves into a new genus.

Apparently, Lenny's last words were "What is this?" (They stand up well against Henry James's "So here it is at last, the distinguished thing," or Cocteau's feebler, "Le bateau sombre.")

The court jester is often an angel of death. Mendy Wager, intimate of the Bernsteins for half a century, played word games in three languages, read Job aloud, and generally commiserated for days, until Lenny, exhausted, unable to breathe, was given another shot. (A shot of what?) His knees buckled, he said "What is this?" and died in Mendy's arms.

It's hard to concentrate on other things. He took up a lot of room. Jules Renard on his fortieth birthday: "I can no longer die young." But Lenny Bernstein died young last Sunday at 72.

Shiva today at six.

Women still, with some justice, complain that they are singled out as second-class citizens. But aren't men, who have no choice in the matter, singled out as cannon fodder? The unknowing faces of adolescent males in the Persian Gulf are as wrenching as the pictures of mutilated boys in our Civil War. Innocent civilians, as opposed to . . . what? Guilty soldiers?

21 Oct.

The 1950s:

They can't cross frontiers: Henri Sauguet, Henri de Montherlant.

A long list on both sides.

At the wake—the Shiva—chez Bernstein on the 16th, as I'm leaving I say to someone in the foyer who's about to enter: "Everyone in there's unfocused, as though waiting for the guest of honor." Harold Brodkey, overhearing, says, "But the guest of honor is dead," then turns to see who'd made the first remark, recognizes me, and rushes away. His remark is startlingly obvious, considering he's a Genius; and his avoidance of me (why?) is leadenly un-European.

Arthur Peters, who is, I guess, heterosexual, says in his adoring preface to *Jean Cocteau and the French Scene*, ". . . Cocteau was all these things, and more. He was also homosexual, and a smoker of opium .. . . " (Like saying that Einstein was "also Jewish and played the violin.") He doesn't realize that to other homosexuals, homosexuality is not exotic, or even apropos.

23 October

Sixty-seventh birthday. I can no longer die middle-aged. Morning, rain, the first fall weather. Got up four times to pee. Dentist in an hour.

Tonight, dine chez Pia Gilbert with JH and the Perles. Tomorrow, drive to Nantucket.

I have no charm. I used to have, but no longer.

This afternoon, rehearse again (maybe) with John Cheek. Then collect photos at Sotheby's. (The two Man Ray portraits, which we'd thought would bring $40,000, brought in nothing.)

What one work would I take to a desert island?

What one work can I not live without? The usual answer is *War and Peace* or the B-minor Mass. Well, I could live without them—the fact of them is in my head and can be revived anytime. I would take my own work-in-progress. (I might take Balzac or Proust, however, since who but a professor reads them clear through seventy times or even thrice, the way one listens infinitely to a musical piece?)

25 October

For *Opera News*:

My least favorite opera? If you mean one from the accepted repertory rather than a passing dud, I elect *Moses und Aron*, for three reasons. First, true opera is never about idea more than about action, and this one displays nothing but raw intelligence. Second, Schoenberg may have had genius, but he hadn't much talent, less charm, and no sense of vocal writing. Third: I balk at unanimous praise. *Moses und Aron* has been everywhere lauded for its difficulty, as though difficulty, once surmounted, revealed unquestioned beauty. But all that's revealed here is the emperor's old clothes.

GOODBYE MY FANCY, A Program Note

Can half a century slide by so fast? Only yesterday, as a Chicago kid, I was being deflowered in many a manner, mainly cultural, in Orchestra Hall where, through a fluke, I was exposed to contemporary music simultaneously with the standard classics. From the start I saw—*heard*—that the present was every bit as vital as the past, a truth made obvious when the two were interlarded, despite Education's efforts to sanctify musical history. 1940 was the Symphony's fiftieth anniversary and conductor Frederick Stock commissioned composers throughout the globe to celebrate. That heady season offered, alongside Brahms and Beethoven, pre-mières by Stravinsky, Chávez, Milhaud, and hometown boys like Sowerby and Carpenter. Had someone asked, "In fifty years will you, a hometown boy, be invited to participate in the centennial?" I'd have said, "Why not?" My self-doubts were never about talent (though like most artists I grow anxious without constant reassurance) but about earning a living. Luck has often been with me during the following decades, after quitting the Midwest in 1943—the year of Bette Davis's movie *Now, Voyager*. That title, borrowed from Walt Whitman ("The untold want by life and land ne'er granted, / Now voyager sail thou forth and find"), is also the title for the first of the three movements in my new oratorio, *Goodbye My Fancy*, commissioned by the Chicago Symphony on the occasion of its hundredth anniversary.

Half of my entire musical output is for chorus, about a hundred pieces, and half of those in turn are based on so-called sacred texts. (Yes, I am an atheist, but if I do not believe in God I do believe in the Belief that has at times spawned good religious art.) Of secular pieces *Goodbye My Fancy* is my twelfth for chorus with orchestra, and, at 55 minutes, my most sizeable single work other than opera. It is also the fourteenth time I've extensively used Whitman texts for music.

The first movement, "Now, Voyager," is divided into seven sections, each the setting of stanzas, mainly optimistic, from Whitman's early years. The second movement, "The Strayed Dead" ("There they lie, strewing the fields, the varieties of strayed dead reaped by the mighty reapers . . . "), is in five sections culled from the prose of Whitman's Civil War diary. The third movement, "The Harvest According" ("Life is the tillage, and Death is the harvest according"), in seven sections, opens with more prose from the diary, "Sunday with the Insane," then returns to the philosophic verse of the poet's old age.

This symphonic scenario is cast for alto and baritone solos, acting alone or with each other, or with the chorus and instruments. On another occasion the alto role might be sung by a man to a more Whitmanesque, if not Roremesque, effect.

Goodbye My Fancy, composed and orchestrated in Nantucket and New York City between March and August 1988, was given its première on 8 November 1990, by the Chicago Symphony in Orchestra Hall, with Wendy White, mezzo, and John Cheek, bass, conducted by Leonard Slatkin with chorus prepared by my dear old friend Margaret Hillis.

12 Nov.

Chicago, welcoming and nostalgic, old friends, old neighborhoods. The four performances were in all ways satisfying—although I never heard the last five minutes, since each time I was rushing from the box to the backstage labyrinths to take a bow. John Corigliano official host, Rosemary and Jim Kendrick star guests.

16 November

Brochure of Matta's paintings states that the artist "insisted on a direct equivalence between his depiction of natural formations and the functioning of the human psyche. 'Inscapes,' as Matta termed them—that is, landscapes of the mind rather than depictions of the phenomenal world—they conformed to the principle of what he termed 'Psychological Morphology.' " Well, well. Inscapes. Is that where Aaron Copland got his title?

And did Christopher Davis get the plot for his first novel, *There Was a Little Girl*, about a raped girl whom everyone turns against including her family, and finally the rapist himself, from Simenon's painful novel *La Mort de Belle* (1952), about a professor in whose house a student is murdered and he, innocent, is accused, even by his wife? Or from Janet Frame's *Yellow Flowers in the Antipodean Room*, about a man who's buried and comes back to life, like Lazarus, and is ostracized? But then, there are only seven plots.

Cocteau's *La Farce du château* depicts two pre-adolescent brothers who dress up in sheets as a joke to scare a friend of their father who was away; but when they arrive at his door, they hear him making love to their mother, and are chastened forevermore. The farce was written in the early 1930s, when Rosemary and I, peeking through the kitchen door, saw Paul Tillich kissing Mother, once when Father was away.

For a Frenchman to practice:
She wound the thread into her wound, / She tried to wind a rose in too. / The wind rose as she choked the Czech, / She brought the tough bough through, / Though it caught upon the sheath.
Style in kids on drugs = poise on boys on poison
Bough bows and boughs bow
Wish beaux bows and beau bows
Winter's everywhere, the whore's all hoar, the rhyme's all rime.

For the NYPL on Nov. 26, 1990:
Who am I to presume to stand here for an hour and command your attention? No one *knows* who he is, but one *can* know *what* he is, and the What might lead us to locate the Who. Yet artists are the sole professionals in our society who cannot be collectively defined; no sooner is a definition coined than along comes some sport to upset the apple cart. Still, since most twentieth-century intellectuals have never met a composer, I will try to depict, through words alone, what it means for this one composer to be a composer.

Obviously a composer is best defined by his music, and you have half-heard some of it during the past few minutes. But I am un-American in that I wear two hats: those of writing and of musicking. I am essentially a composer who writes, however, not an author who composes, the difference being that I earn my living through music, not prose.

I am also a radical to conservatives by being a gay atheistic pacifist, and a conservative to radicals by being an aristocratic believer in tonality as the core of all art.

I am a combination of my mother—who was illogical, instinctive, emotionally unstable, a pessimist who all through life petitioned for equal rights, and who died, as we all do, of a broken heart—and of my father—who was logical, intelligent, emotionally stable, an optimist, a medical economist who in the 1930s co-founded Blue Cross—and who died of a broken heart.

I have two convictions, which on the face of it may seem glib, but which dominate my sense of what is art. The first is:
The Universe as French and German
The second is:
Music of a Country Depends On the Speech of That Country
Much of what I've said has been noted more succinctly in twelve books. Of

these, four are diaries, the others are belles lettres. For the next 25 minutes I'll read to you, not from the diaries (it makes no sense to read aloud from what has been written because it couldn't be spoken), nor yet from set pieces, like, say, portraits of Mussorgsky or Gershwin or Noël Coward, or discussions of trends. Rather, I'll pluck from out of the past three decades, random paragraphs, sometimes mere sentences, about how it feels to be a composer.

After that, we can have questions, if you're willing.

New Year's Eve

The reason for the ever-widening gaps in this diary is that I'm supposed to be writing a memoir for Simon & Schuster. All the material, not to mention the time, that might otherwise go into these pages about today, is going, far more honed, into the melancholy of resurrection.

1991

Abscess on gum. Dentist unavailable. I squeeze out the pus, sleep well, which is rare, and dream, which is standard.

Film shot of man dying alone on desert island, P.O.V. the man. Gulls hover to pluck out his eyes. Bird approaches lens. Pecks. Scarlet spewing, turns to gray, blurs to black. Fade out.

Epistolary exchange with Joel Connaroe about being against the Guggenheim Foundation's soliciting of funds from former beneficiaries. Artists are not in the business of financially supporting one another, and if the Foundation now founders, ask the Vanderbilts or Whitneys, or else just call it a day. Joel disagrees. We have a masterful correspondence.

12 January

Felled by flu, too achy to think or eat but not to watch television. Simultaneous showing of *Death in Venice* and *Lolita*. Flipping channels I stare at these two tales of wise old fools and their sly young crushes. *Lolita* wins hands down. *Death in Venice* is too "shocked and respectful," too heavily meaningful and falsely Mahlerian, with Dirk Bogarde too flimsy to carry much weight. But the Nabokov remains most odd indeed, is tight and senseful, with James Mason wildly strong.

When I mention to, for example, S., who is Jewish, that one of Rosemary's children married a jet black Negro, another married a Chinese, and a third married—consecutively—two Jews, does S. take this as . . . not anti-Semitic, but as my thinking of Jews as The Other? No doubt I do. How often does she (or Ellen, or Eugenie, or any of my cultivated and broadminded straight friends), when "we" leave the room, mention—perhaps not kindly, or maybe even kindly, but still pityingly—things about homosexuality that we might get huffy about?

16 January

War has begun in Iraq.

1 Feb.

In search of a bit of bedtime reading I took *Jeux* off the shelf for the first time in years, and was quickly reminded of what I'd always felt: What a lot of 3/8! (The same effect could be had with 6/8, with half as many barlines.) Since Debussy could do no wrong, I report this as observation, not criticism. But of course he could do wrong. And is *Jeux* really the great unheralded masterpiece it's sometimes called?

7 February

The Beaux Arts Trio, for whom *Spring Music* was written as a gift from Carnegie Hall, have had the music for close to a year without giving a sign of its receipt, much less of whether they like it. Since the première is tomorrow, I swallowed my pride last week and phoned the Trio. It hadn't occurred to them that the composer might want to hear it. Rehearsal yesterday.

Spring Music lasts 31½ minutes—seven minutes longer than I'd projected—and I'm glad: Its imminent public failure will carry more weight.

Axiomatic to state that composers, or any "creative" artists, are self-pollinators. But yesterday, during the ample tryout, it seemed that, although the composer alone conceives and gives birth to his work, that work is nonetheless not fertilized until the performers attack it.

JH, fogged-in in Nantucket, must miss dining with Frankie and Bill Schumann this evening.

16 February

As I was napping, Gloria Vanderbilt phoned out of the blue long-ago. Nothing's changed except her interim tragedies. We've made a lunch date for Mortimer's next Monday. I never go out to lunch but, well . . . Maguerite Lamkin will join us.

Forty minutes after her call, a messenger delivered four books authored by her. They are in breathless prose about rich girl concerns (clothes, men, lunch) in a style nicely satirized by Maggie Paley in *Bad Manners*.

The war goes on. People (Sono Osato) reiterate that Saddam Hussein must be repressed because "he even kills his own people." Does this mean it is okay to kill people across the border? Did we not kill our own people in the Civil War? Who are our people? Aren't the Puerto Rican Catholics down the street our own people? Or the Japs, or Negroes, or indeed the Iraqi, two blocks away?

Complications of Third Quartet (and payment) equal those of the Trio. The standard Guarneri "real-people" groups are as difficult as Mod Music Specialists. In program note for quartet, delineate the 12-note row of each instrument. The first movement *Chaconne* represents (like Debussy's *Nuages*) the indifferent sky (with the neutral second violin) upon which are etched thunderclouds, an airplane, a hawk. But did I know this while composing? The Trio too's based tonally on a row. Find these (obvious) rows in the notebook before they vanish forever.

The speed limit's sixty. A cop arrests her for going sixty-five. She explains that yesterday she went only fifty-five, so doesn't that even things out?

It's only his first murder. Can't he have another chance?

Like *Jeux* the other morning, I grabbed any old book in a rush to the john, to discover upon my lap H. L. Mencken's *Diary*, which for years had sat unread in the shelf. Opening to the index, I sought, as I have by rote for fifty years, the name of Ravel. Of course it wasn't there. Yet on turning inadvertently to page 41 I find this 1931 reference to a Koussevitzky concert: "Willa Cather surprised me by saying that [Mahler's Ninth] Symphony was too much for her, but that she liked the Ravel. The latter was a very cheap piece of trash. I had always thought of La Cather as a musician, but she told me that she really knew very little about music, and thus preferred Ravel's obvious banalities to Mahler's very fine writing." (Three very's in two sentences.) Well, Mahler's not in the index either (although Frank Swinnerton and Louisa Caskey—whoever they may be—each have one entry), which shows us where Knopf's priorities lie. Music's low on everyone's list.

For six weeks now my right elbow joint has ached, sometimes extremely, from either arthritis or tendonitis. For six weeks I've also been pondering a left-hand concerto for Gary Graffman.

18 February

Lunch with Gloria Vanderbilt at Mortimer's on Lexington Avenue. Time stopped when last we met. Today we finished a sentence begun a quarter-century ago, and opened a new paragraph.

Also present: Marguerite Lamkin, like Gloria but less stunning, and Ben Brantley, like me in a black shirt but without a pink tie. Artichokes, soufflé, salad, crême brûlées, strong espressos.

The past few nights I've perused her four books, along with Eugenia Zukerman's. G's are more personal and more "crafted" than I rather dismissively noted last week; like herself they are at once willful and vulnerable, haphazard and unfocused, but finally touching. Eugenia's *Taking the Heat*, far more professional, is equally autobiographical despite her denials, but she is tough where Gloria is tender.

After lunch we leave the others and walk up Lexington to 91st, during which my nipples grow cold and ache. Gloria is skilled in avoiding glances from passersby (mostly well-dressed females, and nobody after 87th Street) by staring at me, or at her green suede shoes. Her new house is less imposing from outside than her others I've known—not unlike my parents' house at 2213 Delancey, which they bought for $20,000 in 1946 and sold for the same price thirteen years later on moving from Philadelphia to Pittsburgh. Inside, though, all is luxury. Ground floor contains a glassed-in studio with her own Matisse-Avery pictures and an adjoining kitchen garden, genre Vermeer. Second floor boasts The Emerald Room; all objects are green (like Alice Tully's crimson room where, like the Masque of Red Death, even the books are chosen solely for their bloody binding). Third and fourth floors have sitting rooms, bedrooms, bathrooms with copious colored tubs in their centers, libraries (Katherine Mansfield, James Salter), and wardrobes with dozens of shoes and sweaters—"But I always end up wearing the same thing." Not a soul in sight, except the darling paper-trained Lhasa named Anna who frisks beside us during the tour. So when Gloria opens a mysterious door on floor five to reveal three women at desks, it is like Joseph K. opening a door onto three hundred typists in *The Trial*. These women are, respectively, curved over Gloria's income tax, her correspondence, and the disordered manuscript of her new novel (about a murdered call-girl named Starr Faithfull) being transcribed into a word processor.

Of Gloria's four sons, two have turned out sorrowfully. Christopher, the younger of the pair by Stokowski, after intensive Thorazine therapy, vanished fifteen years "into Vermont somewhere." Some time later he sent a letter which, because it looked like "the script of a tarantula dipped in black ink," G. took to be a suicide note, but which turned out to be a denial, a total rejection, of his family. Carter, the younger of the pair by Wyatt Cooper, two years ago took his own life, whether by choice or accident Gloria cannot be certain. She reiterates, and reiterates, "the heat that day was oppressive, the suffocating, the sleep, the dreaming," and she cries, but pulls herself quickly together. Carter and she that morning had been reading a story in *The New Yorker* about a man who kills himself, in front of his family, with glass shards in his brain. Carter's asthma attacks presumably required big amphetamine doses. Why would he have returned home in the stifling afternoon, raced upstairs "like an athlete," rushed to the balcony (this was in Gracie Square), hung onto the edge with Gloria frantic in pursuit. "Shall I call your doctor?" "Do you know his number?" But when she returned from the phone he had dropped to his death.

An hour after I reach home, Gloria phones to ask if I heard music in my head all the time. (She seems bemused by my negative reaction to a set of chimes in her dining room, which she had banged into motion.) Well, I guess I'm never not working, even when talking or eating. Surely Stokowski was similar? After another hour, she phones about *The Nantucket Diary*, my lunch-hour gift into which she was already deep. "You had asthma, like Carter . . . Your book is filled with my demon lover!" Who is that? "Harry Benson."

Like Marie-Laure, the only other famous rich woman I've known well, Gloria never pretends not to believe she's the center of the universe. But JH says I'm the same.

20 February

For one embarrassed minute I turned to the Grammy Awards and witnessed Bob Dylan babbling like Donald Duck on *The Gong Show*.

21 Feb.

The Chanticleer male chorus wonderfully sang my *Pilgrim Stranger* at the YMHA, during which there was a bomb scare.

23 Feb.

Ellen Zwilich's new Oboe Concerto—expert, gloomy, theatrical, but without drama. JH feels she can't last. Why? Because there's nothing to oppose—true acceptance comes only after some dose of rejection, while Ellen is nearly everyone's darling and the dissenters are merely indifferent. I feel, however, that her theatricality (without which no art is art, including still lifes) is camouflaged and needs deciphering.

Supper later at the Côte Basque (where as we entered, a female diner was being removed on a stretcher) hosted by the intelligent and affable Martin Segal.

26 Feb.

Snow. JH, in Nantucket since yesterday (he was sole passenger on plane) to check on the new expensive roof, is having trouble returning to New York today. Not just the weather, but more bomb scares.

Massive insomnia. Alone in the house, except for Sonny and the cats. On television, nothing but the war. All the old movies are war movies, and all the new news is suspect reports of flag-waving patriotism. I too am patriotic; it's my country too. Naps, two a day.

Two hours of root canal yesterday, probably unneeded as cure for a vague but persistent ache. Like the inadvertent bombing last week of a civilian bomb shelter.

When *The Advocate* asked me who might portray Ned Rorem on the screen, I unhesitatingly replied "Faye Dunaway," adding that no explanation was necessary. I have since been chided for giving a facetious reply, but I was merely following an old maxim, "Ask a silly question, get a silly answer." In fact, my answer was meant as only half-facetious. Let me set the record straight:

No living or recently dead person can be convincingly portrayed to anyone who knows or cares about them. For example, *Lady Sings the Blues* has little to do with Billie Holiday and much to do with Diana Ross. Ross has too much identity to leave way for Holiday; the latter's tragic career, what's more, is obtainable in two minutes with any of her recordings.

Can one portray oneself? Nobody is more different from oneself than oneself at another time. Sophia Loren demonstrated the point embarrassingly by taking the lead in TV's *The Sophia Loren Story*. (Think of the ego involved.)

If it must be done, best to go against type. Not that Faye Dunaway is so different from me. But if Bernhardt can play Hamlet, etc.

If no one is more different from oneself that oneself at another time, everyone's life is an act. We play ourselves.

27 February

I know all about singing except how to sing.

Taking over Paul Sperry's class in twentieth-century song at Juilliard. Describe how I do this. Setting them at ease. Difference between male & female singers, as distinct from male & female oboists or pianists. Men in women's songs. *Les Bonnes*. Nobody knew Genet's name. Four out of twenty knew Plath's. My usual spiel about how Americans should sing American music. It's all such rote to me now, that only too late did I realize that most of the faces gazing at me were Korean.

Funny Face on television. Dated, pretentious, shrill, and offensive (Kay Thompson's chic preemptive rudeness). Audrey Hepburn's intellectual wimpiness cloys. Nor can I bear Fred Astaire—much less the Casals-like mystique surrounding him—with that nasty smugness that sets the teeth on edge.

Yet on thinking it over, Hepburn's big solo dance in the *cave* is hard to forget (she predates Michael Jackson by 40 years), and the duet between Astaire and Thompson at the party is irresistible. Credit Stanley Donen.

Eight years since I've had sex with another mortal. I do masturbate weekly (doctor's orders), with always more or less the same fantasy. A person kneels (is it me? yet I'm also always observing) before the crotch of a very male unshaven but otherwise shadowy form wearing what the French call *salopettes*. Pungent aroma, sweat, smegma, locker room. One-sided blow job . . . As a youth, I'd be getting fucked, and am forever a "bottom." But the image blurs with the years into something impersonal yet awfully erotic . . .

March

Now that Pauline Kael's left *The New Yorker*, might she find time to compose an essay on movie music? How does music color a scene? Can music that so moved us then, move us now? And are the scores for *The Letter* and *Sunset Boulevard* just fustian today? How has music changed? First use of piano as an orchestra instrument. (*The Fallen Sparrow*.) Does Satie work in *Bad Lands*? Why is Virgil's music so ineffectual in *The Goddess*? Because his sense of Kansas lies in his phony folk tunes, not in the deranged glamour of Hollywood? Why is the music for *Baby Jane* or *The Big Chill* or Kenneth Anger's *Fireworks* so wrong, at least for a musical viewer?

JH: "Brad Gooch got where he is because of his looks. Evans Mirageas got where he is in spite of his looks."

With Gloria: On March 10 in Town Hall to hear my Third Quartet. "You know, I don't think I've ever been here before. And you know, I haven't been to a classical concert since I was married to Leopold."

31 April

To the *Will Rogers Follies* with John Simon. Later I tell JH that the key song, "I Never Met a Man I Didn't Like," seems to have been drawn by Cy Coleman right out of the opening of Barber's *First Essay for Orchestra*.

JH: "I never met a man who didn't bore me."

> *The erect member*
> *So lewdishly cool*
> *In April twixt us,*
> *Glimpsed in December*
> *Seems a pink toadstool*
> *Steaming with mixed pus.*

7 May

My name is in the *Times* crossword again, ROREM, and the clue is "Composer of 'Penny Arcade'" (35 across). Since the song-cycle *Penny Arcade* (1948) is unpublished and nobody remembers its existence except me, how could the editor, Eugene T. Maleska, have . . . ?

With Sondheim the other night: We both agreed that you can't always tell a book by its cover. We both did agree that Hitler hadn't much charm, but I suggested that Saddam Hussein was not without eroticism, while Steve thought that maybe Mengele was likeable looking. Meanwhile, many a saint is a bloody bore, and none of them is sexy. Beginning with Saint Sebastian.

Finished long article on American Opera for July's *Opera News*. About eight thousand words. JH finds it hack journalism and not worthy of putting in a collection.

Bored, testy, critical, can't get interested in the many musical projects that pay the rent, sore Achilles heel still after three months, and nervous prostate. But I feel rather good.

Tomorrow Rosemary's 69th birthday.

Ashbery party, with Gloria chez Plimpton. Also JH chez Gloria. Friday, revival of *The Robbers* after 35 years.

Seldom a word here about the sad world at large. The hundred thousand Iraqi slaughtered, the hundred thousand Bangladeshians drowned, the wayward ways of Bush & Quayle.

Virgil used to say, *Les faits divers*, they're forever the same. And when Gide was criticized for writing of an Arab boy in his bed rather than about the plight of the Arabs, no one replied, "The poor are always with us," but the Arab boy may never come again. Or Gide . . .

Write of Gloria's letter to John Ashbery, of his not answering, get quote from his poem from her . . . And of Plimpton.

9 May

Death of Serkin, who played *Une Barque sur l'océan* (an odd choice) in Carnegie c. 1946.

10 May

I will speak for no more than three minutes, I promise.

All my life I have practiced two professions simultaneously, being a writer as well as a composer (which in America is called spreading yourself thin). My musical reputation seems to center around sung works: over the decades I have set nearly 200 authors to music, some of them many times. So occasionally people ask if I set my own words to music. The answer is no. Whatever my vocal pieces are worth, I flatter myself that I've never used bad literature. Now, if I, the writer, could come up with something good enough to attract me, the composer, I wouldn't need to be a composer. In fact, my prose and my music satisfy different needs, and aim in different directions. The sole exception to all this is *The Robbers*.

During the summer of 1956, long before I'd published a book or had any firm policies about word-setting, I thought it might be fun to do my own libretto. Taking a theme from Chaucer's *The Pardoner's Tale* about three highwaymen who murder a fourth for his money, and who, in a fight over that money, end up killing each other, I confected this cynical little melodrama. The scene is a sordid second-story room of an inn. The three thieves, the corpse at their feet, pass the time bickering as they wait for nightfall when they can go their separate ways without being apprehended.

This gloomy skit, with its musical illustration, seemed tight and telling to me. But that autumn, when I showed it to the canny Marc Blitzstein, he rolled his eyes. "You've gotten lost in libretto-land," said he, "with all those stilted archaic turns of phrase." Without changing a note, he thereupon took it upon himself to translate the entire text "from English to English."

Still, when *The Robbers* was produced by the Mannes School the following year, it flopped. I placed it in a drawer, forgot about it for 34 years, and never again put my own words to music. Then Stephen Radcliffe resurrected a copy from Boosey & Hawkes, which he now presents unstaged. Since I wrote *The Robbers* at age 32, I cannot claim it as juvenilia, nor yet, like Rossini, as a sin of old age. It's a one-shot deal, revived as a museum piece.

It lasts 28 minutes, is cast for three male singers, and scored for 13 instruments. The title page contains this epigraph from Chaucer:

> *Thus ended these two homicides in woe;*
> *Died thus the treacherous poisoner also.*

May, Nantucket

Gloria's voice on the phone: an urgent seductive whisper with a slight stammer, very uppercrust. While the Kurds perish in the hills of Iraq, she talks of taking her doll—the rare and beautiful one that Wyatt gave her—to the Doll Hospital because of a crack in its face. After the expensive repair the doll, formerly a wistful nineteenth-century creature, now resembled Ann Miller. The doctor and nurse had no notion of why Gloria complained.

And there's a leak in her basement. For the past 24 hours (it's the weekend), everyone must refrain from flushing the toilets, and brush teeth in Evian water.

A mammoth fly floats atop the soda in JH's glass, which he left on the kitchen table an hour ago. He flushes it down the sink. Ten minutes later the groggy fly staggers up from the drain. JH is so moved by this instinct of self-preservation that he cups the fly in his hands and flings it out the window.

But last September, though we were at first respectful of the bees in the dining room, we ended by swatting them to death, dozens of them, as they built their hive in the eaves. This was for *our* self-preservation. In theory, this goes against all I believe about pacifism and ecology.

JH says to call my memoirs *As Time Goes By* and quote song.

4 July

This evening as usual after supper we took Sonny to the Children's Beach so that, for fifteen minutes, he could romp without his leash, and exhaust himself for the night. I watched JH as he in turn watched Sonny digging a hole, and thought that JH was as handsome as I've ever seen him in the twenty-four years we've lived together. I know that he thinks I'll die before he does; logic's on his side—I'm nearly sixteen years older. But I feel (and dread) he'll go first.

The anxiety of beauty. (Whose beauty, yours or mine?)

Supersleuth, 1937, ends with "comic" electric chair.

28 July

Visit at 4 to GV to see her pictures—around 25 new lithographic posters, of dolls mostly, and some picnic scenes. More Matisse than Milton Avery, edibly and violently colorful—pumpkin and tangerine cascading with strawberry and lime. She gave me two heavily framed gems, a whimsical cat, which holds its own next to Joe Brainard's huge collage, and a Chagallesque bourgeois scene, which we're taking to Nantucket.

Talk of "truth" in our writing. She doesn't want me to include LSD and her father. Rented house in Southampton for six weeks, $125,000. Inherited $2 million at 20. Lost it all, unscrupulous lawyers. Earned it back.

Stokowski. Bitterness with divorce. He was anti-Semitic. "What was he like?," I ask. "I never really knew him," she answers.

Lunch with Troy Peters re. his copy of my *Left Hand Concerto*. He says most male flutists are gay. (Remember this when discussing Kinsey.)

Haunted by the hideous murders in Milwaukee of young men by a young man, one Jeffrey Dahmer, who tortured and decapitated his many victims, then boiled their heads, the easier to peel the flesh from the skulls, which he retained as trophies. I'm haunted, because in his newspaper photos Dahmer appears, to me, irresistibly seductive.

4 August

Return of JH with Frank. JH plays tape of this morning's service in NY: two of Milhaud's *Chansons Hébraïques* which bring Nell Tangeman into this room after 43 years, and the trio from Bach's *Magnificat* with three of his female singers. JH says he'd admonished them: "Don't perform. The music is just happening." As distinct from opera, which *should* be performed.

Heavy rain after massive drought.

Worried about JH's continuing jaw problem. He will see Dr. Voorhees on Tuesday.

13 August

I, age 67, in shorts and a sweaty T-shirt, take Sonny for his morning walk. On Sunset Hill is parked a truck, the rear-view mirror jutting off to one side. No one is about, so I place the leash-handle over my wrist, stoop to place my face adjacent to the mirror, with both hands begin adjusting my hair, then squeeze a blackhead in my nose as Sonny starts to shit against the wheel. At this moment the truck-driver emerges from across the way and walks swiftly toward me . . .

18 August

Gloomy Sunday. Do you remember that Hungarian song, popularized in the late 1930s by Artie Shaw, Billie Holiday, and others, which was said to have had the same suicidal effect as *Werther* on a whole generation?

JH declares straightforwardly that, despite our sixteen-year age difference, we'll probably both go ga-ga at the same time, in about twenty years (generous estimate!), given our four parents' histories.

Then I declare, wistfully but not bitterly, that in the ken of the public, literary as well as musical, I'm a thing of the past, if not quite forgotten. JH disputes this, which is kind of him, but the facts are clear: my songs are never sung anymore, and my name is never cited in areas (France and Morocco in the 1950s) where . . .

One of the cats' dishes this morning seethed with maggots. I've never seen maggots—tiny white short worms by the seeming hundreds, squirming. I buried them, and cleaned the basement. Sultry heat.

The autobiography is a great chore. I pursue it *à contre coeur* because I can't afford to give back the advance.

20 August

While waiting for Hurricane Bob yesterday, as the dry winds were mounting and the town was battening windows, Previn called to ask if the Beaux Arts had exclusivity for my trio, *Spring Music*, because he's programmed it for next season in Caramoor and elsewhere. This made me feel wanted, for a change. He finds the L.H. Concerto (which he's scheduled to conduct in early '93) v. difficult, very cheatable, i.e., he himself would use two hands if no one were looking.

My name in *Times* crossword puzzle yesterday. I'm always vaguely saddened by this. It means it won't appear again for several months.

The hurricane was—is—devastating. The whole island is a mess, a direct hit, giant trees uprooted obscenely like wisdom teeth torn from the gums—wounds bleeding green in the pavement. Except green no more—the wind was for hours without a drop of rain and left the vegetation etoliated (or however it's spelled). Our property will take fifteen years to reconstruct itself. With money. Rae Gabis, who I called, says that the Vineyard's worse: no water and no electricity, and no idea of when these will resume.

The sound of unapologetic people chewing and swallowing.

5 August

Will Parker has AIDS. He sent this news (not entirely unexpected) in a long handwritten note. Wants me & others (Hoiby, Adams, Harbison, Argento, Hundley) to write songs "about AIDS" for him to sing in a fund-raising (for AIDS) recital. Macabre. Called Lee, also Hundley. Lee still frothing about my review, 18 years ago, of *Summer and Smoke*. Thinks I was getting even with him for something. I said no, I just didn't like the piece. He said (and this is part of his ESTian belief), "If you can't say something good about someone, best to say nothing at all." Which is why I don't talk about Hitler.

Klondike Annie on television. How I remember, indelibly, each frame from the old days, without having realized then, as now, 55 years later, how full of holes is the story, how tame Mae West's *répliques*. For you who never saw the original, a crucial scene is excised toward the start, between Mae's planned escape, and her boarding the boat. Not shown, and properly destroyed, is her Chinese master's saying, in her presence, to a lackey: "Prepare a lime that will burn to nothing the orbs of she who would betray her love." To Mae: "Your eyes are to be burned out." Close-up of Mae's eyes. They embrace. During embrace, she removes the dagger (which we saw in an earlier scene) from its sheath at his waist, and stabs him in the back.

27 August

The hurricane and the Russian Revolution occurred simultaneously, not canceling each other out, but in. Since then the phone lines work sporadically. Both toilets are clogged. The new electric typewriter, I just can't get the hang of. House guests. Break down. (Chas. Horton & weird friend.) Above all, my urinary problems augment—twice an hour or so, and so little comes out, after five dribbly minutes. And the dreary autobiography for S&S! Nothing interests me much anymore.

Dream. The self-sculpting girl. Out of thin air a pair of hands play with each other, mold and scrape each other, arms appear, a torso, an entire body and a pretty head, a statue, a moving statue. The head, smiling, rests its chin upon a platform, covers its self with a sheet, so as not to be recognized when "they" arrive. She stares into a store window. Meanwhile, I am a giant ball of yarn rolling up, then down, a steep hill, between epochs, unreeling the strands into the past, then into the present.

31 August

Nonsense on the *Times* front page about homosexual males having a smaller hypothalamus than heterosexual males. One foresees spats: "My hypothalamus is bigger than yours."

1 September

Alone on the island. JH en route to Kansas City by car for third time, re. ailing parents.

Caught the last eight minutes of *Stand and Deliver*, a "noble" film about barrio students motivated finally to pass, with flying colors, a calculus examination. As victory is announced, hero Olmos walks into the distance, and the rock-music soundtrack swells gloriously. So much for education in America.

8 September

Front page of the *Times Book Review* devoted to Martha Graham, a 3000-word paean on her depth, influence, articulation, and originality, without a word about music, much less naming even one composer among a hundred who helped define her.

Nantucket, 26 September

Heavy sad rains all day, simultaneously nourishing and destroying the vegetation.

Dined with Gloria, Polly, and Stan Stokowski on the 15th. Stan's weird divorce—with Ivy falling in love with a man met by computer. Stan late to GV's because taken in by a scam near the Museum of Mod Art. His handsome vulnerability, as son of two *monstres sacrés*. I gave him tapes of the two pieces of mine (*Eagles* and *Pilgrims*) his father conducted . . . Tea Party Wednesday with Sondheim et al. . . . The dubious Alcalay parents . . . Everything while feeling wretched with prostate aches. Tomorrow the cytoscopy. Will I ever be the same again? And JH goes off to New York.

29 September

Traveling from NY to Philly to Boston (where John Williams conducts my little "Frolic" with the Pops) to Nantucket, but can't get away from my body. I hate my body. No work for weeks, though trying to orchestrate the concerto. Depressed. Can I sweat it out until Friday the 13th of December, when operation is scheduled here?

Nan., 2 October

The huge warm wool comforter JH gave me a year or two ago, is black with speckled crescents on one side, and light with confetti pattern on the other. I always make the bed with the light side up—the dark side is morbid. And the little pillows which decorate the bed, made by Aunt Pearl thirty years ago, are in a checkered pattern on one side, and pink & red velvet on the other. I can no longer bear the pink and red, which recall a slaughterhouse, or the blood in my urine after the cystoscopy last Friday.

Night after night I lie awake in pain and fear, get up and dribble awhile, then back to bed. If JH goes to the store, or for a walk with Sonny, when will he back? I make his life miserable. Having written it, might I feel better soon?

3 October

Going through the motions, including the motions of this pen. Rented Oldsmobile loaded with plants, books, suitcase, Sonny and the two cats, we take the noon ferry to New York for four days. Have orchestrated 59 pages since Monday of the *Concerto*. Reading Britten's huge *Letters & Diaries* to review for Lambda.

Nan., 18 October

Prostate operation. Nantucket Cottage Hospital.

13 Nov.

The pre-voyage angst. Even despair.

Our national heroes are Black today: Anita Hill. Magic Johnson. Clarence Thomas (yes, he's a hero for even Jesse Helms).

Another phrase no Frenchman can pronounce: "Those jabbing thrushes shaved off each last ounce."

Suicide with sleeping pills is more efficient if washed down with whiskey. But what if you're a reformed alcoholic?

Islander = I slander
Co-pilot = Copi – lot

24 November

Letters Department
Sunday Book Review
NYT

A postscript to Henry Louis Gates Jr.'s intriguing essay on "cultural imperson-ators":

I have no argument except with his opening analogy: "The black jazz trumpeter Roy Eldridge once made a wager . . . that he could distinguish white musicians from black ones—blindfolded . . . More than half the time Eldridge was wrong." Gates suggests that this "blindfold test is one that literary critics would do well to ponder, for the belief that we can 'read' a person's . . . ethnic identity from his or her writing runs surprisingly deep." To liken one art to another is already risky; if the arts resem-bled each other we'd need only one. But to go farther and compare performance (in this case music interpretation) with creation (in this case prose writing) is to miss one's own point. The real point would be for Eldridge to assert he could distinguish white *composers* from black ones.

Gates himself elsewhere asks: "If black critics claim special authority as inter-preters of black literature, and black writers claim special authority as interpreters of black reality, are we not obliged to cede an equivalent dollop of authority to our white counterparts?" The answer is no, unless the white counterpart happens to live, say, in a Nigerian village. White people in a predominantly white society are not aware of their whiteness per se.

Twenty years ago a black soprano commissioned me (I am a white composer) to write her a song cycle. For texts I settled on eleven female poets, from Queen Anne Boleyn to Adrienne Rich, but none was black. In those days black poets wrote mostly about the "black condition"; since that condition could never be mine, how could I transfer it to music, albeit for a black singer, without seeming a patronizing type-caster? There's a lot of woman in me, and half my ancestors are female, though none are black. But was I right? Was Gershwin's masterpiece, *Porgy and Bess*, some sort of betrayal in not having been composed by a Negro?

In any case, anyone blindfolded can tell a male from a female singer. And yes, there *is* a black sound in black singers, even the most classically trained, simply by virtue of their background. That difference between white and black becomes pure gold and is a blessing in our otherwise assembly-line society.

Mr. Gates might have added some notes on homosexual artists. Is there, for exam-ple, such a thing as the "Gay Sensibility" (claimed in gay circles), or is that merely a slogan masquerading as an idea, like "Black is Beautiful" or "Feminine Mystique"?

When a Renaissance painter is known to have been homosexual—Caravaggio, Michelangelo—along comes some straight historian like Berenson to show us, after the fact, that the pictures too are gay, usually by pointing out the pretty boys (never the tough soldiers the historian may be less subliminally attracted to). But what about the pretty boys in straight pictures, or the pretty girls in gay ones?

What about the la-di-da effeteness of a heterosexual like Beardsley, or the straightforward ruggedness of a homosexual like Whitman? If no important heterosexual American author has written an intelligent novel wherein the leading characters are gay, 99 percent of gay authors, until recently, wrote novels wherein the leading characters are straight. Only in the past two decades have homosexual authors, like black authors, used their minority status as subject matter.

Back to music. If any blindfolded fool knows the difference between male and female singers, nobody, even without a blindfold and the ears wide open, knows whether the composer of this or that symphony is a man or a woman. Here is a generality, nevertheless: music by women today is often hyper-complex and rough, while many first-rate men have taken to composing delicate tone poems. Women today are inclined to write what was once termed masculine music, while men write feminine music. How empty those terms now seem.

4 December

Write-up a day or so ago by Bernard Holland of Elliott Carter's Violin Concerto. Holland clearly—or rather, obliquely—believes that Carter's garbed in the emperor's clothes, but is deferential, and leaves the benefit of the doubt. Why has no music critic, none ever, blown the whistle on Carter, as literary critics this month are doing on Mailer and Brodkey? Because they're afraid of being proven wrong on the Judgment Day? Andrew Porter's boring eccentricities of introducing E.C.'s name in his every column, whether it belongs or not, is par for the course. But . . . Elliott's music is forever scolding and filled with hate, yet oddly directionless. To claim that it reflects the times we live in is self-evident. So does Poulenc's music, by definition. Nor are our times more vile and hopeless than nineteenth-century London, seventeenth-century Paris, eighth-century Peking, first-century Rome. But they're the only times we know firsthand.

Because JH forbids me to use the lines by William Penn ("They're too preachy, too prosy, too scolding for song") for the Tucker Foundation commission, I'm back at square one, just as I am with the prostate before the operation. Probably I'll opt for Auden.

Première plus three other performances, with the Boston Symphony, of *Swords and Plowshares*, for four singers and orchestra, Hugh Wolff conducting. It's a big piece—50 minutes—and a good one. Why have I written nothing about it here? Plus a trip to Waco, Texas, all during convalescence? Is it because what's most crucial—i.e., my work—I don't talk about, but simply do?

Once again, the Paradox of Charm.

Does Simenon—the greatest writer of our mid-century—have it? His subject matter mostly lacks charm, as do his characters, including Maigret. But he, the novelist, seethes with it.

Does Billie Holiday—the most expressive of mid-century jazz singers—have it? She, the woman had charm, but her singing, while moving you to the core, oddly lacks it, unlike, say, Ella Fitzgerald. Interestingly, Billie's singing had no dynamic nuance: it was—is—all an unshaded mezzo-forte within a tessitura of a deep octave. Given this, the variety was a rainbow paradox.

The time we had to waste (but was it waste? What else should we be doing?). Deciding at least twice a week to have martinis at 3 P.M. and continuing until 3 A.M.

Asie on the tournedisque 80 times at the Bisson Hotel in 1951.

One never knew quite where one stood with Marie-Laure.

Hershey Bar. Which I always read as Heresy Bar, envisioning heretics in a tavern eating chocolate.

Gladly my cross-eyed bear.

Lead me not to Penn Station.

Nantucket, 4 December

Rerun of documentary made six years ago by Vivian Perlis for Copland's 85th birthday in which I have a cameo (don't blink). Sylvia on the phone this morning: "The office says you and Jacob [Druckman, also in film] have changed." In fact, since the operation six weeks ago I've had a *coup de vieux*, physical and mental. No pleasure in mirrors.

Dream. Aaron is telling his audience: "Then suddenly one day it hit me—I had an Aaron Copland in my own back yard."

> *This gave Miss Boulanger*
> *A fit of foul anger.*
> *They said the Giant Sloth was lazy.*
> *The Giant Sloth*
> *Was, though pliant, wroth*
> *To be called lazy.*
> *I do things as I do them,*
> *Prevailing for millenniums,*
> *It's hazy but not hard,*
> *Why there's a Giant Sloth in my own backyard*
> *Munching geraniums.*

Finished Ward Just's novel, cold and hopeless and expert. JH plays a video of *Enemies, A Love Story*, based on I. B. Singer. Expert, cold, hopeless.

Sending Christmas cards for the first time in years, because the years are whirling by, flinging birthdays and obits every which way, and I want to keep in contact with France while the keeping's still good. But who there do I know anymore? Two or three, maybe, and mostly Americans.

Yes, there can be wit without charm. Elliott Stein is one of the most humorously original people on earth, but it's not based on charm. Similarly Evelyn Waugh, and maybe G. B. Shaw (does he even have wit?). Wilde had both charm and wit, like Noël Coward and Mae West, which puts them high among the greats. Charm sans wit? Marilyn Monroe, and a hundred more. There's also charm with sexiness, and sexiness without charm. Sex and wit, however, are anathema.

1992

NY Hospital, New Year's Day,
after second prostate invasion

Gloria on phone tells of her ordeal with a catheter. It remained in for two months. It was like removing an octopus.

An erection with a catheter is something to remember.

21 February

Yesterday, arriving early by cab for appointment with Dr. Agus, I took a brief detour on foot, fell flat on my face on Second Avenue's granite, lacerated both hands, left knee, and broke my right big toe, which turned instantly black and swollen. "How," I ask Dr. Agus a few minutes later, "can you judge your patients as people—you see them always at their worst." And I recount the story I once wrote about a blasé doctor who remained indifferent to a certain female patient, until one day he was forced to operate. On slicing open her abdomen he was so bedazzled by the rainbow of possibility—the saffron liver, the valentine heart, the silver blood, the blue-scarlet nerves—that he fell in love. On sewing her up and bidding her goodbye, he wistfully prayed that her stitches would burst—that she would return to him.

Today my toe being worse (ebony streaked with azure and gold), I returned to have it X-rayed. "My, what beautiful colors!" exclaimed Dr. Agus.

It would have been in 1953 or '54, while anguishing because the Bernanos estate was causing difficulties about the rights of *Dialogues des Carmélites*, that Poulenc took to his bed with stigmata on his palms, and nearly died from liver ailments. For me and José Hell he played the first act of the opera which he claimed was composed literally *"entre deux crises de foie."*

Between the raindrops of agony, I, who have never missed a deadline, have been half-heartedly struggling with a long overdue piece for Columbus. Curtain raiser. Little Prayer. Fanfare.

March

One Jamie James asserts in the *Times* that, despite my being a "gay composer," I didn't dare to "emphasize explicitly [Whitman's] homosexuality, as John Adams did, by setting such a line as 'Many a Soldier's kiss dwells on these bearded lips.' " But if that line implies, to Jamie James, homosexuality rather than human compassion, then James must see Whitman as a gay necrophiliac, or, at least, a dirty old man, and an astonishingly promiscuous and public one at that. For Whitman refers in scores of poems to his embracing of dying youths.

Re. the Saint Patrick's Day Parade, and the Catholic Church's ban on gay marchers, JH feels the church errs, by their own definition. It is not homosexuals of which the church disapproves, but homosexual acts.

JH says the translation of *Bonjour Tristesse* should be *Good Morning, Heartache*. Surely Paul Eluard and Billie Holiday never heard of each other. Am I the only person who knew them both, however slightly? What does "slightly" mean?

Monday morning, 3 Feb.

Anxious, colitis, alone. JH in Nantucket. I go to Philly this aft for 36 hours, there to meet David Diamond, Rosemary, et alia.

Dined chez S. & George Perle last night. I said, "Henry James knew all." George said, "He certainly did not. He knew nothing of music, and didn't have a clue as to why other people liked music." This was, of course, true. Like so many great writers and painters, music meant little to him. (The reverse is seldom the case: No composer ignores the other arts.) What I had meant, however, was that James, like Proust, knew everything about the workings of interhuman relations.

Title: *Reckless Nursemaids*

Certain authors, says JH, should never be read, only reread. Jane Austen, for example. Others should never be read at all. (Dickens.) Others just once. (Melville.) Others often.

For Leonard Raver's memorial—28 March 1992, at the Ascension:

Like all worthy artists he was the sum of his contradictions. The very name, Leonard Raver, suggests one who both roars and raves, while in fact he was soft-spoken, a good listener, endlessly curious, and, though lean, a fabulous cook. Our long relationship too was contradictory, with a calculated start and a sentimental evolution.

In 1975 I had already lived seven years with the organist Jim Holmes without having composed anything for organ, an instrument that left me cool. Cool or not, Jim and I decided pragmatically that I should contribute something major to the organ repertory, and that it would be best to do so with a paid deadline. Since, as a group, organists have a less shameful reputation than other instrumentalists for lenience toward new music, and since Leonard topped the list, I phoned, scarcely knowing him, to ask: Did he want me to write a big work for him? Could he get Alice Tully to commission it specifically for her instrument? And might it then be immediately recorded? He did. She could. It might. So I composed A Quaker Reader, which Leonard premièred in early 1977, then played all over the world.

Jim and Leonard and his George Cree and I grew into staunch acquaintances; as neighbors we saw each other often, not least in the Food Emporium on Broadway, but also on tour, always with colleaguely talk, recipe exchanges, and never a discouraging word.

The instrument that once left me cool now made me warm. During the next decade I wrote five more big pieces for organ, two of which Leonard premièred, including the Concerto, all of which he played—not once, but many times. How could I not feel close to Leonard, almost like a twin, since (and the composers here will understand) as my interpreter, he is an extension of myself.

Composers today are like the homeless. They're not *even* pariahs. Paradox: the mass of young talent today—what's it to do?

Ethel Reiner: "There are only five thousand people in the world, and sooner or later you meet them all." JH puts the figure at *one* thousand, and claims it's not a proportion: There are only one thousand "possible" individuals ever, whether the world population is a million or a billion.

The disputes about which is more crucial, more vital, pop or classical, cannot be resolved, since the two expressions are not flip sides of one coin, but separate languages with separate goals. They've always run parallel, occasionally overlapping but never joining each other. Interestingly, it's pop, which sprang from penniless slave songs, that is today a trillion-dollar business, and classical that goes hungry.

Music has no precise meaning, that is its power. Language has precise meaning, that is its purpose. No one can prove that this or that piece of music, even vocal or programmatic music, has literary connotation beyond what the composer tells you, in words, about it. Music's strength at being able to color, heighten, change, give sense to, a scene in a ballet or movie or some other related art in which it col-laborates, lies exactly in its having no specific sense itself. Anyone can prove that a word, a sentence, or paragraph, has specific connotation—just go to the dictionary if you wish to persuade the Supreme Court. But no dictionary will elucidate the legal or lubricious sense of a modulation from C-major to F-sharp minor, or explain why a dominant resolving to a median is pleasing to some, while to others, like me, a secondary ninth suspended in midair is the ultimate satisfaction, sad and sexy.

What, then, of the madness of song, conjoining the utterly meaningless (music) with the utterly meaningful (poetry)? Because John Ashbery's verse, so far as meaning is concerned, is hopeless beyond the bizarrest dictionary, and because my music, at least to me, has meaning beyond the usual generalities of love, death, and the weather, I like setting his words to music. My music tells me what his words mean—a meaning that he himself ignores.

April

"There are artists who know what they are about, and artists who haven't the faintest idea," begins Richard Sennett in a review of Courbet's letters in the cur-rent *TLS* (April 3, 1992). He goes on: "The former are quite aware of where their art came from; they explain themselves well to their contemporaries; they have a fair estimate of how their work will be discussed when they are gone. Stravinsky was such a composer, Wallace Stevens such a poet, Picasso such a painter. Gustave Courbet seemed to his contemporaries quite the opposite: rough and provincial as a person, obtuse about his own work and ungenerous about the work of others."

As usual, Sennett aims to make a novel case—as his friend Susan Sontag used more solidly to do—on which to base an article. As usual his writing is clumsy in style (two superfluous uses of the adverb "quite") and contradictory in content (if artists who "know what they are about" can "explain themselves well to their contemporaries," does Courbet's seeming "to his contemporaries quite the oppo-site"—the opposite of what?—mean that he couldn't explain himself well?). And as usual Sennett is inconsistent in his examples (if "obtuse" Courbet was ungener-ous about the work of others, so too was the self-aware Stravinsky). More impor-tantly misleading, though, is Sennett's opening premise: One could as correctly state that no artists truly know what they are about, yet all artists think they know.

A certain 12-year-old girl, Minou Drouet, wrote poems so good that her teachers said she couldn't be the author, it must be her father. Eventually, all of France ral-lied, and proclaimed her greatness. Except Cocteau. "All children have genius," said he, "except Minou Drouet."

30 May

Dined chez Daron and his bride, the trumpet-playing Donna, at their new walk-up on West 98th Street, tree-lined and hilly. Troy there too, with Anne, who teaches "problem" children in Philadelphia's inner city. At 6 A.M. this dream:

Young hunters abandon their chief to go to mass. The chief, cleaning his arrows, says to the camera: "They run off to mass, leaving the deer bloody and dying, with one leg chopped off." The others return from mass and savagely beat the chief for being soft-hearted. He dies. I report this to the judge, who tries them, preaches to them, then lets them off, for the judge too is soft-hearted and does not believe in capital punishment. So the young hunters kill the judge for allowing them to go free. And I? A virile angel with his three-day's growth of beard cradles me in his arms while moving to safety through paths of broken glass, for I am only a child, although sixty-eight years old.

In book's Intro.: To CRR on his death bed, add parentheses: (In a whisper: Everything I know was learned from you.)

Culturally we are reentering the dark ages.

2 June

Call from Lucy Shelton: Will I write a little homage for Oliver Knussen's fortieth birthday that she can give to him, with dozens of others, next fortnight in England? Yes, I'll send it directly, don't bother to come by. But I finish it immediately, phone her back. Line busy. Line busy again, and for the next half-hour. Finally I get through (without the sound of a ring) and hear a woman sobbing uncontrollably. "Lucy," I say carefully, "is that you? It's Ned. Are you all right?" But the wails continue, ever louder, it's horrible. "Lucy," I repeat calmly, "are you there?" I don't want to hang up, for fear of being uncharitable, she might need someone. Yet do I really know her well enough to interfere? Quandary. Then the crying stops, she hears me, says, "How did you get on the phone?" "I heard a person crying," I tell her. Is Oliver all right? And you? Yes, yes. Well, I've finished the little homage. It was agreed she'd stop by for it in a couple of hours. Meanwhile I call George Perle to ask: Should I refer to all this when Lucy comes by? When she does come by, fresh and smiling, I don't mention it.

Speak for yourself.

Well, I do speak for myself. But I also speak *to* thousands of others.

His Second Violin Concerto is seldom played. Few second violinists are good enough.

Though I heard Randall Thompson's *A Testament of Freedom* only once, forty-eight years ago in 1944, so vigorous were the rigid repetitions of "The God who gave us life, gave us liberty at the same time, at the same time, at the same time," that the tune remains unforgettable, boring and fascist, belying the Democratic text.

Nantucket, End of June

It won't end. After the two prostate operations last winter, the 8-week paralysis of the herniated disks with accompanying MRI, the broken toe which will never return to normal (ah, those famous feet), the continuing sciatica, the summer flu, and now the befouled bicuspid which, three weeks back in Manhattan I'll have repaired for $5,000, unless (since all the dentists shake their head at the "bone loss") more horrors are discovered in the excavation.

But I have finished the English Horn Concerto for Tom Stacy and the NY Phil., and am trying to get back into the book, now titled *Knowing When to Stop*. Sylvia comes tomorrow. Gloria left a week ago. JH, with his Latin American aides, commutes, the weather is agreeable, and there's some quiet.

"Thou shalt not lie with mankind, as with womankind: it is an abomination." Leviticus, 18, 22 King James version. "Do not lie with a man as one lies with a woman; that is detestable." The same, New International Version (1978). However you slice it—or screw it—both versions evade the issue biologically: men sleep together as men, not as women. Since God's admonishments to Moses are all directed to male behavior, one asks how women's behavior is ever, in any way, illegal or profane. But since the decrees are solely for Jews, all Gentiles are in any case sullied, merely by virtue of being Gentile. So Gentiles need not worry unduly—they simply cannot be saved.

Note for the English Horn Concerto:

> At first I planned to call it *Meditations in an Emergency*, after Frank O'Hara's poem, since half the piece was composed literally in a hospital bed. Indeed, the past winter was one of physical stress; when I worked at all it was through a hazy protestant need to meet deadlines. Later I opted for a straightforward title (saving the ornamental names for the separated movements), for I do not believe that music, especially non-vocal music, necessarily reflects its makers' mood *in medias res*, or that people can agree—as they can with poetry and pictures—that a specific piece is angry or happy or noble, much less that it represents an ocean or an operating room. When a gloomy composer labors on a lengthy project he checks the gloom at his studio door, along with his aches and pains, and functions in a kind of limbo. (A definition of the Artist: One who exists outside himself, and has something to show for it. He is the least egotistical of citizens.)
>
> My sole aim in writing the Concerto for English Horn was to exploit that instrument's special luster and pliability. The literature is slim, maybe because the English horn—or, as the English say, the cor Anglais—cannot hold its own against an orchestra as singularly as a piano or trumpet or cello or flute. To make the sound gleam like an opaline reed through a wash of brass and silver, catgut and steel, I used an orchestra which by Philharmonic standards is hardly huge, with a pair of oboes like nephews often flanking, sometimes goading, their wistful relative.
>
> Each of the five movements is to some degree a passacaglia, a neutral or redundant background, a canvas upon which the soloist will limn his pictures. For what it's

worth, this is my first work ever to have been composed entirely away from a keyboard, and directly onto orchestration parchment. This transpired between December 6, 1991, and June 13, 1992, in New York City and in Nantucket.

25 June

Well, of course nothing is new under the sun. Although depicted as something of a toady to Laurence Olivier, Kenneth Tynan is nonetheless lauded in the current *New Yorker:* "Except for the Shakespearean films, Olivier onstage is best preserved for us in Tynan's prose," says reviewer Lloyd Rose, who then quotes from Tynan's description of a *Coriolanus* production in 1959:

> He is poised now on a promontory some twelve feet above the stage, from which he topples forward, to be caught by the ankles so that he dangles, inverted, like the slaughtered Mussolini. A more shocking, less sentimental death I have not seen in the theater . . .

In 1951 I saw a revival of Sauguet's ballet *La Rencontre* (1948), wherein the choreographer, David Lichine, poses the female Sphinx on a promontory some twelve feet above the stage. When Oedipus correctly answers her question, she surges up in horrific despair, and as the curtain slowly falls she topples forward, to be caught by the ankles so that she dangles, inverted, swinging back and forth— the most spectacular *coup de théâtre* I've ever witnessed.

Could David Horne, age twenty, teach me to play my own music? I may perceive with a finer ear than he the pitfalls in *his* compositions, which is why he remains my pupil; but it's hard to stand outside oneself. No, I don't seek his or anyone's remarks about my music's value, but I wouldn't mind a lesson in how to *play* the stuff. He's a better pianist than I, and even JH feels I often miss the point of my own compositions.

July

Gloria Vanderbilt came to Nantucket for a long weekend, while JH stayed diplomatically in the city. There's no one with whom I feel more comfortable, with our walks in the rain, dining *à deux* in town or at home, visiting my friends or just sitting together. Yet we don't concur about a lot of things, starting with God.

Gloria has her fickle, even dangerous, side. Two people I don't know, Bobby Short and Carol Matthau, she has always spoken of as her dearest friends, describing them with keen alacrity. Now she takes exception to Bobby (the River House incident he adored for the publicity), and to Carol because her new book, which I read and liked and which speaks long and lovingly of Gloria, includes photos Gloria doesn't approve of, and because the jacket, which features a drawing by G., she finds badly reproduced. She has asked the publisher to delete these in the next edition, but has not (she claims) read the book. Oddly she complains that Carol didn't phone her when in town to do publicity.

JH says that the main purpose in my keeping a diary is to impress myself. Well, he's probably right. Probably too that's the purpose in writing a symphony or a play. Certainly that's the purpose in invading a country, or decapitating a criminal.

31 July

Phone call from Gloria, who had awoken from a dream: She sees me at my desk, back to her, beginning an autobiography by contemplating the little cylinder (her word) in which are kept the ashes of my parents.

I told her that, in fact, my memoir does sort of begin that way, in a preamble called "Last Things First" detailing the deaths of Mother and Father in 1988, and taking it from there. Then I asked if she'd read Judy Collins's book, in which Judy quotes me as saying: One way to animate an autobiography might be to examine various mementos around the room, and develop remembrances around the persons who gave the mementos.

I went to sleep and dreamed that I told Gloria: This triad which you see there on the staff is for celesta. Now, a celesta by its nature cannot sustain a chord, yet this triad *is* sustained, as though held by three flutes that are really three drops of water.

"The Second Coming" is a perfect poem in all ways except for its basic premise. Is the "rough beast, its hour come round at last," really so much more horrific than that other slouching toward Bethlehem twenty centuries ago?

A note on JH and the animals, Sonny, Lucille (whom Maggy likens to Rhonda Fleming), and Tom. He sleeps with them.

30 August

Reading Gore Vidal's two new books, *Live from Golgotha* and *Screening History*. In the novel he makes a bid to become America's Salman Rushdie. America's fundamentalists are surely no less adamant than Islam's, and since neither reads books, both will be willing to assassinate on call. But since Gore lives in Italy, where the Holy Family is part of the family, thus open to all sorts of friendly desecration, he's probably safe. I tell JH that the book is a madly disrespectful portrait of Our Lord.

"What are the opening words?" he asks. "Jesus shat?"

Write G.V. (His initials are those of Gloria Vanderbilt and the dreaded Gwen Verdon.) Congratulate on the really good essay on Montaigne in *TLS*. GV in a recent interview mentions Maurice Grosser as the oldest person he knows dead of AIDS. Information from me. Yet all I've cribbed from him! starting with "If everything is art, then nothing is art."

5 September

On the telly last night a statesman, I forget who, said that Family Values and homosexuality are mutually exclusive. I don't see why. My family of a mother &

father & sister & me (one queer out of four) was mutually inclusive: we laughed and cried together, were supportive and caring. Our parents "valued" the notion of providing my sister & me with an intelligent education and a stable hearth. Although my later youth, like that of most people with curiosity and brains, was strewn with wild oats, I have lived for the past 25 years of my life with one man in terms of mutual respect and—I like to think—productive "values." Without JH I could never have had the peace of mind to compose the several hundred hours of music and books that have been so well received in a predominantly heterosexual society. The trouble with Family Values as a monolithic term against which one is judged, is that it's merely a catch-phrase posing as an idea and has never been defined. Just as "pornography" or "gay sensibility" are terms that have never been defined.

Cold summer, insomnia, working slowly on memoir, dreary, dreary.

Nantucket, 30 Sept.

Half my toe amputated yesterday by Voorhees.

JH reads a review in *TLS* on Coleridge as great conversationalist. Like all great conversationalists Coleridge was apparently a soliloquist. (Madame de Staël said he was "a master of monologue, *mais qu'il ne savait pas le dialogue.*") Like all great conversationalists, he repeated himself endlessly. Heaven pity the wife or regular friends who must sit through the same spiel night after night with new guests. I tell JH that Cocteau's repertory was huge, and his sense of improvisation seemed spontaneous, but that sooner or later his best quips were repeated unchanged even to regulars.

JH then says that this is of course the case with all raconteurs, but is it the case, too, with *raconteurs à deux*? He recalls the first time he met Gore Vidal, with whom I was having a long, witty, concerned exchange. The second time he met Vidal, many years later, Vidal and I repeated, word for word, our same long, witty, concerned exchange.

That silly business of the monkey at a typewriter again. (I wrote of this some pages back, no?) Of the zillions of snowflakes in a blizzard throughout the universe, not one crystal in its perfect design is ever identical to another.

Late September

Quick perusal of the feisty and somewhat graceless (considering how successful he is) interview with Spike Lee in *Esquire*. All white people are uncomfortable with all black people. But how does he know, since he's never been white? Between him & me lies more than a difference in color. He's young and I'm old. I've been young but he's never been old, so can't by definition know my perspective no matter how perceptive he is. He's straight and I'm gay, so I can't by definition etc.

There's a wider gap between bright & dull than between black & white, or even between male & female. In a moment of irrational irritation Spike Lee might scream faggot at me (or fruit, or fairy, or whatever is the current epithet), but I doubt if I'd scream nigger at him. I wasn't raised that way, don't think that way, though I might scream you're ugly and unsexy.

"I'll take Sonny out before we go to bed," says JH around about midnight.

"But you took him out just twenty minutes ago."

JH didn't remember this, nor that indeed he and Sonny had exceptionally walked down the back stairs instead of out the front door, and proceeded over the lawn to Wesco Place and stood alone together there in the dark for several minutes. Nothing to worry about—JH is not, like his father, brewing Alzheimer's. On the contrary, his power of concentration, like mine years ago but no longer, is such that he can work for hours at a stretch and hear nothing you say to him, even when the house is on fire.

Mid-October

Flipping the dials on Tuesday we find Marvin Hamlisch, who seems to have published a history of his own genius, chatting with Dick Cavett, and, on a Steinway especially rented for the interview, wisping his accurate fingers over the keys as he explicates the composition of "The Way We Were," his best-known song. Flipping the dials on Wednesday we came across Hamlisch chatting with Charlie Rose, and, on a Steinway especially rented for the occasion, wisping his fingers over the keys while explicating the evolution of "The Way We Were." O well, endless repetition is a foible of even great minds, and since "The Way We Were" is no more and no less than an undefiled mixture of "Tenderly" and "September in the Rain," it merits a twice-told analysis.

26 October

Betwixt New Haven and Hyannis yesterday on the car radio (the classical music station from Hartford is superior to any in Manhattan) we played the usual guessing games to keep us awake at the wheel, JH always being exhausted from his morning masses, and we always drive to Nantucket on Sundays. Overhearing a swooning *in medias res* we ask, What's this? It's endless enough to be Mahler, but not neurotic enough. Probably Bruckner. But when the directionless self-indulgence, without climax, without invention, but with annoying familiarity merged into the last movement, we suddenly recognized Beethoven's Ninth. I've always found that symphony a prolix pompous military bore. All that tonic & dominant in root position! That march-like fascism! That undifferentiated vocal writing (how singers must hate it!), and that cheap insulting repetitious coda. Jim rightly guessed it to be Bernstein's performance at the Berlin Wall, because the strings were so soupy, the sung-parts so rapid. I would not have guessed.

Naïve = Evian
Garden = Nedrag
What does "to diss" mean? (Put on list of pet peeves.)

23 November

The Tucker concert last night, with RR & JH.

I've been "in music" for fifty years, yet saw not one person I know, or even recognized, on the packed stage or in the house of Avery Fisher Hall. The phrases "There is opera and then there is music," "there are singers, and then there are musicians" are quaint and overused only because, like all clichés, they're true. The spectacle last night—a chorus of 220 onstage and an orchestra of 100, plus a dozen second-string soloists, mostly American, who sang operatic blockbusters in every language except English—had nothing of song, everything of selling. When Paul Groves and Craig Rutenberg emerged to present my 4-minute setting of Auden's "Their Lonely Belters" (not an aria, not a pop tune—a *song*), over there in the corner on a near-hidden piano, the audience didn't know what to do, and neither did I when I took a bow. They had been primed to shriek bravo and stamp; my song was a miniature and quiet semi-tragedy.

Enemy territory. Song versus opera.

I got $5,000, but the supper afterward cost surely $100,000. Well, John Kander is next year. Advise him to at least insist on orchestrating his venture, or in having the piano placed where it should be.

JH: "Pigs singing for pigs."

In opera there are no totally heartless villains. The very fact of singing renders the singer sensitive, vulnerable. Claggart and Iago and Scarpia, while contriving evil doings, produce from their bodies such beauty that a layer of strong pity coats them.

I had a green fox. And then I painted him green.

Where have I written here (it's not in the *Nantucket Diary*) of Edward Albee's public persona? Of how on talk shows he apes Gore Vidal's know-it-all, world-weary stance, without Gore's cutting perspicacity or earned despair? Example:

E.A. to Dick Cavett: "You realize, don't you, that under Nixon there was more artistic floraison than under any more-liberal president before or since."

Cavett: "Gee, Edward. Why was that, do you suppose?"

E.A.: "I have no idea."

But the "idea," of course, is that under Nixon we still had capitalist collectors and investors—not least Rockefeller—who still believed that Art was not a dirty word. And art has always flourished better under rich than under more democratic governments.

1993

1 January

If everyone sought to dispense with war, instead of crying discrimination if they can't kill people legally, we'd have a better world. But the better world—how does it grow? When we have enough to eat, all races holding hands, no strife, ubiquitous peace, then what? Is there further need for education? Whence art—since the most lasting art is ever based on conflict? Would the Ideal World be a bland society of pop?

Christianity, in admonishing us to Love Thy Neighbor as Thyself, finds justification for war. So deeply do we loathe ourselves that we take it out on others.

Nantucket, 13 January

The reason I don't write much here is because of the autobiography.

Certain up-to-date terms I do not understand nor want to use: pundit, baby boomer, workplace, to party. (What do the pundits think of baby boomers who party in the workplace?)

Once to Maggy I stated that the physical handicap I most deplore is blindness, the musical form I most deplore is the waltz. How about—she asked—the blind waltzing?

Venue, couch potato, sound bite.

Philadelphia, 4 Feb.

On arriving at Curtis yesterday morning for the final rehearsal of the *Left Hand Concerto*, I was soberly taken aside to Gary's room where André Previn awaited. Would I, he asked, apologize to the student orchestra for having referred to them, in an interview, as slave labor? Mortified, I obeyed. Whereupon they played in a manner to put the city's chief orchestra to shame.

Before the world première tonight in the Academy, Rosemary, with Mike and Rachel, Charity and two kids, dined in my room at the Barclay. Gary has made the piece his own, and whatever the music's worth, I will never complain about this most perfect performance of my career.

Drove back to NY with the Graffmans, Sylvia, and Previn, arriving at 2 A.M. when I pen this paragraph.

6 Feb.

New York première last night with the *L.H. Concerto*, in Carnegie. Dined home beforehand on JH's cuisine, with Gloria Vanderbilt, Frank Benitez, Jerry Lowenthal, and Ellen Adler.

Tomorrow Nantucket. We both nurse colds, plus Jim's bad back and loose tooth.

Because of deadline for the Simon & Schuster book, I'll not write here for a while.

5 September

Although I'm a guest, hardly a conductor, at the choral concert for my birthday next month, in the dream last night I found it difficult to decide what to wear. A severe foot-length wool skirt, perhaps? Or a ball gown. I settled for a vase, yes, a human-size vase of black onyx with a flared brim, like a jonquil, through which head and bare shoulders emerge, and broken at the bottom so that the feet are free.

23 October, spoken at Saint Peter's:

> At two o'clock this morning I became 21,550 days old.
>
> Since I am surely the first person under this roof to have attained that lofty age, let me announce it's not so bad. And I'm touched that you should all be here to share the pleasant trauma. The truth is: I still feel pre-adolescent, and still have nightmares about when I'll grow up and have to go to the office like my father.
>
> Let me talk briefly about the program. Briefly—since brevity is next to godliness, and godliness is the tone tonight.
>
> Half my life's musical work has been for chorus. Half of *that*, in turn, is based on so-called sacred texts. Yet if I do not believe in God, I do believe in Belief, and in the great works that the notion of God has inspired in so many of those poets who are crucial to songwriters. A recent pronouncement, encouraging the performance of non-religious music in churches, argued that all music is religious. I prefer to find all music profane: the pipes of the organ are an outgrowth of the pipes of Pan.

Although I am responsible for each piece tonight, the impeccable Harold Rosenbaum is responsible for the assemblage of pieces, eliminating huge oratorios with diabolical texts, and choosing what befits the nuanced purity of his sixteen madrigalists. The ten works span 43 years. Each is an example of *Gebrauchmusik* commissioned for a specific occasion.

Arise, Shine and *Mercy & Truth* were composed for churches, in Hartford and Delaware respectively, in 1977 and 1983, and the text in each case was suggested by the commissioner.

A Sermon on Miracles, the earliest piece, dates from 1946 and was written for Daniel Pinkham's Christ Church in Cambridge. He specified a 6-minute study for unison chorus with a few solos, accompanied by string orchestra. The text was concocted for the occasion by my friend Paul Goodman. The present reduced version is by my friend Jim Holmes.

In 1988 the Gay Men's Chorus of New York asked various composers to compose something about AIDS. But music is not about politics, I protested, it can't be about the immediate, et cetera; and besides, what words could I use? Then I came across Paul Monette's just-published *Love Alone: Eighteen Elegies for Rog*. Certainly these poems were "about AIDS" while remaining art. So I set the first elegy to music, for piano four-hands, as requested, and for a choir of 300 male voices. Tonight we'll try it with eight.

Te Deum, for large mixed chorus, 2 trumpets, 2 trombones and organ, written the same year as *Love Alone*, was a celebration of Christ Church Cathedral in Indianapolis.

American church music is a specialty within a specialty, on ground that is already specialized to death. Just as there are people in the general population who may have read one of my twelve books but have no idea that I write music, or people who may have heard my music but don't know I write books, so there are those in the musical elite who may know I'm a composer but not a composer of church music. Similarly, there are folks in (say) Branson, Missouri, who sing my hymns on Sunday without even knowing my name.

Since Church Music, like Band Music, is a branch that the average music-fancier doesn't climb, and which never gets reviewed, many multi-faceted composers treat it as a sideline, just as authors such as Joyce Carol Oates or Gore Vidal pseudonymously write murder mysteries or soft-core porn to make extra money.

Not I! I may adopt a style or language according to genre, but I don't do so consciously. Rather, my thinking is more like that of the French, for whom all music is simply music, holy or unholy, and who use the same expressive voice for every kind of piece.

God Is Gone Up, for mixed chorus a cappella, is from "Seven Motets for the Church Year," composed in 1986 for All Saints' Episcopal Church in Fort Lauderdale . . . The *Three Motets*, on poems of Gerard Manley Hopkins, date from 1973 and were written for Saint Luke's Chapel on Hudson Street.

In 1981 Gregg Smith, who loves antiphonal sonorities, requested something for 2-part chorus: all the men in unison counterpointing all the women in unison, with a keyboard between, holding them together as they intone the verses of Ralph Waldo Emerson. The piano part is so radically complex that only I can play it. [I play. The accompaniment consists of two notes, continually repeated.]

The final two pieces, *Truth in the Night Season*, written in 1966 for the Houston Chapter of the American Guild of Organists, and *Praises for the Nativity*, written in 1970 for Saint Patrick's Cathedral on Fifth Avenue, are both, by my standards, thorny. The latter is for four solo voices in English pitted against the other twelve voices in Latin.

25 October

Love can never be politically correct, since love, by its nature, is illogical, selfish, insane. At least Romantic Love—carnal love—is. When love is no longer sexual, it's no longer love—by P.C. standards. *L'amour, c'est l'égoïsme à deux.*

At Joe Machlis's party after the choral concert Bobby Fizdale sidled up confidentially and murmured: "During the past half hour I've overheard you say to three different people, 'I love you more than anyone in the world.'" Me: "Well, I mean it each time I say it."

To the list of Sacred Monsters I Can Do Without (Fred Astaire, Audrey Hepburn, Groucho Marx, Mother Teresa), I now add Frank Lloyd Wright. His architecture has always struck me as frigid, un-homey, pretentious, simple, dangerously jagged.

17 December

JH worse than ever: tobacco withdrawal, Prozac, shingles, painkillers, heart and stomach aches, slight fever, no appetite (except for occasional peanut butter), talks loudly in his sleep, sleeps 17 hours a day, and won't see a doctor—assuming there was one to see. Vaguely delirious, and fault-finding and cranky to everyone including the cats, though not to Sonny.

Despite this, we hied to the Philharmonic to check out Angelina Réaux's Berg and Weill. The moment she opened her mouth, we knew the coast was clear. Her voice is solid, sometimes beautiful, clear, projecting, with good diction and lots of temperament. She does need stage presence. She sings like—but doesn't act like— a star, doesn't seduce the audience when making an entrance or during bows. (Masur hams it up all over the stage, while Réaux stands there like a lost child.) The *Lulu* suite, though sumptuous and O so tonal, seems to me directionless, but JH finds it powerful and frightening. How delicious that the absolutely contemporaneous *Lulu* and *Seven Deadly Sins*, so remote in musical technique, seem so close esthetically to each other, as though Berg and Weill were themselves Anna One and Anna Two. It's their Germanitude: We are what we speak.

What a tight, wonderful, infectious, skillful, original piece, *The Seven Deadly Sins*, which I recall indelibly from the 1958 performances of Balanchine's staging with Lenya and Allegra Kent. The cynical libretto, like all of Brecht, is bitter, yes, and objective and terse and mean and preachy, but the music, like a bridge of honey, spans the fields. Song is the ultimate purgatory, lending an inner glow to even the most despondent story . . . Réaux's black tutu and black satin high heels were perfect . . . Who am I to suggest that Weill, who knew theater like the back of his hand, perhaps missed the chance for a coup at the finish? Shouldn't the recurrent exchange between the two Annas—*Nicht wahr, Anna? Ja, Anna*—be stated unaccompanied at the very end, when the orchestra has stopped? After all, the tale is finished, the "art" is done.

20 Dec.

On the agenda page for next Tuesday he noted: "Don't forget to commit suicide."

An interview is a portrait for which the sitter provides the material, and the painter provides a selective appraisal.

Certain stars, when known through their work, are beloved by us, but when apprehended off-screen lose it. Jeanne Moreau, so magic in the movies, with Charlie Rose acts fake-natural, imperious, charmless, and closed, unable to make herself understood when she errs in English, because she refuses to acknowledge the mistake. ("As an actress I am aside." "You are . . . what?" "Aside. Aside." She means, of course, *à côté*.) Other stars, when known through their work, are bores, but when apprehended on Charlie Rose they glow like a rose. Toni Morrison's prose grandeur escapes me. But as a person she seemed likeable, intelligent, no obvious chips on her shoulder, lucid, patient with "liberal" questions about race she's heard a hundred times.

1994

A generation ago, except for Paul Goodman, Gore Vidal was the only homosexual publicly versed in general politics, as distinct from specific gay-rights politics. With the years he has remained widely versed in the workings of the world, and, indeed, has published best-selling tomes on what he calls "the history of my country." I admire him, agree with him, and learn from him. He *has* had an Achilles Heel, on which he stands above the fray: knowing the sole cures for our planet's ills, he leans back and smiles as we go to pot for not heeding him. His prose too, both fiction and non-, reflects an aloofness that keeps it from soaring, thrilling, inspiring, even repelling. But that's him: his faults conspire to define him, so perhaps they aren't faults at all, but "traits."

Lately, though, his complacency has grown smug. Seer in the broad-heterosexual-world-of-politics though he be, he demonstrates a leaning that can only be termed homosexual (it takes one to know one). Tonight on *The Charlie Rose Show* he likened the tight smile of Inman, Clinton's nominee who has just stepped down "under pressure," to the tight smile of Chicago's Cardinal Bernardin, accused of molesting boys long ago. "It is as though," smirks Gore, proud of his wit, "Bernardin had simply wiped the smile off his own face and lent it to Inman." That's a bitchy remark—a remark one can't imagine from any heterosexual politico, no matter how sleazy. Straight men don't mention each other's looks. Should I add that Gore, so recently the handsome boyish sage, is no longer placed for such a quip, resembling now an all-knowing Buddha in the body of a Lucien Freud portrait?

With all the current fuss around Lucien Freud, no one mentions what he owes to Pavlik Tchelitchew. Pavlik's 1930 painting *Green Venus*, of a sad gross woman whose distended buttocks fill a hammock as wide as it is long, could have been drawn last week by Lucien.

I keep scribbling reminders here of what to write about, but don't. Like the expert interview in *Current Musicology* with Nora Beck. Or the embarrassing fundraiser for the Center for Contemporary Opera. (My songs were sung by Florence Foster Jenkins accompanied on an upright by Harry S. Truman.) Still, it must be noted, for posterity, that G. Vidal in his last letter wrote: "Just acted in a film for Warner's (eat yr. heart out baby), directed by a 28-year-old named Alek Keshishian, whose previous film was a documentary on Madonna, *Truth or Something*. Anyway, *you* are the passion of his life (he did go to Harvard), and he quotes you endlessly, from *The Paris Diary* in particular. He also turned M. on to you so your beach-head at our *fin de siècle* is a powerful one and I see you in some Orpheus Redux, all enigma and myopia, the great androgyne knotted loosely about yr. neck. Was F. O'Hara as ghastly as the book about him? Stuffed culture vulture under a glass bell! Auguri Gore."

    Indeed, a fan in Buffalo sent me a Polaroid of a moment in *Truth or Dare* where Madonna picks up *The Paris Diary* (North Point edition) and flips the pages. It's downhill all the way for me now.

22 Jan.

Insomnia is more pernicious than any torture, and lasts longer than crucifixion. Sleep is a trip on a lake. We set forth each midnight to float directionlessly here & there, pausing, rolling, forgetting, drifting back, awakening. But when the motor doesn't start at the outset, wakefulness, as with Benzedrine, mocks us for 24 hours. (My condition every third night.)

    The—for me—exceeding amount of attention and responsibility these past flattering weeks, plus JH's accumulating maladies, has been taxing. World news meanwhile would seem to center solely on a man whose wife sliced off his dick, an ice skater who paid to have her rival maimed, and Michael Jackson being harassed by an adolescent male who charges—and gets—ten million bucks for a blow job. Meanwhile sub-zero weather maims the East, an earthquake the West, while thousands perish in Yugoslavia.

Reinaldo Arenas's memoir, *Before Night Falls*, in style and content contains little that John Rechy didn't contain a generation ago, yet was written under the constraints of, first, Cuba's thoroughly repressive government and, second, AIDS. It does show that art and beauty, like fire and water, flow out through the bars of any cage to mock, indifferently and from all angles, the will of tyrants. Which is why art and beauty are forever banned, though impotently, by totalitarian societies. Of the AIDS that will kill him he says that nobody really knows what it is, unlike other diseases, which are natural phenomena and thus imperfect and open to cure. "But AIDS is a perfect illness because it is so alien to human nature and has as its function to destroy life in the most cruel and systematic way . . . Such diabolical perfection makes one ponder the possibility that human beings may have had a hand in its creation."

29 Jan.

JH has vomited all over the bed. His diverse diseases prevail. Then abate. Not in twenty years has he cancelled a responsibility. We speak of death. With his shepherding both my parents to the grave, and now his own parents, he wonders what's ahead for him in this small interim. Me too. Have I composed all that's in me? The urge ebbs. The Philharmonic performances are flawless, but the flurry of attention everywhere is more like an obit than a birthday. Unthinkable cold, day after day. The perilous sidewalk seems like Dorchester Avenue sixty years ago where the diamonds—real diamonds—in the cement looked in July as sleet does now in January.

Hateful quarrel with JH, the first in years. The Prozac, or whatever, makes him quick to boil. I told him I was afraid of him—of asking him the simplest question (do you want more salt?) for fear of his sneering impatience. He cried. Then said I was disloyal, that it was part of my history as it is perhaps with all "great" or famous people, that I was disloyal to my lover, my friends, and to my poor mother. Et cetera. Much later he said, "I picture myself hanging from that red rope in your room, out of the sixth-story window, with Sonny in my arms. Probably in a sack." Yesterday he said, "When I die, let Sonny sniff me. That's how animals say goodbye: it keeps them from grieving and seeking in vain." Every day, something like this leaves me without an answer, impotent to penetrate his dark night of the soul.

8 February

There is something unseemly in Harold Brodkey's lament in *The New Yorker* about being stricken with AIDS. Who could wish AIDS on a worst enemy, let alone a lover, which HB was to me for half a year in 1962? Nor does anyone "deserve" it. Yet in appropriating the disease for himself, Harold has not a word to say, either sympathetically or philosophically, about the millions of other AIDS sufferers across the planet. (One can't help but compare his plaint to Susan Sontag's informative and thoughtful *Illness as Metaphor*, written after her mastectomy, in which the pronoun "I" is not once used.) To compound his self-evaluation, Harold informs us—lest we forget—that he is a genius, a major writer, an irresistible sexpot, and not a homosexual—all this with a thudding lack of humor.

Harold longs to be taken seriously by the old-boy network. But his catalogue is short, his content limited to Jewish pre-adolescent navel-gazing, his style mannered, his arrogance charmless (as distinct from, say, Noël Coward's arrogance or Lenny Bernstein's). Of course I realize the accusation of self-absorption is leveled at me. But I am not the content of this paragraph, nor do I review my own books as Harold does. And I do talk occasionally of matters beyond myself.

Nantucket, 10 February
"I feel I know you better than you know yourself," announces the stranger after reading one of my diaries. But I don't pretend to know myself; indeed, the Ned encountered in those diaries, in the rare moments when I turn the pages, strikes me as himself a stranger, remote and pretentious, sometimes amusing, even insightful in a manner which the living Ned is not. And repetitious. JH says my theories (especially those on the state of song, of opera, of sexuality) have, by dint of being so often repeated, turned to rote while the world has passed them by.

Well, I'm seventy now. The world may be passing me by, as well as the theories. But what has been learned is that the world does not learn. The carnage in Bosnia will continue, no matter what, for another ten thousand years, until Homo sapiens evolves into something more sapient, or perishes altogether.

Tomorrow, after a snowbound four days during which I've worked on the untitled quartet for Sharon Isbin et alia—*Songs of Sadness*—and JH has wrestled with painkillers for his heart and shingles and tobacco withdrawal (after four months), sleeping sixteen hours a day, we return by plane & automobile to the city.

Jonathan Holland phoned to say his new orchestra piece, a five-minute waltz inspired by *Who's Afraid of Virginia Woolf?*, has been chosen for the finals of an Afro-American-Composer prize in Detroit. That, plus the Arts & Letters Award I maneuvered for him last month, and feel proud. Plus a pang. Jonathan's eighteen.

14 Feb.
Valentine's Day. JH bought a heart-shaped cake of chocolate meringue at the Soutine, and, except for his modest share, I ate every crumb of it . . . Streets impassable, six-foot heaps of soiled snow still completely hide cars—and, who knows? garbage and rats and human corpses—on each side of the road. Sidewalks slippery. Around 10 P.M., as we stroll slowly east on our block with Sonny and a half-gallon of milk, JH exclaims: "Look at the wall on Number 30! In the twenty-five years we've lived here I've never noticed the ingenious design of the bricks—the way the architect or mason has spaced them, full-size and halves and thirds, so that they make a pattern of diamonds big and little." As we near, the pattern grows diffuse and the bricks seem merely functional. Then we look toward our building. Same design, but different, such useful beauty, the pride of bricklaying artists, the coincidence with my remark (Jan. 29) about childhood diamonds in Chicago's cement.

Truth and Beauty are unrelated. Truth is often ugly. Beauty is generally fancy. Is a Grünewald "Crucifixion" beautiful? Is a Varèse percussion construction ugly? Is *Daphnis et Chloë* Truth? That is all I know, and all I need to know.

15 February

From a sense of duty, of staying *au courant* because I so seldom "take advantage of New York" (as out-of-towners say), and of seeing what the fuss is about, I went alone last night to hear the new Schnittke symphony at the Philharmonic. Well, if the piece were a student's, I'd advice him that it lacks direction. Not only is the meandering unskillful, it's colorless, has no class nor even vulgarity, lacks profile, and is finally less offensive than just plodding. The fuss comes from a need for Greatness in a time of triviality. The claim that Schnittke is Shostakovich's heir makes me giggle with embarrassment. His champions are fellow Russo-Germanophiles (Masur, Rostropovich, Gidon Kremer) and brainwashed critics afraid to signal the Emperor's New Clothes lest they be proved wrong a decade hence.

I'm reminded of the Morley Safer debacle a few months ago. Safer very publicly declared—buttressed by TV cameras focused on certain works of new art—his version of the old canard: "Why, my 8-year-old nephew can paint as well as that." One healthy retort should be for the nephew to go ahead and try; the very act of *doing* is the best art-appreciation. The philistine Safer was invited to confront his elitist accusers on every side. These accusers, in the guise of the Better Art Critics, assembled with their victim on Charlie Rose's talk show, became unstrung in their righteous defense of Modern Art by trying to prove Safer categorically wrong. In fact Safer was right, but for the wrong reasons. Most new art *is* lousy, and it's up to them to have the courage to say so. They are not, after all, writing for the unwashed. If Safer is giving *his* unwashed TV audience an easy way out, exonerating his viewers from any responsibility toward the culture of their time (which they couldn't care less about anyway), it's for the professional critics to . . .

NYC, 17 Feb.

The stillness in the heart of New York. Last night I played through the unbearably gorgeous 5th movement of Messiaen's *Quartet for the End of Time*, the *Louange à l'éternité de Jésus*, the slowest piece ever conceived, and relived my first experience of this music. "Experience" I stress, not "hearing." Unlike most people's initial exposure to the works that most "shape" them—for me *La Mer, Le Sacre, Socrate*—which are passively listened to rather than actively participated in, I first experienced the *Louange* while accompanying Maurice Gendron on the green piano in Hyères in the spring of 1951. I heard it and played it simultaneously—the sound unfolded through my fingers, and through the proximity of Gendron's seamless cello. It changed me. Maurice is dead now. He changed me. Change. The change.

Sunday. Very early this morning JH, before leaving for church, came in my room and said, "I feel much better. Smoking again has helped me." Then he left to pick up the car, so that after church we can drive to Hyannis, board a plane to the island where on Tuesday he'll see Voorhees for lung X-rays.

Yes, after nearly five months of abstaining from cigarettes, during which his physical decline was as horrible as his mental breakdown in the 1970s, Jim started smoking again. Well, we each die in our own way, and maybe tobacco is Jim's motivation for living.

Limbo. By rights we should be en route to the city. But, as on the 11th, we're again snowed in. (*Jamais je ne me souviens d'un hiver aussi terrible.*)

Finished another Simenon, one of his best, circa 1955, *La Boule noire*, the portrait of a mediocre middle-class American in a Connecticut town who, during a week-long crisis, realizes, like Arthur Miller's *Salesman*, that to succeed one must play the game. The secret is to know the rules, then to become more mediocre. It's always fun to see how others see us—Mann in *The Black Swan*, Kafka in *Amerika*, and Simenon glazes our land, despite himself, with a Belgian sordidness while almost never stumbling over facts. (P. 197. Was hanging used in Pennsylvania? Similarly, in *Le Blanc à lunettes*, page 53, the only English quoted anywhere is the thrice repeated ". . . am sorry," a mishearing, I guess, of ". . . I'm sorry.")

JH at my prodding finally had a lung X-ray yesterday. Dr. Voorhees, who's against X-rays anyway, and sort of against attempts to stop cigarettes, found nothing. I almost regret this—". . . am sorry"—since JH has license to smoke up a storm, hiding in the bathroom, or out on the porch.

Galloping insomnia. Hour upon Benzedrine-clear hour I wonder if Billie Holiday and Jean Rhys ever heard of each other. *Good Morning, Midnight* and *Good Morning, Heartache* resonate as more than coincidence.

Sonny will be ten next month. Cute and willful as ever, he is visibly slowing down. Something sad about his unawareness of the inexorable, sadder than with a human. It feeds the insomnia.

Schnittke as placebo. We're told he's great, so we see he's great, because we need him to be great, but he's not great. Who has told us? The learned critics, who need him even more, as they needed Elliott Carter a generation ago. Yet do we, the unwashed, rush out, craving to buy their records? We do buy Gorecki. But neither Górecki nor Schnittke holds a candle to, say, Messiaen, or even (if he would compose theater music) George Perle.

The three young composers at Curtis, Jonathan Holland, Daniel Ott, and Luis Prado, come from Philadelphia for their lessons, usually on Saturdays, when I give them lunch (unchangeably quiche, fruit, cookies, yogurt, decaffeinated coffee). Also I sort of dust the house before their arrival. This morning, while shaking the laden mop out of the sixth-story window over the synagogue, much of the debris blew back into my eyes, and I remember the beautiful last lines of Jimmy Baldwin's *Giovanni's Room* in 1956. I put down the mop, and went to get the moth-eaten novel (price: $2.45) to retrieve the experience. "I take the blue envelope which Jacques has sent me," wrote Jimmy, "and tear it slowly into many pieces, watching them dance in the wind, watching the wind carry them away. Yet, as I turn and begin walking toward the waiting people, the wind blows some of them back on me." The last lines are no longer beautiful but ludicrous when one imagines the waiting people blowing through the wind.

Meanwhile, while scanning the first line of Hortense Calisher's new novel, *In the Palace of the Movie King* (price: $32.50), "You should know that by the last decade of the twentieth century, America—as we in the United States had for over two hundred grandiose if inaccurate years had been calling ourselves . . ." I wonder if indeed we had been calling ourselves America as opposed to Americans, and if years, in themselves, can be termed inaccurate as opposed to terms used by people speaking during those years.

JH, since yesterday, is "on the patch" but smoking anyway. His digestive problems continue, as well as his urinary detention, his fibroid tumors (he calls them) throbbing in his distended rock-hard belly, his debilitating attacks of shingles which prevail after five months, his intimations of Addison's disease (inherited from his mother), and his mercurial temper due, perhaps, to augmenting, at Ellen Adler's suggestion, the Prozac daily dosage from one to two. Otherwise he's thriving. Tomorrow, with the three animals and a trunkful of paraphernalia, we drive to Nantucket for five nights.

(Write of *Songs of Sadness*, three-fourths done, and of Sharon Isbin, the Kathleen Battle of guitarists—to whom Rosalyn Tureck says . . . etc. . . . and the pressures of schools, flattering but frightful.)

12 March

Three-hour Confab for the French Radio on "Paris-New York" at the WNYC studios on this deserted Saturday. The discussion, led by one Jean-Michel Damian, was to be in French. Guests: me, Elliott Carter, plus David Noakes and later Barry Brook, with Dominique Nabokov snapping pictures. I was nervous, not having lived inside the French language for years, and feeling that Elliott might upstage me. As it happened his language sounded accented and rusty, with occasional false agreements and English words thrown in when the French ones seemed elusive (e.g., *decade* pronounced à la française, for *décennie.*)

A shambles. Monsieur Damian based the roundtable on his slanted givens, which weren't necessarily ours. "Since Varèse was, during the 1930s and '40s, the leading musician in New York's French colony, what were your impressions?" But

Varèse was not the leading musician, nor was there a French colony. Nonetheless Elliott droned on for a half-hour about his rapports with Varèse. Would Damian pass the mike to me? Or, since Elliott Carter is God (one doesn't interrupt God), was he waiting for Elliott to nod in my direction? Neither. He played a tape of *Amériques* while the rest of us twiddled our thumbs.

In the exactly fifty years since Elliott and I first met, we've seen each other rarely, except at "functions" where we certainly don't talk French. Still, time counts for something, and I was wondering if I should *tutoyer* him. (It used to seem natural among Americans in Europe to *tutoyer* each other, they being all such innocent infants, etc.) The conundrum was unprecedented. But when I started speaking, *vous* fell naturally onto my tongue. Elliott's unmagnanimous self-importance as usual turned me off. He mouthed Gallic-flavored generalities like "The French lend more character to their music than do the Germans."

"What do you mean by character?"

"Well, they portray things. Only Berlioz" (who in my book is German) "could presume to depict a March to the Scaffold."

"What about Strauss's Till Eulenspiegel's march to the gallows?" I suggest. Elliott harrumphs.

When the host referred to my *Paris Diary* as name-dropping (*"Vous sembliez être collectionneur des gens célèbres."*)—but is that something to say to a guest?—I could only reply that they weren't the trophy, I was, and that anyway I preferred people with brains and talent (in the parlor if not in the bedroom), and that such people were frequently *"célèbres,"* though their fame was incidental to their worth. He seemed disappointed to learn that I was not Poulenc's "type," but intrigued when I said that the 1950s—one sees it now—represented the golden agony of French art, that from then on it went downhill.

Elliott countered with: the serious music of 20th-century France began only in the Fifties.

"What do you mean serious?" I ask. Pause.

"A serious composer," answers Elliott, "is one who puts work before society."

Where does that leave me? Or Haydn? Or Fauré? Or Elliott's dear Nadia Boulanger, who was kept by the rich? Or for that matter Boulez? But we know what he means: Write the unlistenable, avoid pleasure, be a challenge.

Elliott, about whom I once wrote "He is filled with charm although his music has none," no longer has charm. I felt warmly toward David Noakes and Barry Brook, in proportion to the bad odor elsewhere. At least the French Radio promotes such roundtables. Imagine that here.

Taxi uptown with Dominique, always chirpy, whose eye is a camera lens. Stalled in traffic on 10th Avenue and 38th Street, we found ourselves next to a bus, on which were four tableaux of Marky Mark in Calvin Klein underwear. Dominique, who had never heard of Marky Mark (I'm such a name-dropper!), was bedazzled, and took pictures of the pictures.

Surprised—then again, not surprised—that the French, while still up on Bernstein and Gershwin and Jerry Lewis, have not heard of Stephen Sondheim.

Elliott may pooh-pooh the pre-fifties French past. But didn't he, in his 1951
String Quartet, use as a motto Cocteau's device, from *Sang d'un poète*, of opening
the film with a quick shot of a dynamited tower about to crumble and, an hour
later, closing the film with a shot of the tower collapsing on the ground? The film
therefore, like all animate art (music, theater, dance), takes place outside of time,
in a millisecond, like a dream.

12 April
Birthday party at Café des Artistes, planned for S.'s seventieth last night, briskly
cancelled by Eugene for health reasons. So JH improvised a *dîner à quatre* and
the Perles came here instead for lamb chops.

Question of the 18-year-old American sentenced to caning in Singapore. S., and
to an extent JH, are not against this corporal punishment. Break the law—expect
the consequences, he knew what he was getting into, etc. (In fact, if there's no
"crime in the streets" in Singapore, it's not because of good government, but
because everyone, even "the rich," live in fear. So says Anderson Cooper.)

S. extends the proscription even to Salman Rushdie. He, too, knew what he
was getting into, so has no cause for demanding worldwide protection.

Yet if artists complied with government dictation, we'd have no Goya or Wede-
kind, no Mark Twain or Pasternak, no Auden or Shostakovich, even no Mapplethorpe or the pornographer Edith Wharton.

"But Rushdie's no artist," you object.

That's your opinion. Are bad artists to be thrashed and good artists redeemed?
Anyway, questions of artistry are not on the minds of Wildmon or Jesse Helms so
much as questions of perceived image.

April
The need to be up on things. Through childhood, and through the early New York
and Paris years, I went to openings of art exhibits, theater, dance, all events musical of course, and devoured the right books, good and bad. Not from duty but
from lust: what, after all, was the sap of being? It seemed clear that Great Art was
absolute: certain works were eternal facts. (Though already at Curtis, in 1943, I
had to persuade myself that Mozart was more urgent than Ravel.) Even today, if
my teenage students are not up on things, I chide them; if they don't create an
hour's worth of music per week, why live?; if they aren't abreast of Carter's or
Glass's latest quartets (whether or not I am), why call themselves musicians with
curiosity and depth? Yet for the past two decades or so I don't give a damn. I still
read voraciously (less sniffy now than when Virgil said, "I've read the classics.
From now on it's Agatha Christie."), mostly books by friends, and still attend concerts regularly, mostly given by friends. But I rarely go to Broadway on the impulse

of pleasure, and never with bated breath. When, as is rarely the case, I'm seated at a new play, the feeling is "What am I doing here? Who are these TV-oriented hicks squeezed into tight seats, roaring at . . ." No, Great Art has no absolutes; and if I declare Ravel more urgent than Mozart, Berlioz more banal than the Beatles, Jackson Pollock not worth the canvas he's dribbled on, while your eyes widen in disbelief, why are you right where I am wrong? For I do not speak through the lips of an ignorant philistine.

Nevertheless, feeling guiltily out of the swing (but too stingy to spend a whole day in theater), I decided to read *Angels in America*. The fuss about it, like the fuss about Schnittke or Gaddis or Carter, seems to be because it's long, complex, and "says" something. Now, it's *too* long (a sign of youth), not really complex (what is it, with its multiple themes, that a one-track novel of, say, Mary Cantwell, isn't?) and what it says is cant—good cant to be sure, but to be anti-Reagan and pro-gay isn't, by itself, art when it's directionless. Yes, it's theatrical, but that's lipstick, not flesh. Each of the gay characters, all male, calls the others Mary and throws out campy cracks while perishing from AIDS: together their unjust suffering makes up for their lack of intellectuality, etc. The play is sophomoric, soothes the unwashed matinee homophobe by placing these stereotypical queens at a safe distance.

Even if Great Art's an absolute, Great Artists—who might they be?—never concur. Allen Ginsberg (PEN Newsletter #83, March '94) propounds yet again: "First thought, best thought—first thought being primordial thought, flash on your mind." I propound that the stuff of dreams becomes junk in the morning; your notated midnight meditation reads like an adolescent's diary. "Inspiration" is a dangerous goad, and, like sincerity, must be faked to be convincing. Art is not real life, it's art. An artist spends hours, months, honing his first thought so that it will sound like a first thought, tailoring his inspiration so that it will appear inspired. Art is coherence; first thought is blur. Blur is not art, though art, on occasion, simulates blur.

Essay on Elliott Carter (this week's *New Yorker*, May 2) by Griffiths is so defensively sycophantic that it trips over itself. "Simplicity and directness have always been as much his blessings as the vaunted 'complexity.' " Why should this always be introduced as a problem? Who complains of the complexity of a forest? If it is so, as Carter claims, that young composers today are "writing like Brahms and doing it badly," why does Griffiths, a few beats later, state that "Questions of language and style don't arise; history is only what it was. The contemporary composer will do things differently by virtue of being a different person in a different age." If Carter's new *Partita* "occasionally suggest[s] splinters of *Petrushka*," how can his music "since the end of the forties achieve its modernism . . . by never looking back." If Carter never looks back, how is it that in Carter's new piece "one can hear an echo of [Berlioz] in the English-horn solo"? Most amusing is Griffiths' contention that in the pre-concert speech about young composers Carter's "tone was regretful, bewildered, but not bitter: he has too much gaiety of mind ever to turn sour—or, indeed, ever to write like Brahms." Not bitter? Gaiety of mind? Elliott? When Elliott first began to be taken seriously as our Great Composer, Virgil quipped: "When Aaron Copland reached the top, he at least sent the elevator back down."

20 April

To *The Nation*: In his voracious defense of novelist William Gaddis against the review media ("their whining and moaning about . . . what should be a privilege is treated like an affront"), one Steven Marcus declares that "the main charge is 'difficulty,' yet only in literature does this seem to be a sin. One rarely sees a music critic complain that Philip Glass expects too much of his listeners."

But isn't Glass's worldwide popularity due precisely to his eschewing of difficulty, to his return to simplicity? Doesn't it stem from the mortal public's need for an antidote to the convoluted works of Carter, Boulez, et al.? These works, meanwhile, remain beloved by deconstructional music critics who are a majority, and who, like Mr. Marcus, seemingly admire complication for its own sake.

29 April

I was still reading (essays by John Simon in various numbers of *The New Criterion* that he brought over yesterday while out strolling on this first summery day), propped on pillows at around 1 A.M., when JH, long since retired, knocked on the wall that separates our rooms. I went into the darkness of his sleeping area, which for years he has shared with Sonny and the cats. These animals now lay curled among the bedclothes like fur pieces hurled at random by some drunken heiress, and JH lay there with them, inaudibly sobbing. I reclined beside this group in the gloom for half an hour. JH ached for some human contact. He talked subjectively, which he so seldom—in his Midwestern stoicism—does. His father these days is comatose and probably dying, while his mother ministers and is herself mentally shaky, both in the protective halls of Sunset Manor, a retirement home in Kansas, like that of my parents in Jersey, where JH supervised their deaths six years ago.

JH recalled how my father during his last years would weep without apparent reason, then would laugh at this nonsense, only for the laughter to turn again to tears; how Father's long life in "socialized medicine" for the "betterment of man" was now represented by a corrupt cartel; how my music just might last for a while if only because it is mostly vocal and hence transmittable like Gregorian chant (while even the Sistine Chapel, given enough time, turns into pop art); how his own parents are crying—they too—at the meaninglessness of existence; how even stupid people at the end perceive, on some level, that all is vanity.

This insomniac soliloquy was interrupted by one of JH's racking coughs during which, almost daily, he vomits—while holding a lit cigarette in his right hand.

15 May

Alone this afternoon to hear the ACO play Ellen Zwilich's Trombone Concerto. The orchestra, under Dennis Russell Davies, glimmered with unity, but the program was perverse. A harmless Straussian *Tragic Overture* by a turn-of-the-century Chicagoan named Edward Joseph Collins. Then Ellen's piece, so different from her warm and pretty self. The first movement seems cool and directionless, well-scored but without bones. Polite, at least, compared to the pretentious "Einstein's Red/Blue Universe" by one Jane Ira Bloom, who herself played the Soprano Saxophone & Live Electronics. Her hip gyrations suggested she had to pee, so much did she painfully writhe while the orchestra behind (plus eight brass in the left balcony, and eight more in the right) contained players required to rise and blow their horns while turning in complete 360-degree angles. Embarrassing. Her music may have been music, but it was not composition, going nowhere, and being mostly improvised in a manner inferior to, say, Benny Goodman fifty years ago . . . Sessions's Ninth Symphony is hopeless. And it contains one gross miscalculation. Any piece this willfully ugly and gnarled should not have percussion. Percussion is inevitably decorative. Each swish of the cymbal or lick of the xylophone was like rouge and earrings on this sober old professor. Sessions's premise is offensive: "I would prefer by far to write music which has something fresh to reveal at each new hearing than music which is completely self-evident the first time." But who wants to hear his music a second time? Whereas the music of Monteverdi and Messiaen, of Poulenc and Ravel, of Mozart and Chopin, is self-evident the first time, and at least one person longs to hear it again and again. Sessions hints that he could, if he wanted to, compose something self-evident. Well, let him. All music worthy of the name is self-evident.

JH's father is dying in Kansas. Exhausted, JH and Sonny set out by automobile for the Middle West this afternoon. During the concert he was in my mind. In Ellen's slow movement, the icy sadness of the strings, the tone clusters and wisps of aborted melody, made tears well up, and I listened hard, with fists wet and clenched.

2 June

". . . but the style's naïveté is not always faux . . ." states John Updike smartly, if in faulty French (the current *New Yorker*, May 30, p. 109).

For several weeks John and I have corresponded about collaborating on a song short enough to fit onto one page and be adorned by Larry Rivers. This would be one of several joint ventures by other Academy members, to be turned into lithographs and sold expensively for the centennial next year. We've finally opted, not for a new poem, but on the final quatrain from "Somewhere":

> to face one's life and to live solemnly,
> with an eloquence, like a bow being drawn
> across a cello the color of God's cigar —
> to make, of this scuttle and heartbeat, art.

To the oft-posed question, "Why don't you set your own words to music?" I reply: "My writing and my composing answer to two opposed needs, nor have I any gift for penning poems, only prose. I flatter myself that, whatever my songs may be worth, the poems I've used are good literature. If Ned the writer were able to write words good enough for Ned the musician to set, the words wouldn't need music."

What is an "anti-hero"?

Are sugar & starch categorized as French & German, or the reverse?

Nantucket, 8 June

Last January, trepidant, I accepted John Simon's invitation to be an honoree at a fund-raiser for Marymount College on June 7th. Because John's wife, Pat Hoag, is on Marymount's theater staff, I, along with Al Hirshfeld, Tommy Tune, Licia Albanese and others, would be a feather in her cap. The trepidation sprang from not knowing Marymount, from loathing hotel dinners (there would be a lively auction too), and from discomfort when sharing the role of guest-of-honor—not ego so much as deficiency of the crucial ability to interrupt when at a roundtable with extroverts. John assured me I'd not be asked to speak, only to curtsy when accepting the crystal emblem.

The waking reality last evening turned out worse than the anticipatory nightmare.

JH being in Kansas for his father's funeral, Chuck Adams agreed to escort me. The pre-prandial cocktail hour at the swanky Palace mezzanine contained no familiar faces, only loud loud loud rich philistines. John eventually materialized, introduced us to the college president (a hard chic woman with no conversation), then squired us to the dining room, where, to my horror, a thunderous hotel-orchestra was not only at work but working right next to our select table. The din would preclude any coherent talk, although our table was laid for nine by-definition-coherent people: me and Chuck and John and Hirshfeld, talk-show star Jim Ryan and his cousin (a nun), another man (who was to accept an award in absentia for Comden & Greene), the president herself, and Tom Wolfe. Wolfe, whom I've never met—nor were we introduced—sitting three chairs away, arranged for his famous friendly eyes never to cross with mine, which made clear that he would not be extending his hand, nor encouraging me to do so. What, I wondered, have I ever done to him? Ah yes, it must be that crank letter to the *Times*, years ago, when I took to task his review of Cecil Beaton's memoir wherein he twitted queers. Still, is that enough for him to ignore my presence now, rather than, like a suave European, to separate professional feuds from social niceties? He meanwhile might argue he didn't know who I was.

This sophomoric rudeness was as nothing compared to a moment on December 1st, 1989. That afternoon, hieing west on 155th Street toward the Academy where I was to deliver a memorial address on Virgil Thomson, I spotted Alfred

Kazin heading the same way. Knowing him, albeit slightly, from parties and shared panel discussions over the years, I greeted him, and began walking by his side. Like Prince Hal shrugging off old Falstaff he uttered a harrumph, with a look of who's-this-importunistic-nobody. Whereupon, tail between my legs, I detached myself and proceeded alone. When, after my clever and touching memorial address, Kazin came smiling toward me, I, like Tom Wolfe, did not allow our gazes to connect. What had prompted his earlier behavior I do not know, but I felt more insulted than paranoid, and wondered if it were the professional Jew's revenge on the gay goy who appears one rung lower. Probably the goy part is irrelevant: Paul Goodman once wrote that Kazin was sarcastic in referring to his—Paul's—"circle of lads" . . . Were Adam and Eve Jewish?

Anyway. My insecurity was not assuaged when Madame President and John Simon ascended the podium to laud, one by one, the honorees. Alternating in their presentations, they sang the praises of each special guest, after which each special guest mounted the podium and gave an acceptance speech, smarmy and apt. In a sweat I dreaded my turn: unprepared, what could I say? I despised the ease of Tommy Tune's graceful lilt; of Hirshfeld's casual candor; of Albanese's *putasserie* (why the standing ovation for her and for her alone?); of Tune's friend, a coach, whose presence was added at the last moment, and who cleverly announced, "My name's the only one I don't recognize"; of Jim Ryan's expertise. When my time came, after Simon's eulogy, "Ned Rorem is the world's greatest composer of songs" (as Albanese draws a blank), I rose and murmured, "I am touched and thrilled. Thank you," then sat down, inadvertently gulping a swig of wine, which I thought was water, then spat it out. Wolfe gave a disjointed speech on the glories of Marymount, and made an impression that I did not. Should I have said, "I always wanted to be embraced by Catholicism," or "I was asked to be witty as well as brief, and since these two adjectives are synonyms in my vocabulary, I'll . . ." or "How nice to get a good review from John Simon"? But this is just *espirit de l'escalier.*

I hated Wolfe, hated the cheap deafening racket, hated the "social dancing" which should be a prerogative of only the young. Hoarse from small talk, I begged Chuck to leave now with me. Stuffing the crystal emblem in a pocket, we fled. Chuck is low-key and soothing. In the sticky summer air we strolled up Sixth Avenue where, at 57th, he took a subway to Roosevelt Island, and I walked, then, all the way home.

No one, of course, believes I'm shy. But shyness produces diaries wherein one notes what can't be spoken. The purpose of a diary is to evade real life. Yes, actors without scripts are fish out of water, but that doesn't keep them from flipping about on talk shows. The metabolism of group action, as distinct from solo reaction, is anathema to me.

A masterpiece will never be produced by the properly programmed computer for the simple reason that no three wise judges will ever agree on what constitutes a masterpiece. If I, for one, decree that Bach is pap, and that those endless Brahms quartets are merely pompous, why am I wrong and you right?

Do roaches dream? Do mice? Do parakeets?
  Do broaches cream, chew rice, woo parakletes?

Likeness of Britten's *3rd Sonnet of Michelangelo* to Ravel's *Le Paon*.

Nantucket, 8 June

Came here alone by plane, JH being still in Kansas for his father's funeral. The house looks welcome on this painfully lovely afternoon with a great advance in less than a week in the snowballs and peonies. A morose tinge: Before we left here last Thursday JH painted the kitchen floor a glossy enamel and left it to dry, untrampled, for six days. Now I find a daddy long-legs down there, struggling, but unable to advance. When I free him, all of his hair-thin legs remain imbedded. Quickly, to put him out of his misery, smash his brittle little body. He must have been caught there for days.

Nantucket, 9 June

"Oh, the nightmare of insomnia!" moans Archibald.
  "A false image!" retorts Anne-Marie. "Bad dreams require sleep."
  "A true image," Archie sighs. "A sort of oxymoron."
  "So redundant," insists she. "Idiots are by definition bovine."

Gay composers, as discussed in *Queering the Pitch*. Larry Mass won't let me off the hook. Like the now old-fashioned phrase, "gay sensibility," it remains undefined. Possibly, yes, a homosexual writes a certain kind of music because he is that, though it would be hard to demonstrate. But does an affluent rich ugly American WASP buggerer sing the same song as a poor pretty Romanian passive drag queen? What about delicate heterosexuals like Chopin and Beardsley and Leslie Howard, as distinct from the cop who recently raped at gunpoint a series of male cabdrivers? Homosexual is an arbitrary medical term, vaguely legal and very recent. The more interesting question is not what kind of music he or she writes as a result of queerness, but (which is far more rich and strange) what makes that music tick.

David Denby, in June 15 *New York*, re. Dennis Hopper in *Speed*: "Once again, the bad guy is an articulate and malevolent sport (as usual in American movies, intelligence and wit are associated with evil) who . . ." In contrast, Oliver North, who *is* evil, and has just been nominated by Virginia for the senate, is associated by many Americans with good.

A few years ago JH gave me a luscious heavy comforter for the Nantucket bed. One side features somber leaves—ochre and rust and purple—against a jet-black ground, the other side features thousands of light bright dots against a white ground. When I make the bed I alternate the sides every other morning, dreading the gloomy side on odd days, rejoicing in the happy side on even days. Why, you ask, do I not make the bed each day with only the bright side up?

What's the difference between affect & effect, careen & career?

What is:
    The postmodern bottom line
    The cutting edge
    Phenomenology
    Quality time
    Kudo
    Role model
    Workplace
    Baby boomer
    Pundit

Verbs: to party, to bankroll
    The bottom line is the pundits' kudo to baby boomers who party in the work-place, bankrolled by role models giving postmodern quality time.

3 July

Citizen Kane (or snippets therefrom—like everyone else, I flip channels in my superficial haste and short attention span) remains as fresh, novel, and freezing cold as it was 53 years ago. The only moment to shed a tear is, of course, at the very end, but Bernard Herrmann's awful music precludes that. The remarkable and moving revelation of Rosebud, never to be retrieved from the flames, is ruined by the overstated score.

Nantucket, Sunday July 10

"The constant, silent roaring of the sun." That gorgeous pentametrical verse con-cludes the opening sentence of the opening article of today's "The Week In Review," by one George Johnson: "Unless the laws of celestial mechanics are repealed (or have been misapplied), this Saturday, on the very date 49 years ago that the scientists of the Manhattan Project produced the largest manmade sound, Jupiter will be the stage for what some astronomers are billing as the loud-est noise in the solar system, except for the constant, silent roaring of the sun."

JH quotes his pre-adolescent companion of circa 44 years ago: "Have you ever jerked off till you get the heebie-jeebies?"

Friday, Mary Heller's annual exhibit at the Straight Wharf Gallery. Hand-tinted photographs, more than merely professional, sometimes quite moving, despite (maybe because of) the total absence, as in Utrillo, of human personalities. The guests, hovering in the small adjacent garden where Peter Heller hosts at a cocktail table, are typical Nantucket: well-off gentiles, over-scrubbed, the sexless men in shell-pink shorts, the expensive women flawlessly marcelled with self-assured selfish voices pitched like hyenas'.

Correcting proofs of my index, overly detailed, scrupulous, more apt for a biography than for an autobiography, concocted by a possibly would-be writer who feels him-herself every bit as good as me. For instance, this entry:

Jews:
    NR's relationships with, 140, 142, 169
    NR's questionable remarks about, 177, 179–80

Suffocating heat-wave continues. JH, depressed both physically and mentally, returns at 8, on the High-Line ferry, with Cindy Hatcher.

29 June

As is my wont every eight years I'm restudying the quartets of Bartók. Am I allowed to say that they're exasperating? Those unstoppable crunching ostinatos! Those un-lovely too-complex vocalises? Those witty dances that now seem witless! Despite their 31-year *envergure*, the six separate works are really all the same, with the sixth less compelling than the first. Yes, they are unique in the literature, and models for everyone. (The central section of Stravinsky's aria for Jocasta is not so much influenced by as rifled intact from the central section of the last movement of Bartók's first quartet.) But for me they don't add up.

New York, 23 July

Alone in N.Y. during the most paralyzing heat wave of the century.

Went to *Angels in America*, from duty and guilt (I never go to the theater anymore, but am always sounding off about it), and from opportunism and curiosity (maybe Kushner will write me a libretto). Well, you can't laugh it off, and I did sit through till the end. But nothing that long can be all good, and much of it is easily trimmed. Well-acted but unmoving, often vulgar. Not just the endless "fuck you" screams from one and all, but also the pandering to the all-too-willing audience. The queers are all get-you-Mary types. At the end, when the main queer dies theatrically, he, Prior Walter, cries out as the Angel descends in a rumpus, "How very Steven Spielberg." And what does the Angel mean?

Two thefts. A minor one: Talullah Bankhead's unlovely quip to someone who asks if Montgomery Clift is gay, "I wouldn't know: he never sucked *my* cock," is pilfered to no effect when Kushner has a man say it about another man. A major one: The compelling scene in Gide's *Counterfeiters*, where Lillian, after first sleeping with Vincent, tells him of her harrowing escape from the sinking Bourgogne when sailors with hatchets whacked off the hands of drowning survivors crawling aboard the lifeboat. Lillian likens her ensuing life to the scene: she must cut off all those etc. Kushner paraphrases the scene, in the mouth of Prior Walter: same image, same metaphor, same resurgence of his past.

Two recordings of my 1975 *Eight Piano Etudes* are now out (by Walter Cosand and by Frances Renzi) and very well played. JH likes them most of all my music. And they *are* inventive. I couldn't write them today—mainly because I already wrote them yesterday.

Or: I couldn't write it now—mainly because I wrote it then.

1 September

Preamble to a reading from *Knowing When to Stop* at the Atheneum in Nantucket:

There is something contradictory about an author reading aloud from his own book. After all, the prose is there for anyone to mull silently, nor was it primarily written to be heard. Even poetry now is seldom designed for speaking, and when it is spoken the poet is not necessarily the final authority. For example, Elizabeth Bishop sabotages her perfect verse with bland readings, while Dylan Thomas sabotages his with exaggerated histrionics. One can't know how Melville or Emerson once connected with their audience in this very room, but it was probably not through intoning *Omoo* or "Self-Reliance." If they were here tonight, would we want to hear them read, rather than quiz them to see how they tick?

There is something still more contradictory about *my* reading aloud from this new book. My writing, except for occasional objective essays on musical matters, has been in the guise of diaries. Diaries are by nature secret, confessional, subjective in their exuberance about such questions as a broken heart on a Tuesday, a trip to Saratoga, a digestive problem, a professional jealousy. The questions are developed out of frustration at being unable to voice these feelings in public. The contradiction lies in reading aloud to strangers about how shy one is about reading aloud to strangers on subjects that by definition cannot be read aloud to strangers.

Add to this, that I am essentially a musician, not an author: a composer who also writes, not a writer who also composes. Meaning that I earn my living, above all, through music, and that whatever hazy renown I may have as a writer stems solely from whatever hazy renown I have as a composer. In the prose, it is always the composer who speaks. As to whether *music* can depict such exact experiences as a broken heart on a Tuesday or a digestive problem, is moot. Yes, a composer exposes his self as articulately as does a writer or a painter, but no one can explicate that self, including the composer. It's not that music is too vague for words—it's too precise for words. And no composer can be jailed for political subversion like, say, a Goya or a Dostoevsky. A composer can hide behind his notes in a way that another artist cannot hide behind his verbs or paints.

As to the present memoir, it is neither diary nor essay, and was written far from the madding crowd, with the poignancy of retrospect. It would never have occurred to me to write such a book, given my egocentric outpourings available elsewhere, were it not for a publisher's offer too generous to refuse. Once I got going, it was clear that the work would have a beginning, a middle, and a close, for I decided to stop on reaching 1951, the year that the open-ended diary begins.

The choice of extracts I'll now read is based on two premises: 1) Keep it brief, to allow for a few minutes of general discussion at the end. 2) The more anonymous the audience, the easier it is for the speaker to act up; but when he knows and must live with several people here, he will avoid the personal and the salacious, and stick to generalities.

19 September

For Lewis Frumkes's book on favorite words:

As vowels suggest colors to the poet Rimbaud, and as chord-progressions suggest crystal-orange birdsong to the composer Messiaen, so words, all words, are for me no less strong for their dictionary meaning than for their associative textures, mainly of food and various cloth materials.

Thus "one" implies dried blood, "three" is melted butter, "five" is old cherry pie, "twenty" is the taste of a dime.

And thus my favorite word is the omnipresent and humbly useful "the." "The," for me, is the hue and feel of tan-gray goose feathers on a cool summer night.

Il faut être absolument moderne, say the old-fashioned French, citing their authority, the 18-year-old Rimbaud. But I am modern, by definition. I am alive.

Je est un autre, says the same Rimbaud. Why not mix the sayings: *Je est le présent*.

No, you are yesterday.

Oh. Then is Borges's Menard yesterday?

And are the French really old-fashioned—those who are alive? No, but their sayings are.

Knowing When to Stop. I single out Satie as opposed to Bruckner. But when John Cage takes literally Satie's campy metaphoric avviso for his (Satie's) three-minute *Vexations*—repeat 840 times—rents a hall and a relay of pianists to do just that, he goes too far, drawing attention to himself and away from Satie. Or the phrase, "I wish you were dead," which we've all said or thought at least once in passing, and which is taken at face value and acted upon by the madman in *Strangers on a Train*.

Like the verb *to put*, plus a preposition (see *Nan. Diary*), is the infinitive *to make up* (explain it to a Frenchman).

It means *maquiller* (verb).

The composition of (noun), as in the makeup of the soil.

Catch up on, as missed classes.

To be friends again, after a quarrel.

28 Sept.

To Central Park with photographer from *Time*. It was fifty-five years ago that I first wandered these furrows during the 1939 World's Fair, twenty-six years ago since, with JH, I've lived on the edge of this classical expanse. Scarcely a week goes by that I don't cross the Sheep Meadow, or watch the bowlers near the 69th Street entrance. Little has changed in a century. Virgil used to contend that all the bordering buildings on the east side were male, with their purposeful spiky penthouses, and the west buildings were female, with their split-style double towers and bushy gardens a thousand feet in the air. At four A.M. do these structures clash together over the gloomy gracious park?

NYC, 15 October

Tea here with Ellen Zwilich and Eric Lamont (they brought a dozen napoleons, and a dozen small green and russet apples), as well as with David Conte and Conrad Susa. The occasion: to hear tapes of Ellen's two new concertos, one for bassoon, one for trumpet. Collating the sound of the Bassoon Concerto with the sight of the score, which we followed assiduously as suave pros always do when score's around, what we heard contradicted what we saw, the fact of the soloist being more raw than her (for she was a woman) sleek careful line on the page. Since for the Trumpet Concerto no score was supplied, we were forced to absorb the music the way it's said most people enjoy music—simply by listening. Yet I *saw* the sound: Doc Severinsen's instrument became an electric eel slithering rapidly up & down watery buildings of blue-black moiré, and the experience was like drowning in sci-fi silk.

Why do I dislike concertos, and especially the cadenzas—including my own—within concertos? For the same reason I dislike bel canto. They are about performance rather than about what is performed—about the singer, not the song. Cadenzas today (at least I feel, and advise my students) should always be somehow accompanied, with a pedal point, or with intermittent, albeit brief (like coughs), comments. For although my lean French nature prefers style to substance (you've either got substance or you ain't, while style requires cultivation), with a cadenza, when all is style, it's totally predictable, therefore empty of listening appeal.

It could be argued that all music is a cadenza, just as all music is a Theme & Variations (another yawn-making form). But . . .

A few days later. Susa's TV diffusion of *Dangerous Liaisons*. Everything about it is good except *it*. It doesn't add up. Yet, the music is at all times skillful and touching, and the libretto is sound. But is it (what is?) an opera?

27 Oct.

Songs of Sadness. The first noise you hear is of a paintbrush swirling the three instrumental colors into a viable canvas on which, or out of which, or behind which, the baritone melts into focus.

Unsung Eng.-language writers: James Hamilton-Patterson. Denton Welch.

Diaghilev's notorious admonishment to Cocteau, *Etonne-moi*, is forever trans-lated to "Astonish me." More correct, literally and sonorously, is "Astound me."

For the record (I mean the CD), the production of *Miss Julie* at the Manhattan School of Music, with its excellent orchestra and theatrical soloists in Kenward's whittled-down script, is the best the opera will ever need. We are beholden to Marta Istomin.

How the decades Proustianly intertwine, with Martita now the spouse of my best male friend at Curtis 55 years ago.

Nantucket, 17 November

Father's hundredth birthday.

A few days ago—was it in the *Times*?—an "in-depth" article tells us about the high rate of suicide among writers, and trots out the usual suspects. But is the rate so high, really, compared to "real people"? How many of the victims are *failed* authors? Aren't artists, as a whole, finally *less* neurotic than other folks (including bankers and kings) by virtue of deeply knowing what they want to do, being able to do it, and being appreciated for doing it?

Whatever the size of suicide among writers, it's non-existent among musicians. Can you think of one good composer who has killed himself, much less a per-former, still less (among performers) a singer? Something in their nature forbids self-destruction; violence, frequent among painters, skirts creative musicians. True, some wither away, like Charles Naginsky, who drowned in Tanglewood, or Bill Flanagan, whose pills brought about his end. But they are exceptions.

Violence occasionally flirts with the edges of music: Gesualdo was a murderer in 1590, Marc Blitzstein was murdered 400 years later. Other examples don't leap to mind as quickly as, say, raw death among painters and poets (Marlowe was killed and Caravaggio was a killer). But "odd" deaths of composers are more like those of Chausson, who died in a bicycle accident, or Wallingford Riegger, in a tangled dog-leash. Composers have been occasionally wild, drunk, crazy: Mus-sorgsky, Lou Harrison, myself. Or in trouble, and jailed: Henry Cowell. But as a rule they are a calm breed.

Still, not an hour goes by that I don't think of suicide. And of JH's ever-failing health.

(See my notes to Kinsey on who's queer and who isn't in the music world.)

In Harold Bloom's new book on literature: 500-plus pages and not a word about musicians.

20 Dec., nearly Christmas

Tomorrow JH sees urologist Doctor Coleman. Reversal of fortune? He feels his ulcer is due to having quit smoking for 5 weeks.

I know all about acting, except how to act.

Next, or ultimate, project: *Art of Song*.
    Twenty-four pieces for four voices & piano, on American texts.
        Solos   8
        Duos   6
        Trios   6
        Quartets   4

Tried again last night, as I tried 45 years ago when Yves Salgues gave it to me, to read *Siegfried et le limousin*. Couldn't make head or tail of the first chapter. Giraudoux's language is so precious, special, ornate, and my French ear has weakened. Tonight I'll try again. But, like *Le Grand Meaulnes*, it can't cross borders.

On the car radio, between Manhattan and Hyannis, much finer stations than in New York. Always the guessing game: What's this? Is it Mahler or Bruckner? Etc. A Haydn symphony bored us. JH says, "We just don't need Haydn anymore." Those "amazing" modulations and "wrong notes" that musicologists so extol—do they still amaze us the second, the fifty-second, time? *La Valse* is terrific music—if you don't have to listen to it. Like *Boléro*, it's an "idea piece." Yet *Boléro* is more fun.

Philip Johnson and Samuel Ramey on Charlie Rose.
    Despite his canny know-how, Charlie asks the wrong questions. He wonders about "genius" and the "creative" process, and of course Philip Johnson has no answers. Artists make art, they don't make answers; answers are for psychologists, who are generally off-target. To Samuel Ramey he wonders about the one perfect and unforgettable performance the bass may have given. And Ramey, after reflection, recalls such an occasion. But singers, although they may feel good about this or that presentation, really have no notion of how they sound to others. At seventy they'll tell you they're sounding better than ever. The proper question to a creator is: How do you build a building, how do you compose a piece? The proper question to a performer is: How do you approach this sonata, how do you learn that song? All else is blather.

Experience has nothing to do with authority, much less with acumen. Otherwise Tennessee Williams and Gian Carlo Menotti would have grown increasingly better, high-powered producers would never make mistakes, Zeffirelli and Andrew Lloyd Webber would occasionally give us non-commercial marvels, and every high-paid orchestra musician or lower-paid stage-hand would be a penetrating critic.

All art dates, from the moment it is made. Some dates well, some badly. Giotto, *Le Sacre*, the Beatles date well. Beethoven's Ninth, Lautrec, the Rolling Stones date badly. (Pick your own examples: personal taste is risky, even when the argument's solid.)

Last night, having cast aside Giraudoux, I took up Emerson. Imagine, at this late date! Except for the poem "Give All to Love," which I musicalized thirteen years ago, have I ever read Emerson? Well, "Self-Reliance" is purple, smart, brash, and authoritative, but it sure dates—badly or well, I'm not sure. What fun to find phrases like "Do your own thing," from 150 years ago, and "consistency is the hobgoblin of little minds," and "to be great is to be misunderstood." But in urging us to do our own thing, the essay constantly admonishes us to eschew the past. "These roses under my window make no reference to former roses or to better ones: they are what they are; they exist with God today. There is no time to them." Lovely but false: all roses are the same, but not all gods or thoughts or experiences; and every work of art is, by definition, unique.

"Insist on yourself; never imitate," urges Emerson. But two sentences later he asserts: "That which each can do best, none but his Maker can teach him." Then why insist—since it's all in the stars? (Radiguet claimed the reverse: "A true artist can't help but be original. Thus, he has only to copy, to prove his originality.") Be yourself? But how be else?

Emerson dates, if only because there's no audience today for high-minded thoughts, or even a hint that high-mindedness exists.

So I turn to Wendy Lesser's pretty good little quarterly, *The Threepenny Review*. Among the Letters to the Editor, one Mark Jarman takes Alfred Corn to task for stating that Rimbaud shot Verlaine, when in fact Verlaine shot Rimbaud: "It was Verlaine who not only assaulted Rimbaud but also abused his wife, who was the criminal, and not the romantic sort that Alfred had in mind as a French type." Did you know that Rimbaud's wife was a criminal? Elsewhere we are told (by one August Kleinzahler) that the poet Thom Gunn does not have "an aleatory bone in his body. He's Handel, not John Cage." Of course, Handel is not the counterpart to Cage: Elliott Carter is. But Gunn has nothing of Carter. With intellectuals like these, who needs Emerson?

1995

Nantucket, *1 January*

Last year I had six major performances in New York alone: *Anna la bonne*, in January, local première; English Horn Concerto, Jan.–Feb., world première (NY Phil), and played again in July, prior to Far East tour; *The Auden Poems* in May, local première; two short operas: *A Childhood Miracle* and *Three Sisters Who Are Not Sisters*, in Sept. (The Magic Circle); *Songs of Sadness*, in Oct.–Nov., world première; *Miss Julie*, in Dec., revival after 30 years. All this, plus a 600-page memoir, appearing in September. Two of these events (*Anna* and *Auden Poems*) were reviewed by nobody. All the others were attended by Leighton Kerner, who reviewed none of them.

So I open the new year with habitual bitterness, and perpetual insomnia ("Both sides of the pillow / Are already hot"—Akhmatova), the reason for which, as a ploy of God and nature, has no reason.

JH's diverse diseases easing maybe?

Lazy. Un-driven.

The Boarding House with Eugenie, loud and expensive, my last venture into any restaurant.

Saturday *14 Jan.*

Visit from Claire Bloom and Brian Zeger to rehearse the little melodrama *Three Women*, which they'll perform in a couple of weeks at the Y. Cheesecake from the

Soutine, green grapes in blue bowl, pot of tea. Claire, now sixty-three, with her deep wise eyes, looks as handsome as the only other time we met, seventeen years ago. I tell them of my quarrel this morning with our neighbor and ask Claire did she ever lose her temper? She says no, her temperament is mild. But once, with her sister-in-law, with whom she was having altercations, she *played the role* of one who loses her temper. Thereupon she and Brian, for my reaction, performed twice *Three Women*. Claire clearly differentiated twixt the three authors, Jean Rhys, Colette, Elizabeth Hardwick, each deftly framed by my piano score.

JH stopped to hear the second run-through, and made pithy comments, mainly about Americanizing the pronunciation of a few words—"shone" and "birth," etc. We are both very tired.

It's been an interesting pleasure. Care was taken to synchronize music with text (sometimes to the split second), but that's just one way of doing it.

I always like to say that the seven arts are independent of each other; if they could represent each other, we'd only need one art. Words have an exact descriptive sense, while music has only a blurred descriptive sense. Or rather: it's not that music is too vague for words, it's too precise for words. Music cannot, for example, express blue as distinct from green, knife as distinct from fork, or pyramid as distinct from igloo, though it *can* move us inexplicably to tears. Yes, conventions allow music to express Big Notions like Love and Death, but the terms of these conventions shift every generation.

What music *does* do, in relation to spoken or visual theater, is adapt to any situation, and heighten (or support or even change) meanings that are already there. When Copland wrote his background score for *The Heiress*, one very serious scene drew laughs from the audience at a sneak preview; director Wyler pled with the composer to insert some new music "to prevent laughter." When Auric wrote his background score for *Blood of a Poet*, director Cocteau later switched the music intended for this scene with the music intended for that scene; such reversal of intent enhanced the movie's already surreal tone.

Thus, the music for our *Three Women* is not only writ. As the words can stand alone, so can the accompaniment. Indeed, under other circumstances these musical pieces could form a suite extraneous from the stories they now purport to illustrate. Any sequences or silences or repetitions or juxtapositions you may choose to incorporate, after sampling the material, are o.k. with me.

Sunday 15 Jan.
Jim's cough is frightful. Plangent rasping, continuous, nothing helps. Certainly not the three-packs-a-day he smokes, even while soaking in the tub. For a year he's seemed on the edge physically, with the shingles, the hiatal hernia, then the Crohn's disease, which appears to be the crux. Has an arsenal of sedatives & cures, though no steady doctor beyond a woman homeopath somewhere in Maine to whom he talks by phone (for a price), introduced by Judy Collins. High fever. Vomits daily. Today, after yet another hacking sleepless night for him, when he returns

from church, we'll head for a short week on the island, in a rented car with Lucille & Tom (who also vomits), Sonny, and a pile of luggage including my mss, and JH's electric keyboard.

Nantucket, Wednesday 18 Jan.

What shall I do with the rest of my life? Each morning brings an attempt to recover from the shambles of the night. Sleep, such as it is chez moi, never restores.

We both feel wretched. High fever, seeping pores, bloody coughs with cascades of strawberry-colored snot, exhaustion, no appetite, stomach ache. JH continues worse (I had a flu shot last Sept.!) He lies on the parlor sofa twenty hours a day. Upstairs, stretched out in one of the three little rooms, I hear him talk to himself. At 6 A.M. he cries Help! We cough back and forth through the house like monkeys conversing in the jungle. Surreal morbid silence. No reading. No eating. No going forth with Sonny, whom we put on the porch merely. JH pukes several times a day.

Kept awake by the noises in my body: motors squeaking & whirring & wheezing in head & chest. Haven't slept for four days, not even for an hour.

Friday

JH drove alone to NY despite his condition. He'll come back Sunday after church, weather depending. I've cancelled everything for a week, and will stay here in the rain to die.

In 1978 I read Jack Finney's already eight-year-old sci-fi romance, *Time After Time*, which takes off from the Dakota two blocks away. Now a sequel is being advertised. So I re-peruse the original with the same uneasiness as before. In the margins I had noted:

Pp. 106–107: Ray Bradbury wrote a story a generation ago about the world that did change, albeit imperceptibly, after an adventure into the far past. If "that January of 1882 existed out there too," then so did February and March, and 1883, and 1492, and all minutes of all time. 113: If, "In the park we angled across it to the east and south," were "we" visible to people of the present? And (same page) did people say "okay" in 1882? 123: "'Can you do it in half an hour?' 'I don't know,' he said disgustedly.'" What was the driver doing during this half-hour in the "first" 1882? Was he carrying Si & Katie then too? In which case there is no such thing as "going back" in time, since all moments exist in all moments. 138: "I sat forever in Rube's office then, turning the pages of old copies of *Life*, discovering . . ." This book was written 8 years ago, so this page already feels distant. 144: The second paragraph describes a winter scene, while the illustration opposite depicts a summer scene. 224: "A man of no apparent importance, though I'm sure he was important to himself, no longer exists. Never *did* exist, in a very strange yet true sense." Well, do his parents and wife and children exist? The question is not how much the subject remembers of his own background during the debriefing. What about other people who were never born because of his trip to the past? or pieces of music that never got composed? or a race of spiders made extinct by one false step that he was unaware of?

Thirty-five years ago, when I announced to Joe LeSueur that "I've decided to become a nice person," he replied, "Oh? How do you plan to go about it?"

Yes, of course there can be many pasts, even in the ken of one experiencer. Any memoir offers shards of yore, frozen in the present, before they melt into the future. And yes, history depends on where you stand, and shifts each second, according to who "you" are. But all that's metaphoric. The fact: I can never meet and sniff and love, say, Thomas Eakins. Not his painting, but the finite trembling man. I long for his flesh, which was gone before I was born.

JH asks, "Do we know anyone who could be called a Nice Person?" We search long, and in vain. Finally I ask, "Am I a nice person?" "Good heavens, no," says JH.

At 71 have I said all I have to say? I don't feel that the best is yet to come, nor have I retained that boyish élan of so many old artists—especially painters—who feel they've only just begun. By the age of twenty-three I'd written a dozen songs that I've never equaled since. Not that I can't do "as well"; but I can't do it again, because I've done it. Do I await alluringly massive codes to crack? Am proud of my thirteen books, and of the fifty-or-so hours of music in every shape or form. Have I gotten better? Does one "get better," or even different? One repeats oneself in different shapes, large and small and tight and loose forever. An artist speaks his identifiably unique tongue out of everyone's vocabulary.

At four A.M. JH and I, insomniac and wheezing, talk together, suppress tears, allow perspective to whirl about as it always does in the dangerous hours of early morning.

When I turned fifty, Lou Harrison sent me four Sapphic quatrains about that age, including: ". . . a year that I found finest yet of all I lived, / the year in which we know we've likeliest not / another half to live, & thus impatient, / prod to live at last most as we want to, & / slough off false duty."

New York, Saturday 28 Jan.
Returned to the city yesterday afternoon in the requisite seven hours: two on the ferry and five on the road in a rented car, with the three animals, and a couple of stops at McDonald's. Silent trip. One of JH's bad days. Arrived depleted. At 5 A.M., seeing a light beneath his door, I find him listening, through earphones, to Strauss, and with a high fever. He has his own microwave there to heat tea, and to heat wet towels for his belly. My mind was full of chords, stationary and resolving

both. And my room is so stuffed with books and boxes that there's scarcely space for the bed. Cold and bright today. Gloom. Frank will come by for a chicken stew in an hour. The question is whether JH will eat at all. He's lost forty pounds in four months.

Sunday afternoon

At midnight a deafening alarm, from a car parked in front of the synagogue, began to ring, ceaselessly, until two A.M. I put the mattress in the dining room, turned on the fan, and JH, feverish and in pain, came to try to rest beside me for an hour.

Now he is back from church. Ill. I am afraid to write what I think . . .

Waiting for the crew, now, which will proceed with the documentary: Jim Dowell, his friend John Kolomvakis, and the cameraman Scott Barnard. I'm supposed to talk, and will probably say something like this:

Here I sit, on the last Sunday of January in 1995. I am 847 months old, or more precisely 24,812 days old. Tomorrow I'll be one day older, but this film remains fixed, as it will in ten years or a century from now.

The String Quartet came so readily last July at Yaddo, most of the ten movements were written in less than three weeks. Since then, the piece for L.A. has been slow. Preoccupation with JH's health seems so much more important. His delirium, his pain.

Getting through the night. Getting through the day.

31 Jan.

JH could appear to be dying. Stated in the conditional, because his eyes might fall on the phrase; and who knows? *dans un mois dans un an*, he may eventually be in perfect health again. Meanwhile, the 4 A.M. baths, the costly medication, the deep sleep while it lasts (with a look of pinched anguish on his features), and the ubiquitous cigarette. My own flu and phlegm prevail. Am reading the triste novel *Lewis Percy*, by Anita Brookner, about an ordinary life with no rewards.

Because he couldn't, I went alone to the Claire Bloom melodramas last night, sat with Judy Collins and Louis, who thought Lee Hoiby's piece was mine. Took bows with Lee and with Robin Holloway etc. Huge audience, not primarily musicians, but literati, the best sort, from the *NY Review*. My faithful film crew turned up to record my every cough. Do I believe in melodrama? . . . Each day is touch & go, and JH still has no doctor in case of emergency. He lies in the dark overheated bedroom, vaporizer hissing, and groggily watches the O. J. Simpson trial, hour after hour.

When I dream of music, it's not *about* music. I become a chord. I become a sequence, rather than merely feeling a sequence. Become D-flat, am a glass of water, a letter, a mist, not flesh but paper and web and bark and scale.

All is *Rashomon*. Even the perspective of the same person at different times, looking over his shoulder at a long-ago event. A diary is not more truthful than a memoir by virtue of focusing on this morning more than on yesteryear, though it may
be more factual. (Although fact and truth are the same in a court of law. And virtually every event I've ever described in printed prose has been proclaimed
skewed by friends and foes alike.)

With the present diary my entire life is documented, from pre-birth to now.
But the documentation is not consecutive. *The Paris Diary* and *The New York
Diary*, which cover the decade 1951–1961, were first published in the mid-Sixties.
The Later Diaries (which first appeared as *The Final Diary*) covers 1961–1972,
and came out in 1974. *The Nantucket Diary* covers 1973–1985, and came out in
1987. Between these volumes came eight books of belles lettres. Then in 1994 a
big memoir called *Knowing When to Stop*, which relates my first twenty-eight
years, from 1923 through 1951; that is, it ends where *The Paris Diary* starts.

Now, diaries are by definition composed in the heat of the fray, while memoirs
are composed with the introspection of retrospection. A diarist has no plot,
whereas an autobiographer knows beforehand where he's heading. My books are
in my voice, but if they'd been written in another order, or published in other
years, they could remain identical and still give off a different sound.

A biographee is his biographer. The three books on Cocteau that came out in
the 1960s were about three different men; even Robert Phelps's "autobiography"
of the master—a scrapbook made up entirely of JC's words—depicts, through its
order and choice, as much of Phelps as of Cocteau. Similarly, I am at the mercy of
someone named Rorem who presumes to write about me. Is he as far off the track
as those interviewers who come to chat, then publish the result as a portrait of
someone unrecognizable? I've had my Warholian quarter-hour. Yet art belongs to
no one, once it's ejected—not, certainly, to the artist.

Jimmy Merrill died.

JH finally saw the specialist today, and yes, his ills are confirmed; gastric ulcer,
Crohn's disease, and other horrors that will be determined after the analysis of
blood tests. In ten days he'll have a colonoscopy and an endoscopy at the Klingen-
stein Pavillion. Meanwhile, he starves to death.

Last night on channel 37, Martha Graham's try at *The Rite of Spring* embarrassed me no less than when I mentioned it eleven years ago in these pages. But
now, with the suavity of hindsight, one sees it is not just Martha's chutzpah that's ill
advised, but the very dumbness of her gestures. Could she not actually have gone
on from Isadora rather than from Mary Wigman? Dreamed I was the theme from
Buxtehude's fugue that JH was practicing earlier, the same theme Bach used in his
E-flat Three-Part Invention. Dreamed I was the letter G, that I was a chord, a
continually sounding chord, which, though harmonically vertical, reverberates

horizontally forever. I have published perhaps two million words, but am not even a writer. All that preoccupies me is JH's health, the mournful atmosphere throughout the house day after night after day, and the uncertain physical condition of virtually everyone I speak with, young or old.

Glenn Close's lesbian depiction is o.k., yet the whole story looks a touch sentimental and pro-army. Anyway, brava!, in the light of the increasing intolerance within America's dangerously silly society.

He is depressed. Feels he's an albatross around my neck. Is aghast at the mounting medical bills. But he is my life. And what is money for?

12 February

Zero weather. Gary phoned. During his performance of my Concerto last weekend with the Miami Symphony he was assailed by a blaze of light. This, an hour later, was diagnosed as a torn retina, repaired two days after by laser in Philadelphia. O clarity of folly.

Then a California conductor, a Ms. Nan Washburn of Sacramento, sent a tape and program on which she'd included "Love Alone." She asked for Paul Monette's address, which I duly sent. But last night, while speaking with Sandy about the Jimmy Merrill memorial, he asked if I'd seen the Monette obit . . . So Paul too has died, age 49, of AIDS, twenty-two years younger than me, but how much braver!

Glimpsed Peggy Noonan on PBS, about Meaning and Life, etc. A priest speaks about Truth as an absolute. His example states that two and two are always four. (That's not Truth, it's Fact. Besides, two and two make twenty-two.) This he uses as buttress against those who deny God, for such unfortunates are lost and will corrupt the world.

Martha Graham, Ravel, Cocteau for fifty years were idols without flaw. Now, along with Martha's *Rite*, which puts into question whether all her old masterpieces might prove embarrassments too, I reread *Les Parents terribles* with raised eyebrows. Cocteau has a swell ear for dialogue, but his play's too cute, tries too hard, needs trimming. Meanwhile I practice Ravel's little songs on Marot verses (Kurt Ollmann will sing them in a month at Symphony Space) and find them weak. Worse, they're semi-inept, with over-thick harmonies and queasy voice-leading. They do beguile, but they do not seduce. Similarly, the *Chansons Madécasses* (which Kurt intoned expertly last night at the Y) are admirable without being likeable—they *work*, despite too many parallel sevenths that overstay their welcome. As for Bartók's "great" works, they now seem pompous, stuffed, bombastic, next to Stravinsky who, nevertheless, stole much from Bartók.

If today these icons of yore stumble along on feet of clay, who's left? I don't like any of the new books, expert though they are, that come this way. Of course, I'm a walking blue pencil. I want to be moved again. Is *Pelléas* still moving?

Buggery on the sill. Cooing outside the kitchen window. Have the pigeons from the synagogue flown over again for crumbs?

The world is big. Where can you flee to avoid death? Tibet? The apartment is big. Where to hide to avoid death? Behind the refrigerator? The bed is big. Where can you crawl?

Some days are better than others. JH's diet is four pieces of cinnamon toast and tea; he's fearful of taking more, lest it sit in the gut like concrete, motionless. Weekends Frank comes from the Bronx, looking like a corpse, and we fix him a real meal, most of which I eat. I have a cough, piles, immense fatigue, bowels like tan tapeworms, and an anxious heart. JH short-tempered. Smell of gloom. Listens day and night, through earphones, to Carissimi, Tallis, collections of organ solos. (My favorite title is Malengrau's "Tumult in the Praetorium.") No social life. None. Out of duty, maybe a concert, or half of one, every two or three weeks. JH takes no vitamins. We still have our nightly backgammon game. When I compose, it is only an hour a week. And without zeal.

13 Feb., 5 p.m.

Lydia, one of JH's sopranos and a friend, had a psychotic collapse yesterday and was taken, handcuffed, to Roosevelt Hospital. JH is there this minute visiting, with a rose in a little vase. He just phoned, to get the address of two other choir members, and said the doctor, a woman, is a real Nazi. Lydia won't be released until she can explain why she was admitted. As with Joe Machlis a few months ago, one learns the hard way that suicide is illegal . . . Should JH be there now, in his condition?

Apropos of two and two making four, Cocteau in 1953 wrote (in *Des distances*): "*Deux et deux font quatre? J'en doute fort, si j'additione deux lampes et deux fauteuils.*"

16 February

Rushing to the john I grab any old book, which turns out to be Auden's *Secondary Worlds*, essays from 1969. On page 130 he writes: "Poetry is personal speech in its purest form . . . concerned and only concerned with human beings as unique persons . . . As Paul Valéry said: 'In poetry everything that must be said cannot be said well.' It is essentially a spoken, not a written word . . . [Its] meaning is the outcome of a dialogue between the words of the poem and the response of whoever is listening to them." In the margin I noted in red: For dissent see Sontag's *Styles of Radical Will*, p. 30. So I turn to *Styles of Radical Will*, also from 1969: "This tenacious concept of art as 'expression' has given rise to the most common, and dubious, version of the notion of silence—which invokes the idea of 'the ineffable.' . . . It is from this position that Valéry advanced his famous argument . . . that the novel is not, strictly speaking, an art form at all . . . [S]ince the aim of prose is to communicate, the use of language in prose is perfectly straightforward. Poetry, being an art, should have quite different aims: to express an experience which is essentially ineffable; using language to express muteness . . ." In the margin I noted in red: See Auden's *Secondary Worlds*.

Twenty-six years later, I'm awed by how carefully I pondered these and other intellectual statesmen, filling their margins with attentive wisdom and devouring always the new with the old. (Oh, how they *cared* too!) Today, hours once spent with "ideas" are passed in front of a TV screen. Do I help define the dumbing of America, or is it simply that, as Rimbaud wrote (or was it Mallarmé?), "*J'ai lu tous les livres*"? With books, of course, one re-reads far less than one re-hears with music. Yet I've also listened to nearly as much music—including my own—as I'll ever need.

Now there in the television studio sits interviewer Charles Grodin, who manages to make his little eyes look both mean and dead as he pretends to attend to his guest, but who repeats the guest's words as his own, and is ever impatient for his monopolizing monologue. JH meanwhile, during these recent sad dark months, when he's not sleeping, watches Court TV, his overheated bedroom teeming with the vaporizer's fumes mixing with Pall Mall smoke, and the beloved odor of Sonny, Lucille, and Tom. Tomorrow, the tests at Mount Sinai, five hours of endoscopies and colonoscopies and Valium and Demerol, and he is scared for the first time I've known him to be in twenty-seven years. Scared as much for the strangulating discomfort as for what the tests may reveal: bacteria, virus, lesions, more ulcers, cancer, tobacco damage, irreparably twisted intestines, large and small.

It's 8:00 P.M. By tomorrow at ten he will not have eaten for 48 hours. Now he's drinking, over a brief period, a salty gallon of something to clear his innards. Time crawls.

Friday, 17 Feb.

Then time stops, for a strange half-hour.

During a brief period in the waiting room at Mount Sinai (4th floor, Endoscopy), we peered past the glass windows into the recovery area. JH pointed out his doctor, Barry Jaffin, a bearded type who looks like Ron Silver. When JH was summoned for his "procedures," I cabbed back home to feed the cats and Sonny, fix his bed, rest a bit. At noon I returned to find JH in the recovery room, less traumatized than I'd feared, but what he told me was less than Jaffin told me a few minutes later in the waiting room. The Crohn's disease is, for the moment, minor, but there's one huge ulcer (and smaller ulcers), which may be a malignant tumor, he won't know until the biopsies are analyzed next Thursday.

"And the blood test?" I asked.

"Positive," said he.

"You mean HIV positive?"

"Yes." He looked at me quizzically and walked off.

Thus began the strange thirty minutes in the near-empty waiting room. One's focus on everything is changed forever. Did JH know? Why him and not me? He's only 55, while I could prepare to die now without too much bile. This sounds unselfish; in fact, it's pure ego: I want him to take care of me in my old age. What isn't selfish, since all I care about is his comfort? Now there is the sad sad sad sadness.

On leaving the hospital we walked a few sunshiny blocks down Fifth Avenue. JH has known he's HIV positive for some months, but didn't tell me because I'm "obsessive." He feels, though, that if he has a cancer, it's not an opportunistic cancer, but a coincidental ill in his ever more emaciated body.

Sunday morning

He listens continually to music. It sometimes helps his physical strife—the convolutions in his belly. (I lay my hand on his navel, or scratch his back, which he loves, almost as much as he loves the snuggly proximity of Sonny in the bed.) Some music is no help, but the Saint-Saëns Organ Symphony does wonders. He listens, too, to my CDs, as though to implant them on his brain forever. Or take them to the grave. For me, music is no panacea, I like—need—it less and less. (Although last night, while reading the now-dead Jimmy Merrill's lines

> *Crossing the street,*
> *I saw the parents and the child*
> *At their window . . .*
>
> *I have lit what's left of my life.*

with a cello solo in the background blooming, I began to cry.) For me, music has become a mean irony. *La Prieure* of Bernanos declares on her deathbed: *"J'ai médité sur la mort chaque heure de ma vie, et cela maintenant ne me sert de rien!"*

A car alarm that has clanged all night, still clangs.

Reading Georges Bataille's sordid *L'Abbé C*, without pleasure.

20 Feb.

Of Mice and Men. After 56 years Aaron's music for the death-of-the-dog scene remains, in its heartbreaking plainness, the model for us all. Indeed, in the new quartet, I paraphrase it for the final movement ("The Death of the Harlequin"), by going up where Aaron goes down, but leaving his poignant three-part harmonies intact . . . So often in literature too one finds paraphrases. Could Steinbeck, in the moment where Lenny, who doesn't know his own strength, lovingly kills the girl, have been influenced by the Frankenstein movie of 1931, where the monster, who doesn't know his own strength, kills the girl, mistaking her for a flower?

I've not had sex with another creature for twelve years (late April 1983), nor has JH. Yet he tests positive, and I—at least a year or so ago—test negative. Is he, like Ed White, a *sain porteur*, while being afflicted elsewhere so unhealthily? My stomach aches; his woe bounces onto me.

Here's a daily routine. Lights out at midnight. Light sleep, with one or two get-tings-up to pee (or to peek in on JH), until 9 A.M. Unrested. Floor exercises. Breakfast of cold cereal & banana while JH reads the *Times*. An hour's nap, with-out sleep, at 11:30. At 1:00 peanut butter & jelly (apricot) sandwich on whole-wheat toast with a Coke. Year in, year out. Procrastination. Another siesta in midaft. Dine on soup with JH at 6:45, followed by backgammon, year in year out. A little work. A little piano practice. Television: Charlie Rose, the porn channel 35, or spot-checking. Ten minutes reading. Lights out at midnight.

Tuesday 21 Feb.

JH has been playing *Knoxville: Summer of 1915*, the early Steber recording; the whole apartment glistens with nostalgia. Not just nostalgia of the music and prose evoking that "happier time" before the First War when people sat on their porches in the evening, but nostalgia of nearly fifty years ago when I first met Sam in Tangle-wood where he was rehearsing the new piece with Eleanor. There is now a wider space between the evocation and the present, than between the evocation and what is evoked. *Knoxville* is a wonderful piece, so familiar yet so unique in lan-guage, a language which could never be spoken again, at last not with the same honest accent.

In the evening we went to the Village for Dennis Keene's all-American choral concert, including Aaron Copland's *In the Beginning* from 1947—same year as *Knoxville*. Again the space was flooded with wistfulness for another time and speech, so familiar yet so unrepeatable. (For the record, Dennis also led four of my Motets, beautiful in tone but a trifle dispassionate in texture; a very profes-sional triptych by Gregg Smith, no miscalculations and a lot of mystery; and Lenny B.'s *Chichester Psalms* which now, thirty years later, sound unsatisfying, cheap.)

JH says: "If the biopsies Thursday turn out to be malignant, I may look for a healer. Nothing that involves God. God no! Something that involves mind over matter. Why would God want to save me, and not that person down the street? God is not 'fair.' Death is part of His plan, and He likes viruses as much as He likes me. God's supreme triumph is cancer."

JH's silvery hair is maximally short again. He does not complain. But he suffers, and works, and eats sometimes a bit better. I love him more than ever, after nearly twenty-eight years.

The Boys of Saint Vincent, a Canadian TV drama on child molestation in a Catholic orphanage, is smartly acted and filmed, but a touch inflammatory with theatrical misjudgments. The wife of the "villain," for example, makes no stab at understanding. And the girlfriend of the victim whispers exasperatingly in court.

Sonny is aware that when we close the backgammon set after the post-prandial game, year in and year out, it's time to go for a walk . . . Friday, visit to Dr. Agus because of my own stomach ache, herpes, and mainly to talk about Jim. Results of blood test in ten days, including a second HIV (I was negative two years ago, and should be still). From the street at dawn, sound of snow shovels . . . Knees click and ache. Fell on ankle yesterday, black & blue . . . The oft-moaned plaint: Why me? Why my family? Yet, why us? . . . I can't sleep in the same bed—same room— with anyone. But a year or two ago, when JH gave me an odd bathrobe of lilac- and-magenta plaid terry cloth, it was too heavy to wear. So I keep it on my bed all night, and touch it. It is him. Him.

1 March

Each body makes its own rules, out of a trillion possible outcomes. Each body is born to die. But there is never a right time to die.

Every midnight I read another story of Denton Welch.

Ash Wednesday. In an hour I'll leave for JH's 3-hour service at the church. I am already wearier than he allows himself to be.

(Agus phoned. I'm still HIV negative.)

How unfair to write that way about Harold Brodkey! I am not in his shoes, nor do I know how I'd walk if I were. He is an old friend.

Friday 24

Yesterday his diagnoses came through: lymphoma, plus very low T-cell count. That is, stomach cancer aggravated by the non-immunity. Next week, after more tests with the oncologist, Dr. Gruenstein, he'll begin chemotherapy. My life is his, and my duty is to remain stable. What good are tears? Rosemary says: A lot of good.

Monday 27

He looks like a little boy—a *handsome* little boy—as he sits naked on the edge of the bed, sipping the mug of mint tea, and trying to keep it down, ribs showing, so thin, where a year ago he was almost obese. Many people have been told (about the cancer, not about the AIDS, which JH feels is stigmatic and probably irrele- vant), including hallway friends in this very building. Women, for whatever cause, are more sensible, commiserative, and helpful than men. Eugenie in Nantucket forwards the mail, with practical but warm advice (she's been there!); Jim's sister in Oregon who has problems of her own, including their mother now living with her, and short of memory; Sylvia (been there too); Rosemary (the only one aware of the virus); Linda Golding, who has agreed to have Boosey publish JH's expert and beautiful unaccompanied *Stabat Mater*. Plus Shirley, with her Essiac recipes, Pia with her willingness to baby-sit, Lydia in her mad devotion. But Jack Larson, too, calls often, with practical information culled from when Jim Bridges was so ill. "You are," says he to me, "about to begin a roller coaster ride."

JH blames the cancer on his having stopped cigarettes for several months a year ago. The resultant trauma on his system: noxious Nicorette gum infecting his stomach, the massive siege of shingles. He's back to three packs a day, but maybe the damage is done. On the other hand he feels he's in remission, or rather, in reverse, returned to where it all started, with straightforward pain and locked bowels, and, like a movie running backward, it may all vanish. Dr. Gruenstein fortunately does not believe in pain, and prescribed an unlimited dosage of Percadet, which sort of works, but constipates.

Later. The Ash Wednesday service was as effective as any I've attended at Saint Matthew's in twenty years. The choir glowed, sounding as always better in the evening than in a Sunday-morning ritual; in tune, spirited, and with a good program. Jim's own "Miserere mei, Deus," alternating between the Choir and the People, is both inspired and dramatically successful. A fat chunk of Brahms's *Requiem*, which (as Virgil used to say) opened up the gates of heaven and brought down the house. Some smaller twentieth-century works: Randall Thompson, George Oldroyd, and one of my *7 Motets for the Church Year* from tonight's appointed Gospel (Matthew 6:20–21):

> *Lay up for yourselves treasures in heaven, where*
> *neither moth nor rust doth corrupt, and where thieves*
> *do not break through nor steal: For where your treasure*
> *is, there will your heart be also.*

If only I could practice what my texts of choice preach!

After the regular mass came the Spanish mass, which Jim again played, while with Lydia and others I ate lentil soup in the game room. When we came home at 9:30 Ruth Ford was on the phone, calling from her own bed of pain. JH, a wraith and doubled-over with exhaustion, nevertheless spoke with her a minute. "I first fell in love with you," said he, "not when we met, twenty-seven years ago at John Koch's, and you were wearing lavender lamé and waving a cigarette holder, but a few years later when you were acting in Mart Crowley's play. One sees an actor's true nature much more when he's on stage than when he's in the parlor." Wherever did that come from? And where did he find the energy?

Thursday. But of course he *found* the energy, and is paying for it today. After a morning of CAT-scans, he's trying to sleep. Although a moment ago (it's 4 P.M.) I heard him vomiting again. A concerned call from Morris, who claims that two friends of his had complete remissions, thanks to mind over matter.

Why are any hospital's personnel so sullen? Without looking at you, much less a smile, they say, "Here, fill this out." As though you weren't feeling lousy enough. Are manners a question of education? (Yet many illiterates have an innate generosity of spirit.)

Saturday 4 March

Rosemary came up for a day & a night, arriving just as my pupils were arriving (an hour late: an Amtrak derailment in Newark!). So I fixed meals for everyone. JH very manic at supper, telling RR about his symptoms, his optimism. A big chicken stew, his Aunt Jan's recipe.

When they both were a-bed in their separate areas, I finished a section of the

California piece—"More Than a Word"—away from the piano, more by contrivance than by inspiration. Stravinsky said that, when composing, one must always be in contact with *la matière sonore*, that is, the piano. But that *matière* can be in the brain as well as the keyboard. And of course contrivance—educated contrivance—is intrinsically more interesting than inspiration.

Since our parents died I feel closer to Rosemary than in the first sixty years of our lives. Do we accept each other more?

JH on his second day of Essiac. He has faith. Still, in the wee hours comes the terrible sound of the bathwater, meaning he's making hot compresses to ease his stomach. How impotent I feel, watching him eaten alive, immune to painkillers. What I have felt for him over the past three decades (almost) is more than merely love.

Rosemary says, "I don't care for Joyce Carol Oates, although I admire her writing." Reminded of Gloria last year who said, after finishing *Six Exceptional Women* by James Lord, whom she'd never met: "I like his writing but I don't like him."

Calls to inquire about Jim from: Eugene Istomin, Tony Fell in London, Anne Meacham, Morris, Maggie Paley, Ruth Ford, Sharon Isbin.

Sunday

Supper last night, stark and silent. JH isn't digesting, and the new pill causes grogginess. Still, he beat me thrice at backgammon. At this moment he's at church. Would I feel free to type these words if he were at home?

Phone call from a sad-voiced woman on behalf of the National Federation of Music Clubs. Would I be free to accept an honorary award on April 24 in Wichita? "The World—feels Dusty / When We stop to Die— / We want the Dew— then— / Honors taste dry."

Composer auditions at Manhattan School of Music last Tuesday, seven hours of live interviews with the young composers by my ten new colleagues. Impressed with the high level of ignorance.

Twenty minutes daily practice on Debussy's *Ballades* and Ravel's two Clément Marot chansons, prior to performing them later this month with Kurt O. Funny how *Song*, the mystique and the medium, was such an anathema 55 years ago. At fifteen I knew all of Ravel, *except* his songs, which I pooh-poohed. Of course, even today, I'm less taken with singers than with what they sing. In vocal music more than any other, the medium is the message.

He says, when I scratch his back with freshly filed fingernails as I've done regularly for decades, and which he dotes on: "If you draw blood, you'll have to wash your hands."

He says, "I wouldn't care what happens to me if it weren't for you."

Monday 6 March

The first chemo treatment. Dr. Gruenstein turns out to be genial, open, a touch offhand. Results of many tests (bone marrow, etc.) less dire than feared. JH now arranges an array of pills against nausea, pain, pneumonia, and to coat the stomach. Needs weekly blood test. He will now, on top of Prozac and Essiac, ingest fourteen different substances daily, some several times, including Zoffran, Prednisone, Bactrin, Pepcid, and Percocet. Says the chemo treatment, as it drips through a needle into a vein on the back of his hand, resembles a beauty-parlor session, with the several women present, their hands outstretched as for a manicure, discussing coiffures that result from falling hair.

Irony that the piece I'm working so fitfully at, *More Than a Day*, for the Los Angeles Chamber Orchestra with countertenor Brian Asawa (whom I've yet to meet, but have heard with mixed feelings), is based on Jack Larson's verses for Jim Bridges, during their first years, then during Jim's horrific final months.

Brouhaha surrounding new edition of Anne Frank's Diary, "brilliantly translated," says the *Times*, without indicating from what language (Dutch? German? Hebrew?). Anne Frank is not as inherently "wrong" as Mother Teresa, less of a scam, because she doesn't actually hurt people.

8 March

Morbid hour with Kendrick, reconsidering wills, evaluating accounts (JH considerably in debt and ponders bankruptcy so that . . .), other legal things . . . JH overextended, overexcited, touchy, as the Prednisone masks deeper ills, while I again have hemmeroids, or however you spell it.

11 March

His last day of Prednisone. Never rests, house full of people, preparing meals, guests, sweeping. JH plans a concert for his 56th birthday next month at the church. Tomorrow, Nantucket by car, with all the animals, and no sleep, after a long morning of running the church, plus Charles Horton and his friend Sue Arnold, a mezzo. Am I myself getting any work done? any *reflective* work? Does reflection guarantee higher quality than just putting down any old notes? Haven't those notes, in some part of the brain, been reflected too?

Twenty-seven years since I've had a drop of alcohol, or a cigarette. Yet not a day goes by that I don't ponder the danger of one drink, one smoke.

Sunday 12 March

> Our own death is unimaginable; and when we try to imagine it we perceive that we really survive as spectators. At bottom no one believes in his own death; in the unconscious every one of us is convinced of his own immortality.

When setting those sentiments of Freud to music for *The Poets' Requiem* forty years ago, I took the coward's way out, and simply had them spoken against held chords. As for their sense, do I believe that today? Jim, I think, does, although with every hour the rules change. At 2:00 with the animals we'll pile into a rented car and head for Nantucket for the first time in seven weeks. (During our five days there, Charles and Sue will stay here in the apt.)

His agony seems assuaged for the moment. A fool's paradise in the mists of Prednisone? His constant movement, energy, and lack of sleep more urgent than mine. The constipation seems due more to Crohn's than to cancer. His hands shake, barely perceptibly, like incipient Parkinson's, a distant motor. That too could be pills. The church means everything to him: the excellent choir, entirely of his making; the novel and elegant repertory; the internecine feuds; the group of Dominican youths whom he educates solely by example; the mood of *Barchester Towers*. On April 2, his 56th birthday, Jim plans an afternoon choral concert, for his (and my) acquaintances, sacred and profane.

Sunny ice-blue day.

Nantucket, 16 March

Twyla Tharp's rag-doll loose-limbed choreography is all about charm, yet she herself has none. Conversely, Elliott Carter, the man, drips with charm, while his work has none.

Nijinsky's daughter Tamara, whom I've never met, for some reason sent me her father's unexpurgated diaries, in French. Loony but a bit dull. How the fact of him thrilled me in the mid-Thirties! And still thrills.

JH up half the night, every night, in pain and frustration with bowel and stomach. Yet he works all day, and plans his special concert in less than three weeks.

Finished the piano-vocal score of *More Than a Day*. Jim dismisses title as . . .

Saw yesterday (the substitute) Dr. Pearl, female, for my piles, which she doesn't locate. Yet the pain persists. The thought of again undergoing operation as in 1950 is . . . Of course, it could be colon cancer, like Jim Bridges. Or maybe just nothing, except tension because of . . .

Tuesday noon we attended a "Transformational Breathing" session on Main Street, clutching at straws. It would have been an insult if it weren't so inadvertently funny, with gobbledygook about God, emerging from the inexpert Boston-accented lips of an unprepossessing overweight couple.

STOP CIVIC POTS

Like Harold Brodkey, a kind of monster, but not an interesting monster.

New York, Sunday 19 March

The roundtrip to Nantucket was hellish, with JH driving each way, doubled-over in pain, the animals mewling in the back seat, and me with piles that have begun to bleed. Meals were meager and consumed in silence, Jim excusing himself to vomit. Sometimes his hands shake imperceptibly, like Robert Phelps's with Parkinson's. We saw Eugenie twice, but weren't lively company. The driving, too, was passed mutely, with an occasional cassette of Bach on the harpsichord, which can irritate.

Had we made the dangerous trip to stave off dim threats, or simply for a change of heart, and to check on the property? Father used to say that, whatever happens, it won't happen as you imagine. Stendhal, in *I Cenci*, describes the scene of the great execution at which several hundred spectators died before the guillotinings took place, because their grandstand collapsed. And Cocteau, in *Le Grand Ecart*, tells us that we think we have a choice, but all is illusion. He recounts the famous incident (is it the same as "Tonight in Samarkand"?) of the young Persian gardener who says to his prince:

"I saw Death this morning. He made a threatening gesture. Save me. If only by some miracle I could be in Isphahan tonight."

The good prince lent the gardener his horses. That afternoon, the prince too saw Death.

"Why," he asked of Death, "did you make a threatening gesture this morning at my gardener?"

"I did not make a threatening gesture, but a gesture of surprise. For he was so far from Isphahan this morning, and I must take him at Isphahan tonight."

The *petite phrase* of Paul Bowles, which has haunted me over the centuries—the recurring "dying fall" of la-sol-do-sol (see p. 222 of *Knowing When to Stop*)—I realize today was cribbed from the second theme of Ravel's *Pavane*. Whew!! So now that ghost is laid.

Virgil used to say, "We could make pretty noises together."

Monday noon, 20 March

Is the whole of life worth living if the final agony is so protracted? Or: Is life worth living? Period.

At 1:30 A.M., after Jim had had a fairly painless eleven hours, I found him in the kitchen heating up vanilla ice cream, his first meal of the day (except for a cup of pea soup in the evening), his dear emaciated body curved over in pain. "It's a joke," he said, hopeless. He swallowed the last two painkillers then, and lay smoking a Pall Mall in the hot bath. Two hours later, same routine. I went in to see him in the tub, and he "confessed" (as he put it) that he's probably worse than he'd told me.

At the moment he's across the park chez Gruenstein, the oncologist. I worry that the bath will overflow. For, plus the pain, he's foodless, sleepless, and creeps around naked with windows open, and a very low blood count. At 5 A.M. there's no heat.

I too am exhausted. Tonight John Simon will "present" me at the Manhattan Theatre Club, after which I'll read and answer questions. JH says he wants to come—that he wants, after all, to lead a normal life, which is why yesterday after church he insisted we go hear the Stuttgart Chamber Orchestra (Diamond, and a new no-fun Glass symphony), which played like mirthless students.

Later. Jim did not come to the reading. Dr. Gruenstein (who himself, it turns out, has kidney cancer—is that a good advertisement?) wants him to repeat the chemo sooner than planned. I returned home to find him again in agony . . . John S. introduced me lavishly, and I read *Knowing When to Stop* for about thirty minutes followed by questions. Then, with Kendrick, Sharon Mitchell, and John's German friend we had inedible grub at the Sixth Ave. Deli. Is there something not quite human about John? For a man of impeccable letters, he uses "shit" and "fuck" a great deal . . . Light rain. Tomorrow is the first day of spring . . . JH's ailments have dried his cuticle; his toenails are streaked and crusty; his small toe, left foot, has no nail at all, just a half dime-sized clot of crimson. His only reading is the big tome of Symptoms. My own urethral stinging has begun again after all these years. No day passes without my considering a double suicide.

JH, three hours after taking his new, much stronger pain killer: "The mind's alive but the body's dead. And pain still lurks."

Tuesday 21 March

JH, to me, who am on the phone with S: "Tell her I used to send my undying love. Now I send my dying love."

The priorities for this diary now are strictly to monitor JH. Everything else, even composing, seems frivolous. Yet Jim himself perseveres with the work he loves (practicing Messiaen, preparing for the choral program, complaining about the criminally recalcitrant organ tuner), though the new pill knocks him out, almost.

Several afternoon hours, first practicing with Kurt, then discussing selling of archives with Kendrick and a collector, Glenn Horowitz. Then re-sifting the wills of both JH and myself. Plus JH's so-called "living will."

"Have you," asks canny Mr. Horowitz, "a file for, say, Frank O'Hara?" "Sure," I answer, heading to where I thought the file is. Vanished. Now six hours later, after scouring the apartment, there's still no sign of it.

Titles: *Learning to Forget. Remembering to Forget.*

M-L = re. chickens: "*Ils naissent dans leur cercueils*" (They're born in their coffins).

Make an opera of Edith Wharton's *Summer*.

For Symphony Space, 25 March:

Ravel and Debussy, the mother and father of modern French music, were so alike in esthetic and vocabulary that it's become fashionable to claim how different they were. In fact, the differences are superficial: like Comedy and Tragedy they are two sides of the Impressionist mask. Good musicians of the same generation often come in pairs wherein both speak one language, but with divergent accents—of optimism and pessimism, for example, or of concert-hall versus opera-stage. Witness

Mozart & Haydn, Mahler & Strauss, Copland & Thomson, Britten & Tippett, Poulenc & Honegger.

In formal matters everyone agrees that Ravel was a classicist, Debussy a free versifier. Yet the orchestral masterpiece of each one proves the reverse. Ravel's *Daphnis* is a loose rhapsody, Debussy's *La Mer* a tight symphony. Melodically Debussy was short of breath, like Beethoven, while Ravel spun out tunes that were minutes long, like Puccini. Contrapuntally they were, like all the French, unconcerned. Rhythmically they were, like all the French (because of the unstressed national speech from which their music springs), generally amorphous. Harmonically they dealt in the same material of secondary sevenths, except for the whole-tone scale which Ravel avoided. And coloristically they both excelled, making rainbows from a lean palette. Their game could be called Sound, sound taking precedence over shape, over language.

Socially they were strained allies. The younger Ravel paid homage to his semirival by orchestrating certain of his works. The older Debussy paid homage to Ravel by appropriating the device of his *Habañera*, and of certain piano figurations. But Ravel in private felt that Debussy was a thief, while Debussy once called Ravel a trickster—and a trick, he said, can astonish only once. They both had strong personalities and so were inimitable; but they were contemporaries, after all, bearing the same chronological relationship as Liszt to Franck, or as Copland to Barber. (Satie, whom we think of as Papa, actually lay between them, like Lucky Pierre.)

As for their songs, of which we are about to perform five, neither was prolific compared to their German cousins, Debussy having composed ninety, Ravel a mere thirty. Their taste in texts was similar—Mallarmé, for example, among their peers, and a predilection for medieval lyricists.

The Marot *Epigrammes* are early Ravel, dating from 1897 when the composer was 22. The Villon *Ballades* are late Debussy, dating from 1910 when the composer was 48. The poets are both 15th-century, Villon being 55 years older than Marot, even as Debussy was 13 years older than Ravel.

Not Sent
26 March

Dear Alfred Kazin:

I was impressed, and certainly in agreement with, your recent brief essay decrying the increasing lack of manners, even of decency, amongst inhabitants of the same city.

But the perception shifts according to who's perceiving. You have been so dismissively rude to me over the years, during the few times we've been in the same company, that it's caused me mild traumas.

This is the sort of letter that should never be sent, no doubt; but your printed words struck me as contradictory somehow.

Cordially,
Ned R.

Wrote a long recollection of Freda Pastor for the Curtis Institute, to dispel the odor of the above letter. Freda, my piano teacher in 1943, has died, she too.

Wrote a long blurb for the Weill-Lenya correspondence.

". . . an artist is best off concentrating on what's happening inside the rectangle of the canvas and damn the peripheral action . . ." writes Jed Perl of Nell Blaine's painting.

6 April

Since last I wrote here a couple weeks ago little has changed. But Jim's program at the church last Sunday afternoon was a triumph. "Everybody" was there. I myself sat with Rosemary between, on the left, Felicity dell'Aquila, and on the right, Bobby Short and Jean Bach. Mendy said, "I haven't seen so many Jews at a Christian event since the crucifixion." Jim, looking pretty good (up since six, he'd played two morning masses, and fixed a lunch for his choir of twenty-four), introduced every number, and accompanied valiantly on the organ, while the choir blended creamily in, among other things, his own *Ave Verrum* and *Stabat Mater*. Like the last chapter of *Le Temps retrouvé* one saw friends from the farthest past, less pessimistic than exhilarating: Bruce Phemister, Morris Golde, Maggy Magerstadt, Anne Meacham, Ruth Ford, and Charles-Henri Ford, Ellen Adler, and a dozen others from the middle-distance.

For his birthday as usual I composed a wistful vignette. He says to title it "Resignation." Is he better? The woes are the same. My own herpes resemble a grenade or blackberry. The urethral anxiety persists.

Monday at the New School, as guest of Sandy McClatchy (fund-raising for *The Yale Review*). Richard Howard, Joyce Carol Oates, and I each read from our oeuvres to an elderly well-off audience. Richard, very mannered as befits his very verbal verse; Joyce, talking too much about each poem before reading it, and a bit obsequious ("Ned will probably write this up in his diary"); and I, as epilogue, terse and well-prepared, with the blessing of prose to counteract the poetry.

8 April

Then today came a typewritten postcard from Joyce, already so faded that I transcribe it here:

Dear Ned:

What a pleasure to "read" with you, in those odd circumstances (a boutique-sized audience, of whom several of the most elderly had nodded off already even as Richard began his wonderfully energetic first poem!) Although I'd already read and seemed almost on intimate terms with your selections (the "French-German" distinction should become a classic) I was, like Richard, quite enchanted. What a child's innocence (and slyness) you retain! Marvelous work. Thank you. Ray and I are thinking of Jim, and ask to be remembered to him after so many years. (Please excuse this terrible typing.)

With much admiration,

Joyce

Yes, I've always wanted to become an actor (or an actress). Trouble is, I can't act. I can't even play myself—unless life is an act, and we establish our roles as infants.

Such glib wisdom arises from the little Symbiosis Film company having invited Jim to be in the documentary. This afternoon, to my surprise, he consented, but only if I stood with him. There we sat, being "natural," playing ourselves, trying to establish our relationship with the camera, and behaving quite falsely. In a few weeks they'll film me directing a rehearsal of my chamber music. There, too, I'll be playing myself, but with concrete suggestions to the instrumentalists. Are the instrumentalists actors playing roles assigned to them? Is music theater? Do the performers' parts have meaning? *No*: to all this. Music's music and theater's theater. If the arts were all one, we'd only need one.

10 April

If he does swallow a good meal (a few spoonfuls of peas, applesauce, one piece of cinnamon toast, maybe a shred of steak) he vomits it within minutes, including the pain killers and the Zoffran ($26 per pill). Last night in bed, eyes closed, he said he was "fading," doesn't want more chemo or the daily shots (at $300 per shot) for two weeks that will keep his blood count up maybe. We've cooked a new batch of Essiac, and will try that again. Sonny and the cats are company, and problematic, but it's better than without them. My body? Still the same. Mornings are the saddest third of the day. In the dead of night the phone rings, but no one's there. Then rings again, while car alarms clang incessantly throughout our puritan city. During the afternoon, walking with Sonny, I nod at the other so-familiar dog-walkers whose names I don't know, but whose aspect over the years has turned from sexy to unsexy, from fresh to sour.

11 April

Early morning, back from Dr. Jaffin, JH exhausted, having detoured to Woolworth's to buy a lampshade, and where an employee asked if he were a senior citizen . . . Zaidee Dufallo called to say, "Is it true that Jim has AIDS and is going to die?" and in the same breath, "Ned dear, I'm phoning to invite you to ghost-write my memoirs."

Six weeks ago B & H sent proofs of Jim's *Stabat Mater*. Virtually no errors. But he's still not checked them, much less returned them.

Saw my three pupils for their biweekly lunch here today, and feel physically a bit better. Nevertheless will see Dr. Agus tomorrow at dawn.

Nearly finished with orchestration of *More Than a Day*. 131 pages in little more than two weeks. Must start a two-piano piece now for Florida, called perhaps *Blue & White Music*. Tonight, Lorin Lipson's recital at Hunter.

While working on the two-piano piece I heard Jim crying. He never cries. Went to his room where he was desperately clutching Sonny. He said it was the music. That all seems hopeless. We lay for a long time on the bed together. The three of us.

Saturday night, 15 April

Wednesday we went to see Corigliano's opera, the first half. I remember its magic from when, three years ago, John played it—all four hours of it—on a synthesizer. But now, to see it unflawed is to see the flaws, for the better a production the clearer the blemishes. It opens with promising mystery, but soon panders and sags, until the singers sink it with vulgarity. John's music is, in a sense, superior to his opera. The contradiction lies in the medium.

Even in the best of times the end of the Lenten season is a strain on Jim. The planning, the orchestrating, the arrangements, the copying, the rehearsals for the semi-weekly masses, and finally the endless service on Maundy Thursday (which featured his own setting of the 22nd Psalm for four choruses, in different balconies of the church, intoning antiphonally, softer and softer, until the lights are out and the communicants depart in silence); the Good Friday service last night from which I stayed home to read the proofs of Judy Collins's novel *Shameless* (that it is!); the long Spanish service tonight; and tomorrow, replete with brass quintet (Donna Hagen's group), the Easter Service. After which with the animals we will drive to Nantucket and hope to get on stand-by for the evening ferry. Yes, even in the best of times it's a load; but Jim doesn't sleep or eat and has become an obsessed wraith. The apartment grows more scarred by his cigarettes, set down *n'importe où*, for he never uses a tray. At the Thursday service, the Iberian lady on my left burst into tears. Then so did I.

Easter Sunday Afternoon

But we did not drive off to Nantucket. This morning he could scarcely move, excreted green liquid (the chemo? the Essiac?), then went off to the church. He played a Spanish service at eight, then held the 11 o'clock service together for two hours, cohering the mumbo-jumbo and incense with his music. Anne Meacham and Shirley sat with me. Jim shakes like an aspen, with a *low* temperature. At the moment, still fasting, he's taking a nap. It's mid-afternoon.

Now it's mid-evening. He called me into his room, and again burst into tears. So did I. We lay there, holding each other hopelessly. "I've been a failure," said he. "My whole purpose in living was to make things easier for you, and eventually to help you into old age." Although his abdominal pain has abated, he feels already dead ("missing so much," as he puts it), with thorough exhaustion and no incentive. Is it the chemo or the AIDS? He doesn't want more chemo if that's what it does to one. As for the AIDS: how does it kill you? He hasn't even been in the hospital.

Then Jack Larson phoned. I couldn't talk. But he and JH spoke for twenty minutes. Jack, after all, went through much of the same thing with J. Bridges. The utter, utter, utter sadness.

Tomorrow just possibly we may try for Nantucket again, this time taking a plane from Hyannis, with all the animals. But who knows.

Am reading desultorily the *Tibetan Book of the Living and Dead*. It's not written by a writer, is redundant, verbose, a trifle smug ("if you don't believe as we do you're wrong, so of course you'll suffer at the specter of death," or words to that effect). But it has something, and is, of course, True, as it knows too well. Young Ricky Ian Gordon and I yesterday posed for pictures at the AIDS Resource Center, to celebrate a $31,000 check culled from sales of the AIDS songbook. In the taxi back uptown, he suggested the Tibetan oeuvre (which in fact I already had, from Gloria three years ago, but hadn't cracked). His lover, age thirty, has AIDS and has renounced medicine in favor of Positive Thinking and homeopathy.

Penned a shameless blurb for Judy Collins's *Shameless*.

New York 24 April

I never write here when I'm really depressed, because . . . why? And I never write here when I'm truly tired, because . . . how? But today I'm both weary and low, plus, in addition to the groin complaints and a chipped front tooth and an aching molar (tomorrow, the dentist), these woes seem mere barnacles on the . . . to hell with the metaphor . . . compared to Jim's ongoing anguish. His beautiful silver hair is falling; he wears my little fez from Fez, 1949—actually the blue & white skull cap that we'd thought was long since lost. This afternoon: the third of his four chemo treatments.

The mirror these days shows me only Father. I no longer recognize myself.

JH told the interviewers about how we first met, in 1967. He had already known my reputation through pristine songs, and was intimidated. But when he read *The New York Diary*, by the crass Hyde of the lyrical Jekyll, he felt no intimidation about phoning. The two halves are unrelated.

Friday night in Nantucket, the lights went out all over town at about seven P.M. for two hours. When Jim leaned over a row of lit votive candles to light more candles a yard away, his sweater caught fire without his knowing it. I came into the room in the nick of time.

In the new book of essays, include blurbs? No. They're always a trifle dishonest. Yet the dishonesty is *my* dishonesty. So yes, include them.

All-Rorem concert, featuring mostly clarinet, tomorrow night at Bloomingdale's House of Music. Rehearsal fine yesterday. Tom Piercy: *Picnic on the Marne, Ariel, End of Summer*.

Most of my friends are straight women. I don't consciously know any lesbians. I have no composer friends any more, no quotidian buddies like Bill Flanagan, so long ago. Of my precise age group only Lukas Foss and Danny Pinkham remain. I meet, over the months, dozens of young composers. But don't socialize on any regular basis. DDT and Corigliano I see less than once a year.

One quickly grows used to luxury. To poverty—never. Dogs don't appreciate gold & silver, and a vast velvet room is no more fun than a homeless shelter. The boys from Jim's church, the Dominican Republicans, don't actually *see* Nantucket through any comparative historic vision. Their parents did not raise them with nursery rhymes, or grammar, or sense of illusion, to say nothing of irony. They watch television in the King's Chamber as they would in a prison.

I sit typing this diary while in the next room Ms. Randall, the archivist's assistant, sits "appraising" my diary of forty years ago. Forty years ago in Paris, Edouard Roditi, as I was being drunkenly buggered in his little side-bedroom, sat in the parlor reading my diary about being drunkenly buggered. All is artifice. What is not artifice?

Robert Dole claims that the movie *Priest* should be banned, though he has not seen it. Frank Rich claims that one should not make claims about works one hasn't seen. A letter-writer to the *NYT* claims that Rich has no right to make such a statement—that if one morally objects to subject-matter, then a work can be condemned *in absentia*. Well, that takes care of about every masterpiece of the past 2500 years, starting with *Oedipus Rex* and *Hamlet* with their frenzy of incest and patricide.

Being hungry as you are each noon, you prepare a peanut butter and apricot jam sandwich on whole-wheat toast. You are poised for the first lush bite when a thief breaks in and ties you up. During the ensuing ruckus, does your mind turn to the toast getting soggy? Do you hope you soon might get back to your meal? Are you still hungry? (Mendy Wager yesterday was robbed at knifepoint one floor above us.)

"What can we tell the children? How can we explain this horror?" ask parents all over the country re. the explosion in Oklahoma City. But what do we tell the grown-ups? Who can explain this horror?

JH: "I feel like your father during his last months. 'Is this really how it ends, with such petty concerns, after a life of art and variety? Is everyone's death an example of mediocrity, when loved ones and nurses no longer care much?' " But JH combats it as Father did, with humor and logic, although so much younger.

May Day

After-dinner speech for the Saint Wildfrid Club, forty organists, mostly men (but also Janet Hayes: we speak of chemotherapy) in a tiny room at the Sambucca. I read from the 22-year-old "Notes on Sacred Music," then answer questions. Organists hear differently from real people. They hear overtones, registrations, the myriad colors that garb the basic lines. Non-organist composers, like myself, who nevertheless write for the instrument, are miffed when they listen to the result. Where are those clear lines now, those careful triads, those tunes? Composers cannot grasp that the blur is not only part of the performance but has become part of the composition, and never the same on any two instruments.

The section of *Knowing When to Stop* that seems most to have stuck, with the two or three dozen people who read the book, is the one about French & German. (It is a truth universally acknowledged that the entire solar system is torn between two esthetics: French and German. Virtually everything is one or the other. Blue is French, red is German. No is French, yes is German. Formal gardens are French, oceans are German. The moon is French, the sun German. Gay men are French, lesbians German. Crows feet are French, pig knuckles German. Wolff on his good days is French, Berlioz is forever German. Balinese are French, Hawaiians are German. Jokes are French, the explanation of jokes is German. If French is to be profoundly superficial, as when an Impressionist depicts a fleeting vision of eternity, then German is to be superficially profound, as when Bruckner digs ever deeper into one narrow hole. If you agree with all this, you're French. If you disagree, you're German.) Marie Arana asks: "If any concept can be so defined, then which of your two professions, Ned, is French, and which German?" The question stumps me, mainly because I didn't invent it.

Since Americans are German while Europeans are French, am I then a Frenchman trapped in a German body? If prose is German while music is French (although subdivisions of prose, like essays, are French, while subdivisions of music, like symphonies, are German; and Schubert, say, though anatomically Austrian, was, in his economy, Frenchish, while Franck, though biologically Belgian was, in his profligacy, Germanic), then am I, according to my own definition, half & half?

Let me put on my thinking cap. But which one? For I do wear two of them, but never at the same time.

Irony: In the French-German game there is a contradiction where the organ is concerned. The organ is German, being over-rich and hairy. The greatest organ music is contrapuntal. Counterpoint should be French since, by definition, it is economy (single lines against each other weave themselves, without doubling or harmonic reinforcement, into an ice-clear frame), although great French music is never contrapuntal (Debussy). Harmony meanwhile should be German since, by definition, it is extravagance (vertical chords—if that's not a redundancy—with many a doubling and little antiphonal urging, etc.). Thus: Bach's counterpoint when heard on the organ becomes a harmonic flood. Messiaen does compose contrapuntally (i.e., horizontally), but it's mass against mass.

So. Counterpoint is French because it is linear and lean, a bonal structure where each lineament is independent yet, paradoxically, crucial to each lineament. Yet the French don't compose contrapuntally. Harmony is German because it is decorative and plump, a mass of flesh that bestrides the skeleton—and sometimes exists without a skeleton. Yet the Germans do compose contrapuntally; however, it sounds like sheer harmony when played on the organ.

With Debussy you get what you pay for. With Mahler, you get more than you pay for.

TO JH

You are my North, my South,
my Day, my Night.
I thought that love would last forever.
I was right.

Nicholas Fox Weber, intelligent and well prepared, interviewed me for his Balthus biography. In my madness I sold him the priceless little drawing from 1951.

Visit from Ellen Zwilich on May 8. And her music, which I grow to enjoy more and more.

JH played for the funeral on May 12 of Mae Genchek who died Monday of cancer. She had the same doctor as Jim, Dr. Gruenstein.

Should the new book of essays be called *Other Entertainment*? That's my classification by the IRS, who cannot otherwise place a person who claims to be both composer & writer.

15 May

First splendid spring temperature. Green and yellow and lavender have encroached on Manhattan's usual gray hues, now prettier than Paris's. On the slope of Morningside Drive, in front of the building where a party for Wayne Koestenbaum's new book is raging, stands a man with a pig on a leash. Who does not love a pig: their intelligence and cleanliness, their affection? I ask the man a question, but he isn't having any. Shouldn't a man with a pig on the first spring evening be pleasantly resigned to questions?

Despondent, I take the bus down Columbus Avenue, it too quite Parisian, with sidewalk bistros and orange awnings and girls wearing sweatshirts with intellectual slogans. One declares: "To be understood is the sublime achievement.— Emerson." How unFrench of Emerson. I don't want to be understood; I want simply not to be misunderstood. (Gide: Do not be too quick to understand me.) I used to say: If I could cause one heart to break, I should not have lived in vain.

Ubiquitous chatter about Love—"we must learn to love one another." Love is no answer to the world's woes, being essentially self-serving and isolationist. Respect is more valuable than love. At Jim's church, the moment in the service most repellent to me is "The Peace," where each member on left and right and front and back, embraces fellow parishioners. De rigueur: no embrace, no communion.

Along with insomnia I'm burdened with dry mouth and night sweats, changing shirts at least three times before dawn.

In the long run one is more critical of one's friends than of one's foes.

What do I think of Wayne K.'s increasingly visible essays? I'm not an opera queen, since I'm less concerned with the singer than what she sings.

"As one reads history . . . one is absolutely sickened, not by the crimes that the wicked have committed, but by the punishments that the good have inflicted; and a community is infinitely more brutalized by the habitual employment of punishment, than it is by the occasional occurrence of crime."

Wilde, as quoted by Desmond MacCarthy,
as quoted by Christopher Hitchens,
in Vanity Fair, May 1995

Whittled down: Crimes of the bad are less frightful than punishment by the good. Communities are more debased by the regular practice of punishment than by the relatively rare commitment of crimes.

I'll come to your funeral if you'll come to mine.

I'm not intelligent, my books are.

More words that are Greek to me:
Hagiography
Hegemony

Tom Stacy's CD of my English Horn Concerto is a frustration. After performing it (spectacularly) for two seasons with Masur and the NY Philharmonic all over the globe, he recorded it with the Rochester Symphony. The solo instrument sounds great, but at the expense of the orchestra, pinched and distant. The instrumental give-and-take, which I'd so carefully plotted, vanishes.

30 May

Darkness, cold, achy. Alone in the city, JH in Nantucket with Charles and Lassiter. Every day, mostly in the morning, I ponder dying. Living seems . . . uninteresting anymore. Noise here, in the streets, and Perlman's machine. Noise in Nantucket across the lane, the children playing basketball eternally, dogs yelping. The 2-piano piece is lousy, mirthless. JH's illness is not the cause. He hates the talk of double-suicide, and so, I guess, do I, with that looming image from the end of Visconti's *The Damned.* Tonight, Angelina Réaux and I will sing for fifteen minutes on Barrow Street. Tomorrow, I present a class at NYU for Dello Joio's son. *Et après?* Being alone is a luxury, since Jim can only scold me on the phone. But it's a destitute luxury, and a foreboding.

Le jardinier est la plus belle rose de son jardin.
Pompes Funèbres, p. 58

The "Perlman machine" is Itzhak's goddam air conditioner, a whole little hut atop his house across the street. Twenty-four hours a day, twelve months a year, it throbs imperiously—it can be heard a block away. We've had words about this, mostly cool, but since he earns in one evening what I earn in a year, can't he afford to . . . no. Other neighbors don't seem to mind. Triumph of the re-creator over the creator. What he re-creates, *d'ailleurs*, is exhausted nineteenth-century repertory.

In his review of the complex and not bad but too-long new Amis novel, about rivalry between a celebrated bad novelist and an unknown good novelist, Christopher Buckley naïvely quotes Gore Vidal: "Every time a friend succeeds, I die a little." Gore is merely paraphrasing Maugham's "It's not enough that I succeed—my friends must fail." Gore himself, meanwhile, is everywhere succeeding again, by evoking his own grand and querulous past, lest *we* won't evoke it without him. Even as John Simon nearly always masochistically soils an otherwise perfect review by mean remarks about an actress, Gore demeans himself by always—even when uncalled for—mentioning his lineage and his classy connections, by adopting a blasé armor around a splenetic vengeance, and by overusing the dated and unpleasant noun "fag."

In January I wrote Wendy Lesser a letter, of which the postscript—a frequent ploy—was meant to be the pith, with the bulk of the message mere froth. The froth simply comments on the high quality of *The Threepenny Review*, while the postscript went thus:

> I was amused by the grammar, in your Letters column, of one Mark Jarman, who takes Alfred Corn to task for stating that Rimbaud shot Verlaine, when in fact Verlaine shot Rimbaud: "It was Verlaine who not only shot Rimbaud but also abused his wife, who was the real criminal, and not the romantic sort that Alfred had in mind as a French type . . ." Did you know that Rimbaud's wife was a criminal?

In the current issue of the *Review* my letter is reprinted, minus the postscript.

31 May

As guest of Justin Dello Joio I arose at dawn after the usual white night to meet twenty youngish (age median: thirty) composers at NYU at Washington Square. I spoke, read, played music, read some more, spoke again, and sang and danced. Except for a Japanese boy in the front row, defiantly extending his crusty bare feet, they were all impassive, sexless. I raised questions, was contentious, commented on trends and emotions of the past and the present, and generally generalized. But when the moment for exchange arrived, no one uttered a word. So Justin suggested we play more music to fill out the two hours. I said, No, the music is always there but they'll never have me again. So he asked me to talk about the 1940s when his father, Norman, and the rest of us were . . . Then a timid kid wanted to know what the future of music would be—though I only know the present. Etc.

Discouraging. We disbanded before noon.

So I loitered through the Village, past Mother & Father's on Charles Street, then over to 285 West 12th Street where from 1945 to 1949 I lived and loved in the street-level room above the still vital Beatrice Inn. Nothing, nothing has changed, except the broken window pane from a half-century ago has been repaired. And nothing, nothing of the downtown streets is different except the pedestrians. For my pedestrians are all dead. It was the room where I first read *The Idiot* and *Moby-Dick*, and fellated Tony, and reeled with ale, and was twenty-one. The room's identical, but I am not, for I've read *The Idiot* and regurgitated the ale. The utter sensuality of boredom . . .

Last night, too, I was in the Village for the concert with Angelina. Later we drove around, but no tears flowed. Nostalgia is in the heart, not the senses, except sometimes smell, and sadness wells up far less than does boredom. If living is so boring, then why?

It's JH's fourth day in Nantucket, the first time we've been so long apart for years. No, I don't work better in this free space and time. (The 2-piano piece doesn't interest me, mainly because I've no more ideas for anything, nor any urge. "I am empty of desire, and at peace as on a height"—except I'm not on a height, nor at peace. Yes, I do have desire, mainly for sex and desserts.) He'll be back on Saturday for more tests and more chemo, which simply means pumping the system full of artificial poison to vanquish the natural poison, and hoping this won't kill him before that does. He's exhausted, in pain and grumpy on the phone; but, on the whole, of more optimism than I. (Than me?)

2 June

"Art," announces Pat Buchanan to Charlie Rose, "is meant to be uplifting."

What a relief! After all these years I'd never realized that Art had a moral purpose. No more need now to be upset by Shakespeare and Dostoevsky, Picasso and Goya, Stravinsky and Berg, Sophocles and Williams. Pat has clarified the rules, set the noble standard.

4 June

Jim wears many hats. The little blue & white skull cap from Morocco forty-five years ago is the first. But since his hair began falling out, people have given him new ones, gold and azure and rose. Tomorrow, more check-ups; Mooga scans, cat-scans, etc. to see how his heart and blood-count are holding up. He's back in New York from a week in Nantucket with Charles H. and strange JL. Thank God.

My own nocturnal sweats continue, plus an unshakable bronchial cough.

Continuing exchange with I. Perlman about his constant noise.

11 June

Sunday morning. A quick line before running up to the church, thence to Hyannis by rented car.

For the record: finished last night the Six Variations for Two Pianos, weak both technically and content-wise: any old notes strewn forth from snippets of better past pieces (of mainly the 1948 Toccota) . . . Jim's fifth chemo Friday, and he's loaded with the false energy of Prednisone. He'll xerox the Variations to leave on his desk at church, in case the car crashes . . . Spectacular fireworks last night, the most beautiful I've ever seen, after the sinful Disney presentation of *Pocahontas* in Central Park. The display was gorgeously visible from the kitchen window, over the roof of the synagogue . . . Masturbated this morning, as is sort of a ritual on Sundays. I note this as a shred of lagniappe for other septuagenarian prostate-surgery survivors. Not unenjoyable. And I've used the same two or three fantasies for decades. What are they?

12 June (Nantucket)
JH in excruciating pain. Doubled over like a gnome. The worst yet. Nothing helps.

By Bette Davis, embroidered on a pillow cushion: "Old Age Isn't For Sissies."

To Robert DiDomenica, who asks for a reaction to his music: "We speak different languages. But with the same accent."

Rae Gabis, at 101, has died. She made my home away from home into something warm and educational 52 years ago in Philly. Without her, and those surrounding her, I'd be another person today.

Nantucket, 24 June
The current *New Yorker* contains various homages to Mark Twain, including this sentence by one Bobbie Ann Mason:

> Twain's coarse frontier humor and his glib inventiveness with the new American language assaulted the Eastern establishment and changed American literature irrevocably, the way Elvis Presley, born exactly a hundred years after Twain, changed American music.

Again an American literary commentator uses pop instead of "classical" to compare arts from different periods. Is Presley really the proper equivalent to Twain, rather than, say Aaron Copland, or MacDowell or even Charles Ives? Yes, inasmuch as those composers are unknown now to non-musical intellectuals, and history is formed according to what we don't know.

Elvis Presley. He grew famous when I was far away in the Fifties. When I finally heard (and saw) him, the fame seemed bemusing. I don't begrudge his glory, but I don't get the point: banal lyrics, pedestrian tunes, weak face. He *is* slightly more dimensional than his son-in-law, Michael Jackson, hailed last Sunday in the *Times* as one of the world's greatest musicians, whereas he's not a musician at all, but a dancer, and a mouther of other people's lyrics.

During the morning walk with Sonny in Sunset Hill, some workman shingling a roof at no. 33, seeing me pass by, as I do every day, adopted a limp-wrist pose, as though to exclaim: Look at the fairy. But I am 71, gray-haired and (I'd suppose) otherwise featureless. Does an old person exude any sexuality at all—let alone fairyishness—as opposed to being simply invisible to the young? True, I *do* stare, which is relatively harmless in Nantucket, if not in New York.

That paragraph is an invention.

JH flew alone to NY yesterday for 48 hours. (A funeral service this aft., and the church service tomorrow, after which he flies back.) Sonny's at a loss, searching everywhere with his great black eyes, sticking close to me, or waiting at the door for the sound of the truck. Jim is his life. (Johnny Matos is here. Comforting.)

12 July

Review Ishiguro's book for *Vogue*.

JH dejected. It's the AIDS. He doesn't want to die. How long? he wonders.

Glenway's executor sent me a posthumous masterpiece called *Visit to Priapus*. Vastly sexual without being sexy. Perhaps "good writing" can never be pornographic.

27 July

Rosette Lamont last night, in her charming—yes, charming—speech about the Holocaust, at the charming school on Winter Street, mentions that Charlotte Delbo, like so many in the résistance, was a Communist sympathizer until she realized that Russia too had concentration camps. Stalin and Hitler were two sides of the same coin, and thus do (she quotes her beloved Ionesco) extremes always join. *Les extrémités se joignent à la longue.* But the *mot* is empty; for if extreme evils always join, so do opposites, Hitler and Christ for example, and so then, *à la longue*, do all things.

As for Charlotte, Rosette quotes her as saying she, Charlotte, judges all new acquaintances by whether they might help her in an emergency—so great was her suffering and deception in Auschwitz. During my early years in Paris, Mother used to write, "I hope you're attending Quaker meeting" (she enclosed the address, Avenue Mozart, of the Society of Friends) "because they may be helpful someday." But that day may never come, I reasoned; meanwhile why spend time with little gray men while the thrilling Comtesse de Polignac awaits? If today I allow that Mother had a point, I find something vain in Charlotte's sizing up potential friends for their usefulness rather than their poetry. What, after all, is *she* willing to give *them*?

Rothstein's *Emblems of the Mind* is academic to a fault, but has a likeable flavor. I've littered the margins with notes, as usual. He's so able to explain what he feels music is, that I grow . . . not jealous, but wistful. It's a friendly book (unlike

Charles Rosen or Robt. Craft), and full of mathematics. Has he ever read Lautréa-mont? Because there may be no math about art, but there is art about math . . . Why do we weep? Isn't that strictly associative? Seconds and sevenths and sequences . . . but where you may retch, I dissolve . . .

Nantucket, Sunday 20 August
In the truck we keep for Sonny a container of water, which turns quickly fetid in summer. This afternoon, while replenishing the bowl, I perceived from the corner of my eye an early middle-aged man in shorts, not bad looking with a sty in his right eye, approach from the hill. He introduced himself as Paul Tillich's biogra-pher. Might I tell him a bit about my family's ties with the theologian in the 1930s? We chatted a while in the sun (he's staying down the street, he says, at number 45); then I excused myself, asking that he write a letter if he had more questions.

An hour later a voice on the phone introduced itself as a pianist who, with two colleagues, is playing my Trio (with flute & cello) in Cambridge tomorrow. Should those loud chords in the second movement actually drown out the other instru-ments? With him too I spoke for ten minutes.

Once or twice a week I get calls from strangers, and as many letters. These are equally split between inquiries about music and about prose, and between male and female. (In the wake of a new book there is more fuss, but not in the wake of a new piece, performed or published.) One out of five is insane—the person sim-ply wants to know me, and acts silly. Two out of five want me to do their home-work—what "inspired" this or that piece? Few are hostile, none is menacing, as in the old days of *The Paris Diary* when I was more famous and prettier and prey to rape and murder threats.

This is par for the course of most composers, and I don't resent it. But I don't comprehend how a stranger can phone another stranger (I never stoop to asking where they got the number, though I'm usually cold) and expect to have a pleasant conversation.

Letters are relegated either to one of two bins called "Fan Mail" and "Informa-tion Requested." I do not include here the dozens of tapes & scores that arrive from unknown musicians, books from pretty good authors, and the solicitation for blurbs, usually by publishers of friends, which I generally accept. (Russell Baker said the other day, when, at the Nantucket Office Supply Store, I asked him, for lack of anything else to say, if he'd endorse my new collection of essays: "I'll write a blurb for anyone, provided I don't have to read their book.")

Except for autograph seekers, whose self-addressed stamped envelopes I use for my own purposes (even as Thomas Hardy furnished a room with unreturned-unautographed books of his authorship), I answer everything, however briefly. Though when I get answers to my answers, I'm seldom sure who these correspon-dents are. Naturally, they always think they're the only one.

In the evening we looked at the 1985 video of *What Have I Done to Deserve This?* by Almodóvar. I love his films, and have seen this one before, but remember it not at all.

Similarly I remember not at all, on second sighting, the exquisite Danny De Vito's *Other People's Money*. Just the vaguest memory of certain non-crucial frames. As for the title, De Vito cites it in a preliminary soliloquy while leering from the screen: "The only thing I like more than money, is other people's money." When you think of the trillions of dollars, script-writers, and fact-checkers rife in Hollywood, you'd think that a bit of grammatical clarity would impose itself. The clauses don't balance. "Other people's money" is not an alternative, but a subdivision, of the category "money." Should he not have said, "The only thing I like more than *my* money, is other people's money"? The lack of that little "my" throws the whole script out of kilter. At least for me.

21 August

JH's biopsy results are negative.

An aphorism, he says, is a truth encased in a falsehood.

Not to mention Tolstoy's great biography of the British statesman Warren Pease.

Will the clock, the rugs, the dust, remain as they are, silent, un-annoyed, until we come back in a month, in a year? The question deserves no answer. Even poets reply yes. Even if we kick the bucket, the dust and rugs and clock glitter on the bucket as it clatters downhill. And so forth.

Murder in the Nursery. Ur-er ur-er.

Nuclear is unclear.

Venus. Menus.

28 Aug.

Whenever Sonny and I take a walk to the Lily Pond, Tom comes too. He thinks he's a dog, sort of leads the way, is brighter than Sonny, never veers more than a yard or two from us. What peace in the newly cool weather. How soon before there will be only two of us? Then only one? Then none—except in memory? Whose memory? Nobody's even seen us.

30 Aug.

Ferociously erotic dream about . . . Patrick Buchanan.

Nantucket, 31 August

Usually one can at least see what others see in this or that idol whom one, oneself, abhors or is indifferent to. Marlon Brando, for example, always embarrasses me with his slow, slow mimicry, but I do see why others want to find this "great." But

Jerry Garcia? I had never heard of him (which is beside the point) until his death a few weeks ago inspired worldwide mourning. So I've made a point of watching television reruns of his career. What do others see in him? He is not physically ingratiating, has a rasp for a voice, intones tuneless tunes with lyrics (when you can understand them) of stultifying triviality. Likewise the group of Grateful Dead. Likewise Bob Dylan, featured as postscript, whose weasel face, charmless whine, and pseudo-meaningful texts are merely depressing. Depressing, because these folks set standards based more on being With It than on Thought or Beauty or Craft.

The Billie Holiday review for the *NYT* cost me an arm & a leg and will probably, like the *Vogue* review, be rejected. Now that it's done, I've only the brief canticle for Saint Thomas's. After that, not another commission—not even a bagatelle, much less an opera—*for the rest of my life.* I, who twenty years ago was "the world's greatest composer of Art Song" (and, just a week ago, in the *NYT*: "Mr. Rorem has contributed notably to the continuing discourse about what constitutes an effective format for contemporary American opera").

Musicians see with their ears, painters hear with their eyes. I declare this, but what does it mean?

Labor Day, NYC

Is *Time* magazine specious, or careless, or both? Here is the epigraph at the head of the current cover story about "The Evolution of Despair":

> "[I] attribute the social and psychological problems of modern society to the fact that society requires people to live under conditions radically different from those under which the human race evolved . . . "
>
> *The Unabomber*

The text, by one Robert Wright, then begins: "There's a little bit of the Unabomber in most of us." This is insulting and untrue. What Wright probably means is that most of us could agree with the Unabomber's not unusual statement (it could have been uttered by Einstein or Carol Burnett or any observant slumlord) without resorting to his methods. If, in fact, there's a little bit of the Unabomber in most of us—our penchant to identify with a murderer—that has nothing to do with his public statements.

Three petulant reactions that grown-up professionals aren't supposed to own up to:

A year ago June, at the piano, I recorded my 1½-minute "A Christmas Carol" (1951, on anonymous words) with Judy Collins for her *Come Rejoice* CD, which contains fourteen other holiday tunes. That wee song (not to mention my obligatory Local 802 fee of $500 for accompanying) has since pulled in nearly $3,000 in so-called "mechanical rights," more than all my other records of symphonies and operas put together over forty years. Yet, unlike these other records, my name is featured in minuscule type, and only in passing. Of such is the kingdom of pop.

Daron Hagen stopped by to play us a tape of his new piece for the King's Singers, 25 minutes' worth of settings of Daron's in-house poet, Paul Muldoon. The music is solid, expert, and it "sounds." Yet it might as well have been composed by me, so much does it resemble, in technique and device and impact, my own *Pilgrim Strangers*, written for the King's Singers eleven years ago, and for which Daron, as was the custom then, acted as my copyist. It's not elegant to be jealous of one's former student; what, after all, is a student supposed to glean from his mentor? But if imitation is flattery's sincerest form, it is also hard to swallow silently. Like the protagonist in Louise de Vilmorin's *Le lit à colonnes*: A composer condemned (unjustly, of course) to life in prison is treated well by his jailer. But the jailer tells him, as the years float by, that he (the jailer) is now living with the composer's wife. Is sending the composer's daughter to school. Is eating off the composer's plates. And finally, has signed his own name to the composer's opera which is being sung throughout the world.

Edmund White's skilled and crusty story in last week's *New Yorker*, about an adolescent (himself: it's told in the first person) in Mexico where he has a loveless sex encounter, is too close for comfort (at least for *my* comfort) in device if not in choice of words, to my own narration on pages 92–96 of *Knowing When to Stop*. Even as his *Nocturnes for the King of Naples*, in choice of words if not in device, is too close for comfort to the lusher moments of my early diary.

Another title: *The Palace at 4 A.M.*, used by Howard Moss, but taken from Giacometti.

Another pet peeve: toilet tissue placed on the roller so as to unravel from inside and under, not outside and over.

I've never been in Austria or Greece.

All this is noted while, at close to 5 P.M., a wind blows through the apartment on the clearest of summer days, and . . .

Oh, shut up!

The Graffmans and the Istomins are coming to tea. There's a melba cake from the Éclair, plus an egg & avocado salad, brie and camembert and stuff. JH returned yesterday to Nantucket with Jasper. His back is "out" and killing him. I played music all day, weeping at the pith of the texts (death in war, and possibly JH's death) and how my own music becomes eclipsed by Whitman's words. Yet wasn't it the combination of these that provoked the tears? Sylvia says I shouldn't say I've said all I have to say, yet most of us have said all we have to say by the time we're twenty; we just find new ways of saying it. Viz. that sentence.

7 Sept.

Another perfect morning. Disgusting! Month after month of nothing but blue skies and no hint of rain, in either Nantucket or the city.

Alone in New York. JH, feeling better, is with Jasper on the island this week, the first time we've been apart since the illness was diagnosed. So I gave three parties—three *necessary* parties—if you want to call them that.

Monday, the Garys and the Eugenes came for tea, two kinds of berries and nuts (and Naomi brought a homemade plum cake) of which they ate nothing since they all had dinner dates *en ville*. Martita forever young. Eugene almost seventy, not too changed from yesterday in Philadelphia when he was seventeen. We're each old enough to have worked with the conductorial legends, they more than me, by definition. I have been played by, as they have played with, such European monsters as Stokowski (2 pieces), Ormandy (5 pieces, including the commissioned *Sunday Morning*), Reiner (1), Steinberg (3, incl. the Third Symphony on tour, and the Third Piano Concerto commission), Abravanel (4 pieces, plus a record), Paray, Rosenthal, not to mention the dozens of Americans, especially Lenny. But Eugene and Gary seem not to grasp my contention that I don't know what to talk about with conductors. A conductor learns early (one sees this among the kids at Curtis) that he is Absolute Monarch, thus unapproachable, and without conversation except with yes-men. Just in the past two years both Masur and Sawallisch (residues of that continental tradition), though they have, so to speak, "spoken me" by conducting (very well) my music, have also left me speechless socially. What, after all, is a composer? Compared to the soloist, he may as well be dead, usually is, as well as less glamorous in the public eye, and less expensive. Though for Eugene and Gary, such creatures are daily bread.

Tuesday at teatime, leftovers, plus another cake, for the following: Judy Collins, John Kander, Larry Mass, Brian Zeger, and Tony Tommasini, who brought his young medical friend, Ben McCommon and the thousand-page typescript of the Thomson biography which reads smoothly, is outspoken and painstakingly researched. Judy, full of her *Shameless* book and of her trip to Vietnam, practices what she preaches, and I'd feel guilty were it not that I do compose about the war. In proof, played them the Chanticleer CD of *Pilgrim Strangers*, which, whatever else it's worth, is the best performance I have on a record. Judy says the mystique around Jerry Garcia is due not to music but to post-hippy drug solidarity.

After Judy left, discussion of homosexuals as women trapped in men's bodies. Well, I am not a woman, my body is a little boy's, longing to be defiled (not as a woman, as a little boy) by a grown-up, a gentle child-abuser. Tonight, with a hint of misgiving, I will attend alone Terrence McNally's *Love! Valour! Compassion!* Terrible title.

8 September

Saw last night the McNally play. Although I wrote him a letter, mostly truthful, about admiring its shape, with those in-&-out soliloquies that advance the plot without jolting it, and admiring some of its repartee, the repartee in fact is 90% queer quips, pandering to a TV-oriented audience, uttered by "women trapped in men's bodies," each player, by virtue of vocabulary (the requisite forty "mother-

fuckers" per act), indistinguishable from the next. Then there is the unacknowledged debt to *The Boys in the Band* of 1967, plus the blush-making *Swan Lake*
ensemble wherein each character, garbed in a tutu, camps it up, laughing through
his crocodile tears.

But my aim, my motive, is to find within Terrence a librettist. He knows more
than I about opera, repertorially, and his very vulgarity would soften when sung,
turning wistful instead of mawkish.

Nantucket, 12 September
Weak but steady rain began at 3 A.M. and continued until around nine, the first
water after a parched summer throughout the Northeast. But the weather in the
parlor remains fixed, neutral, strained. We've been here, just the two of us, for the
past week, uneventful, except for JH's sieges of depression on alternate days, and
his sore back. Tomorrow, to New York with the cats.

Checking with my review of Terrence McNally's *The Ritz* 21 years ago, it's clear
that my feelings (and word choices regarding them) were then what they are now.
He's an unrepentant panderer writing what the French call Boulevard Comedies.
It's o.k. to give the so-called public what it presumably craves, provided the playwright craves it too. But does Terrence believe what he writes? Is it already three
decades since his single-act *Things That Go Bump in the Night* so transfixed us at
a public reading with its gloomy and honest philosophy ensconced in repartee?

Checking with my review of Charles Rosen's *Classical Style* 23 years ago, it's
clear that my feelings (and word choices regarding them) were then what they are
now. He's still as interested in how many angels can dance on the head of a pin as
he is in the music they're dancing to. With stupefaction one reads the opening of
his new *Romantic Generation*, wherein he goes on about an obvious point (how on
a piano of Beethoven's period the highest notes, especially in slow movements,
decay quickly, and thus the ear must imagine their continuation)—a point that any
good piano teacher would make to any good student, but which in itself is not
interesting, much less world-shattering. In the current (Sept. 21) *NY Review of
Books*, he splits hairs, again on Beethoven as discussed in two recent books, in a
manner that could not interest composers, only performers working from outside,
and non-musical intellectuals who are impressed, as well they might be in this
Philistine age, with Rosen's elegant writing (despite his using "brilliant" three
times in two pages, an adjective now so overemployed as to be meaningless) of
words, words, and he's right and you're wrong.

In the same *NYRB* Linda Asher translates from the French a rambling improvisation by Kundera which sounds like a sophomore on the sacredness of the artist's
impulses.

Should I quote my letter to Linda here? Or write a letter to *NYRB*? What else
have I got to do?

Nantucket, 13 September

Dear Linda

Years have passed. Now what a pleasure to re-find you in the mostly smooth translation of Kundera.

Did he write his essay in French? Does he really know French, like Ionesco did, and Gertrude Stein did not? Or does he have it checked by a native? What was his French for "the annoyance of a performer who cannot tolerate the author's proud behavior and tries to limit his power" with that vague modifier? Or for the scrambled clauses here: "Jealous of her love for Steva, his half-brother, Laca had earlier slashed Jenufa's face; now Jenufa forgives him . . . " ?

Ceci dit, Kundera does write convincingly, doesn't he? And his notions as I best recall them in *Unbearable Lightness* strike home and are original.

But he's terribly off-target with his pieties about an artist's work as unviolable. The approving quotes of Stravinsky re. Ansermet don't convince *me*, at least. *Jeu de cartes* simply isn't as good as *Symphonies of Wind Instruments* and probably deserves to be cut, even as Stravinsky abridged and adopted the works of other composers, without their permission: Pergolesi, Gesualdo, plus oodles of outright plagiarisms from Verdi, Bartók, Mussorgsky. If the urtext is sacred, does Kundera censor Ravel's or Rimsky's orchestration of *Pictures at an Exhibition*, or Ravel's instrumentation of his rival Debussy's *Danse* and *Sarabandes*? Or Debussy's instrumentation of Satie's *Gymnopédies*, or of Schumann's organ etudes? What about Bach and Vivaldi and the constant revamping that they, and others, did with each other's scores, with or without consultation? Or Liszt with Chopin? The examples are endless. Not to mention that any two performances of the same piece—even by the composer herself—are forever at odds with each other.

More to the point, how does Kundera feel about songs?—about the setting to music by a composer, of words by an author who never asked to be set to music? Even the greatest of these composers—Britten (with Hardy), Copland (with Dickinson), Stravinsky himself (with Shakespeare)—take pre-existing poetry and, as though *singing* it were not enough of a betrayal, proceed to shorten, lengthen, eliminate, or repeat words at will. Well, that's a tradition.

As for Broch: never heed an author who reviews his own work. Or who asks to be understood. (Gide: "Don't be too quick to understand me.")

And Brod? ("Ah, Max, Max!") How dare Kundera declare that Brod "loved Janáček . . . but he did not understand that art"! There are as many ways of understanding art as there are people who give a damn. We can't all have Kundera's superior perceptions. He also seems a little off by equating love with understanding, when the reverse could be equally argued. (As soon as you understand your love, the love evaporates.)

His reason for Kafka not destroying his own work is weak. His reason for drawing the curtain against prying eyes being "shame" is against nature, which longs to be alone. (Although his evocation from *Unbearable Lightness* is powerful.) And his equating of Jacques Brel's recoiling before the paparazzi with fascist invasion of privacy is faulty. Brel was a show-biz personality, not a political victim.

Forgive this ill-written outpouring. But if Kundera now rates a C-minus in my book, you rate an A-plus for helping me "understand" him.

How are you? And where? How is Aaron? Will we ever meet again?

Jim Holmes and I will return to New York this weekend, more or less to stay.

Jim's had a hideous winter of chemotherapy. But now he's "in remission" and sturdier, and we keep our fingers crossed. I'm writing music and prose, as always, and taking lots of naps. Am seventy-two next month.

Fondly forever—

Ned

14 Sept.

Why am I so ill-tempered? So critical of what everyone else does? Would I be less cranky if I had what is my due? Probably not. What is "due"?

On September 8, again phoned the Perlman residence. His associate Karen and I are now on a first-name basis, despite having never met during the nearly three years I've been complaining. Life on 70th Street, 24 hours a day, is damaged as a result of that goddamn machine on his roof.

Knees ache and crack.

Present Laughter, for 4-part chorus, brass, and piano, commissioned by the Singing Sergeants, was scheduled for performance last August 25. But neither Boosey & Hawkes nor anyone else knows whether it took place, much less whether it was taped.

Knowing When to Stop is finally out in a Touchstone paperback. Yet despite the final galleys, which incorporate almost a hundred alterations, not one of these alterations appears, unaccountably, in the published edition.

Practicing the piano, fifteen minutes daily, on my *Dances for Cello & Piano*, but making no improvement. The piano part was not conceived for my hands, so I curse the composer. When I compose for the keyboard, knowing that I am to give the first performance, my thinking for the hands is different, though not necessarily more "easy."

How is JH? Sad. His mother, deeply forgetful, now lives with his sister Zoe Ann in Oregon, and is fading. Her past has vanished, says JH, even in thought; her present is too elusive to be useful; and her future by definition doesn't exist. She's "in the prison of [her] days." Jim feels likewise about himself.

Reading quite a bit, when not looking at TV or videos. Last night, Altman's *Ready to Wear*. (Any movie about vacuity cannot itself afford to be vacuous.) William Trevor's *Two Lives* sticks in the memory, especially "Reading Turgenev." Nothing is like it. Edward Rothstein's *Emblems of Mind*, about the "inner life of music and mathematics," is curiously graceful, even friendly. But though we learn that there is mathematics about art, we are not shown that there is art about mathematics. He might have quoted the second Canto of *Les Chants de Maldoror*:

Ô mathématiques sévères, je ne vous ai pas oubliées, depuis que vos savantes leçons, plus douces que le miel, filtrèrent dans mon coeur, comme une onde rafraichîssante. J'aspirais instinctivement, dès le berceau, à boire . . .

. . . and so on for five tight pages.

William Maxwell's short-story collection palls, though he does turn a poignant phrase. As with McNally in a cruder vein, one can't always believe him. For example, in "With Reference to an Incident at a Bridge," he relates, in the first-person singular, a cruel practical joke played on some boys long ago, and tells of now being "sick with shame at the pain I had inflicted." Then lets himself off the hook: "Considering the multitude of things that happen in any one person's life, it seems fairly unlikely that those little boys remembered the incident for very long . . . But I have remembered it. I have remembered it because it was the moment I learned I was not to be trusted." Isn't the reverse more the case? Little boys remember everything, especially fear, even when it doesn't suit Maxwell's purposes. Father used to tell of how, nominated for class president in high school, some idea of sportsmanship compelled him to cast his anonymous ballot for the opponent. He lost by one vote . . . Today into this room comes the stench of male sweat on the arms of those who strangled me in sixth grade, and I grow scared all over again.

NYC, 16 Sept.

Bobby Lewis calls to find out Bowles's address. Bobby rightly feels that, at 86, he'd like to send PB a note. After all, BL directed *My Heart's in the Highlands* way back when. "I'm not old anymore," Bobby says. "I used to be old, but it was just too boring."

17 Sept.

Julie Andrews, discussing her incredible fame and stardom, says to an interviewer, "But really, I go to the bathroom, like everyone else." Well, *I* don't go to the bathroom like everyone else.

In Ed White's hugely good collection of stories, *Skinned Alive*, he refers to "Jouhandeau's 'abjection' amongst butcher boys . . ." In the few times I was with Marcel Jouhandeau, during the mid–1950s, he told me I was just his type precisely because I was not a butcher boy. (To Robert Veyron LaCroix, however, he said I was *"un peu bizarre."*) True, he took up with Jean Lafont in the early 1960s, and Jean, a *manadier* by trade and by renown, was half a butcher boy and half an intellectual.

JH has fallen back a bit, vague discomfort in gut, dizzy, given to restrained hallucinations, not hungry. Will he visit at least one of his docs this week before we return to the island? But what will they tell him? What do they know? Around 1 A.M. I opened his door and found him sitting, smoking, and feeling he was alone in a boat drifting farther and farther away.

Nantucket, 26 September

The gray cloud in which Jim moves, or more often remains still, resembles Mother's. Outsiders cannot pierce the cloud, let alone enter it and peer out—if in fact the inhabitant peers out. Of course, no one ever sees through another's eyes, although with depression the eyes no longer have it. But whereas Mother gave up on life because the world's logic no longer made sense, and God wouldn't heed her advice, Jim has not given up and hopelessly resents dying before his time.

In the city last Thursday he finally saw Dr. Gruenstein about the blood tests. His T-cell count (since the start of the year when he began his chemo) has dropped from 288 to 77. "I was too stunned even to cry," he said on coming home. Has chills, no appetite, feels low. Yes, he functions—that is, does his work—and is in less physical stress than before the treatments. Yet every day might be *the* day when "it" will begin the slow irreversible trek, or crash through the roof.

I feel impotent, but not useless. If his silences for hours on end, while driving to Hyannis for instance, are sinister, at least he has me to be silent with. For the first time ever he mentioned, obliquely, suicide.

Also last week appeared the very real specter of Paul Bowles, the hermit with a hype. Like Medtner, who at the close of his life was patronized by the Maharajah of Mysore, Paul Bowles proves that if you last long enough you can become a household name, if only because an angel could invest in you. With photographs and interviews everywhere, and a pair of expensively produced sold-out orchestra concerts of mainly his music, the reclusive artist had the coverage of Madonna.

He comes off not well. His pose has always been as the inscrutable loner who won't give an inch but who through charm allows minions to run errands through-out the world, minions whom he badmouths once their costly work is done. Sawyer-Lauçanno, for example, one of the scads of biographers, when his vastly researched work was printed, Paul dismissed it as terrible. In the *Times* last Tues-day, Paul chides Bertolucci (whose film *The Sheltering Sky* accounts for Paul's current international acclaim) as someone he tried to discourage from making an unfilmable film. In *The New Yorker* re. the scores of tourists who knock on his African door: "I don't mind meeting people, even though half of them are people I've never seen before and will never see again. Most are lacking in charm." At Monday's press conference, to the question, "Will you see Ned Rorem while you're here?" (this from a New Jersey journalist), he replies, "I'm not really com-fortable with alcoholics." A sower of discord he assesses mutely from afar.

As for the concerts, it's hard to know whether under smoother conditions he might have fared better. His music was the same, but not as good, as the music featured with it (Copland, Revueltas, Stravinsky). The fragile songs, overorches-trated, sounded like Wagner rather than café-conc'; the sprightly Two-Piano Con-certo, originally with just seven instruments, felt waterlogged; and *The Wind Remains*, which changed my life fifty years ago, now embarrassed me as I proudly sat with John Simon, whom I'd hoped would lend a careful ear. I am the first, because the only, commentator to liken Paul's music and his prose (in *The New Republic*, 1972), the music being nostalgic and witty and wearing its heart on its sleeve, the prose being cruel and dark and utterly impersonal. Couldn't a new case be made that, on a deeper level, the music is mean and sarcastic, while the stories are from a frustrated heart crying to be loved? In any event, how much of the huge audience in New York last week, middle-aged and mostly unrecognizable, knew his writing, much less his music? Why were they there?

Indeed, were I thirty years younger, or rather, if I'd never heard of him before, what would I have made of these events? The past can't be unsewn. I've known Paul since I was sixteen, he twenty-nine, and obviously he's been more important to me than I to him. For fifty-four years I was a faithful promoter, seduced by the reticent sexless mystique that makes a hanger-on hang on. Last week was a liberation. The music seems shallow (not in a good way, like Satie), and the prose willful. At least I *know* the prose and music, while Paul's fan club herds together kif-smoking romantics, like Jerry Garcia's.

We chatted at a party Thursday afternoon. He seems truly old now, wheelchair, scarred nose, in pain, deaf, patriarchal, beautiful. I'm finally free. I suppose I'm envious too.

Trying to read *A Man Without Qualities*, which seems smart, loose, stultifying, doggedly heterosexual and sexist (every reference to women is how men perceive them). Thus Musil resembles Faulkner and Hemingway, my two unfavorite geniuses. But I've only reached page 30, with 12 hundred more to go.

On the phone, from California, Brian Asawa asks that the last movement of "More Than a Day" be transposed down a whole step. Well, a computer can do this, and California will pay. Too late to find another singer. Anyway, I'll probably not go. All depends on JH.

28 Sept.

Skimming the *Times Literary Supplement*, London's more orderly answer to our *New York Review of Books*, my name lunged out from the opening phrase in a review of *The Penguin Book of International Gay Writing*:

> "Is a queer queer when out of bed?" Ned Rorem once provocatively asked. "When solving equations?" Irritating though it may seem, his point remains valid: there are plainly aspects of daily life in which other human characteristics—being left-handed, say, or having perfect pitch, or not eating meat—are more relevant than sexuality. And if, as Rorem implies, sexuality has no obvious bearing on mathematical competence, what about "When writing fiction?"

The reviewer, Neil Powell (an Englishman?), must have been delving through dusty *Christopher Street* mags, for these words, which even I had mislaid, date from a 1976 article called "Vocabulary." Rereading that article now, entirely devoted to the notion of gaiety two decades ago, I recall that Father remarked, "It'll be the one essay you'll be remembered for."

In the succeeding issue one David Matthews notes that Britten's "discovery of Rimbaud (to whom Auden introduced him in 1938) resulted in a celebration of his outsiderishness and his homosexuality in *Les Illuminations* far more overt and unrestrained than in his own life." It's hard to think that Britten waited until age 26 to "be introduced" to Rimbaud, whom every schoolboy knows, or to think that Rimbaud was gay, or that Britten "celebrated" this gaiety, or if he did celebrate it, that the celebration was any good for being gay. Matthews then maintains: Britten had "the widest literary taste of any great song composer . . . [The] texts he set to music, apart from operas—360 of them by ninety named poets . . . make a fascinating anthology . . . from medieval carols . . . to Keats and Eliot . . . poems in Latin, French, Italian, Russian . . . [They] remain intact; there is no Tippettian destruction of their verbal music." What about *my* 500-odd songs on texts of over 200 writers, from Sappho to Byron and Ashbery, with poems in Latin, French, Italian, and Ancient Greek? It leaves me out in the cold where I (and, to be fair, most other song writers) have been for two decades. To say that Britten doesn't indulge in Tippetian destruction (Britishers make comparisons just to each other) avoids the fact that Britten lets few texts "remain intact": he repeats words at whim, words not repeated by the poet, for reasons either of emphasis or of onomatopoeia.

Ceci dit, I loved long and long, and grew to be out of fashion like an old song.

Weary of waiting, and leery of seeing the AIDS "specialist" in New York on Monday, JH asked Dr. Voorhees for prescriptions for AZT and DDC. These prescriptions were duly filled this morning at the Island Pharmacy. $400. Spoke with Larry Mass, who approves and who blames the chemo for the immunity breakdown, suggesting Paxil or Effexson for depression, and Megace as an appetite stimulant.

4 October

Yesterday morning and today, rehearsals of my new piece with the Emerson Quartet, in a Kafkian building on West 76 with no visible elevator but with quiet Beethoven piped into a mirthless lobby. (I walked to the fifth floor where the violist, Lawrence Dutton, has a studio.) Well, I thought it a great performance of a great piece, but JH, who came today, as did Jim Dowell and his film crew, found the ensemble confused and off-pitch. I brought along the ten Picasso pix that "inspired" the score. Première's in Pittsfield, Sunday afternoon, where I'll hie with Jennifer Bilfield and Jim Kendrick. The latter says that the Library of Congress has all but agreed to buy the archive, 20% going to the appraiser, and a cut for him, and for the IRS, which leaves . . .

Emerging from the Subway, as I've emerged ten thousand times, the same faces are never there, certainly not in the same configuration. In fifty years this same *bouche du métro* will remain unchanged, but with young men emerging to wonder about the dead . . . Andrew Sullivan, plugging his book on a TV talk show, states that he doesn't know a single homosexual who has not agonized about coming out. Is it his generation? *I* never agonized.

Whole days pass with our only conversation being my questions and his monosyllabic replies. He says he "feels dead inside." Watches O. J. Simpson, who yesterday was freed.

This year he has already paid out more than $30,000 in medical expenses. And is $50,000 in debt to credit cards.

The *Chevalier d'Éon*—man or woman? But what about any male homosexual? Write a sketch in two parts, describing Chuck on a Tuesday, very male at the baths—his mental and bodily processes. And Charles on a Friday (same person) at the baths. Very passive—his bodily and mental processes. Two hats. Unlike Gore Vidal's *A Thirsty Evil*, telling the same sex story twice, à la *Rashomon*, from the angles of two participants, this would be two stories from the vantage of one participant.

For physically Charles seems identical to Chuck, in fact he *is* Chuck (they inhabit the same body), who, with a mere flick of the wrist (I use the term advisedly), becomes Charles. The 1970s, politically correct stance for male gays: You can't bugger another because you mustn't "use" or subjugate another. But a man, unlike a woman, can choose who he will be. Sex is in the head. Even getting fucked or blowing, he controls the situation. A receptacle can snap off the virile member. The Hopi Indians felt the vagina could capture the penis.

I'm attracted sexually to 0% of women.

I'm attracted sexually to perhaps 2% of men seen on the street; the other 98% are as neutral as women.

To Mark L., straight poet at Yaddo 1995: "If you were forced to choose between an elderly female and a robust young male . . . "

"I'd choose the young male."

"What would you do with him?"

"None of your business."

Oct. 20

More fuss about male homosexuality as inherited, genes, hormones, and female DNA. But a gay male is not a woman trapped in a man's body. He is defined by his lusts and longings. The TV shows a playground with little boys "being aggressive," little girls playing with dolls. But many a boy who plays with dolls becomes happily married and sires a dynasty. What about the genes of a virile athlete or coalminer who likes to bugger boys?

Singers never refer to "my voice," always to "the voice," as though it were some disembodied instrument entrusted to their care.

23 October, my birthday

Of the perhaps three-fifths of his skilled and original works that I've read with care, Gore Vidal's new memoir is surely the weakest; it draws so much on what he's already written better and then exhausted, and on other people too. (The very title, *Palimpsest*, echoes Lillian Hellman's *Pentimento*, in sense and in clumsy sound.) Gore's Achilles heel is the need to let us know, for the trillionth time, that the Truly Great are beholden to him. Don't his gifts stand alone? Can one believe for an instant his admission of love for that long dead lad? For if one can love once, then one can love again, but his stance has always been, till now, above all that.

He recalls a conundrum from amongst schoolboys: If God can create anything, can he also, in a trice, create a year-old calf? No, because if the calf is created in a trice, how can it be a year old?

JH clarifies this to poor me: The concept of time is human. God does not exist in time. Even to us, as recently as 150 years ago, train schedules did not exist. Meanwhile, says Jim, God loves everything he has created, including man's concept of time. He loves time, he loves strawberries, he loves agony. "Man invented time to keep everything from happening at once."

So let's turn to Edward Albee's play which, having missed seeing it, I read. What can one learn, how can one change, through *Three Tall Women*? Like Gore's book, this too is about the past, about the irretrievable. "The interwoven sensualities of youth," says the all-knowing James Hamilton-Patterson, "are fully understood only by other adolescents, for whom they are new . . . and free from the corruption of nostalgia." If neither Gore nor Edward is free from the corruption of nostalgia, both are free of warmth. Surely *Three Tall Women* must *play* wonderfully; indeed, every third *répliqué* is followed by a parenthetical indication like *Pause, Under her breath, Loud, Calm, Shuts eyes briefly*, as the non-French Parisian playwrights of the 1950s (Ionesco, Arrabal, Beckett) used to sprinkle their scripts with, and which translate visually well. But tears do not well up, as they do later when on TV is revived *The Heiress*, Aaron Copland's extraordinary movie from 46 years ago, also about miserly bitterness, but with a heart that can shudder. Or Fellini's 8½, which with the years, like *Blood of a Poet*, becomes ever more trenchantly art about art.

We need, in America, geniuses. Not having them, we christen also-rans: Albee, Tony Kushner, Stephen Sondheim, Woody Allen. As for Ishiguro's *The Unconsoled*, which I panned for *Vogue*, it's being praised now all over the United States. The logic is: since it's boring and senseless, yet since it's Ishiguro and also very long (like Kushner), then it must be great, therefore it *is* great, and this deconstruction will prove it. But if Kafka's K. and Lewis Carroll's Alice are sane folk in lands of folly, Ishiguro's dreary hero is mad in a land of madness, thus, at the very least, untheatrical. But we need him too. O boredom of genius!

Today I am 72.

29 October

I will not fly to Los Angeles next week for the première of *More Than a Day*. The reason I gave to the orchestra management, and to Betty Freeman and Jack, is JH's health; in fact, to be away from him for five days seems intolerable. But another reason may be—besides aversion to travel—an intuition about Asawa's narrow gamut of tone and sensibility, and about the conductor Yoel Talmi's imperious iciness on the phone. Jack tells me that the hall will be flooded with movie stars. Yet what if I got there, and there were no movie stars!

Monday 6 Nov.

Every day I tell myself to write here, even listing items to remember or develop: Rabin's assassination; John Simon's call about his review of Gore's book (vengeful); Beethoven's . . .

Tuesday, 7 Nov.

. . . Beethoven's Piano Sonata, Opus 31, No. 3, which is, with its little trills and frills, the campiest thing he ever penned (campy? Beethoven?). Next day the items lose their zest, I too. *Civilization* magazine asked me for an essay on "The Art of the Diary." They should have asked Anus Ninny, who took her jottings more seriously than I take mine. The art? Art has shape. A diary, by definition, does not.

Heard last night at Columbia a live performance of *Le Marteau sans maître*, exactly forty years after attending its première at Aix. At Aix, Boulez having just ascended to absolute monarchy, the brainwashed intelligentsia sat with head in hands and knew that greatness was upon them. Last night no one feared saying how bored they were. Nothing to listen to but relationships whose effects are not subliminal (as with, say, Beethoven who can move the unwashed) but crucial. How quickly propaganda dates. To his credit, Boulez's 1984 *Dérives*, a ten-minute affair that preceded *Marteau*, was quite pretty, even theatrical, straight from the Impressionist tradition, via the Serial Killers.

JH in Nantucket. I have heartburn horribly, and in the night am awakened by spikes thrust into the right heel. Thick rain. Visit from Meryle Secrest about her book on Sondheim. Stayed home alone, then, but didn't work. Haven't worked in weeks. Except for this page. And didn't go to Schuyler Chapin's party.

8 Nov.

The originality, the unexpected, the surprise, are that only once. After the first time these traits, in Haydn as in Stravinsky, must give way to the indefinable lure of the personal. Anyone can be original; only the chosen can be personal. Even this "personal" is not alluring, or even admitted, for all.

The above was elucidated a propos of Sondheim. We need gods, but the gods have gone away. So we anoint *au hasard*. "When half-gods go / The gods arrive." If only.

The meaning of life? The question's as vain as "What is the meaning of art?" since no two proposers will ever concur. A sounder question is: "What is the reason for life?" The reason for life is to seek life's reason. (By definition this applies only to humans, not to Sonny and Tom and Lucille.)

9 Nov.

Oral support of Edmund White at the Academy Meeting. It is important to stress the unimportance of homosexuality in his fiction, given that 95 percent of his characters are gay. Their problems are never those of polemical activists, but simply those of more or less intelligent citizens living and loving in the same world we all inhabit. Edmund White's importance, therefore, lies less in his human subjects than in his extraordinary style—as successfully rich and dangerous as that of Nabokov or of James Hamilton-Patterson.

12 Nov.

Sunday. JH at church. Waiting to go to Rye for Felicity's homage. Unpleasant continuing heartburn. Sleepless night in our noisy city. Tired. Gouty right heel. (The stigmata, perhaps.) Father used to say, "I've enjoyed poor health all my life."

14 Nov.

Nantucket. Second hurricane in a week. Tomorrow the back yard will have become a lake.

In his poem "Aubade," which I'll someday set to music, Philip Larkin states, apropos of dying:

> *. . . this is what we fear — no sight, no sound,*
> *No touch or taste or smell, nothing to think with,*
> *Nothing to love or link with,*
> *The anaesthetic from which none come round.*

Yet if to me too obliteration seems unacceptable, do I *fear* it? In an old song to a poem by (I think) John Clare, David Diamond—who as I write this lies, at 80, in NYU Hospital after a double bypass—asks a singer to intone:

> *This world is not my home,*
> *I'm only passing through . . .*

but of course, that presupposes a promised afterlife. Well, anyway, America today is nothing to be proud of, swamped by an ever-increasing majority of unenlightened anti-art philistines. When they too are gone—for no one's spared—in a year, a decade, a century, the whole globe will be an ant hill.

Last week at the Academy, where I defended my nomination of Ed White before the chamber of immortal homophobes, I later at the loud dinner party found myself between the Shelby Footes, who know a thing or two about the Civil War. I told them of the affinity for Walt Whitman—how I'd set more Whitman (maybe two hours' worth) than any other poet; how Whitman is the most-set writer in the world of music; how, when I learn that other composers are using him, I grow jealous, jealous that Whitman has been unfaithful to me; and how I'll probably never use him again. "You are wrong to want to own him," insist the Footes, "but also wrong in wanting to leave him alone."

"America's two greatest crimes," says Shelby, "were slavery, and the emancipation."

Under "personals" in the Juilliard Newsletter: "Calves would not spend their lives chained in the dark, if you did not eat veal."

Low. A diary is no help when it should be. But if I were "really" low, the rest—which historically is what truly counts—would be silence.

17 Nov.

Father's 101st birthday.

Jim in wintertime sleeps on the parlor sofa with Sonny, not in his basement retreat. Thus I, on the second floor, can hear more clearly his moans and calls. Last midnight he made sounds; I went down; he said he was lonely; we lay together with Sonny for a while. Then the proximity gave him claustrophobia. I returned upstairs to read.

". . . the doctor doesn't hear what I do," writes Mark Doty, "that trickling, steadily rising nothing / that makes him sleep all day / vanish into fever's tranced afternoons, / and I swear sometimes / when I put my hand to his chest / I can hear the virus humming / like a refrigerator."

On the pad at the night table I write "la solitude," avoiding the "loneliness" lest Jim see it. The French word brings back Cocteau's sublimely ridiculous song, which Norris Embry lent me, circa 1942, on a record of Marianne Oswald singing, or rather, reciting (belching): "*Mes soeurs, n'aimez pas les marins, ils vous quittent sans chagrin, . . . La solitude est leur royaume . . . il RIT.*" She screams, dissolves into tears. (Marie-Laure used to quote Picasso, "*Rien n'est agaçant comme une femme qui pleure,*" evoking those portraits of Dora Maar, choked with weeping.) Could that disk still be on the hall shelf, with the disks of Dietrich?

Jim this afternoon has left in the early dark for New York, to return in 56 hours after the Sunday services. He is not communicative. Coughs . . . Go away, quickly, so that you can come back.

There are those who, because of what I may have written about them, will not perform me: Leon Botstein, Michael Tilson Thomas, Itzakh Perlman, Marilyn Horne, a dozen more. Then again, maybe they just don't dig my music.

20 Nov.

Finished a 2000-word prose piece, called *Two Hats*, for the *Washington Post's* "The Writing Life." Mainly recycled cant about being a user of both nouns and neumes. In France, novelists are also playwrights: Montherlant, Cocteau, Gide, Sartre, Duras, Camus, Sagan, how many more! France and America: not their mundane similarities but their thrilling differences. Judy Collins and Leontyne Price both intone my tunes. Awards in both categories from the NEA, back when the NEA dispensed largess to individuals.

27 Nov.

Morton Gould phoned, agog from *Knowing When to Stop*. "Why," he asks, "do you persist in being so honest?"

What is the difference between European and American professionals? Europeans are general practitioners, Americans are specialists. A Parisian doctor who inspects your ears will also be glad to diagnose your arthritis, prescribe for your stomach, and set your broken arm; in the evening you may run across him at a party for a diva where there will also be butchers and bakers and candlestick makers. A New York doctor who inspects your ears will send you across town for your other complaints; nor will you find him at the diva's party—he hobnobs only with physicians.

The same obtains in the arts. A French composer, to make ends meet, must write not only string trios and symphonies but also backgrounds for films, chansons for Piaf, and mood-setters for plays by everyone from Aeschylus to Anouïlh, while his social life is all-inclusive. An American composer who writes string trios might also write symphonies, but won't touch the theater, much less the human voice, and his society is almost strictly musical, containing maybe a few authors, no painters.

The sole area where these generalities are reversed is that of recital singers. Young German or Italian or French sopranos and baritones master the literature of their land first and foremost, often to the exclusion of all other literature; they are proud of their native tongue, in song as in speech. The same obtains to their listeners: German audiences, nursed on *lied*, hear with head in hands; in Italy even the barber and the grocer know their *bel canto* backwards; and the French public, while preferring visual arts to aural, are nonetheless content in their assurance that no music exists beyond their frontiers. Young American singers, meanwhile, learn to sing, albeit unsteadily, in every language but their own. Americans know they're better than the rest of the world in bombs and budgets, but retain a vague inferiority vis-à-vis the musical arts, still feeling that European repertories, not to mention European conductors, are better than ours.

Such was my perception based on a life in France during the 1950s when that country—though we couldn't know it then—lolled in a blazing twilight of cultural activity which would turn to darkness by the decade's close. (As for vocal soloists, my differentiation now seems merely academic, since the art of the song recital has gone the way of the dodo.)

For Americans there is always the suspicion that to practice more than one trade is superficial. "Think what he could do if he didn't spread himself so thin!" people used to say about Leonard Bernstein, who, as we know, never got very far. Did such people consider the jacks-of-all-trades abroad, from Leonardo and Michelangelo to Jean Cocteau and Noël Coward? True, America at the end of the last century did fashion two-faced monuments like the poet Wallace Stevens, born 1879 (a decade before Cocteau), publicly an insurance attorney; composer Charles Ives, born 1874 (twenty-five years before Coward), also publicly in insurance; and writer William Carlos Williams, born 1883, who earned his living as a pediatrician. But that was then, in a time of rugged individualists, nor was their double life divided between various arts. Their words and music were closeted behind mundane professions. They could not exist today.

Nor could audiences today appreciate the diversity, for the simple reason that our audiences are unaware of diversity, at least in music. Serious contemporary concert fare has all but vanished, during the past twenty years, in the ken of even the most educated laymen. Intellectuals who "appreciate" the arts of the past and present know their Dante as they know their Dinesen, and adore Praxiteles as they adore Pollock; but when it comes to music they may thrive on Vivaldi or even Mahler but not on these men's living equivalents. Music today means pop music. Myself and my sisters and brothers—we're not even a despised minority, for to be despised you must exist. Ours is an age of performers, not of creators. A tenor like Pavarotti earns in one evening what a composer is paid to write a three-act opera. And Pavarotti, like 95% of executants, celebrates solely the past. Ironically, there exists a large mass of well-trained, thoughtful, ambitious young composers. What is their future? They will have to invent the rules.

The foregoing was excised by the *Post's* canny editor, Marie Arana, from the *Two Hats* piece. Jim says it's just as well: I've been barking up the same tree for so long I can't hear my yelps anymore; meanwhile, the Song Recital is having a resurgence. (Is it?) But Jim now rides on an excess of energy, gets up early, works all day, doesn't take naps, seems more optimistic. Because of his array of pills? Or because he seeks to be more "alive" before he dies?

There have been no roaches around for many months.

NYC, 3 December
Rosemary is here for 24 hours, always an easy pleasure, especially since JH has gone alone for several days to the island.

There are no more tenors in the world. Baritones, yes, good ones in droves, but no tenors. Ellen Zwilich presses me to find one for *The Auden Poems* in her 1997 series. Since Paul Groves is unavailable, I phone Craig Rutenberg (the only person in the city who knows tenors) about Jerry Hadley, the one American who could be ideal for the job. Craig says he'll call back in fifteen minutes. In fifteen minutes Hadley himself calls from Dallas in a state of profane ecstasy ("I'm so goddamned thrilled at the idea of working with you"), and we chat for half an hour. Nothing in the world could make me happier than that he, an opera star, should want to fold his wings over the dying Art of Song.

Reading Montherlant. (Can anyone else in the USA say the same tonight?) This time it's *Les jeunes filles*, which has all the misogynist meanness of Laclos, and of the only other Montherlant novel I've read, *Pitié pour les femmes*. One year younger than Father, Montherlant killed himself in 1972. I could have known him in Paris, just as I could have known Colette, but by the time I realized their value, they had vanished. Lévesque, who was of the same generation, but joyfully out of the closet, once said that Montherlant liked only toreadors, was guilty about it, and lived in Spain where nobody knew him. Nobody *French*, that is! (Oh yes, there was also his beautiful play from long ago: *Le Royaume dont le prince est un enfant.*)

Again, the irritation of *une femme qui pleure*. No less than Picasso, Montherlant portrays the tiresome poignance of She Who Loves But Is Unloved, the righteous whine, the why why why, like Nicole Simpson's sister weeping for the television, or the duplicitous Mrs. Waldholts of Utah. An unloved lover is divested of character, thus an annoyance. (I reread with a shudder my "Letter to Claude" in *The New York Diary*.) But a laughing woman's pretty awful too: the overreaction, the high decibels which preclude a man's joining in, the phony notion of seduction, oh laughter!, and the cute boys that fall for it.

7 December

I had dreaded Weisgall's *Six Characters in Search of an Author*. He's an old friend, a non-fake musician, with as heady a sense of theatricality as any composer today. But Hugo's language is not mine, and three acts of Germanic thickness might be hard to swallow (though I remember with pleasure—at least with *visual* pleasure—the City Opera's production 35 years ago). But last night at the Manhattan School, everything about the revival turned out to be a joy, albeit a troubling joy. I made a point of greeting Hugo and Nathalie (who introduced me to their big children) before the performance, in case I left in medias res, though when the end came I was still there and clapping. If the show has its flaws (the end is too protracted, the book sometimes too darling), the music is continually alive and surprisingly tuneful. And the two main "characters" were the clear-voiced and sound-acting soprano and baritone, Theodora Fried and Philip Torre, who graced my *Miss Julie* at the same time and place 365 nights ago. Same director, too, and same conductor, James Robinson and David Gilbert. Before the final act Hugo, looking frail at 83, gave a spirited brief speech. I felt wistful, rather than jealous, at his triumph so late in the day. I've lived long enough to be forgotten, but not long enough to be remembered.

For years I've wanted to compose a work called *Art of the Song*, an evening-long work of 24 pieces for four solo voices and piano, on poetry in English by various authors, ranging from birth to death. Contained would be eight solos, six duets, six trios, and four quartets. Who could commission such a piece, and who would perform it where? It's better to write a piece and get paid than to write a piece and not get paid.

9 December

The internationally compulsory total-serial-music rage, launched in the 1950s by Pierre Boulez, stemmed from that composer's personal needs. So powerful was his gift of persuasion (as distinct from his gift of—shall we say—beauty) that, as with Hitler, his dicta became law. Whoever didn't follow was a wimp. The false premise—that one man's perception must become every man's perception—set music back a generation. Yet is music ever "set back?" All is progress, even when it's destructive. The arts are never on the "right track."

New York. Heavy snow. The pupils either will or won't make it from Philadelphia in time for their habitual lunch of quiche, yogurt, fruit juice, and doughnuts.

Meanwhile, into my new agenda for 1996, a sturdy 6 x 8½ red cardboard book with "Daily reminder" stamped on the cover in gold. I enter the few committed dates that are scattered through the coming year: Art Song Festival in Durham, March 2; recital with Réaux in Evanston, March 28; English Horn Concerto in London, August 20th. Things like that. Nowhere do I note that John Doe is in love again, or that so & so died this morning. Empty pages to be filled. Who will survive them? Flipping through this mostly blank paper is like riding a helicopter over the future: hills and valleys are there, waiting, but no landmarks are yet imposed. The past year's agenda, meanwhile, is speckled with "hot weather, noisy neighbors," or "JH says he's not depressed, just feels dead inside."

Moira recalls our first meeting, when she came to interview me in 1964. "You're contradicting what you said twenty minutes ago," she declared. Me: "But I was sitting on the blue sofa then."

Saw part of *The Sheltering Sky* again. What a dreary betrayal of a slightly less dreary book. And Malkovich, with that somnolent ungiving stance, is even drearier than Brando. Or than William Hurt with his lifeless "naturistic" pose.

Insomnia, night after night, mind racing. Racing through blackness. In the next room, what does Jim dream with the new medication, Epivir, racing through his blackness?

More greatness I can't *encaisser*: Henry Roth, Malcolm Lowry, Salinger.

Si je cherchais Dieu, je me trouverais, wrote Montherlant, or words to that effect, which sits well with my atheism. But the phrase could have two senses: 1) If I sought God, I would find only myself; or 2) If I sought God, I would find him in myself. Pascal: *Je ne te chercherais pas si je ne t'avais trouvé.*

Nantucket, 12 December

3 A.M. He talks a great deal about it now. Not dying per se, but about the form it may take. A rapid form: he senses (hopes). Dreads blindness. Gets prescriptions for each new drug touted ever more often in the news, though Dr. Voorhees doesn't know (and admits it) about dosages anymore than does JH himself. The pills alone will come to fifteen thousand a year. Breathes & mutters loudly in his sleep. The money from the Library of C. is for this. For what else? Irony that, except for the chemist at Island Pharmacy, Voorhees is the sole soul in town who knows JH's status; Eugenie, his ex-wife, who comes tonight to dine, does not. We'll have JH's coq au vin, and meringues made à la Virgil. (Put egg whites in a highly heated oven at midnight. Turn off heat. Remove next morning.)

I'm feeling lousy. Petty to mention it in the same paragraph with Jim. Fluey. Right thumb still acts up from when it was smashed in Virgil's door in Paris, 1961. Hemorrhoids and other aches and pains. Aix les pains. Humidifiers buzz throughout the house. Unseasonable cold. Christmas cards. Music continually in the head, all night long. And his sighs, his groans.

Next afternoon. Sun fades by 3:30, we're so far east into the Atlantic. House overheated, snug and safe. Jim has festooned the outdoor evergreen with silver lights.

Late call last night from Larry Rivers, to thank me for thanking him for the huge and complex lithograph, in tangerine nuances, which replicates my song on Updike's verse immortalizing the Academy. We talk of music. Larry is a good musician—plays the saxophone—but doesn't "know" music. (He once asked what was that instrument on a tape of my "Picnic on the Marne." It was a saxophone.) I tell him I spoke with Alice Esty, now 91, on learning of Bobby Fizdale's sad death last week. "The first time I ever saw you at a vocal recital," I add, "was at one of Alice's odd recitals around 1959. Frank O'Hara says it was your first classical outing. Like the young man, in *Catherine Was Great*, who had spent his life in the palace dungeon, and had never seen a woman until he was brought before the mighty empress—in the form of Mae West."

Larry says the one thing that impressed him in the memoir is that I call father Father.

Besides the Updike illustration, Larry has drawn three other images for me: in 1958, at John Myer's coaxing, I posed for a charcoal likeness, to be used as a music cover; in 1979, for the recording of *Miss Julie*, he drew a four-color picture of a left wrist being slashed by a razor; and in 1982, for the private edition of *Paul's Blues*, a double portrait of me & Paul Goodman. But I've never done anything for him.

14 Dec.

Plaintive call from Rosemary in Philadelphia. She's had another dizzy spell of blindness while shoveling snow. Her doctor says it's not a stroke, more likely migraine. Like Jim, she overextends.

From whence the final "s" in Marseilles and Lyons in English, but not in French?

New York, Sunday 17 Dec.

Recital this afternoon by Noël Lee and Ole Böhn playing an all-American program for the Norwegian Embassy. Included were Elliott Carter's *Riconoscenza* for solo violin, and the long Duo. I liked both pieces. (Like is not the word: they *spoke* to me, I got the point for the first time in fifty years.) It was pleasant to tell this to Elliott, who attended the little reception afterward, looking fit for any age. (He's 87.) I was especially struck (I said) by the heart-on-sleeve sentiment of the solo piece (composed for Petrassi, he explained), and by the monolithic spookiness of the Duo, when the piano plays neutral chords every eleven seconds, while the strings twine histrionically around them.

"Yes," says Elliott. "I thought of the keyboard as the inexorable flat side of a mountain, and of the violin as a fearful mountain climber." (Milton Babbitt once declared that he couldn't stand either praise or blame unless the listener could describe, using structural analysis, exactly what he heard.)

"My gosh, Elliott, you still cling to extra-musical images for your impetus—as with your First Quartet, which I heard in Rome in 1954, remember? and felt it sounded like the end of the world—though *you* claimed it existed outside of Time, like the crumbling tower at the beginning and end of *Blood of a Poet*."

"That's what you said then. But you later wrote something quite different. Naughty, naughty."

It never occurred to me that Elliott had ever read a word of mine. In any case, I am glad that at 72 I can experience another *volte-face*.

21 December

The century's most devastating blizzard. By rights we should be in Miami today. Ten teams of finalists for the Dranoff competition were required to play my newly minted Six Variations for Two Pianos this morning, whether they wish to or not, while I, according to the contract, was required to curtsy and speak at tonight's dinner in my honor, and to grace the winner's concert tomorrow night. But after waiting nine hours at JFK last night with Sylvia, Jim and I decided to return to New York. We abandoned Sylvia to the subdued pandemonium of the depot, which had been shut down for most of the day, because she planned to stay on in Florida for a fortnight, visiting relatives etc., and had checked her now irretrievable luggage. As it turns out, when Jim called the airline this morning, our plane took off only at 5 A.M. Which means, had we boarded, we would have arrived, as Auden put it, "unshaved and unshat," and would then have had no sleep for days. I would have suffered a breakdown, and Jim might quite literally have died. (He now supplements AZT with a new "miracle drug," Saquinivar, which may have side effects. He continues to overdo: works all day either at the house or at the church, which, with all its drawbacks, is his life, or at least half of it.) Sylvia, disoriented, may never forgive us. Mrs. Dranoff on the phone, meanwhile, says the hearings of my Variations were dazzlingly rendered this morning.

At the airport, between sleepless naps, I killed time with the galleys of Russell Sherman's arch non-fiction *Piano Pieces*. He may be a major pianist, but he's no writer. His favorite device is metaphor. Since piano playing, like all music, is already metaphor, to discuss it almost solely through metaphor is to confound rather than clarify. I learned nothing.

Nantucket, Friday 29 December

Here in the bitter cold since Monday. Arrived by rented car on Christmas with the animals, Sonny, Lucille, and Tom, plus JH's two protégés from the church,

Dominican Republican adolescents, Jose and Mike. The land is frozen. During the day the sun is of no avail. In the evening, one house in ten has lights. What perfection. Silence. Except for our neighbor Susan's three dogs in the yard across the street, barking incessantly (she and her sons must be off-island) until I take leftovers, which they gobble in snarling hysteria. I do little but read, mainly *The Promise of Rest* by Reynolds Price, a true writer, but in the southern saga vein, not short-winded. Painful, since the narrative concerns a young man, reclaimed by his intelligent estranged parents during his final battle with AIDS. Painful, since a parallel lies under this roof.

Jim has had a small relapse. Already on Christmas Eve, while playing my organ *Magnificat* during the Offertory, he stumbled amongst the notes (I didn't notice; he knows the piece better than I—I only composed it, now forgotten). He feels his coordination has gone awry, is nauseated, dizzy, has diarrhea again, and drowses, snoring loudly, all during the day. And he feels his doctors are indifferent. But his T-cell count is back up to 250 from 71. In another six weeks, we'll learn how the Saquinivar is altering his blood.

Meanwhile, this afternoon I'll visit Dr. Voorhees, because of the little skin tag on the left buttock, the nagging clenched pain in the urethra (still, after fifteen years and two prostate operations), and a bite on the tongue. Petty laments, in view of Jim's muted anxiety.

The cats long to go outdoors, but are not allowed. The boys watch TV and action videos 24 hours a day. Tomorrow, when Jim drives back to the city for the Sunday service, I'll go too, for he should not return here alone on Sunday in the New Year's Eve traffic. If the car is wrecked, at least we'll be together. Father, during his last two decades, frequently refrained: "Your mother and I are here on borrowed time"—partly, no doubt, because his investment annuities, or whatever they're called, were calculated on the principle that most people die at seventy. Well, each day makes its own rules.

Have been leafing through old collections of "American Song" put out by various publishers during their recent house cleanings. How weak and inexpert now are the many songs that seemed so admirable fifty years ago, songs by old friends, and by myself. Two or three I'm not ashamed of: "The Silver Swan," "The Lordly Hudson," "Spring and Fall." But what of those yellowing unpublished drafts that have already been shipped off to the Library of Congress? What, for example, of "Felix Randal"? Like yesterday I can reconstruct the reasoning, musical and intellectual, that went into my setting of those anxious words—the conviction that the physically frail poet longed for the embrace of the now-dead blacksmith.

> *Felix Randal the farrier, O is he dead then? my duty all ended,*
> *Who have watched his mold of man, big-boned and hardy-handsome*
> *Pining, pining . . .*

And Hopkins goes on:

> *My tongue had taught thee comfort . . .*

Wasn't that proof enough? But my dirty mind isn't what made the song good, if it was good. Nor could I do as well today (mainly because I did it yesterday). But I've no copy of the song anymore. In principle, the Library will Xerox whatever is requested. In theory, too, they'll pay the first of the three yearly installments at the beginning of next year, next week. But if the childish federal budget crisis is not settled by then, maybe the money will never come. Meanwhile, the broker has sent a bill for his cut of $70,000.

Call from the *New York Times Magazine*, a Mr. Eric Copage. They're discontinuing the "Last Page," as well as the "Him" and "Her" column, and instituting something called "Mine." Will I (he asks) contribute 900 words, something light but which will make folks think, like, for example, the woman who posed as a housecleaner and reports on what she finds under the bed and on the answering machine? Mr. Copage says he'll fax me more details. But I have no fax, not even an answering machine.

Call from a female saxophone player. She's playing *Picnic on the Marne* next month and wants to know about some possible misprints. Jim asks me if the Alto instrument is the standard Sax for concert fare, as distinct from the Tenor or Baritone or Soprano. I don't know. He says, You're a teacher, you're supposed to know. I say, I know what I know. Like an animal, I don't need to learn new tricks. If I want to hear about the latest thing, I just ask Daron (the latest thing can be taught in two minutes). Jim says I dither, and am bitter.

Reynolds's novel opens strongly. The father, Hutch, a poet and a professor at Duke University, is teaching a class in Milton's "Lycidas." That poem, inspired by Milton's grief at the death by drowning of a young friend, becomes a simile for all that follows. So strong is Reynolds's apology for Milton (greater than Shakespeare, etc.) that I excitedly dragged out the poem for the first time since school. Alas, Milton remains ponderous, silly, impenetrable, dated in the wrong way, and easily caricatured.

Dr. Voorhees excised the little growth on my left buttock. I told him to be less indifferent with Jim, who will come to see him next Tuesday when we're back in Nantucket. Tonight with the boys we dined at the airport (the décor used for a TV series called *Wings*). Afterward, they had a date with A., age 19. Jose came back early, and told us, in his childlike English, that since Mike was going to make love with A., A.'s sister, age 14, suggested Jose do the same with her. He declined. Mike is still out.

This shocks. Are females any less rapacious than males? Neither of the boys has any plans for the rest of their life. A. will get pregnant, try to "use" Mike, who will tell her to get an abortion. Of such is the kingdom of our ever more trivial heaven.

Last week, while filing the letter from Farrar, Straus & Giroux about Russell Sherman's book (they wanted a blurb), I came across another letter from them about
Glenway Wescott's diary, for which I did provide a blurb . . . So I got out "the
Glenway sheaf"—around thirty-five pages, all handwritten on colored paper, and
mostly dating from between 1963 and 1966. (After 1968, nothing. He died in February of 1987.) And I was moved by his being moved by me, the wistful jealousy
that one never imagines an older person has for a younger, until oneself grows
older.

So tomorrow we drive down the East coast. Since when we return in 36 hours,
we may crash, I'll leave these formless pages here. (The fact that I note that we
may crash doesn't preclude the fact that indeed we may.)

1996

Drove back here yesterday, after just 36 hours away. In bed before midnight. Clear and cold now. Days already noticeably longer, which means summer looms when the island's overrun with din. Not that din doesn't dominate the block all winter too, with the endless barking in Susan's empty house across the way.

Documentary on Sistine Chapel ceiling's refurbishing. How breathtakingly great in detail, yet how slightly disappointing to draw back and view the whole. The whole, less than its parts.

2 January

Heavy snow.

JH talks more often and openly about his "condition," his spells of feeling awfully low. Dr. Voorhees tells him that's normal in people with a terminal illness. I find Voorhees's phrase tactless; Jim finds it responsible (doctors shouldn't use euphemisms). But ? We are all terminal. That, of course, is *my* euphemism. Am I more in denial than Jim? We consider the options in case he goes blind, develops pneumonia (though he's been on Bactrin for months), more cancer. Home care? Should we both relinquish Blue Cross and take on Oxford Medicare? I'm eligible, he's not.

New York, 8 January

For 48 hours the century's most massive blizzard has blanketed the eastern third of the nation. Three feet of snow, subzero temperatures, no traffic or mail or "services" anywhere. Beatific paralysis. I have the flu meanwhile with mild fever. In total insomnia I wander, a statue of snot, from room to room. At 4 A.M. a scrape of shovels, and a view of the champagne-colored street lamps around which huge snowflakes dart like disembodied halos. (Or patches of cattle urine in a white field, etc.) I'm not aware of being anything but wide awake for three nights running. Nothing helps. The new vogue, Melatonin, acts like Benzedrine. Teeth ache, cavities or sinus? And the recurring twenty-year-old urethra pain is nearly constant, like an icicle in the penis clamped by a vise. Muscle spasm? Referred pain from a non-existent prostate? (Good title: *Referred Pain.*) There is thunder through the snow. (Does snow cause lightning?) So I reread the stories of Denton Welch, one of the few real writers we (no longer) have. Was he a real man, as a Mailer would say? What's the opposite of a real man? An unreal man? Or a fake man? Anyway, he pulls you into his décor from the very first sentence. (As soon as I entered the room, I drew back in disbelief: a severed head the size of a bushel basket . . . No, he's more dainty than that.)

As for Jim, he's had a sort of relapse, puking again after six healthy months, irritable, mute, and looking pinched. My woes seem curmudgeonly next to his. He seldom complains. I'm in the last third of my life, or the last quarter if I live to a hundred. But he is only 56. My feeling is far deeper than love. (There has been no sex in 25 years.)

11 January

Haven't composed a note since *My Sad Captains* three months ago. Nor do any commissions pend, for the first time in maybe three decades.

The Pulitzer came twenty years ago. Its clout wanes after a while, yet even now, were I to die in a whorehouse, the obit would begin: "Pulitzer Prize winner dies in whorehouse," though the honor no longer pulls down further honors.

CRI is doing an "Out" record of ten gay male composers and asks that they each supply a squib about their feelings *là dessus.*

Is there a perceptible difference between gay and straight composers? Male and female, cute and plain, black and white? Not as much as between good and bad composers, and even that's a matter of opinion. But then so is gay and straight— their music, that is. Are gays inclined to write a *kind* of music? No sooner is the rule made, than it's belied by some genius down the road. Ben Weber, gay as they come, composed twelve-tone music only, and twelve-tone music is dour as they come.

Kay Boyle's poem, "A Defence of Homosexuality," which as adolescents we found so daringly chic, today reads like a put-down: "I speak of it as a thing with a future / As yet badly done by amateurs / Neglecting the opportunity of be discriminating . . . a vocation as engrossing as bee-raising / And as monotonous to the outsider." She posits heterosexuality as the norm by which homosexuals should— but don't—adjust their comportment. Well, might heterosexuality be even *less* engrossing than bee-raising? Given a relaxation of puritan mores, would straights become as promiscuous as (pre-AIDS) gays?

On page 1 of *The Observer* an interview with Bill Buford, new fiction editor of *The New Yorker*. In a mere three columns (of which only a tenth consists of his quotes) he manages to say "fuck," "fucking," and "shit." And he's the new *literary* editor! No doubt my puritan reaction would be met with "That's how people talk today." But writing isn't talking. Art's not life, it's a concentration of life. The F-word should be allowed once in every hundred chapters, but with the dumbing of America, it festoons each page of our better magazines.

Reading the essays of Toni Morrison. Her sentences are long (though graceful), while saying too little. Well, I also relax into America's dumbing by watching television many hours a day, and seldom read. My tastes too are formed by the tube.

This afternoon Jim Dowell brought the transcription of "At Noon Upon Two" wherein two actors (John Myers was one) shriek Charles-Henri Ford's script against my music for piano and flute (played by me and Ralph Freundlich). I had not heard this for *forty-nine years!* Yet every scratch, nuance, "effect," juxtaposition, pause, was as familiar as this afternoon.

12 Jan.

The blizzard starts up again after a two-day hiatus. Snow all morning, streets impassable. But the mail has come.

Letter from James Lord in reply to my inquiry about the survival rate of our old Parisian *dramatis personae*. (It's been twelve years since I saw France, never to return.) Of the nine friends I'd asked about, only two—Suzanne Tezenas and Robert Kanters—are dead. James then adds: "Your list is pretty well. But I suppose you heard of Claude Lebon's suicide. Very sad indeed. Apparently utter melancholy."

But I *hadn't* heard, and have been brooding about it. JH's only comment: "Maybe it was the right thing to do." Maybe it was. JH has his own problems (he's been sleeping all day, awakening only to take his pills every five hours), and anyway has never been . . . what's the word? . . . *effusive* about other people's deaths, especially my ex-lovers'. But poor Claude. Did he do it with pills, like any wise doctor? Was he 66? In bad health? Depressed? More than any other human he caused me to suffer—that overweening year-long anxiety of 1957, from which I emerged, cleansed of the adolescent insanity of Love. (Swann: "All that! For someone not even my type.") I last heard from Claude just two years ago.

La Rochefoucauld: "There are people who would never have been in love if they had never heard of love." Yet by the same token there are people who would never eat truffles if they had never been told that truffles were a delicacy. Or who would never have a notion of right & wrong, or of good taste in clothes or books, or even a sense of musical nuance (and music is *not* a universal language: Moroccans, much less polar bears, can't deal with Chopin or Schoenberg) without the conditioning of education. Such education distinguishes us from animals. Fifty years ago Paul Goodman ended a poem called "The Ford" with Confucius saying:

> ".... *It is impossible*
> *to live with birds and beasts as if they were like us.*
> *If I do not associate with people,*
> *With whom shall I associate?"*

Writing about weeping so as not to weep, at least for the time of writing about weeping. A suicide note delays the suicide by at least a minute or two.

Marie-Laure, with her naughty-girl pseudo-innocence, is cruel in the name of forthrightness. Hearing that Denise Bourdet is diagnosed with cancer, she phones Denise to ask: *Est-ce vrai que vous mourrez?* To me, during my complaints of an awfully retching rectum, longing for advice: *Mais je n'en fais pas le même usage.* Then she pops a Corydrane, of which she swallows twenty daily.

Reading without joy Honor Moore's biography of her grandmother, the painter Margarett Sargeant, who seems to have known everyone I knew, and Dale Peck's un-erotic *Martin and John*, which has a sheen of skill and originality but no charm or vulnerability. Peck would seem to pass off a flabby formal sense as style and daring. Moore's jacket has a photograph by Emlen Etting (did it ever occur to you that Emlen was the Philadelphia parallel of John Koch?), and Peck's a layout by Chip Kidd, Sandy M.'s new boyfriend.

Heraclitus's "You cannot bathe in the same river twice" sounds redundant, since obviously you cannot bathe in the same river even once.

Aversion to answering machines. Supposing you needed someone to help you to the hospital, or to talk you out of suicide. Two out of three times it is impossible with friends, and three out of three times with a "business," to be greeted by a human. When they call you back, you're already dead.

No turns, not urns.

La tonalité est bête.
  L'atonalité hébète.

Father: "It's never how you think it's going to be."

I do not know the meaning of nouns and adjectives when used as verbs, like "downsize" or "off-load" (as in driving cars off the ferry). Or of "resonate" used intransitively (does his poetry resonate for you?). I do not know the meaning of "bumper crop" or "outsource." I do not know the meaning of hermeneutics, much less of the hermeneutics of Beethoven or of hegemony or heuristic or antihero or baby boomer or sound-bite. Or of Modern, much less of Post-Modern—terms thrown out daily by critics, presuming that "we" all speak the same tongue. The encyclopedia is no help. I do not know the meaning of words as metaphors, since all words are, by definition, metaphors, including the word "metaphor." Virgil used to admonish his new colleagues on the *Herald Tribune*: "Use Anglo-Saxon, not Latin. Don't say she had faulty intonation when you can say, 'She sang off-pitch.'"

15 January

Nothing to write about. Or should I say: nothing *more* to write about? Yesterday I made a list of things to note here; they seemed urgent then, because JH and I had quarreled (about my blowing my nose in the kitchen sink; he went to bed without saying good night, I wanted to leave home), while today they're merely burlesque. But when *is* there something to write about?

Why keep a journal? To stop time. To make a point about the pointlessness of it all. To have company. To be remembered. For there is so much to be recalled, with no one to do the recalling. Even *Rashomon*, after 3 or 4 generations, is a blank.

Time is frozen by spelling out the farce of noseblowing, which would otherwise be as forgotten as the skeletons of the finches and slaves and tigers and lovers in Sumatra five thousand years ago—lives, and fractions of lives, as unrecorded as nearly every life today. To emphasize the fact, on paper, of having existed, is to hope the paper lasts a little longer than oneself. Am I my own best company? Is there anything that any of us does—*anything*—that will persist? A diary is less a letter to the world, à la Dickinson, than a letter to oneself at a later time.

JH has another slump. Yet he goes out into the winter to church, with Sonny, Sonny's kennel, and the laundry basket under his arm. I'm at loose ends, weep easily, watch a dark veil enveloping. Too sick to visit the doctor.

Famous phrases I've never understood:
    "Only Connect."
    No doubt this means: "Establish Rapport" (know your fellow man and avoid wars thereby). But why "only"? And why is Forster's phrase complete in itself?

What is it men in women do require
The lineaments of Gratified Desire.

> *What is it women do in men require*
> *The lineaments of Gratified Desire.*

No doubt this means that men and women want the same thing from each other (good sex). But why "lineaments"? Webster defines lineament as outline or feature. Isn't that not quite the word—and anyhow superfluous? Though Blake's *mot* does sound neat.

As for Elizabeth Bishop's most famous phrase, "The art of losing isn't hard to master," no doubt this means one gets used even to death. But is that an art?

Well, I never understand poetry, which is why I set it to music. (Both clauses of that sentence are untrue.)

"'What is truth?' said jesting Pilate, and would not stay for an answer."

Truth, like Love, is not an absolute. There are proofs of Love, but Love itself has no definition. Likewise, when people say Truth, they usually mean Fact; even facts are mostly frozen opinions. Is great art Truth? Why? Can music be untruthful? How? Is a deft forgery of Degas less truthful than an original canvas by a hack?

"Two roads diverged in a yellow wood" should, of course, be "One road diverged in a yellow wood." Otherwise there would be four roads to choose from (assuming Frost had been straddling two roads before he came to the divergence).

The Four Hundred Blows is an incorrect (and meaningless) translation for Truffaut's famous film. The title should be *Raising Hell* or *Wild Oats* or *Off The Deep End* or something like that—not a literal but a parallel rendering of the original. (*The Four Hundred Blows* would have been apt for one of John Rechy's novels, then put into senseless French as *Les Quatre Cents Pompiers*.)

Nantucket, 24 Jan.

"Great comedy is cruel, and therefore is written by the young," says John Lahr, apropos of Congreve.

"Live free or die" is the slogan screaming every year from New Hampshire license plates. Free from what? Why die?

I never open stapled mail for this lacerates the digits and rips the paper.

Rosemary on the telephone: "So last night I turned on the radio and out came a Nielsen symphony, followed by something of Walton. Faceless drek." Rosemary broke some bones in her shin during the Philadelphian ice floes eight days ago.

We rented *Priest*, an Irish movie, tighter if less compelling (because of a weaker hero) than Canada's *Boys of Saint Vincent*. When at the end, Father Greg and Father Matthew respond to the congregation's anti-gay formulaic chastisements, their replies seem equally formulaic. For example, the Bible-quoters' cry of "Thou shalt not lie with another man as with a woman" is met with "Judge not that ye be not judged." Why not answer in modern English? "Thou shalt not lie with another man . . ." how sexist, applying solely to males! Are lesbians then let off the hook?— "as with a woman"—but you can't blow a woman, nor can she bugger you, so the analogy is impossible. What's more the law obtains only to the Old Testament Jews. The minor prophets admonished them not to lie with Gentiles either, nor to eat shellfish, or hobnob with the uncircumcised. Most homophobic Irishmen, like most family-oriented male Texans, are uncircumcised, eat shellfish, and lie with other goyim. So where's the problem? As for me, I judge, and don't mind being judged.

Now that the manuscript for *Other Entertainment*'s in the can, and 100 letters are answered, what shall I do beyond tending to Jim? He wrote a note to *The Inquirer & Mirror* about AIDS treatment on Nantucket, well-worded and pithy. And another to Tina Brown: "Your editorial policies are really a wonderfully fucking piece of shit."

NYC, 27 Jan.

As always, year in year out, when I get up at nine, JH is in the dining room reading the *Times*. "Harold Brodkey died," he announces, and turns the page. Such brief phrases, occurring always oftener, alter the tone of the day. The obit, entirely true, is nevertheless un-apt in its snippiness. Yes, Harold was an insufferable egotistical insecure dissembling pain-in-the-neck, like most people, but on the day of his death perhaps he should be remembered a shade more gently. I am disturbed less than by the news of Claude last week. But I ascertain frigidly how my long chain of marriages, none of which was dissolved in divorce, is now dissolving, link by link, in death. Of course we are all, as James Lord puts it, "on the high sea that leads to shipwreck," and I may be next, even before JH.

Insomnia's such a waste. Exhausted all day, yet can't fall asleep at night. Dread going to bed. Dread getting up.

Nantucket, 31 January

Snowing all night. The world transforms itself, as when Mother came into our bedroom one morning 65 years ago and told us to look out of the window. The snow, with its slow sad fat flakes, evokes that famous last paragraph of "The Dead."

In the preceding paragraph, should "transform" be changed to "purifies" or is "purify" implied? Should "our bedroom" be changed to "Rosemary and my," or is that over-explanatorily clumsy? Does "slow sad fat flakes" contain one adjective too many, or one too few? Should their order be switched for euphony's sake? Should the name of Joyce's story be dropped (although life always imitates art; the sea recalls *La Mer* more than *La Mer* recalls the sea), as distracting from my own feelings and images? Should the parenthetical phrase in the foregoing sentence be deleted—since I've pronounced it elsewhere and often? Should this whole paragraph be deleted, if ever this diary is published?

This diary, some friends protest, does not justify its title because it's slick, worked-over, unspontaneous, whereas a real diary (in their definition—though they don't keep diaries, much less publish them) must arise from the heat of the battle, chaste and inviolable. How might such friends then name my book? It takes a heap of revision to seem impulsive. Every printed diary, good or bad, has been an amalgamation of the author's own selections, retyped by him or her, corrected in page-proofs and re-nudged in galleys, even as the editing crayon is presumably blurred by tears called forth on rereading for the twentieth time about the broken heart or throbbing diarrhea of long ago.

When JH and I first knew each other—it would have been late 1967 or early 1968—we "had sex" one afternoon. After which, while he was in the bathroom, I rolled out of bed and continued writing on an essay about how I once composed an opera. The essay was partly cast in a diary format, with various entries, pre-dated, as though they were penned during the period of musical composition, circa 1963. I now wrote, apropos of Miss Julie and her valet, John: "At the beginning of a love affair they sniff around for strengths and weaknesses, seeking how they can go too far and still come back." Whereupon JH emerged, saw me at work, and became livid: How could I be so practical-minded at such a moment! But I am me, I do what I do, including commemorating an act even as the act is occurring. (Nothing exists in the present except sex and eating, and even sex, for me, exists in the future—what can I write or think about this when it is passed?—while it is transpiring.) The essay, incidentally, was called "Making Miss Julie," and the sentence quoted is on page 115 of the book *Music & People* (Braziller, 1968), for which Jim provided the title and the index. Would I write about him if he died? Sure. But that doesn't mean I'm hardhearted. I probably wouldn't rush to the desk and note "He's dead." But assuming I too didn't die of sheer emptiness, I'd try to explain the sheer emptiness in terms of words or notes. Art is cathartic. Time stops while it is being made.

Meanwhile the snow does continue gleamingly, though every few hours I want to burst out sobbing.

If sex and eating are the only acts that exist in the present, yet if I'm not convinced about sex, neither am I maybe convinced about eating. The Finast here is even more thrilling and vast than the Emporium on 68th and Broadway, with aisle after opulent aisle, like some snug anonymous circus, where no human responsibilities becloud the endlessly nourishing surprises. Desserts! A meal is something to be gotten through. Until the dessert! Is a quick sugar-fix the recovered alcoholic's trademark? Was I as obsessed with desserts than as now, there as here, when drinking as when sober? Marie-Laure's table, twice a day for ten years, had a major *entremets* (never a cheese course); was it there I formed the habit? Anyway, in the Finast's last lane (there are fifteen lanes) toward which we direct our steps, from boring vegetables and fruits, through aspirin and Anusol aisles, to canned soups and cat foods, we find the cakes, those spiritual cakes, amid Sara Lee's pies (quite good too) and Häagen-Dazs's ice creams. My idea of the ultimate culinary satisfaction lies on the shelves of children's birthday cakes. Those mocha layers with thick, thick, vanilla frosting garnished with sky-blue sugar flowers. That yellow batter with pink, pink, strawberry icing bestrewn with rich scarlet sugar birds. The chocolate base with artificially flavored green, green mint sugar leaves.

The Fenice has been destroyed by fire, there where 45 years ago we heard the première of *The Rake's Progress*.

Trying to get through the great James Hamilton-Patterson's disappointing *Griefwork*. I do not know the meaning of software, nor the meaning of Internet, fax, or government (in the sense of "too much government"), nor the meaning of buzzwords. Watching TV. Trying to nap by day to counteract the morbid insomnia by night. No work, and little interest in work.

New York, 5 February

The New Yorker features a spread on Brodkey consisting of two Avedon photographs (the earlier from 1962 when he was robust and horny) with extracts from Harold's own journal—a series of reflections on his impending non-existence. This very timely publicity (clearly he had a pact with the magazine—not a prenuptial but a post-expiration agreement) is nevertheless touching, smart, and rings true. The wise know no more about death than the stupid. So off he swaggered down the lane, taking his big dick with him, along with the final appraisal of his work: "I'm either a genius or a fraud." In fact, he was neither.

Tuesday night, 13 February

Is Jim overdoing it? Increasingly frequent fits of nausea and exhaustion, yet planning a too-ambitious fund-raiser for the Church, and listening constantly to music, Messiaen, Wagner, Bach. Planning also to go by car with Frank & me to Durham next month, and later alone to Kansas for an AGO convention. As though he did not want to die foolish, wants rather to imbue his fading nature with the Beautiful and True. This morning he took off for Nantucket (he didn't go yesterday, staying instead to help me host lunch for the three graces of B & H, Linda and Jennifer and Carolyn) with Sonny, to pick up the mail and be alone for a few days. On arriving he phoned to say he'd been deathly sick the whole way, vomiting both in the car and on the nine-passenger plane. We'd like to think this is not a recurrence of the lymphoma.

15 February

Thursday evening. He's driving back, after just 48 hours on the island, because storms threaten. He called from a café a moment ago (that eerie *Twin Peaks* joint near Danbury) to say that, because he was using the truck, he'd be late, maybe eight o'clock. (It's now 7:50.) I worry always that he'll have a seizure at the wheel, even as he has occasional "accidents"—dysentery—out in society, or that he'll simply burn up or explode, from one of the daily sixty Pall Malls left around burning on tabletops.

Visit yesterday from Terrence McNally, for whom I procured a rosy Valentine's cake from the Éclair, and a dish of large strawberries, plus mint tea. Long warm talk about possible librettos, about *Master Class* which last night I read (and rather liked, thank God!), about our mutual acquaintances from long ago. Also about poor Bobby Drivas who died of Kaposi's sarcoma eight years ago. Terrence spared no details.

Saturday noon, 17 February
Nearly every afternoon I have a visit of some kind, which boosts the morale. For example, since returning from Nantucket on Friday the 2nd: Sunday, Steven Kane, student from Manhattan Music School, with his earring and pony tail, his modest but honest gift, his attentive education. Monday, interview with Paul Kirby, writing a doctorate for CUNY on my non-vocal chamber music from the 1970s (his observations on the music, though always correct, are never cogent, finding tone rows which are probably there, but are not there for *his* purposes, for nothing can be said about music that the music can't say better). Tuesday, interview with a Mrs. Helen Walker-Hill for her "in-depth" study of Margaret Bonds. (Would she be black? I wondered. She's white.) I dredged up every memory about Margaret from sixty years ago, and gave the interviewer a sheaf of xeroxed letters. That evening, JH and I dined in Ellen Adler's pretty new and rugless apartment on 9th Street. Moira and Michael too, and the Gruens . . . Wednesday, the trio of Curtis students, for whom I fix lunch (the inevitable spinach quiche, lemon yogurt, fruit juice, and leftover cake). In the evening, *dîner chez* Sono Osato and Victor Elmahleh on their 31st floor at United Nations Plaza . . . Thursday, nothing, though I practiced and tried to nap, and wrote in the agenda: "JH suicidally low, but gets better as day passes, listening continually to music, and planning carefully a multitude of projects. Both of us abnormally tired." . . . Sunday, Steven Kane again . . . Monday, lunch here for those three muses of Boosey & Hawkes. Bitter cold . . . Tuesday, film session, talking about Milton Babbitt in particular and serial music in general, with one Robert Hilferty and his cameraman. Thence to Cleve Gray's oddly compelling vernissage featuring large oils depicting the Eumenides. Wednesday, as reported, tea with Terrence . . . Thursday, a long unsatisfactory rehearsal of *Last Poems* with soprano Carolann Page and cellist Robert La Rue. Jim returned, this time in the truck, to avoid the blizzard which struck full force yesterday . . . Yesterday, the Curtis students again (an hour late because of the snow between Philly and here), followed by a visit from Paul Sperry . . . Today, at two I'll rehearse *Socrate* with one of the singers (Aaron James) for Virgil's memorial at BAM next month. (Gene Kelly died. Caroline Blackwood died. The greater family tree is losing its leaves to an ever more powerful and indifferent wind.) Then, after floundering through a batch of mediocre applications, I'll visit Gary & Naomi at 5:30 to discuss my future at Curtis . . . Later: too weary to visit the Graffmans, but spoke by phone to GG.

These contacts are for the moments elating, each lasting about two hours. But when I'm alone again, I sag back into the anguished ego, bones aching, stomach gassy, unable to lose consciousness during naps, what with the noise of streets and neighbors, or in the silent night, with that loose manhole cover on the corner which clanks 'neath every passing automobile. JH meanwhile, despite HIV and cancer, acts optimistic and hardworking. I am a worthless burden, uninterested even in music.

Received video of ten performances of the new Six Variations for Two Pianos from Miami in December. All twenty performers are excellent (except the Russians), and at least half the pairs had memorized this not-easy 12-minute vignette. Most were Asian females.

Every morning I perform stretching exercises for twelve minutes (the length of the Variations). One of the exercises was taught me by Guy de Lesseps on the beach of Hyères in 1951. Which means that, year in year out, I think daily of that likeable cipher of yore, when I so seldom think anymore of more crucial influences. Like, say, Paul Goodman, whose *The Grand Piano* I re-examined last night. 55 years old, the little novel remains original, but now seems arch, smart-ass, gimmicky, intellectually "removed," with all the characters talking alike. Paul never had an ear for dialogue. Still, he is America's most unsung master.

13 March

The older I get the less I use percussion. Percussion is an indulgence of the young. In Borodin, say, or Stravinsky's *Histoire*, its overuse is like too much lipstick, too many bracelets. When integral (in Antheil, say, or Elliott Carter's timpani études) it resembles a deaf-mute trying to make himself understood.

Still, after reading the thrilling reviews, I went last night to hear James MacMillan's percussion concerto, titled *Veni, Veni Emmanuel*, with Evelyn Glennie as soloist. Ms. Glennie, as it happens, is deaf.

This is music to see. The battery sections are dramatically placed across the front of the Philharmonic. Ms. Glennie, in barefeet (so as to "hear" the throbbing through her body), steps among the instruments with easy theatricality, and knows a thing or two about how to bang a gong. She is also lovely, with long clean hair and plaid chiffon. But the work itself, if you get rid of all that pounded paraphernalia and reduce it to essentials, resembles all music from the British Isles: harmless modality about hills & dales, folklike, with plainchant thrown in.

Backstage, a gaffe. Introduced to Ms. Glennie, I look into her eyes, carefully mouthing, "I really enjoyed your deftness," while wondering simultaneously why I chose the noun which I've never used before. Did she hear—see—the "t" in "deftness"?

24 April

A nice and vaguely sad Italian meal with Becki Phelps on University Place. Later, chez elle (her own orderly disorder, and loudly empty of Robert), she gave me a batch of Robert's French books, no doubt unprocurable today even in Paris.

Including Paul Léautaud's *Propos d'un jour*. What tripe! I never read this noted contemporary of Jouhandeau and Mauriac in the old days. Did anyone? Banality after smarmy banality, old-hat sexism, and water-logged aphorisms:

> *Les hommes aiment, les femmes se laissent aimer.*
> *L'amour donne toujours du talent.*
> *J'aime la femme. Je n'aime pas les femmes.*
> *Un homme se sent bien bête devant la canaillerie d'une femme.*

That sort of thing.

In *The Eagle Has Two Heads*—wrong translation—Ronald Duncan somewhere has Cocteau state, "There is a little death in every love. Great love is suicide." About as smart as " a little bit pregnant." Great love may well be *l'égoisme à deux* pushed to the limits, but why suicide? Why not murder? Or genius? Or hate? Or, simply, self-perpetuation?

Listened for the first time in years to Lenny's CD of my Violin Concerto. How much more *right* it is than my memory, and so caring. Did I ever tell him—is there still time?—that the third movement, "Romance Without Words," was based on Paul Goodman's "Boy with a Baseball Glove," with the text thrown out and the violin substituting for the human voice?

> *See how the beauty with the glove*
> *And hand on hip and head held high*
> *Arrests me to fall in love*
> *When on an easy way was I.*

"I'll never forget you," said he, as he closed his eyes and died.

27 April

A fifty-minute interview with Rob Schwarz, during which I allowed that all serial music was incomprehensible to me, nor can I comprehend, even objectively, what others purport to see (yes see, not hear) in it. Meanwhile, after the two Donizetti operas at MSM last night, I allowed to Jim that all bel canto music is incomprehensible to me, nor can I comprehend what others purport to hear (yes hear, not see) in it. When everything is intellectual, then nothing is; when everything is decoration, then nothing is. Donizetti is only scales, without invention.

What makes sense? Poetry today versus 12-tone music. Serial music always makes sense: that is its purpose. But does the density, that non-sequiturial clarity of Merrill or Ashbery or even Eliot, make sense? I set poetry to music either to heighten it, or to comprehend it on some terms. But I never know what it "means," except what the music (sometimes decades later) tells me it means, though music itself has no meaning.

Since the pronoun "I" seethes through most poems by most poets today, the poet covets his "inspiration," withholding it from the reader. Auden (except in comic or porno poems) seldom says "I." So he is more easily set to music—at least by me. I mean by I.

Walking up Columbus Avenue, en route to hear *Three Sisters Who Are Not Sisters* at Mannes College, I pass a man on a bench at the planetarium park. Bleary-eyed and sloppy, with a happy smile and a bottle in his hand, he enunciates: "You're . . . a debonair . . . piece . . . of shit." Then, more confident, waving straight at me, he repeats: "You're a debonair piece of shit." I wave back and yell: "Right on!"

The little opera is played well, smoother than at rehearsal. A woman in the row before me introduces herself—"But you'll never remember me"—as Betty Rubinstein who had been on the S.S. *Washington* in May of 1949. Of *course* I remember, she was with a girl named Horowitz, and they taught me, sort of, how to dance the Conga.

Jim's fund-raiser for the church's Community Center last night was a masterpiece of engineering, on which he's labored 12 hours a day for a year. (A year he thought he'd never live through; today he looks more plumply sleek than ever.) Verdi & Puccini choral numbers; coloratura with chorus and organ and flute; solo gospel backed by eight pre-adolescent females; a trio of vocalists doing Sondheim et al.; me, accompanying four prima donnas in fourteen of my songs non-stop; then Judy Collins with "Amazing Grace" and the audience in the palm of her hand. Rosemary and Mary came up for it.

Tomorrow rehearsals all afternoon (Daron, with a clatch from Bard; later Aaron Berofsky and Jon Klibonoff to play *Night Music*). Then in the evening, première at the Y of *My Sad Captains*, which I've not even heard a run-through of.

He's nice and mean.
    Count, countess. Baron, baroness. Earl, . . .

Homer nods. Atlas shrugged. Salomé, where she danced.
    The London derrière.
    Incredulous nuns.

> *Ol' Lew, 'tis Sitwell, O*
> *The peach-colored grief of the formal norns,*
> *Impaled on each reef of the sad fox's horns,*
> *Knows naught of the mad mallard's shrieks re-intoned*
> *By the chic moral daughter, who moaned, who moaned.*

How nicely cold it remains in Nantucket. We're here now for the summer (except for a brief week at the AGO Convention next month), JH having taken a sabbatical. So I write doggerel, when not working crossword puzzles in *TV Guide*, or taking naps.

Beyond a 3-minute trifle (I've already forgotten its name) for the Lancaster Symphony, I've composed nothing in ten months, nor is there one commission in the offing. The only piece I've not heard, *Present Laughter*, will be done without my presence by the Singing Sergeants in Virginia in August. I've finished all the prose that's been asked for—the book *Other Entertainment* and an essay for *Opera News* on the non-state of so-called Art Song in America, both of which come out also in August. So, like an old cow put out to pasture, I confect to stump Frenchmen learning English.

> *John Hathaway Chambers joins throngs of thorough thinkers,*
> *as through the tough boughs, bought though not paid for,*
> *float fruits of fun pharoahs who have read the red readings*
> *of Reading Gaol's reeds, bound but not bowing before cello bowing.*
> *What's that? Both cloth clothes and Brother's other bothers.*

The very short haircut of two weeks ago makes me look like a cross between Falconetti, George Clooney, and Gertrude Stein.

12 June

Sonny turns thirteen next March. After all these years, strictly in the company of sophisticated humans, he has remained a dog.

Nearly every day comes a request to "inscribe a few measures on the enclosed sheet." Nearly every week a stranger phones from Dallas or Topeka or Beloit to say how he agrees with this or that paragraph of mine, and will I be free for lunch when, with the wife, he's on the Cape next month. I am not warm. But cannot bring myself to be unlisted.

I retain the childish conviction that not only am I the center of the universe, I *am* the universe. When I go, you go too, the whole kit & kaboodle, for I invented you all. What's left? The question's superfluous, since I also invented the question.

Maybe I don't *quite* retain that conviction. But if no man is an island, every man's perspective is unique. For each rural Abyssinian who dies, the meaning of E=MC squared is altered, and the world's weight shifts forever. Indeed, it shifts with every millisecond.

Ned Rorem = Red Morne

A WASP who says "nigger" is racist. If he says "wop," what is he? Nationalist?

To describe a past event in the present tense is Jewish. "So I'm walking down the street, and along comes this blonde, and she gives me a look . . ." Or listen to Ira Gershwin. It's because the speaker's forebears learned English incompletely, often mastering (as we all do with a new language) the present tense to the exclusion of all others. The present-tense formula for educated gentiles has long since been discarded.

Straight men don't say "fabulous."

20 June

Jim's T-cell count is now 254. He works strenuously all his waking hours with the boys outside on landscaping and carpentry, and at his desk inside on taxes and my bills. He's monosyllabic and thinks of death, but doesn't speak of it, except ironically. Sleeps fitfully, as do I, and is forever weary. Cold wet weather has turned to cold bright weather; everything's greener and thicker than for many a summer.

1 July

Words, words. This week's bedtime reading, strictly of gardening books, consists of one chapter from Duhamel's *Le jardin des bêtes sauvages* (1932) followed by a chapter from John Berendt's *Midnight in the Garden of Good and Evil* (1994). I never read Duhamel in the old days, and am probably alone in America, even in France, reading him today. A Gidean spinoff, self-important, repetitive, dull. Nor have I read Berendt before, but am told his book is bought by Hollywood. A Capote spinoff, directionless, cast with unloveable southern eccentrics, non-intellectual, and scarcely authentic: The transvestite, Chablis, for example, likes straight men when she's had her female hormone injections, but without these injections has been known to fall for nelly queens. As though the object of one's affections were not in the mind—or how explain the straight men of her acquaintance who long to wear drag?

Meanwhile, George Steiner in his new essay collection, *No Passion Spent*, laments with some reason the decline of reading in our society. But is he part of the solution with sentences like this?

> I cannot arrive at any rigorous conception of a possible determination of either sense or stature, which does not wager on a transcendence, on a real presence, in the act and product of serious art, be it verbal, musical, or that of musical forms.

Jim says this means that any art must "have it" to make sense.

> . . . there is no difference in substance between primary text and commentary, between the poem and the explicator or critique.

That is: words are words.

> . . . the translucency of Kafka's German, its stainless quiet, suggest a process of borrowing at high, very nearly intolerable interest.

That is: Kafka took stylistic risks. Steiner writes of passages from the Old Testament, like the speeches of God from the whirlwind:

> Could there have been degrees of "audition," of a concentrated inward hearing amid silences no longer available to us so intense as to endow consciousness with an

immediacy to metaphor, to imagery, to what I have called "real presence" or a "bodying forth" of meaning, inaccessible since?

Well, yes. But can one know how phrases thousands of years ago were perceived in their time? As for his metaphor about the Last Supper,

> Perhaps I may be forgiven for wondering whether it is only when supping with the Devil that a human being—particularly one out of the house of Jacob—should carry a long spoon.

It's Greek to me. Words, words.

3 July

I spoke too soon. Further into Duhamel's saga, the content and style grow more true and original in their juxtapositions. For example, in Chapter VI, his words do what words cannot do: describe the *sound* of Bach by explicating the author's own reaction to the music at different times of day. Interpersed with these times are experiences of practical discovery, raw and real, which color the musical response, and which finally cause weeping. The chapter is a self-contained gem, each facet independent yet interacting with glimmering purposeful sorrow, or something. The Berendt, though readable, gets worse; he cannot whittle. A portrait that would "tell" in three paragraphs rates three pages. And Steiner? Didn't we correspond in the mid-Fifties, when he had a pretty good story in *Botteghe Oscure*? Twenty years later, didn't he try to arrange a *lieder* concert at the Y, hosted by me and Milton Babbitt, and didn't he suggest I was "arrogant" when I asked why my and Milton's songs shouldn't be programmed along with Schubert's?

Reading this journal, one could seldom date it according to what is told about current events. Well, as Virgil used to say, current events are always with us, while me you have but once. If I don't report on Dole, or abortion, or gays and the Supreme Court, or Bosnia, or bombings in Oklahoma, or even Cézanne at the Met or Wagner at the Met (neither of which I've graced), it's because the greater world's horrors are not on a par with the smaller world's sadness. Jim: relapsing anew, our evening meals accompanied by monosyllables, the sound of clanking forks and swallowing. His diet again consists of cinnamon toast and applesauce, accompanied by nausea, sometimes puke. Yet he fixes elaborate stews for the Dominican boys, Kelvin and Jose and Mike, who do heavy work here for the summer and sleep in the basement. Though I'm mostly idle, Jim works for me too, spending hours planning the week-long exhibit for the AGO Convention to which we hie tomorrow. He strives to help me in all ways (save in demonstrable affection—but what we share is more than love), as though to shore up capital against imminent disappearance.

The *Times* has asked me to do a piece on Zeffirelli, apropos *Carmen*. I will, but don't want to. Don't want to do anything.

A warm letter from Milton Babbitt about my new collection. "I am always pleased to discover how much we agree, for all our apparently different dispositions (only your Francophilia is the irreducible against mine), but your courage, your principled indignation is as reassuring as anything can be in times like these."

Nantucket, 13 August

Call from Russell Oberlin to say that Louise Talma died last night in her sleep at Yaddo. She was 89. Claudette Colbert—dead last week at 92—and Louise had nothing in common beyond being the last of their breed. Louise's breed, profoundly feminine in impulse, was of the masculine musician made flesh, consciously vigorous so as to be on a par with male composers (males often far more languorous, though heterosexual—having nothing to prove), a torch-carrier for Boulanger and the French tradition, so rare here now, and the real thing as an individual. Were I to list fourteen American composers, Louise would be there. When I first beheld her, fifty-two years ago, she strode onto the platform at an ISCM concert in a no-frills black gown, didn't bow, sat down at the keyboard and, without missing a beat, slammed into her Toccata, which brought down the house. When last I saw her, at a Gregg Smith concert—was it last March?—we sat together to hear our pieces, and said nice things to each other. Louise, always abrasive, appeared nonetheless frail and faraway, while trying, trying, trying to keep hold in that ongoing fraternity which, despite the violently dumb talk of national politics all around, speaks almost exclusively of music. Her every allusion is musical. She died in the "Pink Room," in the same bed where many other composers had tossed and turned.

Musical allusions have been far from my ken this past year (unless every breath can, in some way, be construed as that of a composer). The highs and lows in JH's health do not make for creative élan, but for a realization of how idle art seems in time of stress. Summer fades already, wonderfully cold and wet, with nothing accomplished, a few books read.

Yes, I have concocted a trifle called *Waiting*, for the Lancaster Orchestra, and a song for two sopranos, for Joe Machlis's ninetieth birthday in October, based on the final prose lines, in English, of Colette's *L'Etoile vesper* (". . . from here I can see the end of the road."). Yes, we went to Manhattan for a week last month to sit in a booth at the AGO Convention and sell kisses, with the help of Boosey & Hawkes's staff, and Gerre Hancock conducted the première of *Exaltalbo Te, Domine* at Saint Thomas's. From there to New Paltz, during Hurricane Bertha, where JoAnn Falletta in the Old American décor conducted *Sunday Morning*. Yes, the new book, *Other Entertainment*, came out with no fanfare, and total indifference chez Simon & Schuster, though I did do an ill-attended signing here at Mitchell's Book Corner. And yes, the *Times* asked me to come to New York this coming weekend, for a decent fee, to interview Zeffirelli, who will bring his own pasta sauce on the plane from Rome, to pour over the linguini I will provide on Saturday night, with Jim Oestreich and JH as guests with a tape recorder. If we live that long.

But no, the summer has not been otherwise vital. I am not a chronic depressive, as Mother was, and Jim sort of is, but I do dwell in a wistful bubble, and not a morning passes that I don't consider suicide to avoid more dealings with this unpoetic planet. Mostly though it's Jim's shifting health that dominates. Alternate days are "bad" days: he doesn't eat without retching, the wheeze in his chest whirs like a beehive across the parlor, and despite a fevered cough and proto-cancerous stomach he still chain-smokes. (He also is now nearly $100,000 in debt to his credit cards.)

I do read. The usual Simenon, including the dud *Maigret et le voleur paresseux* and the Balzacian masterpiece *Le Petit Homme d'Arkhangelsk*. The short stories of William Maxwell, which, in their plotless *New Yorker*ish idiom, never quite take the plunge, though they move the non-intellectual heart. To re-examine the last of Flaubert's *Trois Contes*, called "Hérodias," is to discover how much of a slave the master was to brand names, like Judaic tribes and types of precious stone; how the story, paradoxically, is high camp without humor; and how Wilde's *Salomé* owes its very existence, if not its superiority, to this narrative.

I note these facts, as Schoenberg announced to his lay audience, in mid-1930s Chicago while chalking on a blackboard a series of exemplary 12-tone rows, "arbitrarily and without inspiration." The summer has been consistently wet & cold, the furnace in mid-August. (What a joy to see the loud tourists' vacation in ruins!) The young Rackham Quartet played my Third Quartet flawlessly at the Old North Church on July 30; indeed, it's one of the 8 or 10 most satisfying performances I've ever had. August 10th was Mother & Father's 75th anniversary—or were they married in 1920? Rosemary & I aren't certain. Insomnia colors my . . . I was going to write "my every waking hour," but that doesn't sound right; there's a vague vindication in learning, through Manuel Rosenthal's perfunctorily useful if falsely opinionated and vaguely homophobic new memoir of Ravel, that Ravel too was similarly afflicted, drifting off only at six A.M., when disgusting chimes from the church down the street, in Monfort l'Amaury, reawakened him. Oliver Stone's film on Nixon is pretty good. Crying infants. If I'd had a child, you'd have read about it in the *Enquirer*: "Dad Slays Tot in Crib." If opposites attract, then love is by definition forever unreciprocated, at least according to the fantasy.

Thursday in Dublin, then in Edinburgh, London (Proms concert), Copenhagen, and Lucerne, Masur and the N.Y. Philharmonic will do my Concerto for English Horn (which in England is called Cor Anglais) with Thomas Stacy. This means, because of the radio there, about 50 million listeners. Yet B & H has yet to put out a score.

JH just came into the room with his IRS forms filled out, and a letter accompanying these to ask for human understanding: he's broke, with medical bills beyond his means. What are these prattling notes of mine compared to . . . He is gone out to lunch with the boys; I play the tape of *Swords & Plowshares* for the first time since 1992, and cry. The words bring the tears. But perhaps the music does not entirely fail.

Always a titillating jolt when, while calmly perusing some swatch of unrelated prose, your own name jumps off the page. Thus when Anthony Hecht, a dozen pages into an essay on Auden, writes, "Ned Rorem has observed, 'Arguably, no artist grows up: If he sheds the perceptions of childhood, he ceases to be an artist,'" I smile. Then I frown when Hecht adds, "That seems to me a ludicrous overstatement." (Why an overstatement, much less a ludicrous one, when I've qualified it with "arguably"?) "It would hardly apply to Hardy, Sophocles, Chekhov, Hawthorne, or Shakespeare." (Because these men all deal with grownup subjects? Couldn't they "arguably" be deemed children? Or maybe not even artists?) He reneges: "Nevertheless, one can think of writers for whom childhood was, however briefly, a state of bliss, all the more cherished because of the requirement suddenly or dramatically to have to give it up. Wordsworth and Proust, Dickens, Dylan Thomas, William Maxwell, and J. D. Salinger all share this feeling with Auden."

Of course I was not speaking of subject matter, but of the bare fact of being an artist—any artist. Hecht will never get my point, for the simple reason that I was uttering a Gallic mot, sufficient unto itself, which he pushes to Germanic explication that never leaves well enough alone.

All this transpires in an obstinate putdown of Richard Davenport-Hines' new biography of Auden, in the July *Yale Review*. Since for Hecht, the biographer is wrong even when he's right, there's no appeal, and humor is cast by the wayside.

I miss you more than I would miss my life if I were dead. That phrase contains three "I"s and one "me." Whoever said love was selfless?

And what would France make of last night's Democratic convention—at least my France of the 1950s—which aims toward a finer America through elimination of tobacco, and which blushes with horror at Clinton's chief advisor, one Dick Morris, who slept with a call-girl, a fact which risks toppling election possibilities?

Hurricane Edouard, the worst in thirty years. Dangerous sounds throttled the house all night; this morning the side & back yards are a 2-foot pond. A seemingly cynical devastation of the series of gentle gardens on which Jim has toiled all summer, and every summer, since 1974. Smashed. Flipped like toothpicks.

(Is this a pathetic fallacy? What kind of etic? A path etic. A pathe tic.)

Jim awakens. "I went to heaven. There I asked an angel: 'Is it possible to meet Jesus Christ?' 'Who?' said the angel."

Sometimes at 4 A.M., when he is muttering loudly in his sleep, I peek into his room. He'll turn toward the door and, in the darkness, tell one of his terrible jokes. "Did you hear about the prostitute with leprosy? Things were going all right until her business fell off." Then he falls back into his anxious dreams. What if I grew sick too? Who would take care of whom? My dreams are wakeful. How can the mind be turned off? I no longer know sleep, much less the intoxication of *drifting* to sleep. Insomnia's an uninstructive illness.

NYC, 11 September, 11 A.M.

In the city alone, because of dozens of appointments put off during the summer, and because JH, now that church has resumed, wants to be here only on weekends. Every morning, thoughts of suicide (how?), which extend ever farther into the day. Doctor Agus. A fistula maybe, which can be a nasty business. And incipient cancer maybe, of the cheek. Managed to get to Philadelphia yesterday, and will go again next Monday. But age precludes these enormous schleps. From now on the students must come here. To them, in the little song class which I held with Loeb's two students (who don't know English), I sang some songs, including Copland's "The World Feels Dusty." All the sleepless night long it persisted. At four A.M. I looked again at the last words in the printed score:

> *Mine be the ministry which thy thirst comes . . .*
> *Dews of thyself to fetch and holy balms.*

Then checked these against the Dickinson collected poems which has it thus:

> *Mine be the Ministry*
> *When thy Thirst comes –*
> *Dews of Thessaly, to fetch –*
> *And Hybla Balms –*

Understandably Aaron wanted to simplify these not very singable lines. Has anyone noticed the disparity?

Soon, when I set to music the final 22 lines of Paul Monette's last elegy, I shall omit these words, ". . . the first straight Pope since the Syllabus of Errors this Polack joke . . .": and substitute the word "one." I've never taken such a liberty with verse (with prose, yes, especially Whitman's), but Paul said I could. Anyway, song is not poetry, it's song.

26 September, Nantucket

Gide and Stravinsky stand chatting in the Champ de Mars. A tourist with a camera asks them politely to step aside, in order to get a clear shot of the Eiffel Tower.

Me, to Marie-Laure, circa 1951, as she prepares a canvas in her studio in Hyères: "What colors don't go with what colors?"

She, applying the first brush stroke in what will become one of her semi-abstract still lifes: "All colors go with all colors (and there is no bad color), it depends how they're used."

Me, to James Lord, circa 1956: "Blue is my favorite color."

He: "Of course it is. Blue is the only color."

Marie-Laure disait "vous" à toute femme sauf à ses deux filles, et tutoyait tous les hommes, sauf son mari, le vicomte. Moi: "Mais comment addressais-tu Charles au lit?" Elle: "Nous ne parlions pas au lit."

Certain great works I will allow, without their being my cup of tea: Beethoven, Milton. Other great works I can't admit even what people find in them: Berlioz, Beckett. Last week I read Seamus Heaney's little collection *The Spirit Level*. Today I reread it and recalled not a single poem. His work had made no impression.

Tomorrow we leave on the new speed-ferry for New York. Early bright autumn, after weeks of flooding rain. We're both depressed.

Rereading *To the Lighthouse*. What marvelous melancholy flow. What a humorless bore.

Rereading Beckett. What a fraud.

Reading Mark Doty's memoir. What patient careful prose for his so painful subject (the ever-nearing death by AIDS of his friend Wally). Almost surely I'll use a long swatch of Doty's verse for *The Art of Song*.

Nantucket, 18 September

Compared to the motionless summer, last week in the city seemed frantic. Monday (the 9th). In a state of more than usual fatigue, hied to Dr. Agus, with fistula, piles, and un-fading irritations on left ear and cheek. Agus advises biopsies . . . From his office, went to Boosey & Hawkes, picked up Sylvia, Steve, and Jennifer, who walked me to A Different Light where I read and signed books for seventy minutes; then, with Arnold Weinstein and Larry Mass, to fill prescriptions and eat soup.

Tuesday. Long day in Philadelphia with Daniel Ott, and the new student, Daniel Kellogg (callow to the eye, but whose music is wildly aggressive and fairly skilled). Gave a class in "song" to these two, plus Loeb's group who know little English. Dined with the good and true young composer Jennifer Higdon & her friend, chez the good and true young composer Robert Maggio & his friend, in one of those tall thin houses in the newly developed area near the river. Train two hours late.

Wednesday. A certain Mel Stewart, making a documentary on Man Ray for PBS, showed up with a crew of three plus a battery of cameras and mikes and lights etc. I spoke for an hour about the great Man Ray (whom I never found great), to be whittled down to five minutes. At 4 o'clock George Plimpton arrived, overlapping with the cineastes (turns out that Stewart had filmed Plimpton years ago), to talk about his ongoing written documentary on Truman Capote. Same format as his long-ago *Edie* collaboration with Jean Stein.

Do a portrait of what could be called the "heterosexual sissy."

Nantucket, 9 October

Just as there is no absolute definition of love, so there is no reality but only perceptions of reality. To say that someone is crazy means merely that his reality is not yours. Thus certain nations are certifiably mad to other nations; but when an "other" nation (our own, perhaps) is viewed through reconstituted eyes (our own, perhaps), that nation too is mad.

An artist's Truth is what he makes up out of whole cloth.

As the ferry enters the Hyannis harbor, I see a huge estate on an estuary to the north, and exclaim: "I've never noticed that big house before." Long pause. Jim considers. Then says, "It's not as big as it looks."

Once a day he'll make a similar Zen-like quip, to me very funny. Once a day he'll be seized by a fit of coughing, after which he vomits. There's little he can keep down, mostly peanut butter, ice cream, mint jelly, nothing that's generally considered healthy. The protease inhibitors, plus the array of other pills imbibed three times daily, he half the time can't keep down. At night I massage the soles of his feet, which, probably due to one of the pills, are without sensation.

What perverse compulsion urged me to sit down with the score & CD of *Winterreise* and re-examine it for several hours, intimately, with both ear and eye? It has never been my cup of tea, I can live without it; hence, I've always routinely poohpoohed it as simply German (does it need my endorsement anyway, when Hahn and Mompou go a-begging?). So the experience was revealing. Each song is flawlessly faceted, in itself, and together they form an inevitable flow. The narration is clearly by a madman (romantic love, in its obsessive indifference to the needs of all others, is by definition mad), probably under twenty, black-haired, suicidal, maybe murderous, one-track-minded, sexless. It's a purging theatrical experience, especially as uttered by Fischer-Dieskau, who knows the language (but overdoes the last two measures), and by Gerald Moore, who is "expressive" in a way that I would never be, and which would never work for, say, Debussy, but is of a period.

Now I don't need to listen again for another twenty years.

13 October

The Editor

NYT Book Review

Re. *The Writer in Prison*, by Joseph Brodsky

The premise of Joseph Brodsky's opening gambit is unarguably wrong. "Prison is essentially a shortage of space made up for by a surplus of time," he writes. "Naturally enough, this ratio—echoing man's situation in the universe—is what has made incarceration an integral metaphor of Christian metaphysics as well as practically the midwife of literature."

But surely man's situation in the universe is a shortage of time in a surplus of space: the length of a life is as nothing against the limitless cosmos.

Since Brodsky goes on to claim, non-sequiturally, that formal poetry can act as therapy for solitary prisoners, while prose is an art rooted in social intercourse, one might conclude that Brodsky's own prose is, in fact, poetry, and need not conform to standard logic.

15 October, Nantucket

Jim is not feeling well. In a week I'll turn 73, while he's only 57, yet he's the one with the irreversible illness, not I. I could outlive him by twenty years. (Of course, it's possible that I could . . . die . . . before I . . . finish . . . this sentence. Whew!)

We quarrel. Not often, not stretching it out. But we do quarrel, mostly about my over-solicitous concern, which he finds mawkish. What do we do? "You learn to *live* with it," he yells. Surely that's the only attitude, more stable than doctors who know so little.

Still, mortal heaviness pervades every space. Saturday we drove to New York for 36 hours. Maybe the "mortal heaviness" would remain in Nantucket, I reasoned. Yet when we arrive on 70th Street, death is already there, lurking in the rugs, in the piano, in the medicine cabinet, and in every crimson leaf of the fantastic October forests along the way.

The three boys, Jose and Mike and Kelvin, went back to the city early this morning; the fence is built, the lawn half-mown, and Jim really did most of the work, except the lifting. His rules are ironclad, the regime is killing, as though everything must be completed before he . . . But nothing is completed. His debts mount, bankruptcy hovers, Gustavo phones from Puerto Rico to borrow money for his starving kids. And Kelvin, penniless, must return in a fortnight to Nantucket for a hearing at the police station about his buying beer for minors.

Late last night I reread "The Snows of Kilimanjaro," which holds up hideously (depiction of over-solicitous mawkish concern!), as downstairs I heard Jim chattering loudly in his sleep, in what sounded like Aramaic.

It is now six in the evening, and already dark. He's been sleeping most of the day, in the basement, with Sonny.

Rosemary, years ago, with her son Paul, Paul's Chinese wife Jacki, and Jacki's father, flew to Peking, traveled up the river 500 miles toward Inner Mongolia where they adopted a baby girl.

Today, in our building on 70th Street, two Caucasian families now have Chinese infants, darling in their buggies in the elevator. The problem is, they'll grow up speaking Chinese.

One often hears that so & so has no sense of humor. Bruckner, Freud, Barbra Streisand. In fact, everyone, like every country, has a sense of humor; it just may not be *your* humor. When the bully asks his victim, "What's the matter, can't you take a joke?" he redefines humor for his own convenience, like a poet saying "The moon is made of green cheese." Of course, if comedy, as distinct from tragedy, is defined as a coin with three sides, then the insane, who are by definition one-track minds, aren't high on humor.

21 October

Handsome Ellen Zwilich, anxious to please, gave a pre-concert analysis of her Triple Concerto to an audience who've never quite seen a "creator" before. (They think it's all meditation, heartbreak, moonlight.) To the question, "Do you agree that painting and music are related," Ellen answers, "Absolutely. Painting, like music, is a time art." Then how long is *Whistler's Mother?* What time will *Guernica* be over? Don't you think Matisse's *The Dance* is better at 25 minutes than at 27?

Everything in the universe exists in time, of course, but certain arts, like music and movies, depend on time; others, like books and pictures, don't.

At six P.M. you leave a note on the kitchen table. "Turn on lights. Bring in cat. Call M.L. Soup on stove, just heat up. Will be back by midnight. I love you." At midnight you return to a dark house. The note is still on the table.

23 October

Today I am seventy-three. When Jim and I first met, in 1967, Father was seventy-three. When William Maxwell received the Gold Medal for Fiction last year at the Academy, he ended his acceptance thus: "At a fairly early age, I was made aware of the fragility of human happiness." I don't necessarily *agree* with this, but certainly I *feel* it.

Jim gave me a Burberry coat—really too lavish, but sorely needed. I shudder to imagine him in Bloomingdale's, so far away, feeling weary as he does.

Can a man (or a woman) have a heart attack while masturbating at 73? How many corpses per year are found in this posture?

Bobby Short: "I'm glad we didn't know each other in Chicago in the old days. You would have broken my heart." (That's the sort of entry that sends "my readers" up the wall.)

31 October

Eugene Istomin throws a party to fête Martita's turning (imperceptibly) sixty. Prior to this, at the Manhattan School where Martita is my boss, I conduct what's laughingly called a Master Class. Which means that for three hours I listen, along with a large audience, to a dozen young singers—only one man, who is also the only Negro ("The host with someone indistinct / Converses at the door apart, / The nightingales are singing near")—as they intone my songs, two apiece, by heart. To set them at ease, I say: "You're probably nervous to be performing for the composer, since you assume he knows what he wants. In fact, the rapport between song and singer is more fluid than between any other instrument and what that instrument performs. The ear cannot distinguish between a male and female pianist or bassoonist, so the composer's attitude is more inflexible; nor is it conceivable that, for the player's convenience, a concerto for bassoon or for piano be transposed. But between a baritone and a soprano, singing the same tune, lies a world of difference, not only in timbre but in temperament, so the composer is more supple, more lenient. The two questions most often asked: 1) How fast should this song go? Answer (quoting Fauré): If the singer is bad, very fast. 2) What does this poem mean? Answer: It means whatever my music tells you it means."

Whereupon a taxi (ten bucks, including tip) whisks me to 303 East 57th. The party, not huge, in full swing, is heavy with *le temps retrouvé*. I recognize neither David Oppenheim nor Peter Gravina, and realize that I too must still be playing the adolescent at 73. The tone is wealthy, cultivated, right-wing. The tone is also musical, but with an emphasis on player, not maker. The composer, from whom all blessings flow, is as anathema to these music lovers as to those sopranos earlier in the day.

Eugene points out various guests, stating almost apologetically, "He's not gay, but . . ." I am made to sit with a group of four who are already in heated converse. These are: Isaac Stern, a married couple (she Swedish, he from Ghana), and another man. Their subject, the creative benefits of Great Music to the suffering masses, so repels me with its let-'em-eat-cake logic, that I instantly say, "What good is Mozart when you're starving?" to which the Ghanese husband takes shocked exception, as to a philistine fool. But I pursue: "Even if art had medicinal powers, it's not Mozart the masses crave, but rock and roll." Isaac, an acquiescent smoothie, declares: "Ned, you're so right." When it's learned that I'm a pacifist, the other man says, "Yes, that's so curious, considering you wrote a book on boxing." I realize he's not kidding, and say: "You've confused me with Joyce Carol Oates." (Back home, checking in *The Nantucket Diary*, I confirm that in 1981, pp. 327–29, I wrote at length about the stupid "Artists to End Hunger" campaign.)

Plates in laps, I spend an hour dining with Isaac as others come and go. With his ex cathedra pronouncements, he does give new meaning to the term "self-involvement"; like Elliott Carter, since he is treated like God, he *is* God. His every statement about music stems from the performer's vantage, and the music is inevitably German classics. The first time I met him, with Eugene at the Rond Point sometime in the fifties, he had the flu, and impressed me by saying: "Even at my worst I must play better than anyone else." The second time, a decade later, I praised his Ravel Trio. "Yes, but it's fluff compared to the Schubert." The last time, at Eugene's own sixtieth-birthday party, he asked to see my Violin Concerto, both orchestral score and tape, which I dutifully had B & H send to him. That was eleven years ago. Tonight I ask if he received the music. Again he declares, "Ned, you're so right, mea culpa," adding no qualification, but avers, without a blush, that he's never commissioned a concerto. "All the works I've premièred have been paid for by groups who raise the money on the strength of my name." Two of these works, by Rochberg and by Penderecki, were "emotionally incomplete" when first presented to Stern, who asked them to rethink certain sections. The composers accordingly came up with "just the right tone" which Stern credits, in the first case, to the death of a son, and in the second, to the death of a father, which led to music "from here" (Stern lifts the napkin hanging from his neck, and taps his heart). This Hollywoodian notion so goes against my conviction of composition as craft—the result of which may move a listener to joy or tears even without the death of a loved one—that I can only giggle. Isaac Stern is not pompous; he's too likeably rotund for that, and is about to marry again, at the age of 76. But we have nothing in common, not even music.

Eugene takes me to the door, helps with my coat, listens as I talk of Jim whom I miss, though he's gone to Nantucket for only a few days. What would you do if Martita died, I ask. "Probably drink myself to death," says Eugene. "I *like* to drink. I'd sit with my feet propped up, glass in hand, and watch ball games on TV."

Back home the empty rooms seem vast. Sleep is, as usual, evasive. (Jim thinks it's because Mother didn't cradle me enough as an infant.) If sleep is a temporary concession to death, my psyche, alas, refuses, in its nightly struggle with Morpheus.

21 November, Nantucket

Words, words. The ever-prolix Arthur Danto is funnier than ever, in the current *TLS* where he criticizes criticism with phrases like "the entire landscape of art has changed, so that modernist as well as traditional art has been opened up in new ways by post-visual art." With endless space at his disposal, he still never defines "modern" or "post-modern" which are now displaced by "contemporary" art, and Andy Warhol (why doesn't anyone just say he's comic bullshit?) is to be academically psychoanalyzed. "Post-modern" may be an accepted coinage, like African-American, but I needn't be forced to change my vocabulary. Sixty years ago we thrilled to old-maid phrases like "this awful modern music," referring merely to Mompou, not even Varèse; yet wasn't the same said of Beethoven and Wagner?

Reading for the first time Dawn Powell (*My Home Is Far Away*), find her paralyzingly coy, and wonder what others see in her. Also *The Wizard of Oz*, which is not too well written. We first read it, Rosemary and I, circa 1930, when Father gave Mother that long overdue engagement ring, a fat diamond surrounded by tiny sapphires in a silver setting. Cost: $350. Mother never removed it. When I phoned Rosemary yesterday to ask whatever became of that ring, she said, "Don't you remember? It was stolen off her hand at Cadbury."

Tony, known as Tiger, champ prizefighter (at least on our block), with that tough mug of his—that cute worried butch mick-wop mug—shoulders like the golden bull of Egypt and biceps to match, could smash your ribs. Instead, he'd whisper in the midst of a fuck, "Hope I'm not hurting you."

1997

I've postponed my suicide.
Too many other deadlines.

More stumbling blocks for francophones:
Have you read what I gave you to read?
He knew the new red books, a few in blue too, and took two to read. Whose?
Those.
A whale of a whore. The whore's horse.
I gave Ralph half for himself. Have you some more at home? Come to Rome
and have a shave. You have to save to halve the glaive.
The leaf's life lives. To live: alive.
Not both sloths!!
A rogue in rouge loves stoves.
When roaches sleep, the rocks awaken.
He soon took the twine and wound up the twin's wound, then combed the
tomb for bombs.

I often think about how seldom I think about liquor.
The devastating floods in California. JH suggests that the Yosemite Valley
could come across as anti-Jewish in rap speech: Yo, Semite!

3 January

Lying abed at 9 A.M. I look forward to the siesta at noon, and again at 3 P.M. Father used to say, "I take a nap before each meal, including breakfast." Which may account for his longevity.

What is the point of a bagel? Step on no pets. Garden = Nedrag.

Wading through poems in search of apt texts for *Art of the Song*. Around 1945 when I scarcely knew of Auden, Paul Goodman spoke of being given the cold shoulder by this fellow writer. "Incomprehensible! After all, he and I are the best poets in English today." Since then I've set to music thousands of words by each. Today I'm rereading their collected works side by side. Who wins?

Paul palls. Half of his poems are laments about being ignored by the world; after the twentieth, we weary of being told he can't be less intelligent than he is, of hearing cold lines about his wife, and of being rebuffed by this or that rugged lad. Yet I need his verse and will use it until death do us part.

In the ideal world, when everyone finally has the equal share that Paul and Auden sing of, culture and finesse, as such elitists now understand those traits, we'll be on a lower plane than ever. The ideal is too glum to contemplate.

24 January

I have no friends. Yes, I "know everyone," and have a certain entrée, thanks to a staying power, real or imagined, not to mention sheer survival. But since JH's diagnosis our day-to-day routine is restricted; and of course, with age, a knack for hanging out, for dinner parties, for catching up by phone with pals (mostly female), sags, and old friends are ever more removed. Their children are now twice the age of those friends when we first knew them. But I have no friends. In an emergency, who would I call—except for Rosemary in Philadelphia? The people in the building, on the block, I know mostly from walking our dogs at the same hours. But at 4 A.M.? What music do I anymore crave? I hear a lot in the line of duty, but not much through choice. The dramas of real illness all around are extensions, in every family, of this homemade horror that emerges hourly and echoes on for weeks. Still, boredom is unhealthy too, and can be tamed. (Is tamed the word?)

Fanatically involved with *Art of the Song*, which, as now envisioned, will contain maybe forty separate texts. This afternoon, a little reunion at Café des Artistes for the 78th birthday of Leon Kirchner (I've made him a silly collage). Tonight, dine chez Gloria Vanderbilt (I'll take her two new CDs). When I come home around eleven, Jim will have returned by rented car from five days in Nantucket where, with Mike and Jose, he's repainted the sideroom's walls. What violent pleasure, always, to see JH!

23 March

Haven't had the urge to write here lately. The eviction trauma has demoralized us both. Nothing to say—when at the end of one's life, one is treated worse than at the start—when one's home, one's total identity, is knocked out from under.

Barbara Grecki, our next-door neighbor, has found us a lawyer, Maddy Tarnowsky.

The last sounds he heard as he lay dying were the throb-throb of the garbage truck down in the street, and the mindless unstoppable screech of a car alarm set off by the truck's vibration.

Title: *Stolen Thunder*.

30 March

Easter service at Saint Matthew's. Jim, as always, keeps things paced with his agile keyboard and adequate chorus. Father Gordon's sermon (not bad, actorishly delivered) centered on the 39 suicides of the Heaven's Gate cult. Then suddenly the high mass turned surreal. Christianity became as daft as the cultists awaiting the spaceship trailing in the wake of the Hale-Bopp comet that would carry them to a higher plane. Is the Bible, is the sermon, more logical? Swing low, sweet chariot.

Bleeding from the rectum again. JH, who leaves by truck for five days tomorrow with Frank, eats almost nothing, vomits, and talks of pain in the gut, like two years ago. (He takes forty pills a day.) Eviction papers may be served Tuesday. The fair weather is to be broken, during Jim's drive north, with snow. Snow.

8 April

At Academy. When I propose James Hamilton-Patterson for nomination in foreign membership, nobody's heard of him. Yet when I read him, as now with his new stories, *The Music*, I feel lucky that there is such writing (I, who am never excited about anything anymore).

Street person, to JH: "Can you spare a dollar? I have AIDS." JH: "So do I." SP: "Yes, but I'm homeless."

13 May

"A clinical depression," says Tancredi, and puts me on Zoloft a week ago. No change, except increased insomnia, increased sadness, increased heartbeat. JH in Nantucket, probably relieved to be without my demoralization.

To get through the day. To get through the night. Yet JH so much worse off than I. Fear his perhaps impending sickness, my own, the eviction, the "piles procedure." Dread the interviews (for BBC about Noël Coward, Lou Harrison, Truman Capote) this week. Dread Spoleto next week. Just walking around the fatal apartment, lying down, never sleeping, body exhausted, mind racing.

Night sweats. Stopped Zoloft after 3/4 mgs a day for 2 weeks. No effect. Never very hungry. Fever 99.5.

Could it be that, in the final analysis, life is a bore.
   Cancelled Spoleto.

Sunday 1 June
Last Wednesday in *Newsday* Liz Smith titled her column "Rorem, Stay Home," and wrote: "New York needs to provide sanctuary and places to live for the world's great artists who inhabit Manhattan. (Just plain ordinary folks deserve sanctuaries, too.) So I consider it very nearly a crime to learn that landlord [she names him] is trying to evict musical genius/erudite diarist Ned Rorem from his rent-controlled apartment on West 70th where he has lived for nearly 30 years." And she continues for five paragraphs. In today's *NY Times*, Lawrence Van Gelder writes a similar piece, complete with photo of JH and me (and Sonny and Tom) working, at the dining room table next to 18 filing cabinets.

The case will be dropped almost surely, and we'll be eternally beholden to Liz and Van Gelder.

Certain beauty—the shimmering forests the car passes, for instance, between Hyannis and Westchester—I cannot enjoy now. I picture Tom Prentiss hanging by his neck from one of those trees.

Art doesn't change us, it makes us more what we already are. Or: Art doesn't change us—certainly not for the better. What about the torturers at Dachau who, after work, played the Haydn quartets? Artist as moralist? Is there any artist who, in human intercourse, is better than he should be? If he is, is his art also better? Art is not ethical. Art does not incite, it reflects. Or if it incites, it's not always art, viz. "The Star-Spangled Banner."

Mother's and Father's ashes in a spice jar on the dresser.

Daniel Mauroc
    Je pars demain pour Hyères
  Or *Je vais demain à Hyères*
           I'm leaving tomorrow for yesterday.
           Tomorrow I go to yesterday.

To downsize the maximized offloading of upgraded software, you must galvanize the watershed.

Nantucket, 10 July

Tête-à-tête with Paul Theroux, who showed up without his wife, refused the iced tea and deviled eggs that JH is famous for, and talked heatedly for two hours, despite the speech he must give about Hong Kong tonight. Because I admire his writing (indeed, he's one of the four—and only four—under-sixty WASP male prose-writers today, each a virtuoso in both fiction and reportage), I spent a preparatory week annotating his very original *My Other Life*, an array of autobiographical fantasies. There is little an author can say in the parlor that hasn't been said more pungently in his book, while a jacket photo is never as telling as the live visage now before you. We were each out to impress the other; but, since I know his work more than he mine (like most well-versed literary and painterly geniuses, he is unembarrassedly innocent about contemporary "classical" music, and asks Music-Lover-type questions like, "What do you listen to?", when in fact—and most composers my age will understand—I don't listen to anything anymore, except students' pieces, and my own inner ear) the advantage is mine. Like his work, the man is long-winded and self-referential (on page 199, for example, the words "me" and "I" or "my" occur 28 times in 24 lines), and anxious to assure you how famous he is (on page 357, about a gang of know-nothing hop-heads who didn't realize movies had scripts, he poignantly notes, "they had hardly heard of me," when in fact they had *not* heard of him), but these traits work in his favor, or almost. No one else resembles him, except maybe me. He's a flirt, and nearsighted . . . At six, the hour he was due at Mimsi's pre-lecture cocktail party, he left for the Jared Coffin House to change clothes, Jim drove him there in the old truck, where Sonny tried to bite him. Jim and I also went to the party, for thirteen minutes, but scarcely said hello to Paul, whose wife Sheila turns out to be . . . well, striking. At eight we also went to his lecture, but decided not to stay.

Since I'd spent so much time nit-picking his sentences, he was maybe justified, when I read aloud from *The Nantucket Diary*, "are pacifists . . . like my own parents who were spit upon . . . cowards?", in saying "The past tense of spit is spat." But is this inflexibly true? Like shat for shit? And did he believe me when I said that I was so insecure that when I open my P.O. box, and there's nothing in it, I quickly shut it, lest glaring strangers think nobody loves me?

(Who, you may ask, are the other three prose-writers? Ed White, James Salter, James Hamilton-Patterson. Of the four, two are straight, two gay. All four travel to non-WASP climes, and three are largely expatriated—like Bowles and Prokosch of yore, and Lawrence of Arabia.)

Before he takes his shower, the horny forty-year-old cop, still in uniform and pungent from a day of giving the third degree to faultless victims (because of which his angry wife won't put out), pushes your face into his steamy crotch.

We read about cloning animals for whatever purpose—their superior meat or eggs or fur. Then comes the question that titillates poor mortals: could we clone another Mozart?

Why is Mozart forever the criterion of absolute genius? If I say he's not a genius, can you prove me false? Until the world can agree as to what et cetera . . .

But let's say that, yes, he was a genius. We have his DNA samples now. We shall clone him. Here comes the clone. Oh! This new Mozart without his father, or, indeed, anything of the 18th century, doesn't seem interested in music. Nudge him, encourage him to learn the "Mozart" sonatas. Still, he can't get the hang of it. Genius, like poetry, is that which cannot be translated—from language to language, or from era to era.

Is genius original? What is original? Originality wasn't a must in Mozart's day. He was like everyone else, only more so. Like everyone else—but no one was like him. Artists don't necessarily feel more deeply than you or me; it's just that they can take the fugitive feelings we all recognize and congeal them into communicable shapes. These shapes, if the artist is true, bear his signature without his half-trying. A true artist cannot *not* be original. To prove it, he has only to copy, and the copy will be as nothing before.

Yet nothing comes from nothing. Every artist is influenced by yesterday. The semi-artist proceeds unaware, and composes postcard music. The complete artist, in his guilt, seeks to cover his tracks. The act of covering his tracks is the act of creation. Aware of his theft, he tries to hide the fact. Poulenc, who never penned an "original" measure in his life, is always quickly identifiable as sheer Poulenc. He knows more than his forebears, and those forebears are what he knows.

These notions, culled from Eliot and Radiguet, are now mine.

25 July

Hurricane Danny rages. Seas of rain plunge from the sky onto soil that hasn't drunk in months. What can a mortal do but read? Here on the *table de chevet* sit a cluster of paperback masterpieces, avoided, yet I feel duty-bound to crack them eventually. Why not now?

Let's start with Emerson's essay on "Self-Reliance": "The soul is no traveler; the wise man stays at home . . . He who travels . . . in Thebes, in Palmyra, . . . carries ruins to ruins . . . Travelling is a fool's paradise." Where does that leave Darwin or Flaubert, Rimbaud or Marco Polo, Paul Bowles or Paul Theroux? So I close the collection forever, finding the writer as stultifying as Milton, with his bromides in archaic English. (But don't forget, Ned, that one of your most telling choral works is based on Emerson's poem "Give All to Love.")

What's E. B. White doing here? As I love bad weather rejoicing in the heavy showers that are the despair of tourists here, so I detest good humor, remaining iron-faced when faced with Groucho or Benchley, or especially S. J. Perelman, whom I begrudged when Mother & Father roared with mirth. Let's give him a try. White & Perelman are pathetically dated. Everything dates, of course. Beethoven and Donatello and Simenon are locked into, and defined by, their periods. But things date well or they date badly. E. B. White's opening four-page essay uses the locution "a man" seven times: "a man from a second-hand bookstore"; "a man could walk away for a thousand mornings"; "goods and chattels seek a man out"; "I had a man once send me"; "a man doesn't like to throw away his good name"; "but if a man doesn't care for that air"; "if a man is hoping to avoid acquisition." His egocentricity, so safe and straight, makes my own pale.

McCourt's *Angela's Ashes* is adept, but full of description, empty of thought. Jorie Graham is a sick joke. No more books.

The Versace murder, an opera in the rough, absorbs us all. The press, while hinting homophobically that Cunanan may have AIDS and, hence, is "a vengeance killer," or that he's hiding out disguised as a woman (it goes without saying that all queers are drag queens), has been fair to the dressmaker, rendering him a noble victim—though gay—and a model for his models.

Call from Charles-Henri Ford. Wants me to be Ruth's executor. (Ruth's lawyer—what a small world—is Regina Sarfaty's husband, Elwood Rickless, now in Santa Fe and stricken with a fatal cancer.) How can I? Ruth needs someone young, un-busy, and in the swim of that special milieu. That special milieu I've been talking about with Charles-Henri's biographer, Marilyn Broe, and with the moviemaker Jim Dowell.

Jim's feet, because of one—which one?—of his twenty medications, have been numb for a year. I massage them nightly, but to what avail? His well-being is more urgent than any music I might plot, but I feel more impotent than . . . Nightly doses of Ambien. Herpes, piles . . . The wind rises. The coming hurricane is sorely needed for the tan and moaning lawns.

26 July

Monday I finished the last of the 36 songs in *Evidence of Things Not Seen*. (Actually, the 36th was written in January; the 34th, on Mark Doty's long poem, is the final one composed here out of sequence.) Jim xeroxed all 165 pages, plus the introductory matter and the 16 sheets of text, made a half-dozen copies, and sent them off to B & H and to the NY Festival of Song. Jim, always careful of expressing value judgments about my work, seems to think this piece, which will require a full evening for performance, holds together, at least intellectually, with its juxtapositions of 24 disparate authors—some used several times—from Auden and Colette to Jane Kenyon and John Wollman. How can I know? The music and words, hot in my brain for a year, seem suddenly forgotten. I remember only what I stole, mainly from myself—from what has proved to work theatrically in former songs. It's all tricks, parasitical attachment to my betters, like Schubert with Heine (he *did* use Heine?), Hahn with Verlaine.

Now I'm supposed to make a double concerto for Jaime & Sharon, and an organ suite for Eileen Hunt, each of whom I trust and admire. Bereft of ideas, I've just tried to prime the pump by listening to my fiddle concerto as played by Gidon Kremer & Bernstein, the English Horn Concerto as played by Tom Stacy and the

Rochester Phil., and the three *Organbooks* as played by Delbert Disselhorst. Again, how can I know? What's good is good—personal, felt, contagious, skillful, or so one hopes—but oh how much is mere filler, weak, corny! Since I never listen to my own music once it's been weaned and thrown in the rink, I don't remember hearing—at least clear through—these CDs. Thus I judge the performances with a clean ear. I'm honored by the fact of the Bernstein-Kremer recording, though neither of them performs according to my metabolism. Gidon swoops like the middle-European that he is, and Lenny "interprets" to within an inch of his life. The concerto was written for Jaime, who did it "right," at least to my French ears. Stacy and Disselhorst, meanwhile, are flawless. So flawless that my flaws shine like fresh wounds. The listening session depressed, rather than stimulated, the so-called creative urge.

Dear Paul Dear Ned (Jim's title), fifty years of correspondence between Paul Bowles and Ned Rorem, preface by Gavin Lambert, is now out in a very costly limited edition from Elysian Press. Does PB now interest me less? If on the surface he's a not especially giving or compassionate man (am I?), he's one of a kind, a loner's loner. Will we ever write to each other again?

Monday 28 July

Ambien, Melatonin, 2 enteric, 2 Tums.

Each late morning, on emerging from a drug-laden half-sleep, I vaguely wonder what sadnesses the day will bring. Another hopeless day in a sleepless body. JH, for whatever reason, works twice as much as I. Currently it's the side deck, plus a little platform next to his bed so that Sonny, now thirteen and the apple of Jim's eye, can climb back more easily after his frequent nocturnal trips around the room. I watch Jim when he's not watching me, knowing how more important he is than anything else, including music, in my ken. His handsome anxious face, his legs. I am him, he is me, he is I, I am he. Who will die first? Look on your globe, at the wee spit of land that is Nantucket, where we, so insignificant, are breathing during the end of the twentieth century. Do you recall looking at the globe 55 years ago at the tiny space of land that was Berlin, where Hitler, so insignificant, was breathing?

Titles: *The Evening News*
       Signed But Not Dictated

Don't just do something. Stand there.

The "Th" of "The" is not the same as "thrust" of "theory." It's like "then." All are unpronounceable to Europeans.

Was it in the summer of 1954 that a touring theater came to Hyères and performed, in the medieval church patio, Alphonse Daudet's *L'Arlésienne* starring the still grand but already deaf veteran, Valentine Tessier? Also featured was a donkey, brought into the setting for a touch of reality. After the show Marie-Laure gave a lawn party, inviting all the cast including the donkey. Asked whether the donkey toured with the play, his keeper answered, "No, he's a local animal, and goes to the slaughterhouse tomorrow." Whereupon Marie-Laure bought the creature. Christened Alphonse, the donkey lived for the next several years in a shed, whence he was brought every dawn by the gardener's son, Maxime, to graze in front of the house. He sported a little bell around his neck, the sound of which meant "rise and shine" to all of us, no matter at what time we had retired. End of story.

1 August

Mid-afternoon, hot with faint breezes that soften the scenery. Sitting alone in the patio which Jim has so prettily refashioned. The others are inside napping. Reading (Simenon's *Le Passager clandestin*), while in the sixty-foot-high elms a flock of crows flap and squawk. Otherwise silence. The haze, the leaves, the flowing sky feel distant. Tom and Lucille purr in slow motion, sniffing, scratching. Calm. No worries. Only the clouds.

This half-hour has now passed, will never come again. During such a tranquil moment how many have died across our globe? How many thousands of humans in China and Texas? How many cheetahs and insects and daisies?

I am rich, I own the world, I own the moon, and could buy the sun if it were for sale. I am in love with Christopher Marlowe. Nothing can bring him here. One can purchase the future, but not the past.

Who's Afraid of Virginia Woolf? on television. How tiresome it now seems, with Burton's and Taylor's histrionics. It means nothing. Yet thirty-seven years ago one never asked, What does it mean? because art *meant*. Freudianly, symbolically. Edward does have a good ear.

The difference between French and Italian chauvinism. A French boy who has a wet dream says, *J'ai fait une carte de France*. The Italian says, *Ho fatto una carta geografica*. Surely I've noted this before? With the decades, I find that most anecdotal entries have been said at least once already, not to mention entries on musical insight, bad health, broken heart. Of course, with each dawning day, the sense of an aperçu shifts, even as we look more dilapidated in the mirror.

Tuesday 5 August

Eerily cold. On the afternoon ferry will arrive the little movie crew for three days. Then tomorrow, Don Bachardy. Others later. August is the cruelest month . . .

Late last night, while massaging JH's feet in the basement bedroom (Sonny and Tom stretched out on the bed too, and Lucille over there on her chair), I said I was depressed from the visit to Doctor Pearl. Pearl had advised no more hemorrhoid "interventions," since they never help, finally, and are painful and gory (don't I know it!); just try to live with it, despite the constant aching tangle lining the rectum. JH said he was sympathetic, adding that he had a disease that was going to kill him. "I didn't tell you," he said, "that the oral surgeon in Hyannis asked me not to touch my partial while in the office, because the saliva on my hands might rub off on a doorknob, or somewhere, and infect everyone. Shades of syphilis and toilet seats." Then Jim said that while proofreading the texts for *Evidence of Things Not Seen*, some verses in Doty's poem, which he'd not read before, hit home:

> . . . *though nothing*
> *shows in any tests, Nothing,*
> *the doctor says, detectable;*
> *the doctor doesn't hear what I do,*
>
> *that trickling, steadily rising nothing*
> *that makes him sleep all day,*
> *vanish into fevered afternoons,*
> *and I swear sometimes*
> *when I put my head to his chest*
> *I can hear the virus humming*
>
> *like a refrigerator . . .*
> *which is what makes me think*
> *you can take your positive attitude*
>
> *and go straight to hell . . .*

In the ensuing and penultimate poem of the cycle, Paul Monette says:

> . . . *if you pass beneath our cypresses*
> *you who are a praying man your god*
> *can go to hell . . .*

Naturally we can't compete about anguish. Jim presses himself, with the aid of Percoden, valiantly, and I don't—or I do, but in my way. He feels I live only for what others think of me, not for what I think of them . . . Now he's in the city for three days. He'll return here with Sylvia. Such stress is no doubt the daily menu for the rest of our short and happy lives.

14 August

What a burden I must be, always kvetching about chronic fatigue, and the sordid melancholy of aging. When strangers materialize in the patio to ask me about page 18 of a score, or to sign a book, I wail. Among Cocteau's unpublished love verse to Jean Marais, one reads:

> *Que me veulent toutes ces pieuvres*
> *Qui fouillent jusque sous mon toit?*

But Jim, whose ills are so much more menacing, and who never complains, feels that cordiality is crucial—that it is not given to everyone to exercise noblesse oblige. As I grow, my patience shortens with just about anyone. Mrs. Depencier, our beloved fourth grade teacher, as of today still thrives on Dorchester Avenue, age 104.

15 August

The one day of summer Marie-Laure most dreaded, when the scorching Mistral discombobulated the whole of Provence. Today, as on all other days of the year, she is in my mind, for the love I had for her (which I did not always show), for the unique wisdom and for the special mad logic she instilled.

A call from Lukas Foss—how kind of him—to say that last night in Bridgehampton he heard my "Mountain Song" (Marya Martin, flute). Have I given this little piece a thought since it was composed, in 1948, as a background for Iris Tree's *Cock-a-Doodle-Doo?* Did I, in fact, steal the tune from a Kentucky folk song? Wasn't it published so as to be intoned by any solo instrument (Seymour Barab played it on cello for the play)? Is it what I wish Lukas to know me by? Can a composer opt for what he will be known by? (Usually he chooses some long and "meaningful" opus.) Has the time come for me to be glad for any crumb? Perhaps crumbs—that is, fragments, songs, those fugitive *mouvements du coeur* that the very young are not yet ashamed of—are what make me me, if I'm lucky enough to be recalled by anything at all.

18 Aug.

Yawn. Cracking Faulkner again, and again finding him numbing. Certain masterpieces I acknowledge, while praying never to hear them again, like Beethoven's Ninth. Others I won't admit, like Bruckner's Ninth. And all of Faulkner. How dated he seems, how long-winded in the style of the non-elliptically "profound" geniuses of the twenties. *The Hamlet* strangles with minutiae. Am I allowed to ask if it is through oversight or for echo that in the novel's second paragraph the word "now" occurs eight times, and on page 7 the word "one" seven times? Am I allowed to throw in the sponge now, after nineteen pages?

Speaking of geniuses, William Burroughs is dead. That would be the best news about him, were it not that he's recollected everywhere. Even at 83, judging by *The New Yorker's* selections from his journal, he was still writing the sophomoric junk that beguiled the non-intellectual beatniks. Of the thousand un-winsome specimens I've ever known over the centuries, Burroughs, whom I met twice—in Tangier in 1961, and at a dinner party chez Ted Morgan in the '70s—wins first prize.

Elsewhere in the same benighted magazine, without once using the requisite "asshole," Paul Goldberger, in a perfectly written essay on a new generation of architects, defines Modernism. I am neither stupid nor ignorant, but have never known to what the ubiquitous term refers. The present is always, by definition, modern. But modernism? And post-modernism? The dictionary, the encyclopedia, have no references. Now Goldberger clarifies the term for little me: "It is an odd irony that modernism, an architectural style that was anything but sentimental, has come to be the object of considerable sentiment . . . Modern architecture was invented to obliterate history, not to make it. When the modern style evolved—in Europe, in the early decades of the century—its goal was to sweep away the clutter of the past, including classical columns and Gothic arches. Modernists were going to invent the world anew and, through the clean simplicity of their buildings, create a better life for all."

Of course, hasn't that been the goal of every generation?

Jim being in Manhattan for 36 hours, I walked alone into the Saturday lanes of Nantucket. What a glut of tourists forcing themselves to have a good time—to have what the French call *le fun* (they have no word for it, just as they have no word for "shallow," or as the Italians have no word for "morbid"). The obligatory handholding of pedestrians, the swarms of unattractive nine-year-olds blocking traffic.

James Hamilton-Patterson, with whom I've inaugurated an ongoing correspondence à la Robert Browning and Elizabeth Barrett (I'm Elizabeth), pleased me with this paragraph: "Schubert's 'heavenly length' (Schumann's phrase, of course, I mean, is that camp or what?) actually bores me quite often. The last movement of the late C-minor sonata is a case in point. I swear it's like watercress: You leave it in the dark and forget about it, and the next time you look it has grown many inches. In fact, I now suspect this sonata is growing & keeps pace with me, and the longer I live the longer it will become—it's an altogether brilliant trick. That, incidentally, is the music on the piano behind the charming picture of your friends the Istomins in *Nantucket Diary*."

Thirty-one years ago when *The Paris Diary* came out, certain people said, "I like everything about it except what you say about me. It simply didn't happen, it's not true." But it did happen, from my viewpoint—it was my truth. Nor was that viewpoint retrospective, like the reader's, but on the spot. I refused to understand these people until I began to find myself in other people's books. For example: I like everything in James Salter's new memoir except what he says about me and Gloria—or what he credits other people as saying. Such sayings are neither revealing nor witty nor factual, and they necessarily discolor all succeeding pages.

Of course, when I read nice things about myself, it's never the *right* nice thing, or *enough* of the nice thing, or, in the case of reviews, the *revealing* right thing. In program notes the analysis is always correct, yet always irrelevant. "Rorem then lets the first theme double back on itself, while the second theme, truncated, is used in retrograde as a cantus firmus. Etc." Did I really do that? I'm flattered that the annotator thinks anyone cares, but can't quite recognize myself in this ingenuity. Well, as Browning said, "When I wrote that poem only God and I knew what it meant. Today only God knows."

There is no Absolute which anyone can state about anyone, even Fact is a matter of individual perception which alters every hour.

"There is no such thing as love," said Picasso (I think it was Picasso), "there are only proofs of love."

12 Sept.

Deaths this past fortnight of Princess Diana and Mother Teresa.

Is the singer of a song on the inside looking out (Patricia Neway's hot frenzy in "Visits to St. Elizabeth's") or on the outside looking in (Phyllis Curtin's recitation of that same song)?

17 Sept.

Carly Simon's half-hour special last night gets low marks. Ostensibly a program of songs from American *films noirs*—that term was not defined, certain numbers were not from films at all, and no song was performed straight through. Then, although a fuss was made over the arranger-conductor, no composers were named, not even the still-vital David Raksin, whose "Laura" served as a theme; yet aren't composers the crux without which our Carly Simons could not exist? Carly herself, to judge from the over-echoey snippets she's allowed to intone, puts herself before the text, with her token dark glasses, and is always slightly off-pitch.

26 Sept.

When JH said, "There's a Mr. Prentiss on the phone from Nova Scotia," I knew instantly that Hatti was dead. Sure enough, when I asked David Prentiss if the news were bad, he confirmed, saying he'd been trying to reach me for days. I burst out crying. Hatti had a stroke last Saturday, was taken to a Dartmouth hospital, and expired, with her sons around her. I'd known her for 72 of her 74 years; we were together in Nursery School on Woodlawn Avenue. Except for Bruce now, she was my oldest friend on earth, with her blind father, her bossy tone, her pursed lips, her opulent body, wearing glasses as she swam in Lake Michigan. Only three months ago we talked by phone about Andrew who had just died. Then two days later, Maggy, who had "roomed" with Hatti in 1941, called from Fish Creek about *her* husband's death.

More leaves are falling from our family tree.

The diaries chez Da Capo.

Reread the Ezra Pound essay, quite good.

Reading Richard Ford. Describe. Joyless, humorless, doggedly heterosexual, painful, acute, original, not "poetic" (unlike, say, Salter), and not without misprints and errors in French. But he *is* a writer.

Re-perusing *The Siegfrid Idyll* for my new students. Nicholas Brown from England, and Bill Rowson from Canada.

Seinfeld on television. Exhausted now.

Paperback gift from Gloria, titled *Death: The Great Adventure*, sort of Tibetan. On the jacket one Alice Bailey proclaims, "There is a technique of dying just as there is a technique of living, but this technique had been lost very largely in the past . . ." How can there be a technique of dying? Dying does not occur in Time; the process requires not even a trillionth of a second. And the difference between almost dead, and dead, is beyond concept. What she means is that there is a technique that can be practiced while alive to prepare us for death.

2 October

Forty-eight years ago this month, after a productive, amorous, illuminating, exotic, and alcoholically abstinent summer in Fez with Guy Ferrand, I went back to Paris for a while, thinking to catch up on God knows what: "contacts," sex, liquor. In fact, I remained in the city eighteen sodden days, then returned to the good life in Africa. But during those eighteen days I met, among a dozen other males I went half to bed with, Yves Salgues, my age, journalist on *Paris-Match*, author of one published novel, nice-looking and aggressively French; monolingually mannerly though drunk and drugged, adamant about the worth of his country's history, ignorant of neighboring cultures, yet hyper-romantic about the fact of an American, that is, myself. I still have his billets-doux delivered nightly to the desk of my little hotel in the rue Jacob. He loved me.

Twenty-four years ago, after we'd met again during a brief trip back to France, in 1973, he gave me another poem, a poem reviving the already dead seasons of Saint-Germain, a poem that today is itself, if not dead, at least frozen, like all art, in time. Because I could never take entirely seriously anyone who loved me (how can they be so deluded!), I never read more than once the various *écrits* from Yves. But this morning, while seeking the file of another friend whose name starts with S, I came across the Salgues sheaf, and reread the poem, this time carefully. It's good. Isn't it good? A real poem, with its tight quintets, unexpected links (love & carnage), and terrific conclusion ("you confused the number with the sum, and hung out with those who didn't want to be anybody").

Yves Salgues—written May 9, 1973

> *1950 – pour Ned Rorem*

> *Il ne reste rien des voyages*
> *que nous fîmes en d'autres temps*
> *à travers des ciels sans nuage*
> *folies d'hiver sages printemps*
> *quand l'amour s'appelait carnage*

> *Il ne reste rien du Paris*
> *qui sut séduire ce jeune homme*
> *arrivé du Mississippi*
> *et qui savait qu'un petit somme*
> *vaut mieux que la plus grande nuit*

Il ne reste rien des soleils
qui à Saint-Cloud entraient en seine
rouge d'or et toujours pareils
et prodiguaient en vrais mécènes
des midis d'azur à créteil

Il ne reste rien des jeunesses
qu'on emmêlait au Montana
de nos vingt ans de nos détresses
mais pour qui donc sonnait le glas
au vendredi saint des Abbesses

Pour les amours désemparés
pour les marins perdus en ville
pour les vents et pour les marées
pour les démons dans les asiles
pour les archanges égarés

Ce gai Paris de l'an 50
a laissé au fond de mon coeur
le rouge d'une lèvre ardente
qui baisait ma bouche en majeur
dans les aurores délirantes

Vous étiez alors beau jeune homme
revêtu du pollen des dieux
un barbare qui fuyait Rome
et qui brûlait avec le feu
confondait le chiffre et la somme

et se mélangeait à tous ceux
qui ne voulaient être personne

Is Yves Salgues alive? Who knows him now in France? Or knows me, for that matter? I did view him, ten or twelve years ago, on Bernard Pivot's *Apostrophes* (which airs here on CUNY TV Sunday nights), with Françoise Sagan and other literary types who had undergone a cure for hard drugs . . . As John Latouche used to say: *Où sont les nègres downtown?*

Over six decades ago, seeing Gloria's tragic-winsome features in the *Chicago Tribune*, I felt we should get married when we grew up. But, of course, we never grew up.

Are we our work? Is the work more interesting than us? Is the painting, the page, the score, more articulate than our throbbing body in the parlor? Hmmm. But no one can fuck our work.

That nun with the buck teeth, who talks likeably about the visual arts on TV, is never stupid and often worthwhile so far as informing the unwashed. But whoever (whomever?) arranges the editing has got it wrong, at least so far as music is concerned. For instance, the segment on surrealism, especially on Dalí, has a score that mickey-mouses the visuals. The artist bustles busily about his studio, to a sound that's busy and bustling; as we see the soft watches, we hear tick-tocking; as the voiceover tells of surrealism's skewered sense of reality, we hear music that is "askew." Because of music's absence of provable concrete sense, it can color any scene in any way. For it to tell us what we already see, is redundant. A more "telling" background for discussions of surrealism could be simply a held chord that shifts slightly its composition every minute or so.

Titles: *Read But Not Signed. Signed But Not Read.*
    Musical title: *Finished But Not Begun.*

Seventy-four. Began (curiously, for the first time) *Les Nourritures terrestres*, and, after 50 pages, couldn't make head or tail of it. Gide, who was always so . . . so *immediate* fifty years ago, seems now blurred and arch. Has my French grown so rusty?

JH, sneering at Sainte Thérèse de Lisieux's musings about how God loves all that He has made (lilies, rabbits, diamonds, champagne, philosophers, jailers), adds: "Yes, and He loves cancer too: It's one of His subtlest creations."

Visit to Dr. Coleman.
    Prostate, internal ejaculation, bladder excretion, 2 trillion dollars if I can impregnate the Princess of Samarkand.

Our liberal state of Massachusetts has voted, 79 to 81, to reinstate the death penalty. Jim says, "If legalized murder deters murder, then why not legalize drugs to deter drug abuse?" Similarly he used to claim, "It's anti-abortionists who are most militaristic. They'd rather wait until the embryo has emerged into a draftable teenager before sending him off to die for his country."

To be Politically Incorrect about oneself.

Alone in the city.
    JH drove off at 4 A.M. with Sonny for Nantucket. Will spend the week commuting to the two Hyannis dentists: he's been four months without front teeth.

His cough: rich and wet and deep, loud with a rattle (can something wet rattle?) followed sometimes by puking, after which the consoling cigarette which has been poised, lit, on the sink's edge . . .

The new organ pieces are weak. What's finished (*si peu*) of the *Double Concerto* is also weak (not interested). Lonely, depressed, uninspired, faint with fatigue, reading Montherlant who reminds me, more slickly, of a reverse Paul Goodman. "I have shaped my literary works and my love-partners with an eye to pleasure, theirs no less than mine. I have never achieved anything else—trained no minds, souls or character . . . I have never experienced any sorrow that half an hour's affectionate copulation has not enabled me . . . to forget . . . religions are all founded on unnatural or unreasonable premises . . . We are born under a layer of superstition and false ideas; we grow up under it, go on living under it, and say to ourselves that we shall die under it, without even, *for one single day in our lives*, having lived otherwise than in subjection to the ideas of idiots and the custom of savages, which we cannot infringe or even denounce without danger to ourselves."

6 November

Business meeting at the Academy yesterday, neatly emceed by Auchincloss. Discussion of nominees. The painters, who know nothing of music, split hairs, promote "avant-gardisme," and crow about their prospective choices. Likewise, but more succinctly, the writers, who also talk of hegemony, talent, technique, deconstruction, message, timeliness. (To her credit, Elizabeth Hardwick did add, regarding Richard Ford, ". . . and he *is* awfully good-looking.") My nominee for foreign membership, James Hamilton-Patterson, didn't even make the ballot, and his name only drew glazed stares. As for Carlisle Floyd, his nominator wasn't present, so I volunteered: "Whatever you think of his operas per se, he did, with Menotti, put the medium on the map in America. For the Academy, it's now or never, since he's not as young as he used to be." "Who is?" Milton Babbitt asked. "Yes, but we're in and he's out."

After the meeting my guest, Nora Sayre, entered with the others, and we heeded the obituaries inexpertly rendered by five doddering members. At the meal, less succulently catered than in former years (though the waiters—out-of-work actors—were cute), I sat twixt Claire Bloom and Francine Gray. Claire wouldn't mind having a male friend of her generation who is both straight and single, but they don't grow on trees. Turns out that, like me, she still thinks of herself as the baby in any situation, and wants to be taken care of.

Nantucket, 23 November

Daily forenoon walk with Sonny on Sunset Hill. Spire on Old North Church framed by the ice-blue sky. For a moment there is a feeling of sheer . . . what? Happiness? Yes, life seems agreeable. Wistful maybe, awesome and unjust, but still agreeable, and I have been given (have *earned*) certain blessings. Though in the end, is there any real point in life? Everything recurrent—philosophy, music, politics, love—conspires to give meaning to something which has none. And yes, it is best to live nicely (I was thinking on the hill, while Sonny shat), eat well, not be sick, read, compose music and be admired for composing it. Still, none of this makes a difference, has a reason, except as construed, like the specter of God, by man.

This elating notion was stilled when the *Times* obits claimed Bobby Lewis. The more one lives, the more one *will* live, there's no right time to die, yet the stars keep falling, and JH is not feeling well.

The newish expensive 834-page *Film Dictionary* by David Thomson is useless. Nobody is represented (Jim Bridges, Lizabeth Scott, Alexis Smith, Gore Vidal, Faulkner, Kenneth Anger, Auric, Roddy McDowall), nor does Thomson's disclaiming epigraph excuse the lacunae. The references are arch, and the preface incomprehensible.

From the Guggenheim, six references required. Only one asked permission. Nor will I back any this year. Annoyance is softened by memory. When Virgil, around twenty years ago, asked for copies of all his letters for the Yale archives, I complied on the condition that he capitulate in kind. Nearly all my early letters asked for a recommendation, likewise those to Copland (did either one of them ever recommend me?—I think not). After a certain age a composer's mailbox is no longer stuffed with mash notes or death threats, but with practical requests from the new crop.

Nantucket, Day after Thanksgiving
Like a racetrack on a day off. The Louvre at 3 A.M. Miss America in solitary confinement.

Everything seems depressing, ominous, bleak. Not just realities like Jim's bowel disorders and recurrent abdominal pain, my debilitating insomnia, the Dominican charges with their sordid travails, or the cold black heaven, but the sad tilt of a lampshade, plaintive cooing of doves in the eaves, the ringing telephone. No incentive to work, although the Concerto for Jaime & Sharon is due soon. Lying around, thumbing magazines that tell the same old stories (ill will in Israel and Iraq, imminent violence for us all—the just and the unjust), trying to get interested in current books. *Angela's Ashes* and the DeLillo novel are too long & too great. But a short *récit*, sent from my fan in Australia, called *Night Letters* by one Robert Dessaix, is original and intelligent; a series of missiles to an unknown person back home, by a Melbourne HIV carrier vacationing in Italy.

At a loss for ideas, let alone for technical facility, I spent two hours yesterday spot-checking old tapes & CDs. How did that younger composer, whose name is the same as mine, make a piece *go*? Every time is the first time. The performance of *Bright Music*, a quintet in five movements by a homosexual (me), recorded in 1989 by five heterosexuals, is perfection, and renders vain the query, "Is there a gay sensibility?" Meanwhile, my Violin Concerto, recorded a year earlier by Gidon

Kremer with Lenny B. and the Philharmonic, is simply wrong, at least for this piece, full of "feeling" and "meaning" where austerity is called for. (We composers are prey to our interpreters; we are judged, not by our music, but by how that music is performed.) Still, I was again envious of how that younger composer (or is he older, having lived longer ago?) was able, so skillfully, to make certain patterns flow. Then, since the mezzo Lorraine Hunt is all over the news, I turned on a tape of her singing *Last Poems of Wallace Stevens* in 1989 (she was a soprano then), which I'd never listened to. Does her irresistible sound of velvet intelligence make the music better than it is? Is music, in itself, good or bad? Can't a lousy pianist get away with more murder in, say, a Ginastera toccata than in a more exposed Haydn sonata? In any case I'd rather my music be played cleanly than sloppily, at least when other people are listening. But what is clean?

The counterpane (I've never used that word, so why now?), a gift from Jim years ago, has on one side a design of dark colors on a black background, and on the other side bright dots against a light background. Each morning when making the bed I alternate the sides. I'm always glad when the light side is up, sad when the dark side is up. Then why not always keep the light side up? (I've written this before? But never on a Friday in November.)

2 Dec.

Alone again and lonely in the city, with JH in Hyannis to see the dentist. Narcolepsy & insomnia. The English student, Nicholas Brown, with whom I'm attentive re. his weird opera, but not weird enough. Listened last night to Donald Gramm singing Didi Cumming's 35-year-old cycle, *We Happy Few*, and the room was filled with the dead come back to life, which only music of all the arts can do. Phoned Didi in Rhode Island at midnight to say (and I meant it) that his setting of Housman's "Here Dead We Lie" is a perfect song. He replied that my 47-year-old setting of "Upon Julia's Clothes" was a perfect setting. I'd all but forgotten it.

Why must American composers forever set Rilke? If we don't create a literature on our own poetry, no one in Europe will do it for us. Rilke, like Berlioz, is meaningless to me, though I admit their vastness. Bruckner, like Eliot, is meaningless to me, and I do not admit their vastness.

And Marlon Brando, so heavy, so one-dimensional, so embarrassing.

Pearl Harbor Day

Reluctantly (because I seldom go out anymore, and never on the spur of the moment) I accepted John Simon's last-minute invitation to attend a recital at Tully by the Austrian mezzo Angelika Kirchschlager, of whom everyone but me has heard. I recognized eleven people in the crowded hall, and settled in for what I felt would be a stultifying afternoon: Schubert, Berg, Mahler (Gustav) and Mahler (Alma), Korngold and Strauss, plus three encores, which add up to the same number, 36, as my cycle next month, *Evidence of Things Not Seen*. The singer, good-looking, likeable, young and with (according to John) very good legs, has an accurate and pleasing voice which "speaks" cleanly, though without sensuality. Indeed, nothing's wrong with her. What's right with her? She has it all except *it*. Not one song—not *one!*—remains in the memory, though her audience, music-lovers all (I am not a music-lover), were agog. Once again I felt the gulf between me & Schubert: the eight letters of that name spell monotony. The Korngold (in English, which she cannot project) seemed worthless, likewise the Alma Mahler.

John gave me *The New Criterion*, for which he now is music critic. How hilariously cranky Hilton Kramer can be: that joyless beating of dead horses, that old-maid fussing about who were Communists, that sophomoric spite of foes (like the *NYT*) who "bleat" and "intone" and "want us to believe" but never simply "say." Can nothing be done to lighten him up? Likewise the other contributors, beating their dead horses, notably Roger Kimball on Paul Goodman, who never tells us *why* Paul's "obsession" with sex is wrong.

So I called Sally Goodman, who hasn't seen the put-down of Paul (nor heard of *The New Criterion*), and invited her also to hear the new songs on Paul's words next month. She says that *Growing Up Absurd* was amongst the Unabomber's belongings, in the shack that's being carted cross-country to Sacramento, as proof that he (the Unabomber) is obviously crazy, for living in such a place.

French book spines, like English car lanes, are ass-backwards. They force you to examine them by cocking your head to the left.

On page 2 of Karlinsky's book about Gogol's homosexuality, Karlinsky states that Gogol despised women intellectually, preferring the company of men. But surely that describes the typical straight male of the period. Gay men like the company of women (except sexually), whose minds and style they esteem, and shun the company of straight men (except sexually). Straight men deplore women socially, if not sexually, and seek to socialize with each other, though not sexually.

9 December

Long schlep to the doc on to the 104 bus. From my window seat, when we turned left on 42nd Street, I began to count the number of men on the sidewalk with whom I'd like to have sex. Between Broadway and Second Avenue there were only two—out of two hundred that seemed vague contenders. If the cross section was varied, the score was perhaps lower than, say, on a college campus. Still, like most male homosexuals, I'm as sexually indifferent to 99% of men as to 100% of women.

Dr. Agus seems to feel that my woes are real but not huge (piles, incipient cancer on left cheek, lightning flashes in feet at night, massive fatigue and insomnia). Not huge, but real.

Jim's Doctor Louie (who took more tests Monday) left a message that Jim's viral load is back up to 90,000. Still more tests must be taken, in case of error, and possibly a change in the protease "cocktail."

On accepting the "Composer of the Year" award from *Musical America*:

> Up through adolescence I assumed that all my classmates went home after school and wrote music. Even today I can't quite grasp that most people just don't care, and that composers are rare birds. Thus, as the years ooze on, bringing with them an occasional trophy of appreciation, I always feel that the trophy was meant for someone more special, bearing the same name as mine. Even with the Pulitzer Prize, my reaction was: "There must be some mistake. First of all, I'm much too young." Indeed, I *was* always The Youngest—growing up would come later. Perhaps all artists feel that way; when the child within disappears, so does the artistic urge. Now suddenly here I stand, the *oldest*, among four fabulous performers. Composer of the Year? Can this be me?
>
> Before I drown in false modesty, let me state that it's an honor to share these honors. Maestro Ozawa, one of the rare musicians to combine intelligence with glamour, is a model for us all. Stanley Drucker's clarinet, robust yet velvety, brings life to our Philharmonic as it once brought life to my own *Water Music*. Martin Katz exemplifies that noble profession, the accompanist, a term sometimes maligned. Yet inasmuch as pianist & singer accompany each other through the adventure of a song (and hope to come out together), the singer too is an accompanist. By extension, all ensemble players are accompanists.
>
> When I was composing a Violin Concerto, I asked my friend, Jim Holmes, if he thought it could be performed by a conductorless orchestra. After a pause, he answered: "That all depends on who's not conducting." Any group that functions convincingly agrees subliminally on a binding force, an ESP, that makes them act as one. The Orpheus Ensemble is the premier of such groups.
>
> As for the magazine that grants these honors today, it may be of interest to note that my first published prose appeared in its pages back in 1949. Perhaps in 1999, if asked nicely, I'll compose a little concertino for the forces present: for soloists Katz and Drucker, plus a conductorless ensemble whose members, while playing, concentrate intensely on the image of Ozawa. And the piece will be called *Musical America*.

If Plimpton's book on Truman Capote succeeds in its novel format, the A&E documentary tonight is a horror. The interviewees gush about Truman's wit, brilliance, charm, though in fact, he never uttered a memorable *mot* that was original with him. Nor was he charming so much as odd and unafraid and fawning. The film was repetitious , visually and textually, with no value judgments beyond leering glances at TC's queerness & alcoholism. The background of jolly jazz was intrusive and incongruous. My own appearance was whittled to 10 seconds, while the supercilious Gray Foy, plus Plimpton and Gary Clarke, simply spouted bromides.

Libby Holman used to call him Gorvy. I don't have Gore V.'s gift for demolishing a specious idea by mockery rather than by indignance.

Emphasis in prose does not come through reiteration but through concision. This does not hold necessarily for music (viz. *Le Sacre*, Beethoven's Fifth, or any sonata or fugue), or architecture (Windows & Pillars), or even poetry (*Reading Gaol*, any villanelle). But in the three Pulitzer Prize novels I've been perusing, all of which unfold exclusively among New Jersey heterosexuals, repetition is a weakener, at least in the first third, which is as far as I got in each case.

New Year's Eve

Jim, toward midnight: "I think I'm dying. I feel myself dying. Maybe I've got 4 or 5 months. Perpetual fatigue. Any energy comes from leftover muscle, not from fat. I get fatter without . . . without what? Without shape?"

Have I myself slept more than 3 hours in the last 3 days, without pills? When Jim leaves for the Hyannis dentist will I cry? Could I die? Will I ever sleep again?

Silent mood. You hear the chewing and ingestion of your tablemates.

Nothing is cloned, because the world is never the same.

Tournier, like all French authors, invokes only other French authors, but only German composers.

There is no right time to die.

1998

Rereading *Gentlemen, I Address You Privately* and recalling almost every word, odd and furtive, of Kay Boyle's style and subject, as fifty-eight years ago.

World première tonight of *Evidence of Things Not Seen*. Sold out—all 270 seats! The dress rehearsal yesterday hung together, or so it seemed, for 95 continuous minutes. But this afternoon in going over what exists of the new Double Concerto, I feel myself no longer a composer.

JH at rock bottom. Exhausted, unhungry, bloody in his cough. Tomorrow he sees Dr. Louie for more tests. Nothing I do seems very necessary now. Certainly not this diary.

Me: "Which parent do I most resemble?"
JH: (pause) "You inherited the worst traits of each."

Nantucket, 28 Jan.
To merge with the glittering Manhattan press last week for the new *Evidence* songs, comes today's report in the *Boston Globe*, by one Richard Buell, on my 1975 *Serenade*, the most dismissive review I've ever had. I don't recall having refused to sleep with Mr. Buell that he should show such spite. Suggesting that it is not "startling" that these settings of five English poems "had taken 20 years plus to get their Boston première," he explains that they are "fatally fluent . . . fashioned to 'tell,' to sound English, and to put on display the rhythmic and emotional

vibrancy such a singer as D'Anna Fortunato could bring to it. And worse, Rorem's songs get onto recital programs! Oh the humanity!" It's a critic's prerogative to dislike a piece, and to explain why. But sarcasm is never instructive, still less when it succeeds two contradictory sentences. (And a critic is allowed one exclamation a month, not two per column.)

29 January
Evening alone with JH (as usual) listening to Scarlatti's ecstatic *Stabat Mater*, its utterly satisfying suspensions & sequences. Heavy rain, back yard flooded. At 2:15 A.M., sounds of massive vomiting. Jim eats what he can (cookies, pizza, no fresh vegs or fruit), but fears a stomach recurrence. Will see doctors again next week while I'm, alas, at Yale. Starving but overweight, his body feeds not on fat but on muscle. The regimen of pills affects the liver irreversibly.

Is it a matter of months? Weeks? A year? (O blessed year.)

3 Feb.
Execution in Texas of Karla Faye Tucker.

February, Friday the thirteenth
Day of contrasts. From 11 to 1, I appraised four youngish composers at MSM, under the unifying eye of Pierre Charvet, who turns out (himself not yet thirty) to be from Fourques, and knew Jean Hugo, Jean Lafont and Valentine Hugo. Or knew *about* them. Of the four young composers, all but one (a Lithuanian woman) seemed pallid, directionless, unsexy.

In the evening, Schuyler Chapin's 75th birthday, celebrated at the Colony Club with perhaps 200 guests, under the unifying eye of his second wife, Catia (sex has never been so great, Schuyler confided a month ago). Shy of entering alone such fêtes. Beverly Sills, zaftig and welcoming, reminded that I once called her a "smart singer of dumb music"—you were quite right, she added. Sat with Naomi Graffman and Jaime Bernstein. A souvenir CD by the four sons. Including Eileen Farrell's difficult-to-resist "Blues in the Night." "My mama done told me, when I was in knee pants, / My mama done told me, 'Son, a woman's a two-faced, a worrisome thing / who'll leave you to sing / the blues in the night!' " Why would a mother tell her son that—or indeed her daughter?

Bowdlerized version of my obit on Allen Ginsberg in *The Advocate*.

I no longer smoke or drink or fuck or use foul words.

Extreme loss of dignity plus extreme physical pain. Two examples:

1. A man can't withdraw from a glory hole because the person in the next booth, instead of giving the man a blow job, pierced his dick with a hat-pin.

2. A woman's vaginal contraction around penis, caused by shock at death of man during intercourse. (Old Jewish joke. A couple, in this posture, are in a taxi.

She: "If you'd screwed me from behind like I asked, we could have economized by walking to the hospital.")

The sophomore piety surrounding Clinton's dalliance, in light of world crises. What can the French be thinking—they who blink at a statesman's mistress who attends his funeral with the wife? Are we the laughingstock of Europe?

People don't listen, except to themselves. (That goes for me too.)
     Wolf flow. A stronger stranger. Germs angered.

Gore Vidal has always chided others for falsifying, especially Truman C. Now that others, and especially, Truman C., are gone, one senses that Gore himself falsifies. (His love affair in the 1940s, his importance on the set of *Ben-Hur,* his intimacy with the political great.) Lest we forget his affiliations, he repeats them tirelessly. JH: "He's a major minor writer, while Mailer's a minor major writer."

25 March
Ash Wednesday service at St. Matthew's. The meaningless masochism of the True Believers. JH, as always, saves the day with his music. The glaring contradiction: Christ admonishes us not to bemoan our sins in public, but in private, for there God will reward us. But isn't to bemoan *so as to be rewarded* as vain in private as in public?

26 Feb.
I'd been to see *L.A. Confidential*, the first public movie I've visited in maybe ten years. [Describe the loudness, the ads, the empty theater, Kevin Spacey, etc.] It's all in one key. The horror has no perspective, since, unlike *Chinatown*, there is no lyric contrast to play against.

Between 6 and 9 Jim had the worst "attack" (he says) since this all began. Unthinkable pain (liver? heart? stomach?) leaving him immobile. At the end he said: "Great clouds of torture hover forever, looking for creatures they can inhabit."
     He said he'd prayed to the saints, the empty saints, he deals with every day. Then to the devil. None of these listened.

4 March
I don't believe in music anymore. I don't believe in "art." I don't believe. The need to write these words may respond to a certain belief, yes, but whoever reads them wants tales of gossip, not of woe. Yet in the light—or dark—of Jim's health, nothing else seems crucial, not certainly the dreary Double Concerto being confected at a snail's pace and sans interest. I believe in the evident insomniac exhaustion.

Bursting into tears he tells me he'd burst into tears during the CAT scan, when the nurse announced they needed a second shot on a certain part of the abdomen. "That means the lymphomas have recurred," he said to her, and she tried to reassure him.

Am I a consolation? It's hard not to be oversolicitous or nagging. Just to *be* there is all that counts. In an emergency would I collapse? Maggy says no—that one draws on invisible forces (Maggy, whose own CAT scan occurred today too, and showed a minor stroke). My every waking and sleeping hour is devoted to concentration on Jim's well being, but what good is that?

Is this entry more self-serving than generous? Luther said, "I can be no other."

6 March

Morning after sleepless morning of sadness. An end is hovering (like JH's clouds) that will change everything, for better or for worse . . . His incontinence.

Discouraged over the Double Concerto, a shapeless rehash, only about 25 pages in five months. Every sin I criticize in students—stodginess, lack of direction, unskilled dramatics, not to mention trite substance—is italicized here: a model of what not to do. The quasi triumph of *Evidence of Things Not Seen* has hexed the very parturition of anything beyond. Embarrassed to show it to Jaime & Sharon.

11 March

Jim's exhaustion. He says, "I could die from one hour to the next. The liver could just give out, send me into a coma, from which I'll never awaken." We wait, like *Cléo de 5 à 7*, for the results of various MRIs and blood tests. Next week, perhaps a biopsy. All that I'm tending to write about is Jim's health, probably because my own so tightly depends on it. *Et encore.*

Then X says, "Yes, but don't you think Man is fundamentally good?"

It seems axiomatic that Man is neither good nor bad, he just *is*, according to the day. What is Good? Are there gradations? Certainly the great do-gooders demand their pound of flesh; Mother Teresa might be considered bad by some (including me), nor does she shun publicity. What is Bad? Can it lie only in evil-doing? Is passive indifference as bad as active torture?

"Outside of love, woman is boring," says Camus (*Notebooks, 1942–51*, page 42). Well, he's no fool, but did thrive, like Socrates, in a pre-feminist era. For feminists (which feminists?), is he bad? For the macho-elite of the American Academy twenty years ago, was he good?

12 March, 6 p.m.

When Jim is away for a while, as he is now, Sonny howls. His small trusting white face—he's nearly fourteen—is so conditioned by Jim that the transiency of the whole animal kingdom (more than the human) becomes heartbreaking.

The core of any student's learning must lie in *direction*—where are you heading? Barbara Kolb's 20-minute *Voyant*, for orchestra with piano obbligato (does she know Sauguet's *La Voyante*?) has the singular quality of being motionless without being directionless; Debussy's *Canope* is the only other example I can think of. Motionless: like a moon that does not revolve, yet which itself is hurtling through space.

Before the concert we chat about the program, which will begin with Roussel. Barbara thinks he's swell. I don't know much about him, except his Third Symphony, which sounds like Ravel, and the haunting *Spider's Feast*. Once in my seat, I read the program note, which begins: "Ned Rorem wrote in 1962 [actually it was 1984], 'Some well-known composers, when they die, become less well-known, enter a sort of limbo, and occasionally never re-emerge . . . One thinks of Roussel, Vaughan Williams, and Hindemith.'" Then, naturally, the annotator, Roger Dettmer, begins to disagree.

Why must we live if we must die?

To Washington for Gershwin panel. The Istomins' warm hospitality, splendiferous apartment, and Ezra Pound collection. Eugene as potential Catholic. The stunning impersonality of the city.

Rain. Rain. Rain. JH discombobulated, awake all night, incontinent, & coughing himself into a hernia. He slept all day, while I went to Dr. Agus.

What will I finally die from? From Apoptosis, says Agus.

Beyond periodicals do I read anymore, rather than watch television two hours a day? A lackluster urge does maintain a perhaps outmoded sense of culture, forcing me, at least for twelve minutes, to peruse this & that.

The book Charvet gave me, Jean Hugo's long *Le Regard de la mémoire*, is, like Marcel Schneider's autobiographical tetralogy, about many souls that I too used to know in France. But Hugo's not really a writer. He doesn't *say* much, beyond anecdotes, about the hearts & minds of those many names he drops, or about himself.

Martin Amis's *Night Train* is an exercise in style, with a cold, mean-minded plot, and all the requisite "fucks." (As in Tina Brown's *New Yorker*, where if a writer, any writer, doesn't not use one "fuck" per page, he's fired.) I don't quite get the point of his glory.

Dreams of My Russian Summers, discussed in hushed tones by the elite of New York—all seven of them—also escapes me. The elite compares Andrei Makine to Proust. But Makine does not merely resemble Proust, he *is* Proust, in subject and device, even to the last line, "What I still had to find were the words to tell it with." It's not quite a bloody bore; indeed, it's "finely wrought" and touching. But not *my* touching.

So then I pick up Philip Roth's new novel at Penn Station. More of the same. Perhaps that could be said also of Chopin or Ravel who, from work to work, didn't change their style much. But style is not the same as subject (in Roth's case, Jew vs. goy), which with the composers comes in many sizes and shapes.

What's left? Do the Great Works hold up? It's been a long time, fifty years in fact, since I've read Dostoevsky. Can he be gone back to—or even Proust? Auden's famous words "About suffering they were never wrong, / The Old Masters . . ." In Brueghel's *Icarus* "the expensive delicate ship that must have seen / Something amazing, a boy falling out of the sky, / Had somewhere to get to and sailed calmly on." A person masturbates with groans and snorts and subsiding whines, while on the bed his cat, facing the wall, yawns. ". . . and the torturer's horse / Scratches its innocent behind on a tree." I was that person an hour ago, at seventy-four years of age.

Reflog noon golfer
    Hysteria = her stereo
    Should good fowl foul souls? Foul bowels foul bowls.
    Fisherman, Fi! Sherman.

". . . this reconstitution of what I must have felt is like a cardboard model that reproduces on a small scale what the buildings, houses, temples, streets, squares and gardens of a submerged town must have been like."

Nathalie Sarraute
Childhood, tr. Barbara Wright, Braziller 1984, p. 154

New York, Sunday 22 March
11 A.M. Snowing all night. Even now the crazy flakes whirl down onto the foot-deep ermine etc. that blankets the city impenetrably. Into this, at 7:30 A.M., Jim ventured, with a heavy suitcase and with Sonny in his wool dog-jacket, to the car rental, thence to the services at church where I'll meet him at 1:00. From there we motor to Nantucket (ice and snow and probably a cancelled plane-shuttle in Hyannis) with two of the boys, Jose and Mike, both of whom have been in NY to face the usual charges about child support and wife-beating. With his deep cough (despite Bactrin), his diverse woes as offshoots of his major plight, and exhaustion from hepatitis A, B & C, he nevertheless pushes himself. Jim hasn't missed an hour of responsible work in the 30 years we've known each other. Sonny, now fourteen, is spry and spoiled as ever. If he "goes," it's hard to foresee JH's reaction.

New York, 27 March
They say that a first trip to India is not so much a dislocation in time or space as a quite new dimension. Likewise a trip back to Chicago's Hyde Park, where so little

has changed and some blocks are identical (not even smaller) to sixty years ago, contains not so much a Proustian sadness as the tedium of repetition. Now my hair is gray; the smells of sex and fright inspired by this or that oak or nook, are flat and faded. In the interim I have shat thirty thousand times with enough exudations of blood, piss, sperm, spit, tears, and sweat to fill the Sunny Gymnasium pool with an odoriferously fecund mash.

Between the islands of Nantucket and Manhattan lie six hours and five laps. From there to here: 10 A.M. taxi to airport, 10:45 plane to Hyannis; rented car to 70th Street (with a stop for gas and another at Twin Peaks for coconut pie); unload at 70th Street, then to 78th to return car; then back home. Jim is the sole driver for these bi-monthly, sometimes oftener, expeditions, plus me and Sonny, plus sometimes the two cats in their boxes, plus occasionally one or two or three of the Dominican boys who room at the house. I haven't driven since high school, having failed the test to renew the license in Hyères in 1961. What if one afternoon the car stalled on the highway, for whatever reason?

Jim is alarmed by his body, by what he calls his "AIDS stomach," distended and without a navel. But yesterday, Dr. Jaffin went over the myriad test results, mainly for the liver, and for uncontrolled bowels. This is all due to the necessary pills, says Jaffin, and don't worry. Today Jim seems less worried, eats better. Tonight we went up to MSM to hear Spano conduct *Sunday Morning*, which he did a month ago, to better effect, with the Curtis students in the Philly Academy. Also tonight, in Zurich, Gary plays the *L.H. Concerto*, which he did a week ago in San Francisco, to weird reviews. (Apparently the conductor, Blomstedt, is an emotive Mahler freak, and hadn't a clue as to how to deal with my "superficiality," though Gary performed grandiloquently.)

To sit with the audience and hear your own music played is to let your mind wander, even when the playing is good, if you've heard the piece before. If the playing is bad, the experience is torment. The audience blames you, not the playing, for how can they know?

A dream as complex as all of Tolstoy transpires in a millisecond, into which the harm of car alarms intrudes and wakens you. I've not had a good night's sleep in thirty years. The astronaut dreams he is walking on the moon.

Party last night chez Maxine Groffsky to fête Sandy McClatchy's two new books. Spoke mainly to Betty Comden, who at 82 remains breathtaking, mainly because of those Garboesque eyes. Those eyes, she says, aren't all hers; they result from cornea transplants, effected some years ago in Pittsburgh, from the bodies of two male criminals. Or so she says. Does she—I ask—see me now as those criminals would have? Yes. However, her reaction is not theirs but hers.

83 degrees. A week ago, a blizzard. I loathe good weather. It means tourists and their transistors.

How about this as a romantic given:

A man named Hyde remembers someone named Jekyll whom he once loved, and spends his life searching for him. Jekyll remembers someone named Hyde whom he once loved, and spends his life searching for him. In the nature of things they will never meet.

Robert Louis Stevenson is on my mind because, as I do twice a year at Christmas and on April 2, I compose a one-page vignette, copy it in various colors, have it framed, and offer it to JH. Today the vignette, called "Sarabande for the Only Jim in the World," turned out to be a weak spinoff of the song, "Requiem," written fifty years ago on Stevenson's famous verses.

Jim's dizziness and cramps. Above all, his depression, his lack of faith in doctors who, if they sense that a patient is washed up, lose interest. He is negative about everyone we know—except Jose—including me. When I side with, say, Ted Hughes or Cocteau (at whom people throw stones because their friends committed suicide) by saying they're not responsible if they attract suicidal types, JH replies it's the same with me, my friends kill themselves (Claude Lebon, Joe Adamiak, Tom Prentiss), I drive people crazy.

Meanwhile, like the asphyxiating eviction problems a year back, now comes a warning from the Town of Nantucket, Dept. of Public Works. If within the next two weeks we don't get rid of the fence and hedge, which impede traffic safety, they'll do it themselves and send us the bill. The marvelous white fence and privet hedge, which Jim spent hundreds of hours constructing over the past two decades.

Tonight, Tobias Picker's and Sandy McClatchy's opera. Tomorrow, reading for the "Favorite Poem" project of the Academy of American Poets at Town Hall. Try to write something about both.

Heat wave. A four-day winter *heat wave*.

Spoken to Academy of American Poets, Town Hall:

It soon became clear that as a fledgling composer I felt less at home when writing so-called abstract music than when writing songs, that is, when setting words to music. Not primarily because I was in love with the human voice as it arched and dipped out of its spoken range, but because I loved poetry and music, and sought to marry these arts. Since the mid–1940s I have used—for soloists, ensembles, choruses and operas—the texts of probably 200 authors, from Homer, King David, and Sappho, to Auden, Sylvia Plath, and Mark Doty, with their screams about the very limits of language, and the melancholy of AIDS. As to how these authors react to my, or any composer's, tampering with their verse is moot. Are they flattered or offended or just bored? For there is no single true way for setting a poem to music; there are as many ways as there are true composers, though none of these ways may jibe with the silent tones the poet first heard in his inner ear. Still, songsmiths, if they are not themselves poets, need poems, and better good ones than bad.

The one contemporary American poet to whom I, as a musician, most often return is an early mentor and friend, the late Paul Goodman. His best poems seem ideal, at least for me, because their content, whether about love or hate or death or the weather, is easy to understand when sung. Typical is this unpublished octet, the first song I composed after going to Paris in 1949. The nicest way for you to hear it, of course, would be if there were a baritone and a piano on this stage. But bear with me. It is called "Rain In Spring."

> *There fell a beautiful clear rain*
> *with no admixture of fog or snow,*
> *and this was and no other thing*
> *the very sign of the start of spring.*
> *Not the longing for a lover*
> *nor the sentiment of starting over*
> *but this clear and refreshing rain*
> *falling without haste or strain.*

April Fool's Day

Dear Tobias,

The highest compliment an opera composer can hear is that his opera *works*. *Emmeline* last night seemed, for me and Jim, a model of theatrical sense. That sense came from contrast, visual and aural, of fast & slow, soft & loud, often at the same time. Most of the music is good, and almost all of it is apt and well-conceived for the highs and lows of the singing voice. Also, I was caught by the horrid tragedy of 19th-century Christian Sanctimony. (Though the silly Lewinsky charade being played out in Washington today is just as insane.)

The epilogue doesn't work. (I felt this too in the TV version.) A redundant anticlimax, it should end 8 minutes sooner.

Best always to Aryeh,

Ned

3 April

Mixed feelings about the "Favorite Poem" thing on Wednesday. Heavy rain. Arrived drenched among "celebrities" I didn't know (Mike Wallace, the charmless Breslin, Geraldine Ferraro), nor was I mentioned in advance publicity or subsequent reviews. Is it a policy of the NYT to keep mum where I'm concerned, viz. the Gershwin readings at the L of C, Tommasini's copious piece on Betty Freeman, etc.? My paranoia knows no bounds.

Anyway, the *American Poet* journal, given as reward to us participants, contains a series of homages to James Laughlin. A lengthy one by Hayden Carruth centers on Laughlin's poems in French. Carruth protests that he, Carruth, is "not a linguist," and has "trouble with native Francophiles," then dissects nuances that presumably even Laughlin ignored. When Laughlin uses the phrase "*une langue très douce et presque / imperceptible . . .* " and, in his own translation renders this "a language that's soft / and almost inaudible . . ." Carruth comments:

It's clear right off that Laughlin is unable to translate his poem any better than anyone else would. [What could *better* be?] *Douce* means much more than *soft*, if only because it's the word one uses to a French child who's being too loudmouthed: "*Douce, douce, chéri.*"

But of course *douce* does not mean more than soft. *Douce* is the feminization of the adjective *doux*, and is never used as an admonishing verb, although the adverb *doucement* is. "*Doucement, chéri*" means "quiet, dear," or "easy does it." But "*Douce, chéri*" is not French, has no meaning whatsoever, unless a boy asks, "What's she like?" and is answered by "She's sweet, my dear."

Elsewhere Carruth twice spells *insaisissable* as *insaissable*. His uppity knowledgeability about his unknowledgeability is another disguise of the academy explicating to us nobodies, in hegemoniacal deconstructionist lingo that garbs their authority.

This afternoon. Trip to Dr. Coleman, urologist.

Uneasy interview of Yo Yo Ma by Charlie Rose. Yo Yo, articulate and affable, spouts bromides. Charlie, in awe of "high art," treads water. Yo Yo, who has played the Bach suites for decades, asks, "How does one get better?" and suggests that collaborating with the Mark Morris company (a clip is now shown of the dancers reacting literally to Yo Yo's cello, unlike Martha Graham who *went against* the music, thereby showing the listener-watcher a new dimension to the score) is one answer. But of course, artists don't "get better"; they are what they are by age twelve, though sometimes as they change, get worse, grow stale. Chopin and Brahms, indeed most composers, never evolve, except in format, throughout their lives, while others, like Beethoven or Stravinsky, do bloom and metamorphose— though are their early works "worse" than the late ones? But Yo Yo is not a composer; he's a performer. Charlie, meanwhile, agog, asks about the secret of "creativity." That word gets thrown around a lot, but always in relation to interpreters, who merely re-create. Where does that leave us poor composers?

Easter Sunday afternoon

Unflawed cloudless weather, a classical Easter. Service at St. Matthew's crowded and musically persuasive because of JH, who moves things along. But the sermon was contradictory. If God (as Father Gordon assures us) loves everyone equally, then why did He authorize (as Father Gordon reminds us) the killing of the first-born in every Egyptian family so that the Jews could "pass over"? How does JH, in his perilous condition, prevail on little sleep, thirty exhausting pills a day, and a crushing schedule—especially at this season, ending thank God with Easter—and leave with Jose and the cats for Nantucket? I'll be alone for a week, and will finish the Double Concerto with an absent heart. The beautiful long afternoons bring thoughts of suicide.

Party last night for Harry Kraut's 65th birthday (I made him a sonic collage) at which I talked to Lauren Bacall, who had waved at me to come over. Did she think I was someone else? Conversation strained. Earlier in the day, three-hour filming for a documentary on James Lord. I note these occurrences for their own sake, without development or interest, but will elaborate if this diary eventually . . .

Maggy's operation.

13 April

To party at DGG offices, with the Emerson Quartet, to fête their new CD of my Fourth Quartet. Gave a speech, then read the program note.

Finished the Double Concerto (except for the mammoth dispassionate chore of orchestration). At 35 mins., it's 15 mins. longer than contracted for.

20 April

On returning last evening from Washington, I lay for a while next to JH (Sonny wriggling between us), exhausted. Then from the silence he said, "Sometimes you look at me as at a smashed bug, wondering how long it will last."

At the Library of Congress, the presentation of *Evidence*, one hundred minutes without pause, was the best performance I've ever had. Each of the four voices, Monique McDonald, Delores Ziegler, Rufus Muller, Kurt Ollmann, and pianists Steven Blier and Michael Barrett, were without ego, inhabiting the texts with emphatic conviction. During these minutes my bodily anxieties were suspended, and the music was engrossing as though by another composer. I wept— and I never weep, at my own or anyone's music. ("Is weeping French or German?" asks Michael later. German, of course.) To my honor, Rosemary and three generations of her family came, Sylvia, Marie Arana, Eugene & Martita, Phyllis Bryn-Julson, Mattiwilda Dobbs . . . Around midnight, a non-prescription sleeping pill, Unisom. No effect on insomnia, but causing dizziness as I staggered hourly to the bathroom. Same madness as the "overdose" of months ago when JH called Emergency. He and Rosemary have made me promise to throw all sedatives away.

Which is when he murmured about the smashed bug. Sadness.

21 April

Sixty years ago today I "lost my virginity" with Perry O'Neill.

Visit to John Kander, three houses down, re. his Academy nomination. Afternoon sun from an outdoor garden illuminates, through glass casements, the indoor garden where we sit and discuss his hesitation to "be a celebrity" in the world wherein he excels (Broadway musicals) as distinct from my world (concert classical) which has no celebrities in that same show-biz sense. Still, he's generous about others. Colette, in her encomium to the late Anna de Noailles, who had said, *"Mais Colette, vous n'aimez pas la gloire,"* has last word. *"Mais si, j'aime la gloire. J'aime la gloire d'Anna de Noailles."*

Later, back home, visit from Judith Malina and Hanon Reznikov, embellished by the verve of Mendy Wager whom I've known (as I've known Judith) for fifty years, and who dwells five yards south and one floor above me, though we seldom meet except in the elevator. Spoke mainly of our common bonds, Paul Goodman, and of Jews versus goys. Judith energizes over the Living Theatre. But the Living Theatre, with all its unique history and value, will never satisfy what she could think of as my effete needs. Art can be about politics, but it can't *be* politics. Name one, just one, work of art that has ever changed people while remaining good art. Of course, if I could compose a march that would make soldiers flee battle rather than wage battle, I'd do so in a trice, and to hell with art.

Monday, interview with a well-informed young Englishman with a sexy cleft chin, Paul Jackson, who's doing a book on modern dance, especially on the collaborations of Martha Graham. In dredging up the past, I asked about Stanley Sussman, who conducted *Dancing Ground*, Martha's 1966 version of my *Eleven Studies*. Yes, well, Sussman was murdered while composing a ballet, the pages of which were spattered with his bloody parts that were confiscated "as evidence" by the police.

23 April

Yesterday in Philadelphia. My *After Long Silence* shared a well-played if loud program at Curtis with David Loeb and Richard Danielpour. Returned with the latter on the late train. The lateness precluded calling JH in Nantucket. But as I came in the door at 1 A.M. the phone was ringing. JH had spent the day writing a rebuke to Charles Rosen who apparently twits me in the *New York Review* for something once said about Elliott Carter. Jim's devotion to my work is moving beyond description—he, who has his own realm, intelligence, and concerns. If he goes, I go.

Heavy rain all day. Fatigue. Cancelled dentist.

Speaking of intelligence, am reading *How Proust Can Change Your Life* by Alain de Botton. Like Makine's *Dreams of My Russian Summers*, it's spoken about with reverence. Subtitled "Not a Novel," it doesn't say much, and he doesn't write too well. (Proust said it all better.)

Current words I do not understand: Mandate, premium, galvanize. Nor do I grasp the mystique around Isaiah Berlin.

Re. Rosen's heavy (because recycled) twitting of those who don't like Carter because they don't understand him. What does understanding music signify? Can Rosen define it? Does it mean to ascribe meaning? Can any non-vocal music be proved to have meaning (i.e., to be about something) that listeners can agree upon? Does to understand automatically mean to like? I understand, for example, Schubert, in that I appreciate and can follow his workings, but I don't like (i.e., need) him. Ditto for Beethoven. I do not understand Debussy, but love him. I understand much current rock music too well, and don't like it. If Rosen dislikes my music, which I presume he does (if only because of its genre, not its peculiarities), is that because he doesn't understand it? Perhaps I don't care for Carter's music precisely because I do understand it.

Among the scattered notes (on books, concerts, friends, wars, sun and rain) meant to be elucidated in these pages, nothing says "Write about Jim." Yet what matters except his well-being? The feeling of impotence in light of his suffering!

Finished, but then withdrew, a review of the biography of Glenn Gould, the thinking man's David Helfgott. This is only the second time I've reneged on a book review (the other was Myrna Loy's biog).

The worst ever. Up a dozen times. At 5:30 began silently to shriek. Peeled herpetic scabs from l. buttock and asked if there's cancer on l. cheek.
    What I've just described—the bug on the bathroom floor—will never come again. Nor is it encoded in anyone's memory but mine. And when I die . . . Still, you, if you're there, who've read this . . . But if I lied . . . My lie is my truth.
    The oddest minutes of my life.

Wrote a glowing nomination of John Kander for the American Academy.
    Of the 43 composer-members, seven are gay (I don't include four others who I know to have had dalliances), or one in six. In literature it's eleven out of 114. Of the artists—as they're called—I really can't say, they're a breed apart. All this apropos of Richard Goldstein of the *Village Voice* wanting statistics.

Astonishingly, after twelve days, we've returned alive from the American Guild of Organists Convention in Denver. Went by automobile, with Sonny and Jose, three days on the road each way, and five in that city. O, flat flat America, flat and asparagus-colored and one-dimensional. The car stalled inexplicably 8 miles out of Toledo, in the midst of nowhere, and we lost half a day. Towns bereft of charm or thought, temporary looking. Stores are "American-owned" and sell ammunition over the counter to anyone. And the heat, the heat. Jim scarcely alive, but functioning admirably; it's he who wants me to shine in his adored organistic milieu where I'm guest-composer-in-residence. Good performances by Eileen Hunt in premiering *The Six New Pieces*, John Obetz playing "Views," Chanticleer singing *Pilgrim Strangers*, and me accompanying Meredith Derr in *The Nantucket Songs*. Meals with Augustus Reed Thomas, David Conte. Ceaseless heat, fireworks, masturbation, anxiety, sadness.
    For the long trek back from Colorado Jim said, "And I have to take care of three babies: Jose and Sonny and you."

He is forever concerned with the well-being of the dark-skinned kids at the church, many of whom he's known since they were toddlers, and who now come to help in Nantucket. They are that part of his life which isn't me.

Nantucket, 12 July

What all would agree is a marvelous Sunday morning: blue and green sky and grass, no humidity, faint wind, and quiet, quiet. Yet for the past few years this is perceived through a scrim, showing things as they are, but cheerlessly. Nothing sparks excitement anymore, not the puerility of Ken Starr, the horrors of Bosnia, the beauties of Debussy. Old people, no matter how dumb, know what young people, no matter how smart, don't know: that life has a term, that we can indeed vanish. I've said, in music and books, pretty much all I have to say. Nobody really cares—Jim maybe, but he'll be gone soon too. How to fill the hours or years that remain to me, to *us!*

NYC, 29 July

Jerry Robbins died today. Been reading his letters to me (1951), and mine to Claude Lebon (1956). They seem valuable. Who will ever know?

Nantucket, 10 Aug.

Jim fixed two huge meals today (halibut plus) for Judy Collins & Louis and entourage, then for Ruth Laredo and Eugenie and entourage. Demoralized by the eternal carpenters across the street. No escape from noise both outside and inside our bodies. Heat.

17 Aug.

Long weekend as Brian Zeger's guest for his Cape & Islands Festival. Cape Cod, with its well-kept WASPy heterosexual upper-class temples and lawns, resembles *The Stepford Wives, The Lottery, The Night of the Living Dead, Invasion of the Body Snatchers.* Adept performance by a mezzo, Mary Phillips, of ten of my songs.

Back here now where JH has fixed two meals a day for all seven members of NYFOS, who will perform *Evidence* tomorrow in Old North Church. Sylvia & Frank here too.

26 Aug.

Indescribable sadness everywhere—the sky, the delicatessen, the doorknob. Windless filthy heat. Hurricane Bonnie approaches from the south.

Correcting proofs for Double Concerto.

JH re. Leontyne's old recording of *La Forza*: "You've got to be crazy to sing like that." The madness of art.

5 Sept.

In the car from Hyannis to Manhattan I read aloud from the *Times*. The 7- and 8-year-old boys accused of killing an 11-year-old girl, hitting her with a rock and asphyxiating her, so as to steal her bike, are acquitted after a lab analysis showed semen on the girl's panties. "Based on the ages of the suspects . . . I understand why they would be incapable of being the source of this semen," said the Police Superintendent. To which Jim coolly adds, "The girl could have had sex with a fourteen-year-old boy, perhaps even willingly, minutes or hours before the murder by the younger kids. After all, it was in what the paper called 'an impoverished neighborhood.'"

16 Sept.

11 P.M. In the dark JH says, "I love you." Pause. "Though what good is it when someone who's dying says, 'I love you'? What a farce." He's been more and more strained, cranky, anguished, eats badly, coughs horrendously, and smokes a lot. But hasn't missed church in 25 years, and next Sunday St. Matthew's celebrates his silver fidelity with a program of all his music.

Tomorrow the first of the Yale flock lands in New York for lunch and their lessons.

My reply, a few minutes later, in the dark: "I'm dying too, and I love you too, and it isn't a farce." This may be metaphoric (though of course we're all dying) but it's honest. Can I do anything? We had been playing Bartók's *Bluebeard*—Boulez's good recording of long ago.

Write about YALE, where I've agreed to teach for the coming scholastic year.

Why do American hotels, even the best, have hall doors that slam?

Why do our airports have no clocks?

Sunday 27 Sept.

As usual on Sundays I got up at 8:15 to see Jim off to church, then returned to bed and jerked off (which the urologist says is fine for any age, though in the case of those whose prostate has been . . . etc.). After which I dozed off and had this dream:

Sitting in my beautiful new room (where?) I gazed up through a high stone window at the framed vista of mountains and castles far away, and thought, "Guy [Ferrand] will love this view when he comes next week." Then, sitting in the fifth row, with perhaps twenty other spectators, we all watched the stage, twenty feet high, where two young actresses performed a scene in which one of them sits in a drawer. But the drawer slips off the stage and both women crash to the floor. Silence. Finally, as "the one in charge," I go forward to inspect the bodies. One is awake, the other dead. The dead body, wrapped up somehow like a cocoon, starts to move. The woman emerges, bright and smiling.

The dream had taken 50 seconds. Much of the scenario seems clear: the windows in Nantucket at dusk are a delight, as I look at the garden while talking to Jim. The girls on the stage are students from Yale who on Thursday gave a pretty good recital. Also, last night, prior to sending Sandy McClatchy another install-ment for our interview about Diaries, I dipped again into Julien Green's *Journal*. On Sept. 26, 1968 (p. 120), he wrote:

> *Il y a dans le rêve une économie de moyens admirable. Tout ce qui n'est pas essen-tiel est éliminé. Le sujet est mis en valeur dans une lumière fulgarante qui rejette dans les ténèbres extérieure l'inutile, le détail, ou alors le détail est isolé dans cet éclairage surnaturel et y prend la toute première place, l'hallucinante première place. Si l'on pouvait écrire et composer ainsi, on ferait de grandes choses.*

But isn't that last sentence the very definition of any worthy novel or sym-phony? The definition—not the hoped-for but unrealizable aim? A work of true music or literature is, like a dream, always shorn of the extraneous. Art is not "real life," it is a concentration of life. (Ravel: "Why can't my critics realize that I am artificial by nature?")

Yes or no.

It's the immutable given before every work of art or science, of every theorem or sexual choice. The universe is conceived on yes or no. Shall I use this note or not? That chord or not? Those texts or not? Do I wish to go to bed with this or this or this person approaching in the street? The decision comes in a split second, as it does with whether you like or are uninterested in the bank teller or the countess up there on the screen. Yes or no—the first and only logic of all creation.

Rewrite, a little more humanly. Begin with: How do we compose a symphony? How do we learn to walk? How do we get through the day?

                                                                                                12 Oct.

JH: "I'm only a third alive."

                                                                                                14 Oct.

In an hour, off to Indianapolis for première of Double Concerto, with Jaime Laredo, Sharon Robinson, and Raymond Leppard. JH simultaneously heads for Nantucket in rented car. His health ("Why must I feel so awful, day after day?") is far more preoccupying than my piece. But I get on his nerves, and maybe these few days apart will . . . In a week I'll turn 75, and various little concerts celebrate this peripheral fact. For I'm no longer a central fact (was I ever?) in New Music. I'm not unproud of what I leave, though it may sink without a trace, like the quadrillions of anonymous souls who lie underground, and who if they still lived and swarmed would blot out the sun.

Arnold Weinstein once said that the phrase he most relished in my Diary was, "Death? Not interested. I'm too old for new experiences." My favorite phrase of his (from *The Red Eye of Love*) is, "Well, life isn't everything."

17

Death of Joe Machlis at 5 A.M. And I phoned him only yesterday.

19

Jim at his very lowest. Eating nothing, but his belly's grown huge. Sleeps continually. Doctor Louie does not return calls. Cirrhosis of the liver.

23 October

> I strove with none, for none was worth my strife,
> Nature I loved, and next to Nature, Art;
> I warmed both hands before the fire of life,
> It sinks, and I am ready to depart.
> > Walter Savage Landor
> > *On His Seventy-fifth Birthday*

Yesterday, all-NR choral concert at Trinity in the afternoon, by Richard Coffey and the Concord Chorale. In tune, wonderful sound, intelligent, "musical," clear diction, good choice of short works. In evening, all-NR chamber concert at Miller Theater, choreographed by Michael Boriskin. Well-rehearsed, good programming, suave and rewarding, including the 50-year-old First Sonata (which Tony de Mare also played last week), *Santa Fe Songs*, and *Bright Music*. JH was not up to either concert (nor were any critics there), which was my sole disappointment.

26 Oct.

Alone, melancholy, no goals.

Review in *The Advocate* of Previn's *Streetcar*, says that the music is so conservative it could have been composed in 1928 rather than 1998. But in 1928 wasn't American music far feistier than today? Meanwhile a feminist letter-writer in the *Times* feels that if Clinton had reciprocated Lewinsky's oral sex there might not be such a fuss, but it's only men who must "be satisfied." The letter-writer sets down the rules, and helps us realize that sexual intercourse, to be valuable, must be shared. This presumably unselfish, but actually puritanical stance, is quite new-fashioned (a century old, only?), and forgets that sex is in the head, and means whatever we feel it means.

4 Nov.

Dr. Louie on the phone to JH: "If you go to the hospital, soon, for a week of 'tests,' we may be able to prolong your life for a year or two."

7 Saturday

He's sorting letters, calling family, etc. as I reluctantly pack for 2 days in Chicago. Monday he may go to the hospital.

The hospital is not a place of repose, with TVs running all night long, three other deranged patients in same ward, inexpert nurses mostly unavailable, and cheerless dementia up and down the halls. JH, depleted, returns home tomorrow, drained of gallons of fluid.

Doctor Pfeffer gives him a year.

If only it were me instead.

22 Nov. (Sunday)

Already dark by 4:30 in Hyannis. As the 12-seater plane is about to take off, we're side by side (with Sonny on our laps) when he says, "I feel like the end of *Midnight Cowboy.*" Meaning, of course, when Joe turns to Ratso and realizes that Ratso is dead.

Dr. Pfeffer: "The end is not pleasant."

Two humans screwing form an octopus.

Great minds do not run in the same channels. They are, by definition, unique.

Thanksgiving, Nantucket

Thanksgiving morning, shifting sunlight, heavy wind, and silence all through the island.

Jim lives in a self-contained hell, a bubble of pain that floats from room to room of the otherwise "normal" house. A year from now, a day from now, will the red sofa, or the five elms out back, still exist if he's not here to see them?

28 Nov.

JH paralyzing cramps, in hand and legs, while driving back with José, Sonny & the 2 cockatiels. Tonight: bleeding scrotum. Vomits, while holding a lit cigarette.

Reread Maurice Gendron's letters. And Robert Veynon-Lacroix's dead. Dead. My address book is a cemetery.

Dec. 1

JH, after 2 days *à jeun*, has switched from AZT to Zerit.

Dec. 2

JH à son pire, le ventre gonflé, les mains engourdies, ne peut à peine bouger.

I went alone to Ellen Zwilich's new and pretty good quartet.

Dec. 3

Coughed all night, perhaps because of acupuncture.

Mother's 102nd (or is it 103rd) birthday?

Corigliano at the Y, the first of three concerts I'm hosting there. I ended my intro by saying "I feel close to his music, possibly because it's not that far from mine. We both wear our hearts on our sleeve, but my heart is colder." (Chuckle from audience.)

Wonderful playing by Joshua Bell and Js. Tocco.

7 Dec.

Jim back in hospital. 263–1517

I had to speak, feebly, at memorial for Joe Machlis, at Juilliard.

8 Dec.

Alone in the apartment with Sonny & the cats. What's left to say, in words or in notes? Jerk off. Bronchitis. JH in the noisy hospital again to have his abdomen drained. Suffers from strictures. As a sleepwalker I negotiated the past two days, hosting Corigliano at the Y Sunday, eulogizing Joe Machlis yesterday. If Jim comes home tomorrow, how long before another return? I write little here, partly because I wouldn't want him to see, and partly because . . . What's left to say?

9 Dec.

Jim must stay there at least another day. All is going wrong. Sonny a strain. Me: bronchitis, exhausted. Cold, clear weather. I am coming apart.

14

JH back from hosp.

Albee's weird party, with our neighbor Barbara Grecki. JH, weak and starved, listens in the dark to Wagner & Strauss. Tomorrow, a wheelchair.

The contretemps between Mailer & Updike vs. Tom Wolfe (two of them homo-phobes and all of them straight) is, in this time of Monicagate triviality, as healthy as the Mauriac-Cocteau feuds on the front page of *Le Figaro* 50 years ago.

16

JH at his most depleted.

Il écoute la musique à travers ses malheurs.

Earphones: Wagner & Strauss, mainly vocal. *Comme si, s'il doit mourir, il veut mourir noyé de musique. L'homme qui rétrécit.*

21 Dec.

JH all afternoon *chez les médecins,* in hired car with hired nurse's aide (a ninety-pound female Hindu to wheel his chair). I, at home, with Rosemary & Sonny, &

later Danny, who did laundry, then Eli for a meal of tofu. Jim says they say there's no hope. He says, "I hate to die." He has stopped all his 20-plus HIV pills, at Dr. Louie's suggestion.

Hospital anew. His roommate, a continually groaning octogenarian, is, like so many there, an orthodox Jew. When he heard Father Gordon at what he felt was a ministration of the last rites, he murmured Kaddish.

Jim has asked that tomorrow I bring all the dozens of receipts and unpaid bills. Also knives, crushed cashews, choc. syrup & bitter choc., etc., so he can make candy. But he still vomits everything he swallows.

Saw *The Dead* again, Huston's great film. In that famous final paragraph Joyce, in a mere hundred words, said everything.

Home from the hospital. He speaks of cremation, of the memorial program. (My songs.) "We are each unique & irreplaceable," I quote from *Nous sommes tous les assassins*. " We are all replaceable clay," he says. Bathtub overflows into apartment below.

2:30 A.M. JH in awful pain.

Diarrhea from—nothing! (He's starving.) Crackers—vomiting. Awful cramps.

4:30 A.M. His shower on the stool in the tub. Asked for a knife to slit his throat.

Afternoon. The hospice worker, a dud. But the "pain patch" perhaps will do some good.

Vast land of hopelessness.

In the middle of the night he'll make his way to the kitchen; with or without the wheelchair, it takes 30 minutes. Then for 30 minutes he nibbles. But cannot keep it down. The liver is shot. (Good name = liver!) He does not give off an odor, as he did, so exceptionally, a month ago. The body has shut down.

1999

New Year's Day

Home Health Aide (Susan Fowler) from 1 to 5.
    Paul & Jackie Marshall at 2:30.
    Talk to Barbara Grecki about her not-bad film script.

2 January

HHA (Kate Clement) 1 to 5.
    At 4 A.M. JH eats caviar. Very, very vague. The patch. In and out of sleep. In pain.
    10:30 A.M. Danny comes to walk Sonny.
    3:00 arrival, Mary Marshall. People coming and going. Frank, plus Lydia from the church.

3 Jan. (Sunday)

1 to 5, Kate Clement. Pain patch # 2.
    Mary still here. Arrival Chris Marshall.
    1:30 Father Gordon and Horace White give communion to Jim. Jim with closed eyes answers the rote ritual. We cry and Kate Clement is comforting. Cabrini Emergency on phone says to change patch. Will send Percocet around 6. High fever. Claudia, another nurse with incomprehensible English, talks incessantly about herself.

11 A.M. Barbara Anderson, an R.N., wise and expedient. Then a new aide, male, from Health Providers. Cruisy and unlikable, 1 to 5.

At 3:00, somewhat incongruously, Claire Bloom and Eugenia Zuckerman and Brian Zeger arrive to rehearse my music for *Romeo & Juliet*, which they perform next week. They felt guilty. But Jim later said he heard them from his faraway bed, even as a month ago he heard (and loved) Marcy Rosen *et al.* rehearsing my 3rd Quartet.

Lydia. The bank.

8 P.M. arrival of a 12-hour nurse, Shade Oyebode, from Nigeria.

5 Jan.

9 A.M. to 8 P.M., another nurse, Stella.

Jim murmurs he was surprised to have woken up alive today . . . Frank. Danny.

6 January, 8:25 a.m.

The dull uncomprehending eyes. Death is in there, trying to get out, like pregnancy, or a bowel movement. The two round-the-clock nurses, Stella and Shade, both from Nigeria, don't stifle the cries, which Joy Fox downstairs hears all night. Mary has been a boon—but must leave today. (Will I break? Will I ever sleep again?) Jim's life has been the sole issue for months. Writing this is all so vain. But there's literally nothing else to do—no reading or writing or music.

11:30 A.M. Father Gordon comes to administer last rites. Frank and Danny and Lydia. Sonny remains continually on the bed. Jim's lovable emaciated body. Can he hear us? I lie beside him. But maybe not enough.

At 1, I go out to get a haircut. Mary must return to Philadelphia. At 3, pain patch again. At 2 and 6 and 10 I administer the morphine myself, with a dropper under the tongue. Waiting. Waiting.

At 9, arrival of Gilda, another round-the-clock HHA.

Daron comes to spend the night.

7 January

Jim died at three this morning.

14 January

Sleet is covering the city. Leaning far out of the sixth-story window, it is still impossible to see the white white park a half-block away. Snug, rather pleasant.

During the week since Jim vanished from the earth, I've functioned mechanically. Before the machine stops it's necessary to describe.

Daron at 3 A.M. came into my sleep-sodden room to say quietly, "We think you should get up." With Sonny and the cats beside him, Jim lay there, wasted, eyes and mouth half-opened, unutterably still. Everything crucial and vivid in him had disappeared forever. I lost control, grew hysterical. Gilda was frightened; Daron gave her $40 for a cab home. I was left alone to be with Jim, but didn't know how to behave. Daron phoned Redden's Funeral Home, as we had been instructed, then took Sonny for a long walk. After three-quarters of an hour two funeral men arrived, looking themselves like the walking dead, *les croque-morts* as the French say, out of central casting. They asked that I wait in the front room as they gathered "the remains." They wheeled their way to the main elevator and said goodbye. The street was dark and empty at 5 A.M. as I looked down, to watch them place the seated body, covered by a dark sheet, into the small ambulance. They drove off toward Central Park, turned right, and that is the last I saw of my golden Jim, the love of my life with whom I lived for thirty-two years.

Daron was perfect. I will remain forever beholden. When he came back with Sonny, we talked for a while. He took charge. At 9 A.M. Frank Benitez came. At 11, Sylvia arrived from Long Island, and while I lay on the floor incoherent they made three dozen phone calls.

I cobbled together a factual obit which Daron delivered by hand to Tony Tommasini uptown. Then downtown to the *Times* with a photograph of Jim. At 2:00 went with Sylvia to Redden's on 14th Street to sign various papers. Both Daron and Sylvia stayed over, he on the sofa, she in JH's room. In the middle of the night I masturbated.

Friday, beautiful obituary with Jim's face smiling at a million readers. Visit at 4 from Shirley and George Perle. Daron cooked supper.

Saturday, Frank came by. Then Rosemary and Jackie at 3:00 to stay for a day or two. At 4:00, visit from Gloria Vanderbilt, wise and cool, and patient with my delirium. A man appeared to reclaim the wheelchair.

Sunday, phone calls from 27 friends (I listed them), visits from Jim Kendrick, from Pia Gilbert (with a lavish casserole), and Chris Marshall. Rosemary ill from the strain. Jackie will take Sonny to live with her and Paul and the children in Lenox. As he was Jim's dog primarily, I could never deal with him here, and feel sadly relieved.

Monday, to Redden's again with Chris, for ashes and death certificate. Visit from Jim Kendrick, from Sylvia as always, and from Naomi and Gary Graffman, with chicken soup and flowers. Insomnia, Melatonin, Ambien.

Wednesday, Father Gordon arranged a large memorial for Jim at Saint Matthew's and Saint Timothy's on 84th. Very well attended with the interracial congregation, my friends, plus Jim's brother Neil with Linda, Aunt Janet and her son Stuart Dalton, all at the Olcott Hotel, and a bit blinded by the big city. The music included much of Jim's *Stabat Mater*.

Now today there is sleet.

18 Jan.

Overwhelming, the support and compassion from family, friends, fellow dog-walkers, and 300 letters from almost-strangers.

13 Feb.

What has Jim missed in the five weeks since? Only the display of concern for him all over. Otherwise nothing.

18 February

Spoken at the "Y":

> This is the second of three programs on which I've been asked to cast light, through conversation and performance, on three American composers: last December, John Corigliano; next April, André Previn; and tonight, myself.
>
> But how does one cast light on oneself?
>
> Once I saw a solo actor interview himself, setting his real-life persona against his stage role. But I am not an actor—I can't even play myself. Nor am I sure that a composer, as distinct from a performer, can say anything about his music that the music can't say better. Except, of course, how it came to be made. So I shall speak briefly about each work, just before it is played.
>
> I want to dedicate this entire program to the memory of my dearest friend, Jim Holmes. Jim was near me during the composition of all four pieces. It was my habit, once a piece was done, to show it to him. He might suggest a cut here, a nudge there, or even that I add a whole new section for balance. I like to believe that his perceptive intelligence helped to make some of my music a little less imperfect.

22 Feb.

The *Times* magazine wants to question me on mourning. These are some ideas.

If my music, like my prose, is not necessarily a new language, it is nevertheless a personal dialect spoken with my own accent. And I like to think that the basic material is unique, if only by virtue of stating age-old notions in a special way.

But when Jim Holmes, my partner for thirty-two years, died last month, my reactions, though brand new, could be expressed only by clichés: "There must be some mistake . . . Why him and not me? . . . What's the point of going on?"

Yes, death is our common fate; the dead from past millennia would blot out the sun. And yes, there are wise books from Tibet that tell of a technique for dying, just as there is a technique for living. Yet how can there be such a technique? Dying does not occur in Time; the difference between being almost dead, and dead, is beyond concept. The only technique, perhaps, is one that might *prepare* us for dying. Yet when that moment comes, all preparation turns to dust.

I'm seventy-five, and have faced the loss of loved ones many times: a childhood friend killed by a car; the war; my parents a mere eleven years ago. And now Jim. None of this has taught me a thing, unless it be that life has no point. We spend our life killing time, while waiting for time to kill us. Nothing seems to matter now, and even Great Art fails.

In the coming months, if I survive them, will I change my tune? Though an atheist, I *have* grown to believe that Jim is "out there" watching. I have no fear in joining him. And yes, finally, I am already planning to compose a huge song-cycle in his memory, based on a poetry of anger and of resignation.

11 March

Doctor Agus says, because of the triglycerides I mustn't eat sweets. But sweets are all I crave now. Am I not allowed at least one hot-fudge sundae per Sunday?

What of the bookish, bespectacled, overweight ten-year-old who, when his classmates taunted, "You big fat sissy, everybody hates you," went home and committed suicide? He was me.

14 March

Sunday. The *Times* printed the piece on mourning today, in a Q & A format.

I continue the classes with the six Yale undergraduates, alternating between here and New Haven, where Jim would pick me up on Fridays, with Sonny, and we'd drive back to New York. Also at MSM and Curtis. But it's rote, dreamlike. Life seems pretty much over, so far as having more to say, or desire for more exposure. Still, the body could last another twenty years . . . I don't believe in life after death, but Jim is watching me, I know.

15 April

Anecdote:

When Gloria asked me to a dinner party for Nancy Reagan, my first impulse was to consult Morris Golde, my most leftist friend. "Of course you must go," said he, "so you can tell us all about it." Then Gloria, nervous hostess, called again to say there'd be eighteen guests, and that I'd be at the head of a table for ten, with Nancy at my right. But what will I talk to her about? "Well, she's met a lot of people, and besides, you have the same initials," was Gloria's reassurance.

Flash back 35 years. Danny Pinkham, passing through New York, phoned to say he'd picked up a butch Italian, named Tony Romano, who was a bit too domineering, and he felt Tony would be right up my alley. Could he give him my number? Sure. So Tony and I hit it off quite well physically, if not literarily, for about two weeks, then drifted apart.

Meanwhile, last evening I arrived late at Gloria's (I'm never late), and was apparently the last guest. My name was phoned up by the doorman. On arriving at the apartment, a swarthy mid-fifties servant said, as he helped me out of my coat, "Mr. Rorem, I presume. Remember me? I'm Tony Romano." As one of four liveried caterers he still looked sexy, and remained solicitous all through the evening ("May I take your glass? . . . A bit more soup?"), like Jupien with Charlus. Very upstairs/downstairs.

As for Mrs. Reagan, she was well dressed in gray with tiny earrings, a jeweled pillbox, much too thin, and easy to talk to, mostly about the movies way back when. (She was Nazimova's god-daughter.) If she'd not heard of, say, John Simon or

Robert Graves, whose names came up in passing, she was full of facts about Ava and Lana and Barbara. On her right sat the chatty Ben Brantley, and on my left sat Leila Hadley and Alex Theroux, all a big boon. The sole mention of the President came when I asked about Dietrich, whom she'd never met. "When Ronnie was shot, Marlene phoned from Paris, and continued to do so over the years. But she'd never permit me to visit when I was in France."

Nancy, who called me Ned, gave me her California address, and we said good-bye. I was the first to leave. Tony helped me on with my coat, gave me his phone number.

End of anecdote.

Out of corner of one eye I'll perceive Jim in the next room, or Sonny rummaging over there by the radiator.

Are they—we—really so anxious to join up and kill people? A gay Quaker speaks: "Instead of 'gays in the military,' why not 'gays to get rid of the military'?"

Because of the fuss, I invested in a CD of the famous Thomas Adès's little piece. Oh, how music is not a common language! Ah, how the nations don't "get" America! As when Ravel or Milhaud start swinging, or Michael Tippett cashes in on unadorned Negro spirituals passed off as his own! Now Mr. Adès, in his setting of Tennessee Williams's hyper-male, homophilic, notorious poem, "Life Story," about two men in bed, enjoins his solo soprano to take Billie Holiday as her model. So the hyper-female voice with an English accent strives to be bluesy, missing the point in a music that, in itself, is already embarrassingly bloodless.

26 April

In the fourteen weeks since he died there has seemed no intellectual motive, much less urge, to write here. Notate a colorless world? define it as the senseless orb we were too interested in Art and Life to see? Not a day that hasn't seemed lost because he's not breathing in it. Today, in yet another vast batch of memorabilia, his diary of 1976 turned up. Unruled pages, neatly inscribed, with thoughts of death, of friends, of me occasionally (did he feel I might see it, and not say "too much"—about, for instance, how I'd appropriated his identity?). He writes a lot on the church, which in fact became his identity, and on his anxiety that the Bible is too laxly interpreted, though he himself . . . But here he is:

> Although Godless, I like others to believe in God. It relieves me from having to do so. Part of Jimmy Carter's appeal is that he believes in God. Margaret Mead's observations on primitive religious customs are strengthened by the fact that she kneels each Sunday at the communion rail. [Mead was a member of JH's Church of Saint Matthew and Saint Timothy.] "Believing in God" is sometimes invigorating mental exercise, like chess, when played according to the rules, except that instead

of an opponent one is matched against theological history. "Believing in Jesus" is far less exciting, except in areas of doctrine such as the Atonement, the Trinity, and Salvation. I can and do enjoy playing make-believe in God and Jesus. But those who Believe, in simply faith, have my deepest respect. Their faith gives me the luxury of being faithless. They keep the sacred flame. Pray for me, Mary, so that I may never suffer the ignom[in]y of praying for myself. Pride groweth fat on prayer.

The principal trouble with Jesus Christ is that he is not likable. No sense of humor chez lui. And certainly "fuzzy on the issues." The picture we have of him was painted by fanatics (the apostles) and suffers accordingly. Why not a collection of the witticisms of J.C.? Who could make them up? And how to avoid a Jesus with humor as being the camp of all time?

May 1

The horror of Kosovo (& Africa & Ireland).
The mass shootings in wealthy Columbine, Colorado, high school.

May 4

Suicide note: "I've gone to find Jim."

May 8

Rosemary's 77th birthday.

During the decade since Itzhak Perlman bought the house across the street, the massive air conditioner on his roof has buzzed loudly 24 hours a day. We've talked about it, first six years ago, in Philadelphia when we were on the same program (Sawallish giving him star treatment while all but ignoring me—I'm only a composer—though the orchestra's performance of *Eagles* was dazzling). Perlman said it would cost $40,000 to replace the machine. So let him give a concert: he earns in an evening what I earn in a year. Today the situation is no better. So, after many an unanswered letter, and chilly phone call to IP's secretary, I'm having windows insulated for $3600. Kendrick says not to send Perlman the bill, just chalk it up to bad faith. A writer-of-music's voice is a cry in the wilderness next to a player-of-music's; my lonely crankiness goes unheard except in these pages. It's not a blank page that I'm longing to fill, but a cluttered mind that I'm anxious to empty.

A 1-act opera on *The Masque of the Red Death*, modernized for AIDS.

Re. Perlman et al. They are not the music. They are the medium through which the music flows. But it enters them by way of the composer. Thus are our priorities skewed. We're the only century since music's existence to celebrate not today but yesterday.

5 July

Phyllis Curtin and I in 1969 performed a Poulenc-Rorem recital in Boston's Gardner Museum. A taped broadcast is now to be issued as a CD, which I've just listened to.

Has it really been thirty years since we gave this program? Soon it will be forty years, then a hundred. The wistful wonder of recording is that the past becomes the present. The dead walk again, though never with the same gait. For life changes meaning even as it's being lived, and the generations are finally irretrievable. Music itself, even to its composer, shifts its own significance with each passing day.

Spent a fortnight trying to write a review for the *TLS* of *The Pale of Words*, a pedantic long essay on the meaning of art. Then sent a 4-page letter to the *TLS* explaining skillfully why I cannot write the review. Unacknowledged. As with the unacknowledged letter re. Glenn Gould, don't they know that my letter *is* the review?

Nantucket, 9 July

Mary has said goodnight and gone upstairs to read. I remain here to revisit snatches from *Of Mice and Men*, Aaron Copland's first movie sixty years ago, and waiting for that "telling" moment when Candy's dog is killed. The men continue their card game, the sound of the gunshot makes Candy turn on his bed, while Aaron's music with tender force italicizes the silence, and my eyes fill with tears. They're all dead now. Jim is dead, too. What further point is there?

Could the same scene, without music, have had an impact? The music, self-contained though it be, certainly imbues the scene. Another *kind* of music could have destroyed it.

Rereading the diary snippets from 1986, to be printed in *The Yale Review*. What does one make of Ned's continual denigration of Elliott Carter? Can this fluctuating from dithyrambs to diatribes over the years be termed hypocrisy? Like Robert Craft, who always denigrates Ned in print but uses Ned's words to publicize his books. Or Ned himself, who uses Elliott's words for that purpose.

Sunday 11 July

When Bill Rowson was here last week with me and Mary, we rented videos for his general education. *L'Avventura* after forty years lacks its first sting but is a flawless movie-as-movie. Like *Picnic at Hanging Rock* a half-generation later, it rightly makes no effort to explain the inexplicable—the disappearance forever of what was just now so utterly here. (Nobody eats in Antonioni's films.)

Visit from Maggie and Frank Conroy. I announce that, without exception, all American poets today use "I," often many times, in nine out of ten of their poems. This apropos of the unlikable Jorie Graham, whom Frank halfheartedly defends, explaining that she is a congenital liar, taking the unreality of existence for the reality of her verse. Or something. But aren't all poets liars, by definition? In the current *New York Review*, Joyce Carol Oates, writing of the Jon Benet Ramsey mystery, says: "Perhaps in the fact-obsessed late twentieth century, the most palatable fictions are those that aren't really fictional but rather 'facts' audaciously reinvented in the language of gifted writers. For what is 'reality' except as it is presented through language?" (Rewrite in my own words, don't credit Joyce, and place in the early "Lies" section of these pages.) Much later she adds: "Presented in emetic bulk, facts can be made to obscure the truth, as a coroner's report presented in scientific detail to the layman, though factually true in every particular, obscures the truth if unanalyzed."

In today's *Times Book Review*, the opening sentence by one James Wood of an otherwise pretty good report on Hemingway reads: "Imitation is not original, thus no original writer is ever really imitable." Have you any idea what that means—or pretends to mean?

As for that "I" in American poets, they leave no space for me as a composer to set their words to music. For who am I in their I-ridden stanzas?

12 July

Call from Sylvia, who says John Ward is dying. Prostate cancer. Call from Gloria who says that Nora's daughter went to doctor with heartburn, but was found to be nine months pregnant. (Well, if pregnancy hides 'neath heartburn, cancer hides 'neath an aching rectum, and we're all on the list. For death, that is, not pregnancy.) She adds that Walter Matthau, her friend Carol's husband, weighs 85 pounds and is dying, he too. Phone calls these days are always about diseases and death, never about love problems.

For some reason I reread "Letter to Claude" for the first time in thirty years. It does have an accumulative energy with its Djuna Barnes-ish obsession with "love" ("Ah, love is impossible, but if it were possible it wouldn't be love"), and the author cannily swerves from abject adoration to abject hate, in an original tone. Perhaps the tone comes from translation: it was first composed in French. I could never write it now, if only because I wrote it then. Are the young today in any way involved with the subject? Do they even write love letters—or hate letters—on the Internet? . . . While reading, I know what a reader then could not know: that Claude would commit suicide thirty years later.

Nightly insomnia: an old friend, or an intimate enemy?

Without a Trace: movie at the Seward Johnsons'. Much too long, easily cut. I, as an actor therein, have the last word. "I don't believe in inexplicable hysterics explicated by magic. But I rather like people who do: opposites attract. My own work is a mystery, to everyone, even me."

[Get exact script from John Johnson.]

Who won?
   Lou won one.
   Boo won one too.
   Pru won two.
   Sue won two too.

Nantucket, 30 July

Saw *The Red Violin* Tuesday at the Gaslight. Later, phoned John Corigliano to say how suave and effective his score was. But John was just short of tears: he'd had his 19-year-old dog put to sleep that morning, and nothing else mattered.

Saw *The Manchurian Candidate* Wednesday on TV. Later, phoned David Amram to say how unusual and supportive his score was. But David was not home: he later called from his new (new to me—we've not seen each other for thirty years) home in Putnam, and we spoke for half an hour, mainly about the good old days of his bohemia.

Alone on the island I try to see people, phone them, write them. While the whole globe is swathed in a record heat wave, Nantucket seems oddly immune. Walking barefoot on the back lawn I'm in awe of Jim's careful work. Everything is Jim, nothing else matters. I still cry about once a week, at the grocery store, at the police station. Work seems superfluous. I've said all I have to say. And except for the new Oboe Pieces (which, at $15,000, are twice what Counterpoint is paying for this new diary, a far cry from the $80,000 paid by S & S for the memoir), I have not one commission. Not one.

When will the cats die? Every morning they snuggle on the bed, Lucille and Tom. They're fifteen years old. Will I ever see Sonny again, now in Lenox? Mary comes back next week, and Kendrick, too. They represent extreme order in an aimless life. I don't *want* to die, but am ready for it. I do want to be again with Jim. His ashes are there in his very own garden.

This entry, inscribed merely for discipline, proves through its aimlessness that the diary is also a thing of the past. In the minutes or decades that remain, there's no longer a need to note it all.

Surely the phrases of Claude Rostand, on pages 344–5 of *The Later Diaries*, are, in their brevity, no less trenchant than the much longer essay called "Thirteen Ways of Looking at a Critic," in describing how a music reviewer should behave. Incidentally, Claude Rostand was said (by Jacques Février) to have had the biggest dick in France's artistic world, even as Robert Shaw was said (by Herbert Kubly) to have had the same in America. And they both were straight. More or less.

Even as Tina Brown in her fatal takeover of *The New Yorker* apparently required of every contributor that the word "fuck" be used at least once per article, so the *TLS* now abuses the term "post modernism." Like the notion of cholesterol or of the catastrophic dangers of nicotine, which were never stressed in my childhood, so postmodernism seems to be something everyone uses without defining it. What have I missed out on? I don't remember that the term modernism was ever used back when—although we did talk with defensive pride about "modern music" (Stravinsky, Copland) if only because that's what it indeed was, just as Mozart was modern music in his day. Well, this very Olivetti on which these words are being typed is now rare as hen's teeth, but I can't use phrases others use just because they . . . Nor have I a fax, nor do I comprehend web sites. Is the world a finer place with these expediencies? Do teenagers now write *billets doux*—and preserve them in cedar boxes?

Sunday night 1 August

Tom's tigerish back and poached egg belly, with eyes the size of Garbo's. He still thinks he's a dog. When Sonny and I used to walk up to Sunset Hill he would trot along with us, never more than a yard or two away. Lucille's apricot fur and sagging belly, with eyes a bit calculating. Maggy once compared her to Rhonda Fleming. The cats now never leave the grounds. They have little humor but much intellect though unaimed at books. They eat well (he, Chef's Blend only; she, salmon Friskies only) but vomit a lot, and sleep. They have their separate country and city stances—as probably we all have. They are part of the house's fabric. And though they once were solely Jim's, today they're mine, *et j'y tiens*.

Gave today a tea party (4 bottles of wine, cheese and tarts from the Gourmet Shoppe, nuts and carrots and cucumbers) for Eugenie, Joyce & Seward Johnson, Susan Sandler & Hugh Conlon, Mary & Peter Heller. Eugenie was cited on the front page of today's *NY Times*, apropos of Nantucket's ever growing fragility under the invasion of moneymakers. Tomorrow Hugh will try to prepare Kelvin for his driver's test. Now I'm alone and sterile. The oboe piece for Lucarelli advances slowly, and is phony and trite.

2 August

"You don't have enough respect for your own music," Jim used to say in reaction to my ho-hum attitude once I'd experienced the thrill (or horror) of a first (or fifth) performance. In fact, my "performances" dwell in the composing; the bringing to life seems always less . . . well, necessary. Jim was every inch a re-creator: he could live with a piece—of Brahms, Fauré, Messiaen, myself—for years, remolding, kneading, whacking it anew every day. The work he did with his beloved church choir for a third of a century involved constant rethinking, friendship, and patience. (Yet he was a composer too. His *Stabat Mater*, especially the fifth movement therein, is as "good" as any other today.) Thus when I received this morning a CD from the Church Foundry of Washington D.C.'s United Methodist Church, which includes "Sing My Soul" and a section from *The Quaker Reader*, I felt obliged to listen, mainly so as to write a polite reply to the conductor, a Ms. Eileen Guenther. But when the music began I dissolved in tears—not from hearing my own music, but from using Jim's ears which no longer function for him. Is he here in this room with us now? Can he read this?

4 Aug.

Do we all, at our age, turn first to the obits? The obits really made a killing today, Richard Olney and Rudy Burkhardt, from the faraway past. Soon there won't be anyone left to condole. Soon there won't be anyone left.

In October I'll turn 76. But I still feel (and behave) like 14.

5 Aug.

When Narayan states that "what is good is always what is new, in both form and content" (p. 14, *NYRB*, 4 March), one thinks of Rimbaud's *"il faut être absolument moderne."* Nothing's new under the sun, etc., and as for being "modern," whatever we do today is by definition modern. Both Rimbaud's and Narayan's statements are *old*. It's more urgent to be "better than" than "different from." Viz. Palestrina, Bach, Debussy & Wagner as opposed to Rebikov, Spohr, Clementi & Hahn.

Do I like "fine writing?" Do I do it? Metaphor bores me, yet all writers use it— *must* use it.

Nightmare of insomnia. Each night seems worse than the last.

17 Aug.

I've always been 100% homosexual (nor is there really such a thing as an honest bisexual, comforting term). I never never appraise a woman sexually, no matter how beautiful or young or "sexy" or old. Of course, only one man in, say, 27 is sexy—the other 26 are as nil as women. But since Jim died seven months ago, I'm hornier than ever. Why? In seven weeks I'll turn 76, but remain dizzy with lust. Because I'm "free" for the first time in 30 years? When no one else cares.

Nantucket, 19 August

Mary has been a help beyond imagination, with papers and taxes and bills, and shopping and housekeeping and driving, and just her silently intense self. So I've decided not to sell the house, despite its every board and wrinkle speaking hourly of Jim. Now I'm alone here, for the past week or two, and luxuriate in the free good of it all. The cats—*Jim's* cats—Tom and Lucille (they came from the local orphanage twelve years ago), preen in the cold sunshine and sleep on my bed. Tom sneezes and coughs like a human. I socialize much more than before, walking twice daily to town, having tea or a meal with acquaintances, and work sporadically. It means less to be "self-expressive" than a year ago. The Oboe Pieces are finished. Now there are dozens of young composers with their gifts and their chutzpah. How I hate to kill things, even flies.

The secret of good translation lies not in knowing the other language but in knowing your own. How I cringe at seeing *triste* rendered as "sad" when it should be "dreary," *sinistre* rendered as "sinister" when it too is "dreary," or *faux amis* like *formidable* and *terrible* rendered as "formidable" and "terrible" instead of "terrific" and "extremely poignant."

Recalling how Jim during his last weeks listened more and more to music, can one know if this was less from a "need for art" than as a distraction from the reality of death? For surely—it now seems—death loomed before him every hour. As it looms before me: nothing else seems urgent anymore.

I should, but haven't the interest to, note what I'm reading and trying to write, whom I'm seeing and what I'm trying to compose, how much I'm masturbating and trying to fill time & space. More engrossing seems to be just the changes in weather, the grass newly mown, the cats who never leave our green but parched half-acre, and the post-prandial dish of strawberry sherbet with chocolate-chip cookies.

21 Aug.

In Turkey 40,000 have died in a 15-second earthquake. In Kosovo, in Ireland, in privileged American schools, still more gratuitous murders en masse. (But here it rains and rains all night, and Jim is dead.) In a more perfect world, a world of peace and mutual respect and enough to eat, would more mediocrity reign? Would we wish to be free to enjoy a world of pop, an unchallenging society of smarmy congratulation?

God, how I hate religion!

A diary can never be a work of art, for it has no shape. By definition, it lacks a beginning and an end—is a perpetual middle. Inasmuch as it's honed and formed, it's no longer a diary.

Life and all that goes with it—sex, art, cooking, war, and astronomy—is a mere matter of killing time while waiting for time to kill us. Religion's a poignant invention to justify life's meaning, when life has no meaning. Order out of chaos is our order, not chaos's.

Father Gordon plans another memorial for early next year, and maybe a plaque on the church wall. But why not also, with the five thousand dollars already contributed toward Jim's memory by church members, start a James R. Holmes scholarship fund, so that his name can be always linked with the music and the kids he so much loved?

Index